Criminal Justice and Immigration Act 2008
A Practitioner's Guide

Criminal Justice and Immigration Act 2008
A Practitioner's Guide

Richard Ward

Vanessa Bettinson

Published by
Jordan Publishing Limited
21 St Thomas Street
Bristol BS1 6JS

Whilst the publishers and the author have taken every care in preparing the material included in this work, any statements made as to the legal or other implications of particular transactions are made in good faith purely for general guidance and cannot be regarded as a substitute for professional advice. Consequently, no liability can be accepted for loss or expense incurred as a result of relying in particular circumstances on statements made in this work.

© Jordan Publishing Limited 2008

All rights reserved. No part of this publication may be reproduced, stored in a retrieval system, or transmitted in any way or by any means, including photocopying or recording, without the written permission of the copyright holder, application for which should be addressed to the publisher.

Crown Copyright material is reproduced with kind permission of the Controller of Her Majesty's Stationery Office.

British Library Cataloguing-in-Publication Data

A catalogue record for this book is available from the British Library.

ISBN 978 1 84661 121 6

Typeset by Letterpart Ltd, Reigate, Surrey

Printed in Great Britain by CPI Antony Rowe

PREFACE

New criminal justice legislation comes along with alarming frequency. Since 1997 there have been at least 38 criminal justice Bills, and a whole raft of immigration provisions. The Criminal Justice and Immigration Act 2008, which received Royal Assent in May 2008, is very different from the Bill that first was introduced into Parliament in October 2007, such were the changes made to it by way of addition and deletion. This is mirrored even now, after Royal Assent, by continued uncertainty about implementation. Commencement is dealt with at **1.5** and in specific parts of the book. But we believe there may be on-going delays in implementation of the allocation and committal for sentence provisions (possibly put back to April 2009, or later) whilst the youth justice provisions may yet see commencement in spring 2009. Of course there is some track record of some provisions of the Criminal Justice Act 2003 never having been brought into force at all!

Even where in force the new Act will not mark the end of the on-going change. Any fond hope that there might now be a pause in the pace of legislative change has been already been dashed by still further proposals for changes to youth justice, and a promised Bill making further provision for victims and witnesses.

This book inevitably has had to be selective in respect of coverage of what was described by one commentator as a 'Christmas tree' Bill, such were the number of matters added, and so diverse are the areas of law dealt with. This is a hotchpotch of an Act. We have concentrated our emphasis on those matters of particular interest to practitioners and given less emphasis to institutional and structural changes. Clearly, some of policy issues that underpin the legislation are major studies in their own right.

We have been greatly assisted by colleagues with whom we have discussed aspects of the changes. In particular Alwyn Jones and Gavin Dingwall, both of Leicester De Montfort Law School, have been sources of encouragement and advice. Needless to say, any errors in the book are the responsibility of the authors alone. We have also been greatly assisted by the team at Jordans, especially Tony Hawitt and Cheryl Prophett, who together have made the publication of the book (if not its writing) as easy as it could be.

Finally, Richard would like to thank Sarah for her support, encouragement and patience whilst this book has been in preparation. Likewise, Vanessa would like to thank John Royal for providing a calm sanctuary during the writing of this book.

The law is stated as we believe it be as at 15 July 2008.

Richard Ward
Vanessa Bettinson
Leicester
July 2008

ABBREVIATIONS

2008 Act	Criminal Justice and Immigration Act 2008
AJA 1999	Access to Justice Act 1999
API	Asylum policy instructions
ASBA 2003	Anti-social Behaviour Act 2003
ASBI	Anti-social behaviour interventions
BA 1976	Bail Act 1976
BBFC	British Board of Film Censors
BIA	Home Office Border Agency
C(S)A 1997	Crime (Sentences) Act 1997
CAA 1968	Criminal Appeal Act 1968
CCRC	Criminal Cases Review Commission
CDA 1998	Crime and Disorder Act 1998
CJA 2003	Criminal Justice Act 2003
CJPOA 1994	Criminal Justice and Public Order Act 1994
CPIA 1996	Criminal Procedure and Investigations Act 1996
CRC	Convention on the Rights of the Child
CYPA 1933	Children and Young Persons Act 1933
DCW	Designated case workers
DPA 1998	Data Protection Act 1998
DPP	Director of Public Prosecutions
ECHR	European Court of Human Rights
HA 1996	Housing Act 1996
HRA 1998	Human Rights Act 1998
HSS	Health and Social Services
IA 1971	Immigration Act 1971
IAA 1999	Immigration and Asylum Act 1999
IAEA	International Atomic Energy Authority
IANA 2006	Immigration, Asylum and Nationality Act 2006
ILPA	Immigration Law Practitioners' Association
IPP	Imprisonment for Public Protection
ISS	intensive supervision and surveillance
ISO	individual support order
JCWI	Joint Council for the Welfare of Immigrants
MCA 1980	Magistrates' Court Act 1980
NASS	National Asylum Support Service

NIAA 2002	Nationality, Immigration and Asylum Act 2002
NM(O)A 1983	Nuclear Materials (Offences) Act 1983
OPA 1959	Obscene Publications Act 1959
PCA 1978	Protection of Children Act 1978
PCC(S)A 2000	Powers of Criminal Courts (Sentencing) Act 2000
PCO	premises closure order
POA 1985	Prosecution of Offences Act 1985
POA 1986	Public Order Act 1986
PSR	pre-sentence reports
SOA 2003	Sexual Offences Act 2003
SRA 2002	Serious Crime Act 2002
TA 2000	Terrorism Act 2000
UNHCR	UN High Commissioner for Refugees
VOO	violent offender order
VRA 1984	Video Recording Act 1984
YDO	youth default order
YOT	youth offending team
YRO	youth rehabilitation order

CONTENTS

Preface	v
Abbreviations	vii
Table of Cases	xv
Table of Statutes	xxi
Table of Statutory Instruments	xxxi

Chapter 1
Introduction

Parliamentary history	1
House of Commons	1
House of Lords	2
Commencement	2
Outline of the Act	3
The passage of the Act	4

Chapter 2
Procedural Changes

Allocation of cases triable either way	5
Commencement	5
Committal for sentence	6
Bail	7
Electronic monitoring condition	7
Children and young persons	7
Persons aged 17 or above	8
Bail for summary offences and other offences tried summarily	8
Trial or sentencing in absence of the accused	9
Contents of accused's defence statement	10
Criminal legal aid	11
Rights of audience in magistrates' courts	13
Background and rationale	14
The detail	15

Chapter 3
Sentencing

Summary	17
Background and wider sentencing context	17
General sentencing matters	19
Pre-Sentence Reports	19

Community sentences	20
Enforcement of sentences – unpaid work requirement for breach of community order	21
Enforcement of sentences – attendance centre requirement on fine defaulter – default order	22
Consecutive terms of imprisonment	22
Example 1	23
Example 2	23
Violent or sexual offenders	23
Background	23
The changes – preconditions for imposition of sentences	25
Dangerousness	27
Indeterminate sentences – determination of tariffs	27
Release and recall of prisoners	30
Credits for remands on bail	30
Home Detention Curfew scheme	31
Release on licence of prisoner serving extended sentence under CJA 2003, ss 227 and 228	32
Release of long-term prisoners	32
Application of licence provisions to prisoners liable to removal from the UK and early removal of prisoners	33
Release of prisoners after recall	35
Background	35
Automatic release	36
Prisoners not eligible or suitable for automatic release	37
Extended sentence prisoners	37
Life prisoners	37

Chapter 4
Young Offenders – General Changes

	39
Summary	39
The wider background	39
Purposes of sentencing offenders under the age of 18	41
Alternatives to prosecution – conditional cautions and other changes	43
Background	43
Reprimands and warnings	44
Youth conditional cautions	44
Preconditions	45
Conditions	46
Code of Practice	47
Non-compliance	47
Restrictions on sentencing on subsequent conviction	47
Referral orders	47
Background	47
The changes	48
Compulsory reference	48
Discretionary reference	48
Power to revoke a referral and changes in length	49

Youth default orders	50
Detention for public protection and extended sentences for violent or sexual offences	51

Chapter 5
Youth Rehabilitation Order — 53

Summary	53
Background	53
The new order	55
Length of the order	56
The requirements that may be imposed	57
Pre-Sentence Reports and other information	58
Making of the order	59
Restrictions on the making of an order	60
The requirements: alternatives to custody	60
YRO with intensive supervision and surveillance (Sch 1, para 3)	61
YRO with fostering (Sch 1, para 4)	62
The requirements: preconditions and detail	63
Activity requirement (Sch 1, paras 6–8)	63
Supervision requirement (Sch 1, para 9)	64
Unpaid work requirement (Sch 1, para 10)	64
Programme requirement (Sch 1, para 11)	65
Attendance centre requirement (Sch 1, para 12)	65
Prohibited activity (Sch 1, para 13)	65
Curfew requirement (Sch 1, para 14)	66
Exclusion requirement (Sch 1, para 15)	66
Residence requirement (Sch 1, para 16)	67
Local authority residence requirement (Sch 1, para 17)	68
Fostering requirement (Sch 1, para 18)	69
Mental health treatment requirement (Sch 1, para 20)	69
Drug treatment requirement (Sch 1, para 22) and drug testing requirement (Sch 1, para 23)	69
Intoxicating substance treatment requirement (Sch 1, para 24)	70
Education requirement (Sch 1, para 25)	70
Electronic monitoring (Sch 1, para 26)	70
Breach, revocation or amendment	71
Breach	71
Revocation and amendment	72
Amendment of the order	72
Powers of a court following conviction	73

Chapter 6
Violent Offender Orders — 75

Summary	75
Background	75
The order	76
The preconditions for the making of a VOO	77
The application and hearing	78

Making of the order	80
When can an order be made?	83
The contents of the order	84
Variation, renewal or discharge	85
Interim orders	85
Appeals	86
Notification requirements	86
Offences	86

Chapter 7
Anti-social Behaviour — **89**

Summary	89
Closure orders in respect of premises associated with persistent disorder or nuisance	89
Who may apply and when may an application be made?	92
The premises closure order	94
Criminal offence	95
Extension and discharge	95
Appeals	96
Reimbursement of costs or compensation	96
Anti-social behaviour orders	97
Background	97
The new provisions	98
Individual support orders	98
Nuisance or disturbance on hospital premises	99
Background	100
The offence	102
Power to remove	103
Guidance	104

Chapter 8
Obscenity and Sexual Offences — **105**

Summary	105
Extreme pornography	105
Background and rationale	105
The offence	108
Image	109
Pornographic	109
Extreme image	112
Grossly offensive, disgusting or otherwise of an obscene character	114
Possession	115
Excluded material	115
Defences	117
Human rights and wider issues	119
Special rules relating to providers of information society services	120
Indecent photographs of children	121
Maximum penalty for publication of obscene articles	122

Sexual offences committed outside the UK	122
Grooming and adoption	123
Information concerning sex offenders	123

Chapter 9
Criminal Offences and Defences 125
Summary	125
Hatred on the grounds of sexual orientation	125
The new provisions	126
Background	127
Sexual orientation	128
The offence – s 29B	128
Reasonable force and self-defence	130
Background	130
The common law defence	131
Abolition of blasphemy	134
Inciting the commission of a nuclear offence	134
Penalty for unlawfully obtaining personal data	136

Chapter 10
Appeals 139
Summary	139
Background	139
Powers to dismiss an appeal following references by the Criminal Cases Review Commission	140
Appeals by prosecution	142
Review of sentence on reference by Attorney-General	143
Other changes	143

Chapter 11
Special Immigration Status 145
Summary	145
Background	145
The new immigration status	147
Is a new legal status necessary at all?	147
Special immigration status – the preconditions	148
The first precondition for the new status – 'foreign criminal'	149
Condition 1 (2008 Act, s 131(2))	149
Condition 2 (2008 Act, s 131(3))	151
Condition 3 (2008 Act, s 131(4))	151
Art 1F(a): Crimes against peace, etc	152
Art 1F(b): Serious non-political crimes	152
Art 1F(c): Acts contrary to the purposes and principles of the UN	153
The second precondition for the new status – 'family member' (2008 Act, s 130(3))	154
The limits on designation (2008 Act, s 130(4), (5)(a) and (b))	156
Right of appeal	157

Effect of designation	157
Conditions (2008 Act, s 133)	158
Failure to comply with the condition (2008 Act, s 133(5))	158
Support	159
End of designation (2008 Act, s 136)	160

Chapter 12
Miscellaneous Changes **161**

Summary	161
Information about child sex offenders	161
Background	161
The new provisions	164
Sexual offences prevention orders: relevant sexual offences	166
Persistent sales of tobacco to persons aged under 18	166
Policing	167
International co-operation	168
Compensation for miscarriages of justice	169

Appendix 1
Statutes **173**
Criminal Justice and Immigration Act 2008   173

Index **447**

TABLE OF CASES

References are to paragraph numbers.

A-G's Reference (No 1 of 2004) [2004] EWCA Crim 1025, [2005] 4 All ER 457, [2004] 1 WLR 2111, [2004] 2 Cr App R 424, [2004] Crim LR 832, [2004] 20 LS Gaz R 34, (2004) *Times*, 30 April, 148 Sol Jo LB 568, [2004] All ER (D) 318 (Apr)	8.25
A-G's Reference (No 11 of 2006) [2006] EWCA Crim 856, [2006] 2 Cr App R (S) 705, (2006) *Times*, 28 March, [2006] All ER (D) 272 (Apr)	3.3
A-G's Reference (No 12 of 2001) [2002] EWCA Crim 353, [2002] All ER (D) 29 (Feb)	10.8
A-G's Reference (No 14 and 15 of 2006) [2006] EWCA Crim 1335, [2007] 1 All ER 718, [2007] 1 Cr App R (S) 215, [2006] Crim LR 943, (2006) *Times*, 20 June, [2006] All ER (D) 47 (Jun)	10.8
AA (Palestine) [2005] UKIAT 00104 ILU, Vol 8, no 12	11.13
Atkins v DPP [2000] EWHC 302 (Admin); [2000] 2 All ER 425, [2000] 1 WLR 1427, [2000] 2 Cr App R 248, [2000] All ER (D) 301, [2000] IP & T 639	8.10, 8.21
B v Chief Constable of Avon and Somerset [2001] 1 WLR 340, [2001] 1 All ER 562	6.8
Beckford v R [1988] AC 130, [1987] 3 All ER 425, [1987] 3 WLR 611, 85 Cr App R 378, [1988] Crim LR 116, 131 Sol Jo 1122, [1987] LS Gaz R 2192, [1987] NLJ Rep 591	9.12
Brutus v Cozens [1973] AC 854; [1972] 2 All ER 1297, [1972] 3 WLR 521, 56 Cr App R 799, 136 JP 636, 116 Sol Jo 647	7.7, 8.19, 9.6
C (Young Person: Persistent Offender), Re [1986] 2 All ER 346	5.15
Davis v Lisle [1936] 2 KB 434, [1936] 2 All ER 213, 34 LGR 253, 100 JP 280, 105 LJKB 593, 30 Cox CC 412, 80 Sol Jo 409, 155 LT 23, 52 TLR 475	7.22
DPP v Brooks [1974] AC 862, [1974] 2 All ER 840, [1974] 2 WLR 899, 59 Cr App R 185, [1974] Crim LR 364, 118 Sol Jo 420	8.21
DPP v Clarke (1991) 94 Cr App R 359, 156 JP 267, 135 Sol Jo LB 135	9.6
DPP v Whyte [1972] AC 849, [1972] 3 All ER 12, [1972] 3 WLR 410, 57 Cr App R 74, 136 JP 686, 116 Sol Jo 583	8.5
Gay News Ltd v UK (1982) 5 EHRR 123	8.28
Gough v Chief Constable of Derbyshire [2002] EWCA Civ 351, [2002] QB 1213, [2002] 2 All ER 985, [2002] 3 WLR 289, (2002) *Times*, 10 April, [2002] All ER (D) 308 (Mar)	6.8
Halford v Brookes [1991] 3 All ER 559, [1991] 1 WLR 428, (1991) *The Times*, 3 October	6.8
Handyside v UK (1976) 1 EHRR 737, [1976] ECHR 5493/72	8.28
Harman v United Kingdom (1984) 38 D & R 53	6.7

Huang v Secretary of State for the Home Department [2007] UKHL 11,
  [2007] 2 AC 167, [2007] 4 All ER 15, [2007] 2 WLR 581, [2007] 1
  FLR 2021, [2007] Fam Law 587, (2007) Times, 22 March, 151 Sol Jo
  LB 435, 24 BHRC 74, [2007] 5 LRC 320, [2007] All ER (D) 338
  (Mar) 11.17

KK (Article 1F(c)),Turkey [2004] UKIAT 00101 .... 11.13
Knuller v DPP [1973] AC 435, [1972] 3 WLR 143, [1972] 2 All ER 898, 6 Cr
  App R 633, 136 JP 728, 116 Sol Jo 545, HL 8.20

McArdle v Egan (1933) 32 LGR 85, 98 JP 103, 30 Cox CC 67, [1933] All
  ER Rep 611, (1933) 150 LT 412 .... 6.7

Nakkuda Ali v Jayarante [1951] AC 66, 94 Sol Jo 516, 66 (pt 2) TLR 214 .... 6.7

Palmer v R [1971] AC 814, [1971] 1 All ER 1077, [1971] 2 WLR 831, 55 Cr
  App R 223, 115 Sol Jo 264, 16 WIR 499, 511 .... 9.12, 9.13, 9.17, 9.18

R (on the application of Clift) v Secretary of State for the Home
  Department, R (on the application of Hindawi and another) v
  Secretary of State for the Home Department [2006] UKHL 54,
  [2007] 2 All ER 1, [2007] 2 WLR 24, (2006) Times, 21 December, 21
  BHRC 704, [2006] All ER (D) 188 (Dec) 3.36
R (on the application of McCann) v Crown Court at Manchester [2002]
  UKHL 39, [2003] 1 AC 787, [2002] 4 All ER 593, [2002] 3 WLR
  1313, [2003] LGR 57, [2003] 1 Cr App R 419, 166 JP 657, [2003]
  Crim LR 269, [2003] HLR 189, (2002) Times, 21 October, 146 Sol Jo
  LB 239, [2002] All ER (D) 246 (Oct), 13 BHRC 482 .... 6.4, 6.7, 6.8, 6.9
R (on the application of N) v M [2002] EWCA Civ 1789, [2003] 1 WLR
  562, [2003] 1 FCR 124, [2003] 1 FLR 667, [2003] Fam Law 160, 72
  BMLR 81, [2003] 08 LS Gaz R 29, (2002) Times, 12 December,
  [2002] All ER (D) 75 (Dec) 6.8
R (on the application of the DPP) v Criminal Cases Review Commission
  [2007] 1 Cr App R 30 .... 10.4
R v Adroikov [2005] EWCA Crim 470 .... 10.2
R v Aman and Watson [2006] EWCA Crim 1680 .... 3.27
R v Appelt (1994) 15 Cr App R (S) 532 .... 3.40
R v Ashes [2007] EWCA Crim 1848, [2008] 1 All ER 113, [2008] 1 Cr App
  R (S) 507, [2008] Crim LR 68, [2007] All ER (D) 374 (Jul) 3.27
R v B [2003] EWCA Crim 319, [2003] 2 Cr App R 197, 147 Sol Jo LB 237,
  [2003] All ER (D) 67 (Apr) 10.2
R v Bartley and others [2007] EWCA Crim 680 .... 3.27
R v Bentley [2001] 1 Cr App R 307, [1999] Crim LR 330, (1998) Times, July
  31 .... 10.4
R v Bowden (unreported) 10 November 1999 .... 8.10
R v Bowler (1993) 15 Cr App R (S) 78, [1993] Crim LR 799 .... 3.40
R v Boyesen [1982] AC 768, [1982] 2 All ER 161, [1982] 2 WLR 882, 75 Cr
  App R 51, 146 JP 217, [1982] Crim LR 596, 126 Sol Jo 308 .... 8.21
R v Brown [1994] 1 AC 212, [1993] 2 All ER 75, [1993] 2 WLR 556, 97 Cr
  App R 44, 157 JP 337, [1993] Crim LR 583, [1993] NLJR 399, [1993]
  3 LRC 707 .... 8.27
R v Brown and Butterworth [2006] EWCA Crim 1996, [2007] 1 Cr App R
  (S) 468, [2007] All ER (D) 29 (Feb) 3.27
R v Calder and Boyars Ltd [1969] 1 QB 151, [1968] 3 All ER 644, [1968] 3
  WLR 974, 52 Cr App R 706, 133 JP 20, 112 Sol Jo 688 .... 8.5
R v Caley-Knowles and Jones [2006] EWCA Crim 1611, [2006] 1 WLR
  3181, [2007] 1 Cr App R 197, (2006) Times, 4 October, [2006] All ER
  (D) 213 (Jun) 10.4
R v Carr-Thompson [2000] 2 Cr App R (S) 335, [2000] All ER (D) 175 .... 5.5

Table of Cases

R v Chalkley [1997] EWCA Crim 3416, [1998] QB 848, [1998] 2 All ER 155, [1998] 3 WLR 146, [1998] 2 Cr App R 79, [1999] Crim LR 214, [1998] 05 LS Gaz R 29, 142 Sol Jo LB 40	10.2
R v Chief Constable for North Wales Police Authority and others, ex p AB and CD [1997] EWHC 667 (Admin)	12.3, 12.4
R v Clarke [2007] EWCA Crim 2532, [2008] 1 Cr App R 403, (2007) *Times*, 29 October, [2007] All ER (D) 120 (Oct)	10.6
R v Clegg [1995] 1 AC 482, [1995] 1 All ER 334, [1995] 2 WLR 80, [1995] 1 Cr App R 507, [1995] Crim LR 418, [1995] 08 LS Gaz R 39, [1995] NLJR 87	9.11, 9.14
R v Cottrell and Fletcher [2007] EWCA Crim 2016, [2007] 1 WLR 3262, [2008] 1 Cr App R 107, (2007) *Times*, 5 September, [2007] All ER (D) 01 (Aug)	10.4, 10.5
R v Cousins [1982] QB 526, [1982] 2 All ER 115, [1982] 2 WLR 621, 74 Cr App R 363, 146 JP 264, [1982] Crim LR 444, 126 Sol Jo 154	9.11
R v Coutts [2005] EWCA Crim 52, [2005] 1 WLR 1605, [2005] 1 Cr App R 517, (2005) *Times*, 26 January, [2005] All ER (D) 191 (Jan) Court: CA	8.3, 8.18
R v Creasy (1994) 15 Cr App R 171	3.40
R v Davis, Ellis and others [2006] EWCA Crim 1155; [2008] UKHL 36, [2008] 3 All ER 461, [2008] 3 WLR 125, [2008] NLJR 932, (2008) *Times*, 18 June, 152 Sol Jo (no 25) 31, [2008] All ER (D) 222 (Jun)	10.2
R v Delamare [2003] EWCA Crim 424, [2003] 2 Cr App R (S) 474, [2003] All ER (D) 127 (Feb)	3.3
R v Durham Constabulary and another, ex p R [2005] UKHL 21, [2005] 2 All ER 369, [2005] 1 WLR 1184, [2006] Crim LR 87, [2005] NLJR 467, (2005) *Times*, 18 March, 149 Sol Jo LB 360, [2005] All ER (D) 278 (Mar)	4.7, 4.9
R v Forsyth [1997] 2 Cr App R 299, [1997] Crim LR 581	6.7
R v Hatton [2005] EWCA Crim 2951, [2006] 1 Cr App R 247, [2006] Crim LR 353, [2005] 44 LS Gaz R 30, (2005) *Times*, 10 November, [2005] All ER (D) 308 (Oct)	9.12
R v Howard [1965] 3 All ER 684, [1966] 1 WLR 13, 50 Cr App R 56, 130 JP 61, 109 Sol Jo 920	8.27
R v Howell [1982] 1 QB 416	7.2, 7.22
R v Kansall (No 2) [2001] EWCA Crim 260	10.4
R v Kennedy [2005] EWCA Crim 685, [2005] 1 WLR 2159, [2005] 2 Cr App R 348, (2005) *Times*, 6 April, [2005] All ER (D) 283 (Mar)	10.4
R v Lambert [2001] UKHL 37, [2002] 2 AC 545, [2001] 3 All ER 577, [2001] 3 WLR 206, [2001] 2 Cr App R 511, [2001] 31 LS Gaz R 29, (2001) *Times*, 6 July, (2001) Independent, 19 July, 145 Sol Jo LB 174, [2002] 1 LRC 584, [2001] All ER (D) 69 (Jul)	8.25
R v Lang (1975) 62 Cr App R 50, [1976] Crim LR 65	8.27
R v Lang and others [2005] EWCA Crim 2864, [2006] 2 All ER 410, [2006] 1 WLR 2509, [2006] Crim LR 174, (2005) *Times*, 10 November, 149 Sol Jo LB 1450, [2005] All ER (D) 54 (Nov)	3.15, 3.27
R v Lobell [1957] 1 QB 547, [1957] 1 All ER 734, [1957] 2 WLR 524, 41 Cr App R 100, 121 JP 282, 101 Sol Jo 268	9.12
R v Martin (Anthony) (2001) TLR, 1 November	9.11, 9.14
R v Metropolitan Stipendiary Magistrate, ex p Choudhury [1991] 1 QB 429, [1991] 1 All ER 306, [1990] 3 WLR 986, 91 Cr App R 393, [1990] Crim LR 711, [1990] NLJR 702	9.19
R v Mijura [2007] EWCA Crim 1249	3.24
R v Mullen [1999] EWCA Crim 278, [2000] QB 520, [1999] 3 WLR 777, [1999] 2 Cr App R 143, [1999] Crim LR 561, (1999) *Times*, 15 February, [1999] All ER (D) 108	10.2
R v O'Brien and others [2006] EWCA Crim 1741, [2006] 4 All ER 1012, [2007] 1 WLR 833, [2007] 1 Cr App R (S) 442, [2006] All ER (D) 200 (Jul)	3.27

R v O'Hare [2006] EWCA Crim 471, [2006] Crim LR 950, [2006] All ER
  (D) 155 (Mar) 10.2
R v Odam [2008] EWCA Crim 1087 .... 5.7, 5.22
R v Orwino [1995] Crim LR 743, [1996] 2 Cr App R 128 .... 9.12
R v Perrin [2002] EWCA Crim 747, [2002] All ER (D) 359 (Mar) 8.5, 8.28
R v Porter [2006] EWCA Crim 560, [2007] 2 All ER 625, [2006] 1 WLR
  2633, [2006] 2 Cr App R 359, (2006) *Times*, 21 June, 150 Sol Jo LB
  396, [2006] All ER (D) 236 (Mar) 8.21
R v Powell (Shane) [1990] 13 Cr App R (S) 202 .... 5.30
R v Rajcoomar [1999] EWCA Crim 447 .... 10.2
R v Ramzan and others [2006] EWCA Crim 1974, [2007] 1 Cr App R 150,
  [2006] All ER (D) 318 (Jul) 10.4
R v Russell [2006] EWCA Crim 470, [2006] All ER (D) 151 (Mar) 10.2
R v Scarlett [1993] 4 All ER 629, 98 Cr App R 290, [1994] Crim LR 288,
  [1993] NLJR 1101 .... 9.12
R v Scarth [2006] Crim LR 775, [2006] EWCA Crim 856, [2006] 2 Cr App R
  (S) 705, (2006) *Times*, 28 March, [2006] All ER (D) 272 (Apr) 3.3
R v Seed and Stark [2007] EWCA Crim 254, [2007] 2 Cr App R (S) 436,
  [2007] Crim LR 501, (2007) *Times*, 16 February, [2007] All ER (D)
  161 (Feb) 3.3
R v Smith [2002] EWCA Crim 683, [2003] 1 Cr App R 212, (2002) *Times*, 23
  April, [2002] All ER (D) 71 (Mar) 8.10
R v Szczerba [2002] Cr App R (S) 86, (2002) *Times*, 10 April, [2002] All ER
  (D) 68 (Feb) 3.25
R v T [1999] 2 Cr App R (S) 304 .... 5.5
R v Taylor [2008] EWCA Crim 465 .... 3.30
R v Thomas [1999] EWCA Crim 1266 .... 10.2
R v Waddon (unreported) 6 April 2000 .... 8.5, 8.10
R v Williams (1993) 15 Cr App R (S) 330, [1993] Crim LR 979 .... 3.40
R v Williams (Gladstone) (1983) 78 Cr App R 71 .... 9.12, 9.13
R v Wolverhampton Coroner, ex parte McCurbin [1990] 1 WLR 719, [1990]
  2 All ER 759, 155 JP 33 .... 6.8
R v Y [2008] EWCA Crim 10, [2008] 2 All ER 484, [2008] 1 Cr App R 411,
  (2008) *Times*, 11 March, [2008] All ER (D) 199 (Jan) 10.6
Randall v R [2002] UKPC 19, [2002] 1 WLR 2237, [2002] 2 Cr App R 267,
  (2002) *Times*, 24 April, [2002] 5 LRC 678, [2002] All ER (D) 88 (Apr) .. 10.2

S v Secretary of State for the Home Department [2006] EWCA Civ 1157,
  (2006) *Times*, 9 October, [2006] All ER (D) 30 (Aug) 11.2, 11.5
Salabiaku v France (1988) 13 EHRR 379, ECHR 8.25
Secretary of State for Justice v Walker and James [2008] EWCA Civ 30,
  [2008] 3 All ER 104, [2008] NLJR 263, (2008) *Times*, 6 February,
  [2008] All ER (D) 15 (Feb) 3.3
Sheldrake v DPP, Attorney General's Reference (No 4 of 2002) [2004]
  UKHL 43, [2005] 1 AC 264, [2005] 1 All ER 237, [2004] 3 WLR 976,
  [2005] RTR 13, [2005] 1 Cr App R 450, 168 JP 669, [2004] 43 LS Gaz
  R 33, (2004) *Times*, 15 October, 148 Sol Jo LB 1216, 17 BHRC 339,
  [2005] 3 LRC 463, [2004] All ER (D) 169 (Oct) 8.25
SW & C v United Kingdom (1995) 21 EHRR 247 .... 6.7

T v Secretary of State for the Home Department [1996] AC 742, [1996] 2
  WLR 766, [1996] 2 All ER 865, [1996] Imm AR 443, 140 Sol Jo LB
  136, HL 11.13

Van der Mussele v Belgium (1983) 6 EHRR 163, [1983] ECHR 8919/80 .. 5.23

Warner v Commissioner of Police for the Metropolis [1969] AC 256 ..... 8.21
Welch v United Kingdom (Application No 17440/90) (1995) 20 EHRR 247,
  ECHR 6.7

Whitehouse v Lemon [1979] AC 617, [1979] 1 All ER 898, [1979] 2 WLR
    281, 68 Cr App R 381, 143 JP 315, [1979] Crim LR 311, 123 Sol Jo
    163 .... 9.19
Wingrove v UK (1996) 24 EHRR 1, 1 BHRC 5098.28 .... 8.28

X v Federal Republic of Germany App No 8410/78 (1980) D & R 216 ..... 5.23

TABLE OF STATUTES

References are to paragraph numbers.

Access to Justice Act 1999	2.19, 2.20
Pt 1	2.18
s 1(2)(b)	2.16
s 18A	2.20
Sch 3	2.18, 2.17
Sch 3, para 7	2.19
Adoption Act 1976	
s 39	8.37
Anti-social Behaviour Act 2003	7.2, 7.3, 7.4
Pt 1	7.4
Pt 1A	7.1, 7.7, 7.9, 7.13, 7.15
s 11A	7.7
s 11A(2)	7.7
s 11A(4)	7.8
s 11A(5)	7.8
s 11A(7)	7.9, 7.12
s 11B	7.7, 7.10
s 11B(3)	7.8
s 11B(8)	7.9
s 11C	7.7
s 11C(2)	7.12
s 11D	7.7
s 11D(1)	7.12
s 11D(2)	7.12
s 11D(5)	7.12
s 11E	7.7
s 11F	7.7, 7.14
s 11F(5)	7.14
s 11G	7.7
s 11H	7.7
s 11I	7.7
s 11J	7.7
s 11K	7.7, 7.11
s 13	7.3
Armed Forces Act 2006	3.24
Asylum and Immigration (Treatment of Claimants, etc) Act 2004	
s 36	11.7, 11.19
s 36(2)	11.19
Bail Act 1976	2.7
s 3	2.7
s 3(6ZAA)	2.7
s 3(6ZAB)	2.7
s 3AA	2.7, 2.8
s 3AB	2.7, 2.9
s 7	2.11
s 9A	2.10
s 9A(2)	2.10
Sch 1, Pt 1	2.11

Bail Act 1976—*continued*	
Sch 1, Pt 1A	2.11
Sch 1, Pt 1A, para 3	2.11
Sch 1, Pt 1A, para 4	2.11
Sch 1, Pt 1A, para 5	2.11
Sch 1, Pt 1A, para 6	2.11
Sch 1, Pt 1A, para 7	2.11
Sch 1, Pt 1A, para 8	2.11
Sch 1, Pt 1A, para 9	2.11
Sch 1, Pt 1A, paras 6A–6C	2.11
British Nationality Act 1981	11.15
s 1	11.9
Children Act 1989	5.32
Children and Young Persons Act 1933	
s 12A	12.9
s 12A(4)	12.9
s 12B	12.9, 12.10
s 12C	12.9
s 12C(1)	12.10
s 12C(2)	12.10
s 12D	12.9
s 44	4.4, 4.5, 7.17
Civil Evidence Act 1995	6.9
Courts Act 2003	
Sch 5	12.13
Crime (Sentences) Act 1997	
s 28(5)	3.25
s 32	3.44, 3.45
s 32(4)	3.45
Crime and Disorder Act 1998	2.22, 4.3, 4.6, 4.7, 7.2, 7.16, 12.5
s 1	7.17, 7.18
s 1(1)	7.19
s 1(2)	7.19
s 1AA	7.4, 7.20
s 1AA(2)	7.20
s 1B	7.18
s 1C	7.18
s 1J	7.18
s 1J(3)	7.18
s 1J(6)	7.18
s 1K	7.19
s 1K(2)	7.19
s 8	2.23
s 37	4.4, 4.5
s 65(2)(b)	4.8
s 65(3)(b)	4.8
s 65(6)	4.8
ss 66A–66H	4.9

Crime and Disorder Act 1998—continued		Criminal Justice Act 2003—continued	
s 66A(2)	4.9	s 148(2)	3.5, 5.10
s 66A(7)	4.10	s 148(3)	3.5
s 66B	4.10	s 148(5)	3.5
s 66C	4.11	s 150	5.5
s 66C(4)	4.11	s 150A	3.6
s 66D	4.12	s 151(2)	3.6
s 66E	4.14	s 152(2)	3.4, 5.38
s 66G	4.13	s 152(3)	3.4
s 66G(2)	4.13	s 153(2)	3.16
s 66H	4.10	s 153(3)(b)	5.10
Criminal Appeal Act 1968	10.4, 10.5	s 156	5.10
s 2	10.2	s 156(2)	5.10
s 16C	10.4, 10.5	s 156(2)(A)	5.10
s 16C(3)	10.5	s 156(4)	5.10
Criminal Damage Act 1971	7.2	s 156(5)	5.10
Criminal Defence Service Act 2006	2.16, 2.17	s 158(1)	3.4
Criminal Justice (Terrorism and		s 158(1)(A)	3.4
Conspiracy) Act 2008	1.4	s 158(1)(b)	3.4
Criminal Justice Act 1967		s 177	5.2, 5.4, 5.22
s 3	9.11	s 181	3.10
s 3(2)	9.11	s 181(5)	3.10
Criminal Justice Act 1987		s 181(7)	3.10
s 9	10.9	s 181(7A)	3.11
Criminal Justice Act 1988		s 183	3.12
s 36	10.8	s 183(4)	3.12
s 36(3A)	10.8	s 199	5.22
s 36(3B)	10.8	s 199(2)	3.8
s 133A	12.15	s 200(3)	5.7
s 133A(6)	12.16	s 202	5.24
s 133B	12.16	s 218(5)	7.12
s 160	8.6, 8.21	s 224	3.15
Criminal Justice Act 1991	3.1, 3.4, 3.34, 3.37	s 225	3.15, 3.17, 3.21, 3.40
s 33	3.35	ss 225–236	3.15
s 33(1A)	3.35	s 225(2)	3.15, 3.21
s 33(1C)	3.35	s 225(2A)	3.19
s 33(1D)	3.35	s 225(3)	3.17
s 33(2)	3.25	s 225(3A)	3.17, 3.18
s 35(1)	3.25	s 225(3B)	3.17
s 37	3.35	s 225(3C)	3.17, 3.19
s 37ZA	3.35	s 225A(6)(b)	3.42
s 46(1)	3.36	s 225A(6)(c)	3.42
s 46ZA	3.37	s 226	3.15, 3.20
s 50(2)	3.36	s 226(1)	3.20
Criminal Justice Act 2003	2.2, 2.4, 2.15, 3.1,	s 226(1)(b)	3.4
	3.2, 3.3, 3.4, 3.8, 3.18, 3.31, 3.34,	s 226(2)	3.20
	3.36, 3.37, 3.40, 4.3, 4.4, 4.7, 4.9,	s 226(3)	3.20
	5.2, 5.3, 5.22, 6.5, 6.9, 7.4, 7.17,	s 227	3.16, 3.21, 3.33
	10.6	s 227(1)(c)	3.21
s 58	10.6	s 227(2)	3.22
s 61	10.6, 10.7	s 227(2A)	3.22
s 61(5)	10.7	s 227(2B)	3.22
s 114	6.8	s 227(2C)	3.16, 3.22
s 140	3.14	s 227(4)	3.16
s 142	4.4	s 228	3.15, 3.16, 3.21, 3.33
s 142A	4.5, 5.8	s 228(1)(b)(i)	3.4
s 142A(3)	4.5	s 228)	3.23
s 142A(4)	4.5	s 229	3.24
s 145	9.5, 9.7	s 229(1)	3.24
s 146	9.4	s 229(2)(aa)	3.24
s 147	5.2	s 229(2)(c)	3.24
s 147(2)	5.2	s 229(2A)	3.24
s 148	3.6, 5.5	s 229(3)	3.24
s 148(1)	3.5	s 229(4)	3.24

Criminal Justice Act 2003—*continued*		Criminal Justice Act 2003—*continued*	
s 231	3.18	s 325A(3)	12.6
s 232	3.18	s 325A(4)	12.6
s 232(1)	3.18	s 325A(5)	12.7
s 240	3.29	s 327	12.6
s 240(3)	3.29	s 327A	12.6, 12.7
s 240(4)	3.29	s 327A(6)	12.7
s 240(5)	3.29	s 327A(7)	12.7
s 240(6)	3.29	s 327B	12.6
s 240A	3.29, 3.30	s 327B(4)	12.6
s 240A(2)	3.29	s 327B(5)	12.6
s 240A(4)	3.29	s 327B(6)	12.6
s 240A(5)	3.29	Sch 3	2.1, 2.2, 2.4
s 240A(12)	3.29	Sch 3, para 8(2)(a)	2.2
s 244	3.36	Sch 3, para 13	2.5
s 244(3)	3.31	Sch 3, para 22	2.4
s 246	3.31, 3.40	Sch 3, para 22A	2.4
s 246(2)	3.32	Sch 3, para 23	2.2
s 247	3.33	Sch 8	3.8, 5.38
s 247(2)	3.33	Sch 8, para 9	3.8
s 250	3.35	Sch 8, para 9(3A)	3.8
s 254	3.33, 3.38	Sch 15	3.18, 3.35
s 254(3)	3.38, 3.40	Sch 15, Pt 1	3.15, 6.5
s 254(4)	3.40	Sch 15, Pt 2	3.15
s 254(5)	3.40	Sch 15A	3.17, 3.18, 3.22
s 254(6)	3.38	Sch 16	3.24
s 255	3.38	Sch 17	3.24
s 255(5)	3.38	Sch 20	3.36
s 255A	3.40	Sch 21	3.3
s 255A(5)	3.40	Sch 24	5.2
s 255A(6)(a)	3.41	Sch 34A	12.6
s 255A(13)	3.40	Sch 34A, paras 1–6	12.6
s 255A(a)	3.40	Criminal Justice and Courts Act 2000,	
s 255A(b)	3.40	s 50	5.27
s 255A(c)	3.40	Criminal Justice and Immigration Act	
s 255B	3.40, 3.41	2008	1.1, 1.2, 1.6, 1.7, 2.1, 2.15, 2.22,
s 255B(1)	3.41		3.1, 3.3, 3.14, 3.16, 3.27, 3.34, 3.36,
s 255B(2)	3.41		3.39, 3.44, 4.1, 4.2, 4.3, 4.5, 4.7,
s 255B(3)	3.41		4.16, 4.22, 5.1, 5.3, 5.4, 5.5, 5.7,
s 255B(4)	3.41		5.8, 5.9, 5.12, 5.15, 5.35, 5.38, 6.1,
s 255B(6)	3.41		6.4, 6.8, 6.10, 6.11, 6.18, 7.5, 7.20,
s 255C	3.40, 3.41, 3.42		7.24, 8.1, 8.7, 8.27, 8.28, 8.38, 9.1,
s 255C(1)	3.42		9.3, 9.4, 9.15, 9.21, 10.2, 10.3, 10.4,
s 255C(3)	3.42		10.5, 11.7, 11.10, 11.17, 12.1, 12.12
s 255C(4)	3.42	Pt 3	10.1
s 255C(5)	3.42	Pt 6	12.13
s 255C(6)	3.42	Pt 7	6.3
s 255D	3.40, 3.43	Pt 9	12.11
s 256	3.38	Pt 10	11.1
s 259	3.33, 3.36, 3.37	s 1	5.8, 5.16
s 259A	3.37	s 1(1)	5.1
s 260	3.36, 3.37	s 1(1)–(4)	5.4, 5.9
S 261	3.37	s 1(3)(a)	5.15
s 262	3.36, 3.37	s 1(3)(b)	5.15
s 264A	3.12	s 1(4)	5.15
s 265	3.13	s 1(4)(b)	5.10
s 272	10.8	s 1(6)	5.5
s 300	3.9	s 1(c)	5.9
s 325	12.4, 12.6	s 4	5.30
s 325(1)	12.6	s 5	5.30
s 325(2)	12.4	s 6	5.21, 5.24, 5.25
s 325(4)	12.4	s 6(2)	6.7
s 325(8)	12.4	s 8(4)	5.8
s 325A(2)	12.6	s 9	4.5, 4.9, 5.8

Criminal Justice and Immigration Act 2008—continued

s 10	3.5
s 11	3.5, 3.6
s 11(4)	3.7
s 11(5)	3.7
s 12	3.4
s 13	3.15, 3.17, 3.26
s 13(2)	3.18
s 14	3.20
s 15(2)	3.21
s 16	3.23
s 16(3)	3.23
s 17	3.24
s 18(1)	3.18
s 18(2)	3.18
s 20	3.10, 3.13
s 20(2)	3.10, 3.11
s 20(3)	3.12
s 20(4)	3.13
s 21	3.28, 3.29
s 23	3.29
s 24	3.28, 3.32
s 25	3.28, 3.33
s 26	1.5, 3.28, 3.35
s 26(4)	3.35
s 26(6)	3.35
s 27	3.36
s 27(1)	3.36
s 28	10.9
s 29	3.28, 3.40
s 31	3.44, 3.45
s 31(4)	3.45
s 33	3.37
s 34	3.37
s 35(2)	4.17
s 35(3)	4.18
s 36	4.20
s 36(2)	4.19
s 36(6)	4.21
s 38	3.8
s 39	4.21
s 40	3.9
s 42	10.4, 10.5
s 44	10.6, 10.7
s 46	10.8
s 48	4.6
s 51	2.6, 2.7
s 52	2.6, 2.10
s 53	1.3, 2.2, 2.3, 2.4
s 54	2.12, 2.13, 12.11
s 54(5)	2.13
s 54(7)	2.14
s 55	2.21, 2.22, 2.23
s 55(4)	2.23
s 56	2.18
ss 56–58	2.16
s 56(10)	2.18
s 57	2.19
s 57(2)	2.19
s 57(3)	2.19
s 58	2.20
s 60	2.15
s 61	12.15

Criminal Justice and Immigration Act 2008—continued

s 62	1.4
s 63	8.1, 8.2, 8.3, 8.10, 8.11, 8.12, 8.13, 8.14, 8.15, 8.17, 8.18, 8.22, 8.25, 8.27, 8.28, 8.30
s 63(1)	8.9
s 63(2)	8.9
s 63(3)	8.11
s 63(4)	8.13, 8.14
s 63(5)	8.14
s 63(6)	8.11, 8.16, 8.19, 8.22
s 63(7)	8.11, 8.16, 8.18
s 63(7)(a)	8.2, 8.27
s 63(7)(b)	8.2, 8.12, 8.27
s 63(7)(c)	8.27
s 63(8)	8.10
s 63(8)(b)	8.13
s 63(9)	8.16
s 64	8.9, 8.22, 8.24, 8.25
s 64(2)	8.22
s 64(3)	8.23
s 64(4)	8.23
s 64(5)(a)	8.22
s 64(6)	8.24
s 64(7)	8.22, 8.24
s 65	8.9, 8.10, 8.25, 8.26
s 66	8.25, 8.27
s 66(3)	8.27
s 67(2)(a)	8.2
s 67(2)(b)	8.2
s 67(3)(b)	8.2
s 68	8.29
s 69	1.4, 8.31
s 70	1.4
s 71	8.32
s 73	8.35
s 74	9.2
s 75	9.20
s 76	9.10, 9.11, 9.15, 9.16
s 76(1)	9.16
s 76(2)	9.16
s 76(3)	9.17
s 76(4)	9.10, 9.16
s 76(5)	9.10, 9.16
s 76(7)	9.17
s 77	1.3, 9.23
s 77(1)	9.23
s 78	9.24
s 79	1.4, 9.19
s 80	12.13, 12.14
s 81	12.13
s 84	12.13, 12.14
s 85	12.13
s 91	12.13, 12.14
s 98	6.3
s 98(2)	6.3, 6.5
s 98(3)	6.5
s 98(4)	6.5
s 99	6.5
s 99(2)(b)	6.5
s 99(2)(c)	6.5
s 99(3)	6.5
s 99(4)	6.5

Criminal Justice and Immigration Act
2008—continued

s 99(5)	6.5
s 100(1)	6.6, 6.7
s 100(2)	6.6
s 100(3)	6.6
s 100(4)	6.6
s 100(5)	6.7
s 101	6.13, 6.16
s 101(3)	6.8
s 101(4)	6.8, 6.13
s 102	6.3, 6.11, 6.16
s 102(5)	6.5
s 102)	6.15
s 103	6.6
s 103(1)(b)	6.17
s 103(3)	6.17
s 103(5)	6.17
s 103(7)	6.17
s 104	6.18
s 104(5)	6.18
s 104(6)	6.18
s 106)	6.19
s 107	6.20
s 108	6.20
s 108(5)	6.20
s 109	6.20
s 110	6.20
s 111	6.20
s 112	6.20
s 113	6.21
s 113(2)	6.21
s 117	6.5
s 118	7.1
s 119	7.1, 7.21, 7.24, 7.25, 7.26, 7.27, 7.30, 7.31
s 119(1)	7.21, 7.24
s 119(4)	7.21, 7.27
s 120	7.27, 7.30, 7.31
s 120(3)	7.30
s 120(4)	7.30
s 120(5)	7.30
s 121	7.31
s 121(2)	7.31
s 121(5)	7.31
s 121(d)	7.24
s 121(e)	7.24
s 121(f)	7.24
s 121(g)	7.24
s 124	7.1, 7.16
s 124(1)	7.20
s 125	7.1
s 126	12.11
s 128	1.3, 12.11
s 130	11.8, 11.20, 11.22
s 130(2)(a)	11.8
s 130(2)(b)	11.8
s 130(3)	11.8, 11.14
s 130(4)	11.14, 11.15
s 130(5)	11.15
s 130(5)(a)	11.13, 11.15
s 130(5)(b)	11.15
s 131	11.7, 11.9, 11.10, 11.16
s 131(2)	11.10, 11.16

Criminal Justice and Immigration Act
2008—continued

s 131(2)(b)	11.9
s 131(3)	11.12, 11.16
s 131(3)(b)	11.12
s 131(4)	11.13
s 131(5)	11.11, 11.12
s 131(6)	11.12
s 132	11.14
s 132(1)	11.18
s 132(2)	11.9
s 132(2)(a)	11.14, 11.18
s 132(2)(b)	11.18
s 132(2)(c)	11.18
s 132(3)	11.9, 11.18
s 132(4)	11.9
s 132(4)(a)	11.18
s 132(4)(b)	11.7, 11.18
s 133	11.19
s 133(2)	11.19
s 133(2)(c)	11.19
s 133(4)	11.19
s 133(5)	11.14, 11.20
s 133(6)	11.20
s 133(7)	11.20
s 133(8)	11.20
s 134	11.21, 11.22
s 134(1)	11.21
s 134(2)	11.21
s 134(2)(a)	11.21
s 134(2)(b)	11.21
s 134(2)(c)	11.21
s 134(2)(d)	11.21
s 134(2)(e)	11.21
s 134(2)(f)	11.21
s 134(2)(g)	11.21
s 134(3)(a)	11.21
s 134(3)(b)	11.21
s 134(3)(c)	11.21
s 134(4)	11.14, 11.21
s 134(5)	11.21
s 134(6)	11.21
s 134(6)(a)	11.21
s 134(6)(b)	11.21
s 135	11.7, 11.21
s 135(1)(a)	11.21
s 135(1)(b)	11.21
s 135(1)(c)	11.21
s 135(2)	11.21
s 135(3)	11.21
s 135(6)	11.21
s 136	11.22
s 136(1)(a)	11.22
s 136(1)(b)	11.22
s 136(1)(c)	11.22
s 136(1)(d)	11.22
s 136(2)	11.22
s 136(3)	11.22
s 137(4)	11.14
s 137(6)	11.12
s 137(7)	11.21
s 138	1.3
s 139	1.3
s 140	12.2, 12.5, 12.6

Criminal Justice and Immigration Act
2008—continued

s 141	12.8
s 143	12.9
s 152	1.1
s 153	1.3
s 153(1)	2.3, 2.4
s 153(2)	1.4, 8.31, 8.32
Sch 1	5.6, 5.8, 5.16, 5.24, 5.26, 5.30, 5.32, 5.36, 5.37
Sch 1, para 2	5.9
Sch 1, para 2(2)	5.37
Sch 1, para 3	5.9, 5.16
Sch 1, para 3(1)	5.6
Sch 1, para 3(5)	5.16
Sch 1, para 4	5.9, 5.17
Sch 1, para 4(2)	5.17
Sch 1, para 4(3)	5.17
Sch 1, para 4(4)	5.17
Sch 1, para 4(5)	5.16
Sch 1, para 6	5.9, 5.19
Sch 1, para 6(2)	5.20
Sch 1, para 6(4)	5.19
Sch 1, para 6(4)(a)	5.19
Sch 1, para 7	5.9, 5.11, 5.19
Sch 1, para 7(3)	5.19
Sch 1, para 7(4)(a)	5.19
Sch 1, para 8	5.9, 5.19
Sch 1, para 8(2)	5.9
Sch 1, para 9	5.9, 5.16, 5.21
Sch 1, para 10	5.9, 5.22, 5.24
Sch 1, para 10(3)	5.24
Sch 1, para 10(7)	5.22
Sch 1, para 11	5.9, 5.24
Sch 1, para 11(2)	5.24
Sch 1, para 12	5.9, 5.25
Sch 1, para 13	5.9, 5.26
Sch 1, para 13(1)	5.26
Sch 1, para 13(2)	5.26
Sch 1, para 14	5.9, 5.16, 5.27
Sch 1, para 14(2)	5.27
Sch 1, para 14(3)	5.28
Sch 1, para 15	5.29
Sch 1, para 15(3)(a)	5.29
Sch 1, para 15(4)	5.29
Sch 1, para 16	5.9, 5.30
Sch 1, para 16(4)	5.30
Sch 1, para 16(5)	5.30
Sch 1, para 17	5.9, 5.30, 5.31
Sch 1, para 17(2)	5.31
Sch 1, para 17(3)	5.30, 5.31
Sch 1, para 18	5.17
Sch 1, para 18(1)	5.17
Sch 1, para 18(2)	5.32
Sch 1, para 18(5)	5.31, 5.32
Sch 1, para 18(7)	5.32
Sch 1, para 19	5.31, 5.32
Sch 1, para 19(1)	5.31
Sch 1, para 19(2)	5.31
Sch 1, para 20	5.9, 5.33
Sch 1, para 20(1)	5.33
Sch 1, para 20(2)	5.33
Sch 1, para 20(5)	5.33
Sch 1, para 21	5.33, 5.34

Criminal Justice and Immigration Act
2008—continued

Sch 1, para 22	5.9, 5.34
Sch 1, para 22(5)	5.34
Sch 1, para 23	5.9, 5.34
Sch 1, para 23(2)(b)	5.34
Sch 1, para 24	5.9, 5.35
Sch 1, para 24(5)	5.35
Sch 1, para 25	5.9, 5.36
Sch 1, para 26	5.9, 5.16, 5.37
Sch 1, para 26(3)	5.37
Sch 1, para 26(4)(b)	5.37
Sch 1, para 26(6)	5.37
Sch 1, para 28	5.10, 5.12
Sch 1, para 29	5.12
Sch 1, para 30	5.7
Sch 1, para 30(4)	5.14
Sch 1, para 31(2)	5.14
Sch 1, para 31(6)(b)	5.20
Sch 1, para 32	5.6, 5.7
Sch 1, para 34	5.13
Sch 1, para 36	5.41
Sch 1, para 36(1)	5.11
Sch 1, paras 6–8	5.16
Sch 1, Pt 3	5.12
Sch 1, Pt 4	5.10, 5.13
Sch 2	5.1, 5.7, 5.38
Sch 2, para 2(2)	5.38
Sch 2, para 3	5.7, 5.38
Sch 2, para 4(2)	5.38
Sch 2, para 4(3)	5.38
Sch 2, para 5(2)	5.38
Sch 2, para 6	5.38
Sch 2, para 7	5.38
Sch 2, para 8	5.38
Sch 2, para 9	5.38
Sch 2, para 18(3)	5.41
Sch 2, para 18(4)	5.41
Sch 2, para 18(5)	5.41
Sch 2, para 18(8)	5.41
Sch 2, para 18(9)	5.41
Sch 2, Pt 3	5.39
Sch 2, Pt 4	5.39
Sch 2, Pt 5	5.41
Sch 3, para 7	2.4, 2.5
Sch 3, para 8	2.4
Sch 4, para 77	5.10
Sch 5	3.18
Sch 6	3.29
Sch 7	4.21
Sch 7, para 5	4.21
Sch 8	10.9
Sch 8, para 2	10.9
Sch 8, para 6	10.9
Sch 8, para 7	10.9
Sch 8, para 10	10.9
Sch 8, para 11	10.9
Sch 8, para 12	10.9
Sch 8, para 13	10.9
Sch 9	4.1, 4.6, 4.9
Sch 9, para 2	4.8
Sch 9, para 2(2)(c)	4.8
Sch 11	2.6, 2.7
Sch 11, para 2	2.7

Criminal Justice and Immigration Act 2008—*continued*	
Sch 12	2.6, 2.10
Sch 12, para 5	2.11
Sch 13	2.2, 2.3
Sch 13, para 7	2.4
Sch 13, para 8	2.5
Sch 13, para 9	2.2
Sch 13, paras 2–5	2.2
Sch 14	8.29
Sch 14, para 1(2)	8.30
Sch 14, para 1(3)	8.30
Sch 14, para 1(4)	8.30
Sch 14, para 1(5)	8.30
Sch 14, para 6	8.29
Sch 15	8.35, 8.37
Sch 17	9.20, 9.22
Sch 17, para 2	9.21
Sch 17, para 3	9.21, 9.22
Sch 17, para 5	9.20
Sch 19	12.14
Sch 19, para 2	12.14
Sch 20	7.1, 7.7
Sch 22	12.11
Sch 23	12.11
Sch 24	12.2, 12.6
Sch 26, para 77	2.3
Sch 28	2.4
Sch 28, Pt 4	2.3, 2.4, 2.5
Sch16	9.2
Criminal Justice and Police Act 2001	7.4
Criminal Justice and Public Order Act 1994	
s 168	8.5
Criminal Procedure and Investigations Act 1996	2.1, 2.15
s 6A	2.15
s 6A(1)	2.15
s 35	10.9
Customs and Excise Management Act 1979	8.6
Data Protection Act 1998	9.24
s 55	9.23
s 55(2)	9.24
s 60	9.23
Domestic Violence Crime and Victims Act 2004	6.2
Environmental Protection Act 1990	7.2
Firearms Act 1968	5.5, 5.26
s 51A(2)	5.5
Housing Act 1996	
s 152	7.3
s 153A	7.3
s 153B	7.3
s 153C	7.3
s 153D	7.3
s 191	7.11
s 196	7.11

Human Rights Act 1998	5.28, 7.22
s 4	3.36
s 6	7.22, 11.8
Immigration Act 1971	11.19
s 1(1)	11.14, 11.15
s 2	11.14, 11.15
s 3(1)(c)(iii)	11.6
s 5(4)	11.14
s 24(1)	11.20
Sch 2, para 21	11.19
Sch 3, para 5	11.19
Immigration and Asylum Act 1999	11.21
Pt VI	11.21
s 4	11.21
s 10	3.36
s 91(1)(b)	11.21
s 96	11.21
s 100	11.21
s 101	11.21
s 104	11.21
s 108	11.21
s 111	11.21
s 113	11.21
s 119(1)(b)	11.21
Immigration, Asylum and Nationality Act 2006	
s 54	11.13
Interpretation Act 1978	5.17
s 1	4.12
s 5	9.3
Sch 1	9.3
Magistrates' Courts Act 1980	
s 11	2.13
ss 11–16	2.12
s 11(1)	2.13
s 11(2)	2.12, 2.13
s 11(2A)	2.13
s 11(3)	2.12, 2.13
s 11(3A)	2.13
s 11(4)	2.12, 2.13
s 13(5)	2.14
s 81	4.21
Sch 2	2.10
Mental Health Act 1983	
s 54	5.33
Misuse of Drugs Act 1971	
s 2	5.34
Nationality, Immigration and Asylum Act 2002	
Pt 4	11.10
s 69	11.19
s 72	11.10, 11.11, 11.12
s 72(2)	11.10
s 72(2)(a)	11.10
s 72(2)(b)	11.10
s 72(3)	11.10
s 72(3)(a)–(c)	11.10
s 72(4)(a)	11.12
s 72(6)	11.11, 11.12

Nationality, Immigration and Asylum Act 2002—*continued*
s 72(7) 11.11
s 72(8) 11.11
s 72(11)(b)(i) 11.12
Noise Act 1996 7.2
Nuclear Material (Offences) Act 1983 9.20, 9.21
s 1 9.22
s 1(1)(a) 9.21
s 1(1)(b) 9.21
s 1(1A) 9.22
s 1A 9.21
s 1B 9.22
s 1C 9.22
s 2 9.22
s 2(3) 9.22
s 2(4) 9.22
s 2(7) 9.22
s 3A 9.20

Obscene Publications Acts 1959 8.5, 8.10, 8.11, 8.15, 8.17
Obscene Publications Acts 1964 8.5

Police Act 1996 12.11
Police and Criminal Evidence Act 1984
s 76 4.10
s 76A 4.10
s 78 4.10
Police Reform Act 2002 12.11
Postal Services Act 2000
s 85 8.6
Powers of Criminal Courts (Sentencing) Act 2000 5.37
Pt III 4.16
s 3 2.4
s 3(2) 2.5
s 3(2)(b) 2.5
s 3(4) 2.5
s 5 2.5
s 16 4.16
s 16(2) 4.16
s 16(4) 4.18
s 17(1) 4.16, 4.17
s 17(1)(c) 4.17
s 17(1A) 4.16, 4.18
s 17(2) 4.16, 4.18
s 17(2A) 4.18
s 17(2B) 4.18
s 17(2C) 4.18
s 17(2D) 4.18
s 26 4.19
s 27 4.19
s 27A 4.19
s 27A(3) 4.19
s 27B 4.20
s 35 4.16
s 36 4.16
s 37 4.16
s 40A 5.2
s 41 5.2
s 46 5.2

Powers of Criminal Courts (Sentencing) Act 2000—*continued*
s 51 5.2
s 52 5.2
s 60 5.25
s 63 5.2, 5.21
s 69 5.2
s 73 5.9
s 73(1) 5.14
s 82(3) 3.25, 3.30
s 82A 3.19, 3.25
s 82A(2) 3.27
s 82A(3) 3.25, 3.27
s 82A(3A) 3.27
s 82A(3B) 3.27
s 82A(3C) 3.27
s 82A(4) 3.27
s 84A(4) 3.25
s 87 3.25
s 89 4.21
s 100(2) 5.15
s 110(2) 5.5
s 111(2) 5.5
s 150(1A) 3.7
s 150(2) 3.7
s 151(2) 3.7
s 161 3.5, 5.2
s 162 3.4
s 163 5.2
s 221(2) 5.25
Sch 1, para 1(2) 4.19
Sch 1, Pt 1ZA 4.20
Sch 1, Pt 1ZA, para 9ZB(2) 4.20
Sch 1, Pt 1ZA, para 9ZB(4) 4.20
Sch 2 5.30
Sch 2, para 8 5.29
Sch 6 5.33
Sch 6, para 5 5.31
Prevention of Terrorism Act 2005 11.19
s 1(4) 11.19
s 41 6.8
Prosecution of Offences Act 1985
s 7A 2.21, 2.22, 2.23
s 7A(2) 2.22, 2.23
s 7A(5) 2.23
s 7A(6) 2.23
Protection from Harassment Act 1997 9.4
s 5 2.23
Protection of Children Act 1978 8.1, 8.7, 8.10, 8.31
s 1 8.6
s 1B 8.31
s 1B(1)(b) 8.31
s 7(4) 8.31
s 7(4A) 8.31
s 7(7) 8.31
Public Order Act 1986 7.2, 7.24, 8.1, 8.19, 9.1, 9.3, 9.4
Pt 3A 9.2
s 4 9.4, 9.6
s 5 7.22, 9.4, 9.6
s 29AB 9.3, 9.7
s 29B 9.2, 9.3, 9.5, 9.6, 9.7, 9.8, 9.9
s 29C 9.3

Table of Statutes

Public Order Act 1986—*continued*	
s 29E	9.3
s 29F	9.3
s 29G	9.3
s 29J	9.9
s 29JA	9.3, 9.9
s 29L(1)	9.3
Racial and Religious Hatred Act 2006	9.4
Rehabilitation of Offenders Act 1974	4.7, 4.16
Serious Crime Act 2007	6.4, 7.4, 9.20
s 2	6.2
Sch 1	6.2, 7.4
Sexual Offences Act 2003	8.1, 8.35, 8.37, 12.5, 12.6
s 15	8.36
s 64	8.37
s 65	8.37
s 72	8.33, 8.34
s 72(2)	8.34
s 72(3)	8.34
s 72(4)	8.34
s 74	8.27
s 75	8.27

Sexual Offences Act 2003—*continued*	
s 76	8.27
s 106	12.8
Sch 2	8.33
Sch 3	12.8
Sch 3, para 32(b)	5.7
Sch 5	12.8
Supreme Court Act 1981	
s 81	10.9
Terrorism Act 2000	
s 1	11.13
Sch 1	9.21
Theft Act 1968	
s 12A	2.10
UK Borders Act 2007	11.7, 11.19
s 16	11.6, 11.7
Video Recordings Act 1984	8.24
s 4	8.22, 8.24
s 4A	8.24
Youth Justice and Criminal Evidence Act 1999	4.16

TABLE OF STATUTORY INSTRUMENTS

References are to paragraph numbers.

Criminal Justice and Immigration Act 2008 (Commencement No 1 and Transitional Provisions Order) 2008		Immigration (European Economic Area) Regulations 2006, SI 2006/1003	11.16
SI 2008/1466	1.5	Nationality, Immigration and Asylum Act 2002 (Specification of Particularly Serious Crimes) Order 2004, SI 2004/1910	11.11, 11.12
Criminal Justice and Immigration Act 2008 (Commencement No 2 and Transitional and Savings Provisions) Order 2008			
SI 2008/1586	1.5	Parole Board (Transfer of Functions) Order 1998	
Sch 2, para 2	3.28	SI 1998/3218	3.36

Chapter 1
INTRODUCTION

1.1 This book deals with the provisions of the Criminal Justice and Immigration Act 2008 which apply to England and Wales.[1] Its purpose is to explain and comment on the provisions of the Act, to explain their rationale and to set them in context. The book does not, directly, consider the merits of the policies that underpin the Act, although those polices are explained and commented on where appropriate.

References to 'the Act', 'the new Act', 'the 2008 Act' or to any section are to the Criminal Justice and Immigration Act 2008, unless otherwise indicated directly or by the context. References to other statutory provisions are to those provisions as amended by legislation other than the new Act. For the sake of both brevity and clarity, the amending legislation has not been referred to unless this is essential to explain the point being made.

PARLIAMENTARY HISTORY

1.2 The gestation of the Act was long. The Bill that has now become law was first introduced in the 2006/07 parliamentary session. Its parliamentary passage not having been completed during that session, it was carried over into session 2007/08. The parliamentary debates can be found at www.parliament.uk/business/bills_and_legislation.cfm.

House of Commons

2nd Reading (2006/07)	8 October 2007
Committee (2006/07)	16 October–25 October 2007
2nd Reading (2007/08)	7 November 2007
Committee (2007/08)	20 November–29 November 2007
Report	9 January 2008
3rd Reading	9 January 2008
Consideration of Lords' Amendments	3 and 4 May 2008

---

[1] Section 152 prescribes the extent of the Act.

House of Lords

2nd Reading	22 January 2008
Committee	5 February–12 March 2008
Report	26 March and 2 April 2008
3rd Reading	30 April 2008
ROYAL ASSENT	8 May 2008

COMMENCEMENT

1.3 By s 153 of the new Act, some provisions came into force on the date of Royal Assent (8 May 2008). They are indicated in the appropriate parts of this book. In summary, the main such substantive provisions are as follows:

- s 53 and associated provisions (allocation of either way offences);

- s 77 (penalty relating to unlawfully obtained personal data);

- s 128 (financial assistance for police); and

- s 138 (part) and s 139 (industrial action by prison officers).

1.4 Other provisions came into force on 8 July 2008 (see s 153(2)). The main substantive provisions that came into effect on that date are:

- s 62 (repeal of requirements in respect of Annual Reports on the Criminal Justice (Terrorism and Conspiracy) Act 2008);

- s 69 (criminal offence relating to indecent photographs of children);

- s 70 (increase in maximum penalty for publication of obscene articles); and

- s 79 (abolition of common law offence of blasphemy).

1.5 Other provisions come into effect on such days as may be appointed by order.

Two Orders have been made as at the date of going to press:

- Criminal Justice and Immigration Act 2008 (Commencement No 1 and Transitional Provisions Order) 2008, SI 2008/1466: this commences s 26 and related provisions on 9 June 2008, subject to certain transitional provisions. Section 26 imposes a duty on the Secretary of State to release certain long-term prisoners serving sentences of imprisonment of at least 4 years (see **3.34**).

- Criminal Justice and Immigration Act 2008 (Commencement No 2 and Transitional and Saving Provisions) Order 2008, SI 2008/586: this commences a wide range of provisions on 14 July 2008, and one minor provision on 15 July 2008. It contains transitional provisions. References are made to commencement at the relevant parts of this book.

OUTLINE OF THE ACT

1.6 The Act is the latest in a long line of criminal justice legislation. Some 39 such Acts have been passed since 1997.[2] It also takes the opportunity to continue to address immigration matters that are a source of ongoing problems in the light of the Government's anti-terrorism strategy.

In July 2006 the Government stated its commitment to 'delivering an effective criminal justice system' in a White Paper *Rebalancing the criminal justice system in favour of the law-abiding majority*. It sought ways to cut crime, reduce re-offending and to protect the public. A wide-ranging piece of legislation, at its heart is a desire to increase protection of the public, promote the rehabilitation of offenders and 'further strengthen confidence in the criminal justice system'.[3] The Government identified key areas of action:

- to ensure that the needs of victims are at the heart of what the criminal justice system does;

- to toughen up trial processes when a defendant fails to appear without good reason;

- the creation of new powers to tackle anti-social and violent behaviour;

- the creation of new criminal offences, including the offence of possession of extreme pornographic images;

- the creation of a new, generic community sentence for young offenders;

- achieving clearer sentencing decisions;

- changes in the way convictions are overturned and offenders released on appeal; and

- changes in the compensation scheme for those wrongly convicted, to bring them into line with compensation paid to victims of crime.

However, the Act is not simply addressing pure criminal justice provisions. It contains important provisions relating to immigration, particularly the new, and important, Special Immigration Status that is created to address limitations on the conduct of those persons who are designated.

---

[2] The figure quoted by Jack Straw, Secretary of State for Justice and Lord Chancellor, HC 2nd Reading, col 59 (8 October 2007).
[3] Lord Hunt, Parliamentary Under-Secretary of State, Ministry of Justice, HL 2nd Reading, col 27 (22 January 2008).

As appears inevitable in the context of criminal justice statutes, the Government has taken the opportunity to include a wide variety of procedural and miscellaneous matters. These include:

- changes to the rules relating to allocation of either way offences;

- changes to legal representation and criminal legal aid;

- changes to the international enforcement regime for financial penalties; and

- changes involving police and prison service management.

THE PASSAGE OF THE ACT

1.7 Some comment on the passage of the Act is called for. Criminal Justice Bills typically change, usually by expanding, as they pass through Parliament. However, the journey of this Bill through Parliament was remarkable in many different ways. Significant chunks of what is now known as the Act were not in the original Bill.

Provisions relating to incitement of hatred on the grounds of a person's sexuality, disclosure of details relating to sex offenders, the abolition of the crime of blasphemy and the law relating to self defence each made their first appearance at Committee or Report stage. Other provisions relating to appeals and the release of prisoners after recall were subject to significant amendment.

It is also notable to see elements of the initial Bill that were withdrawn by the Government. Part 4 of the original Bill contained provisions that would have established a Commissioner for Offender Management and Prisons. In the absence of an agreed way forward about the independence of the proposed office-holder, this was withdrawn by the Government.[4] This is another controversial part of the Bill that did not make the statute book. Clauses 71 to 73 related to prostitution; these met widespread opposition and criticism and were not persevered with. Both matters may well reappear, in some form, in future legislation.

We cannot avoid the conclusion that legislating in this way is neither conducive to proper scrutiny nor conducive to having clear, relatively simple and well thought out legal rules.

---

[4] See the comments of Lord Hunt, ibid, HL 2nd Reading, col 129 (22 January 2008). For the detailed reasons for withdrawal, see HL Committee, col 953 (5 February 2008).

Chapter 2

PROCEDURAL CHANGES

2.1 The Act introduces a variety of procedural changes. These include the following:

- detailed changes are made to Sch 3 to the Criminal Justice Act 2003 (allocation of either way offences);

- the powers of a magistrates' court to try or sentence a defendant in his absence are amended;

- the powers of non-legal staff to conduct proceedings in the magistrates' court are extended;

- changes are made in respect of criminal legal aid to allow a provisional grant of the right to legal representation, and powers to require disclosure of information in respect of criminal legal aid changed;

- minor changes are made to the provisions relating to defence disclosure under the Criminal Procedure and Investigations Act 1996 (CPIA 1996).

ALLOCATION OF CASES TRIABLE EITHER WAY

2.2 The rules relating to the allocation of either way offences were the subject of major change in the Criminal Justice Act 2003 (CJA 2003), and are to be found in Sch 3 to that Act. Section 53 of, and Sch 13 to, the new Act amend those provisions. Some of these changes simply tidy up Sch 3.[1] Thus, obvious errors in Sch 3 (such as the reference in Sch 3, para 8(2)(a) to 'trial on indictment' rather than 'summary trial', and the reference in para 23 to a 'court committing a specified offence to the Crown Court') are corrected.[2] The fact that such corrections are necessary is a reminder of the sheer complexity of legislative drafting of criminal justice legislation. Other changes are consequent upon decisions as to the implementation, or non-implementation, of earlier changes relating to allocation decisions and committal for sentence.

Commencement

2.3 The changes introduced by s 53 of, and Sch 13 to, the new Act took effect on 8 May 2008, the day of Royal Assent (s 153(1)). So too do the provisions in Sch 26, para 77, and the repeals in Sch 28, Part 4 which relate to committal for sentence. Other changes came into force on 14 July, and are identified at the appropriate parts of this chapter.

---

[1] 2008 Act, Sch 13, paras 2, 3, 5.
[2] 2008 Act, Sch 13, paras 4, 9.

Committal for sentence

2.4 Schedule 3 to the 2003 Act introduced a new scheme of sending for trial, linked to changes relating to the sentencing powers of magistrates' courts. Paragraph 22 of that Schedule had effectively limited the right of a magistrates' court to commit to the Crown Court an either way offence that had been tried summarily. That limitation was justified in the light of the scheme relating to the sentencing powers of a magistrates' court, designed to seek to achieve a higher proportion of either way cases where dealt with summarily.[3] That scheme has not yet, in fact, been implemented. The change made by the CJA 2003 restricting committal for trial is reversed by Sch 13, para 7, of the new Act: the power to commit for sentence remains, albeit with the amendments discussed below (see **2.5**).

With effect from 8 May 2008, Sch 3, para 22 of the 2003 Act is repealed (2008 Act, s 53; Sch 28, Part 4; s 153(1)). Paragraph 22 had inserted a new s 3 into the Powers of Criminal Courts (Sentencing) Act 2000 (PCC(S)A 2000), dealing with committal for sentence on an indication of a guilty plea to a serious offence triable either way. This change was never brought into force. Now, the effect of Sch 3, para 7 and Sch 28 is to repeal that change. Schedule 3, para 8 of the new Act amends Sch 3 to CJA 2003, by inserting a new para 22A into that Schedule. The effect of this complicated example of legislating by cross-reference is that, when Sch 3 to CJA 2003 is in force, the power to commit for sentence remains, but is amended. Different preconditions for committal for sentence will apply under an amended s 3 of PCC(S)A 2000.

2.5 Under the pre-existing law, the power exists to commit for sentence a person aged 18 or over who has been convicted of one or more offences on summary trial. One or more of the preconditions in s 3(2) of PCC(S)A 2000 must be satisfied. These are:

'(a) that the offence or the offence together with any associated offence is so serious that greater punishment should be inflicted for the offence than the court has the power to impose; or

(b) in the case of a violent or sexual offence, that a custodial sentence for a term longer than the court has the power to impose is necessary to protect the public from serious harm from him.'

The offender may not be committed for sentence in a case where the value involved is small (PCC(S)A 2000, s 3(4)). This last limitation was removed by the never-implemented provisions of Sch 3, para 13 of CJA 2003, which is now, itself, effectively repealed (2008 Act, Sch 3, para 7 and Sch 28, Part 4). So, this low value limitation on committal for sentence remains in the revised law, which is set out below.

Under the new, amended, provisions, the power continues to remain to commit an offender in custody or on bail to the Crown Court for sentence.[4] As a result of the change made by Sch 13, para 8, of the new Act, the power to commit may be exercised where the court is of the opinion:

---

[3] See R Ward and O Davies *Criminal Justice Act 2003: A Practitioner's Guide* (Jordan Publishing, 2004) at 8.41. For further analysis of the policy issues see Herbert 'Mode of Trial and Magistrates' Sentencing Powers' [2003] Crim LR 315.

[4] In accordance with PCC(S)A 2000, s 5.

'(a) that the offence or the combination of the offence and one or more offences associated with it was so serious that the *Crown Court should, in the court's opinion, have the power to deal with the offender in any way it could deal with him if he had been convicted on indictment*;[5] or

(b) in the case of a violent or sexual offence, that a custodial sentence for a term longer than the court has the power to impose is necessary to protect the public from serious harm from him.'

Thus, under the new wording, shown by italics, it will not be necessary to show that the level of punishment should exceed what the magistrates' court could have imposed.

BAIL

2.6 Sections 51 and 52, together with Schs 11 and 12, make detailed changes relating to bail. The power to require the electronic tagging of a person released on conditional bail is specifically created. The rules relating to bail for certain value-linked offences are also changed. In all cases the rationale for change is simple: a desire to try and reduce offending whilst the accused is on bail and, clearly, to increase the number of individuals who may be released on bail.

Electronic monitoring condition

2.7 Section 3 of the Bail Act 1976 (BA 1976) deals with requirements relating to bail. Section 3(6ZAA) provided that a child or young person could be required to comply with requirements imposed for the purpose of securing his compliance with any other bail requirement. That is repealed. Instead, new provisions are substituted by Sch 11, para 2. A new s 3(6ZAA) and s 3(6ZAB) have the effect of permitting a court to impose an electronic monitoring requirement. An amended s 3AA deals with the preconditions that apply in respect of children and young persons and a new s 3AB deals with similar matters in relation to adults.

The electronic monitoring provisions in s 51 and Sch 11 are not in force as at the date of going to press.

Children and young persons

2.8 The effect of the amendments is to rework the four preconditions that must be satisfied before a court imposes an electronic monitoring requirement. The new s 3AA provides that:

(1) the child or young person must be at least be 12 years of age;

(2) the child or young person must be charged with, or convicted of, a violent or sexual offence, or an offence punishable (in the case of an adult) with 14 years or more, or be charged with or convicted of one or more imprisonable offences which, together with any other imprisonable offences of which he has been convicted, amount to a recent history of repeatedly committing offences while on bail while remanded to local authority accommodation. These are the preconditions for a secure remand;

---

[5] Italics added indicating new changed wording. PCC(S)A 2000, s 3(2)(b) is deleted.

(3) the court must be satisfied that the necessary arrangements for persons released on bail are currently available; and

(4) a youth offending team must have informed the court that the imposition of an electronic monitoring requirement will be suitable in the case of the child or young person.

Persons aged 17 or above

2.9 The new s 3AB creates the following new preconditions:

(1) the court must be satisfied that without the electronic monitoring requirement the person would not be granted bail;

(2) the court is satisfied that the necessary arrangements for dealing with the individual can be made; and

(3) if the individual is aged 17, the youth offending team must indicate that it considers the case to be suitable for electronic monitoring.

Bail for summary offences and other offences tried summarily

2.10 Section 52 of, and Sch 12 to, the new Act inserts a new s 9A into BA 1976. It applies where a court is making a pre-trial bail decision in relation to an accused aged under 18 charged with a scheduled offence. A 'scheduled offence' is an offence that falls within Sch 2 to the Magistrates' Court Act 1980 (MCA 1980). These are offences in respect of which the value involved is relevant to the mode of trial. The relevant offences are criminal damage, excluding an offence caused by destroying or damaging property by fire, or aiding, abetting, counselling or procuring any such offence, or offences of aggravated vehicle taking under s 12A of the Theft Act 1968. Such offences are classed as either way offences but, if the value is £5,000 or less, must be tried summarily.

The new s 9A(2) requires a court, before deciding whether or not to grant bail, to consider, having regard to any representations made by the prosecutor or the accused, whether the value exceeds the specified sum (ie exceeds £5,000). If it does not the court must formally determine that bit does not do so.

Section 52 and Sch 12 came into force on 14 July 2008 (see **1.5**).

2.11 If there is no such determination (in other words, if the value exceeds £5,000) the more stringent provisions of Sch 1, Part 1 continue to apply, as now. If, however, there is a determination then Part 1 does not apply: instead a new, more flexible bail regime under a new Part 1A applies (2008 Act, Sch 12, para 5). The defendant need not be granted bail if the exceptions to the right to bail in Part 1A apply. They are as follows:

- if it appears to a court that, having been granted bail in criminal proceedings, he has failed to surrender to custody in accordance with obligations under the grant of bail, and the court believes that, in view of that failure the defendant, if released on bail, (whether or not subject to conditions) would fail to surrender to bail (BA 1976, Sch 1, Part 1A, para 3);

- if the court is satisfied that there are substantial grounds for believing that the defendant, if released on bail, whether subject to conditions or not, would commit an offence whilst on bail involving conduct of a certain type. That conduct is conduct which would, or which would be likely to, cause physical or mental injury to any person other than the defendant, or cause such a person to fear physical or mental injury (BA 1976, Sch 1, Part 1A, para 4);

- if the court is satisfied that the defendant should be kept in custody for his own protection, or, if he is a child or young person, for his own welfare (BA 1976, Sch 1, Part 1A, para 5);

- if he is in custody in pursuance of a sentence (BA 1976, Sch 1, Part 1A, para 6);

- if, having been granted bail in connection with the proceedings, he has been arrested under s 7 of BA 1976,[6] and the court is satisfied that there are substantial grounds for believing that the defendant, if released on bail and whether or not subject to conditions, would fail to surrender to custody, commit an offence while on bail, or interfere with witnesses or otherwise obstruct the course of justice (whether in relation to himself or another person) (BA 1976, Sch 1, Part 1A, para 7);

- if the court is satisfied that it has not been practicable to obtain sufficient information for the purposes of taking the decisions required by Part 1A of BA 1976 for want of time since the institution of the proceedings against him (BA 1976, Sch 1, Part 1A, para 8);

- in addition, the restrictions contained in paras 6A to 6C of Part 1 (exceptions applicable to drug users in certain areas) also apply (BA 1976, Sch 1, Part 1A, para 9).

TRIAL OR SENTENCING IN ABSENCE OF THE ACCUSED

2.12 Section 54 of the new Act creates a presumption that if a defendant fails to attend the trial of an information in the magistrates' court, without good cause, magistrates will use their powers to try the defendant in his absence. The reason for the changes is that it is considered that the powers that exist are not being exercised uniformly across the country.[7] It is hoped that, in cases where the accused fails to attend court, more trials will go ahead in the absence of the accused: not turning-up should not be a way to delay the case.[8]

The changes came into effect on 14 July 2008 (see **1.5**).

The powers to try a defendant in his absence are contained in ss 11–16 of MCA 1980. Section 11(2) of MCA 1980 permits a court to try an information in the absence of the accused if it is proved to the satisfaction of the court that the summons was served on the accused within what appears to be a reasonable time before the trial, or the accused

---

[6] Liability for arrest for absconding or breaking conditions of bail.
[7] David Hanson, Minister of State, Ministry of Justice, HC Committee, cols 486–494 (22 November 2007).
[8] Maria Eagle, MP, Parliamentary Under-Secretary of State for Justice, HC Committee, col 27 (16 October 2007).

has appeared on a previous occasion to answer the information. There are limits on the sentences or orders that may be imposed (MCA 1980, s 11(3) and (4)).

2.13 The amendments made to s 11 by s 54 include a new s 11(1). By the new s 11(1) if the accused is aged under 18 the court may proceed in his absence, but if the accused is 18 or above the court *shall* proceed in his absence unless it appears to the court to be contrary to the interests of justice to do so. The court must be satisfied of the matters set out in s 11(2).

The new provisions contain additional safeguards. A new s 11(2A) prohibits the court from proceeding in the absence of the accused if it considers that there is an acceptable reason for his failure to appear. Arguably, this new provision is unnecessary, because if there was an acceptable reason for the accused's failure to appear then it would be contrary to the interests of justice to proceed in any event. However, the rationale is to build into the provision explicit safeguards.

As noted above, s 11(3) and (4) restrict the imposition of certain sentences and orders in the absence of the accused. These are not explicitly amended, but the effect of s 54(5), which creates a new s 11(3A), appears to be that if the court does impose such a sentence or order it will not take effect until the offender is brought before the court. It is the intention that there should be a power to sentence the accused in his absence.[9] This change has been made in a very opaque way. Nonetheless, when the accused is, eventually, before the court he will have an opportunity to explain his absence and, if he thinks an injustice has been done, seek a rehearing.[10] Whether a court will, or should, grant such an application is a different matter, though it would be difficult to resist *if* an injustice has been done.

2.14 Section 13(5) of MCA 1980 required a court to consider whether the attendance of the accused was necessary, or whether, having been given an opportunity to attend court, the magistrates should proceed to deal with the offender. That subsection is now repealed (2008 Act, s 54(7)).

CONTENTS OF ACCUSED'S DEFENCE STATEMENT

2.15 The new Act takes the opportunity to amend further the provisions relating to defence statements under CPIA 1996 (2008 Act, s 60). This change had not been brought into force as at the date of going to press.

CJA 2003 substantially amended the obligations of an accused under CPIA 1996. Section 6A of CPIA 1996, added by CJA 2003, required additional matters to be included in the defence statement that the accused has to give, on pain of having an inference drawn from a failure to disclose, or properly disclose. The additional matters were the particular defences relied on, the matters of fact on which issue is taken with the prosecution, and any points of law (including admissibility) on which the accused intends to rely.

---

[9] Maria Eagle, MP, Parliamentary Under-Secretary of State for Justice, HC Committee, col 27 (16 October 2007).
[10] Maria Eagle, MP, Parliamentary Under-Secretary of State for Justice, HC Committee, col 27 (16 October 2007).

The small but important change made by the new Act is to require a statement of the 'particulars of the matters of fact on which he intends to rely'.

Section 6A(1) of CPIA 1996 will now read:[11]

'(1) ... a defence statement is a written statement—

(a) setting out the nature of the accused's defence, including any particular defence on which he intends to rely,
(b) indicating *particulars* of the matters of fact on which he takes issue with the prosecution,
(c) setting out, in the case of each matter, why he takes issue with the prosecution,
(ca) *setting out particulars of the matters of fact on which he intends to reply for the purposes of his defence, and*
(d) indicating any point of law (including any point as to the admissibility of evidence or an abuse of process) which he wishes to take, and any authority on which he intends to reply for that purpose.'

Now, not only must the accused indicate the facts on which the prosecution intends to rely and with which the defence takes issue, but must also indicate the defences relied on. The accused must now set out the particular facts that underpin his defence. This is a significant change. It marks a further step away from the original intention behind CPIA 1996. The Royal Commission on Criminal Justice had recommended that defence disclosure should be of a relatively brief type.[12] When the Act was passed there were clear limits as to the level of detail expected.[13] However, clearly the intention now is to require quite specific statements of fact. The defence will have to disclose, in effect, the factual basis underpinning the defence, not simply the defence itself. This may be at a time when these may not be clear, or even known, or in circumstances where it may be thought unwise to disclose that factual basis. However, arguably the change does not go so far as to require the names of witnesses to be disclosed.

CRIMINAL LEGAL AID

2.16 Sections 56–58 of the new Act make significant changes to the system of legal aid in criminal cases. They came into force on 14 July 2008 (see **1.5**).

The Criminal Defence Service was established under s 1(2)(b) of the Access to Justice Act 1999 (AJA 1999), and further regulated by the Criminal Defence Service Act 2006. It has a role of securing advice, assistance and representation to persons involved in criminal investigations or proceedings. Criminal legal aid is available for representation in cases where it is in the interests of justice for it to be granted (the merits test). In addition, applicants must pass a means test.

The changes made by the new Act introduce the power to grant provisional representation rights at an earlier stage. They also potentially will secure information flows from HM Revenue and Customs and the Department of Work and Pensions to enable accurate means assessment. It also facilitates the setting up of pilot schemes.

---

[11] Words in italics added by 2008 Act.
[12] Royal Commission on Criminal Justice (1991), para 68, p 99.
[13] See HC 1995/1996 Standing Committee B of CPIA 1996, col 68 et seq (4 April 1996 to 21 May 1996). See R Card and R Ward *Criminal Procedure and Investigations Act 1996* (Jordan Publishing, 1997), at para b2.57.

It should be noted that the new Act itself merely provides the legal framework. It is intended that there should be extensive consultation with the legal profession and others prior to the making of regulations and detailed implementation.

2.17 The rationale for the changes is to ensure that potential causes of delay are reduced, bearing in mind that some solicitors will not be willing to act until a representation order is made.[14] It was clearly and fully explained in June 2007 by Vera Baird, then Minister for Legal Aid, in a letter to various interested bodies:[15]

> 'First, we are intending that applications for representation orders be made and processed during the actual investigation into the offence, rather than waiting for the point of charge. This would allow the financial eligibility test to be carried out, and a decision made on the "Interests of Justice" (IOJ) test, in cases where it is clear what charge(s) or range of charges a suspect is likely to face. Upon charge, the representation order would be formally confirmed, or if the charge differs from that anticipated, an amendment to the IOJ section of the application can be submitted. Enabling the forms to be completed, submitted and processed earlier in the life of a case will minimize the risk of delay and help ensure representation orders are in place ahead of first hearings.
>
> Second, we propose to make it possible for a representation order to be granted before formal charges have been laid in certain specified cases. This could be particularly advantageous in those cases, such as VHCC (very high cost case) fraud, where much work is often conducted pre-charge. Clearly, careful thought needs to be given to the specific conditions which would attach to such an order, including the type of work, the appropriate level of representation authorised to undertake such work, and the correct fee structure. We will work closely with stakeholders from the legal profession and from CJS agencies in developing the detail of these proposals before any new scheme is implemented. The Attorney General has already established a Working Group to take forward a recommendation of the Fraud Review that a framework for early plea negotiations in fraud cases should be devised. This change would help facilitate such negotiations.
>
> We are also proposing to introduce an express power to pilot schemes relating to the grant of representation orders. This will ensure that future changes can be fully tested and evaluated before being rolled out – including Crown Court implementation of the Criminal Defence Service Act 2006 and the earlier grant of representation orders referred to above. The power would extend to all Criminal Defence Service schemes governed by secondary legislation, and would allow us to test in greater detail the wider impact on the CJS of changes to the legal aid regime. Any pilots under this power would have effect only for a specified period, not longer than 12 months unless extended by regulation (and in any case no more than 18 months). We would also like it to be possible to extend a pilot scheme if that is necessary to cover a gap between the end of the pilot and its possible rollout on a more comprehensive basis. Pilots could apply in relation to one or more prescribed areas or locations (which could include particular court buildings or other locations such as custody suites at police stations), types of court (ie magistrates' courts or the Crown Court), offences or classes of person (such as persistent young offenders).
>
> Lastly, in response to practical concerns raised about the working of the real time link between courts and the DWP to process means test applications from those in receipt of "passportable" benefits, it is proposed to introduce a statutory gateway to ensure applications are dealt with as swiftly and accurately as possible. While we have already made some changes to the system to minimise error and improve functionality, the current

---

[14] See speech of Vera Baird, Minister of State, Minister of Justice to London Criminal Courts Solicitors' Association Conference (2006), reported at www.lccsa.org.uk.
[15] Cited at HC Research Paper 07/95, to be found at www.parliament.uk/commons/lib/research/rp2007/rp07-065.pdf.

framework will not adequately address the issues that have arisen since implementation. Therefore, the best long-term solution is for staff to be able to search the DWP database and access information about the benefit status of the individual. The statutory gateway would only allow the sharing of relevant information for the specific purpose of administering the grant of legal aid (a function of the Legal Services Commission under schedule 3 of the Access to Justice Act 1999).'

The detailed provisions of the 2008 implement these changes.

2. 18 Section 56 provides for the provisional granting of representations, amending Part 1 of AJA 1999. It enables regulations to be made which will regulate the stages of investigations or proceedings at which such a provisional grant could be made, the circumstances when a provisional grant would become a full grant or be withdrawn. It is not intended that there should be a right of appeal against refusal to make a provisional grant (see 2008 Act, s 56(10), amending AJA 1999, Sch 3).

2.19 Section 57 provides for the disclosure of information by the Department of Work and Pensions or the Commissioners of Revenue and Customs, amending AJA 1999 for the purpose. The information that could be requested and disclosed is identified by s 57(2) and (3). It includes details of name and address of the applicant, date of birth, national insurance number, benefit status, details relating to the name and address of an employer, and other information of a type that may in due course be identified in regulations.

A new Sch 3, para 7 of AJA 1999 is inserted by s 57 of the new Act, and deals with restrictions on disclosure of information supplied under these provisions. It allows disclosure by the relevant authority which has received the information, to persons when it is necessary or expedient to do so for the making of relevant decisions on legal aid, but creates a new criminal offence of unauthorised disclosure.

2.20 Section 58 amends AJA 1999 by creating a new s 18A. The effect of this new section is to enable pilot schemes to be run in respect of specified localities, or types of court, or types of offences, or types of person, selected, if appropriate by reference to specified criteria or on a sampling basis. As is common, development of the criminal legal aid scheme will be driven by the success or otherwise of pilot initiatives, clearly with the intention of maximising value for money and reducing delay to a minimum.

RIGHTS OF AUDIENCE IN MAGISTRATES' COURTS

2.21 Section 55 amends s 7A of the Prosecution of Offences Act 1985 (POA 1985), by extending the powers of designated non-legal staff. Designated case workers in the CPS will be able to conduct summary trials in the magistrates' courts, deal with certain matters, such as bail applications, even in cases which will be tried or otherwise dealt with at the Crown Court, conduct applications or other proceedings relating to civil preventative orders (such as ASBOs) and conduct non civil proceedings assigned to the Director of Public Prosecutions (DPP).

Section 55 came into force on 14 July 2008 (see **1.5**).

Background and rationale

2.22 Section 7A(2) of POA 1985 authorises the DPP to designate members of staff of the Crown Prosecution Service (CPS) who are not legally qualified to conduct certain proceedings. Originally, designated case workers (DCWs) had all the powers of a Crown Prosecutor in relation to an application for, or relating to, bail. However, following a recommendation in the Narey Report[16] the powers of DCWs were significantly extended by the Crime and Disorder Act 1998. A new s 7A of POA 1985 extended the powers of DCWs beyond bail to include the conduct of proceedings in the magistrates' court other than trials. The powers granted did not extend to any proceedings relating to an offence triable only on indictment.

The use of lay presenters in magistrates' courts was not new: local authorities and other organisations and bodies have often been represented by non-legally qualified presenters. Further, non-legally qualified presenters, in the form of police officers, were common in the days preceding the establishment of the CPS. Nonetheless, the role of the CPS is, now, crucial to ensuring fairness in the process. As one commentary observed:[17]

> '... criminal proceedings in the magistrates' court are not necessarily formal or straightforward. Decisions by prosecutors can require judgments about what is an acceptable plea or an acceptable basis for plea. They can involve difficult decisions with implications for the accused, for victims of crime and for the running of the court. Unexpected points can crop up, as when the court clerk notices that someone has decided on a plea which is not appropriate. A *Newton* hearing on disputed facts relevant to sentence may have to take place.'

Some 10 years on, the use of DCWs is generally accepted. The Law Society 'recognise that the deployment of paralegals in appropriate circumstances ... will result in the time of legally qualified prosecutors being more productively used'.[18] However, both the Law Society and Bar Council strongly opposed the scope of the extension of powers for DCWs now contained in the 2008 Act.[19] So, too, did some in Parliament,[20] articulating concerns about a non-legally qualified DCW not having the same background or expertise as his or her legally qualified defence colleague. At the heart of the opposition was concern about non-legally qualified staff to conduct trials, including in respect of imprisonable offences. Considerations relating to training, complexity of issues, advocacy skills and independence were all matters of concern:[21]

> 'The proposal is not aimed at improving the quality of the service provided to victims of crime and witness, but rather the Law Society is concerned that the proposal is an expedient means to save money which may have a very detrimental effect on due process. In particular, we are concerned that no qualified lawyer may be involved with a case in the magistrates' court in which the defendant is facing an imprisonable offence.'

This last concern has been met by amendments which now form part of s 55. The CPS has argued that effective training and supervision would ensure that the input of experienced DCWs would permit qualified lawyers to concentrate on more serious cases.

---

[16] *Review of Delay in the Criminal Justice Process* (Home Office, 1997).
[17] R Card and R Ward *Crime and Disorder Act 1998 A Practitioners Guide* (Jordan Publishing, 1998), at para 6.8.
[18] *Parliamentary Brief: Criminal Justice and Immigration Bill Second Reading*, 23 July 2007.
[19] 'Wider role for CPS caseworkers "not in the public interest"' *Law Society Gazette*, 19 July 2007.
[20] See, eg, HC Committee, cols 486–494 (22 November 2007).
[21] *Parliamentary Brief: Criminal Justice and Immigration Bill Second Reading*, 23 July 2007.

The detail

2.23 The effect of s 55 is to amend s 7A of POA 1985.

The amended s 7A now states, in s 7A(2), the following permitted designation for DCWs:

'(a) the powers and rights of Crown Prosecutors in relation to:
- (i) applications for, or relating to, bail in criminal proceedings;
- (ii) the conduct of criminal proceedings in magistrates' courts other than trials of offences triable either way or offences which are punishable with imprisonment in the case of persons aged 21 or over;
- (iii) the conduct of applications or other proceedings relating to preventative civil orders;[22]
- (iv) the conduct of proceedings (other than criminal proceedings) in or in connection with the discharge of functions assigned to the Director.'

A DCW can thus conduct all matters in the magistrates' court other than trials of either way offences or of any offence punishable with imprisonment in the case of an adult. Section 55(4) removes the restriction contained in s 7A(6) in relation to offences triable only on indictment. That means that a DCW can deal with all matters in respect of such cases, but not, of course, conduct trials – DCW do not have rights of audience in respect of trials in the Crown Court.

---

[22] Defined by a new s 7A(5), and which includes anti-social behaviour orders, restraining orders under the Protection from Harassment Act 1997, s 5, or parenting orders under the Crime and Disorder Act 1998, s 8.

Chapter 3

SENTENCING

SUMMARY

3.1 The new Act contains significant changes relating to sentencing. Some of these specifically relate to youth justice, and are discussed in Chapter 4. The Act creates a new Youth Rehabilitation Order, discussed in Chapter 5. In this chapter we deal with a wide range of other sentencing provisions:

- public protection sentences are reformed to increase judicial discretion and refocus them on the more dangerous offenders;

- credit is to be given to offenders who spent time on bail subject to an electronically monitored curfew, in a similar way to the credit currently given in respect of time spent on remand;

- release and recall arrangements are changed, by bringing the arrangement for the recall of prisoners sentenced under the Criminal Justice Act 1991 (CJA 1991) into line with the arrangements for those sentenced under the Criminal Justice Act 2003 (CJA 2003). Release arrangements for non-dangerous offenders sentenced under CJA 1991 to a sentence of 4 years and over, are also aligned with the release provisions of CJA 2003;

- the Act provides for a fixed 28-day recall period for non-dangerous offenders who breach the terms of their licence;

- the availability of community sentences is restricted to imprisonable offences only.

Many of the provisions are now in force. Commencement is referred to at the relevant part of this chapter.

BACKGROUND AND WIDER SENTENCING CONTEXT

3.2 The sentencing provisions relating to adult offenders are intended to build on the framework created by CJA 2003, and reflect the experience of the operation of those changes that have been brought into effect (although some have not yet been brought into effect).[1] The changes also have to be understood in the light of the general trend of government penal policy, and of the increasing number of offenders being sent to prison. The detailed changes dealt with in this chapter, and in Chapters 4 and 5, can largely be explained by reference to this wider picture.

---

[1] HL 2nd Reading, col 128 (22 January 2008).

CJA 2003 introduced major changes in sentencing, as well as, for the first time, setting out the purposes of sentencing. Those changes were based largely on the recommendations of the *Halliday Report*.[2] Its focus was to seek to concentrate the use of custody as far as possible on offenders who present some risk to the public, especially through the new sentences for dangerous offenders, coupled with seeking to strengthen community punishments, through the new generic community order. A review of sentencing in 2006[3] and 2007 found that further change was necessary. The growth of custody rates was a matter of concern: during the period 1996 to 2006 the custody rate for indictable offences increased from 7% to almost 15%. In the Crown Court the equivalent figures show an equivalent increase from 53% to 61%, with average sentence lengths in the Crown Court increasing by some 6.6 months to an average of 27 months. The *Carter Review*[4] identified a 60% increase in the prison population since 1995.

3.3 The use of the range of sentences is another matter of concern. The Review stated:[5]

> '... the courts have made good use of the new sentences for dangerous offenders. The shorter sentences which were anticipated for non-dangerous offenders ... have not, however, materialised. Early evidence also that the new Suspended Sentence Order may be used in cases where a community order would be appropriate ... The evidence so far is that the courts are not using community orders as fully as they might. The anticipated switch to these new community sentences from short terms of imprisonment that was envisaged has not happened ... Less serious offenders should be fined rather than given low-level community sentences. These are now much better enforced, hit offenders in the pocket and save taxpayer money. The use of fines has decreased significantly in the last 10 years (for indictable offences). Rebuilding the use of the fine will avoid probation being overloaded by low-level offenders serving community sentences ...'

The general direction of the analysis is clear, and is reflected in many of the measures in the new Act: fine enforcement is strengthened, the threshold for community sentences raised, and attempts were made, but abandoned by the Government, to modify the suspended sentence order by abolishing their use for summary offences.[6]

A further pressure driving change is allied to the growth of custody, and is the pressure on available prison places. In 2007 the *Carter Review*[7] stressed the rapid growth in custody and its impact on the prison estate. There have been some 66 pieces of criminal justice legislation since 1995, all with a range of sentences and sanctions: legislation seeking to increase the length of sentences for some offenders; and new sanctions for dangerous offenders, increasing the average time served.

---

[2] *Making Punishment Work: A Report of a Review of the Sentencing Framework of England and Wales* (Home Office, July 2001). For a critique, see Baker and Clarkson 'An Evaluation of the Halliday Report on Sentencing in England and Wales' [2002] Crim LR 81.
[3] *Making Sentencing Clearer: A Consultation* (Home Office, November 2006): see responses at www.cjsonline.gov.uk; *Rebalancing the criminal justice system in favour of the law abiding majority. Cutting crime reducing reoffending and protecting the public* (Home Office, July 2006).
[4] *Securing the Future: proposals for the efficient and sustainable use of custody in England and Wales* (Ministry of Justice, 2007), to be found at www.justice.gov.uk/docs/securing-the-future.pdf.
[5] Ibid, at 6.
[6] Originally contained in the Bill but abandoned by the Government following considerable parliamentary opposition.
[7] *Securing the Future* (Ministry of Justice, 2007).

This pressure on prison places can be seen as one motivator for changes relating to early release, recall of prisoners and length of sentence. During the passage of the Act, the Minister of State observed:[8]

> 'The Government will always ensure sufficient prison places to accommodate those serious and dangerous offenders on whom the courts see fit to pass a custodial sentence. Over the last 10 years we have increased prison capacity by more than 20,000 places and, following the review by ... Lord Carter ... we will see capacity by a further 15,000 places by 2012. [His] remit was not just to look at the supply of prison places, but at the other side of the equation – demand. We need to ensure that prison and probation resources are properly focused on serious, dangerous and violent offenders, with public safety coming first ...'

The pressure on prison places also has an impact on judicial approaches to sentencing. In *Seed and Stark*[9] Lord Bingham CJ observed:[10]

> 'Once again judges who have to sentence offenders are confronted with the fact that the prisons are full. When they impose sentences of imprisonment – and very often the nature of the offence will mean that there is no alternative to this course – the prison regime that the offender will experience will be likely to be more punitive because of the consequence of overcrowding and then opportunities for rehabilitative intervention in prison will be restricted ...
>
> The numbers of those in prison are as a product of the numbers of custodial sentences imposed and the length of those sentences. Parliament has not given judges a free hand ... It is of course the duty of the judge to follow those requirements. Requirements of the Criminal Justice Act 2003 dealing with the sentencing for serious offences may well have the effect of increasing the size of the prison population. The requirement of Schedule 21 making provision for the determination of the minimum term in relation to mandatory life sentences may well ... be seen to have that effect. Figures in relation to those serving indeterminate sentences for public protection suggest that these sentences may already be making a significant contribution to the rise in prison numbers ...'

Further, the pressure on prison places may have the effect of undermining the very measures put in place by Parliament. In *Secretary of State for Justice v Walker and James*[11] a challenge to the legality of detention of individuals subject to an imprisonment for public protection (IPP)[12] revealed 'a systematic failure on the part of the Secretary of State to put in place the resources necessary to implement the scheme of rehabilitation necessary to enable the relevant provisions of the 2003 Act to function as intended',[13] and potentially giving rise to a breach of Art 5 of the ECHR.

GENERAL SENTENCING MATTERS

Pre-Sentence Reports

3.4 The rules relating to Pre-Sentence Reports (PSR) were re-enacted[14] in CJA 2003 with minor amendments. Section 158(1) of that Act defined a PSR as a report which:

---

[8] HL 2nd Reading, col 128 (22 January 2008).
[9] *R v Seed and Stark* [2007] EWCA Crim 254.
[10] For other exhortations, see *Attorney-General's Reference No 11 of 2006 (R v Scarth)* [2006] Crim LR 775; *R v Delamare* [2003] EWCA Crim 24.
[11] [2008] EWCA Civ 30.
[12] See **3.15**.
[13] Lord Phillips CJ at para 72.
[14] Formerly PCC(S) A 2000, s 162.

(a) with a view to assisting the court in determining the most suitable method of dealing with the offender, is made or submitted by an appropriate officer, and

(b) contains information as to such matters, presented in such a manner, as may be prescribed by rule made by the Secretary of State.'

The amendment made by s 12 of the new Act adds a new s 158(1A). This allows a court, subject to any rules made under s 158(1)(b), to accept an oral report. This clearly has real benefits in assisting courts to dispose of cases and avoid adjournments for written reports where that is possible and appropriate. It permits oral 'stand down' reports which were permissible before PSRs were introduced by CJA 1991. Of course, it will be important that oral reports are only accepted in appropriate cases; particularly where a community sentence is being considered, a report may be extremely important in determining the combination of requirements to be included under the scheme created by CJA 2003.

This change does not apply to a young offender in certain circumstances (2008 Act, s 12, inserting a new s 158(1)(A)). A written PSR will be needed before the court forms the opinion that the seriousness of the offence potentially warrants a custodial sentence (CJA 2003, s 152(2)), before determining the length of any custodial sentence (s 152(3)), or before coming to the opinion that detention for life (s 226(1)(b)) or an extended sentence(s 228(1)(b)(i)) if there is a significant risk to members of the public of serious harm occasioned by the commission by the offender of further serious or specified offences.

This change came into effect on 14 July 2008 (see **1.5**).

Community sentences

3.5 Sections 10 and 11 amend the restrictions on making a community order. The changes came into effect on 14 July 2008 (see **1.5**).

Section 148(1) of CJA 2003 states the general restriction on imposing a community sentence. A court must not pass a community sentence on an offender unless it is of the opinion that the offence, or the combination of the offence and any associated offences,[15] is serious enough to warrant it. The restriction reflects the hierarchical nature of the sentencing regime: community sentences are appropriate where lesser disposals, such as discharges, fines, referral orders cannot be made or are inappropriate. The severity of the sentence should be proportionate to the offence for which the offender is being sentenced.[16]

Section 148(2) requires that a community order must be suitable for the offender and also commensurate with the seriousness of the offence. Any restrictions on liberty must be commensurate with the offence (s 148(3)).

Section 10 creates a new s 148(5) of CJA 2003. This simply has the effect of reinforcing what has always been the position. If the threshold for a community sentence has been crossed it does not mean that a court is obliged to impose a community sentence and although the court has the power to impose a requirement which reflects the seriousness of the offence it does not mean that it must impose it. In short, a court can impose a

---

[15] PCC(S)A 2000, s 161.
[16] See the Halliday Report, *Making Punishment Work: A Report of a Review of the Sentencing Framework of England and Wales* (Home Office, July 2001): available at www.homeoffice.gov.uk/documents/312280.

sentence which is lesser in severity than the seriousness of the offence would justify. Of course, in all these matters the court will be mindful of Sentencing Guidelines.

3.6 The second change is made by s 11, creating a new s 150A of CJA 2003. It effectively prohibits the making of a community order in respect of an offence which is not punishable by imprisonment or to cases where s 151(2) applies. Again, the purpose of the change is to reduce the making of community orders for less serious offences.

In deciding whether an either way offence is imprisonable, regard is had to the court which is dealing with the offence. If the court that is dealing with the offence has the power to impose a term of imprisonment then the new s 150A does not apply. But if, for example, the case is being dealt with by a magistrates' court but only if the Crown Court has power to impose a term of imprisonment, s 150A will apply. For these purposes, s 148 is disregarded: the fact that a court could, by virtue of s 148, impose a community sentence instead of a term of imprisonment does not alter the fact that, for this purpose, it is or is not an imprisonable offence. Of course, if the offence does not reach the community sentence threshold then s 150A is irrelevant in any event.

3.7 Even though the community sentence threshold has not been reached, s 151(2) of PCC(S)A 2000 permits the making of a community order for a persistent offender aged 16 or over who has, since he attained 16, on at least three separate occasions had a fine (and only a fine) imposed on him. Even if the community order offence seriousness threshold has not been crossed, a court may nonetheless make a community order. However, the effect of s 11(4) and (5) is to significantly limit its operation.

Section 11(4) of the 2008 Act limits this power to cases where the offender was aged at least 16 when convicted of the offence for which the court is now sentencing, and that offence is imprisonable (see **3.6**). A further complication is created by s 11(5): this permits the application of the s 150(2) power, by creating a new s 150(1A). Although the offence before the court may not be imprisonment, a court can use the s 150(2) power if the offender is aged at least 16, and he or she has been fined (and only fined) on at least three occasions in respect of offences committed since the offender attained the age of 16.

Enforcement of sentences – unpaid work requirement for breach of community order

3.8 Section 38 of the new Act amends parts of Sch 8 to CJA 2003 (enforcement of community sentences). Paragraph 9 of Sch 8 is one of the provisions that relates to what a magistrates' court may do where it is proved that an offender has failed without reasonable excuse to comply with any of the requirements of a community order. One of the things it may do[17] is amend the order by imposing more onerous requirements which the court could include if it was then making the order.

A new para 9(3A) is inserted into Sch 8: the power to impose an unpaid work requirement exists. However each requirement is subject to any limits the 2003 Act imposes generally in respect of any such requirement. One of the particular limits imposed on a requirement is contained in s 199(2) which relates to unpaid work

---

[17] The other choices are to deal with the offender for the offence in respect of which the community order was made as if the court were then making the order (with such sentencing powers as it would then have), or the imposition of a term of imprisonment not exceeding 51 weeks.

requirements. That section sets the minimum length of an unpaid work requirement to not less than 40 hours. In cases such as this, where a court is using its powers following breach of a community order, that period is reduced to 20 hours, but only if no unpaid work requirement had been attached to the relevant order. A short period of unpaid work may be an effective way of emphasising for a particular offender that failure to comply with a community order is a serious matter. If there had been an unpaid work order in the original order, para 9 allows that requirement in any event.

The changes came into effect on 14 July 2008 (see **1.5**).

Enforcement of sentences – attendance centre requirement on fine defaulter – default order

3.9 Section 300 of CJA 2003 provides for the making of a default order in respect of a person aged under 25. It permits the imposition of a curfew requirement or an unpaid work requirement by a magistrates' court, instead of issuing a warrant for commitment for failure to pay a fine. The amendment made by s 40 of the new Act enables a court to make an attendance centre order in respect of such a person aged at least 16 or under 25.

The change came into effect on 14 July 2008 (see **1.5**).

Consecutive terms of imprisonment

3.10 Section 20(2) makes changes in respect of consecutive terms of imprisonment under s 181 of CJA 2003. Section 181 provides for a scheme of 'custody plus', although its introduction has been deferred. The changes came into effect on 14 July 2008 (see **1.5**).

The essence of the scheme created by s 181 of CJA 2003 is that, in respect of prison sentences of less than 12 months, the maximum term for a single offence is 51 weeks, provided that does not exceed the maximum for the offence. The minimum sentence length is 28 weeks. The sentence comprised two elements – the *custodial period* and the *licence period*. The former is the period that must actually be served, to be followed by a licence period that runs from the date of the end of the custodial period until the end of the total sentence length. The custodial period must be not less than 2 weeks, or more than 13 weeks (s 181(5)). The licence period must not be less than 26 weeks in length.

Section 181 sets a different maximum limit in respect of consecutive orders. The maximum consecutive length must not be more than 65 weeks, and the aggregate length of the custodial periods must not exceed 26 weeks (s 181(7)). It is how these limits are calculated that is the subject to the change made by s 20.

3.11 Section 20(2) inserts a new s 181(7A) into CJA 2003. For calculating whether consecutive sentences exceed 65 weeks, the aggregate length is not to be taken as exceeding 65 weeks if the aggregate of all the custodial periods and the longest of the licence periods in relation to those terms is not more than 65 weeks. This change clarifies the pre-existing position, and brings sentences within the bounds of the custody-plus regime which would not otherwise be possible. It has the potential therefore to permit a court to make consecutive custody-plus orders where, because of the restriction, a court might have considered a longer term to be necessary.

The effect can be seen from the following two examples:

Example 1

Court imposes terms of 51 weeks and 40 weeks consecutively, with the maximum custodial periods (25 weeks and 14 weeks). The total sentence length for this purpose is 25 weeks + 14 weeks + 26 weeks (longest licence period) = 65 weeks. Permissible sentence.

Example 2

Court imposes two terms of 40 weeks and one of 35 weeks consecutively, with the maximum custodial periods (each of 14 weeks). The total sentence length for this purpose is 14 weeks + 14 weeks + 9 weeks +26 weeks (longest licence period) = 63 weeks. Permissible sentence.

3.12 Section 264A of CJA 2003 deals with consecutive terms of intermittent custody, as is amended by s 20(3). Intermittent custody was introduced by s 183 of CJA 2003, and is a sentence expressed in weeks, being not less than 28 weeks and not more than 51 weeks in length (s 183(4)). The custodial period is served intermittently. For that reason the court specifies the number of days to be served in custody, being not less than 14 and, for one offence, no more than 90. The court must specify the number of days that the offender must serve in prison before being released on licence, and specify the periods the offender is to be released on licence.

In respect of consecutive sentences the aggregate number of custodial days must not be more than 180, and the aggregate sentence length must not exceed 65 weeks.

The changes made by s 20(3) amend s 264A and have the effect of clarifying the extent to which consecutive orders can be made. The effect is, that in respect of consecutive orders, the offender must serve all the custodial periods and the total licence period in respect of all the offences for which consecutive terms are passed.

3.13 Section 20(4) amends s 265 of CJA 2003. That section prohibits a court from directing that a sentence is to commence on the expiry of any other sentence of imprisonment from which the defendant has been released early. The change made by s 20 makes it clear that this restriction does not apply to sentences of intermittent custody. Even though an offender has been released on periods of licence a consecutive term of custody may be imposed.

VIOLENT OR SEXUAL OFFENDERS

Background

3.14 The new Act makes significant changes to the rules relating to dangerous offenders. The changes came into effect on 14 July 2008 (see **1.5**). These changes were made in order to reduce the numbers of such sentences being imposed, which have led to the 'silting up' of the prisons.[18] Between 2005 and 2007 over 2,000 sentences of

---

[18] Christine Laurie, Chief Executive, Probation Boards Association, HC Committee, col 102 (16 October 2007).

imprisonment for public protection were imposed.[19] The changes now introduced will increase judicial discretion and refocus them on the most dangerous offenders.[20]

Another aspect of protecting the public from dangerous offenders is the disclosure of information about the convictions of child sex offenders, which is addressed by s 140. This is dealt with in Chapter 12.

3.15 Sections 225–236 of CJA 2003 created new indeterminate sentences in respect of dangerous offenders, whether adults or juveniles. Where a person aged 18 or over is convicted of a serious offence,[21] as defined by s 224, and the court is of the view that there is a significant risk[22] to members of the public of serious harm occasioned by the commission of further specified offences, it must either impose a life sentence or a sentence of imprisonment for public protection (IPP) (CJA 2003, s 225). Equivalent provisions, in respect of detention for life or for public protection, of an offender aged under 18 are contained in s 226.

Which of the two sentences has to be imposed depends on whether the preconditions in s 225(2) are satisfied. These are that the offence must be punishable by a term of life imprisonment, and the court considers that the seriousness of the offence, together with any associated offences, justifies the imposition of a sentence of life imprisonment. If it does not then the court must impose a sentence of IPP. Under the pre-existing law the court was required to impose such a sentence in respect of a serious offence if it did not impose a term of life imprisonment. It is these provisions relating to requirements to impose a sentence of IPP that are changed by s 13.

Section 226 contains provisions relating to detention for life or for public protection in respect of a serious offence offender aged under 18. As with adults, a court is required to impose a sentence of detention for life in certain circumstances. Those circumstances are equivalent to those in respect of adult offenders (see above). They are that the offence must be punishable by a term of detention for life, and the court considers that the seriousness of the offence, together with any associated offences, justifies the imposition of such a sentence. If it does not then the court must impose a sentence of detention for public protection, but only if the extended sentence provisions in s 228 would not be adequate for the purposes of protecting the public from serious harm occasioned by the commission by the offender of further specified offences. Under the pre-existing law the court was required to impose such a sentence if it did not impose a term of life imprisonment. Again, it is these provisions relating to requirements to impose a sentence of IPP that are changed by s 13.

3.16 Sections 227 and 228 of CJA 2003 deal with extended sentences of imprisonment (in the case of offenders aged 18 or over) or detention (in the case of offenders aged under 18).

---

[19] *Penal Policy – A Background Paper* (Ministry of Justice, 2007).
[20] Lord Hunt, Parliamentary Under-Secretary of State, Ministry of Justice, HL 2nd Reading, col 127 (22 January 2008).
[21] Defined by CJA 2003, s 224: an offence is a 'serious offence' if it is a specified offence and is punishable with life or with a determinate period of 10 years or more. An offence is a 'specified offence' if it is a specified violent offence or a specified sexual offence. A specified violent offence is one falling within CJA 2003, Sch 15, Part 1. A specified sexual offence is one falling within CJA 2003, Sch 15, Part 2.
[22] See on this, and generally *Lang and others* [2005] EWCA Crim 2864.

Section 227 applies to those specified offences which do not fall within the definition of 'serious offences'. How such offences are dealt with changes under the new Act (see **3.21**). If the court considers that there is a significant risk to members of the public of serious harm occasioned by the commission by the offender of further specified offences, it must impose an extended sentence of imprisonment. An extended sentence comprises an *appropriate custodial term*[23] and an *extension period*, for which the offender is to be subject to a licence of such length as the court considers necessary for the purpose of protecting members of the public from serious harm occasioned by the commission by him of further specified offences. The extension period must not exceed 5 years (in the case of a specified violent offence) or 8 years (in the case of a specified sexual offence) (CJA 2003, s 227(4)).[24]

Similar provisions apply to persons aged under 18 in respect of specified offences (CJA 2003, s 228).

The changes – preconditions for imposition of sentences

3.17 The preconditions for the imposition of a sentence of IPP on an adult[25] are amended by s 13 of the new Act. Section 13 does not change the requirements relating to imprisonment for life, but replaces the existing provisions relating to IPP, inserting into s 225 a new s 225(3), (3A), (3B) and (3C). Under the new law a sentence of IPP is not now mandatory: the new s 225(3) uses the word 'may' as opposed to the use of 'must' in the pre-existing s 225(3). A sentence of IPP may be imposed if the preconditions in s 225(3A) or (3B) are satisfied. The effect of the changes is to restrict the categories of offence where the court may impose a sentence of IPP or detention for public protection, restricting it to more significant cases. In future, it will be restricted to cases involving the commission of a serious offence where a minimum custodial term of 2 years is called for, or where the offender has already been convicted of a Sch 15A offence. This will, it is hoped, restrict those being imprisoned under an sentence for IPP for relatively less serious offences, and go some way to address the problems identified at **3.10**.

3.18 Section 225(3A) creates the first of the new alternative preconditions. This is that, at the time when the offence for which the offender is now being sentenced was committed, the offender had already been convicted for an offence falling within Sch 15A to CJA 2003. Schedule 15A is new.[26] The new Sch 15A identifies some 52 different serious violent or sexual offences, which may have been convicted in one of the three jurisdictions identified.[27] However, the range of offences identified in Sch 15A is narrower than that contained in Sch 15 and which applies to the definition of specified offences.[28] So, IPP will now not be available in respect of *all* specified offences.

The fact of conviction of a Sch 15A offence will be proved by a certificate issued by the court which sentenced the offender for that offence (CJA 2003, s 232, as amended by 2008 Act, s 18(2)). It is important for that court to state the fact that it is a conviction of

---

[23] Defined by CJA 2003, s 227(4) (read with CJA 2003, s 153(2)) as the shortest term, not exceeding the maximum permitted term for the offence, which is commensurate with the seriousness of the offence and any associated offences. If that term is less than 12 months, the custodial term is 12 months.
[24] See s 227(2C).
[25] See CJA 2003, s 225.
[26] Inserted into CJA 2003 by s 13(2) of, and Sch 5 to, the 2008 Act.
[27] England and Wales, Scotland, Northern Ireland.
[28] See **3.17**.

a Sch 15A offence (see CJA 2003, s 232(1)). In a case where that conviction is later quashed on appeal, s 231 of CJA 2003 (as amended by s 18(1) of the 2008 Act) applies.

3.19 The second, alternative, precondition is contained in s 225(2A), and is that the notional minimum term must be at least 2 years in length. The 'notional minimum term' is defined by the new s 225(3C). It is the part of the sentence which amounts to the tariff for the offence (the minimum period to be served for the purpose of punishment, under s 82A of the Powers of Criminal Courts (Sentencing) Act 2000 (PCC(S)A 2000)). In calculating this period of 2 years, any credits for remand must be disregarded (see **3.21**). If the offender is entitled to credits for time spent on remand (see **3.30**), the period after those credits must be at least 2 years in length.

3.20 Equivalent provisions relate to detention for public protection (CJA 2003, s 226). Section 14 amends s 226. The criteria for the imposition of a sentence for life or detention for public protection in s 226(1) and (2) remain unchanged. If the seriousness of the offence is such as to justify a sentence of detention for life, then a court must impose it. In other cases, a new s 226(3) applies. The precondition for the sentence of detention for public protection is, again, that the notional minimum term is at least 2 years, calculated in the same way as for adults (see **3.17**).

3.21 Sections 227 and 228 of CJA 2003 provide for the imposition of extended sentences for certain violent or sexual offences. As already noted (see **3.16**) s 227 applies where a person aged 18 or over was convicted for a specified offence other than a serious offence. That is changed by a textual amendment made by s 15(2). The words 'other than a serious offence' are deleted and are replaced by a new s 227(1)(c). This makes it clear that the power to impose an extended sentence potentially arises (subject to the preconditions that apply) where the court is not, under s 225(2), obliged to impose a life sentence (see **3.15**). The effect of this is that s 227 can now apply to some cases where an offender is being sentenced for a serious offence as well as a specified offence. If the offender's offence justifies a life term it 'must be imposed' by virtue of s 225. If it does not, the court 'may' impose a sentence of IPP under s 225 if the preconditions are satisfied (see **3.18**). If the preconditions for IPP are not satisfied, or if the court decides not to impose such a sentence, it may now impose an extended sentence, but, again, only if the preconditions are satisfied.

3.22 These preconditions are contained in an amended s 227(2) and new s 227(2A), (2B) and (2C). The *obligation* to impose an extended term (in s 227(2)) is changed to a *power* to do so (the word 'may' replacing 'must'). There are two preconditions: these are alternatives.

The first is contained in the new s 227(2A), and is that at the date of conviction for the offence for which the offender is being sentenced, he must have already been convicted of an offence specified under the new Sch 15A (see **3.18**). The second (contained in the new s 227(2B)) is that it must be the case that if the court were to impose an extended sentence the term that it would specify as the custodial term would be at least 4 years.

3.23 Equivalent provisions relate to extended sentences for certain violent or sexual offences for persons aged under 18 (CJA 2003, s 228): s 16 amends s 228. Section 228 applies to where a person aged 18 or over was convicted for a specified offence. The amendments made by s 16(3) replace the duty to impose an extended term with a power ('must' being replaced by 'may'). The precondition for an extended sentence under s 228 is now that the appropriate custodial term would be at least 4 years.

Dangerousness

3.24 As noted above (**3.15**) the risk of harm to members of the public must be 'significant'. That excludes minimal risks.[29] The court must decide whether the specified offences involve a significant degree of risk of serious harm to members of the public. In determining that question, s 229 of CJA 2003 applies (s 229(1)): s 17 of the new Act amends s 229. The current s 229 distinguishes between cases where the offender had not previously been convicted of any relevant offence, and cases where the offender had been convicted of a relevant offence (s 229(3) and (4)). That distinction is abolished, as are the provisions in s 229(4), and Schs 16 and 17 to CJA 2003 which dealt with the definition of 'relevant offence'.

The amended s 229 provides that the court, in making the assessment of significant risk (contained in s 229(1)):

'(a) must take into account all such information as is available to it about the nature and circumstances of the offence;
(aa) may take into account all such information as is available to it about the nature and circumstances of any other offences of which the offender has been convicted by a court anywhere in the world;
(b) may take into account any information which is before it about any pattern of behaviour of which the offences mentioned in (a) or (aa) forms part;
(c) may take into account any information about the offender which is before it.'

A new s 229(2A) includes within the meaning of conviction in s 229(2)(aa) findings of guilt in service disciplinary proceedings, and service convictions.[30]

Thus, a court may take into account a pattern of offending even if based in whole or in part upon convictions in other parts of the world. For example, in deciding the levels of risk posed by an individual who is before the court for a sexual offence, regard can be had to convictions for sexual assaults in a foreign country. These are clearly matters of relevance to the determination of dangerousness. Arguably, they are matters to which regard could be had under s 229(2)(c), but the amended provision puts the matter beyond any doubt.

INDETERMINATE SENTENCES – DETERMINATION OF TARIFFS

3.25 On the imposition of an indeterminate sentence, the judge must set the minimum period justified for the seriousness of the offence itself ('the tariff'). By s 82A of PCC(S)A 2000, when that date has elapsed the prisoner may be considered for release on licence, that issue being determined by the Parole Board.[31]

The tariff is set by the court in accordance with s 82(3), which states:

'The part of his sentence shall be such as the court considers appropriate taking into account—

---

[29] By analogy from a different statute, see *Mijura* [2007] EWCA 1249.
[30] Within the meaning of the Armed Forces Act 2006.
[31] PCC(S)A 2000, s 82A(3); Crime (Sentences) Act 1997 (C(S)A 1997), s 28(5).

(a) the seriousness of the offence, or of the combination of the offence and one or more offences associated with it;
(b) the effect of any direction which would have been given under section 87 below (crediting periods of remand in custody) if it had sentenced him to a term of imprisonment; and
(c) the early release provisions as compared with sections 33(2) and 35(1) of the Criminal Justice Act 1991.'

Thus, the tariff is the sentence that would have been imposed if the indeterminate sentence had not been imposed, but, instead, a fixed term custodial sentence was imposed. It must take into account appropriate credit if a guilty plea is given.[32] The length of sentence is determined by the seriousness of the offence, and does not incorporate any element relating to any future risk the offender may pose, because that is dealt with by the indeterminate sentence itself. The effect of (c) should be noted. Section 33(2) and 35(1) of CJA 1991 create an entitlement to release after the offender has served one-half of the custodial term. Thus, because a fixed-term prisoner would normally serve one-half of that term before release on licence, the notional term is then halved, although, wholly exceptionally, s 84A(4) permits a variation from this.[33] Finally, from the resulting term is, usually, deducted the period of time spent on remand in custody.

3.26 The application of these rules has caused controversy. One such case was that of Craig Sweeney,[34] who was convicted of four charges of kidnapping of a 3-year-old girl, three of sexual assault and one of dangerous driving. In 2003 he had been convicted of indecently assaulting a 6-year-old child. He was sentenced to a discretionary life sentence, with a tariff of 10 years. The effect of the tariff was, after making the calculation described above, that he will be eligible for parole after 5 years 108 days. Of course, it does not follow that an application for release on licence will be successful. The sentence and its political effects caused a political furore. The then Home Secretary himself was 'concerned that the tariff Craig Sweeney had been given does not reflect the seriousness of this crime and is writing to the Attorney-General to ask him to consider referring the sentence to the Court of Appeal as unduly lenient'.[35] No such reference was made, no doubt partly due to the fact that the trial judge had correctly applied the legislation which required him to give credit for a guilty plea, for time spent on remand in custody and the half-sentence deduction.

In its White Paper *Rebalancing the Criminal Justice System in favour of the law-abiding majority: Cutting crime, reducing reoffending and protecting the public*[36] the Government stated:

'... very few offenders on unlimited sentences will be released at the halfway point ... But it gives the public the impression that dangerous people might be released after a very short time; and we believe it is wrong to automatically apply this principle to "halving" the sentence tariffs for dangerous offenders ...'

---

[32] See *Reduction in Sentence for a Guilty Plea* (Sentencing Guidelines Council, Revised 2007).
[33] But see *Szczerba* [2002] Cr App R (S) 387.
[34] Swansea Crown Court, 12 June 2006.
[35] Home Office spokesperson, *Guardian*, 12 June 2006 at www.guardian.co.uk/uk/2006/jun/12/ukcrime.immigrationpolicy.
[36] *Securing the Future: proposals for the efficient and sustainable use of custody in England and Wales* (Ministry of Justice, 2007), to be found at: www.justice.gov.uk/docs/securing-the-future.pdf.

It is this aim that s 13 is addressing, albeit in language described in Parliament as 'gobbledegook'.[37]

3.27 The effect of the changes in the 2008 Act is that the provisions contained in s 82A(3) (set out above) are to be subject to new s 82A(3A), (3B) and (3C). Section 82A(3A) and (3B) define *Class A* and *Class B* respectively. If the case falls within either Class A or Class B then it is to be dealt with in accordance with the provisions of a new s 82A(3C):

> '*Case A* is where the offender was aged at least 18 when he committed the offence, and the court is of the opinion—
>
> (a) that the seriousness of the offence, together with any associated offences, is exceptional, but not such that the court proposes to make an order under s 82A(4),
> (b) and that the seriousness of the offence would not be adequately reflected by the tariff period that the court would otherwise specify under s 82A(2).
>
> *Case B* is where the court is of the opinion that the period which it would otherwise specify under s 82A(2) would have little or no effect on the time spent in custody, taking into account all the circumstances of the particular offender.'

This is particularly likely to be the case where the indeterminate sentence is being served at the same time as determinate sentences, with the minimum term expiring before the expiration of the fixed term. Generally, the court should avoid indeterminate sentences consecutive to determinate sentences. In *O'Brien and others*[38] Hooper LJ observed:

> 'Given the difficulties that may be encountered already in determining when a prisoner must be released or is eligible for parole, it seems to us much easier to compound those difficulties by making indeterminate sentences consecutive to other sentences or periods in custody.'

The court should impose a concurrent term which takes into account the time remaining to be served on the existing determinate sentence but also has regard to the additional period the court is minded to impose on the term of IPP.[39]

In cases where either Case A or Case B applies, the court, in having regard to the effect of the comparison required by s 82A(3) (with the length of a determinate sentence), may, instead of reducing that period by one half:

> 'In *Case A* reduce it by such lesser amount (including nil) as the court may consider appropriate according to the seriousness of the offence; or
>
> In *Case B*, reduce it by such lesser amount (but not by less than one-third) as the court may consider appropriate in all the circumstances.'

In short, the 50% reduction that applies to determinate sentences can be reduced. In Case A, there might be no reduction at all. In Case B, the size of the reduction is a matter for the court but will not be less than one-third. This reflects the approach taken

---

[37] Edward Garnier MP, HC Committee, col 344 (20 October 2007).
[38] [2006] EWCA Crim 1741, [2007] 1 Cr App R (S) 75. See also *Lang* [2005] EWCA Crim 2864; *Aman and Watson* [2006] EWCA Crim 1680; *Brown and Butterworth* [2006] EWCA Crim 1996; *Bartley and others* [2007] EWCA Crim 680.
[39] See *Ashes* [2007] EWCA Crim 1848.

in *Lang*[40] and other cases that the determinate sentences should be shorter than the indeterminate term. There will always be a one-third reduction. Clearly, given the different powers in s 82A(3C) that relate to Case A and Case B, it will be important for the court to identify precisely into which of those the case falls. It might even conceivably be that a case before the court falls within both. Care will therefore need to be taken as to how these provisions are to be applied. There will also be a need to develop appropriate principles governing the exercise of these powers. There is a danger that Case A may in fact be used routinely, as the default position.[41] It also means that the length of time served under a determinate and indeterminate sentence may differ despite the nominal period to be served for punishment being identical: a danger that may increase with the changes to the requirements as to the imposition of sentences for dangerous offenders.[42]

RELEASE AND RECALL OF PRISONERS

3.28 A significant number of provisions deal with the length of the period a prisoner will serve, their early release and their recall to prison:

- s 21 deals with credit for periods of remands on bail;

- s 24 deals with the minimum conditions for early release;

- s 25 deals with release on licence of prisoners serving extended sentences;

- s 26 deals with release of long-term prisoners; and

- s 29 deals with release of prisoners after recall.

Section 26 and related sections came into force on 4 June 2008, subject to certain transitional provisions (see **1.5**). Sections 24, 25 and 29 came into force on 14 July 2008 (see **1.5**) subject to transitional provisions in respect of s 25 and 29 (see Criminal Justice and Immigration Act 2008 (Commencement No 2 and Transitional and Savings Provisions) Order 2008, SI 2008/1586, Sch 2, para 2. Section 25 does not apply to any person sentenced before 14 July 2008. Section 29 does not apply to any person recalled before 14 July 2008. Section 21 is not yet in force.

The changes are made in the context of overcrowding in prisons and a lack of sufficient prison places. One result of that is the changes to the dangerous offender provisions so that only the most dangerous offenders are given an indeterminate term (see **3.14**). Another is to change the rules to reduce the growth of recall prisoners and to facilitate the removal of foreign prisoners.

Credits for remands on bail

3.29 Section 240 of CJA 2003 provides for credit to be given for periods spent in custody, when determining how long the offender should serve having been sentenced to

---

[40] [2005] EWCA Crim 2864.
[41] See the concerns of Prison Reform Trust, cited by HC Research Study 07/65 *The Criminal Justice and Immigration Bill* (August 2007).
[42] See evidence of Gareth Crossman, Policy Director, Liberty, HC Committee, col 244 (18 October 2007).

a term of imprisonment or, if aged under 18, detention. Subject to the exceptions contained in s 240(4), the court must direct that the number of days for which the offender was remanded in custody in connection with the offence, or any related offences,[43] is to count as time served by him as part of the sentence (s 240(3)). Despite the seemingly clear words of s 240(3) it is open to a court to make a direction as to a lesser number of days if the test in s 240 is satisfied ('where it is just in all the circumstances not to give a direction …'). That flows clearly both from the terms of s 240(5) and (6).

Section 21 of the new Act creates a new s 240A of CJA 2003. It applies in respect of offences committed on or after 4 April 2005 (the commencement date for s 240). Transitional arrangements in respect of offences committed prior to that date are contained in s 23 and Sch 6. Section 21 has not been brought into force as at the date of going to press.

The new s 240A applies where the offender was remanded on bail after the commencement date of s 21 and which was subject to an electronic monitoring condition. Where those preconditions are satisfied the court must order the credit period to count as time served, subject to the limitation in s 240A(4). The number of days, the subject of the direction, must be stated in open court.

Just as with s 240, this permits such time not to count to the extent that rules so provide, or, if the court considers it just, in all the circumstances not to give a direction under s 240A(2). Amongst the factors the court must take into account is whether the offender broke any electronic monitoring condition.

The 'credit period' is one-half of the number of days on which the offender's bail was subject to an electronic monitoring condition. As with s 240, a court can make a direction for a lesser period of time (s 240A(5)).

3.30 The new s 240A of CJA 2003 (see above) is extended to cases involving mandatory or discretionary life sentences, detention and training orders, prisoners being sentenced at a re-trial and International Criminal Court sentences. That may have the effect of simplifying the sentencing regime. In respect of sentences of IPP the provisions of s 82(3) of PCC(S)A 2000 provide that the judge must take into account periods spent on remand when determining minimum terms.[44] The changes means that, when in force, s 240A will apply to such cases.

Home Detention Curfew scheme

3.31 Section 246 of CJA 2003 re-enacted, with significant amendments, the scheme first introduced in 1991 to release some, although not all, short-term prisoners on licence to serve part of their sentence at home. The 2003 Act extended the scheme to most fixed-term sentences, departing from the principle that it ought not to apply to those serving longer sentences. CJA 2003 extended the potential number of days left to be served to 135 days.

---

[43] An offence, other than the offence for which the sentence is imposed (offence A) with which the offender was charged and the charge for which was founded on the same facts or evidence as offence A: see now s 240A(12).
[44] *Taylor* [2008] EWCA 465.

Home detention curfew did not apply to a prisoner unless the length of the requisite custody period was at least 6 weeks, and the offender had served at least 4 weeks of his sentence and one-half of the requisite custody period.[45] The one exception to this is the case of prisoners serving intermittent custody, where the number of required custodial days is at least 42, and the prisoner has served at least 28 of those days and at least one-half of those days.

3.32 Section 24 of the new Act amends s 246(2). The effect of the amendment is to change the precondition for release. The 6-week period becomes 4 weeks. The requirement for the prisoner to have served one-half of the requisite custodial period remains.

Release on licence of prisoner serving extended sentence under CJA 2003, ss 227 and 228

3.33 Section 247 of CJA 2003 brought prisoners serving extended sentences into the Home Detention Curfew scheme. As soon as a prisoner who is serving an extended sentence has served one-half of the custodial term, and the Parole Board has directed his release, the Home Secretary must release him on licence. The licence lasts throughout the remainder of the sentence (s 259). The Parole Board may not give a direction for release unless it is satisfied that it is no longer necessary for the protection of the public that the prisoner should be confined (s 247(2)).

The change made by s 25 of the new Act is to remove the requirement that the Parole Board must direct release. The effect of deleting para (b) from s 247(2) is to make release automatic on the offender having served one-half of the custodial term, irrespective of any perceived risk in terms of public protection. However, that release is on licence and subject to the recall provisions contained in s 254 of CJA 2003.

Release of long-term prisoners

3.34 CJA 2003 introduced a new scheme for the release on licence of prisoners[46] which came into effect in respect of offences committed on or after 5 April 2005 (the relevant date of commencement). It applied to fixed-term prisoners, where the prisoner had served the requisite custodial period. In respect of a term of 12 months or more the custodial period is one-half of the term imposed. In respect of terms less than 12 months, the 'custody plus' provisions (see **3.10**) mean that the offender has to serve the custodial sentence. In all cases the actual time served under the sentence may be affected by credit for time spent on remand in custody, or, following the changes in the 2008 Act, on bail but subject to electronic monitoring requirements.[47]

Prisoners sentenced in respect of offences committed prior to 4 April 2005 remained on the old regime pursuant to CJA 1991. That scheme drew a distinction between short-term and long-term prisoners. In relation to the former (persons serving up to 4 years) the prisoner served half the sentence, with the remainder on licence, subject to release on the Home Detention Curfew scheme. In respect of long-term prisoners (those

---

[45] Defined by CJA 2003, s 244(3) by reference to the determinate sentence in the case of 'custody-plus' (see **3.10**), the length of the custodial period and in the case of intermittent custody (see **3.12**) by the number of days which are not part of the licence period.
[46] For the reasons for change see Halliday Report, para 4.15.
[47] See **3.29**.

sentenced to a term of 4 years or more) the prisoner served half the sentence before becoming eligible for release on licence following a decision of the Parole Board. Automatic release occurred at the two-thirds sentence point, and licence continued until the three-quarters sentence date. The difference between short-term, and long-term prisoners could be explained on the basis that long-term prisoners were likely to include those who might be a danger to the public and the different release and supervision arrangements needed to be put in place.

3.35 The changes made by the new Act, and contained in s 26, affect the position of some, but not all, long-term prisoners. It will apply only to those who have not reached the halfway point of their sentence at the date of commencement of these provisions.[48]

Amendments are made to s 33 of CJA 1991, the effect of which is to require the Home Secretary to release on licence some long-term prisoners after the prisoner has served one-half of his sentence (CJA 1991, s 33(1A)). The group of long-term prisoners who do not fall within this change are those serving a term for an offence under Sch 15 to CJA 2003 (violent or sexual offences).[49] The role of the Parole Board in respect of non-violent or sexual offences is abolished.

The duration and conditions of the licence under which the long-term offender is released is governed by a new s 37ZA of CJA 1991, created by s 26(6) of the 2008 Act. It is this section, rather than the pre-existing s 37 of CJA 1991 that will govern these matters (2008 Act, s 26(4)). This provision requires the licence to continue to the end of the sentence, subject to standard conditions issued by the Home Secretary under s 250 of CJA 2003, and which are applicable to post 4 April 2005 offences. Section 250 requires the Home Secretary to have regard to the protection of the public, the prevention of re-offending and to the securing of successful reintegration of the prisoner into the community.

Application of licence provisions to prisoners liable to removal from the UK and early removal of prisoners

3.36 Foreign prisoners comprise some 14% of the prison population.[50] Schemes for transfer out of the UK exist: in 2006 the number of prisoners so transferred was 2,784. As part of the measures attempting to reduce the population, the Act addresses two issues.

The first is the question of the grant of licence. Some prisoners are liable to being removed from the UK on their release. These are non-UK citizens, who are liable to deportation, or who have been refused leave to enter the UK, or liable to removal under s 10 of the Immigration and Asylum Act 1999.[51] In such cases, they may be removed early from the UK during a period of 135 days ending with the day on which the prisoner will have completed the custodial part of his sentence (CJA 2003, s 260).[52]

The right of long-term prisoners to be released on licence following a recommendation from the Parole Board has in the past been limited in respect of offenders serving a fixed

---

[48] See **3.28**.
[49] Including various service offences: see CJA 1991, s 33(1C) and (1D) inserted therein by the 2008 Act, s 26.
[50] David Hanson, Minister Of State, Ministry of Justice, HC Committee, col 359 (20 October 2007).
[51] CJA 2003, s 259.
[52] See, now **3.34**.

term of 15 years or more.[53] It was also the case that the Parole Board did not have the power to recommend the release of prisoners who are liable to removal from the UK. That was a matter for the Home Secretary. Both these restrictions did not survive the passage of CJA 2003,[54] the terms of which apply to offences committed after 4 April 2005 (the commencement day for the relevant provisions).

However, those changes do not apply in respect of offences committed before that date. In *R (on the application of Clift) v Secretary of State for the Home Department, R (on the application of Hindawi and another) v Secretary of State for the Home Department*[55] both principles were challenged by prisoners who had committed offences prior to 4 April 2005. The appeal of C, a UK citizen serving a term longer than 15 years, failed, but that of H, a non-UK national liable to deportation, succeeded, on the ground that it was discriminatory in applying the rule (no role for the Parole Board in the case of non-UK nationals), and thus there was a breach of Art 14 of the ECHR in conjunction with Art 5. A declaration of incompatibility was made.[56] The rule was 'an indefensible anomaly ... no longer capable of rational justification';[57] Lord Brown stated:[58]

> 'Under the 2003 Act the [Home Secretary] has surrendered his discretion (save in respect of 135 days) with regard to all determinate sentence prisoners whose offences were committed after 4 April 2005 ie those subject to removal no less than nationals. The anomaly ... has similarly become yet more plainly indefensible. Given that the House is now to declare the legislation which still affects these two applicants to be incompatible with their Convention rights, the [Home Secretary] will surely wish to consider whether the time has now come to leave all future decisions as to the release on licence ... exclusively to the Parole Board.'

Although the role of the Parole Board is reduced generally (see **3.34**), the 2008 Act takes the opportunity to make the change necessary following the decision of the House of Lords in *Hindawi*.

The change is made by s 27, which repeals s 46(1) and s 50(2) of CJA 1991 (the early release provisions which excluded the role of the Parole Board). They are now to be treated in the same way as other prisoners (the effect of the reference in s 27(1) to 'the 1998 Order').

3.37 The second set of changes is in relation to the Early Removal Scheme. This is governed by ss 259–261 and s 262 of CJA 2003, with equivalent provisions in CJA 1991 in respect of offences committed prior to the commencement of the 2003 Act provisions. These confer a power to remove a person from the UK. The effect of s 33 of the 2008 Act is to insert a new s 46ZA into CJA 1991 and s 34 inserts an equivalent s 259A into CJA 2003. These new sections define the category of persons to whom the power applies as 'a person [who] has the settled intention of residing permanently outside the United Kingdom if removed from prison'. That person must not be liable to removal. He or she could be a British citizen who has that settled intention. Existing limitations on certain categories of prisoner are removed.

---

[53] See Parole Board (Transfer of Functions) Order 1998, SI 1998/3218.
[54] See CJA 2003, ss 244, 259, 262 and Sch 20.
[55] [2006] UKHL 54.
[56] Under the Human Rights Act 1998, s 4.
[57] Lord Bingham at para 38.
[58] At para 69.

RELEASE OF PRISONERS AFTER RECALL

Background

3.38 Significant concern has arisen about the operation of the recall system in respect of prisoners who breach their licence conditions. Sections 254–256 of CJA 2003 re-enacted, with amendments, the recall provisions contained in earlier legislation. The essence of those provisions is that the Secretary has discretion (not a duty) to recall prisoners and revoke his or her licence. An obligation to refer such cases to the Parole Board arises after recall (CJA 2003, s 254(3)). If the Parole Board recommends the prisoner's immediate release, the Secretary of State is under an obligation to release that prisoner.

Section 255 deals with early release (see **3.34**). If the prisoner fails to comply with any condition attached to that early release or licence, or the prisoner's whereabouts cannot be electronically monitored at the place specified in a curfew condition in his licence, again, the Secretary of State has the power to revoke the licence and recall the prisoner. In this situation, there is no right of reference to the Parole Board, but the Secretary of State is under an obligation to consider representations from the prisoner.

In either situation, on revocation of licence and recall, the prisoner is detained pursuant to his or her licence (ss 254(6) and 255(5)). Section 256 confers a duty on the Secretary of State to fix a date for release, or fix a date for the review of release, if the Parole Board recommends release under s 254(3).

3.39 This 'trapdoor to prison'[59] has led to a significant increase in the population, from around 3,400 in April 2005 to nearly 5,000 in February 2007.[60] About 800 a month are being returned to prison for breaking the terms of their licence.[61] These numbers increase the pressures on the prison estate, but also on the Parole Board. The background paper on *Penal Policy*[62] proposed 'new arrangements so that in appropriate cases non-dangerous prisoners can be given a fixed term, punitive recall to prison for 28 days'. That is what the 2008 Act implements. 'Automatic release' occurs after this 28-day period, in cases to which it applies. The purpose of the change is that, if the prisoner is assessed as not presenting a risk of harm any recall will be for a maximum period of 28 days. This is intended to ensure that recall is not a punitive measure, but a measure of protection for the public, removing the prisoner from 'often rapidly deteriorating situations, and placing them in secure environments'.[63] It also may have the effect of not having lots of people who have been recalled to custody for what in effect are minor breaches.[64]

Probation officers will be able to review the licence conditions and, if appropriate, recommend additional restrictions. Swift and effective enforcement of licence conditions is regarded as extremely important, and has significantly improved in recent years.[65]

---

[59] Lord Phillips CJ, *Guardian*, 3 May 2007.
[60] Figures cited in *Penal Policy – a background paper* (Ministry of Justice, 2007) at p 9, available at: www.justice.gov.uk/docs/Penal-Policy-Final.pdf.
[61] Lord Phillips, *Guardian*, 3 May 2007.
[62] See *Penal Policy – a background paper* (Ministry of Justice, 2007), available at www.justice.gov.uk/docs/Penal-Policy-Final.pdf.
[63] David Hanson, Minister of State, Ministry of Justice, HC Committee, col 369 (20 November 2007).
[64] Edward Garnier MP, HC Committee, col 373 (20 November 2007): supporting the proposals by reference to the experience of a similar scheme in New York.
[65] 33% enforcement in 1997, 91% in 2006: David Hanson, HC Committee, col 369 (20 November 2007).

There is the risk that the effectiveness of recall may be watered down. In evidence to the HC Committee, the Chief Executive of the Probation Boards Association observed:[66]

> 'The probation service originally would have been quite uncomfortable about the idea of recall being such a central part of our professional work, but it changed its views ... There was a real threat – if people did not comply, they knew they were going back – and that helped the work of probation officers in making their relationship with that prisoner stick. Our concern is that, prisoners will know that it almost does not matter – that you can behave badly or re-offend when you are on licence and have a 28-day window of opportunity when you can maybe persuade the parole board to let you out, and you will certainly be out within 28 days. That makes it more difficult for probation staff to have an authoritative relationship with those offenders ...'

Nonetheless, the proposals attracted widespread support.

Automatic release

3.40 Section 29 removes the provisions in s 254(3)–(5) of CJA 2003, and inserts into CJA 2003 new ss 255A, 255B, 255C and 255D.

The new s 255A provides for automatic release of certain, but not all, offenders following recall. Eligibility for automatic release does not extend to an extended sentence prisoner (see **3.16**) or a specified offence prisoner (see **3.17**). Nor does it apply to cases where the offender is recalled under s 246 having been granted early release, or where, during the same term of imprisonment already been given an automatic release or released under the new s 255C. In short, the broad effect is to confine automatic release to non-dangerous offenders who have not been recalled before (see s 255A(a)–(c)).

When a prisoner who is eligible is recalled he must be told whether he is considered suitable for automatic release. The prisoner is 'suitable' only if the Secretary of State is satisfied that the prisoner will not present a risk of serious harm to members of the public if he is released at the end of that period (s 255A(5)). 'Serious harm' means death or serious injury, whether physical or psychological (s 255A(13)). The term 'risk' must be contrasted with 'significant risk' in s 225 of CJA 2003. If that difference is anything other than a drafting omission, the potential exists for a very strict approach to suitability, although given the motivation for the change, it is perhaps unlikely that this will in fact be the approach taken. The definition of serious harm is not limited to cases where the danger of serious harm is obvious and has actually been caused in the past. The key test is the risk of serious harm in the future. An indecent assault on a young girl may well lead to serious psychological injury. It will include the risk of serious harm to those who are vulnerable or less robust than average.[67]

The risk of serious harm must be in respect of harm to members of the public. This is a broad term, which is not defined. It is wide enough to include the public generally, particular sections of the public or even individual members of the public, such as family members, individuals against whom the prisoner has a grudge or ex-partners in respect of whom the prisoner may threaten, or inflict, violence.

---

[66] See Probation Boards Association, HC Committee, col 102 (16 October 2007).
[67] For approaches to the concept of serious harm see *Bowler* (1994) 15 Cr App R (S) 78; *Appelt* (1994) 15 Cr App R (S) 532; *Williams* (1994) 15 Cr App R (S) 330; *Creasy* (1994) 15 Cr App R 171.

The level of risk posed will be for the Secretary of State to determine, with no independent input from the Parole Board or others. Whilst the prisoner will have a right to appeal to the Parole Board if he is refused release, there is no independent input into a decision that in fact grants release. The success of the scheme will depend on the risk assessment done at the time of recall. This is likely to be the only risk assessment and will determine whether the automatic release provisions discussed above apply, or whether further assessments are needed before the exercise of discretion, discussed at **3.35**.[68]

3.41 If the prisoner is suitable for automatic release, s 255B applies (not suitable s 255A(6)(a)). The prisoner must be told that he will be released under s 255B, and be released after 28 days (s 255B(1)). However, the Secretary of State may release him earlier than 28 days if he considers that it is not necessary for the protection of the public that he should remain in prison until the end of the 28-day period (s 255B(2), (3)). A prisoner has the right to make representations before the end of the 28-day period, and, if this happens, they must be referred to the Parole Board (s 255B(4)). If the Board recommends immediate release, this must be given effect to (s 255B(6)). Special rules apply to prisoners serving a term of intermittent custody (s 255B(6)).

If the prisoner is eligible for automatic release, but considered not to be suitable, s 255C applies. This is dealt with at **3.42** below.

Prisoners not eligible or suitable for automatic release

3.42 In respect of prisoners who are not eligible or suitable for automatic release, other than extended sentence prisoners,[69] s 255C applies (s 225A(6)(b), (c) and s 255C(1)). These are prisoners who pose some risk either because of the nature of the offence, the decision of the Secretary of State or already having benefited from automatic release. The power to release exists at any time after return to prison, provided the Secretary of State is satisfied that it is not necessary for the protection of the public that he should remain in prison (s 255C(3)). If the prisoner makes representations before the end of 28 days, or if the prisoner has not been released at the end of 28 days the case must be referred to the Parole Board (s 255C(4)). If the Parole Board recommends the prisoner's immediate release, that must occur (s 255C(5)). Special rules apply to those serving a term of intermittent custody (s 255C(6)).

Again, as noted above (**3.35**) the risk assessment will be crucial. It is intended that the decision of the Secretary of State will be informed by 'up-to-date' risk assessments.[70]

Extended sentence prisoners

3.43 On recall, the case of an extended sentence prisoner must be referred to the Parole Board. The Secretary of State must give effect to that recommendation (s 255D).

Life prisoners

3.44 The revocation of the licence of a life prisoner is governed by s 32 of C(S)A 1997. Prior to the new Act, s 32 provided that the Secretary of State may revoke the licence of

---

[68] See evidence of Christine Laurie to HC Committee (16 October 2007).
[69] See **3.34**.
[70] David Hanson, Minister of State, HC Committee, col 369 (20 November 2007).

a prisoner serving a life sentence who has been released on licence, and recall the prisoner to prison: (a) if recommended to do so by the Parole Board, or (b) without such a recommendation, where it appears to the Secretary of State that it is expedient in the public interest to recall the prisoner before such a recommendation is practicable. If, therefore, it was practicable to obtain a consideration of the Parole Board it was necessary to do so.

Section 31 of the 2008 Act abolishes the requirement for a recommendation by the Parole Board. The matter is now one for the Secretary of State. Section 31 does not specify any criteria limiting in any way the exercise of that discretion.

3.45 The reason for change appears to be real concerns about dangerous prisoners re-offending whilst on licence. A House of Commons Research Paper[71] cites the case of Anthony Rice, a discretionary life prisoner who killed whilst on licence. Clearly decisions on risk, dangerousness and the public interest are difficult issues. The review quoted by the Research Paper suggests that, perhaps, the emphasis has shifted to an increasing focus on the human rights of the prisoner prior to release rather than by issues of public protection. The change made by s 31 enables the Secretary of State to take the primary role in assessing these risks and wider public interests. However, nothing in s 31 specifically states on what criteria this power is to be used, or what the safeguards are for the prisoner. The position of the life prisoner after recall will be governed by s 32 of C(S)A 1997, with the Secretary of State under a duty to refer the case to the Parole Board (C(S)A 1997, s 32(4) and the 2008 Act, s 31(4)).

---

[71] HC Research paper 07/65, at p 30. The Research Report cites extensively the resultant report *HM Inspectorate of Probation Serious Further Offence Review: Anthony Rice*.

Chapter 4

YOUNG OFFENDERS – GENERAL CHANGES

SUMMARY

4.1 The new Act makes significant changes in respect of young offenders and youth justice.[1] The creation of a new Youth Rehabilitation Order is discussed in Chapter 5. The changes related to sentences of extended detention were discussed with similar changes relating to adults, in Chapter 3. However, other changes are just as significant:

- the Act defines the purposes of sentencing offenders aged under 18;

- it changes the restrictions on the imposition of a community order;

- the rules applicable to referral orders are changed;

- detailed changes are made to youth default orders;

- changes are made to how young offenders are dealt with by the criminal justice system, with Sch 9 introducing a power to issue conditional cautions.

THE WIDER BACKGROUND

4.2 The provisions of the new Act are the latest in a long line of provisions intended to address the question of offending by children and young persons. Much time, and significant resources, have been invested. Yet, despite this, the success or otherwise of a strategy aimed specifically at reducing youth crime remains contentious amongst politicians, commentators, practitioners and academics. One commentator is said to have observed:[2]

> 'Youth justice in the past 10 years is a tale of the ineffectiveness of custodial crackdowns that ignore the broader welfare context which is absolutely necessary.'

A report published in late May 2008 by the Centre for Crime and Justice Studies[3] concluded that, since the beginning of 2000, spending on youth justice had increased in real terms by 45% but had had no discernible effect on cutting offending rates. The Report concluded that nearly all the targets set, relating to youth offenders'

---

[1] For an interesting contextual overview, see Ball 'Youth Justice: Half a Century of Responses to Youth Offending' [2008] Crim LR 28.
[2] Frances Crook, Director of Howard League for Penal Reform, quoted in *The Observer*, 1 June 2008.
[3] *Ten years of Labour's youth justice reforms: an independent audit* (Centre for Crime and Justice Studies, King's College, London, May 2008): available at www.crimeandjustice.org.uk.

accommodation, education, training, employment, substance abuse and mental health, have not been met. Youth Justice Board statistics show that in the last 3 years offences committed by young offenders have risen to almost 300,000, with offences by girls up by 25% and violent offences up by 50%.[4] These statistics are not regarded by the Government as showing the whole picture and, like all statistics, perhaps do not tell the full story. Offending rates overall remain stable with offending by under 16s declining. Most additional disposals by the youth courts were community-based rather than custodial. Indeed the increased levels reported may reflect changes in official responses to low-level criminality as opposed to changes in the amount of criminal behaviour itself. Yet, it is in this context that a further raft of measures is being introduced by the new Act.

4.3 The background to these particular provisions was set out in Chapter 1 (see **1.6**). The basis for the Government's youth justice strategy was set when it came to office, taking account of a striking picture of youth crime identified by the Audit Commission.[5] Its strategy was identified by the White Paper *No More Excuses: New National and Local Focus on Youth Crime*,[6] which formed the basis for the Crime and Disorder Act 1998 (CDA 1998). Since then there has been, of course, a flow of analyses, policy documents, initiative and pilot schemes, underpinned by a range of legislative provisions, not least in the Criminal Justice Act 2003 (CJA 2003).

More recently, the White Paper *Rebalancing the criminal justice system in favour of the law-abiding majority* followed on the heels of a Government Green Paper, *Every Child Matters*,[7] published in 2003, which addressed the risks faced by children by proposing a wide range of services, interventions and improved child protection and support procedures. Alongside that, as a companion document, *Youth Justice – The Next Steps*[8] launched a consultation process with regards to possible changes to the youth justice system. The current provisions are in principle, though not necessarily in detail, based on the approach identified in that document, informed by the responses to that consultation.[9]

Yet fundamental issues remain. The question is whether further legislative intervention can impact on the issues. In its Report, the Centre for Crime and Justice Studies asks whether the expectations of what the youth justice system can achieve have been too high, and whether more effective solutions could be achieved through social rather than legal solutions. There is some evidence that a major new review of approach will be adopted during 2008 and beyond. Indeed, the *Youth Crime Action Plan 2008*[10] identifies a wide range of measures designed to 'address the root causes of their behaviour, [including] supporting and challenging their parents to meet their responsibilities'.[11] The proposed actions include the following:

---

[4] 158 NLJ 719 (23 May 2008): see www.new-law-journal.co.uk.
[5] See *Misspent Youth: Young People and Crime* (Audit Commission, 1996); *Misspent Youth '98: The Challenge for Youth Justice* (Audit Commission, 1998). See also *Tackling Youth Crime: Reforming Youth Justice* (Labour Party, 1996).
[6] Home Office, 1997.
[7] Cm 5860 (TSO, September 2003). The Report was a response to the Laming Report into the death of Victoria Climbie.
[8] Home Office, May 2003.
[9] *Youth Justice – The Next Steps: Summary of Responses and the Government's Proposals* (Home Office, 2004).
[10] Published 15 July 2008, to be found at www.justice.gov.uk/youth-crime-action-plan.pdf.
[11] See ibid, 5, para 6.

- more searches and search equipment to help take weapons off the streets: everyone over the age of 16 who is found carrying a knife can expect to be prosecuted, and those under 16 can be expected to be prosecuted for a second offence;

- increasing the proportion of ASBOs accompanied by a parenting order;

- expanding provision of youth centres;

- using existing police powers more, including measures to tackle anti-social behaviour and under-age drinking;

- making permanent exclusion from school a trigger of assessment;

- greater use of parenting orders;

- getting the public to identify reparation work.

The longer-term initiatives proposed include the implementation of some of the key powers conferred by the 2008 Act.

PURPOSES OF SENTENCING OFFENDERS UNDER THE AGE OF 18

4.4 Section 142 of CJA 2003 states that a court when dealing with an offender must have regard to the punishment of offenders, the reduction of crime (including by deterrence) the reform and rehabilitation of offenders, the protection of the public and the making of reparation by offenders to persons affected by their offences. It was introduced because of the mixed messages that were sometimes sent as to what sentencers were trying to achieve. In the case of adult offenders, until CJA 2003 there had not been any statutory statement of the principles a court should adopt.

By contrast, s 37 of CDA 1998 states that 'the principal aim of the youth justice system [is] to prevent offending by children and young persons'. It is the duty of all those working within the youth justice system to have regard to this aim, although the use of the phrase 'principal aim' indicates that this was not to be regarded as the sole aim. Another legitimate aim is the welfare of the offender. Thus, s 44 of the Children and Young Persons Act 1933 (CYPA 1933) requires a court, in fulfilling its duties, to take account of the welfare of the child or young person before the court, and to take steps to remove him or her from undesirable surroundings. It must also secure proper provision for his or her education.

Clearly there is a tension between the general duty in s 37, and the specific duty in s 44 of CYPA 1933 relating to the individual child or young person. That tension is, perhaps, highlighted by the range of provisions in international law. In particular, the Convention on the Rights of the Child[12] is relevant. Article 3 provides that in all actions concerning children, their best interests are to be a primary consideration. The Convention recognises that the use of custody for children should be a last resort.[13] Again, note may

---

[12] TS No 44 (No 2) Cm 17976, adopted by United Nations General Assembly 20 November 1989.
[13] TS No 44 (No 2) Cm 17976, Art 37(b). See **5.3**.

be taken of, in international law, the Beijing Rules.[14] Rule 5 requires a juvenile justice system to be proportionate to both the offence *and* the offender.

4.5 The new Act revisits these issues. Section 9 inserts a new s 142A into CJA 2003. It had not been brought into effect as at the date of going to press.

It requires a court, when sentencing an offender aged under 18 to have regard to the principal aim of the youth justice system contained in s 37, and to the welfare of the offender, under s 44. The effect of that is to make the prevention of re-offending the first regard. The court must now have regard to the purposes of sentencing, unless the sentence the court may impose is limited in the way identified by s 142A(4). These are stated by the new s 142A(3) as:

'(a) the punishment of offenders,
(b) the reform and rehabilitation of offenders,
(c) the protection of the public, and
(d) the making of reparation by offenders to persons affected by the offences.'

The question arises as to whether this approach is compatible with the Convention on the Rights of the Child (CRC). Article 3 of that Convention imposes an obligation to ensure that the best interests of the child is a primary consideration in all actions concerning them. The Government believes that in this respect the new law is Convention-compliant, in that Art 3 does not require the best interests of the child to be *the* primary consideration, but only *a* primary consideration.[15] The Joint Committee on Human Rights recommended that the Bill be amended to give effect more explicitly to the requirement that welfare issues are a primary consideration. However, no such amendment was made. Under the Act, the welfare of the child is a consideration to which a court must have regard, but is not *the* primary aim.

The importance of recognising that the welfare of the offender is fundamental is not only derived from a desire to comply with the CRC. One of the key objectives of this legislative change, and associated executive actions, is to reduce the numbers of children and young being taken into custody. The Chairman of the Children's Society[16] observed during the passage of the Act that such a decrease should not be expected to occur unless the youth justice system takes into account the welfare and well-being of children. At the moment, some £280m a year is spent on sending children into custody.[17] The tensions that may arise become clear when one examines the choices open to a court under the new youth rehabilitation provisions (see **5.8**).

It might be thought that, given the complexity of the role of the court in dealing with young offenders, there should be a general right to legal representation for children in criminal proceedings. That was certainly the view of the Joint Committee on Human Rights.[18] It stated:

'We are surprised to learn that there is not a presumption that children are entitled to publicly funded legal representation in criminal proceedings, given the seriousness of the

---

[14] United Nation Standard Minimum Rules for the Administration of Juvenile Justice, adopted by United Nations General Assembly 29 November 1985.
[15] Joint Committee on Human Rights, 5th Report, para 1.27.
[16] Bob Reitemeier, in evidence to the HC Committee, col 88 (18 October 2008).
[17] Simon Hickson, Policy Adviser, Children's Society in evidence to HC Committee, col 91 (18 October 2007).
[18] 5th Report, para 1.24.

consequences for them and the complex and intimidating nature of those proceedings ... We recommend ... that the Government amend the Bill to provide for a general right of legal representation for children ...'

Unsuccessful attempts were made to achieve this during the passage of the Act. Although legal representation is a precondition in certain limited situations, it is not generally required as a prerequisite. This remains a live issue.

ALTERNATIVES TO PROSECUTION – CONDITIONAL CAUTIONS AND OTHER CHANGES

4.6 Section 48 of, and Sch 9 to, the new Act amend the Crime and Disorder Act 1998 (CDA 1998) to permit the giving of youth conditional cautions to children and young persons. They also make minor amendments to the scheme of reprimands and final warnings created by CDA 1998. These changes had not been brought into effect as at the date of going to press.

Background

4.7 CDA 1998 introduced a system of reprimands and final warnings for young offenders, replacing the then existing system of police cautions. The system permits the giving of a reprimand or final warning where the offender admits the offence, and it is not in the public interest that the offender be prosecuted. The reprimand or warning does not amount to a conviction, would not be recorded by the police and would not be covered by the Rehabilitation of Offenders Act 1974. The rationale for the scheme was to attempt to divert first-time young offenders from the criminal justice system, but within a system that recognised that the impact of this diversion became less effective the more it was used for repeat offending.[19]

The main features of the scheme are as follows. A first offence may attract a reprimand provided it is not serious, but any further offence should result in either a warning or prosecution. In no circumstances should an offender receive two reprimands. If the first offence results in a warning, any subsequent offence should normally lead to prosecution. Only where 2 years have elapsed since a warning, and the subsequent offence is minor should prosecution not follow for an offence subsequent to a final warning. The police, if a child or young person is prosecuted, should always refer him or her, subject to a warning, to a youth offender team.

In CJA 2003 a scheme of conditional cautions was introduced for adult offenders. A conditional caution is a caution which is given in respect of an offence committed by the offender, and which has conditions attached to it with which the offender must comply. Failure to comply with those conditions renders the offender liable to be prosecuted for the offence in respect of which the caution was given. The new Act extends this approach to children and young persons.

---

[19] *No More Excuses – New National and Local Focus on Youth Crime* (Home Office, 1997). For a convenient review of the history and purpose see Lord Bingham in *R v Durham Constabulary and another, ex p R* [2005] UKHL 21.

Reprimands and warnings

4.8 Schedule 9, para 2 makes detailed changes to the provisions relating to the conditions for the giving of a reprimand or warning.

The first changes the preconditions in s 65(2)(b) of CDA 1998 relating to the evidential basis that must exist. The old wording required the police officer to consider that 'the evidence is such that, if the offender were prosecuted for the offence, there would be a realistic prospect of conviction'. The new amendment simply requires the officer to consider that there is sufficient evidence to charge the offender. This makes it clear that the officer simply has to consider the evidential basis without regard to any wider questions as to the likelihood of conviction. That said, if the evidential basis is not such as to provide a reasonable prospect of convicting there is surely insufficient evidence to charge.

The second change is consequential upon the introduction of youth conditional cautions. Under the amended provisions, the officer has to be satisfied that it is not in the public interest for the offender to be prosecuted 'or given a youth conditional caution'.[20] Thus, in this and related amendments,[21] it is made clear that reprimands and warnings remain at the bottom of the hierarchy of available actions in respect of young offenders, and certainly below youth conditional cautions.

Youth conditional cautions

4.9 As noted at **4.7**, CJA 2003 introduced a scheme of conditional cautions. Section 9 of, and Sch 9 to, the new Act, creates a largely similar scheme in respect of young offenders. It does so by creating a series of sections (ss 66A–H) which are inserted into CDA 1998. Nothing in the new Act gives clear guidance as to the interrelationship between the conditional cautioning scheme, and the scheme for reprimands and warnings.

A conditional caution is, for these purposes, a caution which is given in respect of an offence committed by the offender and which has conditions attached to it with which the offender must comply (CDA 1998, s 66A(2)). Breach of any of the conditions can lead to prosecution for the offence in respect of which the caution was given. The conditions attached to the caution must:

(a) facilitate the rehabilitation of the offender;

(b) ensure that the offender makes reparation for the offence; or

(c) punish the offender.

The first two criteria replicate those in respect of adults; the third is new, reflecting the principal aim of the youth justice system and the fact that the main emphasis now is not intended to be the welfare of the individual offender.

---

[20] Sch 9, para 2(2)(c).
[21] To CDA 1998, s 65(3)(b) and s 65(6).

In response to criticisms that this was, in effect, 'dumbing down' justice[22] (especially for 16 and 17 year olds) the Minister explained the purpose of the provisions:[23]

> 'The aim ... is to reduce the number of children being taken to court for relatively low-level offences by creating an alternative, robust mechanism for bringing young offenders to account, and to address some of the causes of their behaviour. The conditions ... must help the rehabilitation of the offender ... In general terms we are trying to reduce the number of people who go into custody by putting in place an alternative to custody which will provide rehabilitation, introduce some effective measures and help to prevent reoffending by young people ...'

Despite this emphasis on rehabilitation, some evidence exists to suggest that the majority of conditional cautions (80%) given to adults have been reparative rather than rehabilitative.[24] A system which operated, in the context of young offenders, in this way might be open to challenge under various international requirements as to the rights of the child,[25] although, probably, not in breach of the ECHR.[26] Further issues will arise about the extent to which rehabilitative conditions relating perhaps to drugs or alcohol, can be resourced and the speed at which the whole system can and will operate. Conditional cautioning is potentially a complicated process. There also remains the basic issue of whether individuals who ought to be brought before a court are not being so, even for 'quite serious offences'.[27] There is no formal requirement in the legislative scheme for involvement by a youth offending team (YOT), which would of course happen if there was a guilty plea by a first time offender. However, it is likely that a YOT would in reality be involved where appropriate.

Preconditions

4.10 There are five preconditions that must be satisfied (CDA 1998, s 66B). These replicate the preconditions that apply in respect of adults. They are:

(1) the 'authorised person' (defined by s 66A(7)) has evidence that the offender has committed an offence;

(2) a 'relevant prosecutor' (defined by s 66H) decides that there is sufficient evidence to charge the offender and that a youth conditional caution should be given to the offender in respect of the offence;

(3) the offender admits to the 'authorised person' that he committed the offence. An offender may in reality be willing to accept a caution, even if he did not actually commit the offence, because it may be a more palatable solution than going to court, with the risks that might involve. Alternatively, the individuals who are most likely to be those to whom these provisions are applied 'tend to be unskilled and inexpert in dealing with these types of engagements. They are very used to dealing with the police, but they cannot make judgments about whether they are in a situation where perhaps they ought to be pleading not guilty and going to court.

---

[22] David Burrows, MP, HC Committee, col 26 (16 October 2007).
[23] David Hanson, Minister of State, Ministry of Justice, HC Committee, col 26 (16 October 2007).
[24] David Hanson, Minister of State, Ministry of Justice, HC Committee, col 26 (16 October 2007).
[25] See **4.4**.
[26] See the dissenting speech of Baroness Hale in *R v Durham Constabulary and another, ex p R* [2005] UKHL 21, at para 48. See also **4.4**.
[27] Sally Dickinson, Chief Executive, Magistrates' Association, in evidence to HC Committee, col 47 (16 October 2007).

They may be putting themselves in a situation where they allow themselves to be cautioned when perhaps they should not'.[28] However, the admission is important, because it will be admissible evidence of the commission of the offence in any subsequent proceedings;

(4) the 'authorised person' explains the effect of the caution and warns him that failure to comply with any of the conditions may result in the offender being prosecuted for the offence. If the offender is 16 or under that explanation or warning must be given in the presence of an 'appropriate adult' (as defined by s 66H);

(5) the offender signs a document which contains details of the offence, an admission that he committed the offence, consent to being given a conditional caution, and the conditions attached to the caution. Precision in this document, especially in the drafting of the conditions, is crucial. Breach of the conditions will give rise to potential for prosecution for the original offence, not the breach of conditions. If the offender accepts a caution for causing criminal damage on condition that he cleans up graffiti within 7 days, but then changes his mind or fails to comply with the condition, he might be prosecuted for the original offence of criminal damage, though this might simply result in a referral order being made (see **4.16**). The admission contained in the caution document could be used to prove guilt in the unlikely event of a plea of not guilty. The admission would be subject to the same preconditions as apply generally in respect of confessions and admissions.[29]

The power to give a conditional caution is not limited by the legislative provisions relating to offence seriousness. Whilst guidance will no doubt confirm that conditional cautions will be appropriate for less serious offences, there is no legal reason why they cannot be administered for offences which would attract a community order if they went to court, or even in theory which cross the custodial sentence threshold. In that regard it may be noted that the Minster spoke of 'alternatives to custody' (see **4.8**).

Conditions

4.11 The conditions that are to be imposed will be determined by a 'relevant prosecutor'. Under the terms of s 66C of CDA 1998 no condition imposing a financial penalty can be attached, unless the offence is one that has been prescribed by an order made by the Secretary of State. No such order had been made as at the date of going to press. The terms of s 66C limit the maximum financial penalty to £100.[30] If a prosecutor authorises a condition requiring a financial penalty condition, he will determine when and to whom it is paid.

Apart from the above the nature of conditions that may be attached to a youth conditional caution is not generally limited, perhaps only by general concepts of reasonableness and proportionality. However, because the offender agrees to conditions that are being imposed, in the sense that he is agreeing to the caution and therefore, by implication to its contents, it is going to be an unlikely case where any sustainable grounds of challenge arise. After all, there is no obligation on the offender to agree, although the consent must be genuine.

---

[28] Christine Laurie, Chief Executive, Probation Boards Association, in evidence to HC Committee, col 47 (16 October 2007).
[29] See Police and Criminal Evidence Act, ss 76, 76A and 78.
[30] Subject to variation of this maximum by order: CDA 1998, s 66C(4).

The nature of the conditions will also be subject to Ministerial guidance in general, and the provisions of a Code of Practice in particular (see **4.13**).

4.12 The conditions can be varied by the 'relevant prosecutor' (s 66D). This can include the modification or omission of any of the conditions, or by adding a condition. Normal rules of statutory interpretation[31] mean that this might involve the addition of more than one condition, because there is nothing in the overall context of the legislation to rebut the normal presumption.

Code of Practice

4.13 A new s 66G imposes a duty on the Secretary of State to prepare a Code of Practice. The matters that may be the subject of its provisions are identified by s 66G(2). It will deal with things such as when a conditional caution will be appropriate, the procedure to be followed, the types of conditions to be attached and how the conditions are to be defined, implemented and monitored.

Non-compliance

4.14 As noted at **4.9**, failure to comply with the conditions can lead to prosecution for the offence in respect of which the caution was given (s 66E). That is subject to the failure being without 'reasonable excuse'. That will be for the responsible officer to determine, but ultimately might be a matter for the court if it was submitted that, because there was reasonable excuse, there was no right to commence the proceedings. If prosecuted for the breach the conditional caution ceases to have effect. The burden of proof in respect of the original offence will remain on the prosecutor, but, as already noted, the admission of the offence at the time will in reality confine the real live issues in the vast majority of cases to how the offender should be dealt with.

Restrictions on sentencing on subsequent conviction

4.15 Where an offender has been given a youth conditional caution, the sentencing powers of a court are limited. If that court deals with the offender within 2 years of the giving of a conditional caution, it may not order a conditional discharge unless it is of the opinion that exceptional circumstances exist that justify this course of action. Obviously, this will be a restriction that will apply to a court dealing with an offender for the original offence for which a conditional caution has not been complied with.

REFERRAL ORDERS

Background

4.16 Referral orders were introduced by the Youth Justice and Criminal Evidence Act 1999,[32] and are now dealt with by Part III of the Powers of Criminal Courts (Sentencing) Act 2000 (PCC(S)A 2000). They were introduced to provide a means whereby first-time offenders had their offending behaviour addressed by a youth offending team with the intention of diverting the offender from further offending

---

[31] See Interpretation Act 1978, s 1.
[32] See, generally, Field 'Early Interventions and the "New" Youth Justice: a Study of Initial decision-making' [2008] Crim LR 172.

behaviour. They now form the biggest proportion of orders made by the youth court, and have one of the largest success rates.[33] The power to make a referral arises in respect of an offence where the sentence is not fixed by law, and the court is not proposing to impose a custodial sentence or a discharge (PCC(S)A 2000, s 16). It lasts for the specified period and is to be regarded as a conviction, but one which is spent on expiration of the contract period.[34]

In some circumstances, defined by s 16(2) of PCC(S)A 2000,, referral is compulsory by virtue of the compulsory referral conditions contained in s 17(1). Where they do not apply, there is nonetheless the right to make discretionary referral if the conditions in s 17(1A) and (2) are satisfied.

The new Act amends the referral conditions (s 35). It also amends the power to revoke a referral order (s 36) and deals with questions relating to extension of the period during which the youth offender contract has effect (s 37). These changes had not been brought into effect as at the date of going to press.

The changes

Compulsory reference

4.17 Section 35(2) of the new Act amends the compulsory referral requirements contained in s 17(1) of PCC(S)A 2000. The effect of the deletion of s 17(1)(c) is that the pre-existing exclusion from compulsory reference, of those who had in the past been bound over to keep the peace or be of good behaviour, is removed. This change is justified by the relatively good success rate of the referral order.[35] However, the changes do not alter the basic rule that a first-time offender who pleads guilty must be the subject of a referral order. There is no scope for a high-end youth rehabilitation order (**see 5.8**). This means that there is no middle course: it is either referral or custody, a position some find unsatisfactory.[36]

Discretionary reference

4.18 Section 35(3) of the new Act amends the discretionary referral requirements by substituting a new s 17(1A) and (2) of PCC(S)A 2000, and creating a new s 17(2A)–(2D). Under the redrafted provisions discretionary referral powers exist in respect of an offence punishable with imprisonment, where the powers of compulsory referral do not apply, and the offender pleads guilty to the offence or one of any connected offences.[37] In addition one of the three conditions created by s 17(2A), (2B) or (2C) must be satisfied. These are:

(1) that the offender has never been convicted in the UK of any offence except for the offence (and any connected offence) for which he is being dealt with (s 17(2A)).

---

[33] See Brendan Finnegan, Director of Strategy, Youth Justice Board, in evidence to HC Committee, col 97 (18 October 2007).
[34] Under the Rehabilitation of Offenders Act 1974, as amended.
[35] 44.7% re-offending rate, compared with 57.6% for discharges (the next lowest re-offending rate for community sentences): see *Reoffending of juveniles: results from the 2004 cohort* (Home Office, June 2006).
[36] See Cindy Barnett, Chair, Magistrates' Association, in evidence to HC Committee, col 46 (16 October 2007).
[37] Defined by PCC(S)A 2000, s 16(4): 'an offence is connected with another if the offender falls to be dealt with for it at the same time as he is dealt with for the other offence'.

The limitation is in respect to *any* offence, and is not limited to prior conviction in respect of an offence punishable with imprisonment;

(2) the offender has been dealt with for such an offence, on one previous occasion, but was not referred to a youth offending panel (s 17(2B));

(3) the offender has been dealt with on one or more prior occasions, has been referred to a youth offending team on *one* occasion, is now recommended as suitable for a referral by an 'appropriate officer',[38] and the court considers there are exceptional circumstances which justify ordering a referral on this occasion (s 17(2)).

In short, it increases the discretion of the court. Hitherto, there was no power to make a discretionary reference in respect of an offender with one or more previous convictions. There now will be such a power. It reflects the desire to engage in restorative justice with as wide a range of young offenders, and a desire to avoid driving young offenders further up the hierarchy of disposals. These changes are expected to lead to the increased use of referral orders, because of their good record in reducing re-offending.[39]

Power to revoke a referral and changes in length

4.19 Section 36(2) inserts a new s 27A into PCC(S)A 2000. Neither s 26 or s 27 of this Act contained a power for the youth offender panel to refer an offender back to a court as a result of good progress, other than at the insistence of the offender himself. That gap is now remedied. The new s 27A confers powers on a youth offender panel to refer the offender back to the appropriate court[40] where it is in the interests of justice for the referral order (or each of them if there are more than one) to be revoked. The new subsection does not limit the circumstances in which such reference back may be made. However, those circumstances *include* the offender's making good progress under the contract (s 27A(3)).

The decision whether or not to revoke is that of the court, not that of the panel. If the court does not agree, the panel may not make a further similar referral to the court without that court's consent.

4.20 Section 36 also inserts a new s 27B into PCC(S)A 2000. There was no power under that Act to extend the period of the youth offender contract. That gap is now filled. The new s 27B permits a panel to refer back to the court a referral of less than 12 months, even though that period has not ended. The panel must consider that, having regard to the circumstances which have arisen since the contract took effect it appears to be in the interests of justice that the length of the period be extended. That period of extension requested cannot exceed 3 months.

Faced with such a reference back, the appropriate court[41] will act in accordance with a new Sch 1, Part 1ZA to PCC(S)A 2000. It will consider a report from the panel, and extend the period of the order for no more than 3 months if it considers that to be in the

---

[38] Defined by PCC(S)A 2000, s 17(2D) as: 'a member of a youth offending team; an officer of a local probation board; or an officer of a provider of probation services'.
[39] See Regulatory Impact Assessment that accompanied the Bill, citing a reconviction rate of 44.7%.
[40] Defined by PCC(S)A 2000, Sch 1, para 1(2).
[41] Defined for this purpose by PCC(S)A 2000, Sch 1, Part 1ZA, para 9ZB(2) as, in the case of a referral over a person aged under 18 at the date of reference back, a youth court acting for the area in which the offender resides, or otherwise a magistrates' court for that area.

interests of justice, having regard to circumstances that have arisen since the contract took effect. It is those circumstances that matter, and does not give the court the right to reassess its own previous judgments or decisions as to the appropriate period of reference.

The procedural requirements in para 9ZD(4) must be satisfied. There is no requirement that the offender be represented.

YOUTH DEFAULT ORDERS

4.21 A young offender cannot be committed to prison for failure to pay a fine (PCC(S)A 2000, s 89). If the court would have had the power, but for s 89, to commit for failure to pay a fine, the court can proceed under s 81 of the Magistrates' Court Act 1980. This permits the making of one of two orders against a parent or guardian. Under the changes made by s 39 of the new Act, a youth default order (YDO) is created. These provisions had not been brought into effect as at the date of going to press.

This new order means that a court can impose an unpaid work requirement on an offender,[42] if the offender is aged 16 or 17. Alternatively, in respect of any young offender it can impose an attendance centre order or a curfew requirement, which may be combined with an electronic monitoring requirement.[43]

The length of the requirements under a YDO are subject to the detailed provisions contained in Sch 7 to the new Act. These can be summarised as follows:

Unpaid Work	**Minimum**: 20 hours
Amount	**Maximum hours**
Not exceeding £200	40
Exceeding £200 and not exceeding £500	60
Exceeding £500	100
Attendance Centre Requirement – age 14 or over	**Minimum**: none
Amount	**Maximum hours**
Not exceeding £250	8
Exceeding £250 and not exceeding £500	14
Exceeding £500	24

---

[42] See **5.22**.
[43] See **5.37**.

Attendance Centre Requirement – age under 14	No minimum
Amount	**Maximum hours**
Not exceeding £250	8
Exceeding £250 and not exceeding £500	10
Exceeding £500	12
Curfew requirement	No minimum number of days
Amount	**Maximum days**
Not exceeding £200	20
Exceeding £200 and not exceeding £500	30
Exceeding £500 but not exceeding £1,000	60
Exceeding £1,000 but not exceeding £2,000	90
Exceeding £2,000	180

It is not entirely clear why the financial limits appertaining to attendance centre requirements should be different from the other requirements.

A YDO which imposes such requirements is subject to various provisions relating to the imposition, detail and enforcement of requirements in a Youth Rehabilitation Order (see s 36(6) and the relevant parts of Chapter 6), subject, in the case of enforcement, to the modifications contained in Sch 7, para 5.

The order ceases to have effect on payment of the whole sum due. Where there is part payment the number of hours under the order is reduced proportionately.

DETENTION FOR PUBLIC PROTECTION AND EXTENDED SENTENCES FOR VIOLENT OR SEXUAL OFFENCES

4.22 The new Act contains provisions relating to young offenders. These are dealt with at **3.23**.

Chapter 5

YOUTH REHABILITATION ORDER

SUMMARY

5.1 The 2008 Act abolishes a range of existing community orders. These are: curfew orders, exclusion orders, attendance centre orders, supervision orders and action plan orders. In their place the Act creates a new youth rehabilitation order (YRO), which can be made in respect of an offender who is aged under 18. It replaces those provisions that permitted a youth community order to be made in respect of those aged 16 or 17.

A YRO may contain one or more requirements (s 1(1)). Many of these requirements reflect the powers under pre-existing law, but there are detailed changes, as well as a power to impose a fostering requirement as part of a YRO. Enforcement of the order is in accordance with the provisions of Sch 2.

No date for commencement had been published at the date of going to press.

BACKGROUND

5.2 The Criminal Justice Act 2003 (CJA 2003) contained provisions which significantly restructured the scheme of community orders applicable to offenders aged 16 or over. Section 147 of CJA 2003 created a single, unified community sentence comprising either a 'community order', as defined by s 177, or, in the case of a person aged 16 or over, one or more 'youth community orders', as defined by s 147(2). These changes, following on from the recommendations of the Halliday Report,[1] were intended to create one generic community order, the punitive weight of which would be proportionate to the offence (and any associated offences),[2] which would comprise the ingredients best suited for meeting the needs of crime reduction and reparation and which address the causes of the offending behaviour. Section 177 contains a list of requirements, one of more of which may be included as requirements in a community order.[3] CJA 2003 did not address the regime of orders for young offenders in any fundamental way, although it made some detailed changes to action plan orders.[4] Consequently, the existing regime in respect of young offenders was, in this context, broadly unchanged. The power, in respect of an offender aged 16 or over, to make a

---

[1] The Halliday Report, *Making Punishments Work: Report of a Review of the Sentencing Framework for England & Wales* (Home Office, July 2001), available at: www.homeoffice.gov.uk/documents/312280.
[2] Defined by the Powers of Criminal Courts (Sentencing) Act 2000 (PCC(S)A 2000), s 161.
[3] Unpaid work requirement; activity requirement; programme requirement; prohibited activity requirement; curfew requirement; exclusion requirement; residence requirement; mental health treatment requirement; drug rehabilitation; alcohol treatment requirement; supervision requirement; an attendance centre requirement (in the case of a person under 25). For the effect of community orders, see *Penal Policy – A Background Paper* (Ministry of Justice, May 2007).
[4] CJA 2003, Sch 24.

community rehabilitation order, a community punishment order and a community punishment and rehabilitation order existed under pre-existing law.[5] So, too, with the drug treatment and testing order.[6] The range of youth community orders comprised curfew orders, exclusion orders, attendance centre orders, supervision orders, and action plan orders.[7] The separate power to make a reparation order also existed.

5.3   As noted at **4.3**, in CJA 2003 the Government published a Green Paper, *Every Child Matters*[8] which addressed the risks faced by children by proposing a wide range of services, interventions and improved child protection and support procedures. Alongside that, as a companion document, *Youth Justice – The Next Steps*[9] launched a consultation process specifically concerning changes to the youth justice system. The current provisions are in principle, though not necessarily in detail, based on the approach identified in that document, informed by the responses to that consultation.[10]

The Consultation Paper proposed the replacement of nine juvenile non-custodial sentences with one, an action plan order, which would comprise a menu of options, including a range of requirements, along with discharges and referral orders. Responses to this consultation were generally supportive. Some who responded thought that the power to select a variety of interventions from a list would effectively enable tailored orders to be made which addressed the particular individual needs of the offender.[11] Some concerns were expressed about whether the 'bite' of increasingly more severe orders would be lost, with offenders failing to realise that a later sentence was any different or more severe than those that preceded it.[12] The Government's response following the Consultation Paper proposed that the reparation order and the referral orders should each remain as distinct, separate, orders, a position reflected in the new provisions. By contrast, attendance centre orders would be subsumed into the new order.

One proposal in the Consultation Paper that has not found its way directly into the new Act is that for child behaviour contracts. It had proposed that '[Youth Offender Teams should] be encouraged to make child behaviour contracts with young offenders to strengthen their commitment to changing their behaviour'.[13] Its conclusion, following consultation, was to modify that original proposal, instead encouraging the use of acceptable behaviour contracts 'with positive requirements as part of the early intervention work by Youth Inclusion and Support Panels'.[14]

The result of this consultation process is to be found in the new YRO created by the new Act. It is intended to simplify the sentencing structure, and to enable the courts to tailor sentences to individual risks and needs,[15] addressing the multiple needs of the young offender.[16] The hope, the House of Lords was told, is that offending will be reduced, and there will be achieved a reduction in the numbers of young offenders sent into

---

[5]   See PCC(S)A 2000, ss 41, 46 and 51, all prospectively repealed by CJA 2003.
[6]   PCC(S)A 2000, s 52, prospectively repealed by CJA 2003.
[7]   See CJA 2003, s 147; for the individual orders, see PCC(S)A 2000, ss 163, 40A, 63 and 69.
[8]   Cm 5860 (TSO, September 2003). The Report was a response to the Laming Report into the death of Victoria Climbie.
[9]   Home Office, May 2003.
[10] *Youth Justice – The Next Steps: Summary of Responses and the Government's Proposals* (Home Office, 2004).
[11] Ibid, para 16.
[12] Ibid, para 15.
[13] Ibid, para 19.
[14] Ibid, para 11.
[15] Lord Hunt, HL 2nd Reading, col 127 (22 January 2008).
[16] Graham Robb, Acting Chair, Youth Justice Board, HC Committee (18 October 2007).

custody. The Government expect that youth offending teams 'will work with the courts to provide them with appropriate information that [the courts] can use to help them decide which requirements should be attached to the orders'.[17] It was explained by the Minister of State at the Ministry of Justice as follows:[18]

> '... we are trying to simplify the sentencing structure, building on and learning from our experiences with existing sentencing and tailoring sentences to individual risk and need. I accept that some measures now in place are, in part, replicated in the new youth rehabilitation order. We are trying to pull these measures together into a generic sentence and to put in additional capability, particularly relating to residential sentences ...'

The Minister stressed the strategy of stronger community penalties as alternatives to custody. In particular the 'key new element' in the YRO is intended to be the requirement to participate in specified activities or residential exercises for 90 days or more (see **5.16**).

Some evidence exists that certain available orders or requirements, in particular attendance centre and drug treatment requirements, are not widely used at the moment because of their relative lack of availability.[19] Clearly, the practical success of the new order in meeting its objectives depends fundamentally on the levels of resource available to support the different schemes, activities or actions that can potentially form part of the requirements imposed on a young offender.

The new order

5.4 A youth rehabilitation order is a community sentence[20] which may be made in respect of a person aged under 18 at the date of conviction for an offence. There is no minimum age limit.

An order may be made by the court that convicts for the offence, whether that be a magistrates' court or Crown Court. It will impose on the offender one or more of the requirements specified in s 1(1)–(4) of the new Act, subject to any limitations the Act imposes.

5.5 Nothing in the 2008 Act affects the general rules relating to restrictions on the imposition of a community sentence. Sections 148 and 150 of CJA 2003 apply (2008 Act, s 1(6)). Section 148 of CJA 2003 states that a court must not pass a community sentence on an offender unless it is of the opinion that the offence, or the combination of the offence and one or more offences associated with it, was serious enough[21] to warrant such a sentence. Section 150 prohibits the making of a community order in respect of an offence for which the sentence is fixed by law, or where a term of custody is required by statute.[22] Further, the restrictions recognised by the court relating to community sentences will continue to operate. In particular, it will continue to be wrong to combine a community sentence with a custodial sentence, whether for one or more

---

[17] Lord Hunt, HL 2nd Reading, col 127 (22 January 2008).
[18] David Hanson, MP, in evidence to the HC Committee (16 October 2007).
[19] Centre for Crime and Justice Studies, cited by Nick Hurd MP, HC Committee (16 October 2007). The concerns relating to lack of available resources were echoed by the evidence of the Magistrates' Association, HC Committee (16 October 2007).
[20] See CJA 2003, s 177.
[21] As to which, see *T* [1999] 2 Cr App R (S) 304.
[22] Under the Firearms Act 1968, s 51A(2); PCC(S)A 2000, s 110(2) or s 111(2); CJA 2003, ss 225–228.

than one offence.[23] On the other hand the new generic sentence will permit the combination of requirements that fall within it, subject to the totality of the package being appropriate. It is important that requirements are not imposed to such extent as to amount to 'tariff inflation'.

Length of the order

5.6 There is no reason why a court should not make concurrent or consecutive orders. However, Sch 1 contains restrictions on which requirements may be combined with each other, or as to which may be consecutive (Sch 1, paras 3(1) and 32 (see **5.7**)).

5.7 An order must specify a date by which all the requirements in it have been complied with (2008 Act, Sch 1, para 32). That date must be no later than 3 years after the date 'on which the order takes effect'. That is not the date of the making of the order, but the day after (Sch 1, para 30).

The Act does not state a minimum or maximum length of the order itself. Instead, Sch 1, para 32 states that a court must specify a date by which all the requirements of the order must have been complied with. That date must be no more than 3 years from *the day after* the making of the order, although the court can specify a shorter period if it wishes. It is crucial that, when the requirements of the order are set, it is clear that they can be fully complied with within a 3-year period.[24] The position is further complicated by the fact that Sch 2 (which deals with breach, revocation or amendment of an order)[25] simply refers to breach provisions before a court 'while a youth rehabilitation order is in force' (Sch 2, para 3). The intention of Parliament is that an order should not last longer than 3 years,[26] but that is not quite what it says. If requirements can be completed within the 3-year period, but are not, the order remains in force, although it is difficult to envisage a case where enforcement action has not been taken under Sch 2. On the other hand if the failure is due to the management of the order, then reasonable excuse for failure to comply would exist.

The order will end when its requirements have been complied with. Unless care is taken, that may have unintended consequences. In *Odam*[27] the court indicated, in the context of an adult community order, that a work requirement order came to an end when the requirement was completed.[28] The requirement was completed within less than 12 months. It followed that the notification requirements under the Sexual Offences Act 2003 (SOA 2003) did not apply.[29] It is the length of the order *as made* that is important, not how soon it is completed. However, since an unpaid work requirement order (where that is the only requirement) should only state the number of hours to be worked, the notification requirement under SOA 2003 may operate only if the order is such that, at the time of its being made, it lasts for a minimum of 12 months.

---

[23] *Carr-Thompson* [2000] 2 Cr App R (S) 335.
[24] David Hanson, MP, Minister of State, Ministry of Justice, HC Committee (23 October 2007).
[25] See **5.38**.
[26] David Hanson, MP, Minster of State, Ministry of Justice, HC Committee (23 October 2007).
[27] [2008] EWCA Crim 1087.
[28] See CJA 2003, s 200(3).
[29] Sexual Offences Act 2003, Sch 3, para 32(b): a person is only subject to a notification requirement if sentenced to a community order of at least 12 months.

The requirements that may be imposed

5.8 The requirements that may be imposed are specified by s 1 of the new Act, supplemented by the provisions in Sch 1. There are no general restrictions on the combinations of requirements that may be imposed, but certain specific restrictions apply. These are discussed at the appropriate parts of this chapter.

The overall effect and impact of the order should also be borne in mind. Arguably, the totality of the order should not be disproportionate to the offence in respect of which the offender is being dealt with. The position is somewhat complicated by the changes made by the 2008 Act as to the purposes of sentencing. Section 9 introduces into CJA 2003 a new s 142A, which states that, when a court is dealing with an offender aged under 18, the court must primarily have regard to the prevention of offending, which is the principal aim of the youth justice system (see **4.4**). It might be argued therefore that it is proper to impose whatever combination of requirements is necessary to achieve this. Nonetheless, s 8(4) also specifies other 'purposes of sentencing', and it is submitted that nothing in the 2008 Act affects the basic principle that a sentence should be proportionate to the offence or offences in respect of which it is being imposed. This is consistent with the intention of the Government that the YRO provisions should be regarded as a hierarchy, with reparation at the lowest level and custody at the highest when no other disposal is appropriate.[30] Thus, for example, the intensive supervision and surveillance (ISS) requirements (see **5.16**) are intended to be high-end alternatives when custody would otherwise be justified. Indeed, the Government stated that 'intensive supervision and surveillance would be the first option and custody would be the second option only where the offences were so serious that only a physical restriction of liberty could be justified'.[31] Despite a recommendation from the Joint Committee on Human Rights that the Bill be amended to explicitly state that a YRO with ISS should always be tried before custody, unless the offence is so exceptionally serious that a custodial sentence is necessary to protect the public, no such safeguard found its way into what is now the Act.

5.9 The requirements *potentially* available are specified by s 1(1), and are as follows:

Requirement	Detailed provisions of 2008 Act
Activity	Sch 1, paras 6–8
Supervision	Sch 1, para 9
Unpaid work (16 or 17 year olds)	Sch 1, para 10
Programme	Sch 1, para 11
Attendance centre	Sch 1, para 12
Prohibited activity	Sch 1, para 13
Curfew (usually with electronic monitoring requirement)	s 1(2); Sch 1, paras 2 14, 26
Exclusion (usually with electronic monitoring requirement)	s 1(2); Sch 1, paras 2, 15, 26
Residence	Sch 1, para 16

---

[30] Lord Hunt, Parliamentary Under-Secretary of State, Ministry of Justice, HL Committee, col 975 (5 February 2008); Lord Bach, HL Committee, col 979 (5 February 2008).
[31] In evidence to the Joint Committee on Human Rights 2007/2008, cited at para 1.16.

Local authority residence	Sch 1, para 17
Mental health treatment	Sch 1, para 20
Drug treatment	Sch 1, para 22
Drug testing	Sch 1, para 23
Intoxicating substance treatment	Sch 1, para 24
Education treatment	Sch 1, para 25
Intensive supervision	s 1(3); Sch 1, para 3
Fostering	s 1(4); Sch 1, para 4

The Act contains restrictions on the combination of several requirements. Section 1(c) only permits an unpaid work requirement to be made if the offender is aged 16 or 17 at the date of conviction. Further restrictions are imposed in respect of ISS requirements (see s 1(4), and **5.16**).

The Act does not contain powers that enable a court to impose a reparation requirement. That was an omission that caused considerable debate during the passage of the Act.[32] The power to make a reparation order exists,[33] and continues to do so even after the passage of the new Act. Critics argued that the failure to include the potential for a reparation requirement deprived the courts of a complete choice of available options. However, the Minister stressed that the reason for reparation being retained as a separate sentence was 'so that [the courts] do not have to resort to a youth rehabilitation order simply to ensure that reparation is made'.[34] The reparation order 'is designed to reinforce personal responsibility and learning about the consequences of the damage the offender has caused to the individual and the community'.[35] A reparation order falls beneath the YRO in the new sentencing hierarchy, and evidence received by the House of Commons Public Bill Committee supported the retention of the reparation order as a separate order.[36] It permits a court to order the making of reparation in cases which are not of sufficient justification to justify the making of a YRO. In any event, the powers of the courts when making a YRO extend to requiring reparation. An activity requirement may 'consist of, or include an activity whose purpose is that of reparation, such as an activity involving contact between an offender and persons affected by the offences in respect of which the order was made' (Sch 1, para 8(2)).

Pre-Sentence Reports and other information

5.10 Key procedural provisions are contained in Sch 1, Part 4. Before making an order the court must first obtain and consider information about the offender's family circumstances and the likely effect of such an order on those circumstances (Sch 1, para 28). That does not of itself require a court to consider a Pre-Sentence Report (PSR).

---

[32] See HL Committee, cols 979–980 (5 February 2008); HC Committee (16 October 2007).
[33] See PCC(S)A 2000, s 73.
[34] Lord Bach, HL Committee, col 980 (5 February 2008).
[35] Lord Bach, HL Committee, col 980 (5 February 2008).
[36] Chief Executive of the Youth Justice Board, HC Committee, col 109 (18 October 2007).

Section 156 of CJA 2003 contains the relevant provisions relating to the need for a PSR in respect of young offenders. As amended,[37] s 156 provides that a court, in deciding the question as to whether an offence is serious enough to warrant a community sentence, or whether a YRO with intensive supervision or with a fostering requirement should be made,[38] must take into account 'such information as is available to it' about the circumstances of the offence, or offences associated with it, including any aggravating or mitigating factors. In addition, in deciding what particular requirements are, commensurate for the offender, whether singly or together, the court may take into account 'any information about the offender that is before it' (CJA 2003, ss 156(2), 148(2), Sch 4, para 77).

The court is only *required* to consider a PSR before imposition of a community sentence or YRO in determining offence seriousness, whether the restrictions on liberty contained in any order are commensurate to the offence seriousness,[39] or whether a YRO with ISS or with a fostering requirement should be made (CJA 2003, s 156(3)(b)). Even that is, as before, subject to the very limited exception contained in s 156(4).[40] However, the reality is that a court will not be able to determine what requirements, either singly or in combination, are the most suitable for the offender (CJA 2003, s 156(2)(a)), and what is the appropriate length of the order, unless it does consider a PSR and other relevant reports. The PSR will be crucial in identifying what the multiple needs of the young offender are, in the context of addressing both the welfare of the young offender and the primary aim of preventing re-offending.[41]

Making of the order

5.11 An order may be made by either a youth court or Crown Court. If a Crown Court makes an order, it may include a direction that any further proceedings in relation to the order are to be in a youth court or magistrates' court (Sch 1, para 36(1)). Such a direction will thus generally, but not always, vest all further proceedings relating to amendment, revocation, modification or discharge of the order in the youth or magistrates' court (Sch 2, para 7; see **5.39**).

5.12 Before making an order a court must do the things specified in Sch 1, Part 3:

- it must obtain and consider information about the offender's family circumstances (Sch 1, para 28); and

- it must consider whether requirements to be imposed are compatible with each other and avoid conflict with religious beliefs, educational requirements or any other order to which the offender may be subject (Sch 1, para 29).

There is no *general* requirement that the offender be legally represented before a YRO is made. Given the significance of the new YRO in the sentencing hierarchy, this is perhaps a significant omission. Amendments to require this were unsuccessfully proposed during

---

[37] 2008 Act, Sch 4, para 77.
[38] CJA 2003, s 156 (as amended by the 2008 Act, Sch 4, para 77), 2008 Act, s 1((4)(b)). See **5.32**.
[39] In combination with any associated offences.
[40] Section 156(4) provides that a PSR need not be obtained if the court considers that it is unnecessary to obtain such a report. But that is subject to s 156(5): in respect of young offenders the court must obtain such a report unless there is a previous PSR and the court has had regard to the information in that report, or, if more than one such report, the most recent report.
[41] See **4.5**.

the passage of the Act, and thus the requirement of legal representation only applies where a fostering requirement is being imposed.

5.13 Sch 1, Part 4 deals with the content of the order. It contains detail regarding information about the relevant local justice area for the offender that must be specified, and the service of copies of orders (para 34). Crucially, it must specify the length of the order (see **5.6**).

RESTRICTIONS ON THE MAKING OF AN ORDER

5.14 Certain restrictions relate to the imposition of particular requirements. These were noted at **5.9** and are also referred to in dealing with individual requirements. However, there are restrictions on the making of a YRO itself.

First, a court may not make a YRO on an offender who, at that time, is subject to another YRO, or to a reparation order,[42] unless it revokes the earlier order or orders (Sch 1, para 30(4)).

Second, if the offender is being dealt with for two or more associated offences, a court can only make an order of one particular type. If it makes a YRO, it may not make a YRO with ISS, or a YRO with fostering. So, too, with the other two types of orders. The three types of order cannot be combined (Sch 1, para 31(2)). A YRO with ISS and a YRO with fostering can only be combined with other such orders. There are also restrictions on when these two types of order can be made (see **5.9**).

THE REQUIREMENTS: ALTERNATIVES TO CUSTODY

5.15 Many of the provisions relating to requirements in YRO mirror powers in the pre-existing law relating to adult offenders, and powers that already existed to impose requirements in a youth community order.

The selection of the appropriate requirements will be for the court in accordance with the objectives of sentencing, in particular the objective of preventing re-offending. Arguably the totality of the requirements imposed should not be disproportionate to the offence in respect of which the offender is being dealt with. Indeed, as already noted, there is a danger that the YRO might create the risk of 'tariff inflation', in the sense that the number and nature of the requirements might be out of proportion to the offence under consideration. The Convention on the Rights of the Child (CRC) requires that a variety of disposals shall be available 'to ensure that children are dealt with in a manner appropriate to their well-being and proportionate to their circumstances and the offence'.[43] No explicit requirements for proportionality are contained in these provisions, although arguably are to be implied. The impact of the requirements on the well-being of the child is, of course, a consideration but one that has to be viewed in the wider context of the principal aim of the criminal justice system (see **4.4**). There is a

---

[42] Under PCC(S)A 2000, s 73(1).
[43] Art 40(4).

potential danger that the imposition of a wider range of requirements than necessary may have the result of 'setting the child up to fail'.[44]

At the outset, the availability of two particular requirements should be noted. They are at the top of the hierarchy of seriousness. The Act confers power to recognise the power of the court to make a YRO with ISS, under s 1(3)(a), and the power to make a YRO with fostering, under s 1(3)(b). These are significant orders, emphasised by the fact that a YRO with ISS cannot be combined with any other form of YRO (see **5.14**). So too with a YRO with a fostering requirement (see **5.15**). The use of these two orders is restricted by s 1(4). By s 1(4) one of these two orders may only be made if:

> '(a) the offence for which the offender is being sentenced is punishable by imprisonment;
> (b) the offence, together with any associated offences, was so serious that a custodial sentence would be appropriate but for the power of the court to make one of these two orders, or in the case of an offender aged under 12 at the date of conviction, would have been appropriate had the offender been at least 12 at the date of conviction;
> (c) if the offender was aged under 15 at the date of conviction, the court is of the opinion that the offender is a persistent offender.'[45]

In short, these two orders are intended to divert from custody those whose offences cross the custody sentencing threshold. Unsuccessful attempts were made during the parliamentary passage of the Act to restrict the imposition of a custodial sentence to circumstances where an offender had already been the subject of a YRO with ISS. Attempts were also made to require legal representation of the offender before a YRO is made, again without success.[46]

YRO with intensive supervision and surveillance (Sch 1, para 3)

5.16 These provisions create a statutory basis for the informal ISS programme which has been developed by the Youth Justice Board and implemented by youth offending teams. Where the preconditions set out above apply, and a court is imposing an activity requirement (see **5.19**) it may impose an 'extended activity requirement', of more than 90 but not exceeding 180 days. If it does so, it must also impose a supervision requirement, and a curfew requirement, accompanied, where appropriate, with an electronic monitoring requirement. But such an order cannot contain a fostering requirement (Sch 1, para 4(5)).

Such an order is to be known as a 'youth rehabilitation order with intensive supervision and surveillance' (Sch 1, para 3(5)). The making of such an order, with the mandatory requirements described above, does not prevent a court from imposing any further requirements permitted by s 1, subject to any general sentencing restrictions that may apply (see **5.5**).

---

[44] Prison Reform Trust, cited at HC Research Paper 07/65 *The Criminal Justice and Immigration Bill* (August 2007): to be found at http://services.parliament.uk/bills/2007-08/criminaljusticeandimmigration.html.
[45] The term 'persistent offender' is not defined by PCC(S)A 2000, s 100(2), and is a question of fact to be determined by his past course of conduct. See, eg, *Re C (Young Person: Persistent Offender)* [1986] 2 All ER 346.
[46] HC Committee (23 October 2007).

If made the provisions of Sch 1 relating to activity requirements (paras 6–8), supervision requirements (para 9), curfew requirement (para 14) and electronic monitoring requirement (para 26) each apply. The detail of these requirements is discussed later in this chapter (see **5.19**, **5.20**, **5.26** and **5.26**).

YRO with fostering (Sch 1, para 4)

5.17 Where the preconditions set out in **5.15** apply a court may make a YRO with fostering. This is an order which imposes a fostering requirement, of not longer than 12 months, defined by Sch 1, para 18 as a requirement that for a specified period the offender must reside with a local authority foster parent (Sch 1, para 18(1)). If an order imposes a fostering requirement, it must also impose a supervision requirement (Sch 1, para 4(4)).[47] The detail of such requirements is discussed at **5.32** and **5.21**.

Before a court imposes a fostering requirement it must be satisfied of the matters set out in Sch 1, para 4(2). The court must be satisfied:

'(a) that the behaviour which constituted the offence was due to a significant extent to the circumstances in which the offender was living, and
(b) that the imposition of such a requirement would assist in the offender's rehabilitation.'

Before it makes such an order it must, if it is practicable to do so, consult the offender's parents or guardians (Sch 1, para 4(3)). This refers to 'parents' in the plural. Whilst of course the general rule of interpretation is that the singular includes the plural,[48] the use of the plural here does suggest that if it is practicable to consult *both* parents it should do so. Whether it is practicable is a matter of fact, ultimately to be decided by the court in the light of the overall family context and circumstances. However, practicability is not the same as desirability: there may be situations when consultation is practicable but undesirable. It is difficult to imagine a court requiring consultation with both as a precondition in such circumstances, no doubt taking a broad purposive approach to the concept of practicability.

The court must also consult with the local authority which is to place the offender with a local authority foster parent. Theoretically, the court does not need the *consent* of the local authority before the making of the requirement. However, it inconceivable that a court would impose a fostering requirement without the agreement of the local authority.[49]

5.18 The extent to which a court will use this new fostering requirement is a matter of conjecture. It is intended to be used at the higher end of offence seriousness, and as an alternative to custody, with a presumption that the offender will return to his or her family. The intention is 'for the state to work with the child and the family to repair the harm, fix the issues and reduce the likelihood of reoffending'.[50] The Chair of the Magistrates' Association, in evidence to the Public Bill Committee, observed that 'if there are overwhelming welfare needs the matter ought to be transferred to the family proceedings court'.[51] She accepted that, in some extreme cases, this new power could be useful in addressing a welfare need.

---

[47] See **5.21**.
[48] Interpretation Act 1978.
[49] See David Hanson, Minister of State, Ministry of Justice (23 October 2007).
[50] Brendan Finnegan, Director of Strategy, Youth Justice Board, HC Committee (18 October 2007).
[51] Cindy Barnett, HC Committee (16 October 2007).

The key feature of the new regime is *intensive* fostering. A pilot has been supported by the Youth Justice Board: the early results are said to be encouraging,[52] but 'there are issues with sustaining its development at local and national levels'. One of those may be the extent to which sentencing courts take account of the welfare and well-being of children in the determination of sentences and orders.[53] Without such a welfare-focused approach there must be some doubt whether the Government's intention of reducing reliance on custody can be achieved (see **5.3**).

THE REQUIREMENTS: PRECONDITIONS AND DETAIL

Activity requirement (Sch 1, paras 6–8)

5.19 The activity requirement is a requirement that the offender do any or all of the following:

(a) participate in activities at a specified place or places. This permits the court to identify the place where activities will take place. The activities themselves can be identified by the court itself under (b), or by the responsible officer under (d);

(b) participate in a specified activity or activities. This permits the court to identify the activities which will take place. The place where these are to be performed can be identified by the court itself under (a), or by the responsible officer under (d);

(c) participate in one or more residential exercises for a continuous period or periods comprising a specified number of days. The order must specify either the place or the activity (Sch 1, para 6(4)). The use of the word 'or' in Sch 1, para 6(4)(a) suggests that the court must not specify both, although the reason why the court should not do so is not entirely clear. This leaves the responsible officer to identify either the place or activity under (d);

(d) engage in activities in accordance with instructions given by the responsible officer, on such number of days as may be specified by the order. The total number of days is for the court, not the responsible officer, but the place and nature of the activities will be a matter for the responsible officer. Amongst the things that may be done, this provision enables the responsible officer to require participation in a residential exercise for a period of not more than 7 days, provided the consent of a parent or guardian is given (Sch 1, para 7(3), (4)(a)). If participation at one or more residential activities for a period exceeding 7 days is considered appropriate, such a requirement must be imposed by the court, not the responsible officer.

5.20 There is an overall maximum time-limit for the number of days specified in the order: that is 90 days (Sch 1, para 6(2)). Within that, of course, there may be different numbers for different activities, or any combination of activities. For example, a 10-day residential exercise might be combined with 60 days of other specified activities.

---

[52] Graham Robb, Acting Chair, Youth Justice Board, HC Committee (18 October 2007). The pilot schemes have been in Staffordshire, Hampshire and London: 13 places were available, with a throughput of 35 people.
[53] Rob Reitemeier, Chief Executive, Children's' Society, HC Committee (18 October 2007).

A court may make concurrent or consecutive orders. In that situation, the days specified are applicable to each order, but the total number of days of activities must not exceed 90 (Sch 1, para 31(6)(b)).

Supervision requirement (Sch 1, para 9)

5.21 A supervision requirement is what was known as a supervision order.[54] It amounts to a requirement that during the period during which the order remains in force (see **5.7**), the offender must attend appointments with the responsible officer, or another person specified by that officer, at such times and places as that officer may direct.

Unpaid work requirement (Sch 1, para 10)

5.22 CJA 2003 permitted the making of an unpaid work requirement in a community order in respect of those aged 16 and 17, as well as adults.[55] Schedule 1, para 10 now permits an unpaid work requirement to be included in a YRO for such individuals, although this provision does not explicitly refer to the 16 and 17 age group.[56]

It is a requirement that the offender perform unpaid work for, in aggregate, a minimum of 40 hours, and a maximum of 240.[57] The work must be performed within 12 months of the commencement of the YRO (see **5.7**). The order may continue in any event after the unpaid work requirement, but even if that is not the case, it remains in force until the work requirement has been completed (Sch 1, para 10(7)). If the requirement is the only requirement in the order, the order ends when the work requirement is completed, which may have unforeseen consequences.[58]

5.23 The issues arise in respect of whether such a requirement is compliant with Art 4 of the ECHR, which prohibits forced or compulsory labour. It is a limited right, and does not extend, inter alia, to forced work in the course of detention, or service or work which forms part of normal civil obligations. Article 4 is likely to apply in limited circumstances where there is compulsory work or service, and 'where the requirement ... is unjust or oppressive or the work itself involves avoidable hardship'.[59] The factors to be take into account were identified in *Van der Mussele v Belgium*:[60] a requirement to undertake work is likely to be Convention-compliant if it is justified, necessary and proportionate, and required in the public interest in fulfilment of a legitimate social objective. The purpose of an unpaid work requirement is for the offender to make reparation for the wrongdoing in a way that confers benefit on the community. At the higher end of the hierarchy of offence seriousness it may also assist the court in avoiding a custodial sentence. On that basis, the ability to impose a requirement of itself is unlikely to infringe Art 4. That leaves it open in an individual case to argue, perhaps only in a wholly exceptional case, that the particular unpaid work requirement was disproportionate given the nature of the offence committed. That is unlikely to be the case given the condition set out below.

---

[54] PCC(S)A 2000, s 63, abolished by 2008 Act, s 6.
[55] See CJA 2003, ss 177, 199.
[56] See David Hanson, Minister of State, Ministry of Justice, HC Committee (23 October 2007).
[57] Compared with the 300 hours maximum in CJA 2003, s 199.
[58] See *Odam* [2008] EWCA Crim 1087; see **5.7**.
[59] *X v Federal Republic of Germany* App No 8410/78 (1980); D & R 216, at 219.
[60] (1983) 6 EHRR 163.

Programme requirement (Sch 1, para 11)

5.24 Schedule 1, para 10 provides the power to make a programme requirement, in substantially the same terms as set out in CJA 2003, s 202, which is repealed.[61] The effect of a requirement is that the offender must participate in a systematic set of activities ('a programme') at a specified place on a specified number of days. The requirement may require residence at any place for the purpose of completing the activities (Sch 1, para 11(2)).

The programme in question must be recommended by a member of a youth offender team, officer of a local probation board or an officer of the provider of probation services as suitable for the offender, and that a place for the offender is available. If the co-operation of another person is required, that other person must consent.

The requirement is particularly suitable for addressing behavioural causes of offending – teaching life skills, anger management and other similar programmes. There are, in Sch 1, no limits on the length of period of attendance. The order will specify the programme and the number of days but leave detailed implementation to the responsible officer. Care should be taken to ensure the totality of the requirement is one which is not disproportionate given the nature of the offence, and the age and characteristics of the offender.

The requirement must only be imposed if the court is satisfied that the offender is a suitable person to perform such a requirement, and that appropriate arrangements can be made (Sch 1, para 10(3)).

Attendance centre requirement (Sch 1, para 12)

5.25 The attendance centre requirement in para 12 replaces the provisions in s 60 of PCC(S)A 2000, which is repealed.[62] The key provisions relate to the aggregate number of hours for which the offender may be required to attend an attendance centre:[63]

Age	Number of hours
Aged under 14 at date of conviction	No more than 12
Aged under 16 at date of conviction	No less than 12
	No more than 24
Aged over 16 at date of conviction	No less than 12
	No more than 36

Prohibited activity (Sch 1, para 13)

5.26 Schedule 1 permits a court to impose a requirement that the offender abstain from participating in specified activities on a day or days specified, or during a specified

---

[61] 2008 Act, s 6. It was in fact never brought into effect.
[62] 2008 Act, s 6.
[63] As defined by PCC(S)A 2000, s 221(2).

period. This may include a requirement that the offender does not possess, use or carry a firearm.[64] It is not clear whether this last provision in any way detracts from the generality of para 13(1); arguably there is no reason why it should not be used to impose, say, a similar prohibition against the carrying of a knife during a prescribed period.

Paragraph 13(2) imposes duties of consultation prior to the imposition of such a requirement. The court cannot impose such a requirement without first consulting a probation officer, a member of a youth offending team or an officer of a provider of probation services.

Curfew requirement (Sch 1, para 14)

5.27 The effect of such a provision as a curfew requirement in an order is to require the offender to remain, for the period specified in the order, at a place specified in the order.

The ability to impose a curfew order was introduced in 2000.[65] It is based on the wish to keep offenders away from the opportunities to commit crime at the times when they are likely to do so. The limits of any curfew requirement are set by Sch 1, para 14(2): in any given day, the curfew period may not be less than 2 hours or more than 12 hours. The periods specified and the place specified may be different for different days, but not, probably, for periods of curfew within any one day. The curfew period must not fall outside the period of 6 months from the date the requirement comes into effect. That will often be, but is not necessarily, the date the YRO comes into effect. Thus a YRO might commence in March, but, if factually appropriate, might contain a curfew requirement during mid-June when a particular football tournament, music festival or other focus of potential offending for the individual offender occurs.

5.28 Because of the Human Rights Act 1998 implications relating to the Art 8 rights to respect for private and family life for both the offender and those whom the offender is with when subject to the curfew, care needs to be taken to ensure that the requirement is both necessary and proportionate. The procedural requirements specified in para 14(3) must be satisfied: the court must obtain and consider information about the place proposed to be specified, and the attitude of those likely to be affected by the enforced presence of the offender at that place.

Exclusion requirement (Sch 1, para 15)

5.29 The exclusion requirement effectively re-enacts Sch 2, para 8 of PCC(S)A 2000. The power to make a separate exclusion order will no longer exist.

The requirement may prohibit the offender from entering a place specified in the order, for a period of not more than 3 months. It is clear from the wording of para 15(3)(a) that this means 3 months in total, not one period not exceeding 3 months. The order may specify different places for different periods or days, and may specify that the prohibition may operate only during the periods specified.

---

[64] As defined by the Firearms Act 1968.
[65] PCC(S)A 2000, Sch 2, para 7, as amended by Criminal Justice and Courts Act 2000, s 50.

The term 'place' means not only an individually identifiable address or location, but also an area (para 15(4)). Thus a requirement might, for example, exclude from part of a town centre, neighbourhood shopping concourse, from the area around a town or village green or open space, or from an area round a particular club or public house, or football ground. Theoretically, there is no limit on the place that can be subject to a restriction: it would be theoretically possible for an offender who has been convicted of an offence of violence at his or her place of residence to be excluded from that: however, that would have major human rights implications and should not usually be used in that way. Again,[66] issues of necessity, proportionality and reasonableness arise.

An exclusion order may well be enforced and monitored through an electronic monitoring requirement, discussed at **5.37**.

Residence requirement (Sch 1, para 16)

5.30 Schedule 1 re-enacts the residence requirement provisions formerly found in Sch 2 to PCC(S)A 2000. Where such a requirement is imposed the offender can be required to live with a specified individual (but only if that individual agrees), or at a specified place (if the offender was aged at least 16 at the date of conviction).[67] There is no age restriction in respect of a requirement that specifies residence with an individual as opposed to residence at a specified place.

An order may specify a place of residence provided the offender is aged 16 at the date of conviction. Nonetheless, the responsible officer[68] may permit residence other than that specified in the order (para 16(5)). In all circumstances, regard must be had to the home surroundings of the offender. It might be that the specified place is a hostel or other regulated environment, although often that may often fall within the scope of a local authority residence requirement (see **5.31**). Nothing in Sch 1 deals explicitly with the relationship of the two provisions. However, there are restrictions contained in Sch 1, para 17(3) that are not applicable to residence requirements under para 16. It is submitted that where the residence requirement is one where the offender must reside in local authority accommodation,[69] the requirement should be imposed by virtue of para 17, not para 16; any other conclusion would render the restrictions in para 17 unnecessary and pointless.

If the place of residence is a regulated environment, then no doubt offenders will need to comply with that regime. It would be open to a court to impose a provision in an order requiring compliance with such a regime, but there is no necessity to do that, given that s 5 of the new Act requires the offender to comply with arrangements put in place and instructions given by the responsible officer. In any event such a power might be implied.[70]

The requirement must specify the period of residence, but does not limit the length of the period, which is thus limited solely by what is reasonable, necessary and proportionate. The stated period, like any other details in a requirement, must be sufficiently precise and specific. If, for example, there is uncertainty as to the precise

---

[66] See also **5.15**.
[67] Sch 1, para 16(4).
[68] As to whom see 2008 Act, s 4.
[69] Accommodation provided by or on behalf of a local authority.
[70] See, by analogy, *Powell (Shane)* [1990] 13 Cr App R (S) 202.

period of residence that is suitable for the offender, the order should specify what the sentencing court considers appropriate at the time of sentence, with any variation or amendment dealt with as such (see **5.39**).

Local authority residence requirement (Sch 1, para 17)

5.31 The predecessor to the local authority residence requirement was that contained in Sch 6, para 5 of PCC(S)A 2000, conferring a power to impose such a requirement as part of a supervision order. It is a requirement to reside in local authority accommodation[71] for a specified period. Such a requirement may be combined with a requirement that the offender is not to reside with a specified person (Sch 1, para 17(2)). The specified period must not be for a period longer than 6 months, and must not extend beyond the date when the offender becomes 18.

This power raises important questions. Removing an offender from the home raises issues under Art 8 of ECHR. Such an interference with private or family life must be necessary and proportionate, but if it is in the best interest of the offender to remove him from circumstances that encourage or facilitate offending behaviour, the interference with the Art 8 right may be justified. It is for these reasons that para 17(3) restricts the making of such an order until the court is satisfied that the behaviour which constituted the offence was due to a significant extent to the circumstances in which the offender was living, and that the imposition of the requirement will assist in the offender's rehabilitation. In addition, of course, the detail of the requirement not to live with a named individual will be important in the context of whether such a requirement is proportionate. Such a requirement in respect of a parent or individual with whom the offender is in a relationship would be an extremely severe restriction and need compelling justification. Indeed, in the case of a parent arguably a fostering requirement might, in many cases be a more appropriate response, although, as noted earlier, a fostering requirement is a 'high end' requirement involving intensive work with the offender. However, the effect of para 18(5) is that a local authority residence requirement does not preclude the local authority placing the offender with a foster parent. This by implication surely means that it is considered inappropriate for the court to combine this requirement with a fostering requirement. Placing an offender in foster care is to place an offender in accommodation provided 'on behalf of' the authority for the purposes of this provision. The requirements and restrictions relating to the two orders are similar, but not identical.[72] Further, the wording of para 18(5) gives implicit confirmation, if it is needed, that the right to require residence in accommodation is distinct from a requirement of fostering.

The order can only be made after consultation with a parent or guardian, unless it is impracticable to do so, and with the relevant local authority responsible for the area where the offender resides or is to reside. Further, the provisions of para 19(1) apply; generally no order can be made unless the offender is legally represented at the time the order is made.[73]

---

[71] See **5.30**.
[72] See para 19 for identical requirements, but compare para 17 which applies only in respect of local authority residence requirements.
[73] For the limited exception, see para 19(2).

Fostering requirement (Sch 1, para 18)

5.32 The fostering requirements in Sch 1 are new. A fostering requirement is a requirement to reside with a local authority foster parent[74] for a specified period no later than 12 months after the coming into effect of the requirement. It cannot extend beyond the date when the offender becomes 18 (para 18(2)). The relationship between this requirement and a local authority residence requirement has already been discussed (see **5.30**).

The order will specify the local authority who is responsible for the fostering, which will be the local authority for the area in which the offender resides or will reside. Clearly, appropriate fostering arrangements must exist (para 18(7)). If they exist when the order is made, but later become unavailable then the order operates as a requirement for local authority residence (para 18(5)). The offender must generally be legally represented at the time the fostering requirement is imposed (para 19).

Mental health treatment requirement (Sch 1, para 20)

5.33 The power to impose a mental health requirement in a supervision order was contained in Sch 6 to PCC(S)A 2000. Such a requirement in the new generic YRO is defined by para 20(1) and permits either residential or non-residential treatment as specified in the order in accordance with the terms of para 20(2). The order must not specify the nature of the treatment beyond its type as defined in para 20(2). The responsible officer will supervise the offender who is subject to a residential requirement only to the extent necessary for revoking, or amending the order.

The court must be satisfied[75] that the mental condition requires and is susceptible to treatment, that arrangements for it can be made, and that the offender is willing to comply with the requirement.

The treatment will be at a place or by the practitioner specified in the order in accordance with para 20(2). However, para 21 deals with treatment otherwise than as stated in the order. The effect is that the relevant practitioner may make other arrangements for part of the treatment if he or she considers that treatment can be better or more conveniently given at a non-specified place or institution, or by a non-specified practitioner.

Drug treatment requirement (Sch 1, para 22) and drug testing requirement (Sch 1, para 23)

5.34 The power to impose drug testing and drug treatment requirements was made available to a court in respect of young offenders in 2003, and is now contained in paras 22 and 23. A 'drug treatment requirement' imposes an obligation, during specified periods which are not time-limited other than during the currency of the order, to submit to treatment with the view to the reduction or elimination of the offender's dependency on, or propensity to misuse, controlled drugs.[76] A 'drug testing requirement' is a requirement that, for the purpose of ascertaining whether there is any drug in the

---

[74] Defined by the Children Act 1989.
[75] Proved in accordance with the Mental Health Act 1983, s 54: see 2008 Act, Sch 1, para 20(5).
[76] Within the meaning of Misuse of Drugs Act 1971, s 2: see 2008 Act, Sch 1, para 22(5).

offender's body during any treatment period, the offender must, during that period, provide samples as instructed by the responsible officer.

The two requirements are linked; a testing requirement cannot be imposed without a treatment requirement (para 23(2(b)). The treatment requirement, which cannot be imposed without the consent of the offender, is subject to the preconditions set out above, and prescribes treatment whether residential or non-residential. A requirement cannot be imposed unless it has been recommended to the court by a member of a youth offending team, an officer of the local probation board, or an officer of a provider of probation services.

The testing requirement sets out, for each month, the minimum number of occasions on which samples are to be provided, and may specify the times at which and circumstances in which the responsible officer or treatment provider may require samples, and the description of the samples which might be required.

Intoxicating substance treatment requirement (Sch 1, para 24)

5.35 The Act in its original form when introduced into Parliament did not contain a specific provision relating to alcohol. This was the subject of significant and substantial criticism, and as a result the Government introduced an amendment which is now para 24 of Sch 1. It is, in terms, similar to the provisions relating to drug treatment, only, of course, relating to intoxicating substances. The definition of 'intoxicating substance' in para 24(5) goes beyond alcohol to include substances or products (other than drugs) which are themselves, or the fumes from which, capable of being inhaled or otherwise used for the purposes of causing intoxication. Glue and lighter fuel are two obvious examples.

The treatment may be residential or non-residential. A requirement can only be imposed on the recommendation of a member of a youth offending team, probation officer or an officer of a provider of probation services.

Education requirement (Sch 1, para 25)

5.36 The power to impose an education requirement is re-enacted by Sch 1. A court may require the offender, if of compulsory school age, to comply with such arrangements for his or her education as may from time to time be made by the offender's parent or guardian, the arrangements being such as have been approved by the Local Education Authority (LEA). The LEA must be consulted and be satisfied that arrangements exist for education suitable to the offender's age, ability and aptitude, and to any special educational needs that may exist. The court must be satisfied that the requirement is necessary for securing the good conduct of the offender or for preventing the commission of further offences.

Electronic monitoring (Sch 1, para 26)

5.37 The power to impose electronic monitoring has existed under the PCC(S)A 2000, and is re-enacted by Sch 1. It is a means for ensuring the offender's compliance with other requirements, such as a curfew requirement or exclusion requirement, and must be imposed unless a person whose consent is necessary (see below) does not consent, if the facilities to monitor are not available (Sch 1, para 26(3) and (6)) or, in the particular circumstances of the case the court considers it inappropriate for the order to do so (Sch 1, para 2(2)).

Any person, other than the offender, whose co-operation is necessary to secure that the monitoring takes place must consent (para 26(4)(b)). The order must specify the period during which monitoring is to occur.

BREACH, REVOCATION OR AMENDMENT
Breach

5.38 Schedule 2 to the new Act deals with this in Part 2. It creates a scheme of some similarity to that introduced by CJA 2003, Sch 8. In summary, it provides for breach to be dealt with as follows:

- the responsible officer must issue a warning where he is of the opinion that the offender has failed without reasonable excuse to comply with the YRO (Sch 2, para 3). The contents of the warning are stated in para 2(2). It is intended that the warning should be in writing;[77]

- it is open to the responsible officer to proceed to enforcement in a youth or Crown Court (para 4(3));

- if an offender is given two warnings and, within the period of 12 months from the first, he or she fails, without reasonable excuse,[78] to comply with the YRO, the responsible officer must commence proceedings, unless he or she considers there are 'exceptional circumstances' that justify not commencing breach proceedings in court (para 4(2)).
This process might be open to criticism for limiting the discretion of the responsible officer (and was criticised for that reason), but the House of Commons was told:[79]

> 'This is a reasonable approach to ensure that young people are formally encouraged through a series of warnings before a third breach ... the provisions reflect the Youth Justice Board's national standards for breaches and have been put into [the Act] specifically to ensure that there is clear evidence that breaches will be pursued rigorously and consistently ...'

Nonetheless there is a real danger that this regime, introduced 'to maintain confidence in community sentences'[80] may have the effect of 'accelerating into custody' young offenders, not because of the seriousness of their offending but because of persistent failure to comply with the terms of the requirements imposed.[81]
The term 'reasonable excuse' requires the responsible officer and, later perhaps, the court to make a finding of fact as to what the reason was for the failure to

---

[77] David Hanson, Minister of State, Ministry of Justice, HC Committee, col 276 (25 October 2007).
[78] The burden of proof of showing an absence of reasonable excuse is on the prosecution.
[79] David Hanson, Minister of State, Ministry of Justice, HC Committee, col 263 (25 October 2007).
[80] Government evidence to the Joint Committee on Human Rights 2007/2008, cited at para 1.21.
[81] Joint Committee on Human Rights, ibid at 1.21.

comply and whether that reason was objectively reasonable, having regard to the characteristics and circumstances of the offender:

- in respect of a Crown Court order the breach proceedings will be in the Crown Court unless that court has made a direction otherwise (para 5(2); see **5.11**));

- applications in respect of breach will otherwise be to the relevant youth court (if the offender is then under 18) or (if over 18) to the magistrates' court;

- if a youth or magistrates' court finds that there is a failure to comply without reasonable excuse, it can fine the offender,[82] amend the order or deal with the offender for the original offence (para 6). Schedule 2, paras 6 and 9 contain detailed provisions relating to the powers of the court. Importantly, if the court finds that the breach is wilful and persistent it can impose a YRO with ISS. If the order in question is a YRO with ISS, it may impose a custodial sentence despite any general restrictions on the imposition of a custodial sentence contained in s 152(2) of CJA 2003;

- if a Crown Court order comes before a youth court or magistrates' court, that court can send the offender to the Crown Court, but is not obliged to do so (para 7);

- the powers of the Crown Court are similar to those of the magistrates' court or youth court, save only that the Crown Court may deal with the offender in any way it could have dealt with the offender for the original offence. Paragraphs 8 and 9 contain detailed provisions relating to the powers of the court.

Revocation and amendment

5.39 Parts 3 and 4 of Sch 2 deal with revocation or amendment of a YRO. Both the Crown Court and the youth court are given power to revoke an order where it is in the interests of justice to do so. A court can either revoke an order, or revoke and deal with the offender for the original offence in accordance with the powers that that court had. The court must have regard to the progress of the offender or how he or she has responded to treatment. If the offender is being dealt with for the original offence the court must have regard to the extent of compliance with the order.

Amendment of the order

5.40 Power to amend the order is vested in the youth or magistrates' court (if aged 18) unless the Crown Court (in the case of a Crown Court order) has not made a direction (see **5.4**).

One aspect of the right to amend should be noted: a court may wish to amend a fostering requirement. If it so wishes it can extend the period of fostering by substituting a new fostering requirement for the old provided it does not extend beyond 18 months from the date of the first requirement. Given that the fostering requirement is itself an interference with the right to family life, it is suggested that such powers of extension be used cautiously, and only where the circumstances manifestly warrant it.

---

[82] Maximum £1,000, or, if the offender is aged under 14, £250.

Powers of a court following conviction

5.41 Powers of a court following conviction are dealt with by Part 5 of Sch 2. The convicting court may revoke the order and deal with the offender for the original offence if it considers that it is in the interests of justice to do so (para 18(3) and (5)). Paragraph 18(8) deals with the question of whether the convicting court can deal with the offender where the YRO is a Crown Court order. When making an order the Crown Court can make a direction that further proceedings relating to the order be in a youth court or other magistrates' court (Sch 1, para 36). If an offender is brought before a youth court and magistrates' court for a further offence, and a direction has been made, that court may revoke the order, and deal with the offender for the original offence in any way it could have dealt with him for that offence (Sch 2, para 18(4)). But they may choose to send the case to the Crown Court, and they have the power to do so (Sch 2, para 18(9)).

Chapter 6

VIOLENT OFFENDER ORDERS

SUMMARY

6.1 The 2008 Act creates a new civil order, the Violent Offender Order (VOO). A person who qualifies can be made the subject of an order which lasts not less than 2 or more than 5 years. The order is designed to prevent serious violent harm to the public. An order is made following an application to a magistrates' court by the relevant chief officer of police, and will contain appropriate prohibitions, restrictions and conditions. Breach of these is a criminal offence.

The power to make an interim order is created, as are notification requirements.

The provisions are not in force as at the date of going to press.

BACKGROUND

6.2 The problem of violent crime is one of the key issues that the Government's criminal justice strategy is seeking to address. Its importance in the context of the sentencing provisions has already been noted (see **3.14**) especially with the IPP and extended sentence provisions. The new order (VOO) is another strand designed to assist in the prevention, or reduction, of violent crime. It is intended to 'provide a means of continuously protecting the public from some of the most dangerous violent offenders who still present a high risk at the end of their sentence, when there are no other means for public protection authorities to manage their risk. Violent offender orders will therefore be an essential risk management tool by enabling the closure of the gap in supervision arrangements'.[1]

That 'gap' could arise in several ways. The IPP provisions might not have been available in respect of the offender, because they might not have been in force at the date he committed the offence for which he was sentenced. Alternatively, the risk the offender poses may have increased since he was convicted of his criminal offence, or the period of licence on his custodial sentence may have come to an end.

However, the case for a further order has to be made; some consider that it has not been.[2] When they apply, the licence provisions of an IPP sentence[3] are extensive, and can provide potentially effective means of ongoing supervision of the actions of released

---

[1] Lord Hunt, Parliamentary Under-Secretary of State, Ministry of Justice, HL 2nd Reading (22 January 2008).
[2] See, eg, HC Committee, cols 592–596 (28 November 2007) citing, in particular, the representations of *Liberty*.
[3] As to which see **3.15**.

prisoners. However, the preconditions for the making of a VOO do not confine it to cases where an IPP sentence has been imposed. Other means of protection are anti-social behaviour orders (ASBOs), sex offender prevention orders, foreign travel orders, risk of sexual harm orders, or control orders made under the anti-terrorism legislation. There is also the potential for the making of non-molestation orders, with their new criminal sanction for breach;[4] although non-molestation orders are only of value where the threat or danger of violence is against a named individual. The serious crime prevention orders[5] are likely to be of limited value in the contexts where the VOO is potentially going to be of value.

The use of civil orders with criminal sanctions for breach is now well established and believed, at any rate by some, to be successful.[6] The VOO scheme follows the model of ASBOs in that respect. The question as to whether a further weapon is needed in this increasingly large armoury of powers is important, not simply because of a need to avoid unnecessary legislation. It may have the potential to increase the prison population when the aim of the Government is the reverse.[7] The Minister estimated that 'a small number – about 100 people – might breach orders and be subject to a term of imprisonment', and requiring 20 additional prison places, figures which are at odds with the estimate of a need for 3,000 additional prison places made by the National Association of Probation Officers.[8]

The order

6.3 Part 7 of the new Act contains the relevant provisions in respect of a VOO. Section 98 defines a VOO as an order made in respect of a qualifying offender which:

> '(a) contains such prohibitions, restrictions or conditions authorised by section 102 as the court making the order considers necessary for the purpose of protecting the public from the risk of serious violent harm caused by the offender, and
> (b) has effect for such period of not less than 2, nor more than 5, years as is specified in the order(unless renewed or discharged).'

The reference to 'protecting the public' refers to the public in the UK or to any particular members of the public in the UK (s 98(2)). 'Serious violent harm' means 'serious physical or psychological harm caused by that person committing one or more specified offences'. We return to what has to be proved at **6.8**.

6.4 Questions arise about the nature of the order. It is civil in nature, like ASBOs, control orders and the other orders referred to above. That raises issues about compatibility of the VOO powers with the ECHR, as well as the desirability of addressing criminality through the use of civil order.

In *R (McCann) v Crown Court at Manchester*[9] the House of Lords held that the making of an ASBO did not amount to the determination of a criminal charge for the purpose of Art 6, although a court should apply the criminal standard of proof. A variety of

---

[4] See Domestic Violence Crime and Victims Act 2004.
[5] See Serious Crime Act 2007, s 2 and Sch 1.
[6] See Vernon Coaker, Parliamentary Under-Secretary of State for Home Department, HC Committee, col 596 (28 November 2007).
[7] See **3.3**.
[8] HC Committee, col 599 (28 November 2007).
[9] [2002] UKHL 39, [2003] 1 AC 787.

factors pointed to the conclusion that these were not criminal proceedings for the purposes of deciding whether the criminal fair trial standards apply: there was no formal accusation of a criminal offence; the proceedings were commenced by a civil complaint; it was unnecessary to establish criminal liability; the purpose of the order was preventative; and the making of an ASBO was not a conviction or a finding that the person subject to the application was guilty of an offence.

Clearly VOOs are distinguishable from ASBOs in major respects: a precondition for the making of a VOO is that the individual has been convicted of a 'specified offence'. No such prior conviction is a precondition for the making of an ASBO. The definition of a 'specified offence' is such that VOOs potentially will only be available where the individual has committed a serious offence of violence. The Joint Committee on Human Rights had real concerns.[10] It considered that, because of the requirement for such a conviction, the severity of the restrictions that could potentially be imposed, and the possible length of the order, it is likely to amount to the determination of a criminal charge for the purposes of Art 6. Those requirements may affect working arrangements, family life, travel and the right to visit premises, and are left to the discretion of the court.[11] These could potentially impact significantly on the individual and, in one sense flow from the first precondition, namely conviction for a serious violent offence.

The Government rejected this analysis, pointing out the purpose of the VOO was preventative, looking at potential future risk, not looking backward to add to the punishment of the original offence.

However, the Committee regretted the fact that the criminal standard of proof was not spelt out explicitly in the Act,[12] a change unsuccessfully proposed during the passage of the Act. The Joint Committee also followed the logic of its conclusion by recommending that a full adversarial hearing be a prerequisite to the making of an order (see **6.7**). Other concerns relate to interim orders (see **6.18**) and the potential retrospective operation that might in some cases occur, potentially in breach of Art 7 (see **6.5**).

The preconditions for the making of a VOO

6.5 The person who is to be the subject to a VOO must be a 'qualifying offender', defined by s 99. That person (P) must be aged 18 or over; original proposals that this should extend to under-18s were dropped. P must have been convicted in the past of a 'specified offence', as defined by s 98(3), and, in addition, one of three preconditions must apply (see below). Section 99 does not impose any requirement that a VOO must be made within a specified period of time after the conviction, or after the completion of any sentence imposed or served. The conviction could be many years prior to the application for a VOO. The legislation envisages that a VOO can be sought whilst P is in custody, perhaps, but not necessarily, for the specified offence (see, for example, s 102(5)). The length of time since the conviction may affect how the court dealing with the application for a VOO assesses risk, but even an old conviction is sufficient to satisfy the offence criterion set by s 99.

'Specified offences' are serious violent offences: manslaughter, soliciting murder, wounding with intent, malicious wounding, attempting or conspiring to commit murder,

---

[10] 5th Report 2007/2008 at para 1.90.
[11] See **6.16**. In this regard, cf Serious Crime Act 2007.
[12] 5th Report 2007/2008 at para 1.95.

or a relevant service offence (s 98(3)).[13] This is a much more narrow definition than was used in the Criminal Justice Act 2003 (CJA 2003) for the purposes of the indeterminate sentence provisions.[14] The applicant for a VOO does not have to show that the offence of which P has been convicted is directly related to the risk of serious violent harm against which the VOO is intended to protect. Thus, if P has been convicted of malicious wounding, this precondition for the making of a VOO is satisfied if there is a risk, for example, of soliciting murder, even if there was no direct link between the malicious wounding and the conduct of serious violent harm now apprehended. In short, what the specified offence does is show a propensity to serious violence. However, evidence of a link between the type of conduct which the specified offence comprised and the future risk apprehended may be extremely cogent in persuading the court as to the need for, and terms of, a VOO.

Apart from the requirement for a prior conviction for a specified offence, there are three preconditions (s 99(2), (3) and (4)), one of which must be met: the first is that a custodial sentence[15] of at least 12 months was imposed, or P was made subject to a hospital order; the second is that the individual has been found not guilty of a specified offence by reason of insanity, provided the court made a hospital order or a supervision order (s 99(2)(b), (3)); and the third is that the individual is found to be under a disability and to have done the act charged in respect of a specified offence, again, providing the court has made a hospital order or a supervision order (s 99(2)(c) and (3)).

An individual is also a qualifying offender if s 99(5) applies. This extends the scope of 'qualifying offenders' to those who are convicted of a relevant offence[16] or are subject to an equivalent finding in a jurisdiction outside England and Wales. The effect of s 99(5) is that it does not matter how that offence is described in the law of the relevant jurisdiction: what matters is the nature of the facts alleged, whether they are unlawful in the law of that jurisdiction, and whether they would constitute a specified offence if that had occurred in England and Wales. That last question is to be presumed, if the person to whom the application relates denies that a notice must be served on the applicant stating the reasons why P considers the precondition in s 99(4) is not met and requiring the applicant to prove that it is.

The application and hearing

6.6 An application may be made to a magistrates' court by a chief officer of police for the area (a) where the person resides, or (b) where the chief officer believes that P 'is in, or is intending to come to, that area' (s 100(1)). Rules may provide for other persons to have the power to make an application, and may specify the circumstances in which such applications may be made (s 100(4)). No such rules had been made as at the date of going to press.

The wording of s 100(1) does not completely put beyond doubt the question of the meaning of the words in (b). However, arguably the belief in (b) does not mean that that belief has to be that P is in, or coming to, the chief officer's area for the purpose of residence. That conclusion is given some support by the absence of any reference in (b) to P intending to reside, and by the drafting of s 103, which envisages three possible scenarios, only one of which explicitly refers to residence. Therefore it follows, for

---

[13] As to which see s 98(4).
[14] See CJA 2003, Sch 15, Part 1.
[15] Defined by the 2008 Act, s 117. It includes a suspended sentence of imprisonment.
[16] See s 99(5).

example, that a chief officer who believed that P was intending to visit an ex-spouse in his (the chief officer's) area (that being an area in which P did not reside) with the intention of causing her serious physical harm could make an application provided that the chief officer holds the belief set out in s 100(2).

The application is to be made to any magistrates' court for the area of the applicant chief police officer (see above) or for any place where the conduct occurs that gives rise to the reasonable cause to believe that it is necessary for a VOO to be made (s 100(3)). No power to make a VOO is conferred on a sentencing court: the Crown Court has no power to make a VOO, nor does a magistrates' court exercising criminal jurisdiction.

6.7 An application can be made if it appears to the relevant chief officer that P is a qualifying offender and, since the appropriate date (defined by s 100(5) by reference to the date of conviction of the specified offence) P had acted in such a way as to give reasonable cause to believe[17] that it is necessary for a VOO to be made in respect of that person (s 100(1)).

This raises possible issues of retrospectivity under Art 7 of ECHR, which prohibits the retrospective operation of a criminal offence, and prohibits the imposition of a heavier penalty than the penalty available at the time the criminal offence was committed.[18]

An offender is potentially liable to the imposition of a VOO even though the conviction for a specified offence pre-dated the commencement of the VOO provisions. The Government does not consider that Art 7 is even engaged, arguing that P is not being convicted of a criminal offence. A VOO is not a punishment but a preventative measure. There was no question of retrospective punishment. The criminality in regards to a VOO occurs only where there is a breach of the VOO (see **6.21**). It is not the specified offence that gives rise to the VOO, but the later conduct of P. The Government's arguments are perhaps also supported by the decision in *McCann*[19] where the House of Lords concluded that proceedings to obtain an ASBO do not amount to the determination of a criminal charge.

The Joint Committee on Human Rights was unconvinced,[20] particularly in the context of onerous restrictions and conditions. Indeed, one might argue that these obligations may be preventative, but they do amount effectively to additional punitive and restrictive measures that were not available to a court when P was convicted. Some support for those concerns surely comes from the responses by the Government to the concerns of the Joint Committee, when it asked what the difference was between VOOs and sentences for public protection. The Government's responses indicated that VOOs would be a means of protecting the public where IPP was not available because the qualifying offence was prior to the commencement of the IPP legislation, where the individual risk level for IPP was not considered, at the time, sufficiently great, and where the IPP sentence had expired.[21] In other words, if the preventative powers had existed or

---

[17] Belief is something more than suspicion: *Forsyth* [1997] Crim LR 589: 'Reasonable cause to believe' means the person concerned must actually, believe, and on evidence that belief must be objectively reasonable. This is decided in all the circumstances disclosed by the evidence. See *McArdle v Egan* (1933) 150 LT 412; *Nakkuda Ali v Jayarante* [1951] AC 66.
[18] See *Harman v United Kingdom* 38 D & R 53; *Welch v United Kingdom* (1995) 20 EHRR 247; *SW & C v United Kingdom* (1995) 21 EHRR 247.
[19] [2002] UKHL 39, [2003] 1 AC 787.
[20] 5th Report 2007/2008 at para 1.102.
[21] Ibid, para 1.87.

been considered necessary at the time they would have been imposed. If they had, that would indeed have been punitive in nature even if it was also imposed for the future purpose of public protection.

The hearing at the relevant magistrates' court will be in person. It has already been noted that, arguably, the VOO engages with criminal fair trial provisions.[22] The applicant should be present, so, too, should P, if P wishes to be heard (s 6(2)). For that reason, if P is in custody and wishes to be heard there appears to be no power to proceed until he is present. Issues also arise in respect of the making of interim orders (see **6.18**).

Making of the order

6.8 A court may make an order if it is satisfied that P is a qualifying person and that, since the appropriate date, P has acted in such a way as to make it necessary to make a VOO for the purpose of protecting the public from the risk of serious violent harm caused by P. In deciding whether to make an order the court must have regard to whether P would, at any time, when such an order is in force, be subject under any other enactment to any measures that would operate to protect the public from serious harm (s 101(3) and (4)).

The court has to be 'satisfied'. The burden of proof is on the applicant. The standard of proof is likely to be the criminal standard despite the fact that the proceedings are civil in nature. That is the effect of the House of Lords decision in *R (McCann) v Chief Constable of Manchester*.[23] The courts have consistently stressed that the civil standard of proof traditionally, on the balance of probabilities is a flexible standard, and may even extend to the high criminal standard 'beyond reasonable doubt',[24] particularly where there are allegations of misconduct in respect of the individual who is subject to the application. In civil proceedings to obtain ASBOs,[25] sex offender orders[26] and football banning orders,[27] it has been held that the standard of proof required for such purposes is indistinguishable from the criminal standard.

Whether there are in fact two standards, or simply different levels of proof which vary according to what has to be determined, is debatable.[28] However in *R (on the application of McCann) v Manchester Crown Court*, which concerned the making of ASBOs, the House of Lords considered it impractical to leave individual magistrates to determine precisely what was required by a 'heightened civil standard' of proof; in the interests of pragmatism Lord Steyn concluded that the standard in all such cases should be the criminal one.[29] However, it also concluded that since the proceedings were civil in nature (see **6.4**) civil rules of evidence applied, which at that time was particularly significant in the context of the rules dealing with hearsay evidence.[30]

---

[22] See **6.4** and **6.7**.
[23] [2002] UKHL 39.
[24] *R v Wolverhampton Coroner, ex parte McCurbin* [1990] 1 WLR 719, [1990] 2 All ER 759; *Halford v Brookes* (1991) *The Times*, October 3.
[25] *R (on the application of McCann) v Manchester Crown Court* [2002] UKHL 39, [2003] 1 AC 787, [2002] 4 All ER 593.
[26] *B v Chief Constable of Avon and Somerset* [2001] 1 WLR 340, [2001] 1 All ER 562.
[27] *Gough v Chief Constable of Derbyshire* [2002] EWCA Civ 351, [2002] QB 1213, [2002] 2 All ER 985.
[28] *R (on the application of N) v M* [2002] EWCA Civ 1789, [2003] 1 WLR 562, [2003] 1 FLR 667.
[29] [2002] UKHL 39 at [18].
[30] See the changes made by CJA 2003, s 114.

During the passage of the Act attempts were made to explicitly write into it a requirement that the standard of proof for the making of a VOO was the criminal standard. Oddly, that was rejected by the Government, even though it accepted that the criminal standard was appropriate[31] and even though a precedent for defining the standard of proof explicitly is to be found in s 41 of the Prevention of Terrorism Act 2005. Despite this, a magistrates' court should apply the criminal standard of proof when dealing with an application for a VOO.

6.9 Although the standard of proof is effectively the criminal standard, the rules of evidence are not: the civil rules of evidence apply.[32] In particular it will be the civil rules relating to hearsay, and how witness statements should be handled,[33] not the different rules and standards contained in CJA 2003. Particularly in this regard the decision relating to whether the proceedings are criminal in nature for the purposes of Art 6 of ECHR (see **6.4**) is important. If the courts maintain the position taken in respect of ASBOs, there will not be any right to require witnesses whose factual testimony is the basis for concluding that the requisite risks exist to attend for cross-examination.

The applicant will have to prove the following:

- that P is a qualifying person. To that end the applicant will prove the relevant conviction, by certificate of conviction or other appropriate evidence;

- that since the qualifying date (the date of conviction) P has *acted* in a way to give rise to the risk described below; and

- that it is necessary to make an order for the purpose of protecting the public from the risk of serious violent harm *caused by P*.

Several aspects of this merit discussion.

6.10 The applicant has to prove the fact and date of conviction of a specified offence. That is a factual matter, easily proved. The applicant does not have to establish the facts of that offence, or offences, and arguably those facts are only relevant if they provide the context for assessment of risk. Of course, in many cases they may do so, but despite the intention of Parliament that the VOO is intended to be a means of supervision of offenders who have shown themselves to be a risk there is no connection as such *as required by law*. For example, P may have many years ago committed a specified offence. He is now considered, for unrelated reasons, to pose a risk in the way envisaged by the Act. That risk may not relate in any way to the specified offence, but the preconditions are potentially satisfied. The details of the specified offence may have no evidential value, and there is no *requirement* for them to be heard. On the other hand, the detail of the offence may be absolutely vital in demonstrating the level of risk.

6.11 The applicant must prove that, since the date of conviction for a specified offence, P has acted in a way that gives rise to the risk. The parliamentary debates were often couched in terms of ongoing protection against risk, and indeed that is the context of the provisions. But unless the statute is to be read widely, and purposively, there must be something other than the conviction itself. The conviction itself may show that P

---

[31] HC Committee, col 607 (28 November 2007).
[32] See the *McCann* case.
[33] See Civil Evidence Act 1995.

poses a significant risk to the public, which may be ongoing, but that is not enough. There must be an act or acts beyond the specified offence. It follows that if an application were to be made before or on release from, the custodial sentence being served for that specified offence (as is possible under the Act[34]) such an application should fail unless there was conduct during the service of that sentence that amounted to evidence that was sufficient to justify the making of the order. The point is theoretical rather than real, because on release from custody such an offender will be on licence in any event. However, the point becomes less academic if, when the licence period is expiring the police consider there to be a real continuing risk of serious violent conduct. Again, that belief must be based on evidence of acts and not justified solely by the specified offence itself.

The use of the term 'acted' suggests positive actions, not negatives, unless 'acted' is given the wider meaning of 'failed to act'. Given the consequences of a VOO the wording of the statute should be construed strictly. A failure to follow advice or to seek advice, counselling or behaviour management activities should not, of themselves, be regarded as 'actions'. Nonetheless, the scope of the term is very wide. Obviously actual violence, threats of violence, targeting of victims suffice. But the conduct does not have to be unlawful. Visiting premises where violence may occur, or where P's presence is likely to lead to violence is an 'act' (but see **6.14**). Outbursts of rage and temper might of themselves be lawful, but coupled with the criminal history of violence may give rise to a belief in the existence of the requisite risk. Drinking to excess may not, of itself, be unlawful, but if there is a history of alcohol-fuelled violence it may, again, give rise to the risk. It will be important that the risk assessment on which the application is based identifies the actions on which the risk assessment can validly conclude that the relevant risk arises.

6.12 The making of the order must be 'necessary' to protect the public from a risk of serious violent harm. Arguably the term 'necessary' does not mean that this must be the only way of addressing that risk. There will be few situations where this is the *only* way of dealing with the problem. If a court considers that, of the alternatives open to the applicant, or the court, a VOO is an appropriate way of addressing the risk, then the making of the VOO is 'necessary'. However, if there are alternatives of equal utility the court is entitled to ask why a VOO is needed in preference to other courses of action, and in that regard the restrictive or coercive nature of the order will need to be taken into account. Of course, it may be that it is the very power to impose restrictions and conditions that makes the VOO 'necessary'. In that case it is the order with the restrictions and conditions that must be 'necessary'. If that necessity can be addressed with lesser, or no, restrictions and conditions then that is what the court should do.

6.13 The order must be necessary to protect the public from the risk of serious violent harm caused by P. It is not only the actual harm which is being prevented, it is protection from the risk of that harm. Of course, often the two cannot be separated. What amounts to 'serious violent harm' is not defined. It could, of course, have been defined by reference to 'specified offences' (see **6.5**), but the fact that it is not suggests very strongly that it is meant to be very much wider. In the absence of a definition, it is a particularly wide power, and left to the court determining the application to make a judgment. It will obviously include the major offences against the person: murder, attempted murder, grievous bodily harm and other significant wounding. How far it applies to assaults is debatable. For example, although the VOO is not intended as an

---

[34] See s 102.

alternative to a non-molestation order, can a VOO be used to prevent ongoing assaults in a domestic violence context? Although s 101(4) requires a court to have regard to what the protections under other legislative provisions exist, it does not explicitly require a VOO to be issued only where there are no other alternative protections (see **6.12**). The question arises as to how 'serious' is to be defined. A pattern of assaults in a domestic context might well justify the adjective 'serious'. In its operation, s 101 may also be wider than might be assumed. For example, those who go to a public demonstration intent on causing violence may well be causing a risk of serious violent harm. The potential for the making of a VOO in such a situation exists, although important issues relating to freedom of expression under Art 10 of ECHR might well arise.

The term 'risk' should not be confused with 'danger'. Risk relates the probability that a harmful event or behaviour will occur. 'Danger' describes the actual exposure to harm, or the propensity to present harm.[35] In the case of a VOO we are looking at the probability that serious violent conduct will occur. This should be based on an up-to-date risk assessment which takes into account the behaviour that gives rise to the application (see **6.11**). It should be noted that the word is not qualified by an adjective such as 'significant', 'substantial' or 'real'. Despite that, and given the nature of the order, a court should be slow to make a VOO on remote or slight risks. But patently one has to ask the question: risk of what? The greater the *danger* (ie of serious violent harm) the lower the level of *risk* that may suffice to justify the making of the VOO.

Given that the risk assessment will be evidence based, there may be a need to seek an interim VOO (see **6.18**).

6.14 The risk must be of serious violent harm *caused*. The term 'caused' should bear its ordinary and natural meaning. The order is designed to prevent serious violent harm by P. Any other conclusion would lead to unacceptable breadth. For example, violence may occur *as a result* of P being at a particular place, for example a known sex offender being in a neighbourhood in a high state of tension because of recent sex offences. Violence might result, but it will not have been caused by P unless he actually engages in it, or, possibly, incites it.

When can an order be made?

6.15 A VOO may not be made to come into force whilst P is subject to a custodial sentence for *any* offence, is on licence for part of the time of such a sentence, or is subject to a hospital order or supervision order. So a VOO can subsist concurrently with licence for a custodial sentence. There appears to be no restriction on the making of a VOO whilst a community sentence is in operation. However, that might cause the prospect of double jeopardy for breach of requirements under such an order and under a VOO, and in many cases be an undesirable combination.

Although a VOO cannot come into effect during a custodial sentence, an application may be made during that time (s 102). Thus an application can be made whilst P is in custody to take effect once he comes out, provided he is not subject to a licence condition. However, there must always be acts of P subsequent to the conviction for the specified offence that give rise to the reasonable belief in the existence of the risk (see **6.8**).

---

[35] See H Kemshall *Reviewing Risk* (Home Office, 1996).

The contents of the order

6.16 The order may contain prohibitions, restrictions or conditions preventing the offender:[36]

(a) from going to any specified premises or any other specified place (whether at all, or at or between any specified time or times);
(b) from attending any specified event;
(c) from having any, or any specified description of, contact with any specified individual.

Any restrictions contained in an order made by a court may apply to Scotland or Northern Ireland.

It is clear that the order can prohibit, restrict or regulate but cannot impose positive obligations. It is also self evident that the restrictions, prohibitions or conditions must be for the purpose of preventing serious violent offences being committed by P. The prohibitions, restrictions and conditions must be part of the order; they cannot be left to be determined by some other person. Section 102 also appears to be specific about what may or may not be included in an order: there are no words of generality that might indicate that the matters specified in (a), (b) or (c) above are intended to be examples, without prejudice to the generality. Construed strictly, as s 102 should be, it appears to identify categories of prohibitions, restrictions and conditions that may be imposed.

Other than the above, there appear to be few restrictions on the nature of those prohibitions, restrictions or conditions. They must be necessary for the purpose of protecting against the risk. Although the purpose of the VOO is clear, its terms are in no way confined to that purpose, and are potentially wide enough to engage with a wide range of activities. The fact that P must have been convicted of a specified offence, narrowly drawn, is some limitation. But the order may be unrelated to the specified offence (see **6.11**). The terms of the order might involve a prohibition with contact with a particular individual, say, an ex-girlfriend or group of individuals who are known members of a particular gang, provided the order specifies the individuals. They might prohibit visits to certain premises or localities, either totally or at particular times. Theoretically prohibitions could be used to prohibit access to the place where P resides, or has resided. They might prevent attendance at a particular event such as a football match, or identifiable event. They might regulate the basis on which conduct is permitted, for example, a prohibition against carrying a knife in certain, or possibly all, situations. Prohibitions could be used to prevent attendance at a demonstration or other event where it is believed P might engage in serious violent crime.

The one main restriction that exists, other than that they are relevant to the purpose of the order is that they are necessary and proportionate. Proportionality is important in the context of ECHR. Prohibitions, restrictions or conditions which interfere with the otherwise lawful acts of an individual must be proportionate to the harm that is sought to be prevented. Extreme orders, such as requiring P not to visit property at which he lives, not to go to a particular locality or street, are draconian in effect and would need high levels of justification. A court will need to assess the level of risk, and then balance the effect of the prohibition, restriction or condition against that risk in the light of the alternative means of reducing or preventing that risk. Some restrictions may raise particular problems: interferences with private and family life engage with Art 8; prohibitions or restrictions relating to public order situations raise important freedom of

---

[36] Section 102 creates a 'Henry VIII clause' which gives power to the Secretary of State to amend s 101.

expression issues under Art 10; and restrictions which affect P's freedom to participate in religious belief or activity raise clear problems under Art 12.

Variation, renewal or discharge

6.17 An application, by complaint, may be made to the appropriate magistrates' court[37] to vary or discharge a VOO, or to renew it for a period of not more than 5 years. An application may be made by the offender, the chief officer of police who applied for the order, or the chief officer of police for the area where the offender resides, or the chief police officer who believes that the offender is in, or intending to come to, his police area. Given that there is no power to make an order of less than 2 years in length; this power might appear to be a useful way of dealing with short-term risks. However, an order may not be discharged within a 2-year period without the consent of the offender and by the relevant chief officer of police.[38]

A VOO may only be renewed or varied so as to impose additional prohibitions, restrictions or conditions on the offender if the court considers that it is necessary to do so for the purpose of protecting the public from the risk of serious violent harm caused by the offender and any renewed or varied order may contain only such prohibitions restriction or conditions as the court considers necessary for this purpose (s 103(5)). Section 103(1)(b) limits the length of any renewal to 'such period of not more than 5 years'. There is no express provision limiting renewal to within the original potential 5-year maximum, and the wording of s 103(1)(b) provides a time-limit on the 'renewal'. The 5-year maximum is a clear indication that such orders are not intended to be indefinite in nature. However, it would of course be open to a relevant chief police officer to seek a new order, on exactly the same as would need to be satisfied on an application for renewal.

Interim orders

6.18 If an application for a VOO has not been determined, an application made is made for an interim complaint or a further complaint by the person making the application. The preconditions are stated in s 104. If it appears to the court:

'(a) that the person to whom the main application relates ("P") is a qualifying offender,
(b) that, if the court were determining that application, it would be likely to make a violent offender order in respect of P, and
(c) that it is desirable to act before that application is determined, with a view to securing the immediate protection of the public from the risk of serious violent harm caused by P.'

The restrictions on the making of an order apply equally to an interim order (s 104(5)). It ceases to have effect at the period stated in the order, and, in any event ceases to have effect when the court grants the main application, or when the application is withdrawn or when the court determines the application (s 104(6)).

The criteria stated in the original Bill (if the court considers 'it just' to grant such an order) were the subject of much criticism,[39] and were redrafted to include paras (b) and (c) above. The court is expected to determine what is 'likely'. However, by definition the

---

[37] See s 103(3).
[38] See s 103(7): if the offender makes the application, the chief officer for the area where the offender resides.
[39] See, eg, HC Committee, col 609 (28 November 2007).

evidence that will justify the making of the VOO will not be before the court, for otherwise an application for a full order, rather than an interim order, would be before the court. The need for the order is obviously urgent, in the light of the terms of (c), yet the safeguards that apply are unclear. Such an application can only be made if notice of the hearing has been given a reasonable time beforehand. But there is no obligation, in the statute, to make a full application, if one has not already been made, within a specific period of time, and there appears to be no safeguard against repeated orders in terms of the length of interim orders other than the discretion of the court to refuse to grant repeat interim orders. That would be a significant erosion of the protections that the Act puts in place in respect of a final order.

Appeals

6.19 Appeal lies to the Crown Court. The Crown Court may make such orders as may be necessary to give effect to its determination, and may also make such incidental or consequential orders as appear to it to be just (s 106).

Notification requirements

6.20 Sections 107–112 create a raft of provisions relating to notification requirements. Reference should be made to these long provisions for the relevant detail. In summary, an offender who is subject to a VOO, or an interim order, is subject to notification requirements (s 107). Within 3 days of the making of an order, or interim order, the offender must supply the following information to the police: date of birth, national insurance number, name or names used at the relevant date and at the date when notification was given, home address[40] on the date when notification was given, addresses or addresses where the offender regularly resides or stays, and any prescribed information. In determining the time-limit, the time spent in custody or outside the UK is to be disregarded.

Section 109 imposes requirements to inform the police of changes to name, address, the expiry of any period when the offender was in custody or outside the UK, any prescribed change of circumstances or release from custody.

Offences

6.21 Section 113 creates a range of offences. If P fails, without reasonable excuse, to comply with any prohibition, restriction or condition contained in:

(a) a violent offender order; or

(b) an interim violent offender order,

P commits an offence, punishable on trial on indictment with a term of imprisonment not exceeding 5 years or a fine, or both, or on summary conviction to a term of imprisonment not exceeding 12 months, or a fine not exceeding the statutory maximum, or both.

---

[40] Defined by s 108(5).

The question of 'reasonable excuse' raises issues as to whether the court is prepared to imply into this legislation a legal burden of proof on the defendant, or whether this will be construed as an evidential burden.[41]

A similar offence is committed if there is a breach of notification requirements, including a potential penalty of 5 years' imprisonment (s 113(2)).

---

[41] See **8.25.**

Chapter 7

ANTI-SOCIAL BEHAVIOUR

SUMMARY

7.1 Section 118 of, and Sch 20 to, the 2008 Act insert a new Part 1A into the Anti-social Behaviour Act 2003 (ASBA 2003), which deals with the making of closure notices in respect of premises associated with persistent disorder or nuisance. Sections 124 and 125 amend provisions relating to anti-social behaviour orders (ASBOs) and individual support orders (ISOs). Section 119 creates a new criminal offence of causing nuisance or disturbance on NHS premises.

These provisions had not been brought into force as at the date of going to press.

CLOSURE ORDERS IN RESPECT OF PREMISES ASSOCIATED WITH PERSISTENT DISORDER OR NUISANCE

7.2 Over the last 10 years or so the government has brought forward a range of legislative provisions designed to deal with the problem of anti-social behaviour. The ASBO was introduced by the Crime and Disorder Act 1998 (CDA 1998)[1] with the intent of allowing 'ordinary people to live their lives free from fear and intimidation'.[2] A civil order, with criminal sanctions for breach, it was intended to provide additional measures to deal with anti-social conduct, whether lawful or unlawful. Those pre-existing protections included protections under public order legislation,[3] the Criminal Damage Act 1971, the Environmental Protection Act 1990 and the Noise Act 1996. Common law provisions relating to breaches of the peace[4] are relevant to the prevention of anti-social behaviour. Despite this wide range of powers, use of ASBOs has grown rapidly: they are 'helping individuals address their behaviour and have shown how communities and agencies can come together to take back control of their neighbourhoods'.[5] However, the growth in numbers can serve to highlight some of the basic concerns about the approach of using civil orders to deal with what, in the view of some, should be dealt with by the criminal law: the lack of clarity and definition of criminal, and 'anti-social behaviour', the use of civil powers when the criminal law ought to be used if the conduct is, or should be, criminal, and the potential to criminalise, though breach proceedings a wide range of individuals, including children.[6] Enforcing the orders has often proven difficult, so to encourage the public to take an active role recipients are frequently

---

[1] See now ASBA 2003.
[2] *Community Orders, A Consultation Paper* (Home Office, 1997), at para 1.
[3] Principally, the Public Order Act 1986.
[4] Defined in *Howell* [1982] QB 416 as harm or the threat of harm to a person or, in his presence, to his property.
[5] *Strengthening powers to tackle anti-social behaviour: Consultation Paper* (Home Office, 2006), to be found at: www.homeoffice.gov.uk/documents/cons-asb-powers/asb-powers-consultation?view=Binary, at p 4.
[6] See the concerns of Liberty at www.liberty-human-rights.org.uk/pdfs/policy04/anti-social-evidence.pdf.

'named and shamed'.[7] Between April 1999 and December 2004, 4,649 ASBOs were issued in England and Wales and that number rose to some 7,356 in 2006. Some 43% of these were made in respect of juveniles.[8] In February 2007, the government, in response to a freedom of information request, revealed that 47% of these orders had been breached.

7.3 Nonetheless, the trend to use these and similar powers has continued. ASBA 2003 built on this framework by strengthening the legal powers available, particularly in the context of housing. There had been a power in s 152 of the Housing Act 1996 (HA 1996) to allow a local authority to make an application to High Court or county court seeking an injunction prohibiting a person from engaging or threatening to engage in conduct causing, or likely to cause, a nuisance or annoyance to a person residing in, visiting or otherwise engaging in a lawful activity in residential premises to which s 152 applied or in the locality of such premises; from using or threatening to use residential premises to which s 152 applied for immoral or illegal purposes; or entering residential premises to which s 152 applied or being found in the locality of any such premises. Section 152 was introduced to combat the menace and nuisance caused by young persons, often gangs, on local authority estates. However, it was replaced by s 13 of ASBA 2003, which inserted new ss 153A–D into HA 1996. This created the anti-social behaviour injunction. The provisions apply to conduct:

'(a) which is capable of causing nuisance or annoyance to any person, and
(b) which directly or indirectly relates to or affects the housing management functions of a relevant landlord.'

On the application of a relevant landlord the court may grant an injunction (an anti-social behaviour injunction) if both of the following two conditions are satisfied. The first is that the person against whom the injunction is sought is engaging, has engaged or threatens to engage in conduct to which s 153B applies. The second is that the conduct is capable of causing nuisance or annoyance to any of the following:

'(a) a person with a right (of whatever description) to reside in or occupy housing accommodation owned or managed by the relevant landlord;
(b) a person with a right (of whatever description) to reside in or occupy other housing accommodation in the neighborhood of housing accommodation mentioned in (a);
(c) a person engaged in lawful activity in or in the neighborhood of housing accommodation mentioned in (a);
(d) a person employed (whether or not by the relevant landlord) in connection with the exercise of the relevant landlord's housing management functions.'

Section 153B created the power to obtain an injunction against unlawful use of premises.

7.4 Part 1 of ASBA 2003 introduced closure orders (known colloquially as 'crack house orders') in respect of premises which a senior police officer[9] has reasonable grounds for believing:

---

[7] See, eg, www.statewatch.org.
[8] Home Office, reported at: http://news.bbc.co.uk/1/hi/uk/4935606.stm, BBC News, 23 April 2006.
[9] Of at least the rank of superintendent.

(a) that at any time during the relevant period the premises have been used in connection with the unlawful use, production or supply of a Class A controlled drug; and

(b) that the use of the premises is associated with the occurrence of disorder or serious nuisance to members of the public.

Still further powers were introduced by ASBA 2003. These include dispersal powers, whereby police can designate an area and then disperse groups within it, ISOs, introduced by the Criminal Justice Act (CJA 2003),[10] and fixed penalty notices for disorder introduced by the Criminal Justice and Police Act 2001. More recently, the Serious Crime Act 2007 (SCA 2007) introduced serious crime prevention orders. The High Court may make an order if satisfied that a person has been involved in serious crime[11] (whether in England and Wales or elsewhere); and has reasonable grounds to believe that the order would protect the public by preventing, restricting or disrupting involvement by the person in serious crime in England and Wales. An order may contain such prohibitions, restrictions or requirements; and such other terms as the court considers appropriate for the purpose of protecting the public by preventing, restricting or disrupting involvement by the person concerned in serious crime in England and Wales.

7.5 In 2006 the Government published a Consultation Paper, *Strengthening powers to tackle anti-social behaviour*[12] which in part drew on the work of the Respect Task Force, established in 2005 to support local agencies and residents.[13] It observed:[14]

> 'Tools and powers such as ASBOs and ASBIs[[15]] have a proven track record in bringing much needed respite to victims of anti-social behaviour ... The preventative approach involves setting boundaries to behaviour that do more than enforce the standards of the law-abiding majority, so that everyone can give, earn and enjoy respect, and live in peace with their neighbours.'

It identified three possible areas for extension of powers: (i) extended police intervention powers; (ii) new premises closure powers; and (iii) the power to issue deferred penalty notices. The first and third have not, for the moment, been proceeded with. The second, additional closure powers, forms the basis of the new provisions in the 2008 Act.

In a Consultation Paper in 2003, the Government wrote:[16]

> 'We have to close down these properties from which drug dealers operate, or new dealers will simply move in. These dealers are sophisticated and devious in their methods. They can prey on vulnerable people compelling them to give over their property whilst they deal and use

---

[10] CJA 2003 creates a new s 1AA of CDA 1998. If the relevant conditions are satisfied an ISO can require the defendant to comply, for a period not exceeding 6 months, with such requirements as are specified, and to comply with any directions given by the responsible officer. The preconditions are that an ISO would be desirable in the interests of preventing repetition of conduct that led to the making of the ASBO, and that the individual is not already subject to an ISO.
[11] Defined by SCA 2007, Sch 1, and includes drug trafficking, people trafficking, arms trafficking, child sex, prostitution, armed robbery, money laundering, fraud, blackmail, and inchoate offences.
[12] *Strengthening powers to tackle anti-social behaviour: Consultation Paper* (Home Office, 2006).
[13] See www.respect.gov.uk.
[14] At p 6.
[15] Anti-social behaviour interventions.
[16] *Respect and Responsibility – Taking A Stand Against Anti-Social Behaviour*, Cm 5778 (Home Office, 2003), at p 40.

drugs, and intimidate both the residents and neighbours, sometimes making them too frightened to speak out for fear of retribution.'

In 2006 the Consultation Paper[17] commented:

'We know that crack house closures and licensing and disorder-related closures are working well and are welcomed by communities for bringing immediate relief to their neighbourhoods. Visible, accountable and speedy justice of this kind, with all the necessary court and judicial safeguards, shows that the needs of the law-abiding majority come first and is an example of a new balance between rights and due process.'

The new premises closure order (PCO) is intended to address nuisance and anti-social behaviour that is not drug related, or related to licensed premises. Conduct that may be within its ambit might include excessive noise and rowdy behaviour with frequent drunken parties; high numbers of people entering and leaving premises at all times of day or night; anti-social residents intimidating or threatening their neighbours; or criminals running illegal businesses from their properties.[18] Some of these may already be criminal. Other such conduct may, of course, be symptomatic of other criminal conduct which, for one reason or another, cannot be proved to a criminal standard of proof. They are intended to close premises, but are not intended simply to be powers of eviction. It is, said the Government (drawing on experience from similar provisions piloted in Scotland), 'about giving immediate respite to communities ... and providing means with which to engage the perpetrator(s), tackle the underlying causes and put an end to their nuisance behaviour'.[19] It is also intended to be part of a 'holistic response' aimed at addressing underlying causes: 'Practitioners in Scotland report that their use of closure orders has led to a change in behaviour.'[20]

7.6 The Consultation Process drew broad, but not universal support, for its proposal, with some 86% of respondents supporting the proposal. One concern was expressed by Liberty:[21]

'The Government's consultation emphasised that closure would only be considered as a last resort and would require multi-agency involvement. It also stated that the safety of the young and vulnerable would not be compromised; the implication being that a court would not have the power to make an order unless satisfied that proper arrangements were in place to protect their interests ... That safeguard appears to be absent. It appears that an entire family could be displaced due to the disruptive and nuisance behaviour of one child or parent. Home closure remains a drastic step.'

The Youth Justice Board also aired concerns, pointing to the need for a strong multi-agency approach.

Who may apply and when may an application be made?

7.7 Schedule 20 inserts new Part 1A into ASBA 2003, with new ss 11A–J. Applications can be made by a senior police officer[22] or a local authority, who will serve

---

[17] *Strengthening powers to tackle anti-social behaviour: Consultation Paper* (Home Office, 2006), at p 14.
[18] These are examples given by the 2006 Consultation Paper, ibid, at p 14.
[19] Ibid, at p 17.
[20] Explanatory Notes, Regulatory Impact Assessment.
[21] See HC Research Paper 07/65, at p 87.
[22] An officer not below the rank of superintendent.

a premises closure notice. In either case the relevant police officer or local authority must have reasonable grounds for believing:

> '(a) that at any time during the relevant period a person has engaged in anti-social behaviour on the premises, and
> (b) that the use of the premises is associated with significant and persistent disorder or persistent serious nuisance to members of the public.'

The 'relevant period' is the period of 3 months ending on the date when the appropriate officer or authority considers whether to issue a notice. That is not the same date as the date of the issue of the notice, and it is possible that a delay may intervene. Given the nature of the time it will be important for the relevant police officer or local authority to have proper records, given that a decision to issue a notice can be taken and given verbally.

'Anti-social behaviour' is defined as behaviour by a person which causes or is likely to cause harassment, alarm or distress[23] to one or more other persons not of the same household as the person.

'Premises' is broadly defined by the new s 11K and includes land or any other place (whether enclosed or not) and outbuildings which are used as part of the premises. The scope of the new closure order could thus include open land used, legally or not, for festivals, motor bike riding, entertainments, public demonstrations, or encampments by gypsies, travellers and other groups of individuals. Although the new closure order may not be targeted at such groups, and although it may be unlikely that the order will be used to prevent legitimate activity, the scope gives a very wide discretion indeed. That appears to be intentional.[24]

In each case the relevant police officer must consult the local authority, or vice versa (s 11A(2)), and have taken reasonable steps to establish the identity of any person who lives on the premises or who has control of, or responsibility for, or an interest in, the premises. Authorisation may be given verbally or in writing, but if verbally must be confirmed in writing.

The closure notice gives notice that application is being made for a PCO, states that access to the premises by any person other than a person who habitually resides in the premises or the owner of the premises is prohibited; and specifies the date and time when, and the place at which, the application will be heard. It must explain the effects of a PCO, state that failure to comply with the notice amounts to a criminal offence, and give information about relevant advice providers. This means that the notice must contain information about the names of, and means of contacting, persons and organisations in the area that provide advice about housing and legal matters.

The notice may allow a resident of the property to stay in the property whilst alternative accommodation is arranged, pending the court hearing. It is for that reason that the notice must provide information about contacts for housing or legal advice.

---

[23] These terms bear their ordinary natural meaning: see *Brutus v Cozens* [1973] AC 854; [1972] 2 All ER 1297.
[24] See Vernon Coaker, Parliamentary Under-Secretary of State for Home Department, HC Committee, col 623 (27 November 2007).

The premises closure order

7.8 Application for a PCO may be made to a magistrates' court either by a constable or the local authority (depending on who authorised the issue of the notice). The application must be heard by the magistrates' court not later than 48 hours after the notice was served (s 11B(3)).

The court may make a PCO if, and only if, it is satisfied that each of the following preconditions are satisfied (s 11A(4)):

(a) a person has engaged in anti-social behaviour on the premises;

(b) the use of the premises is associated with significant and persistent disorder or persistent serious nuisance to members of the public; and

(c) the making of the order is necessary to prevent the occurrence of such disorder or nuisance for the period specified in the order.

If these preconditions are satisfied, a PCO can be made. This is an order that the premises in respect of which the order is made are closed to all persons for such period (not exceeding 3 months) as is specified in the order (s 11A(5)). The order may include such provision as the court thinks appropriate relating to access to any part of the building or structure of which the premises form part. It may extend to the whole or any part of the premises.

7.9 Although a closure notice has already been served, inter alia giving notice of the making of the application, it is clear from s 11A(7) that the matter can be dealt with in the absence of those affected. Nevertheless, the court may adjourn the hearing on the application for a period of not more than 14 days to enable the occupier of the premises, the person who has control of or responsibility for the premises, or any other person with an interest in the premises, to show why a Part 1A closure order should not be made. If it does so, the closure can continue in operation but only if it so orders (s 11B(8)).

7.10 If a magistrates' court makes an order under s 11B, a relevant person[25] may enter the premises, and do anything reasonably necessary to secure the premises against entry by any person, or to carry out essential maintenance. Reasonable force may be used. That relevant person seeking to enter the premises for that purpose must, if required to do so by, or on behalf of the owner, occupier or other person in charge of the premises, produce evidence of his identity and authority before entering the premises.

7.11 Despite the intention of the Government as expressed during the consultation process that appropriate safeguards for families (especially children) would be in place,[26] there is no express requirement that a court must consider such matters, although clearly it is unlikely that a court would not address such matters in determining whether to make an order. No doubt guidance will be clear on this point.[27] Nor is the existence of satisfactory accommodation a precondition to the making of an order. A person who is

---

[25] This means a constable or a person authorised by the appropriate chief officer; or a person authorised by the local authority, depending on who gave the notice and made application for the order.
[26] See **7.5**.
[27] The power to issue guidance is contained in s 11K. See also statement by Vernon Coaker, Parliamentary Under-Secretary of State for Home Department, HC Committee, col 621 (27 November 2007).

homeless because of their own anti-social behaviour could be deemed to be intentionally homeless and thus not liable to benefit from a duty on a local authority[28] to secure accommodation for them.

However, reliance on guidance and on a non-specific discretion of the court may not be either satisfactory or sufficient. The power potentially interferes with Art 8 of ECHR: the right to respect for private and family life. Any limitation of that must be necessary and proportionate. The Joint Committee on Human Rights had concerns.[29] It considers that both for reasons of legal certainty and proportionality safeguards should appear on the face of the Act. It was disappointed 'that the Government does not propose to include, on the face of the Bill, the requirement that a premises closure order only be imposed as a last resort, and that the needs of children and vulnerable adults are taken into account'. In Scotland, such safeguards do exist. The sheriff must have regard to the ability of any person who habitually resides in the premises to find alternative accommodation, and to the vulnerability of any such person who has not been engaged in anti-social behaviour in the premises.[30] It is not wholly clear why the preferred approach of the minister was to indicate that these matters could be dealt with by guidance, and by representations as to whether an order should be made.[31]

Criminal offence

7.12 Section 11D(1) of ASBA 2003 makes it an offence for a person to remain on or enter premises in contravention of a closure notice. Section 11D(2) makes it an offence to obstruct a person acting under s 11A(7) or 11C(2) (see **7.10**), to remain on closed premises, or to enter closed premises. In either case a defence exists of reasonable excuse for entering or being on the premises.

In either case the offence is triable summarily. A person convicted is liable on conviction to imprisonment for a period not exceeding 51 weeks,[32] or to a fine not exceeding level 5 on the standard scale, or to both.

Extension and discharge

7.13 At any time whilst the order is in force an application may be made to a justice of the peace by a constable (if it is a police closure order) or the local authority (if it is a local authority closure order). In a similar way to the original decision-making process (see **7.7**) the relevant senior officer or local authority must have reasonable grounds for believing that it is necessary to extend the period for which the order has effect, for the purpose of preventing the occurrence of significant and persistent disorder, or persistent serious nuisance to members of the public, and the appropriate consultation (with the police officer or local authority as appropriate) has taken place.

If the court is satisfied that the order is necessary to prevent the occurrence of significant and persistent disorder or persistent serious nuisance to members of the

---

[28] Under HA 1996, ss 191 and 196.
[29] HC Committee 2007/2008, 5th Report, at para 110.
[30] See David Burrows MP, HC Committee, col 620 (27 November 2007).
[31] Vernon Coaker, Parliamentary Under-Secretary of State for Home Department, HC Committee, col 621 (27 November 2007).
[32] This provision is on the assumption that CJA 2003, s 218(5) is in force, until it is the relevant period is 6 months: see s 11D(5).

public for a further period, it may make an order extending the period the order has effect by a period not exceeding 3 months. However, a closure order cannot take effect for more than 6 months.

A relevant police officer, local authority or an individual on whom notice relating to the closed premises was served (see **7.7**) may make an application to a justice of the peace for discharge of the closure order. The justice may then require the constable or authority to appear before the magistrates' court to answer to the complaint. The court may not make an order discharging a Part 1A closure order unless it is satisfied that the Part 1A closure order is no longer necessary to prevent the occurrence of significant and persistent disorder or persistent serious nuisance to members of the public.

Appeals

7.14 Appeal against the making or refusal of an order lies to the Crown Court before the end of the period of 21 days beginning with the day on which the order or decision is made (s 11F(5). On an appeal under s 11F the Crown Court may make such order as it thinks appropriate.

Reimbursement of costs or compensation

7.15 A police authority or a local authority which incurs expenditure for the purpose of clearing, securing or maintaining the premises, in respect of which a Part 1A closure order has effect, may apply to the court which made the order for an order for costs. The court may make such order as it thinks appropriate in the circumstances for the reimbursement (in full or in part) by the owner of the premises of the expenditure. Such an application can only be made before the end of a period of 3 months starting with the date on which the closure order ceased to have effect.

An application can be made for compensation by a person who incurs financial loss in consequence of the issue of a closure, or because a closure order has effect. It must be made within a period of 3 months starting with a decision not to make a closure order, or dismissal of an appeal against a refusal to make a closure order, or the date when a closure order ceases to have effect. The court may order the payment of compensation out of central funds if it is satisfied:

(a) that the person is not associated with such use of the premises;

(b) if the person is the owner or occupier of the premises, that the person took reasonable steps to prevent such use of the premises;

(c) that the person has incurred financial loss; and

(d) having regard to all the circumstances it is appropriate to order payment of compensation in respect of that loss.

ANTI-SOCIAL BEHAVIOUR ORDERS

7.16 The nature and purpose of ASBOs has already been discussed (see **7.2**). Section 124 provides for the review of ASBOs in respect of individuals aged under 17 by inserting new sections into CDA 1998.

Background

7.17 An ASBO can be made against an individual aged 10 years or over (CDA 1998, s 1). At the time s 1 was passed, it was considered that the use of the ASBO power against juveniles (and certainly young juveniles) was intended to be exceptional,[33] yet by 2006 some 43% of orders had been made in respect of juveniles.[34] Although not criminal in nature it has potentially criminal consequences if breached. Because it is not made in criminal proceedings (except where it is imposed when the child or young person is being sentenced for a criminal offence), it is by no means clear that the duty under s 44 of the Children and Young Persons Act 1933 (to have regard to the welfare of the child) applies.[35] The purpose of making the order is, of course, to seek to prevent anti-social behaviour, but as a result of the changes made by CJA 2003, an ASBO must contain an ISO[36] if the court takes the view that it would help prevent further anti-social behaviour. This does not apply on the making of an ASBO following criminal conviction, because the sentence passed by the court will be intended to address the offending behaviour.[37]

Guidance as to the use of ASBOs was issued in 2006. It states:[38]

> 'Orders issued to young people should be reviewed each year, given young person's continually changing circumstances, to help to ensure that they are receiving the support they need to prevent breach. The review should be administrative rather than judicial, and should be undertaken by the team that decided on the initial application. Where practicable, the YOT should provide the group with an assessment of the young person. Depending on progress towards improved behaviour, possible outcomes will include an application to discharge the order or a strengthening of the prohibitions ... The overriding considerations remain the safety and needs of the community, and the review would have to incorporate the community's views on the order's effectiveness.'

In 2005, Hazel Blears said:[39]

> 'The one year review of ASBOs for young people is an important safeguard and will ensure that the young person is receiving the support they need to prevent them breaching the terms of their ASBO and causing further harm to the community. We also recognise that patterns of behaviour may have changed significantly in a year – and this measure provides that check and balance.'

---

[33] See R Card and R Ward *Crime & Disorder Act 1998: A Practitioners' Guide* (Jordan Publishing, 1998) at para 5.39.
[34] Home Office Statistics, reported at: http://news.bbc.co.uk/1/hi/uk/4935606.stm, BBC News, 23 April 2006.
[35] For this, and the general duties owed under the youth justice system, see **4.4**.
[36] See **7.20**.
[37] See **4.4**.
[38] *A guide to anti-social behaviour orders* (Home Office, August 2006), at p 45 at: www.crimereduction. homeoffice.gov.uk/antisocialbehaviour/antisocialbehaviour55.pdf.
[39] Minister of State, Home Office, reported at: www.yjb.gov.uk/en-gb/News/ OneYearASBOReview.htm?area=Corporate, 20 December 2005.

The new provisions give statutory effect to that review process. They are intended to achieve the aims set out above, but also have the effect of enabling a structured process whereby those who are the subject of the ASBO are no longer at the risk of criminalisation if they breach an order that has wholly or substantially served its purposes. Indeed it has been said that in many cases the use of ASBOs on juveniles 'demonises' young individuals, dealing with matters that sometimes could be better dealt with outside the criminal justice system.[40] Some requirements imposed by courts have been described as 'unrealistic'.[41] The opportunity for formal review in the way described above is clearly an opportunity to take into account not only changes of circumstances but also the very requirements of the order and the progress made by the individual in compliance with them and in personal development.

The new provisions

7.18 A new s 1J of CDA 1998 applies the new provisions to ASBOs made under ss 1, 1B and 1C of CDA 1998 in respect of a person aged under 17. The section imposes a duty to review the operation of the order, before the end of the review period. That is defined as (s 1J(3)):

'(a) the period of 12 months beginning with—
(i) the day on which the order was made, or
(ii) if during that period there is a supplemental order[42] (or more than one), the date of the supplemental order (or the last of them);
(b) a period of 12 months ... [after a previous review period].'

Section 1J(6) requires that the review that takes place must include consideration of:

'(a) the extent to which the person subject to the order has complied with it;
(b) the adequacy of any support available to the person to help him comply with it;
(c) any matters relevant to the question whether an application should be made for the order to be varied or discharged.'

7.19 A new s 1K identifies responsibility for, and participation in, these reviews, if it is to be carried by the relevant authority that applied for the order,[43] although in some circumstances it may be conducted only by the appropriate chief officer of police.[44] The relevant local authority and chief police officer must consult and co-operate in the review.

INDIVIDUAL SUPPORT ORDERS

7.20 Section 124(1) of the new Act amends s 1AA of CDA 1998, which deals with ISOs. These have not been the success hoped for when they were introduced in 2003.[45] The new Act does so by making the section apply to cases where:

---

[40] See reported comments of Prof Rod Morgan, Chair, Youth Justice Board, at: http://news.bbc.co.uk/1/hi/uk/4935606.stm, BBC News, 23 April 2006.
[41] Paul Cavadino, Chief Executive of NACRO, 12 November 2006.
[42] A variation to the order, or the making of an ISO.
[43] 'Relevant authority' means the council for the relevant local government area, or the relevant chief officer of police (CDA 1998, s 1(1), (2)).
[44] For the detail, see CDA 1998, s 1K(2).
[45] See Vernon Coaker, Parliamentary Under-Secretary of State for Home Department, HC Committee, col 631 (28 November 2007).

'(a) an anti-social behaviour order has previously been made in respect of a defendant;
(b) an application is made by complaint to the court which made that order, by the relevant authority which applied for it, for an order under this section; and
(c) at the time of the hearing of the application—
 (i) the defendant is still a child or young person, and
 (ii) the anti-social behaviour order is still in force.'

In that situation the court must consider whether the individual support conditions are fulfilled and, if satisfied that they are, *must* make an ISO. The nature of that order is defined by s 1AA(2). If the relevant conditions are satisfied an ISO can require the defendant to comply, for a period not exceeding 6 months, with such requirements as are specified, and to comply with any directions given by the responsible officer. The preconditions are that an ISO would be desirable in the interests of preventing repetition of conduct that led to the making of the ASBO, and that the individual is not already subject to an ISO.

The effect of this is to require the making of a further ISO for a young person who is subject to an ASBO. The rationale is, as before, to provide ongoing support to address the factors that led to the anti-social behaviour. The further ISO cannot last longer than the remaining period of the ASBO, and in any event not longer than 6 months.

The amendments also allow an ISO to be attached to an order granted on conviction or in the county court.

NUISANCE OR DISTURBANCE ON HOSPITAL PREMISES

7.21 Section 119 of the new Act creates a new criminal offence of causing nuisance or disturbance on NHS premises,[46] which is triable summarily.

The provisions had not been brought into force as at the date of going to press.

Section 119(1) states that a person commits an offence if:

'(a) the person causes, without reasonable excuse and while on NHS premises, a nuisance or disturbance to an NHS staff member who is working there or is otherwise there in connection with work,
(b) the person refuses, without reasonable excuse, to leave the NHS premises when asked to do so by a constable or an NHS staff member, and
(c) the person is not on the NHS premises for the purpose of obtaining medical advice, treatment or care for himself or herself.'

---

[46] Defined by s 119(4):
'"English NHS premises" means—
(a) any hospital vested in, or managed by, a relevant English NHS body,
(b) any building or other structure, or vehicle, associated with the hospital and situated on hospital grounds (whether or not vested in, or managed by, a relevant English NHS body), and
(c) the hospital grounds,
"hospital grounds" means land in the vicinity of a hospital and associated with it,
"NHS premises" means English NHS premises or Welsh NHS premises,
"NHS staff member" means a person employed by a relevant English NHS body, or a relevant Welsh NHS body, or otherwise working for such a body (whether as or on behalf of a contractor, as a volunteer or otherwise)'.

The offence is punishable on summary conviction to a fine not exceeding level 3 on the standard scale.

Background

7.22 In a Consultation Paper in 2006,[47] the Government estimated the financial cost of assaults on NHS staff as anything between £10m to £270m, depending on the degree of absenteeism due to sickness that can be attributed to assaults. In a survey some 20% of NHS staff surveyed did not feel that the NHS provided them with a safe and secure environment for work. There needed, said the Consultation Paper, to be emphasis placed on the prevention of crime, including assaults on staff. So, too, with nuisance or disturbance behaviour, due to its impact on staff and patients, and because of the potential for escalation.

The Consultation Paper considered existing powers to be inadequate:[48]

> 'These existing powers do not always provide NHS bodies with sufficient protection from those who behave in a disruptive manner on NHS premises ... Currently, NHS bodies have two options open to them ... The first is to seek the assistance of the police to remove offenders. However, if the behaviour in question falls short of the existing public order and anti-social behaviour offences it may not be appropriate for the police to respond. Where this is the case NHS security personnel will have no power to remove the person from NHS premises. This creates the atmosphere which makes the occurrence of a more serious incident more likely and gives both staff and patients the misleading impression that the NHS tolerates such behaviour.'

It considered an increase in security staff to be an insufficient response to the problem, because of their lack of legal power. The idea that NHS security staff have insufficient power to remove individuals is debatable but, arguably, sufficiently opaque as to justify legislation. The NHS has the power, as does any property owner, to remove trespassers from its land,[49] and arguably those who engage in nuisance or disturbance behaviour can be asked to leave. However, if such individuals are at the premises for treatment or medical investigation then this may raise human rights issues, the NHS being a public body for the purposes of the Human Rights Act 1998 (HRA 1998).[50] The new statutory power to remove individuals can be justified as a legitimate response to these uncertainties. Whether a new criminal offence is needed, given the breadth of public order legislation,[51] and other offences, is very debatable.[52]

Responses to the Consultation Paper were broadly, but not universally, supportive. However, concerns were expressed about how these provisions would affect the mentally ill. Mencap also observed that the limits of the offence might in fact serve to exclude the vast majority of people who cause a nuisance or disturbance from their scope.[53]

---

[47] *A Department of Health Consultation Paper: Tackling nuisance or disturbance behaviour on NHS healthcare premises: a paper for consultation* (Department of Health, 2006), to be found at: www.dh.gov.uk/en/Consultations/Liveconsultations/DH_4130745.
[48] Ibid, at p 7.
[49] See, eg, *Davis v Lisle* [1936] 2 QB 434.
[50] See HRA 1998, s 6.
[51] See Public Order Act 1986, s 5 (threatening abusive or insulting words or behaviour or disorderly conduct, likely to cause harassment alarm or distress). Note also preventative powers in relation to breach of the peace: see *R v Howell* [1982] 1 QB 416.
[52] See comments of Edward Garnier MP, HC Committee, col 625 (28 November 2007).
[53] See HC Research Paper 07/65, at p 91. David Heath MP, HC Committee, col 624 (28 November 2007).

7.23 A person cannot commit this offence if on the NHS premises for the purposes of obtaining medical advice, treatment or care for him or herself. It is intended that the 'authorised officer' (see **7.30**) should be a medical practitioner.[54] A person who is there seeking to obtain medical advice, treatment or care for another (say a spouse or life partner, child, friend or colleague can commit the offence). A person ceases to be on NHS premises for the purpose of obtaining medical advice, treatment or care for him or herself once the person has received the advice, treatment or care. A person is not on NHS premises for the purpose of obtaining medical advice, treatment or care for him or herself if the person has been refused the advice, treatment or care during the last 8 hours.

7.24 The Joint Committee on Human Rights[55] had concerns that the s 119 offence and the power to remove could adversely affect the ability of some vulnerable people (such as those with mental health problems) to access medical treatment. This potentially raises ECHR issues under Arts 2 (the right to life) and 8 (right to private and family life), as well as the right not to be discriminated against in the enjoyment of Convention rights (Art 14 in conjunction with Arts 2 and 8). The concern centred largely on the possible effect of deterring individuals from seeking access to medical advice and treatment. It commented:

> 'In addition, given the Government's positive duties to protect life and prevent ill-treatment and the possibility that an individual might avoid seeking help for medical problems, including those that are life threatening, for fear that s/he would face a criminal sanction, we asked the Government to indicate the steps that it proposed to take to ensure that it complied with its positive obligations.'

The justification for the offence given in response pointed to gaps in current legal protection:[56]

> '(a) Existing anti-social behaviour law is inadequate to deal with low level nuisance and disturbance occurring on hospital premises, in particular because it requires a court order and therefore cannot be used to deal with an incident as it occurs;
> (b) Existing criminal offences such as drunkenness and Public Order Act offences are relevant, but require a police response to arrest and remove the person committing the offence, leaving hospital staff to deal with the offender unless and until the police arrive;
> (c) Hospitals may apply for civil law injunctions against individuals, but this is time-consuming, slow and costly and is not appropriate for dealing with an incident as it occurs.'

The Minister concluded:[57]

> 'There is no existing offence dealing with nuisance or disturbance behaviour, with an attendant power of removal exercisable on the commission of the offence conferred on persons other than police officers. There is a need for both the offence, and a power of removal by an authorised NHS staff member where a person has committed or is committing the offence. It will meet the dual objectives of ensuring that persons who cause a nuisance or disturbance on NHS premises to NHS staff and refuse to leave when asked to do

---

[54] See Vernon Coaker, Parliamentary Under-Secretary of State for Home Department, HC Committee, col 631 (28 November 2007).
[55] Joint Committee 2007/2008, 5th Report, at para 1.113.
[56] See Joint Committee 2007/2008, 5th Report at para 1.114.
[57] Ibid, at para 1.115.

so by NHS staff members can be prosecuted for that specific offence ... and NHS staff can be empowered to take immediate action against offenders by exercising the power of removal.'

The Joint Committee were ultimately satisfied as to the need for this new offence.[58] It stated that 'the proposed new offence appears to attempt to strike a balance between the desire for staff and patients not to suffer nuisance and disturbance and the needs of those requiring medical attention to be treated'. However, it was concerned that some of the safeguards were to be contained in guidance rather than on the face of legislation. In particular it asserted:

'... we suggest that the [Act] should be amended to include express provisions on the matters currently covered by [section 121(d)–(g)] as the exercise of the powers in relation to these issues has the capacity to seriously interfere with an individual's Convention rights. We recommend that the [Act] set out an indicative list of the factors which would constitute a reasonable excuse for the purposes of [s 119(1)]. Whilst the Government has told us that nuisance or disturbance caused by an individual suffering a mental or physical condition will prevent the commission of an offence or removal, it is unclear whether this would include behaviour due to an addiction (e g to drugs or alcohol).'

The offence

7.25 For the s 119 offence to be a proved, the prosecutor will need to show:

(a) that the defendant caused a nuisance or disturbance to an NHS staff member who was working there or was otherwise there in connection with work;

(b) that the defendant was on NHS premises;

(c) that the person refused, without reasonable excuse, to leave the NHS premises when asked to do so by a constable or an NHS staff member; and

(d) that the person is not on the NHS premises for the purpose of obtaining medical advice, treatment or care for him or herself.

7.26 'Nuisance' and 'disturbance' are ordinary words, not defined, and will be given their ordinary and natural meaning.[59] The Shorter English Dictionary defines nuisance as 'injury hurt, harm, annoyance; anything injurious or obnoxious . . .'. It defines disturbance as 'the interruption of tranquility, peace, rest or settled condition; agitation (physical, social or political) interruption of mental tranquility; discomposure; interference with the course of any due action or process; molestation'.

Clearly physical assault or threats of assault are not necessary, although clearly these will fall within this, and several other, criminal offences. The use of abuse, lengthy haranguing of staff, abuse and swearing can amount to either, or both, nuisance and disturbance. The loud playing of music, live or recorded, singing, inappropriate use of mobile phones may well be such conduct. Drunkenness may well found a basis for the offence if manifested in ways that are considered to cause disturbance or nuisance. It will be a matter for the court in each case to determine given the words or conduct and

---

[58] Ibid, at para 1.122.
[59] See Rosie Winterton, Minister of State, Department of Health, HC Deb, col 676 (20 February 2007), cited by HC Research Study 07/65 at p 92.

the context in which they were used or it occurred. Even conduct which might be regarded as understandable, such as the over-zealous complaining or demands of a stressed relative might theoretically fall within the actus reus of the offence, although might, on occasion, fail to satisfy the criterion of being 'without reasonable excuse'.

The term used in s 119 is 'causes'. Clearly there has to be a causative link between the conduct of the individual and the disturbance or nuisance. It does not follow that that person has to intend to cause a nuisance or disturbance. The relative who shouts and swears and refuses to take 'no' for an answer may not intend to cause nuisance or disturbance but intend to do the things that objectively cause nuisance. So, too, with the drunk, the individual under the influence of substances or the mentally ill person who might not be aware of the effect of their conduct. However, the objective is to prevent conduct by the person, and arguably does not extend to conduct which is not caused by that person but arises from someone else.

7.27 The offence extends to nuisance or disturbance caused to NHS staff on NHS premises. These terms are fully defined by s 119 and s 120.[60] Premises extend to hospitals and land and structures that are part of them. The new offences do not apply to the surgeries of general practitioners, where problems of proof may arise because of the general lack of CCTV or security services.[61]

7.28 The conduct must be without reasonable excuse. The problem common to such offences as to where the burden of proof of this lies applies here as it does to other such offences.[62] Certainly there will be an evidential burden on the defendant and perhaps a legal burden given that the facts that give rise to the reasonable excuse may well be best known, and most easily proved by, the defendant. Matters that might amount to a reasonable excuse include committing nuisance or disturbance because of a mental health condition or another condition which affects behaviour and there will be examples in the guidance. Other examples include receiving distressing news or a communication problem due to language barriers.

7.29 The person in question must not be at the hospital for diagnosis or treatment. Whilst refusal to treat is easily proved (provided the hospital has kept proper records) disputes about this criterion may arise. Obviously the police office who attends will not be able to judge the need for treatment. The problem will obviously turn on the medical assessment that the hospital makes.

Power to remove

7.30 Section 120 confers a power to remove a person causing nuisance or disturbance. If a constable reasonably suspects that a person is committing or has committed an offence under s 119, the constable may remove the person from the NHS premises concerned. An 'authorised person' (defined by s 120(5) as a person authorised by the relevant NHS body) also has powers to remove. If that authorised person has such a reasonable suspicion, that officer may remove the person from the NHS premises concerned, or authorise an appropriate NHS staff member to do so.

---

[60] Defined by s 119(4).
[61] See Vernon Coaker, Parliamentary Under-Secretary of State for Home Department, HC Committee, col 628 (28 November 2007).
[62] See **8.25**.

The constable or authorised person who is removing an individual may use reasonable force in doing so (s 120(3)).

One important limitation is contained in s 120(4), and applies to an authorised person (but not a constable):

> 'An authorised officer cannot remove a person . . . or authorise another person to do so if the authorised officer has reason to believe that—
>
> (a) the person to be removed requires medical advice, treatment or care for himself or herself, or
> (b) the removal of the person would endanger the person's physical or mental health.'

Guidance

7.31 Section 121 empowers the 'appropriate national authority'[63] to issue guidance. It may relate to the matters identified by s 121(2), although that does not appear to limit guidance on matters that are not within the matters specified in s 121(2), because of the use of the words 'in particular'. Those matters are:

> '(a) the authorisation by relevant NHS bodies of authorised officers,
> (b) the authorisation by authorised officers of appropriate NHS staff members to remove persons under section 120,
> (c) training requirements for authorised officers and persons authorised by them to remove persons under section 120,
> (d) matters that may be relevant to a consideration by authorised officers for the purposes of section 120 of whether offences are being, or have been, committed under section 119,
> (e) matters to be taken into account by authorised officers in deciding whether there is reason to believe that a person requires medical advice, treatment or care for himself or herself or that the removal of a person would endanger the person's physical or mental health,
> (f) the procedure to be followed by authorised officers or persons authorised by them before using the power of removal in section 120,
> (g) the degree of force that it may be appropriate for authorised officers or persons authorised by them to use in particular circumstances,
> (h) arrangements for ensuring that persons on NHS premises are aware of the offence in section 119 and the powers of removal in section 120, or
> (i) the keeping of records.'

---

[63] See s 121(5).

Chapter 8

OBSCENITY AND SEXUAL OFFENCES

SUMMARY

8.1 The 2008 Act creates a range of new criminal offences. Some of its provisions deal with pornography, indecent images and sexual offences. In particular, s 63 makes unlawful the possession of extreme pornographic images. The Protection of Children Act 1978 (PCA 1978), relating to indecent photographs of children, is amended. Changes are made to the law relating to commission of sexual offences outside the UK. Other changes are made to the Sexual Offences Act 2003 (SOA 2003).

A new offence of hatred on the grounds of sexual orientation is introduced into Public Order Act 1986. This is discussed in Chapter 9.

Some of these provisions came into effect in July 2008. Commencement is dealt with at the relevant part of this chapter.

EXTREME PORNOGRAPHY

8.2 Section 63 creates the criminal offence of possession of an extreme pornographic image. It is an either way offence punishable on summary conviction, by a term of imprisonment not exceeding 12 months, or by a fine not exceeding the statutory maximum, or both (s 67(2)(a)). If it is tried on indictment, it is punishable with a term of imprisonment, or a fine, or both (s 67(2)(b), (3)(b)). The maximum term of imprisonment that can be imposed following conviction on indictment depends upon the nature of the image the defendant possessed, in cases to which s 63(7)(a) or (b) apply, the maximum is 3 years; in other cases, it is 2 years.

No order for commencement had been made as at the date of going to press.

Background and rationale[1]

8.3 The impetus for this change appears initially to have come as a result of a campaign led by a mother whose daughter was murdered by an individual who was addicted to violent sexual pornography.[2] The Government's consultation paper, *On the possession of extreme pornographic material*, published in 2005, identified public concern

---

[1] For discussion of the background and some of the policy issues see: McGlynn and Rackley 'Striking a Balance: Arguments for the Criminal Regulation of Extreme Pornography' [2007] Crim LR 677; Rowbottom 'Obscenity and the Internet: Targeting the Supply and Demand' [2006] Crim LR 97.

[2] There was evidence that the individual, ultimately convicted following a retrial, had been accessing websites such as 'rapepassion', 'hanging bitches' and 'deathbyasphyxia'. For confirmation of the effect of the campaign, see Jack Straw, Minister of Justice, HC 2nd Reading, col 60 (8 October 2007). For details of the particular case, see *Coutts* [2005] EWCA Crim 52.

about extreme pornographic material involving adults, especially in the light of the growth of the internet.[3] Legislation had addressed the downloading and possession of pornographic photographs and pseudo-photographs of children (see **8.6**), but the criminal law addressed such material in relation to adults only through the relevant legislation relating to obscene and indecent publications (see **8.5**).

The consultation elicited some 379 or so responses reflecting polarised opinions. Whilst there was a consensus that the protections relating to children were necessary and appropriate, much greater disagreement arose in respect of laws targeting 'sexual violence', 'serious sexual violence' or 'serious violence in a sexual context'. This was partly because of vagueness of concepts and problems of definition, and partly due to the extent to which such a law might interfere with legitimate artistic or creative freedom, or with the criminalisation of possession of images of consensual sexual activity.[4] Human rights issues, particularly under Arts 8 and 10 of ECHR were also engaged.

In August 2006 the Government published its responses to the consultation paper.[5] It is that response, subject to many detailed changes, that finds its way into law through s 63 and its associated sections.

8.4 The rationale for the new offence can only be appreciated by examining first the concept of extreme pornography, and then by an overview of the wider framework of law.

'Extreme pornography' is not material that is likely to be legal, even without the new offence. This type of material also goes beyond that classified for the cinema or for sale in licensed sex shops. The consultation paper referred to material which is violent and abusive, featuring activities which are illegal in themselves, and where the participants may, in some cases, have been the victims of criminal offences. It stated that:[6]

> '... there are hundreds of internet sites offering a wide range of material featuring the torture of (mostly female) victims ... These acts are usually presented in a sexually explicit context so that it is clear that the purpose of the material is sexual gratification, although the violence itself may not be sexual ... There is also extensive availability of sites featuring violent rape scenes ...'

The material in question goes beyond depictions of:[7]

> '... consensual sexual activity [or] the milder forms of bondage and humiliation which are commonplace in pornographic material. It depicts suffering, pain, torture and degradation of a kind which we believe most people would find abhorrent. The underlying premise is that this material should have no place in our society. The fact that it is widely accessible over the internet does not legitimise it.'

Publication of such material is already illegal (see **8.5**). The further criminalisation of such material is not considered to directly affect those who deal with sexual material

---

[3] The new legislation is intended to mirror that relating to images or pseudo-images of children: see *Consultation: On the possession of extreme pornographic material* (Home Office, 2005) at p 5, para 1.
[4] See, eg, 'Harmful viewing' NLJ (2 February 2007), p 170.
[5] See www.homeoffice.gov.uk/documents/cons-extreme-porn-3008051/Gvt-response-extreme-porn2.pdf?view =Binary.
[6] *Consultation: On the possession of extreme pornographic material* (Home Office, 2005) at p 5, para 5.
[7] Ibid, at p 6, para 11.

within the boundaries of the existing pornography laws. The mischief the new offence is seeking to address is internet publication and access which, the Government consider, cannot be controlled or prevented within the current legal framework.

8.5 Existing protections and criminal constraints in respect of adult material focus mainly on the Obscene Publications Acts of 1959 (OPA 1959) and 1964. It is a criminal offence to publish for gain, or have for the purposes of publication for gain an obscene matter. The definition of obscenity for the purposes of OPA 1959 is that it must, taken as a whole, tend to deprave and corrupt a significant proportion of persons who are likely to read, see or hear it.[8] There must be a publication, in the sense of giving, hiring, lending and selling, distributing or circulating. Although possession of adult obscene material is not, of itself, unlawful under OPA 1959, uploading or downloading images, even to an overseas based website does amount to 'publication' and thus can be the subject of an OPA 1959 prosecution.[9] In *Perrin* a successful prosecution was brought in respect of a French national based in England who uploaded obscene material to a US-based website. This was so even though the major steps to 'publication' were taken out of the English jurisdiction; the Court of Appeal rejected submissions that the legality of the 'publication' should be judged by the legal requirements of the jurisdiction where the internet site was based and managed. It is perhaps because of this broad approach that there is a lack of UK-based internet obscene material.[10]

The extreme material at which the new offence is aimed will often fall foul of the tests of obscenity under OPA 1959. However, OPA 1959 has distinct limitations: the publisher may be, and for this type of material usually is, abroad and therefore outside the jurisdiction. The use of OPA 1959 has declined as it has proved increasingly more difficult to obtain convictions.[11]

8.6 A range of other offences exists. Taking an indecent photograph, pseudo-photograph or film of a person aged under 18, or possessing it with a view to sale, showing or distributing it is an offence under s 1 of PCA 1978. Section 160 of the Criminal Justice Act 1988 makes it an offence to possess an indecent photograph or pseudo-photograph of a child. Section 85 of the Postal Services Act 2000, criminalises the sending by post of indecent or obscene articles. Powers of forfeiture exist in respect of those who import articles for gain.[12]

8.7 It is clear that whilst the existing criminal law can deal, to greater or lesser degrees of effectiveness, with the problem relating to extreme sexual images, convenient law enforcement aimed at the dissemination of such pornography and those who wish to view it would be enhanced by a criminal offence along the line of that that applies to children, if properly drafted and appropriately narrow. For the Government, and many commentators, the purpose of the new law is clear. The growth of internet use over the last few years[13] makes the issue of potential accidental or legitimate contact one of

---

[8] The number must be significant, in the sense of a minimal number: see generally *Calder and Boyars Ltd* (1968) 52 Cr App R 706; *DPP v Whyte* [1972] AC 849; *Perrin* [2002] EWCA Crim 747.
[9] *Perrin* [2002] EWCA Crim 747, citing with approval *Waddon* (unreported) 6 April 2000. See the Criminal Justice and Public Order Act 1994, s 168 amending OPA 1959.
[10] See H Fenwick *Civil Liberties and Human Rights* (Routledge-Cavendish, 4th edn, 2007), at p 585 and sources therein cited.
[11] See *Consultation: On the possession of extreme pornographic material* (Home Office, 2005) at p 7, para 15.
[12] Customs and Excise Management Act 1979.
[13] For data on this, see *Consultation: On the possession of extreme pornographic material* (Home Office, 2005) at p 6, para 6.

concern. It is not the Government's intention that the new offence should be to penalise individuals who come across material accidentally, but, rather, to set a benchmark for unacceptable material.

The new offence criminalises possession, and mirrors PCA 1978 offences. It fills a gap in respect of absent publications relating to adults, where *simple* possession without an intent to publish for gain is not unlawful. The Government's argument is that society should be protected from the corrosive effect on individuals and relationships that interest in violent or aberrant sexual behaviour is believed to create.[14] However, the Government drew back from actually confirming the likely long-term impact of such material, and the evidence is ambivalent. This was an area of some debate during the passage of the Act, with some questioning whether there was in fact a causal link between images and acts of violence.[15] Indeed, it is interesting that it is only sexually arousing extreme images that fall within the new offence, not wider images of extreme violence. The rapid evidence assessment[16] undertaken by the Government suggested that there was *some* link and *some* evidence of harm. These included development of pro-rape attitudes, beliefs and behaviours, and men who are predisposed to aggression are more susceptible to the influence of extreme pornographic material.

8.8 The new offence raises controversial issues about whether it is needed, whether it is drawn in suitably narrow terms, with its compatibility with Art 10 of ECHR, and whether it potentially might criminalise lawful conduct between consenting adults. For that reason, it underwent significant change even after being introduced into Parliament.

The offence

8.9 By s 63(1) it is an offence for a person to be in possession of an extreme pornographic image.

The concept of 'extreme pornographic image' is an image which falls within s 63(2), however, certain images are excluded by s 64 (see **8.10** and **8.22**). Further, there is a defence created by s 65 in respect of legitimate reason to possess unsolicited images and being unaware (with no cause to suspect) that he was in possession of such an image.

For the offence to be committed the prosecution will need to prove that:

(a)   the item in question is an image;

(b)   it is pornographic; and

(c)   the pornographic image is extreme.

---

[14]   Ibid, at pp 9–10, paras 27–31 contain an analysis of the harm considered by the Government to be potentially caused by such material. See further details in *The evidence of harm to adults relating to exposure to extreme pornographic material: a rapid evidence assessment* Ministry of Justice Research Series 11/07 (Ministry of Justice, September 2007), available at: www.justice.gov.uk/publications/research280907.htm.
[15]   See HC Committee, col 518 (22 November 2007).
[16]   Cited by Joint Committee 2007/2008, 15th Report at para 2.10.

Image

8.10 The term 'image' means a moving or still image (produced by any means) or data (stored by any means) which is capable of conversion into an image (s 63(8)). This is broadly drawn, and of course includes photographs, video, CD and any other form of visual representation. The word 'image' in its ordinary and natural meaning would exclude depiction by words alone. Literature that, in text, depicts fictional scenes of torture, rape and murder of women and children does not fall within the parameters of the new s 63 offence, and may not even be prosecuted as an obscene publication under OPA 1959.[17]

However, it is not confined to what might be termed 'real' images: constructed images are just as much images as video clips downloaded from the internet. So, too, are drawings and cartoons, although these may not in fact fall within s 63 for the different reason that the portrayal of extreme images must be realistic and explicit. For further discussion, see **8.16**.

Data stored by the defendant on a computer hard drive is an 'image' even though it has still to be converted on computer screen to visual form.[18] The decision in *Atkins v DPP*[19] does not negate that proposition. In that case the charge was one of possession of indecent images of children, contrary to PCA 1978. The Divisional Court concluded that, as the appellant was not aware the data was automatically saved to the 'cache' on the hard drive of the computer, that he was not in possession of that data. That, however, goes to the issue of 'possession', not, in these circumstances, to the definition of 'image'. Further, it is clear from s 65, as it was in *Atkins*, that displaying the image on screen would amount to possession for the purposes of the offence.

The term 'image' is not in any way confined to electronic images, despite the emphasis given in the consultation paper and subsequent debate to the internet issues that justify the creation of the offence. Thus, hard copy photographs will potentially fall within the offence, as well as, probably, being obscene within the terms of OPA 1959. In such circumstances a prosecutor might well consider that the scope of the new offence provides a more realistic prospect of conviction than the uncertainties of an obscenity prosecution under OPA 1959.

Pornographic

8.11 The purpose of s 63 is to catch material which would normally be caught by OPA 1959 were it to be distributed or published.[20] However, the term 'pornographic' for the purposes of s 63 does not mean the same as 'obscene' for the purposes of the obscenity laws. An image is pornographic if it is of such a nature that 'it must reasonably be assumed' to have been produced solely or principally for the purposes of sexual arousal (s 63(3)). It is the *purpose* that matters, not the effect. The fact that an image has caused, or is likely to cause, sexual arousal is of itself not sufficient, though might provide some evidence as to what the *purpose* of the producer was.

---

[17] For example, see the case of Marquis de Sade's *Juliette*, where, in 1991, the DPP declined to commence prosecution proceedings against its publisher Arrow Books under OPA 1959.
[18] *Bowden* (unreported) 10 November 1999.
[19] [2000] EWHC Admin 302; see also *Waddon* (unreported) 6 April 2000; *Smith* [2003] 1 Cr App R 212.
[20] Lord Hunt, Parliamentary Under-Secretary of State, Ministry of Justice, HL Committee, col 893 (3 March 2008).

Nor is the intention of the producer directly relevant. When the then Bill was first introduced into the House of Commons, the definition of 'pornography' required an element of judgment as to the intention of the producer, with the phrase 'if it appears to have been produced solely or principally for the purposes of sexual arousal'. Following concerns raised at Committee stage in the House of Commons, amendments were made in the Lords to allow 'a jury [to] simply take a view by reference to the nature of the material before them. It is not a question of the intentions of those who produced it'.[21]

The pornographic nature of the image is therefore not to be judged by its content, but by the *probable* purpose for which the image was produced judged on the material itself. The point is a real and not a theoretical one: an offence is committed if a pornographic image is extreme. But an extreme image is not unlawful under s 63 if it is not pornographic, though might well, of course, be unlawful under other provisions such as OPA 1959.

It might be thought that the purpose for which the image was produced will be self evident from the image itself. The 2008 Act requires it be judged in that way, and in fact in many cases that will be so. However, the definition of 'extreme' in s 63(6) and (7) extends beyond images of acts that are *of themselves* necessarily sexual in depiction (see **8.16**).

The court will need also to distinguish between the assumed purpose and the actual intention. Often they will go hand in hand. Section 63 is clearly framed so as to avoid the prosecution having to prove actual intention. The actual content may be so overtly sexual as to lead to an irresistible conclusion that that was the intended purpose for it being produced. But what, for example, of a film or photograph (or series of photographs) where the producer argues, nevertheless, that the primary purpose for production is artistic and not for the purpose of sexual arousal? Arguably, in such a case the offence is made out if the court is satisfied of the assumed purpose. On the issue of 'pornography', evidence of actual intention is irrelevant and is, on that issue, inadmissible. It might be argued that a defendant might wish to adduce evidence of actual intention in an attempt to provide an evidential basis for the court to conclude that it *should* not be assumed that it was not created principally for the purpose of sexual arousal. But by then the court will have decided that it can reasonably be assumed that it is for that purpose, for otherwise no case to answer would exist. For that reason, it is argued that evidence of actual intent is generally irrelevant.

8.12 The test is, at any rate partly, objective. The court will have to decide what can be reasonably assumed as to the reasons for production, not how the image is in fact, or might be, received. However, since what the court is being asked to decide is judgmental, how it is received or, likely to be received, is of course one important way in which the purpose of the producer can be gauged. As with all other elements of the offence, the burden of proof of showing that purpose is to the criminal standard. The court will have to be satisfied so that it is sure. In the vast majority of cases it will probably not be difficult to reach a conclusion on the purpose. The examples given during debate and in accompanying evidence were clearly sexual in content and intent. However, difficulties may arise in the context of images which might not overtly have a sexual context but

---

[21] Lord Hunt, Parliamentary Under-Secretary of State, Ministry of Justice, HL Committee, col 892 (3 March 2008).

which nonetheless have the potential to create sexual arousal. Or, indeed, images that may be sexual in content but nonetheless were not produced wholly or principally for the purposes of sexual arousal.

Examples given by those critical of the new laws raise the point. Classic works of art may depict sexual material: for example *Ledar and the Swan* or *The Rape of Europe* may depict bestiality. In drama, the *Romans in Britain* depicted anal sex. The murder of Gaveston in Marlowe's *Edward II* would almost certainly engage with s 63(7)(b) if explicitly depicted on film or DVD. The new law is not intended to criminalise such works or drama, unless they were unlawful under the Obscene Publication legislation. Section 63 is not intended, of itself, to criminalise such work, and, indeed, such images are potentially excluded from its scope (see **8.22**). The same applies to explicit images of actuality, for example news footage of atrocities. It may depict life threatening images but the depiction is not for any purpose of sexual arousal.

It is the purpose of the producer of the *image* that matters. The production of a play may be lawful or a DVD of the film may be lawful given the assumed purpose of the makers, but the assumed purpose is likely to be judged by the content and context. It is the intention of the artist or producers that matters, but arguably such works fall outside the scope of s 63 because it cannot be assumed that the images were produced for the purpose of sexual arousal.

The question also arises as to whether in appropriate cases expert evidence may, or should, be called. In the context of obscenity, expert evidence on that very question is not permitted. By analogy one can argue that this is for the court to determine on a purely factual basis. However, by definition this type of material is likely to be material with which a jury is unfamiliar and may not fully understand the potential context and purpose. In such cases there is some logic that a court should admit expert evidence if the prosecution should wish to tender it.

8.13 The question also arises as to who is the 'producer' in answering the question as to what was the purpose, or principal purpose of the production. The creator of a film, video clip, photograph or other image is the producer. So, too, is the creator of data that falls to be regarded as an image by reference to s 63(8)(b) (see **8.10**). It is his purpose that matters. However, if the defendant has printed off a copy, or downloaded a copy onto hard disk, or burnt a copy onto DVD, he is the producer of the *copy*. Is he, though, the producer of the *image*? If s 63 were to be interpreted as the latter, it would be his purpose that matters. Thus, if it is printed off for his own sexual arousal, then the offence is, in this regard, theoretically made out. Arguably, that conclusion cannot be correct. The defendant will probably also be in possession of the image made by the original producer, and in that case it is the purpose of that producer that matters. It would be absurd if, in respect of two identical copies, a person was criminally liable in respect of one but not in respect of another. It is the purpose of the creator of the image that matters. Any other conclusion would make the provisions in s 63(4) unnecessary.

8.14 However, it may be that the defendant has made alterations to an original image. Then different considerations apply. He is the creator of *that* image. This might be by being in possession of part only of a series of images – a series of photographs perhaps. The legality will have to be judged in the light of s 63(4):

'Where (as found in the person's possession) an image forms part of a series of images the question whether the image is of such a nature . . . [as for it to be reasonably assumed that it was produced solely or principally for the purpose of sexual arousal is] to be determined by reference to—

(a) to the image itself, and
(b) (if the series of images is such as to be capable of providing a context for the image) the context in which occurs in the series of images.'

This is explained by s 63(5) which begins with the words: 'So, for example, …'. The use of examples in statutes is not new, but nonetheless they can be no more than an example to assist in explaining and clarifying, but not limiting, the meaning, breadth and scope of s 63(4).

The example given in s 63(5) relates to where an image forms part of a narrative constituted by a series of images. In that set of circumstances if, having regard to those images as a whole, they are not of such a nature that they must reasonably be assumed to have been produced solely or principally for the purpose of sexual arousal, the image may, by virtue of being part of that narrative, be found not to be pornographic even though it might be found to be pornographic if taken by itself.

So a film or video which contains one image which is 'pornographic' will not, of itself, fall to be regarded as pornographic for the purpose of s 63, if the overall context shows that the series was not produced wholly or principally for the purpose of sexual arousal. Of course, it may escape s 63 in any event if it is excluded (see **8.22**). A book containing a series of photographs pursuing a medical or artistic theme would not be pornographic within the meaning of s 63 if it could reasonably be assumed it was produced for artistic or medical purposes, not for the main or principal purpose of sexual arousal.

8.15 Issues arise if an individual is in possession of one of a series of images, which has been printed, downloaded, or posted as a clip on an internet site. Although the image may originally have been part of a series of images it is not in those circumstances ('as found in the person's possession') part of a series which provide the context for assuming that in that situation possession of the series would not contravene s 63, though might raise OPA 1959 issues, but possession of the extract might well do so.

Extreme image

8.16 An extreme image is an image that falls within s 63(7) *and* is grossly offensive, disgusting or otherwise of an extreme character (s 63(6)).

The matters that fall within s 63(7) are, unlike earlier proposals, quite precise and detailed, avoid judgments as to what amounts to 'serious violence' and make it absolutely clear that matters such as mental injury are excluded. This level of specificity is intended to ensure that individuals 'can be aware of what material is illegal to possess before they go about seeking to acquire it'.[22]

The matters that go to determine whether an image is 'extreme' are those which portray in an explicit and realistic way:

---

[22] Lord Hunt, Parliamentary Under Secretary of State, Ministry of Justice, HL Committee, col 894 (3 March 2008).

'(a) an act which threatens a person's life;
(b) an act which results, or is likely to result, in serious injury to a person's anus, breasts or genitals,[23]
(c) an act which involves sexual interference with a human corpse;
(d) a person performing an act of intercourse or oral sex with an animal, whether dead or alive,

and a reasonable person looking at the image would think any such person or animal was real.'

8.17 The use of the word 'portray' is important, in its ordinary sense it has an extended range of meanings: 'to represent in a painting, drawing, sculpture; to make a portrait of; to make a verbal picture; depict in words; play the part of ...'.[24] The context of s 63 is clearly such as to exclude the written word. Its meaning is 'show'. It is intended to include visual representations of actual acts and of realistic depictions of such acts.[25]

The portrayal must be 'explicit' and 'realistic'. Portrayals which are discreet, not overt or by inference are not extreme images for the purpose of s 63. This will be a matter of judgment, which should, arguably, be judged in the light of the purposes of the legislation, namely to punish possession of extreme pornography, not challenging sexual and violent matter in films and DVDs.[26] What the matters are which are being depicted, and whether they are explicit and realistic, are issues of fact to be judged by the magistrates or jury. The images must also make a reasonable person think that any such person or animal was real. Of course, sadly, it may be real, and for the reasons set out above that is within the scope of s 63. However, it may be a simulation, in which case the standard used is that of the reasonable person. Again, this will be a judgment for the particular bench of magistrates or jury to make. However, in looking at what are extreme images and at the scope of the legislation, note should be made of the fact that the image may in fact be an image of lawful conduct. Actual commission of acts is not required, for otherwise prosecutors would face formidable evidential problems. A realistic and explicit depiction of an act which threatens a person's life, by participants who fully and freely consent is not, of itself, unlawful, depending on how the courts interpret the words 'realistic' and 'explicit'. Nor would possession of images of that depiction by *adults* infringe OPA 1959 if not for the purposes of gain. In short, s 63 criminalises the depiction of conduct which it is lawful to participate in and to watch. The conduct depicted will be abhorrent to most people, but that, of itself, may not be sufficient to justify legislative intervention through the criminalisation of possession.

8.18 It is not necessary here to give graphic examples of the types of conduct that will fall within the circumstances set out in s 63(7). However, some issues do arise. Presumably the act which 'threatens a person's life' has to be life-threatening (or a realistic and explicit depiction of life-threatening acts), not simply a threat to take life. Routinely drama contains threats to life, but drama also routinely depicts life-threatening acts. No doubt this is one reason why s 63 is confined to images with the purpose of sexual arousal. No doubt many acts can threaten life, if taken to extremes.

---

[23] In this context see s 63(9): it includes a part of the body which has been surgically reconstructed.
[24] *Collins Complete English Dictionary* (2003).
[25] Lord Hunt, Parliamentary Under Secretary of State, Ministry of Justice, HL Committee, col 895 (3 March 2008).
[26] See the example of Marlowe's *Edward II*.

This might include physical beating, or asphyxiation.[27] The latter certainly is intended to be within the scope of the legislation, and indeed, as noted above, was the initial cause of the campaign that ultimately led to s 63.

Similarly with the likelihood of serious injury being caused; the term is not defined. In some cases, such as severe cutting, beating or mutilation the conclusion may be obvious, but in others perhaps less so. As drafted, it is judgmental and subjective, permitting individual judgments that might vary wildly, and possibly impact on those who wish to engage in conduct in private consensually. The concerns of the Joint Committee on Human Rights have not, in this respect, been met. The Committee recommended that the term be given a less subjective meaning and should mean 'permanent physical harm'.[28]

Grossly offensive, disgusting or otherwise of an obscene character

8.19 The image must be 'grossly offensive, disgusting or otherwise of an obscene character', as contained in s 63(6). Whether the image is obscene will depend upon whether it fits the definition of obscenity already identified (**8.11**). Certainly anything that is obscene will be grossly offensive or disgusting. However, the opposite is not necessarily true: an image can be offensive or disgusting without being obscene.

The word 'grossly' attaches to and qualifies 'offensive': it is not clear whether it similarly attaches and qualifies 'disgusting', arguably it does, for any other conclusion has little sense. It is not entirely clear what, exactly, is the difference between 'offensive' and 'disgusting'. These are ordinary words to be given their ordinary and natural meaning, like the words 'threatening, abusive and insulting' in the Public Order Act 1986.[29] One dictionary defines 'offensive' as: 'unpleasant or disgusting; causing anger or annoyance'. Words such as revolting, repulsive, sickening, ghastly or sordid also come to mind. The same dictionary[30] defines 'disgusting' as 'repugnant'. Perhaps 'offensive' relates to feelings whilst 'disgusting' refers to taste. These terms are vague, wide and subjective and this vagueness may lead to challenge under the principle of legal certainty. An individual may not regard his sexual tastes as 'disgusting' even though most people might. In that context the law is coming close to criminalising an individual simply because of sexual aberrant taste. A court will have to judge whether images are disgusting or offensive in the light of its own perceptions of what the words actually mean. Yet an individual who is minded to download such material will not be able to predict, with accuracy, what conclusion a court might reach, with only limited defences. The use of such words also raises the question: if the intention of Parliament is to equate extreme images with the obscenity legislation, why has it gone beyond that concept in s 63(6)? There will be some material that falls within the ambit of extreme images that is not obscene, unless one regards the words 'grossly offensive, disgusting or otherwise' as superfluous.

8.20 The terms 'offensive' and 'disgusting' echo, perhaps, concepts of outrage or disgust for the purposes of laws relating to indecency.[31] In *Knuller v DPP* some doubt was cast on whether these were appropriate concepts on which to create a basis of criminality.[32] It might be argued that to extend such concepts to circumstances which

---

[27] See the sexual context in *Coutts* [2005] EWCA Crim 52.
[28] Joint Committee 2007/2008, 15th Report at para 2.16.
[29] See *Brutus v Cozens* [1973] AC 854.
[30] Collins *Complete English Dictionary* (2003).
[31] See *Knuller v DPP* [1973] AC 435.
[32] See Lord Reid at [1973] AC at 456.

are not, of themselves unrelated to public order, or the protection of groups of individuals, is to create a vague offence of uncertain scope and which simply criminalises the particular tastes of the individual.

Possession

8.21 The prosecution must prove that the defendant was in possession of the extreme pornographic images. The wording and structure of this new offence mirrors that in respect of possession of indecent photographs or pseudo-photographs of a child, under s 160 of CJA 1988.

The term 'possession' is not without difficulty.[33] For an individual to possess something, he must have it in his custody.[34] It is also clear from *Atkins v DPP*[35] that knowledge by an individual that he has it in his custody is key. These principles are relatively straightforward in a case involving hard copy images, but more troublesome in respect of computer images; one of the key problems that the new offence is addressing. In *Porter*[36] the Court of Appeal used the concept of 'having custody or control of the images' as the appropriate approach to possession for the purposes of the s 160 offence. Thus files that were stored in a 'temporary files' cache were in the possession of the appellant. But other images had been deleted both from the mail files and from the 'recycle bin'. In respect of such images, if the individual cannot retrieve or gain access to an image he was no longer in possession of it, even if it remained on hard disk. Just because he was in possession of the computer and hard disk did not mean he was in possession of images if he could not access them. This was a matter of fact for the jury to consider on the particular facts of the case:[37]

> 'Thus images which have been emptied from the recycle bin may be considered to be within the control of the defendant who is skilled in the use of computers and in fact owns the software necessary to retrieve such images, whereas such images may be considered not to be within the control of a defendant who does not possess those skills and does not own such software.'

Thus, an element of subjectivity is inherent in the concept of possession for the s 160 offence, and by analogy with this new offence. On the fact of *Porter* some of the images under consideration could only be accessed with the use of specialist forensic techniques and equipment provided by the US Federal Government. What matters is whether the images are within the control of the defendant.[38]

Excluded material

8.22 Section 63 does not apply to excluded images (s 64), defined by s 64(2) as an image which forms part of a series of images contained in a recording of the whole or part of a classified work. The term 'recording' includes any disc, tape, or other device capable of storing data electronically and from which images may be produced (s 64(7)). In deciding whether something is a recording of the whole or part of a classified work, any alteration attributable to a technical defect is to be disregarded. So, too, any defect

---

[33] See the observations of Lord Pearce in *Warner v Commissioner of Police for the Metropolis* [1969] AC 256.
[34] *DPP v Brooks* [1974] AC 862; *Boyesen* [1982] AC 768.
[35] [2002] 2 Cr App R 248, a decision in respect of a charge under CJA 1988, s 160.
[36] [2006] EWCA Crim 560.
[37] Per Dyson LJ.
[38] Ibid, at para 24.

caused by inadvertence by any person (s 64(5)(a)). The inclusion in the recording of any extraneous material, such as advertisements, is also to be disregarded. So, a DVD of a film that includes advertisements or other material, or which for technical reasons is not a complete and true version of the original work, would nonetheless be able to fall within the definition of 'classified work' for the purpose of this exclusion.

'Classified work' is defined by s 64(7). It means a video work in respect of which a classification certificate has been issued by a designated authority.[39] The fact that a classification certificate application to the British Board of Film Censors is pending, or that an appeal to the Video Appeal Committee against refusal of a certificate is irrelevant: the terms of s 64(7) make it quite clear that either the certificate has been issued or it has not. Section 64 is not explicit as to when such certification should exist. Is it at the date when the defendant was found in possession of the extreme pornographic image, or is it at the date of trial? Arguably, it is the former. The effect of s 64 is to disapply s 63 in certain circumstances where a person is in possession of such an image. At the date of being found to be in possession of the image if no certification exists the offence is committed, and what happens thereafter is irrelevant to criminal liability although perhaps not irrelevant as to whether a prosecution should proceed, the mode of trial if it is started or the punishment to be imposed following a conviction. Of course the point is probably theoretical because if a certificate was issued it is scarcely conceivable that the constituent elements of the offence (particularly those in s 63(6)) are satisfied.

8.23 Even if an image is contained within a recording of, or extract from, a classified work, it will not be an 'excluded image' if it is of such a nature that must reasonably be assumed to have been extracted (whether with or without other images) solely or principally for the purposes of sexual gratification (s 64(3)). There are also provisions in s 64(4) that apply the same rules to a series of images that are extracted from a classified work as apply to non-classified images (see **8.22**).

This means that the court must judge the legality of an *extract,* or a series of extracts, from a classified work by reference to whether it *must* reasonably be assumed that it has been extracted solely or principally for the purposes of sexual arousal. The word 'must' means the possibility that the purpose of extraction is for the purposes of sexual arousal is not enough. The nature of the material must surely be of such a nature to make such a purpose inevitable to any reasonable person (see **8.12**).

The real importance of this provision must be in some doubt. It is clearly aimed at preventing extreme images being extracted from a classified work out of context and circulated by email or posted on websites. However, for the offence to be committed the images must be 'extreme' (see **8.16**).

8.24 The relevant legislation for classification of videos, DVDs and other digital works such as digital games is the Video Recordings Act 1984 (VRA 1984).[40] The 'designated authority' under s 4 of VRA 1984[41] is the British Board of Film Censors (BBFC). Given the nature of 'extreme images', and the intent of Parliament in criminalising such images, it is scarcely likely that certification would be granted by the BBFC in respect of films or video recordings containing significant elements of such

---

[39] Under Video Recordings Act 1984, s 4.
[40] See generally Munroe 'Sex, Laws and Videotape: The R18 Category' [2007] Crim LR 957.
[41] See the 2008 Act, s 64(7).

conduct. Indeed, it is relied on not to issue a certificate in respect of material that is obscene.[42] Therefore, the fact that there is an exemption for classified works must provide some confirmation that the legal scope of the new offence goes beyond matters which are in law obscene, although that may not have been the Government's intention.

The BBFC has routinely been refusing certification to types of material which might be thought to be within the scope of the new offence. The Annual Report for 1998, for example, shows that certification was refused to *Boy meets Girl*, which depicted scenes that clearly would fall within the scope of the new offence, assuming that the purpose of its producers was sexual arousal.[43] The 2005 Guidelines issued by the BBFC stated that the following were not acceptable: material in breach of the criminal law; material likely to encourage interest in sexually abusive activity; portrayal of sexual behaviour involving lack of consent, whether real or simulated; infliction of pain or physical harm.

By s 4A of VRA 1984, the BBFC must have 'special regard' to *harm* that may be caused to potential viewers or, through their behaviour, to society by the manner in which the film deals with criminal behaviour, illegal drugs, violent behaviour or incidents, horrific incidents or behaviour, or human sexual activity. Of course, shock, horror, offence or disgust are not the same as *harm*. Although theoretically one could argue that there might be some instances of conduct falling within the definition of 'extreme image' which do not, in one sense, 'harm', in fact one should more readily conclude that it is difficult to envisage the certification of extreme images. Nothing in s 64 is to be taken as requiring BBFC to certificate a film containing such images (s 64(6)). If that is correct, the number of cases of extreme images benefiting from the exemption will be few in number. Perhaps the main purpose of s 64 is to provide legal reassurance that the new offence is *not* intended to criminalise acceptable films, videos and images.

Defences

8.25 Even if the prosecution can prove the integral elements of the offence as defined in s 63 and s 64, there are, nonetheless, three defences created by s 65, and a defence in s 66. In each case the relevant wording states that it is a defence for the person to prove (in the case of s 65) or the defendant to prove (in the case of s 66) the relevant defence. Arguably, that is an evidential burden, and not a legal burden which the defendant has to satisfy on the balance of probabilities. Whether a statutory provision imposes a legal or evidential burden will depend on whether the interference with the normal presumption of innocence is necessary and proportionate.[44] In the context of the s 63 offence, the harm potentially caused by possession of such images is regarded by the Government, and Parliament, as significant, it is possession itself that is criminalised, and the person or defendant (as the case may be) is the person best placed to be able to prove the matters contained in s 65 or s 66. However, the principles relating to reverse onus provisions have been determined on a case-by-case basis, and it remains to be seen how a court will apply these principles. It should also be remembered that the burden of proof on a defendant is only in respect of the defence, and the prosecution is under the overall duty to prove guilt in respect of the constituent elements of the offence.

---

[42] See Edwards 'The VAC and the Standard of Legal Pornography' [2001] Crim LR 305.
[43] 90% of the work was set in a torture chamber where a man was tortured to death.
[44] See *Lambert* [2001] 3 All ER 577; *Attorney-General's Reference (No 1 of 2004)* [2004] 1 WLR 2111; *Sheldrake v DPP, Attorney General's Reference (No 4 of 2002)* [2005] 1 All ER 237. The principles set out in these cases are compatible with the right to a fair trial in Art 6 of ECHR, as stated in *Salabiaku v France* (1988) 13 EHRR 379.

8.26 Under s 65, it is a defence for the person charged to show one of the following:

(a) that the person had a legitimate reason for being in possession of the image concerned. For example a police officer investigating an offence will be in possession of an extreme image and thus have a legitimate reason for being in possession of it; so, too, a legal representative of such a person, or a CPS solicitor considering prosecution. It will be a question of fact in each case. Thus whether an academic could claim that the image was possessed for then purposes of 'research' will depend on the context, nature of the research and research methodology. Arguably, courts will apply this narrowly, requiring convincing justification for the possession of such images;

(b) that the person had not seen the image concerned and did not know, nor had any cause to suspect, it to be an extreme pornographic image. Again, this is a narrow defence: if the individual does not know he has the image at all, then he is in most cases not in 'possession' of it, and there is no need for a defence at all. It will apply in the narrow set of circumstances where the person is aware he is in possession of data, but is unaware of its nature and has no reason to suspect that it contains an extreme image. It will perhaps also be of value in respect of computers which are shared, say, between husband and wife. One of the individuals may have no knowledge of particular material on the computer. A court will have to determine the possession and of knowledge of the images on the particular facts; or

(c) the person was sent the image concerned without any prior request having been made by or on behalf of the person, and did not keep it for an unreasonable time.

8.27 The defence in s 66 applies where a person is charged with an offence under s 63, provided that it is an offence that involves the portrayal of an image under s 63(7)(a), (b) or (c) of the new Act (see **8.16**). In such a case it is a defence for the defendant to prove:

(a) that the defendant directly participated in the act or any of the acts portrayed; and

(b) that the act or acts did not involve the infliction of any non-consensual harm on any person; and

(c) in the case of an image depicting sexual interference with a human corpse, that what is portrayed as a human corpse, was not in fact a corpse.

The justification for this defence, added during the parliamentary passage of the 2008 Act, is so as not to interfere with and potentially criminalise images of private, sexual activity, no matter how extreme. Of course, on a literal reading of s 66, the defence is applicable to possession by the *defendant,* and in no way protects possession by any other person who was not participating consensually in the conduct, the subject of the charge. A photographer who was present during consensual activity of this type arguably would not be 'directly [participating]' in any of the acts portrayed, unless a wide interpretation is given to those words, making *his* possession of extreme images unlawful.

Whether this is too narrow an interpretation remains to be seen. The Joint Committee on Human Rights[45] recommended that the definition of the offence be refined to

---

[45] Joint Committee 2007/2008, 15th Report at para 2.17.

exclude images created by consenting adults, where there is no significant harm to any participant and no intention to distribute the material beyond the participants involved. It also recommended that guidance should be drawn up identifying factors that should be taken into account in determining whether participants consented, including whether or not they received payment. The terms of s 66 do not go that far. Arguably, the narrow approach to 'participant' ought to be rejected, to meet the objective of non-criminalising the possession of images of those who, in the wider sense, were 'participating'. Such an approach is consistent both with the intention of Parliament not to penalise lawful, consensual conduct in private, and with the objective of preventing the dissemination of harmful material that may undesirably influence others.

The issue of consent is, for this purpose, dealt with by s 66(3). Harm which is inflicted on a person is non-consensual if:

'(a) the harm is of such a nature that the person cannot, in law, consent to it being inflicted on himself or herself; or
(b) where the person can, in law, consent to it being so inflicted, the person does not in fact consent to it being inflicted.'

Thus, s 66 looks not simply at whether consent was given, but also whether the law will permit such consent to be given. Possession by a participant of images of unlawful conduct, such as that in *Brown*,[46] would not benefit from such a defence even though the conduct was said to be consensual, and thus be potentially unlawful.

The fact of consent will therefore be dealt with in accordance with wider legal principle, principally, ss 74–76 of SOA 2003. Section 74 of SOA 2003 states:

'... for the purposes [of Part 1] a person consents if he agrees by choice, and has the freedom and capacity to make that choice.'

The principles developed by the courts will continue to apply. Thus, a person of limited understanding may not have consented.[47] A person who is grossly intoxicated is unlikely to be held to have given genuine consent. In the context of the type of images, the potential subject of s 63, consent can be vitiated by violence, fear or threats. Particularly in respect of private violent images there is a real danger that claimed real consent was in fact genuine.

Human rights and wider issues

8.28 The justification, scope and purpose of the offence are key issues for lawyers seeking to answer the question as to whether the new offence is Convention-compliant. The Government believes that the new offence is compatible with Arts 8 and 10 of ECHR. Article 8 protects the right to private and family life, home and correspondence, subject to the limitations permitted in Art 8(2). Any limitations on the right have to be prescribed by law, necessary, and proportionate.[48] Article 10 protects the right to freedom of expression, subject again to exceptions of a similar type and principles.

---

[46] [1994] 1 AC 212.
[47] *Lang* (1975) 62 Cr App R 50; *Howard* [1965] 3 All ER 684.
[48] *Handyside v UK* (1976) 1 EHRR 737; *Wingrove v UK* (1996) 24 EHRR 1; *Gay News Ltd v UK* (1982) 5 EHRR 123.

Parliament has identified the problem it is seeking to address, and it is 'prescribed by law', although the question remains whether the definitional problems relating to the original proposal have been wholly solved by the amendments made by the Government during the passage of the Act. As already noted, key vagueness and uncertainties remain.

But the fact that the offence is a legitimate response is insufficient.[49] The question remains whether the response is also proportionate. To demonstrate that, a key requirement is to show that the restrictions of the rights of the individual are necessary and proportionate to a pressing social need. The fact that the Government cannot show a proven link between the possession of extreme sexual images and violent sexual behaviour, and that, arguably, the new offence goes beyond the scope of the existing obscenity legislation, are all matters which might make it hard to show that the offence is a proportionate response that necessitates an extension of the pre-existing law, which has the effect, as drafted, of going beyond the particular purpose of regulating internet obscene material.

Human rights issues also potentially arise if the legislation goes too far. In its original form the tests adopted were both vague and subjective. It would have proved difficult to satisfy the test of legal certainty, whereby an individual can gauge in advance the legality of his conduct. There were also concerns about it interfering to an unjustifiable extent with private freedoms. One organisation, Backlash, which was created in 2005 for the purpose of campaigning against aspects of the legislation wrote:[50]

> 'The central issue here is not whether violent and abusive behaviour is defensible. It is not, as everyone agrees. Rather, the issue is whether the proposal will criminalise non-abusive activities engaged in by consenting adults ... The question that immediately follows is this: if the activities/material in question are not abusive, should they be outlawed because (even most) people find them distasteful?'

However, the issue is not whether the *activities* themselves are criminalised (though many of them are); rather, it is whether the criminalisation of their depiction can be justified. Nothing in the current legislation criminalises *conduct* which is not otherwise criminal, except in regard to possession of images of that conduct. The principle of regulating possession of images of conduct is established. The question is whether the case has been made out that the need to criminalise this possession in the way s 63 does is in fact necessary. The changes made in the passage of the 2008 Act through Parliament go some way to protect against the criminalisation of private conduct and of possession of legitimate films and images.

Special rules relating to providers of information society services

8.29 Section 68, by reference to Sch 14 of the new Act, relates to the issue of information society services. These are defined by Sch 14, para 6, by reference to E-Commerce Directive 2000/31/EC, and basically relates to the provision of any service normally provided for remuneration, at a distance, by means of electronic equipment for the processing (including digital compression) of storage of data, and at the individual request of a recipient of a service.

---

[49] Cf *Perrin* [2002] EWCA Crim 747.
[50] Briefing note cited at HC Research Paper 07/65.

8.30 The effect of para 1(2) of Sch 14 is to apply s 63 to a domestic service provider who is in possession of an extreme pornographic image in an EEA state[51] other than the UK. There are restrictions on when s 63 can be used against a non-UK provider but established in the EEA. The purpose of the provisions is to ensure that s 63 is consistent with the E-Commerce Directive.

Paragraphs 3, 4 and 5 provide exemptions from s 63 in limited circumstances such as where they are acting as mere conduits for such material or are storing it as caches or hosts.

INDECENT PHOTOGRAPHS OF CHILDREN

8.31 Section 69 of the new Act amends PCA 1978. The change came into force on 8 July 2008 (see s 153(2)).

It does so in a minor way by extending the exemption contained in s 1B(1)(b) for members of the Security Service to include members of the Secret Intelligence Service. It is therefore a defence for a member of the Secret Intelligence Service to show that the photograph or pseudo-photograph was made for the purposes of the prevention, detection or investigation of crime, or for the purposes of criminal proceedings, in any part of the world.[52]

Further changes are made by s 69 to the definition of 'photograph' in s 7(4) of PCA 1978. It does so by inserting a new s 7(4A). The pre-existing definition extends to photographs or pseudo-photographs.[53] The change made reflects the fact that images of children can be created in a variety of ways, and in ways that go beyond depictions that appear to be photographs. The mischief the change is addressing is the creation of images of children that need protection under PCA 1978 by tracing, whether by hand, using tracing paper, or electronically. Child welfare groups report a growing increase in interest in images of this type, and are concerned that 'these images could fuel the abuse of real children by reinforcing abusers' inappropriate feelings towards children. These images, particularly as they area cartoon or fantasy style format could be used in 'grooming' or preparing children for sexual abuse.[54]

The new s 7(4A) states that references in PCA 1978 include:

'(a) a tracing or other image, whether made by electronic or other means (of whatever nature)—
(i) which is not itself a photograph or pseudo-photograph, but
(ii) which is derived from the whole or part of a photograph or pseudo-photograph (or a combination of either or both) . . .'

A 'photograph' also includes data stored on a computer disk, or by other electronic means, which is capable of conversion into a photograph or pseudo-photograph. So, it follows that, if the tracing is electronic it is caught by the amended prohibition.

---

[51] European Economic Area.
[52] PCA 1978, s 1B, as amended.
[53] A pseudo-photograph means an image whether made by computer graphics or otherwise, however, which appears to be a photograph (PCA 1978, s 7(7)).
[54] See www.homeoffice.gov.uk/documents/cons-2007-depiction-sex-abuse.

MAXIMUM PENALTY FOR PUBLICATION OF OBSCENE ARTICLES

8.32 Section 71 increases the maximum penalty on conviction on indictment for publication of obscene articles from 3 years to 5 years. This provision came into force on 8 July 2008 (see s 153(2)).

SEXUAL OFFENCES COMMITTED OUTSIDE THE UK

8.33 One of the main changes made by SOA 2003 was to attempt to tackle the problem of 'sex tourism'. Section 72 of SOA 2003 effectively created extra-territorial jurisdiction. Its effect is to make it unlawful in the UK to engage in any act which, if done in England, Wales or Northern Ireland would constitute a sexual offence to which s 72 applied. The offences to which s 72 applied were specified by Sch 2 of SOA 2003.

This criminalisation of extra-jurisdictional conduct applied to a person who was a British citizen as at 1 September 1997 or who later became one.

8.34 Section 72 of the new Act replaces the pre-existing s 72 of SOA 2003 with a new s 72. Patently the Government wishes to have effective provisions in place to prevent sex tourism, in preparation for ratification of the new European Convention on the Protection of Children from Sexual Exploitation and Abuse.

The Minister of State, observed:[55]

> 'We already have some of the toughest sex offences legislation in the world but we are determined to do everything we can to protect the most vulnerable, at home and abroad ... anyone who commits an offence against children abroad will face the prospect of prosecution for the same offence here even though it may not have been an offence in that country.'

To that end, the new s 72 extends the categories of persons to which it applies beyond UK citizens, to include a UK resident (SOA 2003, s 72(2)) and any individual who, although not a UK national or resident at the time when such an act is done, has rights of residence or rights of nationality at the 'relevant time' (SOA 2003, s 72(3)). The change came into force on 14 July 2008 (see **1.5**).

What is the 'relevant time' is defined by SOA 2003, s 72(4) as the time when the proceedings are brought. Effectively, therefore, a person who had no direct connection with the UK at the time when the offence was committed can be prosecuted for that offence at some time in the future, when he or she has acquired rights of residence. This is not to be regarded as infringing any rights of retrospectivity, because a precondition is that the act done constitutes an offence under the law relating to the place where the act was done.

---

[55] Vernon Coaker, Parliamentary Under-Secretary of State for Home Department, 14 July 2008 at www.press.home office.gov.uk/press-releases/Stopping-Sex-Offenders.

GROOMING AND ADOPTION

8.35 Section 73 of, and Sch 15 to, the new Act, make detailed amendments to the provisions relating to grooming, and amends SOA 2003 in a detailed way in respect of adoption. The changes came into effect on 14 July 2008 (see **1.5**).

8.36 Section 15 of the SOA 2003 creates an offence of grooming. It states that:

'A person aged 18 or over (A) commits an offence if—

(a) having met or communicated with another person (B) on at least two earlier occasions he—
  (i) intentionally meets B, or
  (ii) travels with the intention of meeting B in any part of the world,
(b) ... [intending to do anything which is] a relevant offence,
(c) B is under 16, and
(d) A does not reasonably believe B is 16 or over.'

Plainly the scope of that offence can be avoided if the prosecution cannot show that A travels with the intention of meeting B but can nonetheless *show* that A has arranged to meet B in any part of the world; after all A may have already travelled. It can also be avoided if it is B who travels with the intention of meeting A. The amendments to s 15 rectify this problem and close these loopholes.

8.37 Other provisions in Sch 15 deal with the question of the meaning of 'adoption' or 'adopted' in the SOA 2003, and do so by reference to the Adoption Act 1976, s 39. This effectively means that those who fall within the terms of s 39 will be familial members for the purposes of the offences under s 64 or 65 of SOA 2003 (sex with an adult relative, etc).

INFORMATION CONCERNING SEX OFFENDERS

8.38 The new Act deals with how, and in what circumstances, information about sex offenders is communicated to individuals. This is dealt with at **12.2**.

Chapter 9

CRIMINAL OFFENCES AND DEFENCES

SUMMARY

9.1 In Chapter 8 we examined changes in the criminal law relating to obscenity and sexual offences. Other important changes made by the new Act are as follows:

- the introduction of a new offence of hatred on the grounds of sexual orientation into Public Order Act 1986;

- the law of blasphemy is abolished; and

- the law relating to reasonable force for the purposes of self-defence is placed, at least in part, on a statutory basis.

Additional changes relate to unlawfully obtaining personal data to the protection of nuclear material and facilities.

HATRED ON THE GROUNDS OF SEXUAL ORIENTATION

9.2 Section 74 of, and Sch 16 to, the new Act create a new offence of hatred on the grounds of sexual orientation. These provisions have not yet been brought into force.

Unhelpfully, s 74 creates the new offence by significant and detailed amendment of Part 3A of Public Order Act 1986 (POA 1986) (which deals with hatred against persons on religious grounds) to extend that legislation to include hatred on the grounds of sexual orientation. The Government resisted attempts to create a completely new provision which would have been more accessible.[1] The relevant parts of the section are, for convenience, reproduced at **9.3**, with the words added shown in italics.

Under a new s 29B of POA 1986, it is an offence whether by words or acts, for any person to do, or incite any other person to do, any act with the intention of causing physical or mental harm to any person or group of persons on the basis of hatred of their sexual orientation or presumed sexual orientation.

---

[1] See Maria Eagle, Parliamentary Under-Secretary of State, Ministry of Justice, HC Committee, col 687 (29 November 2007).

The new provisions

9.3 Section 29AB of POA 1986 defines 'hatred on the grounds of sexual orientation'. This means 'hatred against a group of persons defined by reference to sexual orientation (whether towards persons of the same sex, the opposite sex or both)'.

Section 29B, as amended, now reads:

> '(1) A person who uses threatening words or behaviour, or displays any written material[2] which is threatening, is guilty of an offence if he intends thereby to stir up religious hatred *or hatred on the grounds of sexual orientation.*
> (2) An offence under this section may be committed in a public or a private place, except that no offence is committed where the words or behaviour are used, or the written material is displayed, by a person inside a dwelling and are not heard or seen except by other persons in that or another dwelling.
> (3) *[Omitted by new Act]*
> (4) In proceedings for an offence under this section it is a defence for the accused to prove that he was inside a dwelling and had no reason to believe that the words or behaviour used, or the written material displayed, would be heard or seen by a person outside that or any other dwelling.
> (5) This section does not apply to words or behaviour used, or written material displayed, solely for the purposes of being included in a programme service.'

Section 29C now provides:

> '(1) A person who publishes or distributes written material which is threatening is guilty of an offence if he intends thereby to stir up racial hatred *or hatred on the grounds of sexual orientation.*
> (2) References in this Part of the Act to the publication or distribution of written material are to its publication or distribution to the public or a section of the public.'

The offences below are extended to include not only religious discrimination, but also hatred on the grounds of sexual orientation:

- s 29E: distributing, showing or playing a recording;

- s 29F: broadcasting or including programme in programme service;

- s 29G: possession of written material which is threatening, or a recording of visual images or sounds which are threatening, with a view to its being displayed, published, or included in a programme service whether by himself or another, or (in the case of a recording, being distributed, shown, played or included in a programme service, whether by himself or another, and in either case he intends religious hatred or hatred on the grounds of sexual orientation.

A new s 29JA of POA 1986 states that 'for the avoidance of doubt, the discussion or criticism of sexual conduct or practices or the urging of persons to refrain from or modify such conduct or practices shall not be taken of itself to be threatening or intended to stir up hatred'.

---

[2] '"Writing" includes typing, printing, lithography, photography and other modes of representing or reproducing words in visible form' (Interpretation Act 1978, s 5 and Sch 1).

If convicted of an offence, the accused is liable to imprisonment not exceeding 7 years or a fine, or both (on indictment) or a term not exceeding 12 months (formerly 6 months prior to the 2008 Act changes) or a fine not exceeding the statutory maximum.

The Attorney-General has to consent to the commencement of any prosecution (POA 1986, s 29L(1)).

Background

9.4 The criminal law already gives significant protection to prevent the incitement to hatred on various grounds. In recent years Parliament has legislated to prevent the use of threatening, abusive or insulting words or behaviour to incite racial hatred.[3] In 2006, the Racial and Religious Hatred Act was passed, introducing the offences, set out above, of inciting religious hatred by the use of threatening behaviour. The provisions on hatred on the grounds of sexual orientation mirror those, the Government using the model of the incitement to religious hatred agreed by Parliament in 2006.

There is a large body of other law that is relevant and may well catch incitement to hatred on the grounds of sexual orientation as well as other forms of incitement. Sections 4 and 5 of POA 1986 criminalise the use of threatening, abusive and insulting words and behaviour which is likely to cause harassment, alarm or distress, and which can (and has) been used against individuals making homophobic comments. Offences of assault or wounding, or incitement to such, are punishable under the normal criminal law. Breach of the peace powers continue to exist. Section 146 of the Criminal Justice Act 2003 (CJA 2003) increases sentence severity for offences motivated by the victim's sexual orientation. Harassment on these grounds can be tackled under the powers available in the Protection from Harassment Act 1997. So why a new offence?

The answer was given by Maria Eagle, Parliamentary Under-Secretary of State for Justice, as follows when introducing these provisions as amendments to the Bill:[4]

> '... there is a lacuna, in that there are already offences dealing with hatred leading to violence against an individual; it is an aggravating feature to be motivated by hating gay and lesbian groups. The lacuna relates to the fact that it is not presently unlawful to incite hatred of a group of people, without picking out an individual on the basis of their sexuality. The new provisions seek to deal with that lacuna.'

Despite the opinion of the Minister, in many cases the use of homophobic words or behaviour when aimed at a group of people because of their sexuality will result in the commission of an offence under s 4 or s 5 of POA 1986. The explanation given to the House of Lords was more graphic:[5]

> '[We] have seen evidence ... that gay people are the target for threatening words and behaviour which stir up hatred ... it shows extreme political parties trying to whip up hatred against the gay community by associating homosexuality with child abuse or with the spread of disease. Recent BNP campaign literature distributed to voters in north Wales featured photographs of child murder victims and claimed that a majority vote by mainstream parties to equalise the age of consent indicated that MPs were trying to legalise child sex step by step. Violently homophobic lyrics in some reggae and rap songs urge the torture and murder

---

[3] See now POA 1986.
[4] Parliamentary Under-Secretary of State for Justice, HC Committee, col 663–664 (29 November 2007).
[5] Lord Hunt, Minister of State, Ministry of Justice, HL Committee, col 940 (3 March 2008).

of lesbians and gay men. Stonewall[6] has commented that while some artists and their record producers have said that the songs in question will not be performed in the future, other artists have refused to make such a commitment, and no legal action has been taken to prevent the sale and distribution of such material in Britain.'

A wider rationale was given by the Joint Committee on Human Rights,[7] which welcomed the proposed new offence as a 'human rights enhancing measure'. It concluded that there was considerable evidence that 'gay people in particular are often the subject of material inciting people to violence against them'. There was a positive obligation under ECHR to ensure that adequate measures were in place to protect individuals from such harm.

The new offences caused considerable debate and disagreement during the passage of the Act,[8] not about the unacceptability of such conduct, but rather about whether a new offence was needed, its effects on legitimate debate and expression on what are sensitive issues on which individuals and religious bodies, and because of what some[9] see as over-zealous approaches, by the police and others to what is perceived as homophobic comments. Underpinning all of these concerns were issues relating to how far it was necessary or appropriate to restrict freedom of speech. However, arguably, the issue of principle in respect of such legislation was settled in 2006 by the extension of the incitement to hatred laws.

Sexual orientation

9.5 The term 'sexual orientation' is not defined. Nor was it defined in s 145 of CJA 2003, dealing with aggravation in terms of offence seriousness and sentence. Clearly it includes heterosexual, homosexual and lesbian sexual orientation. It includes bisexuals, but not transgender individuals (because there is no evidence of a problem).[10] Unlike the Northern Irish equivalent legislation it does not refer anywhere to 'presumed sexual orientation', but arguably that is unimportant because this provision is aimed at hatred against groups, not individuals.

Beyond that, the scope of the provision is uncertain. Arguably one can distinguish between 'sexual orientation' and 'sexual preference' or 'sexual taste': it would be surprising if, for example, paedophilia was regarded as 'sexual orientation', and there is no evidence that the Government intended to cast the net for this offence wider than the well-recognised and lawful sexual orientation groups. Those individuals who in public threaten child sex offenders will fall to be dealt with under the wider provisions of the criminal law, not the specific provisions of s 29B.

The offence – s 29B

9.6 The offence under s 29B, set out above, cannot be committed unless there is threatening words or behaviour. The Joint Committee on Human Rights[11] concluded

---

[6] Campaigning group representing gay and lesbian individuals. For its evidence, see HC Committee (16 October 2007).
[7] Joint Committee 2007/2008, 5th Report at para 1.62.
[8] See HC Committee, cols 658 et seq (29 November 2007); HL Committee, cols 920 et seq (3 March 2008).
[9] See, eg, Lord Waddington, HL Committee, col 925 (3 March 2008).
[10] Maria Eagle, Parliamentary Under-Secretary of State for Justice, HC Committee, col 666 (29 November 2007).
[11] Joint Committee 2007/2008, 5th Report at para 1.64.

that confining the ambit of the offence in this way gave an appropriate degree of protection for freedom of speech, allowing criticism but not threats. Abusive or insulting words or behaviour are insufficient, and in this respect the offences of incitement to religious hatred and hatred on the grounds of sexual orientation differ from the offence of incitement to racial hatred. They also differ from the wider public order offences under s 4 or s 5 of POA 1986. These provisions are specifically aimed at the mischief of groups being threatened because of their sexual orientation. The wider offences have sufficient scope to catch words or behaviour which is simply abusive or insulting.

The term 'threatening' is to be given its ordinary and natural meaning,[12] and whether words or behaviour are threatening is a matter of fact in each case. It is impossible to do other than assess that question except on a case-by-case basis. The question as to whether words or behaviour *are* threatening does not of itself turn on the question as to whether the group *felt* threatened, although arguably the fact that a group *felt* threatened is cogent evidence that they *were* in fact threatened. This is not simply a matter of semantics: a group may feel threatened by quite legitimate criticism or debate (see **9.9**).

The offence can be committed in either a public or private place. However, it cannot be committed if the words or behaviour are in a dwelling and only can be heard or seen by a person in the same dwelling. If, therefore, words are heard by someone in another dwelling, or in the common areas of flats, then the limitation does not apply.

9.7 The offence under s 29B is not committed if the threats are aimed at an individual and not a group (see s 29AB). Words or behaviour aimed at a specific individual should be dealt with under the wider public order legislation, and the offence will be aggravated by the context (CJA 2003, s 145). However, drawing this distinction may not always be easy. A threatening homophobic comment addressed to an individual may well encompass the speaker's homophobic views on gay people generally. After all, the individual is in that sense a member of that group. Nor should criminal liability be avoided under s 29B in the (theoretical) event by an accused claiming that his threat was individual: that conclusion would be both absurd and unacceptable. However, that said, despite the types of words or behaviour used the subject of the charge will be being prosecuted because, whoever they are aimed at, they are being aimed at that person because of his membership of a group defined by sexual orientation.

9.8 Section 29B requires an intention to stir up hatred on the grounds of sexual orientation. So, the accused must intend the words or behaviour, and must also intend, or be reckless to, the stirring up of hatred on the grounds of sexual orientation. This targets the offence of those who intend to incite hate, not those who are insensitive or thoughtless. Likelihood is not enough. Obviously, that will be for the court to judge in the light of what is said, where and in what context, but it is the state of mind of the particular accused that matters.

9.9 Words or behaviour are not to be regarded as threatening or intended to stir up hatred if, taken of themselves, they amount to discussion or criticism of sexual conduct or practices or amount to the urging of persons to refrain from or modify such conduct or practices (s 29JA). This is the equivalent freedom of expression provision to that contained in s 29J for the purposes of incitement to religious hatred. Section 29JA is intended to protect the right of freedom of expression that is inherent in Art 10 of

---

[12] *Brutus v Cozens* [1973] AC 854; *DPP v Clarke* (1991) 94 Cr App R 359.

ECHR. Those who for religious or other reasons disapprove of homosexual conduct are entitled to say so. Those who wish sexual practices, of which they disapprove, to stop are entitled to do so. However, whether such conduct will be lawful within s 29B will depend on tone, the words or behaviour used and the context. The scope this protection offers *ought* to be sufficient to protect honest expressions of opinion or criticism put reasonably. However, some fear that the provision may have a 'chilling effect'.[13]

REASONABLE FORCE AND SELF-DEFENCE

9.10 Section 76 clarifies the operation of the common law defence of self-defence. The question of whether the amount of force used is reasonable in the circumstances is to be decided by reference to the circumstances as the defendant believed them to be. Section 76(4) and (5) make further provision as to how the reasonableness of the degree of force used is to be assessed. The force used must not be disproportionate to the circumstances as the defendant believed them to be.

The provisions came into force on 14 July 2008 (see **1.5**).

Background

9.11 The adequacy of the law relating to self-defence has been a live issue for many years, particularly since the conviction and jailing of a Norfolk farmer, Tony Martin, for the murder[14] of a teenage burglar. The issues highlighted by this case involve more than simply the technical application of the defence: they involve moral issues as to moral culpability, the protection of property and the extent to which persons acting in good faith should be prosecuted. However, at the outset it is important to remember that the scope of the defence of self-defence goes far beyond individuals who are seeking to protect themselves, family and property. It applies to those, including state agents (such as, for example, police firearms officers seeking to apprehend a suspected terrorist).

The framework of the law is, in one context, based on statute. Section 3 of CJA 1967 authorises a person to use such force as is reasonable in the circumstances in the prevention of crime, or in effecting or assisting in the apprehension in the lawful arrest of offenders or suspected offenders or of persons unlawfully at large. So, if these are the purposes for which the force is used, the limits in s 3 apply, to the exclusion of the common law (CJA 1967, s 3(2)).[15] In other circumstances the common law defence of self-defence applies. It is this common law defence that is affected by the changes made by s 76.

---

[13] Edward Garnier MP, HC Committee, cols 667–668 (29 November 2007).
[14] Later reduced to manslaughter on the grounds of diminished responsibility. Martin had a paranoid personality disorder, probably made worse by an earlier invasion of his property by burglars. For news comments on the issues at the time, see http://news.bbc.co.uk/1/hi/uk/724416.stm (for 24 April 2000) and www.guardian.co.uk/uk/2001/oct/30/tonymartin.ukcrime. See, generally, *Martin (Anthony)* TLR, 1 November 2001.
[15] For comment on s 3 and its purpose see Kaye 'Excessive force in self-defence after R v Clegg' (1997) 61 *Journal of Criminal Law* 448 at 451. But cf *Cousins* [1982] QB 526.

The common law defence[16]

9.12 At common law 'self-defence ... provides a complete defence to any charge of fatal or non-fatal violence'. It is a defence, but it may be noted that the burden of proof of the offence is on the prosecution. Once the defence has adduced evidence to make this a 'live issue' it is for the prosecution to prove that the defence did not apply and that the case is made out.[17]

> 'A person (D) whose conduct and state of mind falls within the parameters of the defence does not act unlawfully and so is not guilty of any offence. Conversely, a person whose conduct and/or state of mind does not fall within the defence acts unlawfully and therefore stands to be convicted.'[18]

The defence applies where a person charged with an offence (D) uses force in defence of himself, or another, from what he perceives to be an actual or imminent unlawful assault. Two questions arise: the reasonableness of the use of force in self-defence, and the reasonableness of the level of force used. The tests are partly subjective, partly objective. Whether D is entitled to use force in self-defence must be judged in the light of the circumstances as he perceived them to be (subjective). However, the level of force used must be reasonable (objective).[19]

The subjective element permits a defendant to justify his or her intervention by way of self-defence by what he or she thought and believed. Provided the belief is honest and genuinely held, the defendant may be judged on that basis,[20] unless that belief was generated by intoxication.[21] The belief does not have to be objectively reasonable, although the reasonableness or otherwise of the belief may help the jury decide whether the belief was actually and genuinely held. So, the jury must decide whether the conditions justifying force existed genuinely in the mind of the defendant. In *Williams (Gladstone)* the court concluded that the belief was genuinely, but mistakenly held. He was entitled to rely on the defence of self-defence. If the belief is not genuinely held, then the defence fails, for that reason.

9.13 Even if the jury is satisfied that the belief in the need to use force in self-defence is genuinely held by the defendant, the defence is not made out unless the force used is objectively reasonable in the circumstances as the defendant believed them to be. In *Palmer*[22] the Privy Council concluded that a person who is attacked may defend him or herself, but only to the extent that is reasonably necessary. If the person does not achieve that, there is no halfway house.

A proportionate response is clearly required by the law. An imminent threat of fatal force can justify high levels of force in self-defence, even fatal force. By contrast, threats of non-fatal force may not necessarily be such as to justify a response which involves fatal force. Ultimately, it comes down to questions of fact in the particular case. The state of mind of D will be relevant; the court in *Palmer* did observe:

---

[16] See, generally, Law Commission *Partial Defences to Murder (Consultation Paper)* [2003] EWLC 173(9).
[17] *Lobell* [1957] 1 All ER 734.
[18] Law Commission *Partial Defences to Murder (Consultation Paper)* [2003] EWLC 173(9), at para 9.1.
[19] *Orwino* [1995] Crim LR 743; *Scarlett* [1993] 4 All ER 629.
[20] *Williams (Gladstone)* (1983) 78 Cr App R 71; *Beckford* [1987] 3 WLR 611.
[21] *Hatton* [2005] EWCA Crim 2951.
[22] [1971] AC 814.

'If there had been an attack so that defence is [reasonably[23]] necessary it will be recognised that a person defending himself cannot weigh to a nicety the exact measure of his necessary defensive action. If a jury thought in a moment of unexpected anguish a person attacked had only done what he had honestly and instinctively thought was necessary that would be the most potent evidence that only reasonable defensive action had been taken.'

The conclusion reached by the Law Commission in its consultation paper was as follows:[24]

'A jury which conscientiously applied such an approach would be slow to convict D where they were of the view that the acts in question were undertaken in self-defence and may have been an instinctive response to the perceived level of risk. It would only be possible for such a jury to convict if it was sure that the level of violence used instinctively was utterly disproportionate to the level of risk perceived by D.'

The Law Commission regarded this as an important factor diminishing the concern that the 'all or nothing' approach is too restrictive. Yet the generous approach is in reality a departure from a *strict* test the court itself set out in *Palmer* and has applied in other cases.

9.14 One such case was *Clegg*[25] where a fourth fatal shot fired by a soldier at a car could not objectively be held to be reasonable, because it was excessive; the speeding car passing through a checkpoint was already speeding away from the life-threatening danger that the soldier believed existed. There was no partial defence that would reduce the conduct from murder to manslaughter. Another was *Martin (Anthony)*.[26] Martin, whose farm had previously been burgled, was disturbed during the night by the noise of burglars. He armed himself with a pump-action shotgun. The prosecution alleged he lay in wait for the burglars. Without warning he discharged the gun three times wounding one in the legs and fatally shooting the other in the back. His argument that his conduct should be considered in the context of his mental state was, in respect of the defence of self-defence (but not in respect of diminished responsibility), rejected by the court.

Arguably, both *Clegg* and *Martin* are cases where the court considered the level of force to be such as to be totally disproportionate to the needs of self-defence. In *Martin* the court said that the jury could take into account the physical characteristics of D, suggesting that even an objective approach had to have some regard to context.[27] However, the rejection of submissions that for the purpose of self-defence, the court should consider medical evidence as to his state of mind and mental characteristics is entirely consistent with rejections of a subjective approach.

9.15 The Law Commission consultation paper, and, indeed, the provisions of s 76, should be viewed in the context of two earlier proposals for change. In 1980 the Criminal Law Revision Committee recommended that the defence of self-defence should reduce a charge from murder to manslaughter if at the time he honestly believed that the force used was reasonable, but was objectively excessive. A similar approach was taken by the Law Commission in its Draft Criminal Law Code. The change in the law made by s 76 does not do this. It maintains the 'all or nothing' approach. However, the main impetus for the change in the new Act is very much based on public opinion, and

---

[23] The words 'reasonable' no longer represents the law: see *Williams (Gladstone)* above.
[24] Law Commission *Partial Defences to Murder (Consultation Paper)* [2003] EWLC 173(9), at para 9.7.
[25] [1995] 1 AC 482.
[26] See **9.11**.
[27] But, see **9.13**.

the Government seeking to reassure the public that the criminal law will not engage if property owners reasonably defend themselves and their property. The changes followed a review in autumn 2007 'aimed at ensuring that those who seek to protect themselves, their loved ones and their homes, as well as other citizens, have confidence that the law is on their side'.[28] It was for that reason that what is now s 76 was inserted into the Bill during its passage. Prosecution policy has also reflected this attitude. A CPS spokesman observed in 2008[29] that 'the law protects the law-abiding, and the Director of Public Prosecutions is determined to ensure that those who use reasonable force in defending themselves will enjoy the full protection of the law'.

9.16 The provisions in s 76 apply where an issue arises as to whether a person charged with an offence (D) is entitled to rely on a defence within s 76(2) and the question arises whether the degree of force used by D against a person (V) was reasonable in the circumstances (s 76(1)). Section 76 does not change the nature of self-defence as an absolute defence: it remains an 'all or nothing' defence. Nor does s 76 change the first question that has to be asked, namely, is it reasonable to use force in self-defence (see **9.12**)? That is, as now, a subjective question, save only in the context of intoxication (s 76(4) and (5)).

Section 76(4) states that if D claims to have held a particular belief as regard the existence of any circumstances, the reasonableness of that belief is relevant to the question as to whether D in fact held it; if he did in fact genuinely hold it, D is entitled to reply on that whether or not it was mistaken, or, if it was, irrespective of whether the mistake is reasonable. This formulation has been criticised,[30] as over-complex, but arguably in reality it is not, if one focuses on its purpose. That is to determine what D believed, and does not really assist on the main question as to whether the response was reasonable. Section 76(5) prevents D from relying on a mistaken belief caused by voluntary intoxication. Again, that reflects existing law.

9.17 The changes in the law (if that is what they are) are in respect of the second question, namely, whether the levels of force used are reasonable. When in force, s 76(3) will require a court to decide the question whether the degree of force used by D is reasonable to be determined by reference to the circumstances as he believed them to be. In deciding that question, s 76(7) is relevant. The court must take into account the following factors, insofar as they are relevant to the facts of the case:

'(a) that a person acting for a legitimate purpose may not be able to weigh to a nicety the exact measure of any necessary action; and
(b) that evidence of a person's having only done what the person honestly and instinctively thought was necessary for a legitimate purpose constitutes strong evidence that only reasonable action was taken by that person for that purpose.'

This is, in effect, reducing the approach in *Palmer*[31] to statutory form. The effect of *Palmer* was that a jury should consider the levels of force understanding that D could not be expected nicely to weigh alternatives. As the Law Commission observed, it was only where the force used was totally disproportionate (objectively judged) to the situation honestly believed by D to exist was that force in self-defence was likely to be

---

[28] Jack Straw, Minister for Justice, 2006/2007, 1 October 2007. The changes were introduced at Report Stage.
[29] See (2008) 172 JP 123: no charges to be brought against a shopkeeper who fatally stabbed an armed robber, who died from a single stab wound.
[30] See AJT at (2008) 172 JP 281.
[31] See **9.13**.

held unlawful. However, as also noted above, the *Palmer* approach was not a strict rule of law, but rather an appropriate direction to a jury that a 'conscientious jury' would follow.

9.18 The effect of the change may therefore be regarded as clarification and confirmation of an approach that was in reality taken by the courts. It makes no significant real change in the law, but conveniently restates it. Cases will continue to turn on their particular facts as to what is objectively reasonable in the light of the judgments D has to make at the time. Even objective judgments have to be made in the light of the contexts in which the force in self-defence was used. It does not address the concerns some commentators[32] have about a gender bias, actual or perceived, in the way the test operates. What is clear is that the approach in *Palmer* is very much at the heart of this legislative response.

ABOLITION OF BLASPHEMY

9.19 One of the striking changes made by s 79 of the new Act is the abolition of the common law offence of blasphemy and blasphemous libel. This ancient common law offence, which protected Christianity (but not any other faith)[33] was largely a dead letter, inappropriate in a modern multi-faith society and probably, in 2008, in breach of ECHR. The Law Commission recommended its abolition as far back as 1985.[34] Yet this change was not even in the Bill as originally introduced into Parliament, but was one of many additions during its passage.

Blasphemy was in reality little used. The modern laws of incitement to religious hatred (see **9.4**) and other public order offences in reality provide effective legal processes to deal with the expression of religious comment which goes beyond legitimate criticism and comment.

INCITING THE COMMISSION OF A NUCLEAR OFFENCE

9.20 Section 75 and Sch 17 create new criminal offences, and extend existing ones under the Nuclear Material (Offences) Act 1983 (NM(O)A 1983). These changes which are necessary in order for the UK to ratify amendments made in 2005 to the Convention on the Physical Protection of Nuclear Material. The changes are intended to bring UK law into line with certain changes made by the Convention.[35] They are intended to be transitional changes until such time as the Serious Crime Act 2007 comes into force.

---

[32] See: Schneider 'Equal Rights to Trial for Women: Sex Bias in the Law' (1980) 15 Harvard Civil Rights-Civil Liberties Law Review 623; Taylor 'Provoked Reason in Men and Women: Heat of Passion Manslaughter and Imperfect Self-defence' (1986) 33 UCLA Law Rev 1679; McColgan 'In Defence of Battered Women who Kill' (1993) 13 Oxford Journal of Legal Studies 24.
[33] See *R v Metropolitan Stipendiary Magistrate, ex p Choudhury* [1991] 1 All ER 306.
[34] *Offences against Religion and Public Worship*, Law Com No 145 (1985). For case-law see *Whitehouse v Lemon* [1979] AC 617, and for comment on its recent history see Parpworth 'The Abolition of the Blasphemy Law' (2008) 172 JP 164.
[35] Maria Eagle, Parliamentary Under-Secretary of State for Justice, HC Committee, col 574 (27 November 2007). The following explanation relies on the explanation given by the Minister.

The Convention, which does not apply to military activities or facilities,[36] was concluded under the auspices of the International Atomic Energy Authority (IAEA) in 1980 with the UK signing the Convention in 1980. Some 130 or so states have signed the Convention. It was ratified in 1991, but only about 10 to 15 states have ratified it,[37] of which the UK is one. The Convention requires each state party to establish, implement and maintain an appropriate physical protection regime for civil nuclear material and facilities under its jurisdiction, with the aim of protecting against theft, recovering missing or stolen material, protecting material and facilities against sabotage and mitigating or minimising the radiological consequences of sabotage. It also provides for co-operation between states in the event of nuclear sabotage. It also incorporates a longer list of nuclear offences than the original.

A diplomatic conference of 2005 marked the end of a process initiated by calls for amendment of the convention from the IAEA director general in 1999 and given impetus by enhanced concern for nuclear security following the terrorist attacks in the US in 2001.

9.21 The provisions in the new Act (which excludes military activities)[38] create a new criminal offence, and also amend the list of 'Convention offences' in Sch 1 to the Terrorism Act 2000. Schedule 17, para 2 amends NM(O)A 1983 and creates a new offence by inserting therein a new s 11(1A). This provides that if:

'(a) a person, whatever his nationality, does outside the United Kingdom an act directed at a nuclear facility (which includes on civilian facilities and not facilities used for military purposes), or which interferes with the operation of such a facility;
(b) the act causes death, injury or damage resulting from the emission of ionising radiation or the release of radioactive material, and
(c) had he done that act in any part of the United Kingdom, it would have made him guilty of an offence under s 1(1)(a) or (b) of the 1983 Act,

the person shall in any part of the United Kingdom be guilty of such of the offences mentioned in s 1(1)(a) or (b) as he could have been convicted of if the acts were convicted in that part of the United Kingdom.'

The effect of this provision is to make the offences set out in **9.22** below extra-territorial. The penalties for misusing nuclear material are increased by a new s 1A to the NM(O)A 1983 (see 2008 Act, Sch 17, para 3).

This new offence is, breathtakingly wide in its scope, although, perhaps, few would argue at the need to have effective mechanisms to avoid problems of jurisdiction to avoid incompatible legal rules in addressing a clear potential problem. The offence has universal application. It can be prosecuted in any jurisdiction of the UK. Unusually, it can be committed by anyone anywhere, no matter where in the world the offence was committed. Nor does the alleged offender have to be a British national or resident. That clearly raises jurisdictional issues about which jurisdiction takes responsibility for the

---

[36] Whether in respect of the offences the matters relate to military facilities or activities is a matter determined conclusively by a certificate issued by the relevant Secretary of State: see NM(O)A 1983, s 3A inserted by Sch 17, para 5.
[37] Maria Eagle, HC Committee, col 574 (27 November 2007).
[38] See n 36 above.

trial of the offence. In an appropriate case the government would wait to see whether a prosecution was being undertaken in the jurisdiction where the event in question took place.[39]

9.22 The other offences dealt with by Sch 17 include: misusing nuclear material here or abroad, intending damage to the environment or being reckless about whether it will be caused (NM(O)A 1983, s 1B);[40] doing something outside the UK that involves moving nuclear material into or out of a state without lawful authority (NM(O)A 1983, s 1C); attacking a nuclear facility here or abroad intending that damage will be caused to the environment by radiation or to exposure to radiation, or being reckless about whether such damage will be caused; attacking a nuclear facility abroad and intentionally or recklessly causing death, injury or damage to property as a result of exposure to radiation; attacking a nuclear facility here or abroad intending that death, injury or property damage will be caused by exposure to radiation or being reckless about whether that is the outcome, even if no such injury or damage occurs. All of the latter offences are extended to extra-jurisdictional operation by the terms of s 1 of NM(O)A 1983, as extended by the new s 1(1A) (see **9.21**).

The scope of the changes is further increased by the creation of a new s 2 in NM(O)A 1983. It makes the receiving, holding or dealing with nuclear material a criminal offence if done with the intent to cause, or for others to cause, relevant injury or damage by means of that material, or being reckless as to that. Doing an act directed at a nuclear facility, intending to cause damage or injury, or being reckless falls within s 2(3) of NM(O)A 1983. The making of threats to cause relevant injury or damage, or damage to the environment, or threaten to obtain material for any of these purposes are each offences under s 2 (see NM(O)A 1983, s 2(3)–(7)). Furthermore, attempting, conspiring, inciting or aiding and abetting, counselling or procuring such offences is unlawful. In such cases it must be proved that the individual intended or believed that the offence would be committed (NM(O)A 1983, s 2(4)).

PENALTY FOR UNLAWFULLY OBTAINING PERSONAL DATA

9.23 Section 77 of the new Act increases the penalties for an offence under s 55 of the Data Protection Act 1998 (DPA 1998). That section creates the offence of unlawfully obtaining personal data. The penalty under s 60 of DPA 1998 was a fine.

In 2006 the Government consulted on increasing the penalties.[41] Despite concerns from some that the changes would have a 'chilling effect'[42] on investigative journalism, the Act raises the penalties to such period of imprisonment designated by order made under s 77(1). The maximum periods that may be designated are (in the case of summary conviction) 12 months and (following conviction on indictment) 2 years.

9.24 Following the concerns noted above, what is now s 78 was introduced. Section 55(2) of DPA 1998 contains four defences, relating to: (i) the disclosure, obtaining or procuring of data for the prevention or detection of crime; (ii) acting on

---

[39] Maria Eagle, HC Committee, col 578 (22 November 2007).
[40] Inserted by the 2008 Act, Sch 17, para 3.
[41] Department for Constitutional Affairs Consultation Paper CP 9/06 *Increasing penalties for deliberate and wilful misuse of personal data* (DCA, 2006).
[42] See Edward Garnier MP, HC Committee, col 409 (25 October 2007).

reasonable belief that the individual had the right to disclose the data; (iii) reasonable belief that the individual had consent to disclose the data; and (iv) in the particular circumstances the obtaining, disclosing or procuring was in the public interest.

Section 78 of the new Act inserts a fifth defence into s 55(2) of DPA 1998. This is that he acted for the special purposes, with a view to the publication by any person of any journalistic literary or artistic material, and in the reasonable belief that obtaining, disclosing or procuring was justified as being in the public interest. This permits a journalist to act on reasonable belief (as he or she can do in connection with civil liability under DPA 1998) as opposed to having to depend on an objective conclusion that he or she acted in the public interest. The anomaly is thus removed.

Chapter 10

APPEALS

SUMMARY

10.1 Part 3 of the new Act deals with appeals. It confers power on the Court of Appeal (Criminal Division) to dismiss an appeal despite the fact that the law has changed since the conviction under appeal. It amends the powers of the court on an appeal by the prosecution, and also the powers of the court in dealing with reviews of sentence on reference by the Attorney-General.

BACKGROUND[1]

10.2 The provisions remaining in the Act relating to appeals owe their origins to a consultation process during 2006 and 2007. In September 2006 the Office of Criminal Justice Reform published a consultation paper: *Quashing Convictions – Report of a Review by the Home Secretary, Lord Chancellor and Attorney General*.[2] The consultation was concerned that the Court of Appeal (Criminal Division) was required, under current law, to quash a conviction even if it was satisfied that the appellant was in fact guilty. This could occur because a conviction might be quashed not because the court had any real doubt about whether the defendant committed the offence charged, but because of procedural errors or misuse of power before or at the trial. The Auld Review in 1999[3] had identified this as an issue but did not make any recommendations.

The essential issue relates to the use of the courts' powers under s 2 of the Criminal Appeal Act 1968 (CAA 1968), which states that a conviction should be quashed if 'they think that the conviction is unsafe'. A series of cases developed divergent approaches as to the question of whether a conviction should be quashed where there had been major error in, or abuse of, the pre-trial or trial process,[4] or perhaps for other reasons not involving fault.[5] In *Mullen* the Court of Appeal quashed a conviction for pre-trial abuse of process despite the fact that it considered that the trial itself was fair. The appellant had been brought into the UK jurisdiction unlawfully. The court considered that,

---

[1] For background discussion in respect of the role and powers of the Court of Appeal see: O'Connor 'The Court of Appeal: Retrials and Tribulations' [1990] Crim LR 615; Spencer 'Does our Present Court of Appeal System Make Sense?' [2006] Crim LR 677.
[2] Available at www.homeoffice.gov.uk/documents/cons-2006-quashing/cons-2006-quashing-convictions2?view=Binary or www.cjsonline.gov.uk/downloads/application/pdf/quashing_convictions_consult.pdf.
[3] *Review of the Criminal Courts*.
[4] See *Chalkley* [1997] EWCA Crim 3416; *Rajcoomar* [1999] EWCA Crim 447; *Thomas* [1999] EWCA Crim 1266; *Mullen* [1999] EWCA Crim 278.
[5] See *B* [2003] EWCA Crim 319.

contrary to the approach taken in *Chalkley*,[6] a broad approach to the term 'unsafe' should be taken. In *Randall*,[7] Lord Bingham observed:

> 'It is not every departure from good practice which renders a trial unfair. But the right of a defendant to a fair trial is absolute. There will come a point when the departure from good practice is so gross, or so persistent or so prejudicial, or so irremediable that an appellant court will have no choice but to condemn a trial as unfair and quash a conviction as unsafe, however strong the grounds for believing the defendant to be guilty.'

Of course, the case-law shows that it is not every procedural error or abuse that leads a court to conclude that a conviction which is otherwise fair should be regarded as unsafe because of procedural error or abuse. Nonetheless the Government considered the position to be unsatisfactory. The law should not allow people to go free where they were convicted and the court is satisfied that they committed the offence.[8]

10.3 Responses to the consultation are to be found in the *Summary of Responses* published in October 2007.[9] They were overwhelmingly negative, because, apart from any other reason, it is only in exceptional cases that the court quashes the conviction of a plainly guilty individual.[10] Some respondents also were concerned about a possible violation of Art 6 of ECHR, right to a fair trial. Despite the doubts of many of the respondents, the Government pressed ahead with changes, albeit in a tentative spirit.[11] Its proposals, in what were originally clauses 26 and 27, were badly received in Parliament. They would have required the Court of Appeal to dismiss an appeal if it considered there was no reasonable doubt of guilt. Concessions were made that would have allowed a conviction to be quashed if it would seriously undermine the proper administration of justice to allow the conviction to stand. However, the combination of parliamentary hostility and time pressure on Parliament, due to an urgent need to achieve Royal Assent by May 2008[12] forced the Government to abandon these two flagship clauses designed to implement the principle that 'guilty' individuals should not have their convictions quashed.

However, the lesser changes which now form part of the Act were less controversial. It is those that are discussed below.

Powers to dismiss an appeal following references by the Criminal Cases Review Commission

10.4 Section 42 of the new Act inserts a new s 16C into CAA 1968. It came into force on 14 July 2008 (see **1.5**).

---

[6] [1997] EWCA Crim 3416.
[7] [2002] 1 WLR 2237; see also *Adroikov* [2005] EWCA Crim 470; *O'Hare* [2006] EWCA Crim 471; *Russell* [2006] EWCA Crim 470; *Davis, Ellis and others* [2006] EWCA Crim 1155, and now [2008] UKHL 36.
[8] Office of Criminal Justice Reform: *Quashing Convictions – Report of a Review by the Home Secretary, Lord Chancellor and Attorney General* (2006) at para 31.
[9] See www.cjsonline.gov.uk/downloads/application/pdf/Quashing%20Convictions%20Consultation%20 Response.pdf or www.homeoffice.gov.uk/documents/cons-2006-quashing/quashing-consultation-responses? view=Binary.
[10] *Summary of Responses to the Consultation Paper and Response of HM Government* (CJS, October 2007), p 4.
[11] Ibid, p 5.
[12] See Lord Hunt of Kings Heath, Parliamentary Under-Secretary of State, Minister of Justice, HL Committee, col 659 (27 February 2008).

Under CAA 1968, the power is given to the Criminal Cases Review Commission (CCRC or the Commission) to refer cases to the Court of Appeal. The criteria are, first, that there must be a real possibility that a conviction would not be upheld if a reference was made; secondly, the reason for this must be that an argument or evidence was not raised at trial or appeal; and finally, an appeal must have been heard or leave to appeal refused.

One problem the Commission faces is what to do where the law has changed since the date of conviction. A series of cases confirmed that the Court of Appeal was obliged to apply the law as it stood at the time of the second appeal following reference, not the old law, Lord Bingham in *Bentley*[13] stated:

> 'When between conviction and appeal there had been significant changes in the common law (as opposed to changes effected by statute) or in standards of fairness, the approach ... requires the court to apply legal rules and procedural criteria that were not and could not have been applied at the time.'

The position was often complicated, in the context of whether the Commission should make a reference given the traditional approach of the courts to refuse leave.[14] The Divisional Court in *R (on the application of the DPP) v Criminal Cases Review Commission*[15] suggested that the Commission should ignore any aspect of the law or practice of the court when deciding whether to make a reference. That view was rejected by the Court of Appeal in *Cottrell* and *Fletcher*.[16] That Court decided that, except where exceptional circumstances exist, a conviction should not normally be referred to the Court of Appeal on the basis of a change in the law, flagging up that further difficulties still remained unresolved, and should be resolved by statute. The new Act does just that.

10.5 The new s 16C sets out what the court should do if there is a reference before it. It may dismiss the appeal if:

(a) the only ground for allowing it would be that there has been a development in the law since the date of conviction, verdict or finding that is the subject of the appeal; and

(b) the condition in s 16C(3) is met.

That condition is that the court would not, had a reference been made, think it appropriate to give leave to appeal out of time.

The effect of the change is that the Court of Appeal is no longer obliged to consider references for the reason that there have been changes in the common law. It is a matter for its discretion, on the facts of the particular case. The clause was introduced in the light of the Divisional Court's ruling discussed above, and some considered that since the effect of that decision had been disapproved, *obiter*, by the Court of Appeal in *Cottrell* and *Fletcher* the clause was unnecessary and should be deleted.[17] However, that

---

[13] [2001] 1 Cr App R 307; see also *Ramzan and others* [2006] EWCA Crim 1974.
[14] See *Kansall (No 2)* [2001] EWCA Crim 260; *Kennedy* [2005] EWCA Crim 685; *Caley-Knowles and Jones* [2006] EWCA Crim 1611.
[15] [2007] 1 Cr App R 30.
[16] [2007] EWCA Crim 2016.
[17] See, eg, Lord Lloyd of Berwick, HL Committee, col 589 (27 February 2008).

view did not find favour with the Government: the provision was necessary to remove the difficulty of both the CCRC and the Court of Appeal.[18]

The effect of this is to make it more unlikely that the CCRC will refer cases to the Court of Appeal, because there is increased likelihood that the Court of Appeal will decline to take into account changes in the law since the date of conviction. The change does not prevent the Court from taking into account such changes, but it is the normal practice to decline to grant leave to appeal out of time in change-of-law cases. The condition created by s 16C(3) (see above) has, therefore, the effect of permitting the court, within its discretion, to dismiss an appeal whether leave was actually required or has received a reference from CCRC under the CAA 1998 even though an unsuccessful appeal has in the past already occurred. However, the tensions between the approaches of the CCRC and Court of Appeal, discussed above, will not completely disappear, because the Court still has the right to quash a conviction on the basis of change in the law. No guidance is given in the Act as to how the discretion preserved by s 42 is to be exercised. No doubt it will remain the case that the Court of Appeal will continue to look at change-of-law cases exceptionally, where there are compelling reasons in the interests of justice.

Appeals by prosecution

10.6 The Criminal Justice Act 2003 (CJA 2003) introduced the right of the prosecution to appeal against a ruling made by a judge on trial on indictment. This power, and the preconditions for its exercise are contained in s 58 of CJA 2003. The types of rulings envisaged to be within the s 58 power are what was described as 'terminating rulings', although CJA 2003 does not use that phrase anywhere. They include stays for abuse of process, successful arguments for *autrefois acquit* or *autrefois convict*, a successful submission of no case to answer, an adverse public interest immunity ruling, or a ruling that the facts alleged do not disclose an offence known to law.

The Court of Appeal has the power under s 61 of CJA 2003, to confirm, reverse or vary any ruling to which an appeal under s 58 relates.[19] It is that power that is changed by s 44 of the 2008 Act.

10.7 Section 44 amends s 61 of CJA 2003, by substituting a new provision for the pre-existing s 61(5). That pre-existing provision permitted the Court of Appeal to acquit the defendant, to refer the case back to the trial court for the proceedings to be resumed, or for a fresh trial to be commenced. It stated that the Court of Appeal may not make an order that the Crown Court proceedings be resumed, or that a fresh trial take place, unless it considered that it was necessary in the interests of justice to do so. Now, the revised provision says that the court may not make an order acquitting the defendant of the offence which is the subject of the ruling unless it considers that the defendant could not receive a fair trial if an order were made that the hearing be resumed, or should be the subject of a fair trial.

---

[18] Lord Davidson of Glen Clova, HL Committee, col 589 (27 February 2008).
[19] For guidance as to how these powers should be used, see *Clarke* [2007] EWCA Crim 2532; *Y* [2008] EWCA CA 10.

The change is made clearly in pursuance of the principle that where at all possible, a defendant should not be acquitted simply because of legal technicalities, issues or mistakes where it is possible to continue with trying the defendant for the offence charged.

Review of sentence on reference by Attorney-General

10.8   Section 46 of the new Act amends s 36 of CJA 1988. Section 36 deals with the power of a court to deal with an over-lenient sentence when it is referred to it. Concern has arisen about the fact that a court may take into account the fact that the defendant is being sentenced for a second time when determining the minimum term for a discretionary life sentence. This practice of allowing a 'double jeopardy discount', which hitherto has applied to all cases other than a mandatory life sentence, has had the effect that the court would not increase the sentence (if that was what it considered it appropriate to do) as much as it would otherwise do, because of the distress and anxiety of going through the process a second time.

The change made by the insertion of a new s 36(3A) and (3B) requires the Court of Appeal to disregard the fact that the individual is being sentenced for a second time. In 2003 the practice was prohibited for mandatory life sentences by s 272 of CJA 2003. The prohibition is now extended to discretionary life sentences and indeterminate sentences. The practical effect of the change may not be particularly significant. In *A-G's Reference (No 14 and 15 of 2006)*[20] the court stated that where an offender has a substantial part of a long determinate sentence, or a discretionary life sentence, the principle of double jeopardy has limited effect. Some discount was to be made,[21] but not much because the overall length of the sentence is not affected by the decision of the court. The main effect in reality may be to bring consistency of treatment between mandatory and discretionary non-determinate sentences.

Other changes

10.9   A range of other detailed changes are made by s 28 of, and Sch 8 to, the new Act. In summary, these are as follows:

- *Time for issue of certificates for fitness to appeal (Sch 8, para 2)* – increased to 28 days to mirror the period of bail available to a Crown Court judge under s 81 of the Supreme Court Act 1981.

- *Powers of Court of Appeal to re-sentence (Sch 8, para 6)* – following the quashing of a conviction, the Court of Appeal will now be able to re-sentence for any other offence which was passed on the same day, or treated by the court below as substantially one sentence. The Explanatory Notes that accompanied the Bill to the House of Lords give the example of where a conviction for an offence is quashed, and in respect of which an indeterminate sentence for public protection was given. If at the same time a sentence was passed for a determinate offence the level of seriousness would have been reflected in the tariff for the indeterminate term rather than in the determinate sentence. In future the Court will be able to reflect the true level of seriousness by re-sentencing for the other offence.

---

[20]   [2007] 1 All ER 718.
[21]   The range was typically 12% to 30%: see Lord Phillips CJ in *A-G's Reference (No 12 of 2001)* [2002] 2 Cr App R (S) 382, at para 59.

- *Interim hospital orders (Sch 8, para 7)* – extends and rationalises the powers of the Court of Appeal in respect of hospital orders.

- *Evidence (Sch 8, para 10)* – extends the powers of the Court of Appeal to compel the production of documents and compel the attendance of witnesses. The Court will now be able to compel both, at both an actual appeal and also an application for leave to appeal.

- *Powers of single judge (Sch 8, para 11-12)* – these are extended to allow grant of leave in certain interlocutory appeals relating to preparatory hearings under s 9 of CJA 1987 or s 35 of the Criminal Procedure and Investigations Act 1996. The power to issue directions which cannot be appealed is extended.

- *Detention of defendant pending appeal to Supreme Court (Sch 8, para 13)* – where the Court of Appeal allows an appeal but the prosecution successfully appeals to the Supreme Court. At the moment the Court has to automatically release the successful appellant. Under the amended provisions, the Court can provide for his continued detention or release on bail. Only if the appellant is released without bail will he be immune from being required to complete his period of detention should the prosecution succeed in the Supreme Court.

Chapter 11

SPECIAL IMMIGRATION STATUS

SUMMARY

11.1 Part 10 of the new Act introduces an additional category of immigration status. This new status will enable the Home Secretary to attach additional restrictive conditions to designated individuals. The Government intends that this new status will apply to foreign criminals who are not considered suitable to be granted discretionary leave to remain in the UK because of their own conduct in committing serious crimes.

The new status enables the Home Secretary to impose conditions on a 'designated person' in relation to residence, employment, and reporting to the police. By these means the Home Office Border Agency expects to be able to keep a close track on a designated person's whereabouts. In addition further conditions can also be attached in relation to support.

The special immigration status provisions had not been brought into effect as at the date of going to press.

BACKGROUND

11.2 The Government has admitted that the current immigration system, and the legal rules within which it operates, are very complex, which means that it is costly in both legal and administrative terms. This complexity also contributes to a lack of public confidence in the system as a whole, a fact acknowledged in June 2007 when the Home Office Border and Immigration Agency released a consultation paper *Simplifying Immigration Law: An initial consultation.*[1] This stated an aim to 'radically ... simplify immigration law, rules and guidance'.[2] With this objective of moving towards a simplification of immigration laws, the introduction of yet another category of immigration status to what is already an over-complicated system is one criticism of these new provisions.[3]

However, the Government considered it necessary to create a further immigration status as a result of the decision in *S v Secretary of State for the Home Department.*[4] The Court of Appeal held that the Secretary of State for the Home Department had acted unlawfully by creating rules changing the Asylum Policy Instructions (API). Without parliamentary authority, he created a new category of temporarily admitted persons,

---

[1] To be found at www.ukba.homeoffice.gov.uk/sitecontent/documents/aboutus/consultations/closedconsultations/simplification1stconsultation.
[2] At para 1.2.
[3] HC 2nd Reading, cols 84–85 (8 October 2007).
[4] [2006] EWCA Civ 1157.

which enabled him to grant 'temporary admission or temporary release' to individuals who ought otherwise to be granted discretionary leave to remain.

The new status is intended to give effect to a scheme similar to those introduced, unlawfully, by the Home Secretary, and successfully challenged in *S*.

11.3 The case itself concerned a number of Afghanis who hijacked an aircraft of the Afghan national airline from Kabul, and forced the pilot to fly to Stansted Airport. Criminal charges were brought against them in the UK for, inter alia, hijacking an aircraft. They were convicted after a retrial, although their convictions were set aside following the Court of Appeal's ruling that the trial judge had misdirected the jury on the defence of duress of circumstances. A retrial was not ordered because their sentences were either near completion or had been completed.

The respondents were then able to apply for asylum. The adjudicators ruled that the respondents did not qualify for refugee status because of the exclusion clause governed by Art 1F of the Refugee Convention 1951. This provision operates where there are serious reasons for considering that a person 'has committed a serious non-political crime outside the country of refuge prior to his admission to that country as a refugee'. Article 1F has the effect of preventing the grant of refugee status, after the individual's claim for refugee status has been assessed under Art 1A of the Refugee Convention. The decision, that the respondents did not qualify for asylum, was not contested by the applicants. However, the adjudicators did agree that, in the current climate, returning the respondents to Afghanistan would violate Art 3 of the ECHR (the right to be protected against inhuman or degrading treatment or torture). Again, this finding was not challenged by the Secretary of State.

11.4 The Secretary of State for the Home Department was then required to give effect to the adjudicators' ruling and apply to the respondents the existing published API. In 2003 the API stated that humanitarian protection was not available to persons, in respect of whom there were serious reasons for believing that they had committed a serious crime in the UK or overseas. However, if, despite their conduct, such persons were unable to be removed because of ECHR considerations, then they ought to be granted a period of discretionary leave.[5] The API also state that in that situation a period of 6 months should be granted.[6] As an excluded category those subject to discretionary leave are only eligible for settlement after 10 years. Even then, the grant of the right of settlement could still be denied in any event, if the Minister considered that it would not be conducive to the public good.[7]

Despite the fact that the respondents were entitled to a grant of discretionary leave the Home Secretary did not grant this to the respondents. Instead, in 2005 he changed the API. The changes gave him wider discretionary powers. The essence of the changes was that the Home Secretary would have the power to deny discretionary leave to those in the respondents' position where he felt it would be inappropriate to grant any leave. Instead, such persons would be placed on 'temporary admission or temporary release'.[8] The respondents were finally notified that they could remain, on the basis of temporary admission, more than 12 months after the adjudicators' decision.

---

[5] API, para 2.7.
[6] API, para 5.
[7] API, para 8.4.
[8] API, para 2.6, amended August 2005.

11.5 On an application for judicial review, Sullivan J ruled that the decision to keep the respondents on temporary admission was unlawful. The amendments made by the Home Secretary to the API were not within his powers to make unless approved by Parliament. The Court of Appeal agreed, concluding that it was not for the Home Secretary to confer a new status upon the respondents where it was not part of the statutory scheme.[9] The court specifically stated that it would be 'open to Parliament to confer power on the Secretary of State to introduce a regime similar to the regime he sought to introduce through the August 2005 Discretionary Leave API (so long as the arbitrary elements of it are removed)'.[10]

THE NEW IMMIGRATION STATUS

Is a new legal status necessary at all?

11.6 The purpose of the new special immigration status is to enable the Home Secretary to accommodate persons who he feels should be denied any discretionary leave on account of their criminal conduct. Such individuals are excluded from eligibility for settlement under the discretionary leave requirements, and are subject to stringent conditions. A failure to comply with those conditions amounts to a criminal offence.

The Immigration Law Practitioners' Association (ILPA) argues that the new special immigration status will be unnecessary when s 16 of the UK Borders Act 2007 comes into force.[11] The relevant part of s 16 states:

> 'After section 3(1)(c)(iii) of the Immigration Act 1971 (limited leave to enter or remain: conditions) insert—
>
> "(iv) a condition requiring him to report to an immigration officer or the Secretary of State; and
> (v) a condition about residence."'

This provision gives the Home Secretary powers to place restrictions on those with discretionary leave, so as to ensure that the immigration service can maintain contact with individuals who may have committed serious crimes, or who may pose a threat to the UK. However, the Government clearly considered that it was necessary to create further discretionary powers to enable the Home Secretary to attach even more onerous conditions to an individual who he thinks is a foreign criminal. It certainly does 'send a clear signal that foreign criminals and terrorists cannot expect to secure a settled status in this country'.[12]

11.7 Until the new immigration status is brought into effect, individuals who successfully establish that their removal from the UK would violate Art 3 of ECHR (because they would face a real risk of torture, inhuman or degrading treatment or punishment upon removal) are granted 6 months' discretionary leave. This can be renewed for periods not exceeding 6 months. If the Art 3 considerations in relation to

---

[9] See *S v Secretary of State for the Home Department* [2006] EWCA Civ 1157, at para 46.
[10] Ibid, at para 47.
[11] See the ILPA website at www.ilpa.org.uk.
[12] Criminal Justice and Immigration Bill Overarching Regulatory Impact Assessment (Ministry of Justice, 2007), p 14, available at: www.justice.gov.uk/docs/reg-impact-assess-june07.pdf.

the individual's case change, and thus no Art 3 consideration prevents removal, then removal can take place. However, whilst the individual is here on the basis of discretionary leave, he or she is entitled to take paid employment and access welfare services.[13] However, the new status created by the 2008 Act will offer an alternative to the grant of discretionary leave in cases where the individual is a foreign criminal. Paid employment and access to welfare benefits will not be permitted or available, despite the fact that the UK Borders Act 2007 would permit the imposition of limitation, and permit regulation by condition.

The justification for the creation of this new status is so that the category of individuals to which it applies can be denied discretionary leave to remain. By virtue of s 132(4)(b) such individuals may not be granted temporary admission to the UK, because of their own criminal conduct. In addition, this new status aims to attach greater conditions than is currently applied to grants of discretionary leave. Clearly, these will impact on a designated person's private and family life. If they do, then, under Art 8(2), such conditions must be prescribed by law and necessary in the interests of national security, public safety or for the prevention of disorder and crime. The conditions that can be attached to this new status (under s 135) will enable the Government to monitor serious foreign criminals who are unable to be removed on human rights grounds. Arguably, the creation of this new status is not necessary for the legitimate aims it is seeking to achieve, because, as already noted,[14] existing legislative powers exist that can be used to achieve the aims of the Government. Section 16 of the UK Borders Act 2007 enables the Home Secretary to attach to a grant of discretionary leave restrictions to residence and regular reporting to immigration officials. These are clearly intended to improve monitoring of individuals, where that is considered necessary. The new restrictive status created by the 2008 Act gives greater discretionary power to the Home Secretary or an immigration officer who will be able to also add conditions in relation to employment and electronic monitoring under s 36 of the Asylum and Immigration (Treatment of Claimants, etc) Act 2004. To justify such onerous measures, the threat to national security and public safety ought to be great. However, when one considers the wide definition of the term 'foreign criminal' (as defined by s 131) and also the fact that the new special immigration status can attach to family members of a designated foreign criminal, it is by no means certain that the new provisions will always be Convention compliant. It is debatable whether, given their potentially far-reaching ambit, the conditions that can be imposed are necessary in a democratic society and proportionate to a legitimate aim.

Special immigration status – the preconditions

11.8 Section 130 of the new Act gives to the Home Secretary the power to designate a person with the new special immigration status, where he or she satisfies one of the relevant preconditions. The individual does not have to satisfy both preconditions.

The first condition is that the individual is a 'foreign criminal' (s 130(2)(a)) and would be liable to deportation if the provisions of s 6 of the Human Rights Act 1998 (HRA 1998) did not apply (s 130(2)(b)). Section 6 of HRA 1998 requires a public authority to act in accordance with rights under ECHR (s 130(2)(b)). Clearly, the Home Secretary is a

---

[13] The API are available at: www.ind.homeoffice.gov.uk/sitecontent/documents/policyandlaw/asylumpolicyinstructions.

[14] See **11.6**.

'public authority'. Thus, the 'foreign criminal' cannot be deported if the deportation would infringe Art 3 of the Convention because of the threat of torture that the foreign criminal would face if deported.

The second condition is that the person is a member of the family of a person who satisfies the first condition (s 130(3)).

The first precondition for the new status – 'foreign criminal'

11.9 A 'foreign criminal' is defined by s 131. The individual concerned must not be a British citizen. Section 1 of the British Nationality Act 1981 provides British citizenship to people born in the UK, and at the time of birth at least one parent is a British citizen or settled in the UK. A British citizen has a right of abode in the UK and clearly is not subject to immigration controls.

The individual must also satisfy one of the three conditions contained in s 132(2), (3) or (4). The use of the word 'any' in s 131(2)(b) confirms that only one of these conditions need to be satisfied.

Condition 1 (2008 Act, s 131(2))

11.10 The first condition in s 131(2) is that the designated person falls under s 72(2)(a) and (b) or (3)(a)–(c) of the Nationality, Immigration and Asylum Act 2002 (NIAA 2002). Both sections state that there is a presumption that 'a person shall be presumed to have been convicted by a final judgment of a particularly serious crime and to constitute a danger to the community of the UK' if, under s 72(2), he has been convicted in the UK and sentenced to a term of imprisonment of 2 years or more, or if, under s 72(3), he has been convicted outside the UK with such a sentence.

The scope of the new status depends on the scope of s 72; if that latter section is too wide, or contains insufficient safeguards, then the provisions in the 2008 Act are also too wide and lacking in safeguards. If s 72 is liable to challenge under international treaty provisions, then so too is the new status under the 2008 Act.

Section 131 cross-references to s 72 of NIAA 2002. The reason s 72 was passed was to give effect in English law to Art 33 of the Refugee Convention. Article 33(1) prohibits the expulsion or return of a refugee to their country of origin where their life or freedom would be threatened on account of their race, religion, nationality or membership of a particular social group or political opinion. This is termed 'non-refoulement' and entitles any individual to make a claim for asylum. However, Art 33(2) relieves the state of this non-refoulement obligation where there are reasonable grounds for considering the refugee to be a risk to national security or, following conviction for a particularly serious crime, is a risk to the indigenous community. It does not remove all of the other protections within the Convention, only that of non-refoulement. The non-refoulement requirement cannot be denied to a person simply because he or she has a criminal conviction for a particularly serious crime.[15] The denial of non-refoulement must be proportionate to the risk to national security or to the seriousness of the crime. Goodwin-Gill observes:[16]

---

[15] See G S Goodwin-Gill *The Refugee in International Law* (OUP, 1996), p 140.
[16] Ibid.

'The offence in question and the perceived threat to the community would need to be extremely grave if danger to the life of the refugee were to be disregarded, although a less serious offence and a lesser threat might justify the return of an individual likely to face only some harassment or discrimination.'

Section 72 of NIAA 2002 incorporates Art 33(2) into domestic legislation. Part 4 of NIAA 2002 creates a power to detain and remove a 'serious criminal'. Section 72 defines 'serious criminal', the establishment of which will lead to the issuing of a deportation order. In short, a 'foreign criminal' under this first precondition in the 2008 Act is a 'serious criminal' under s 72. The decision that the individual is a 'serious criminal' has to be taken before any consideration of 'foreign criminal' applies. Note that for the special immigration status to be granted under the new legislation it is necessary to be a foreign criminal subject to deportation and therefore the consideration of whether the individual is a foreign criminal will have taken place prior to the decision to designate.

As noted above, Art 33(2) of the Refugee Convention requires states to apply proportionality when considering whether an individual constitutes a particularly serious threat to the host state's community. However, it is by no means clear that this concept is inherent in s 72 itself. One commentator[17] points out that s 72 does not in its terms incorporate this concept of proportionality. If s 72 is deficient in that way, then so is s 131 of the new Act.

11.11 As already noted, there is a presumption that an individual who is sentenced to a minimum term of 2 years' imprisonment following conviction in the UK is a serious criminal. So, too, in respect of convictions outside the UK for a similar offence which would carry a 2-year custodial term if the individual was convicted of an equivalent offence in the UK. However, under s 131(5) there is an element of proportionality incorporated by s 72(6), which provides that the presumption that a person is a serious criminal is rebuttable. The grounds on which rebuttal of the presumption can occur are contained in s 72(7)[18] and s 72(8). However, these are specifically excluded from applying in the case of this precondition (1) (and also precondition (2) – see **11.12**). That in itself raises the prospect that the application of the new status by reason of this precondition potentially is in breach of the Convention. However, unlike the terms of the ECHR, the Refugee Convention is not directly enforceable in English law.

The Joint Council for the Welfare of Immigrants (JCWI)[19] raised a concern about the impact of s 72 and therefore the wide ambit it will give the Home Secretary to designate a person with the new special immigration status. It pointed out that the effect of s 72 is that of an exclusion clause, in that it prevents a claim for refugee status in respect of an individual who has committed a serious crime and is considered to constitute a danger to the community. In their opinion there is no proportionality assessment to be made under s 72, but instead an automatic presumption. The crimes do not need to be particularly serious, nor does the danger posed to the community need to be 'very serious'.[20] Its concern that the effect of s 72 and the relevant Order[21] is incompatible with the Refugee Convention is shared by the Joint Committee on Human Rights which

---

[17] G Clayton *Textbook on Immigration and Asylum Law* (OUP, 2nd edn, 2006), p 501.
[18] Under s 72(7) the presumption will not apply whist a conviction or sentence is pending or could be brought.
[19] Joint Council for the Welfare of Immigrants, Criminal Justice and Immigration Bill Parliamentary Briefing, HC 2nd Reading (8 October 2007), to be found at www.jcwi.org.uk/news/news.html.
[20] Ibid.
[21] The Nationality, Immigration and Asylum Act 2002 (Specification of Particularly Serious Crimes) Order 2004, SI 2004/1910.

felt that the inclusion of offences that are not particularly serious crimes made the Order unlawful and expressed doubts as to the compatibility of s 72 with the Convention.[22]

Where the presumption is successfully rebutted, the individual is entitled to the protection of refoulement, and to have his or her asylum claim considered. Such a claim could lead to refugee status. Thus the person would clearly not be subject to a deportation order, and thus not potentially subject to designation under these provisions. Alternatively, the same conclusion can be reached by the simple logic that if the individual is not a serious criminal (because the presumption in s 72 has been rebutted) he or she is not a foreign criminal within the meaning of this first precondition.

Condition 2 (2008 Act, s 131(3))

11.12 The second condition in s 131(3) applies where a person has been convicted (either within or outside the UK) of a crime specified by an order made by the Secretary of State under s 72(4)(a) of NIAA 2002. The Nationality, Immigration and Asylum Act 2002 (Specification of Particularly Serious Crimes) Order 2004, specifies 183 crimes. The list of specified crimes that are covered by s 72 is far-ranging, from particularly serious crimes to less serious crimes. Under s 131(3)(b) the convicted person must also have been sentenced to a term of imprisonment. The section does not require a term of imprisonment to be of any particular minimum length. This raises concerns that the designation under the new status, and its onerous restrictions that may impair daily life, can be imposed where an individual is 'imprisoned to any term of imprisonment however short'.[23]

Section 131(3)(b) specifies that the person under this condition must have been sentenced to a 'period of imprisonment'. Under s 137(6) the period of imprisonment is to be construed in accordance with s 72(11)(b)(i) and (ii) (see above). This means that individuals who receive a suspended sentence will not be viewed as being sentenced to a period of imprisonment unless at least 2 years are not suspended. Persons who are detained in an institution other than a prison such as a young offenders institute or hospital will be considered to have been sentenced to a period of imprisonment.

Interestingly, under s 131(5) the presumption in relation to conditions 1 and 2 are not rebuttable as it states that the rebuttal of presumption available under s 72(6) of NIAA 2002 has no effect. This removes the potential to apply a proportionality exercise when considering whether to designate the individual. Section 131(6) allows an individual to be designated with special immigration status where a criminal appeal is pending or could be brought.

Condition 3 (2008 Act, s 131(4))

11.13 The third condition in s 131(4) relates to where a person is excluded from refugee status because of the protections provided by the Refugee Convention by virtue of Art 1F. The purpose of Art 1F is to exclude a person from the protection of the Refugee Convention where his or her acts have caused the circumstances that create refugee

---

[22] House of Commons Joint Committee on Human Rights, The Nationality Immigration and Asylum Act 2002 (specification of Particularly Serious Crimes Order 2004: Joint Committee 2003/2004, 22nd Report, p 16.
[23] ILPA, *Memorandum of Evidence to Public Bill Committee*, available at www.ilpa.org.uk, at para 22.

flows. In recent years the use of this exclusion has increased in the UK, however, the United Nations High Commissioner for Refugees (UNHCR) has issued guidelines (UNHCR 2003 Guidelines) on the application of exclusion clauses.[24]

The exclusion operates in three situations. These are where there are serious reasons for considering that a person has committed:

(a) a crime against peace, a war crime, or crime against humanity as defined in international instruments;

(b) a serious non-political crime outside the country of refuge prior to admission to that country as a refugee; and

(c) acts contrary to purpose and principles of the UN.

Art 1F(a): Crimes against peace, etc

This category is used less frequently than the other two. There is little UK case-law available on this issue, but the UNHCR 2003 Guidelines provide for the interpretation of these crimes.[25] These guidelines refer to several international instruments for interpretation. Article 6 of the Charter of the International Military Tribunal (the London Charter) defines a crime against peace as 'planning, preparation, initiation or waging of a war of aggression, or a war in violation of international treaties, agreements or assurances'. The UNHCR 2003 Guidelines state that war crimes 'can be committed in both international and non-international armed conflicts. The content of the crimes depends on the nature of the conflict. War crimes cover such acts as wilful killing and torture of civilians, launching indiscriminate attacks on civilians, and wilfully depriving a civilian or a prisoner of war of the rights of fair and regular trial'.[26]

Crimes against humanity are acts that form a 'systematic attack directed against the civilian population' such as genocide or rape. It is not enough that there be only one isolated incident.[27]

Art 1F(b): Serious non-political crimes

The second exclusion under Art 1F(b) has been used more frequently in UK case-law than the other two categories. It only applies to serious acts that took place outside the host state. Case-law in this area has tended to widen the meaning of serious non-political crime. In *T v Secretary of State for the Home Department*[28] the House of Lords followed the approach taken in the UNHCR Handbook[29] that, for the purposes of Art 1F, a serious crime 'must be a capital crime or a very grave punishable act'.[30] The

---

[24] *Guidelines on International Protection: Application of the Exclusion Clauses: Article 1F of the 1951 Convention relating to the Status of Refugees* (UNHCR, 4 September 2003), available at www.unhcr.org/publ/PUBL/3f7d48514.pdf.
[25] Ibid, at paras 10–13.
[26] Ibid, at para 12.
[27] For further discussion see G Clayton *Textbook on Immigration and Asylum Law* (OUP, 2nd edn, 2006), pp 491–492.
[28] [1996] 2 All ER 865.
[29] Handbook on Procedures and Criteria for Determining Refugee Status under the 1951 Convention and the 1967 Protocol relating to the Status of Refugees, HCR/IP/4/Eng/REV.1 Reedited, Geneva, January 1992, UNHCR 1979 , paras 151–161. This is now superseded by the UNHCR 2003 Guidelines.
[30] Ibid, at para 155.

UNHCR 2003 Guidelines specifically state that serious offences include murder, rape and armed robbery but exclude theft (para 14). To determine whether the crime is of a political nature the court looks at whether there is a sufficient link between the desired political purpose and the criminal act carried out. Lord Lloyd considered that a political crime must be committed for a political purpose and that there must be a 'sufficiently close and direct link between the crime and the alleged political purpose. In determining whether such a link exists, the court will bear in mind the means used to achieve the political end, and will have particular regard to whether the crime was aimed at a military or governmental target, on the one hand, or a civilian target on the other, and in either event whether it was likely to involve the indiscriminate killing or injuring of members of the public'.[31] The real difficulty in the interpretation of the phrase 'non-political' occurs when an individual's acts are termed 'terrorist'.

Although there is no international definition of the term 'terrorism', s 1 of the Terrorism Act 2000 (TA 2000) provides a UK definition. Section 1 states that 'terrorism' means the use or threat of action where it:

'(a) involves serious violence against a person,
(b) involves serious damage to property,
(c) endangers a person's life, other than that of the person committing the action,
(d) creates a serious risk to the health or safety of the public or a section of the public, or
(e) is designed seriously to interfere with or seriously to disrupt an electronic system.'

It also includes the use or threat of violence which is designed to influence the government or to intimidate the public or a section of the public, and where the use or threat is made for the purpose of advancing a political, religious or ideological cause.

This definition of terrorism invariably links terrorism to a certain purpose including political. Where a crime is very serious, such as murder or rape, it will outweigh a purported political purpose for it.[32] This is clear from the UNHCR 2003 Guidelines that state:[33]

'Where no clear link exists between the crime and its alleged political objective or when the act in question is disproportionate to the alleged political objective, non-political motives are predominant.'

However, the JCWI point out that s 1 of TA 2000 'includes actions that could be considered to be legitimate political activities within a democratic state or indeed a non democratic state, and actions that do not attack the very basis for the international community's coexistence'.[34] In this sense the UK's interpretation of Art 1F goes beyond the spirit of the Refugee Convention.

Art 1F(c): Acts contrary to the purposes and principles of the UN

According to the UNHCR 2003 Guidelines this category ought to be read narrowly, and should only be applied in rare extreme circumstances, because the scope of its terms are broad and therefore unclear (para 17). However, the UK judiciary's response has been to

---

[31] *T v Secretary of State for the Home Department* [1996] 2 All ER 865, at 787.
[32] For a full discussion of the case-law in this area see G Clayton *Textbook on Immigration and Asylum Law* (OUP, 2nd edn, 2006), ch 14.
[33] UNHCR 2003 Guidelines, at para 15. This is in line with para 152 of the UNHCR Handbook.
[34] Ibid.

adopt a wider approach.[35] The courts have ruled that acts that come within s 1 of TA 2000 come within Art 1F(c), as the UN condemns terrorism. Section 54 of the Immigration, Asylum and Nationality Act 2006 (IANA 2006) seeks to incorporate this wide interpretation of Art 1F(c) into domestic legislation.[36]

The legislation appears to reject the UNHCR's view that Art 1F(c) should only be 'triggered in extreme circumstances by activity which attacks the very basis of the international community's coexistence. *Such activity must have an international dimension'*.[37] As noted above, s 1 of TA 2000 does not limit its definition to 'international terrorism'. This may mean that the basis adopted by the UK at judicial and executive levels to determine whether or not an individual is a foreign criminal for the purposes of s 131(4) is not in line with the Refugee Convention. Where a wider interpretation of Art 1F(c) is applied, such as that in s 54 of IANA 2006, it could be said that the subsequent designation of the individual is contrary to the Refugee Convention and would be curtailed by s 130(5)(a). The concern of the ILPA is that some individuals can potentially fall within the ambit of the special immigration framework where they 'have been wrongly excluded from the Refugee Convention due to inappropriate and unlawful interpretations of that Convention introduced by UK domestic law; and include individuals who have been convicted of relatively minor offences ... whether or not there is any reason to think they may re-offend'.[38]

Under condition 3, s 131(4) of the 2008 Act is not referred to. Given that s 54 of IANA 2006 has yet to come into force this perhaps is unsurprising.

The second precondition for the new status – 'family member' (2008 Act, s 130(3))

11.14 The second precondition to designation of special immigration status is controversial. Section 130(3) states that where 'the person is a member of the family of a person who satisfies Condition 1' (see **11.10**) designation may occur. By virtue of s 130(4) it may only be attached to family members who do not have the right of abode in the UK. Section 1(1) of the Immigration Act 1971 (IA 1971) explains that the right of abode means the person has the right to enter the UK 'without let or hindrance'.[39] In accordance with s 137(4) the right of abode has the meaning given by s 2 of IA 1971. Section 132(2)(a) expressly states that the person, once designated, is subject to immigration control. The term 'family' bears the same meaning as set out in s 5(4) of IA

---

[35] See *KK (Article 1F(c)), Turkey* [2004] UKIAT 00101 and *AA (Palestine)* [2005] UKIAT 00104 ILU, Vol 8, no 12.

[36] IANA 2006, s 54: '(1) In the construction and application of Article 1(F)(c) of the Refugee Convention the reference to acts contrary to the purposes and principles of the United Nations shall be taken as including, in particular—
(a) acts of committing, preparing or instigating terrorism (whether or not the acts amount to an actual or inchoate offence), and
(b) acts of encouraging or inducing others to commit, prepare or instigate terrorism (whether or not the acts amount to an actual or inchoate offence).
(2) In this section—
"the Refugee Convention" means the Convention relating to the Status of Refugees done at Geneva on 28th July 1951, and
"terrorism" has the meaning given by section 1 of the Terrorism Act 2000.'

[37] UNHCR 2003 Guidelines, at para 17, emphasis added.

[38] ILPA, *Memorandum of Evidence to Public Bill Committee*, at para 44.

[39] See G Clayton *Textbook on Immigration and Asylum Law* (OUP, 2nd edn, 2006), ch 2 for the history and development of nationality and the right of abode.

1971. Section 5(4) of IA 1971 states that for the purposes of deportation the following shall be those who are regarded as belonging to another person's family:

'(a) Where that other person is a man, his wife and his or her children under the age of eighteen; and
(b) Where that other person is a woman, her children under the age of eighteen.

And ... an adopted child, whether legally adopted or not, may be treated as the child of the adopter and, if legally adopted, shall be regarded as the child only of the adopter; an illegitimate child (subject to the foregoing rule as to adoptions) shall be regarded as the child of the mother; and "wife" includes each of two or more wives.'

The inclusion of family members in the new legislation has been attacked for being inappropriate and unnecessary for the protection of the community against crime. One Member of Parliament was concerned in particular that designation of family members would restrict 'the activities, chances and income of children ... in their growing independence'.[40] Another concern that arises over the Secretary of State's ability to designate family members is that the special status (the very reason for which is to closely monitor foreign criminals) may be attached to those who have not participated in criminal activity. These measures could potentially violate Art 8 of ECHR (right to respect for private and family life, etc). Although the measures might be for the pursuit of a legitimate aim, such as the interests of national security or public safety, designation of a person who has not been shown to have committed any criminal conduct would be difficult to justify as necessary in a democratic society. The ILPA also pointed out that imposing severe restrictions that impact upon a person's 'capacity to engage in normal activities and conduct a normal life would itself be a violation of Art 8'.[41] However, the Government responded that it is the policy of the Home Office Border Agency that an application for leave as a dependent of another person relies on the outcome of the principal applicant's success.[42] A family member is entitled to apply for leave in their own right. However, that does not explain why this second precondition is an alternative precondition and not one consequent upon the designation of another (on whom this individual is dependent).

Another reason provided for the addition of family members to the new special immigration status framework is that it may 'prevent a foreign criminal from establishing links with this country which might constitute an additional obstacle to his eventual deportation'.[43] Arguably, even where the family member is not subject to the special immigration status themselves, they will be affected by the status attaching to the designated person. The exclusion from employment and other restrictive conditions that can be attached to the new status by virtue of s 132, which includes limits on ordinary welfare, will cause financial strain to the family. They may be stigmatised given that the support that they may receive can be in the form of vouchers (s 134(4)) and they will also be under strain from the indefinite nature of the status.[44] In addition failure to comply with any of the conditions attached to the special status is a criminal offence

---

[40] Harry Cohen, HC Committee, col 637 (27 November 2007). See Research Paper 07/93, Criminal Justice and Immigration Bill: Committee Stage Report: Bill 1 of 2007-08 (House of Commons Library, 2007), p 29 and 30, available at www.parliament.uk/commons/lib/research/rp2007/rp07-093.pdf.
[41] ILPA, *Memorandum of Evidence to Public Bill Committee*, at para 18.
[42] See Research Paper 07/93, p 29 and 30.
[43] Ibid.
[44] ILPA, *Memorandum of Evidence to Public Bill Committee*, at para.

under s 133(5). The JCWI have expressed concerns that the special immigration status and its conditions will put strain on previously law abiding individuals economically and further criminalises immigrants.[45]

The limits on designation (2008 Act, s 130(4), (5)(a) and (b))

11.15 The limits on designation are contained in s 130(4)and (5). Designation cannot be made in respect of a person who has the right of abode in the UK. Those with the right of abode are not subject to immigration control and therefore have the right to enter the UK 'with or without hindrance' (IA 1971, s1(1)). Section 2 of IA 1971 (as amended)[46] provides the right of abode to British citizens and Commonwealth citizens who, immediately before the commencement of the British Nationality Act 1981, had a right of abode in the UK under the previous s 2.

The second limitation on the power of the Home Secretary to designate a person with the new special immigration status is contained in s 130(5). Designation is not permitted where the Secretary of State thinks that the effect of the designation would breach the Refugee Convention (s 130(5)(a)) or the individual's rights under the Community treaties (s 130(5)(b)). Section 130(5)(a) requires the Secretary of State to refrain from designating a person to this new status where he 'thinks' there may be a breach of the UK's obligations under the Refugee Convention. The term 'thinks' is remarkably broad and seemingly completely subjective. It suggests that provided the Secretary of State acts in good faith his mental state cannot be challenged. Whilst, of course, this does not matter if the individual is given the benefit of the doubt, this wholly subjective test *does* matter if the Secretary of State, honestly but wrongly, concludes he does not consider that there may be a breach of the Convention. It is unclear whether this was in fact the intention of the Government, which clarified to the Joint Committee that the Secretary of State's designation would be unlawful if, *in the opinion of a court,* the effect of designation would breach the UK's obligations under the Convention,[47] however, that is not what the section says.

11.16 Under the Refugee Convention proviso, it seems that it would be difficult for an individual to prove that their rights have been breached given the wide interpretation that the UK courts have given to the exclusion clauses. Therefore, there is significantly less possibility that an EEA national will be subject to designation, because of the rights granted to them under European free movement laws.[48] One minister stated that EEA nationals cannot be designated[49] because the Secretary of State is not able to designate a person where it would amount to a breach of the rights granted under the Community treaties. Currently the public policy exception to the freedom of movement rights for EU workers are governed by Directive 2004/38 in force in April 2006 and implemented in the Immigration (European Economic Area) Regulations 2006.[50] These public policy grounds include public health and security and where applicable can allow a state to refuse entry or provide grounds for deportation.

Article 27.2 of the Directive provides:

---

[45] JCWI, Criminal Justice and Immigration Bill Parliamentary Briefing, HC 2nd Reading (8 October 2007).
[46] By the British Nationality Act 1981.
[47] Joint Committee 2007/2008, 5th Report at para 1.125.
[48] EEA nationals include EU nationals and nationals of Iceland, Liechtenstein and Norway.
[49] See Research Paper 07/93, p 31.
[50] SI 2006/1003.

'Measures taken on grounds of public policy or public security shall comply with the principle of proportionality and shall be based exclusively on the personal conduct of the individual concerned. Previous criminal convictions shall not in themselves constitute grounds for taking such measures.'

This Directive differs greatly from the conditions that establish the meaning of a 'foreign criminal' under s 131 of the new Act. As discussed above,[51] conditions 1 and 2 under s 131(2) and (3) do not promote a test of proportionality in determining whether a person is a 'foreign criminal' for the purpose of designation. The Directive on the other hand does require proportionality, and this is evident where the issue of personal conduct is concerned. Article 27.2 continues:

'The personal conduct of the individual concerned must represent a genuine, present and sufficiently serious threat affecting one of the fundamental interests of society. Justifications that are isolated from the particulars of the case or that rely on considerations of general prevention shall not be accepted.'

Clearly it might arise that an EEA national could be designated with the new status where their personal conduct posed a specific and sufficiently serious affect on a fundamental interest of society such to justify designation. However, at the same time there would also be the fact that deportation was not possible on account of Art 3 of ECHR considerations, which are unlikely to occur in the case of EU nationals given that all the member states are signatories to the ECHR. This new special immigration status therefore further creates the impression that some 'foreign nationals' are more 'foreign' than others and can be dealt with more severely. This may give rise to questions of discrimination under Art 14 of ECHR in conjunction with Art 8 or alternatively Art 1 of Protocol 1 (right to property).

Right of appeal

11.17 There is no right to appeal against the designation of a person contained in the Act. Judicial review remains an option, because designation is clearly an administrative decision. Unlawfulness and arbitrary decision making may be found where it can be established that the Secretary of State has breached an individual's rights either under the Refugee Convention or the Community Treaties. The decision to exclude a right of appeal against designation, however, emphasises the great discretionary power of the executive in the area of immigration law and policy. The extent to which the courts will be willing to interfere with the exercise of this discretion may also be a matter of concern.[52]

Effect of designation

11.18 Section 132(1) states that a designated person does not have leave to enter or remain in the UK, and are subject to immigration control (s 132(2)(a)). They are not to be treated as an asylum seeker (s 132(2)(b)) or a former asylum seeker (s 132(2)(c)), after all they have already had their asylum applications determined, and they are not in the UK in breach of immigration laws. Section 132(3) refers to the government's desire to prevent those who are suitable for designation from any future settlement rights. Under this section it is clear that any period of time spent in the UK as a designated person will

---

[51] See **11.11**.
[52] See some of the issues discussed at length in *Huang* v *Secretary of State for the Home Department* [2007] UKHL 11, [2007] 2 AC 167, [2007] 4 All ER 15.

not be considered for the purposes of nationality regardless of the fact that they are present in the UK and not in breach of immigration laws. It is clearly established that a person with special immigration status will not have discretionary leave under s 132(4)(a) or temporary admission under s 132(4)(b).

Conditions (2008 Act, s 133)

11.19 A designated person will receive a written notice detailing the conditions imposed upon them by either a Secretary of State or immigration officer. What these conditions can relate to is defined by s 133(2): there can be residence, employment, and reporting restrictions. Therefore, designation goes further than existing legislation because it seeks to limit the right to work, a limitation not included in the UK Borders Act 2007. The use of the term 'relates to' suggests the powers of the Secretary of State are 'exceptionally wide'. The ILPA have pointed out that this will allow for conditions akin to those attached to control orders under s 1(4) of the Prevention of Terrorism Act 2005 to be used.[53] However, where the conditions are restrictive upon the designated person's liberty they may fall foul of Art 5 of ECHR (the right to liberty and security of persons), although deprivation of liberty can be justified under Art 5(1)(f) where the detention is of a person against whom action is being taken with a view to deportation.

In addition to any conditions being imposed by the Secretary of State under s 133(2), s 36 of the Asylum and Immigration (Treatment of Claimants, etc) Act 2004 will also apply. This provides for electronic monitoring associated with a residence restriction.[54] Therefore a designated person 'may be' required to co-operate with electronic monitoring. This appears to be somewhat onerous given that the person is not serving a sentence for any further offence, it could create greater stigma of the individual in a society/area they have not chosen and quite possibly is unfamiliar. Further, it is a concern that as family members can be designated, this section also applies to them. However, it must be remembered that whether electronic monitoring will be imposed upon a designated person is subject to the Secretary of State's discretion as expressed by the term 'may be required'.

Another issue is conditions that impose a requirement of reporting to the police. Section 133(4) states that s 69 of NIAA 2002 applies in relation to a condition made relating to reporting to the police, the Secretary of State or an immigration officer in accordance with s 133(2)(c).[55]

Failure to comply with the condition (2008 Act, s 133(5))

11.20 Where a designated person does not comply with the conditions attached to the written notice conferring special immigration status and has no reasonable excuse for non-compliance they will have committed a criminal offence under s 133(5). Section 133(6) states that the offence leads to a summary conviction punishable by a fine

---

[53] ILPA, *Memorandum of Evidence to Public Bill Committee*, at para 33.
[54] Section 36(2) states that where a residence restriction is imposed on an adult: (a) he may be required to co-operate with electronic monitoring, and (b) failure to comply with a requirement under paragraph (a) shall be treated for all purposes of the Immigration Acts as failure to observe the residence restriction. Where a reporting restriction could be imposed on an adult: (a) he may instead be required to co-operate with electronic monitoring, and (b) the requirement shall be treated for all purposes of the Immigration Acts as a reporting restriction.
[55] These apply in the same way as restrictions imposed under IA 1971 under para 21 of Sch 2 or para 5 of Sch 3 to that Act (pending deportation).

not exceeding level 5 on the standard scale and or imprisonment for up to 51 weeks. This appears excessive where family members are concerned and could raise issues of proportionality under Art 8 of ECHR. Could it successfully be argued that it is necessary and proportionate to designate a person who has no prior convictions, with a status that failure to comply leads to a criminal conviction in order to protect law and order and public safety? Under s 133(8) the maximum sentence for non-compliance is 6 months' imprisonment. The provisions of s 24(1) of IA 1971 apply to the offence of failing to comply with conditions attached to a s 130 order as stated by s 133(7).

Support

11.21 Section 134 defines the level of support that will be available to a designated person. Section 134(1) states that the level of support for a designated person and their family members will be applied as it is for asylum seekers, contained in Part VI of the Immigration and Asylum Act 1999 (IAA 1999). This enables the Government to exclude designated individuals from working and receiving social security for the duration of designation. There are differences between the level of support intended for designated persons compared to asylum seekers and these are contained in s 134(2). This section lists the provisions in the IAA 1999 that will not apply in terms of support for those with special immigration status.[56] Instead the Secretary of State can provide support to the designated person under the more flexible provisions provided by s 134(3)(a)–(c). Under these provisions the Secretary of State must provide what appears to him or her to be adequate accommodation and essential living needs and other support that he or she thinks is necessary 'to reflect exceptional circumstances of a particular case' (s 134(3)(c)). These provisions provide less detail than is provided under their counterparts in IAA 1999.

Under s 134(4) the support 'may not be provided wholly or mainly by way of cash' and s 137(7) states 'a voucher is not cash'. Therefore the support received by designated persons is likely to take the form of vouchers. This was not fully supported by ministers at the debate stages given that the voucher scheme had not proven practicable in the past.[57] The ILPA added that the voucher system will add further stigmatisation of the family.[58] Oddly the government appears to have recognised these concerns by adding to s 134(4) that the Secretary of State can alternatively provide support by way of cash if he or she thinks it is appropriate 'because of exceptional circumstances'. The Secretary of State also has the power under s 135(6) to repeal, modify or disapply (to any extent) by way of an order s 134(4). This again emphasises the wide discretion being given to the Secretary of State.

Under s 134(5) the provision of accommodation under s 4 of IAA 1999 is not applicable to a designated person. Section 4 provides that the Secretary of State should arrange accommodation for people who are temporarily admitted or released from detention. This provision therefore further emphasises that the new special immigration framework is distinct from the framework available to those who have been temporarily admitted.

Section 134(6) specifies that a designated person is not subject to immigration control for the purpose of s 119(1)(b) of IAA 1999 which relates to homelessness provisions in

---

[56] 2008 Act, s 134(2)(a–g). See IAA 1996, ss 96, 97(1)(b), 100, 101, 108, 111, 113.
[57] PBC Deb, cols 640, 649 (27 November 2007).
[58] ILPA, *Memorandum of Evidence to Public Bill Committee*, at para 19.

Scotland and Northern Ireland (s 134(6)(a)) and are not 'a person from abroad who is not eligible for housing assistance' (s 134(6)(b)).

Section 135 provides supplemental information relating to support of designated persons. Section 135(1)(a)–(c) states when s 134 will be included in a reference to s 96 of IAA 1999. Section 135(2) requires the Secretary of State to have regard to 'the nature and circumstances of support' rather than the 'temporary nature of support' under Part VI of IAA 1999.

Section 135(3) enables a designated person to make appeals concerning support under rules created by s 104 of IAA 1999. The ILPA states that these clauses 'create a whole new area of support appeals by adopting the sections in IAA 1999 establishing what is now the Asylum Support Tribunal'.[59] It is also noted that further complexity is added to the system of support when the Secretary of State uses his or her powers to makes new provisions in relation to National Asylum Support Service (NASS) support. Section 134(4) enables the new provisions to apply or not to designated persons.[60]

End of designation (2008 Act, s 136)

11.22 This section determines when the s 130 order ceases and consequently the individual ceases to have special immigration status. Under s 136(1)(a) designation will cease where the individual is granted leave to enter or remain. This caters for individuals who may be granted the special immigration status whilst awaiting their appeal of conviction or sentence. Designation lapses under s 136(1)(b) if the person is notified by the Secretary of State or an immigration officer of a right to residence in the UK by virtue of the Community Treaties; under s 136(1)(c) if the person leaves; or under s 136(1)(d) if the person is able to be deported. Under s 136(2) support provided under s 134 may be stopped unless the individual has been granted leave to enter or remain or has a right of residence in the UK. In these circumstances s 136(3) allows support from the date the designation lapsed until a date specified in an order by the Secretary of State. Support may also be provided where the individual is appealing the decision to deport until after the appeal on a date specified by order of the Secretary of State.

---

[59] Ibid, at para 40.
[60] Ibid, at para 41.

Chapter 12

MISCELLANEOUS CHANGES

SUMMARY

12.1 In this chapter we deal with a variety of changes made by the 2008 Act. These include:

- disclosure of information about convictions of child sex offenders;

- amendments to the provisions relating to sexual offences prevention orders;

- creation of new powers to deal with persistent sales of tobacco to persons aged under 18;

- changes to police regulation and disciplinary process;

- international co-operation; and

- compensation for miscarriages of justice.

INFORMATION ABOUT CHILD SEX OFFENDERS

12.2 Section 140 of, and Sch 24 to, the new Act implement proposal in respect of disclosure of information about child sex offenders. They form part of a raft of legislative and administrative changes dealing with sex offenders, following various reviews, culminating in a *Review of the Protection of Children from Sex Offenders* published by the Home Office in June 2007.[1] Many of the proposals contained in that Review are outside the scope of this book.

These provisions came into effect on 14 July 2008 (see **1.5**).

Background

12.3 Public interest in disclosure of information about child sex offenders was heightened in 2001 by a campaign led by the mother of Sarah Payne, an 8-year-old murdered by Roy Whiting, who murdered the 8-year-old some 5 years after abducting another girl. The issue as to the boundaries of disclosure of information was not new. In

---

[1] See *Review of the Protection of Children from Sex Offenders* (Home Office, June 2007), to be found at: www.homeoffice.gov.uk/documents/CSOR/chid-sex-offender-review-130607?view=Binary.

1997, a Divisional Court clarified the applicable legal principles,[2] and the Home Office subsequently issued Guidance reflecting that decision.

The campaign for what became known as 'Sarah's Law' sought to achieve the right for parents to have access to lists of paedophiles living in their area. The proposal was based on 'Megan's Law', the approach adopted in various ways in the US. 'Megan's Law' itself came into being following the murder of a 7-year-old by a convicted child offender who lived with two other sex offenders. Implementation of the principle that individuals have the right to know details of paedophiles in their community takes various forms. In some states details are posted on the internet. In other states, details are posted at local police stations and libraries. Elsewhere, homes within the immediate vicinity are posted with leaflets giving relevant details.[3]

12.4 Such widespread disclosure has not, hitherto, been the approach adopted in the UK. In *R v Chief Constable of North Wales Police, ex p AB and CD*[4] a Divisional Court held that the existing Guidelines were lawful and compatible with the ECHR. In summary, they were as follows:

(1) There is a general presumption that information should not be disclosed, such a presumption being based on recognition of: (a) the potentially serious effect on the ability of the convicted people to live a normal life; (b) the risk of violence to such people; and (c) the risk that disclosure might drive them underground.

(2) There is a strong public interest in ensuring that police are able to disclose information about offenders where that is necessary for the prevention or detection of crime, or for the protection of young or other vulnerable people.

(3) Each case should be considered carefully on its particular facts, assessing the risk posed by the individual offenders; the vulnerability of those who may be at risk; and the impact of disclosure on the offender. In making such assessment, the police should normally consult other relevant agencies (such as social services and the probation service).

The approach of confining information to those who need to receive it for the purposes of managing risk has been clearly adopted. Since the implementation of s 325 of the Criminal Justice Act 2003 (CJA 2003), multi-agency approaches to managing risk have been formalised, and proved to be effective. Section 325(2) of CJA 2003 created a formal structure for arrangements for the purpose of assessing and managing the risks posed in any particular area by relevant sexual and violent offenders, and others who, by reason of offences committed by them, are considered to be persons who may cause serious harm to the public. The powers given to these multi-agency public protection arrangements authorities (MAPPA) include and involve the sharing of information (CJA 2003, s 325(4)).

Under the guidance, which has until now governed the use and disclosure of information, the police have disclosed information:[5]

---

[2] *R v Chief Constable for North Wales Police Authority and others, ex p AB and CD* [1997] EWHC (Admin) 667.
[3] See *Review of the Protection of Children from Sex Offenders* (Home Office, June 2007), to be found at: www.homeoffice.gov.uk/documents/CSOR/chid-sex-offender-review-130607?view=Binary, at p 10.
[4] [1997] EWHC (Admin) 667.
[5] CJA 2003, s 325(8).

'... in a controlled way. Consideration must be given in each case to whether information about an offender should be disclosed to others to protect victims, staff and others in the community.'

The review of strategies relating to sex offenders, and dealt with in the Consultation Paper, found that the extent of disclosure varied from area to area.[6] Head teachers, leisure centre managers, employers, landlords and parents are all potential recipients. The website operated by Child Exploitation and Online Protection Centre[7] contains details of high risk offenders who have gone missing. However, the overall picture shows uneven implementation between different areas. In addition, this controlled use of information did not address the occasional public clamour for a more open, Megan's law type approach. That had been considered and rejected consistently by the Government.[8]

12.5 The Review considered, but rejected a simple Megan's Law type approach. It stated:[9]

'There is a risk, which is supported by evidence from the US, that offenders' details were automatically available to all members of the public, a proportion would no longer comply with the notification requirements[[10]] and could disappear, leaving the authorities unsure of their whereabouts and unable to monitor them. Also some US states have a high proportion of offenders registering as "homeless", suggesting that they either are not being truthful with the authorities or are choosing to live rough to avoid having their whereabouts published. In either case the risk they pose increases.'

The risk of vigilantism was noted by the Consultation, with some justification. In 2002, the *News of the World* conducted a 'name and shame' campaign, leading to vigilante groups mounting protests outside the homes of suspected sex offenders. Two men suspected of sex offences against children committed suicide, and others fled their homes in Portsmouth.[11]

The Review concluded that there was justification for a greater degree of controlled disclosure to those who need to know 'for example a single mother who might be sharing a home with a registered offender'. Indeed it used a hypothetical example of such an instance.[12] The new provisions are intended to facilitate that, although whether they will lead to significantly increased disclosure of information beyond that already occurring is a matter of conjecture. What might be regarded as unclear is the *reason* for the changes. The Consultation Paper examines why implementation of Megan's Law is undesirable. It does not state what is unsatisfactory about the pre-existing system, or why change is necessary. Some consider that the changes are driven by a simple desire to be seen to be 'doing something'[13] or even 'tabloid-driven and politically driven'[14] in the

---

[6] Review, at 10.
[7] See www.ceop.gov.uk. See also Review, above.
[8] See, eg, www.news.bbc.co.uk, 16 December 2001, and more recently comments by the then Home Secretary, reported at www.independent.co.uk/news 'Reid unveils "Sarah's Law" proposals'.
[9] Review, above, at 10.
[10] Under Crime and Disorder Act 1998, as amended by Sexual Offences Act 2003.
[11] See www.guardian.co.uk/theissues 'Sarah's Law explained'.
[12] Review, at 12.
[13] See David Heath MP and Edward Garnier MP, HC Committee, col 700 (29 November 2007).
[14] Edward Garnier MP, ibid.

face of on-going public concerns. Indeed, the Minister accepted that the change was partly about 'reassurance of the public'.[15] In the House of Lords the Minister observed:

> 'We wish to ensure the effective protection of children from sex offenders while wishing to guard against the perils of inappropriate and unduly widespread disclosure ... Our aims ... are to extend the use of controlled disclosure where it is an appropriate and necessary response to a risk of serious harm to a child or children to ensure that there is consistency ... in the practice of disclosure and to ensure that the decision to disclose results from a formalised and auditable process.'

However, it is not entirely clear why this cannot be achieved within pre-existing arrangements. There are also wider concerns about the scheme introduced by s 140, which are discussed later.

The new provisions

12.6 The relevant change made by s 140 of the new Act is to insert a new s 327A and 327B into CJA 2003. This states that the responsible authority[16] for each area (ie MAPPA) must, in the course of discharging its functions under arrangements established by it under s 325 and s 327, consider whether to disclose information in its possession about the relevant previous convictions of any child sex offender managed by it to any particular member of the public. This duty arises only in respect of actual convictions (but including any cautions)[17] and does not arise in respect of any wider information relating to persons who have not been convicted, or in respect of information other than the relevant convictions of relevant individuals. These are individuals who fall within the scope of (a) or (b) below. These are where the responsible authority for the area has reasonable cause to believe that:

(a) a child sex offender[18] managed by it poses a risk in that or any other area of causing serious harm[19] to any particular child or children or to children of any particular description; and

(b) the disclosure of information about the relevant previous convictions of the offender to the particular member of the public is necessary for the purpose of protecting the particular child or children, or the children of that description, from serious harm caused by the offender.

In such cases a presumption arises that the responsible authority should disclose information in its possession about the relevant previous conviction of the offender to

---

[15] Vernon Coaker, Parliamentary Under-secretary of State for the Home Department, HC Committee, col 708 (29 November 2007).
[16] Defined by CJA 2003, s 325(1) as, in respect of any area, the chief officer of police, the local probation board for that area and the Minister of the Crown exercising functions in respect of prisons, acting jointly.
[17] See CJA 2003, s 327B(4) and (5).
[18] Defined by s 327B(4): '"Child sex offender" means any person who—
 (a) has been convicted of such an offence,
 (b) has been found not guilty of such an offence by reason of insanity,
 (c) has been found to be under a disability and to have done the act charged against the person in respect of such an offence, or
 (d) has been cautioned in respect of such an offence.'
[19] Defined by CJA 2003, s 327B(6): 'References to serious harm caused by a child sex offender are references to serious physical or psychological harm caused by the offender committing any offence listed in any paragraph of Schedule 34A other than paragraphs 1 to 6 (offences under provisions repealed by Sexual Offences Act 2003).'

the particular member of the public (CJA 2003, s 325A(2), (3)). This is irrespective of whether or not such disclosure is requested (s 325A(4)).

The duty is a duty to *consider* disclosure of data, not a duty to make actual disclosure. Nonetheless, authorities may be under some pressure to explain why disclosure is not being made, especially where the presumption applies. Even in the circumstances where the presumption outlined above is made, it is only a presumption. In other words, that is the starting point for the consideration by MAPPA, which, of course, may be outweighed by other factors if they are sufficiently strong. Disclosure is not automatic. However, despite the fact that the Minister considered that MAPPA would not be subject to an absolute duty in such circumstances, it is difficult to see how disclosure could, or should, be refused where the presumption applies. The fact that the criteria are satisfied if disclosure is necessary for child protection ought to mean that the presumption in favour of disclosure ought to be decisive. It is difficult to see how MAPPA could reach any other conclusion other than appropriate disclosure if the presumption that disclosure is 'necessary' for the purposes of child protection is met. To argue that disclosure may not be in the child's interests is a difficult position if MAPPA has already concluded (as it must for the presumption to operate) that disclosure is necessary to prevent serious harm to that child. Of course, MAPPA must also consider whether the disclosure is proportionate for the purposes of Art 8 of ECHR, for disclosure does presumptively interfere with the Art 8 rights of the sex offender (right to private and family life, home and correspondence). However it will be a rare case where the presumption applies and the authority does not give effect to the necessary child protection action of disclosure.

On the other hand the presumption is also limited in scope, in its requirements in respect of serious harm to a particular child or group of children. The harm has to be 'serious', a word added during the passage of the Act through Parliament. The fact that the harm must be 'serious' recognises that the imperatives in favour of disclosure must be substantial and must outweigh the harm, in relation to the offender, that might ensue.

The offences (or cautions in respect of offences) to which the provisions relating to disclosure apply are identified and set out in the new Sch 34A to CJA 2003 (see 2008 Act, Sch 24).

12.7 The new s 327A(5) provides for disclosure. Where the responsible authority (ie MAPPA) makes a disclosure under s 327A:

(a) it may disclose such information about the relevant previous convictions of the offender as it considers appropriate to disclose to the member of the public concerned; and

(b) it may impose conditions for preventing the member of the public concerned from disclosing the information to any other person.

Any disclosure under this section must be made as soon as is reasonably practicable having regard to all the circumstances, and specified records kept (s 327A(6) and (7)).

What these provisions do not do is provide any sanction for breach of any limitations on communication passed on by the person or organisation to whom disclosure is made. What is the person who receives the information to do with it? A civil action might be appropriate, and indeed was envisaged by the Minister.[20] but is scarcely going to be brought against a non-media individual. This was an issue that concerned the Joint Committee on Human Rights.[21] It recommended that there be a presumption in favour of notifying an individual in advance that the authorities intend to make a disclosure and provide an opportunity for an individual to make representations as to whether or not the disclosure should take place, and the manner in which it would be made. No such safeguard has found its way into the legislation.

SEXUAL OFFENCES PREVENTION ORDERS: RELEVANT SEXUAL OFFENCES

12.8 Section 141 of the new Act amends s 106 (supplemental provisions about sexual offences prevention orders) of the Sexual Offences Act 2003 (SOA 2003). The effect of the changes is to remove certain thresholds in Sch 3 to SOA 2003 as to the age of the victim, age of the offender and/or sentence length for a sexual offences prevention order to be made. This will have the effect of giving the court the same power to make a sexual offences prevention order in respect of those convicted of a sexual offence under Sch 3 as it currently does in respect of violent offences under Sch 5 of SOA 2003.

The thresholds relating to sentence length/type and the age of the offender or victim set out in Sch 3, will continue to apply for the purposes of determining whether an offender is subject to the notification requirements ('the sex offender's register').

PERSISTENT SALES OF TOBACCO TO PERSONS AGED UNDER 18

12.9 Section 143 of the new Act inserts into the Children and Young Persons Act 1933 new ss 12A–D. It creates what was described as a 'negative licensing scheme'.[22] It permits the making of 'restricted premises orders' following the persistent sale of tobacco to under-18s. It is intended to be a means of discouraging such sales following the raising of the legal age for purchase of tobacco products from 16 to 18, which came into effect in October 2007.

The power to do so applies where a person ('the offender') is convicted of a tobacco offence ('the relevant offence'). The person who brought the proceedings for the relevant offence may by complaint to a magistrates' court apply for a restricted premises order to be made in respect of the premises in relation to which that offence was committed ('the relevant premises'). The effect of the order is to prohibit any further sale of tobacco or cigarettes on those premises to *any* person. That prohibition extends to sales in person or by machine (s 12A(4)).

The order may not last for more than 12 months.

---

[20] Vernon Coaker, HC Committee, col 706 (29 November 2007).
[21] See Joint Committee 2007/2008, 15th Report at para 2.64.
[22] See Vernon Coaker, HC Committee, col 713 (29 November 2007).

12.10 The court may make the order if (and only if) it is satisfied that:

(a) on at least two occasions within the period of 2 years ending with the date on which the relevant offence was committed, the offender has committed other tobacco offences in relation to the relevant premises; and

(b) the applicant has given notice to each person appearing, after reasonable enquiries, to be a person affected by it.

Under a new s 12B, a restricted sales order may restrict sales by particular individuals.

By s 12C(1):

'If—

(a) a person sells on any premises any tobacco or cigarette papers in contravention of a restricted premises order, and
(b) the person knew, or ought reasonably to have known, that the sale was in contravention of the order,

the person commits an offence.'

A person who fails to comply with a restricted sale order is also guilty of an offence (s 12C(2)).

It is a defence for a person charged with an offence under s 12C(2) to prove that the person took all reasonable precautions and exercised all due diligence to avoid the commission of the offence. The burden of proving that defence is on the balance of probabilities.[23]

A person guilty of either offence is liable, on summary conviction, to a fine not exceeding £20,000.

POLICING

12.11 Part 9 of the Act deals with general policing matters as follows:

- Section 126 of, and Sch 22 to, the new Act amend the Police Act 1996 to make provision for or in connection with disciplinary and other proceedings in respect of the conduct and performance of members of police forces and special constables. These provisions came into force on 14 July 2008 (see **1.5**).

- Schedule 23 amends the Police Reform Act 2002 to make provision about the investigation of complaints of police misconduct and other matters.

- Section 128 amends the powers of the Secretary of State to provide financial assistance.

---

[23] See **8.25**.

- Section 54 deals with amendments to the powers of inspectors of constabulary.

12.12 The provisions relating to police discipline owe their origin to the *Review of Police Disciplinary Arrangements Report* (the Taylor Review 2005).[24] It recommended the creation of a Code of Professional Standards; the introduction of new disciplinary arrangements, and the creation of new procedures for unsatisfactory performance. The detailed development of these proposals followed on-going dissatisfaction with the existing regime.[25] The provisions in the new Act are intended to provide a framework for detailed regulatory change. Regulations will be made to identify when a police officer has the right to legal representation, to allow police tribunals to have the power to do anything that the original hearing could have done, to specify the circumstances in which a case might be dealt with without a hearing, and to remove the power to make a finding of 'required to resign'.

INTERNATIONAL CO-OPERATION

12.13 Part 6 of the Act deals with international co-operation. It seeks to implement obligations agreed in 2005[26] in respect of the mutual recognition of financial penalties, and is part of an on-going process of cross-border co-operation on law enforcement involving the European Arrest Warrant, and execution of freezing orders.

Section 80 amends Sch 5 to the Courts Act 2003 in respect of collection of fines imposed by a court in England and Wales. Following the issue of a certificate by the court requesting enforcement under the Framework Decision on financial penalties; it will be enforced by the court in the other jurisdiction. A certificate requesting enforcement under the Framework Decision on financial penalties may only be issued where:

(a) the sum due is a financial penalty (defined by s 80); and

(b) it appears to the fines officer or the court that the person is normally resident, or has property or income, in a member state other than the UK.

A certificate requesting enforcement may be issued where: (a) a person is required to pay a financial penalty; (b) the penalty is not paid in full within the time allowed for payment; (c) there is no appeal outstanding in relation to the penalty; (d) Sch 5 to the Courts Act 2003 does not apply in relation to the enforcement of the penalty; and (e) it appears to the designated officer that the person is normally resident in, or has property or income in, a member state other than the UK.

The procedure to be followed if a certificate is issued is set out in s 81 of the new Act.

The system is intended to work in a reciprocal way. Section 84 deals with requests from other jurisdictions. When a certificate is received from the court in that jurisdiction, it is

---

[24] To be found at http://police.homeoffice.gov.uk/publications/human-resources/Discipline_review_report_FI1.pdf?view=Binary.
[25] For a detailed resume of the history, see HC Research Paper 07/65 at www.parliament.uk/commons/lib/research/rp2007/rp07-065.pdf.
[26] See Framework Decision, 2005/214/JHA.

passed to the enforcing officer in the court in England and Wales. The procedure to be followed is set out in s 85. In this context s 91 is important.

12.14 Section 91, in combination with Sch 19, sets out the circumstances when an court may decline to refuse to enforce a penalty, even though a certificate has been issued under s 80 or s 84. These circumstances are where there is double jeopardy, in the sense that the offender has already been dealt with for the same offence in the other jurisdiction, or the absence of dual criminality[27] unless the offence is one which is identified by Sch 19, para 2. These offences are wide-ranging, and include offences of absolute severity including murder, terrorism, trafficking, racism and xenophobia. It remains to be seen whether the non-applicability of the principle of absence of dual criminality will operate unfairly given that, for example, an offence such as racism or xenophobia might well not be unlawful in the UK.

Enforcement can also be refused if the criminal act took place outside the territory of the court which imposed the financial penalty, where the age of criminal responsibility is not met in the executing state (ie the state enforcing the certificate), or when the penalty is less than €70.

COMPENSATION FOR MISCARRIAGES OF JUSTICE

12.15 Section 61 of the new Act imposes a 2-year time-limit within which claims for compensation for miscarriages must be brought. Section 61 inserts a new s 133A into CJA 1988. It had not been brought into force as at the date of going to press.

In assessing so much of any compensation payable under s 133 as is attributable to suffering, harm to reputation or similar damage, the assessor[28] must have regard in particular to:

(a) the seriousness of the offence of which the person was convicted and the severity of the punishment suffered as a result of the conviction; and

(b) the conduct of the investigation and prosecution of the offence.

The new Act allows (but does not require) the assessor to make deductions that the assessor considers appropriate by reason of either or both of the following:

(a) any conduct of the person appearing to the assessor to have directly or indirectly caused, or contributed to, the conviction concerned; and

(b) any other convictions of the person and any punishment suffered as a result of them.

In exceptional circumstances the compensation may be nominal only. In any event the total amount of compensation payable to or in respect of a person must not exceed the overall compensation limit.

---

[27] The principle that orders are not enforced unless the conduct with which they deal is unlawful in both states.
[28] Criminal Injuries Compensation Commission Authority.

12.16 The overall compensation limit is set at £500,000. However, if s 133B applies the limit increases to £1m. That limit may be increased by order, but is related very broadly to economic circumstances (see CJA 1988, s 133A(6)). Section 133B applies where the person has been detained in a prison or hospital for at least 10 years when the conviction is quashed or pardon granted. Detailed provisions in s 133B govern how this period of 10 years is to be calculated.

12.17 The rationale for limiting the amount of compensation payable to individuals who, by definition, should not have been detained is difficult fully to explain. The Government did so when introducing these provisions by stressing the need 'to put victims' interests at the heart of the criminal justice system'.[29] However some may consider cost to be the driving force. The then Home Secretary stated:

> 'Claims for compensation have increased in complexity in recent years and may drag on for several years. This reflects the absence of time limits on the process, as would be expected if the case had come to court, lack of clarity about the maximum amounts payable, and the absence of limits on legal fees, which are reimbursed at private work rates. Currently, applicants are invited simply to submit their claims for compensation and to detail their financial loss. Compensation payments for miscarriages of justice have increased sharply over the last few years and are now running at an average of well over £250,000, with more than ten per cent of that amount also paid in legal fees. In contrast, no legal costs are payable under the scheme for victims of crime, and the average amount received by each victim is less than one fiftieth of what is paid to those eligible under the miscarriages of justice scheme.'

Deductions for the conduct of the applicant are already made. Typically, such deductions have been modest, ranging in most cases from around 5% to no more than 20%. In contrast, reductions in payments to victims of crime are much higher, ranging up to 100% in serious cases.[30]

The Minister of State[31] stated:

> '... a victim of a miscarriage of justice receives, on average, 50 times more compensation than a victim of violent crime and we do not believe that is right.'

However some challenge the validity of any link between the two matters, and the fairness of the cap.[32]

In 2006, the then Home Secretary announced changes in dealing with legal costs being introduced by the Assessor:

> 'The Assessor has also decided that legal costs in relation to applications for compensation will, with immediate effect, be paid by reference to the fees for publicly funded civil cases as provided for in the Legal Help contained in the Community Legal Service (Funding) Order 2000. This change will apply to all existing cases (both under the statutory and discretionary scheme) which are currently awaiting a decision from the Assessor on the amount of compensation, as well as to all existing cases (both under the statutory and discretionary scheme) where the question of eligibility for compensation is being considered by the Office for Criminal Justice Reform, and to all new cases for compensation under the

---

[29] Charles Clarke MP, the then Home Secretary, Home Office Press Release (19 April 2006).
[30] See Press Release, above.
[31] Maria Eagle MP, HC Committee, col 507 (22 November 2008).
[32] See, generally, HC Committee (22 November 2007).

statutory scheme received by the Office for Criminal Justice Reform. However, in the case of applications already received by the Office for Criminal Justice Reform or already under consideration by the Assessor, the change will apply only in relation to legal costs incurred after today and compensation in respect of legal costs before today will be paid on the same basis as before.'

It is clear that the rationale goes beyond saving money. The announcement of a review of the powers of the Court of Appeal's powers was made at the same time. It was the changes that resulted from the recommendations of that Review were, controversially introduced as part of the Bill and ultimately abandoned.[33]

---

[33] See **10.3**.

Appendix 1

STATUTES

CRIMINAL JUSTICE AND IMMIGRATION ACT 2008

Chapter 4

ARRANGEMENT OF SECTIONS

PART 1
YOUTH REHABILITATION ORDERS

Section		Page
1	Youth rehabilitation orders	179
2	Breach, revocation or amendment of youth rehabilitation orders	180
3	Transfer of youth rehabilitation orders to Northern Ireland	180
4	Meaning of "the responsible officer"	180
5	Responsible officer and offender: duties in relation to the other	180

Supplementary

6	Abolition of certain youth orders and related amendments	181
7	Youth rehabilitation orders: interpretation	181
8	Isles of Scilly	183

PART 2
SENTENCING

General sentencing provisions

9	Purposes etc. of sentencing: offenders under 18	183
10	Effect of restriction on imposing community sentences	184
11	Restriction on power to make a community order	184
12	Pre-sentence reports	184

Custodial sentences

13	Sentences of imprisonment for public protection	184
14	Sentences of detention for public protection	185
15	Extended sentences for certain violent or sexual offences: persons 18 or over	185
16	Extended sentences for certain violent or sexual offences: persons under 18	185
17	The assessment of dangerousness	186
18	Further amendments relating to sentences for public protection	186
19	Indeterminate sentences: determination of tariffs	187
20	Consecutive terms of imprisonment	187

Release and recall of prisoners

21	Credit for period of remand on bail: terms of imprisonment and detention	188
22	Credit for period of remand on bail: other cases	188
23	Credit for period of remand on bail: transitional provisions	188
24	Minimum conditions for early release under section 246(1) of Criminal Justice Act 2003	190
25	Release on licence under Criminal Justice Act 2003 of prisoners serving extended sentences	190
26	Release of certain long-term prisoners under Criminal Justice Act 1991	190
27	Application of section 35(1) of Criminal Justice Act 1991 to prisoners liable to removal from the UK	191

28	Release of fine defaulters and contemnors under Criminal Justice Act 1991	191
29	Release of prisoners after recall	191
30	Further review and release of prisoners after recall	192
31	Recall of life prisoners: abolition of requirement for recommendation by Parole Board	192
32	Release of prisoners recalled following release under Criminal Justice Act 1991	192

Early removal of prisoners from the United Kingdom

33	Removal under Criminal Justice Act 1991	192
34	Removal under Criminal Justice Act 2003	193

Referral orders

35	Referral conditions	194
36	Power to revoke a referral order	194
37	Extension of period for which young offender contract has effect	194

Enforcement of sentences

38	Imposition of unpaid work requirement for breach of community order	195
39	Youth default orders	195
40	Power to impose attendance centre requirement on fine defaulter	195
41	Disclosure of information for enforcing fines	195

PART 3
APPEALS

Appeals by defendant

42	Power to dismiss certain appeals following references by the CCRC: England and Wales	196
43	Power to dismiss certain appeals following references by the CCRC: Northern Ireland	197

Appeals by prosecution

44	Determination of prosecution appeals: England and Wales	197
45	Determination of prosecution appeals: Northern Ireland	197

Miscellaneous

46	Review of sentence on reference by Attorney General	198
47	Further amendments relating to appeals in criminal cases	199

PART 4
OTHER CRIMINAL JUSTICE PROVISIONS

Alternatives to prosecution

48	Alternatives to prosecution for offenders under 18	199
49	Protection for spent cautions under Rehabilitation of Offenders Act 1974	199
50	Criminal conviction certificates and criminal record certificates	199

Bail

51	Bail conditions: electronic monitoring	201
52	Bail for summary offences and certain other offences to be tried summarily	201

Proceedings in magistrates' courts

53	Allocation of offences triable either way etc.	202
54	Trial or sentencing in absence of accused in magistrates' courts	202
55	Extension of powers of non-legal staff	203

Criminal legal aid

56	Provisional grant of right to representation	203
57	Disclosure of information to enable assessment of financial eligibility	203
58	Pilot schemes	204

Miscellaneous

59	SFO's pre-investigation powers in relation to bribery and corruption: foreign officers etc.	204
60	Contents of an accused's defence statement	204
61	Compensation for miscarriages of justice	204
62	Annual report on Criminal Justice (Terrorism and Conspiracy) Act 1998	205

PART 5
CRIMINAL LAW

Pornography etc.

63	Possession of extreme pornographic images	205
64	Exclusion of classified films etc.	205
65	Defences: general	205
66	Defence: participation in consensual acts	205
67	Penalties etc. for possession of extreme pornographic images	206
68	Special rules relating to providers of information society services	206
69	Indecent photographs of children: England and Wales	206
70	Indecent photographs of children: Northern Ireland	206
71	Maximum penalty for publication etc. of obscene articles	207

Sexual offences

72	Offences committed outside the United Kingdom	209
73	Grooming and adoption	210

Hatred on the grounds of sexual orientation

74	Hatred on the grounds of sexual orientation	210

Offences relating to nuclear material and nuclear facilities

75	Offences relating to the physical protection of nuclear material and nuclear facilities	211

Self-defence etc.

76	Reasonable force for purposes of self-defence etc.	211

Unlawfully obtaining etc. personal data

77	Power to alter penalty for unlawfully obtaining etc. personal data	212
78	New defence for purposes of journalism and other special purposes	212

Blasphemy

79	Abolition of common law offences of blasphemy and blasphemous libel	213

PART 6
INTERNATIONAL CO-OPERATION IN RELATION TO CRIMINAL JUSTICE MATTERS

Recognition of financial penalties: requests to other member States

80	Requests to other member States: England and Wales	213
81	Procedure on issue of certificate: England and Wales	214
82	Requests to other member States: Northern Ireland	215
83	Procedure on issue of certificate: Northern Ireland	216

Recognition of financial penalties: requests from other member States

84	Requests from other member States: England and Wales	216
85	Procedure on receipt of certificate by designated officer	217
86	Modification of Magistrates' Courts Act 1980	217
87	Requests from other member States: Northern Ireland	217
88	Procedure on receipt of certificate by clerk of petty sessions	217
89	Modification of Magistrates' Courts (Northern Ireland) Order 1981	218
90	Transfer of certificates to central authority for Scotland	218

Recognition of financial penalties: miscellaneous

91	Recognition of financial penalties: general	218
92	Interpretation of sections 80 to 91 etc.	218

Repatriation of prisoners

93	Delivery of prisoner to place abroad for purposes of transfer out of the United Kingdom	219
94	Issue of warrant transferring responsibility for detention and release of an offender to or from the relevant Minister	220
95	Powers to arrest and detain persons believed to fall within section 4A(3) of Repatriation of Prisoners Act 1984	220
96	Amendments relating to Scotland	220

Mutual legal assistance in revenue matters

97	Power to transfer functions under Crime (International Co-operation) Act 2003 in relation to direct taxation	221

PART 7
VIOLENT OFFENDER ORDERS

Violent offender orders

98	Violent offender orders	221
99	Qualifying offenders	222
100	Applications for violent offender orders	222
101	Making of violent offender orders	223
102	Provisions that orders may contain	223
103	Variation, renewal or discharge of violent offender orders	224
104	Interim violent offender orders	224
105	Notice of applications	225
106	Appeals	226

Notification requirements

107	Offenders subject to notification requirements	226
108	Notification requirements: initial notification	227
109	Notification requirements: changes	227
110	Notification requirements: periodic notification	228
111	Notification requirements: travel outside United Kingdom	228
112	Method of notification and related matters	228

Supplementary

113	Offences	229
114	Supply of information to Secretary of State etc.	229
115	Supply of information by Secretary of State etc.	229
116	Information about release or transfer	230
117	Interpretation of Part 7	231

PART 8
ANTI-SOCIAL BEHAVIOUR

Premises closure orders

118	Closure orders: premises associated with persistent disorder or nuisance	232

Nuisance or disturbance on hospital premises

119	Offence of causing nuisance or disturbance on NHS premises	232
120	Power to remove person causing nuisance or disturbance	233
121	Guidance about the power to remove etc.	234
122	Nuisance or disturbance on HSS premises	234

Anti-social behaviour orders etc. in respect of children and young persons

123	Review of anti-social behaviour orders etc.	234
124	Individual support orders	234

Parenting contracts and parenting orders

125	Parenting contracts and parenting orders: local authorities	235

PART 9
POLICING

Misconduct procedures etc.

126	Police misconduct and performance procedures	236
127	Investigation of complaints of police misconduct etc.	237

Financial assistance

128	Financial assistance under section 57 of Police Act 1996	237

Inspection

129	Inspection of police authorities	237

PART 10
SPECIAL IMMIGRATION STATUS

130	Designation	238
131	"Foreign criminal"	239
132	Effect of designation	239
133	Conditions	240
134	Support	240
135	Support: supplemental	241
136	End of designation	242
137	Interpretation: general	242

PART 11
MISCELLANEOUS

Industrial action by prison officers

138	Amendment of section 127 of Criminal Justice and Public Order Act 1994	242
139	Power to suspend the operation of section 127 of Criminal Justice and Public Order Act 1994	243

Sex offenders

140	Disclosure of information about convictions etc. of child sex offenders to members of the public	244
141	Sexual offences prevention orders: relevant sexual offences	244
142	Notification requirements: prescribed information	245

Persistent sales of tobacco to persons under 18

143	Persistent sales of tobacco to persons under 18	245

Penalties for serious contraventions of data protection principles

144	Power to require data controllers to pay monetary penalty	246

Armed forces legislation

145	Amendments to armed forces legislation	246

Automatic deportation of criminals

146	Convention against human trafficking	247

PART 12
GENERAL

147	Orders, rules and regulations	248
148	Consequential etc. amendments and transitional and saving provision	249
149	Repeals and revocations	249
150	Financial provisions	249
151	Effect of amendments to criminal justice provisions applied for purposes of service law	250
152	Extent	250
153	Commencement	251
154	Short title	252

Schedule 1 – Further Provisions About Youth Rehabilitation Orders	252
Part 1 – Provisions To Be Included In Youth Rehabilitation Orders	252
Part 2 – Requirements	253
Part 3 – Provisions Applying Where Court Proposes To Make Youth Rehabilitation Order	253
Part 4 – Provisions applying where court makes youth rehabilitation order etc.	253
Schedule 2 – Breach, Revocation Or Amendment Of Youth Rehabilitation Orders	254
Part 1 – Preliminary	254
Part 2 – Breach Of Requirement Of Order	255
Part 3 – Revocation Of Order	255
Part 4 – Amendment Of Order	256
Part 5 – Powers Of Court In Relation To Order Following Subsequent Conviction	256
Part 6 – Supplementary	257
Schedule 3 – Transfer Of Youth Rehabilitation Orders To Northern Ireland	257
Part 1 – Making Or Amendment Of A Youth Rehabilitation Order Where Offender Resides Or Proposes To Reside In Northern Ireland	257
Part 2 – Provisions Relating To An Order Made Or Amended Under Part 1	258
Schedule 4 – Youth Rehabilitation Orders: Consequential And Related Amendments	258
Part 1 – Consequential Amendments	258
Part 2 – Related Amendments	259

Schedule 5 – Offences Specified For The Purposes Of Sections 225(3a) And 227(2a) Of Criminal Justice Act 2003	259
Schedule 6 – Credit For Period Of Remand On Bail: Transitional Provisions	260
Schedule 7 – Youth Default Orders: Modification Of Provisions Applying To Youth Rehabilitation Orders	260
Schedule 8 – Appeals In Criminal Cases	261
Part 1 – Amendments Of Criminal Appeal Act 1968	261
Part 2 – Amendments Of Criminal Appeal (Northern Ireland) Act 1980	262
PART 3 – AMENDMENTS OF OTHER ACTS	262
Schedule 9 – Alternatives To Prosecution For Persons Under 18	262
Schedule 10 – Protection For Spent Cautions Under Rehabilitation Of Offenders Act 1974	263
Schedule 11 – Electronic Monitoring Of Persons Released On Bail Subject To Conditions	263
Schedule 12 – Bail For Summary Offences And Certain Other Offences To Be Tried Summarily	263
Schedule 13 – Allocation of cases triable either way etc.	264
Schedule 14 – Special Rules Relating To Providers Of Information Society Services	264
Schedule 15 – Sexual Offences: Grooming And Adoption	264
Schedule 16 – Hatred On The Grounds Of Sexual Orientation	264
Schedule 17 – Offences Relating To Nuclear Material And Nuclear Facilities	265
Part 1 – Amendments Of Nuclear Material (Offences) Act 1983	266
Part 2 – Amendments Of Customs And Excise Management Act 1979	266
Schedule 18 – Penalties Suitable For Enforcement In England And Wales Or Northern Ireland	266
Schedule 19 – Grounds For Refusal To Enforce Financial Penalties	266
Part 1 – The Grounds For Refusal	267
Part 2 – European Framework List (Financial Penalties)	268
Part 3 – Interpretation	269
Schedule 20 – Closure Orders: Premises Associated With Persistent Disorder Or Nuisance	269
Schedule 21 – Nuisance Or Disturbance On HSS Premises	270
Schedule 22 – Police Misconduct And Performance Procedures	282
Part 1 – Amendments Of Police Act 1996	284
Part 2 – Amendments Of Ministry Of Defence Police Act 1987	286
Part 3 – Amendments Of Railways And Transport Safety Act 2003	286
Schedule 23 – Investigation of complaints of police misconduct etc.	287
Schedule 24 – Section 327A of Criminal Justice Act 2003: meaning of "child sex offence"	292
Schedule 25 – Amendments To Armed Forces Legislation Part 1 Courts-Martial (Appeals) Act 1968	294
Part 2 – Armed Forces Act 2006	296
Part 3 – Transitional Provisions	298
Schedule 26 – Minor And Consequential Amendments	300
Part 1 – Fine Defaulters	300
Part 2 – Other Amendments	304
Schedule 27 – Transitory, Transitional And Saving Provisions	306
Part 1 – Youth Justice	306
Part 2 – Sentencing	325
Part 3 – Appeals	329
Part 4 – Other Criminal Justice Provisions	329
Part 5 – Criminal Law	329
Part 6 – International Co-Operation In Relation To Criminal Justice Matters	331
Part 7 – Violent Offender Orders	332
Part 8 – Anti-Social Behaviour	333
Part 9 – Police	333
Part 10	334
Special Immigration Status	335
Part 11	338
Miscellaneous	338
Schedule 28 – Repeals And Revocations	341
Part 1 – Youth Rehabilitation Orders	343
Part 2 – Sentencing	344
Part 3 – Appeals	348
Part 4	349
Other Criminal Justice Provisions	351
Part 5 – Criminal Law	353
Part 6 – International Co-Operation In Relation To Criminal Justice Matters	354
Part 7 – Anti-Social Behaviour	355
Part 8 – Policing	356

PART 1
YOUTH REHABILITATION ORDERS

1 Youth rehabilitation orders

(1) Where a person aged under 18 is convicted of an offence, the court by or before which the person is convicted may in accordance with Schedule 1 make an order (in this Part referred to as a "youth rehabilitation order") imposing on the person any one or more of the following requirements –

- (a) an activity requirement (see paragraphs 6 to 8 of Schedule 1),
- (b) a supervision requirement (see paragraph 9 of that Schedule),
- (c) in a case where the offender is aged 16 or 17 at the time of the conviction, an unpaid work requirement (see paragraph 10 of that Schedule),
- (d) a programme requirement (see paragraph 11 of that Schedule),
- (e) an attendance centre requirement (see paragraph 12 of that Schedule),
- (f) a prohibited activity requirement (see paragraph 13 of that Schedule),
- (g) a curfew requirement (see paragraph 14 of that Schedule),
- (h) an exclusion requirement (see paragraph 15 of that Schedule),
- (i) a residence requirement (see paragraph 16 of that Schedule),
- (j) a local authority residence requirement (see paragraph 17 of that Schedule),
- (k) a mental health treatment requirement (see paragraph 20 of that Schedule),
- (l) a drug treatment requirement (see paragraph 22 of that Schedule),
- (m) a drug testing requirement (see paragraph 23 of that Schedule),
- (n) an intoxicating substance treatment requirement (see paragraph 24 of that Schedule), and
- (o) an education requirement (see paragraph 25 of that Schedule).

(2) A youth rehabilitation order –

- (a) may also impose an electronic monitoring requirement (see paragraph 26 of Schedule 1), and
- (b) must do so if paragraph 2 of that Schedule so requires.

(3) A youth rehabilitation order may be –

- (a) a youth rehabilitation order with intensive supervision and surveillance (see paragraph 3 of Schedule 1), or
- (b) a youth rehabilitation order with fostering (see paragraph 4 of that Schedule).

(4) But a court may only make an order mentioned in subsection (3)(a) or (b) if –

- (a) the court is dealing with the offender for an offence which is punishable with imprisonment,
- (b) the court is of the opinion that the offence, or the combination of the offence and one or more offences associated with it, was so serious that, but for paragraph 3 or 4 of Schedule 1, a custodial sentence would be appropriate (or, if the offender was aged under 12 at the time of conviction, would be appropriate if the offender had been aged 12), and
- (c) if the offender was aged under 15 at the time of conviction, the court is of the opinion that the offender is a persistent offender.

(5) Schedule 1 makes further provision about youth rehabilitation orders.

(6) This section is subject to –

- (a) sections 148 and 150 of the Criminal Justice Act 2003 (c. 44) (restrictions on community sentences etc.), and
- (b) the provisions of Parts 1 and 3 of Schedule 1.

2 Breach, revocation or amendment of youth rehabilitation orders

Schedule 2 makes provision about failures to comply with the requirements of youth rehabilitation orders and about the revocation or amendment of such orders.

3 Transfer of youth rehabilitation orders to Northern Ireland

Schedule 3 makes provision about the transfer of youth rehabilitation orders to Northern Ireland.

4 Meaning of "the responsible officer"

(1) For the purposes of this Part, "the responsible officer", in relation to an offender to whom a youth rehabilitation order relates, means –

- (a) in a case where the order –
  - (i) imposes a curfew requirement or an exclusion requirement but no other requirement mentioned in section 1(1), and
  - (ii) imposes an electronic monitoring requirement, the person who under paragraph 26(4) of Schedule 1 is responsible for the electronic monitoring required by the order;
- (b) in a case where the only requirement imposed by the order is an attendance centre requirement, the officer in charge of the attendance centre in question;
- (c) in any other case, the qualifying officer who, as respects the offender, is for the time being responsible for discharging the functions conferred by this Part on the responsible officer.

(2) In this section "qualifying officer", in relation to a youth rehabilitation order, means –

- (a) a member of a youth offending team established by a local authority for the time being specified in the order for the purposes of this section, or
- (b) an officer of a local probation board appointed for or assigned to the local justice area for the time being so specified or (as the case may be) an officer of a provider of probation services acting in the local justice area for the time being so specified.

(3) The Secretary of State may by order –

- (a) amend subsections (1) and (2), and
- (b) make any other amendments of –
  - (i) this Part, or
  - (ii) Chapter 1 of Part 12 of the Criminal Justice Act 2003 (c. 44)

(general provisions about sentencing), that appear to be necessary or expedient in consequence of any amendment made by virtue of paragraph (a).

(4) An order under subsection (3) may, in particular, provide for the court to determine which of two or more descriptions of responsible officer is to apply in relation to any youth rehabilitation order.

5 Responsible officer and offender: duties in relation to the other

(1) Where a youth rehabilitation order has effect, it is the duty of the responsible officer –

- (a) to make any arrangements that are necessary in connection with the requirements imposed by the order,
- (b) to promote the offender's compliance with those requirements, and
- (c) where appropriate, to take steps to enforce those requirements.

(2) In subsection (1) "responsible officer" does not include a person falling within section 4(1)(a).

(3) In giving instructions in pursuance of a youth rehabilitation order relating to an offender, the responsible officer must ensure, as far as practicable, that any instruction is such as to avoid –

- (a) any conflict with the offender's religious beliefs,

(b) any interference with the times, if any, at which the offender normally works or attends school or any other educational establishment, and
(c) any conflict with the requirements of any other youth rehabilitation order to which the offender may be subject.

(4) The Secretary of State may by order provide that subsection (3) is to have effect with such additional restrictions as may be specified in the order.

(5) An offender in respect of whom a youth rehabilitation order is in force –

(a) must keep in touch with the responsible officer in accordance with such instructions as the offender may from time to time be given by that officer, and
(b) must notify the responsible officer of any change of address.

(6) The obligation imposed by subsection (5) is enforceable as if it were a requirement imposed by the order.

Supplementary

6 Abolition of certain youth orders and related amendments

(1) Chapters 1, 2, 4 and 5 of Part 4 of (and Schedules 3 and 5 to 7 to) the Powers of Criminal Courts (Sentencing) Act 2000 (c. 6) (curfew orders, exclusion orders, attendance centre orders, supervision orders and action plan orders) cease to have effect.

(2) Part 1 of Schedule 4 makes amendments consequential on provisions of this Part.

(3) Part 2 of Schedule 4 makes minor amendments regarding other community orders which are related to the consequential amendments in Part 1 of that Schedule.

7 Youth rehabilitation orders: interpretation

(1) In this Part, except where the contrary intention appears –

"accommodation provided by or on behalf of a local authority" has the same meaning as it has in the Children Act 1989 (c. 41) by virtue of section 105 of that Act;
"activity requirement", in relation to a youth rehabilitation order, has the meaning given by paragraph 6 of Schedule 1;
"associated", in relation to offences, is to be read in accordance with section 161(1) of the Powers of Criminal Courts (Sentencing) Act 2000 (c. 6);
"attendance centre" has the meaning given by section 221(2) of the Criminal Justice Act 2003 (c. 44);
"attendance centre requirement", in relation to a youth rehabilitation order, has the meaning given by paragraph 12 of Schedule 1;
"curfew requirement", in relation to a youth rehabilitation order, has the meaning given by paragraph 14 of Schedule 1;
"custodial sentence" has the meaning given by section 76 of the Powers of Criminal Courts (Sentencing) Act 2000;
"detention and training order" has the same meaning as it has in that Act by virtue of section 163 of that Act;
"drug treatment requirement", in relation to a youth rehabilitation order, has the meaning given by paragraph 22 of Schedule 1;
"drug testing requirement", in relation to a youth rehabilitation order, has the meaning given by paragraph 23 of Schedule 1;
"education requirement", in relation to a youth rehabilitation order, has the meaning given by paragraph 25 of Schedule 1;
"electronic monitoring requirement", in relation to a youth rehabilitation order, has the meaning given by paragraph 26 of Schedule 1;
"exclusion requirement", in relation to a youth rehabilitation order, has the meaning given by paragraph 15 of Schedule 1;

"extended activity requirement", in relation to a youth rehabilitation order, has the meaning given by paragraph 3 of Schedule 1;
"fostering requirement", in relation to a youth rehabilitation order with fostering, has the meaning given by paragraph 18 of Schedule 1;
"guardian" has the same meaning as in the Children and Young Persons Act 1933 (c. 12);
"intoxicating substance treatment requirement", in relation to a youth rehabilitation order, has the meaning given by paragraph 24 of Schedule 1;
"local authority" means –
- (a) in relation to England –
    - (i) a county council,
    - (ii) a district council whose district does not form part of an area that has a county council,
    - (iii) a London borough council, or
    - (iv) the Common Council of the City of London in its capacity as a local authority, and
- (b) in relation to Wales –
    - (i) a county council, or
    - (ii) a county borough council;

"local authority residence requirement", in relation to a youth rehabilitation order, has the meaning given by paragraph 17 of Schedule 1;
"local probation board" means a local probation board established under section 4 of the Criminal Justice and Court Services Act 2000 (c. 43);
"mental health treatment requirement", in relation to a youth rehabilitation order, has the meaning given by paragraph 20 of Schedule 1;
"programme requirement", in relation to a youth rehabilitation order, has the meaning given by paragraph 11 of Schedule 1;
"prohibited activity requirement", in relation to a youth rehabilitation order, has the meaning given by paragraph 13 of Schedule 1;
"residence requirement", in relation to a youth rehabilitation order, has the meaning given by paragraph 16 of Schedule 1;
"the responsible officer", in relation to an offender to whom a youth rehabilitation order relates, has the meaning given by section 4;
"supervision requirement", in relation to a youth rehabilitation order, has the meaning given by paragraph 9 of Schedule 1;
"unpaid work requirement", in relation to a youth rehabilitation order, has the meaning given by paragraph 10 of Schedule 1;
"youth offending team" means a team established under section 39 of the Crime and Disorder Act 1998 (c. 37);
"youth rehabilitation order" has the meaning given by section 1;
"youth rehabilitation order with fostering" has the meaning given by paragraph 4 of Schedule 1;
"youth rehabilitation order with intensive supervision and surveillance" has the meaning given by paragraph 3 of Schedule 1.

(2) For the purposes of any provision of this Part which requires the determination of the age of a person by the court, the Secretary of State or a local authority, the person's age is to be taken to be that which it appears to the court or (as the case may be) the Secretary of State or a local authority to be after considering any available evidence.

(3) Any reference in this Part to an offence punishable with imprisonment is to be read without regard to any prohibition or restriction imposed by or under any Act on the imprisonment of young offenders.

(4) If a local authority has parental responsibility for an offender who is in its care or provided with accommodation by it in the exercise of any social services functions, any reference in this Part (except in paragraphs 4 and 25 of Schedule 1) to the offender's parent or guardian is to be read as a reference to that authority.

(5) In subsection (4) –

"parental responsibility" has the same meaning as it has in the Children Act 1989 (c. 41) by virtue of section 3 of that Act, and

"social services functions" has the same meaning as it has in the Local Authority Social Services Act 1970 (c. 42) by virtue of section 1A of that Act.

8 Isles of Scilly

This Part has effect in relation to the Isles of Scilly with such exceptions, adaptations and modifications as the Secretary of State may by order specify.

PART 2
SENTENCING

General sentencing provisions

9 Purposes etc. of sentencing: offenders under 18

(1) After section 142 of the Criminal Justice Act 2003 (c. 44) insert –

> (1) This section applies where a court is dealing with an offender aged under 18 in respect of an offence.
>
> (2) The court must have regard to –
>
> (a) the principal aim of the youth justice system (which is to prevent offending (or re-offending) by persons aged under 18: see section 37(1) of the Crime and Disorder Act 1998),
>
> (b) in accordance with section 44 of the Children and Young Persons Act 1933, the welfare of the offender, and
>
> (c) the purposes of sentencing mentioned in subsection (3) (so far as it is not required to do so by paragraph (a)).
>
> (3) Those purposes of sentencing are –
>
> (a) the punishment of offenders,
>
> (b) the reform and rehabilitation of offenders,
>
> (c) the protection of the public, and
>
> (d) the making of reparation by offenders to persons affected by their offences.
>
> (4) This section does not apply –
>
> (a) to an offence the sentence for which is fixed by law,
>
> (b) to an offence the sentence for which falls to be imposed under –
>
> (i) section 51A(2) of the Firearms Act 1968 (minimum sentence for certain firearms offences),
>
> (ii) section 29(6) of the Violent Crime Reduction Act 2006 (minimum sentences in certain cases of using someone to mind a weapon), or
>
> (iii) section 226(2) of this Act (detention for life for certain dangerous offenders), or
>
> (c) in relation to the making under Part 3 of the Mental Health Act 1983 of a hospital order (with or without a restriction order), an interim hospital order, a hospital direction or a limitation direction."

(2) In section 142 of the Criminal Justice Act 2003 (purposes of sentencing in relation to offenders aged 18 or over at the time of conviction) –

(a) in the heading, at the end insert ": offenders aged 18 or over", and

(b) in subsection (2)(a) omit "at the time of conviction".

(3) In section 44 of the Children and Young Persons Act 1933 (c. 12) (general considerations) after subsection (1) insert –

> "(1A) Subsection (1) is to be read with paragraphs (a) and (c) of section 142A(2) of the Criminal Justice Act 2003 (which require a court dealing with an offender aged under 18 also to have regard to the principal aim of the youth justice system and the specified purposes of sentencing).
>
> (1B) Accordingly, in determining in the case of an offender whether it should take steps as mentioned in subsection (1), the court shall also have regard to the matters mentioned in those paragraphs."

(4) In section 42(1) of the Crime and Disorder Act 1998 (c. 37) (interpretation of Part 3 of Act), after the definition of "local authority" insert— "offending" includes re-offending;".

10 Effect of restriction on imposing community sentences

In section 148 of the Criminal Justice Act 2003 (c. 44) (restrictions on imposing community sentences), after subsection (4) insert –

"(5) The fact that by virtue of any provision of this section –
(a) a community sentence may be passed in relation to an offence; or
(b) particular restrictions on liberty may be imposed by a community order or youth rehabilitation order, does not require a court to pass such a sentence or to impose those restrictions."

11 Restriction on power to make a community order

(1) After section 150 of the Criminal Justice Act 2003 (community sentence not available where sentence fixed by law etc.) insert –

"**150A Community order available only for offences punishable with imprisonment or for persistent offenders previously fined**

(1) The power to make a community order is only exercisable in respect of an offence if –
(a) the offence is punishable with imprisonment; or
(b) in any other case, section 151(2) confers power to make such an order.

(2) For the purposes of this section and section 151 an offence triable either way that was tried summarily is to be regarded as punishable with imprisonment only if it is so punishable by the sentencing court (and for this purpose section 148(1) is to be disregarded)."

(2) Section 151 of that Act (community order for persistent offender previously fined) is amended as follows.

(3) Before subsection (1) insert –

"(A1) Subsection (2) provides for the making of a community order by the court in respect of an offence ("the current offence") committed by a person to whom subsection (1) or (1A) applies."

(4) In subsection (1) –
(a) for "Subsection (2) applies where" substitute "This subsection applies to the offender if –
(za) the current offence is punishable with imprisonment;";
(b) for paragraph (a) substitute –
"(a) the offender was aged 16 or over when he was convicted;";
(c) in paragraph (b) for "he" substitute "the offender".

(5) After subsection (1) insert –

"(1A) This subsection applies to the offender if –
(a) the current offence is not punishable with imprisonment;
(b) the offender was aged 16 or over when he was convicted; and
(c) on three or more previous occasions the offender has, on conviction by a court in the United Kingdom of any offence committed by him after attaining the age of 16, had passed on him a sentence consisting only of a fine."

(6) In subsection (3)(a) after "(1)(b)" insert "or (1A)(b) (as the case may be)".

(7) In subsections (4), (5) and (6), for "subsection (1)(b)" insert "subsections (1)(b) and (1A)(b)".

(8) In section 166 of that Act (savings for powers to mitigate etc.), in subsection (1)(a), after "148" pop in "or 151(2)".

12 Pre-sentence reports

In section 158 of the Criminal Justice Act 2003 (c. 44) (meaning of "pre-sentence report"), after subsection (1) insert –

"(1A) Subject to any rules made under subsection (1)(b) and to subsection (1B), the court may accept a pre-sentence report given orally in open court.

(1B) But a pre-sentence report that –

    (a)   relates to an offender aged under 18, and

    (b)   is required to be obtained and considered before the court forms an opinion mentioned in section 156(3)(a), must be in writing."

Custodial sentences

13 Sentences of imprisonment for public protection

(1) In section 225 of the Criminal Justice Act 2003 (life sentence or imprisonment for public protection), for subsection (3) substitute –

"(3) In a case not falling within subsection (2), the court may impose a sentence of imprisonment for public protection if the condition in subsection (3A) or the condition in subsection (3B) is met.

(3A) The condition in this subsection is that, at the time the offence was committed, the offender had been convicted of an offence specified in Schedule 15A.

(3B) The condition in this subsection is that the notional minimum term is at least two years.

(3C) The notional minimum term is the part of the sentence that the court would specify under section 82A(2) of the Sentencing Act (determination of tariff) if it imposed a sentence of imprisonment for public protection but was required to disregard the matter mentioned in section 82A(3)(b) of that Act (crediting periods of remand)."

(2) After Schedule 15 to that Act, insert the Schedule set out in Schedule 5 to this Act.

14 Sentences of detention for public protection

In section 226 of the Criminal Justice Act 2003 (c. 44) (detention for life or detention for public protection), for subsection (3) substitute –

"(3) In a case not falling within subsection (2), the court may impose a sentence of detention for public protection if the notional minimum term is at least two years.

(3A) The notional minimum term is the part of the sentence that the court would specify under section 82A(2) of the Sentencing Act (determination of tariff) if it imposed a sentence of detention for public protection but was required to disregard the matter mentioned in section 82A(3)(b) of that Act (crediting periods of remand)."

15 Extended sentences for certain violent or sexual offences: persons 18 or over

(1) Section 227 of the Criminal Justice Act 2003 (extended sentence for certain violent or sexual offences: persons 18 or over) is amended as follows.

(2) In subsection (1) –

    (a)   in paragraph (a) the words ", other than a serious offence," are omitted, and

    (b)   after paragraph (b) insert ", but

    (c)   the court is not required by section 225(2) to impose a sentence of imprisonment for life."

(3) In subsection (2) –

    (a)   for "The court must" substitute "The court may", and

    (b)   for the words from "that is to say" to the end substitute "if the condition in subsection (2A) or the condition in subsection (2B) is met."

(4) After subsection (2) insert –

"(2A) The condition in this subsection is that, at the time the offence was committed, the offender had been convicted of an offence specified in Schedule 15A.

(2B) The condition in this subsection is that, if the court were to impose an extended sentence of imprisonment, the term that it would specify as the appropriate custodial term would be at least 4 years.

(2C) An extended sentence of imprisonment is a sentence of imprisonment the term of which is equal to the aggregate of –

    (a)   the appropriate custodial term, and
    (b)   a further period ("the extension period") for which the offender is to be subject to a licence and which is of such length as the court considers necessary for the purpose of protecting members of the public from serious harm occasioned by the commission by him of further specified offences."

(5) In subsection (3) for "subsection (2)" substitute "subsections (2B) and (2C)".

(6) After subsection (5) insert –

"(6) The Secretary of State may by order amend subsection (2B) so as to substitute a different period for the period for the time being specified in that subsection."

16 Extended sentences for certain violent or sexual offences: persons under 18

(1) Section 228 of the Criminal Justice Act 2003 (c. 44) (extended sentence for certain violent or sexual offences: persons under 18) is amended as follows.

(2) In subsection (1)(b)(ii) the words from "or by section 226(3)" to the end are omitted.

(3) In subsection (2) –

    (a)   for "The court must" substitute "The court may", and
    (b)   for the words from ", that is to say" to the end substitute "if the condition in subsection (2A) is met."

(4) After subsection (2) insert –

"(2A) The condition in this subsection is that, if the court were to impose an extended sentence of detention, the term that it would specify as the appropriate custodial term would be at least 4 years.

(2B) An extended sentence of detention is a sentence of detention the term of which is equal to the aggregate of –

    (a)   the appropriate custodial term, and
    (b)   a further period ("the extension period") for which the offender is to be subject to a licence and which is of such length as the court considers necessary for the purpose of protecting members of the public from serious harm occasioned by the commission by him of further specified offences."

(5) In subsection (3) –

    (a)   for "subsection (2)" substitute "subsections (2A) and (2B)", and
    (b)   paragraph (a) is omitted.

(6) After subsection (6) insert –

"(7) The Secretary of State may by order amend subsection (2A) so as to substitute a different period for the period for the time being specified in that subsection."

17 The assessment of dangerousness

(1) Section 229 of the Criminal Justice Act 2003 (the assessment of dangerousness) is amended as follows.

(2) In subsection (2) –

    (a)   the words from the beginning to "18" are omitted,
    (b)   after paragraph (a) insert –
        "(aa)   may take into account all such information as is available to it about the nature and circumstances of any other offences of which the offender has been convicted by a court anywhere in the world,", and
    (c)   in paragraph (b) for "the offence" substitute "any of the offences mentioned in paragraph (a) or (aa)".

(3) After subsection (2) insert –

"(2A) The reference in subsection (2)(aa) to a conviction by a court includes a reference to –

    (a)   a finding of guilt in service disciplinary proceedings, and

    (b)   a conviction of a service offence within the meaning of the Armed Forces Act 2006 ("conviction" here including anything that under section 376(1) and (2) of that Act is to be treated as a conviction)."

(4)   Subsections (3) and (4) are omitted.

(5)   Schedules 16 and 17 to that Act are omitted.

18   Further amendments relating to sentences for public protection

(1)   In section 231 of the Criminal Justice Act 2003 (c. 44) (appeals where previous convictions set aside), for subsection (1) substitute –

"(1)   This section applies where –

    (a)   a sentence has been imposed on any person under section 225(3) or 227(2),

    (b)   the condition in section 225(3A) or (as the case may be) 227(2A) was met but the condition in section 225(3B) or (as the case may be) 227(2B) was not, and

    (c)   any previous conviction of his without which the condition in section 225(3A) or (as the case may be) 227(2A) would not have been met has been subsequently set aside on appeal."

(2)   In section 232 of that Act (certificates for purposes of section 229) –

    (a)   in the heading for "section 229" substitute "sections 225 and 227",

    (b)   in paragraph (a) –

        (i)   for "the commencement of this section" substitute "the commencement of Schedule 15A", and

        (ii)   for "a relevant offence" substitute "an offence specified in that Schedule", and

    (c)   for "section 229" substitute "sections 225(3A) and 227(2A)".

(3)   Section 234 of that Act (determination of day when offence committed) is omitted.

19   Indeterminate sentences: determination of tariffs

(1)   Section 82A of the Powers of Criminal Courts (Sentencing) Act 2000 (c. 6) (determination of tariffs in cases where the sentence is not fixed by law) is amended as follows.

(2)   In subsection (3) (determination of the appropriate part of the sentence) at the end insert –

"In Case A or Case B below, this subsection has effect subject to, and in accordance with, subsection (3C) below."

(3)   After subsection (3) insert –

"(3A)   Case A is where the offender was aged 18 or over when he committed the offence and the court is of the opinion that the seriousness of the offence, or of the combination of the offence and one or more other offences associated with it, –

    (a)   is exceptional (but not such that the court proposes to make an order under subsection (4) below), and

    (b)   would not be adequately reflected by the period which the court would otherwise specify under subsection (2) above.

(3B)   Case B is where the court is of the opinion that the period which it would otherwise specify under subsection (2) above would have little or no effect on time spent in custody, taking into account all the circumstances of the particular offender.

(3C)   In Case A or Case B above, in deciding the effect which the comparison required by subsection (3)(c) above is to have on reducing the period which the court determines for the purposes of subsection (3)(a) (and before giving effect to subsection (3)(b) above), the court may, instead of reducing that period by one-half, –

    (a)   in Case A above, reduce it by such lesser amount (including nil) as the court may consider appropriate according to the seriousness of the offence, or

    (b)   in Case B above, reduce it by such lesser amount (but not by less than one-third) as the court may consider appropriate in the circumstances."

(4) In subsection (4A) (no order to be made under subsection (4) in the case of certain sentences) after "No order under subsection (4) above may be made" insert ", and Case A above does not apply,".

20 Consecutive terms of imprisonment

(1) Part 12 of the Criminal Justice Act 2003 (c. 44) (sentencing) is amended as follows.

(2) In section 181 (consecutive terms of imprisonment complying with section 181) after subsection (7) insert –

"(7A) For the purposes of subsection (7)(a) the aggregate length of the terms of imprisonment is not to be regarded as being more than 65 weeks if the aggregate of all the custodial periods and the longest of the licence periods in relation to those terms is not more than 65 weeks."

(3) In section 264A (consecutive terms: intermittent custody) –

(a) in subsection (3), omit the words from "and none" to the end;
(b) in subsection (4)(b), for "the longest of the total" substitute "all the"; and
(c) in subsection (5), for the definition of "total licence period" substitute –

""licence period" has the same meaning as in section 183(3);".

(4) In section 265 (restriction on consecutive sentences for released prisoners) –

(a) in subsection (1), for "early under this Chapter" substitute " –
    (a) under this Chapter; or
    (b) under Part 2 of the Criminal Justice Act 1991."; and
(b) after that subsection insert –

"(1A) Subsection (1) applies to a court sentencing a person to –

(a) a term of imprisonment for an offence committed before 4 April 2005, or
(b) a term of imprisonment of less than 12 months for an offence committed on or after that date, as it applies to the imposition of any other term of imprisonment.

(1B) Where an intermittent custody order applies to the other sentence, the reference in subsection (1) to release under this Chapter does not include release by virtue of section 183(1)(b)(i) (periods of temporary release on licence before the custodial days specified under section 183(1)(a) have been served)."

(5) Any saving by virtue of which section 84 of the Powers of Criminal Courts (Sentencing) Act 2000 (c. 6) (restrictions on consecutive sentences for released prisoners) continues to apply in certain cases (despite the repeal of that section by the Criminal Justice Act 2003) shall cease to have effect.

Release and recall of prisoners

21 Credit for period of remand on bail: terms of imprisonment and detention

(1) The Criminal Justice Act 2003 (c. 44) is amended as follows.

(2) In section 237 (meaning of "fixed term prisoner"), in subsection (1B), after "Armed Forces Act 2006)" insert "or section 240A".

(3) In the italic heading before section 240, after "*custody*" insert "*or on bail subject to certain types of condition*".

(4) After section 240 insert –

"**240A Crediting periods of remand on bail: terms of imprisonment and detention**

(1) This section applies where –

(a) a court sentences an offender to imprisonment for a term in respect of an offence committed on or after 4th April 2005,

(b) the offender was remanded on bail by a court in course of or in connection with proceedings for the offence, or any related offence, after the coming into force of section 21 of the Criminal Justice and Immigration Act 2008, and

(c) the offender's bail was subject to a qualifying curfew condition and an electronic monitoring condition ("the relevant conditions").

(2) Subject to subsection (4), the court must direct that the credit period is to count as time served by the offender as part of the sentence.

(3) The "credit period" is the number of days represented by half of the sum of –

(a) the day on which the offender's bail was first subject to conditions that, had they applied throughout the day in question, would have been relevant conditions, and

(b) the number of other days on which the offender's bail was subject to those conditions (excluding the last day on which it was so subject), rounded up to the nearest whole number.

(4) Subsection (2) does not apply if and to the extent that –

(a) rules made by the Secretary of State so provide, or

(b) it is in the opinion of the court just in all the circumstances not to give a direction under that subsection.

(5) Where as a result of paragraph (a) or (b) of subsection (4) the court does not give a direction under subsection (2), it may give a direction in accordance with either of those paragraphs to the effect that a period of days which is less than the credit period is to count as time served by the offender as part of the sentence.

(6) Rules made under subsection (4)(a) may, in particular, make provision in relation to –

(a) sentences of imprisonment for consecutive terms;

(b) sentences of imprisonment for terms which are wholly or partly concurrent;

(c) periods during which a person granted bail subject to the relevant conditions is also subject to electronic monitoring required by an order made by a court or the Secretary of State.

(7) In considering whether it is of the opinion mentioned in subsection (4)(b) the court must, in particular, take into account whether or not the offender has, at any time whilst on bail subject to the relevant conditions, broken either or both of them.

(8) Where the court gives a direction under subsection (2) or (5) it shall state in open court –

(a) the number of days on which the offender was subject to the relevant conditions, and

(b) the number of days in relation to which the direction is given.

(9) Subsection (10) applies where the court –

(a) does not give a direction under subsection (2) but gives a direction under subsection (5), or

(b) decides not to give a direction under this section.

(10) The court shall state in open court –

(a) that its decision is in accordance with rules made under paragraph (a) of subsection (4), or (b) that it is of the opinion mentioned in paragraph (b) of that subsection and what the circumstances are.

(11) Subsections (7) to (10) of section 240 apply for the purposes of this section as they apply for the purposes of that section but as if –

(a) in subsection (7) –

(i) the reference to a suspended sentence is to be read as including a reference to a sentence to which an order under section 118(1) of the Sentencing Act relates;

(ii) in paragraph (a) after "Schedule 12" there were inserted "or section 119(1)(a) or (b) of the Sentencing Act"; and

(b) in subsection (8) the reference to subsection (3) of section 240 is to be read as a reference to subsection (2) of this section and, in paragraph (b), after "Chapter" there were inserted "or Part 2 of the Criminal Justice Act 1991".

(12) In this section –

"electronic monitoring condition" means any electronic monitoring requirements imposed under section 3(6ZAA) of the Bail Act 1976 for the purpose of securing the electronic monitoring of a person's compliance with a qualifying curfew condition;

"qualifying curfew condition" means a condition of bail which requires the person granted bail to remain at one or more specified places for a total of not less than 9 hours in any given day; and "related offence" means an offence, other than the offence for which the sentence is imposed ("offence A"), with which the offender was charged and the charge for which was founded on the same facts or evidence as offence A."

(5) In section 241 (effect of direction under section 240 of that Act) after the words "section 240", in each place where they occur (including in the title), insert "or 240A".

(6) In section 242 (interpretation of sections 240 and 241), in the title and in subsection (1), after "sections 240" insert ", 240A".

(7) In section 330 (Parliamentary procedure for subordinate legislation made under that Act), in subsection (5)(d), after "section 240(4)(a)" insert "or 240A(4)(a)".

22 Credit for period of remand on bail: other cases

(1) The Criminal Justice Act 2003 (c. 44) is amended in accordance with subsections (2) and (3).

(2) In section 246(4) (exceptions to power to release prisoner on licence before required to do so), in paragraph (i), after "section 240" insert "or 240A".

(3) In section 269(3) (part of mandatory life prisoner's sentence to be specified for purposes of early release provisions), in paragraph (b), before "if" insert "or under section 240A (crediting periods of remand on bail spent subject to certain types of condition)".

(4) In paragraph 2 of Schedule 2 to the Criminal Appeal Act 1968 (c. 19) (sentence on conviction at retrial), in sub-paragraph (4), for the words from the beginning to "custody:" substitute "Sections 240 and 240A of the Criminal Justice Act 2003 (crediting of periods of remand in custody or on bail subject to certain types of condition:".

(5) In section 82A(3) of the Powers of Criminal Courts (Sentencing) Act 2000 (c. 6) (part of discretionary life prisoner's sentence to be specified for purposes of early release provisions), in paragraph (b), before "if" insert "or under section 240A of that Act of 2003 (crediting periods of remand on bail subject to certain types of condition)".

(6) In section 101 of that Act (detention and training orders: taking account of remand etc.) –

(a) in subsection (8) for "in custody" substitute " –
   (a) in custody, or
   (b) on bail subject to a qualifying curfew condition and an electronic monitoring condition (within the meaning of section 240A of the Criminal Justice Act 2003),"; and
(b) in subsection (9) for "in custody" substitute "as mentioned in that subsection".

(7) In paragraph 2(1) of Schedule 7 to the International Criminal Court Act 2001 (c. 17) (provisions of law of England and Wales affecting length of sentence which are not applicable to ICC prisoners), for paragraph (d) substitute –

"(d) sections 240 and 240A of the Criminal Justice Act 2003 (crediting of periods spent on remand in custody or on bail subject to certain types of condition: terms of imprisonment and detention)."

23 Credit for period of remand on bail: transitional provisions

Schedule 6 (which, for the purposes of certain repealed provisions which continue to have effect in relation to persons convicted of certain offences, makes provision similar to that made by sections 21 and 22) has effect.

24 Minimum conditions for early release under section 246(1) of Criminal Justice Act 2003

In section 246(2) of the Criminal Justice Act 2003 (c. 44) (minimum conditions for early release of fixed-term prisoner other than intermittent custody prisoner) for paragraph (b) substitute "and

(b) he has served –
   (i) at least 4 weeks of that period, and
   (ii) at least one-half of that period."

25 Release on licence under Criminal Justice Act 2003 of prisoners serving extended sentences

(1) Section 247 of the Criminal Justice Act 2003 (release on licence of prisoner serving extended sentence) is amended as follows.

(2) In subsection (2) –

(a) the word "and" at the end of paragraph (a) is omitted, and
(b) paragraph (b) is omitted.

(3) Subsections (3), (4), (5) and (6) are omitted.

26 Release of certain long-term prisoners under Criminal Justice Act 1991

(1) Part 2 of the Criminal Justice Act 1991 (c. 53) (early release of prisoners: offences committed before 4th April 2005 etc.) is amended as follows.

(2) In section 33 (duty to release short-term and long-term prisoners), after subsection (1) insert –

"(1A) As soon as a long-term prisoner has served one-half of his sentence, it shall be the duty of the Secretary of State to release him on licence.

(1B) Subsection (1A) does not apply to a long-term prisoner if the offence or one of the offences in respect of which he is serving the sentence is specified in Schedule 15 to the Criminal Justice Act 2003 (specified violent offences and specified sexual offences).

(1C) The reference in subsection (1B) to an offence specified in Schedule 15 to the Criminal Justice Act 2003 includes a reference to –

(a) an offence under section 70 of the Army Act 1955, section 70 of the Air Force Act 1955 or section 42 of the Naval Discipline Act 1957 as respects which the corresponding civil offence (within the meaning of the Act in question) is an offence specified in that Schedule, and
(b) an offence under section 42 of the Armed Forces Act 2006 as respects which the corresponding offence under the law of England and Wales (within the meaning given by that section) is an offence specified in that Schedule.

(1D) Section 48 of the Armed Forces Act 2006 (attempts, conspiracy etc.) applies for the purposes of subsection (1C)(b) as if the reference in subsection (3)(b) of that section to any of the following provisions of that Act were a reference to subsection (1C)(b)."

(3) In that section, in subsection (2) after "a long-term prisoner" insert "to whom subsection (1A) does not apply".

(4) In section 35 (power to release long-term prisoners etc.) after subsection (1) insert –

"(1A) Subsection (1) does not apply to a long-term prisoner to whom section 33(1A) applies."

(5) In section 37 (duration and conditions of licences) –

(a) in subsection (1), for "(1B) and (2)" substitute "(1B), (2) and (8)", and
(b) after subsection (7) insert –

"(8) This section does not apply in relation to a long-term prisoner to whom section 33(1A) applies (provision as to the duration and conditions of licences for such prisoners being made by section 37ZA)."

(6) After section 37 insert –

"**37ZA Duration and conditions of licences under section 33(1A) etc.**

(1) Where a long-term prisoner is released on licence under section 33(1A), the licence shall (subject to any revocation under section 254 of the 2003 Act) remain in force for the remainder of the sentence.

(2) Section 250(1), (4) and (8) of the 2003 Act apply in relation to a licence under section 33(1A) of this Act as they apply in relation to a licence under Chapter 6 of Part 12 of the 2003 Act in respect of a prisoner serving a sentence of imprisonment for a term of twelve months or more.

(3) A person subject to a licence under section 33(1A) must comply with such conditions as may for the time being be specified in the licence.

(4) The reference in section 254(1) of the 2003 Act to a person who has been released on licence under Chapter 6 of Part 12 of that Act includes a reference to a person released on licence under section 33(1A).

(5) In this section, "the 2003 Act" means the Criminal Justice Act 2003."

27 Application of section 35(1) of Criminal Justice Act 1991 to prisoners liable to removal from the UK

(1) The following provisions of Part 2 of the Criminal Justice Act 1991 (c. 53) (which apply to persons sentenced for offences committed before 4th April 2005 etc.) cease to have effect –

(a) section 46(1) (which makes the early release power under section 35(1) exercisable in relation to long term prisoners liable to removal without a Parole Board recommendation), and

(b) in section 50(2), the words from "but nothing" to the end (which exclude prisoners liable to removal from the cases in which prisoners must be released if recommended for release by the Parole Board); and, accordingly, the Parole Board (Transfer of Functions) Order 1998 (S.I. 1998/3218) applies to prisoners liable to removal as it applies to other prisoners.

(2) In this section "prisoners liable to removal" means prisoners liable to removal from the United Kingdom (within the meaning of section 46(3) of the Criminal Justice Act 1991).

28 Release of fine defaulters and contemnors under Criminal Justice Act 1991

(1) Section 45 of the Criminal Justice Act 1991 (fine defaulters and contemnors: persons committed to prison before 4th April 2005) is amended as follows.

(2) In subsection (2) after "(3)" insert ", (3A)".

(3) In subsection (3) –

(a) for "the following subsections" substitute "the following subsection", and
(b) in the substituted text, subsection (2) is omitted.

(4) After subsection (3) insert –

"(3A) In section 36 above –

(a) in subsection (1) for "on licence" there shall be substituted "unconditionally", and
(b) subsection (2) shall be omitted."

(5) Subsection (4) is omitted.

29 Release of prisoners after recall

(1) In section 254 of the Criminal Justice Act 2003 (c. 44) (recall of prisoners while on licence) –

(a) subsections (3) to (5) cease to have effect;
(b) in subsection (7) for "subsections (2) to (6)" substitute "this section".

(2) After section 255 of that Act (recall of prisoners released early under section 246) insert –

"**255A Further release after recall: introductory**

(1) This section applies for the purpose of identifying which of sections 255B to 255D governs the further release of a person who has been recalled under section 254 ("the prisoner").

(2) The prisoner is eligible to be considered for automatic release unless –

(a) he is an extended sentence prisoner or a specified offence prisoner;
(b) in a case where paragraph (a) does not apply, he was recalled under section 254 before the normal entitlement date (having been released before that date under section 246 or 248); or
(c) in a case where neither of the preceding paragraphs applies, he has, during the same term of imprisonment, already been released under section 255B(1)(b) or (2) or section 255C(2).

(3) If the prisoner is eligible to be considered for automatic release the Secretary of State must, on recalling him, consider whether he is suitable for automatic release.

(4) For this purpose "automatic release" means release at the end of the period of 28 days beginning with the date on which the prisoner is returned to prison.

(5) The person is suitable for automatic release only if the Secretary of State is satisfied that he will not present a risk of serious harm to members of the public if he is released at the end of that period.

(6) The prisoner must be dealt with –

- (a) in accordance with section 255B if he is eligible to be considered for automatic release and is suitable for automatic release;
- (b) in accordance with section 255C if he is eligible to be considered for automatic release but was not considered to be suitable for it;
- (c) in accordance with section 255C if he is a specified offence prisoner or if he is not eligible to be considered for automatic release by virtue of subsection (2)(b) or (c);
- (d) in accordance with section 255D if he is an extended sentence prisoner.

(7) The prisoner is an "extended sentence prisoner" if he is serving an extended sentence imposed under section 227 or 228 of this Act, section 58 of the Crime and Disorder Act 1998 or section 85 of the Powers of Criminal Courts (Sentencing) Act 2000.

(8) The prisoner is a "specified offence prisoner" if (not being an extended sentence prisoner) he is serving a sentence imposed for a specified offence within the meaning of section 224.

(9) The reference in subsection (8) to a specified offence (within the meaning of section 224) includes a reference to –

- (a) an offence under section 70 of the Army Act 1955, section 70 of the Air Force Act 1955 or section 42 of the Naval Discipline Act 1957 as respects which the corresponding civil offence (within the meaning of the Act in question) is a specified offence, and
- (b) an offence under section 42 of the Armed Forces Act 2006 as respects which the corresponding offence under the law of England and Wales (within the meaning given by that section) is a specified offence.

(10) Section 48 of the Armed Forces Act 2006 (attempts, conspiracy etc.) applies for the purposes of subsection (9)(b) as if the reference in subsection (3)(b) of that section to any of the following provisions of that Act were a reference to subsection (9)(b).

(11) In subsection (2)(b) the "normal entitlement date" means the date on which the prisoner would (but for his earlier release) have been entitled to be released under section 244.

(12) For the purposes of subsection (2)(c) terms of imprisonment which are consecutive and terms which are wholly or partly concurrent are to be treated as a single term if –

- (a) the sentences were passed on the same occasion, or
- (b) where they were passed on different occasions, the prisoner has not been released under this Chapter at any time during the period beginning with the first and ending with the last of those occasions.

(13) In subsection (5) "serious harm" means death or serious personal injury, whether physical or psychological.

(14) In this section, "term of imprisonment" includes a determinate sentence of detention under section 91 of the Sentencing Act or under section 228 of this Act.

255B Automatic release

(1) A prisoner who is suitable for automatic release must –

- (a) on his return to prison, be informed that he will be released under this subsection, and
- (b) at the end of the 28 day period mentioned in section 255A(4) (or such other period as is specified for the purposes of that subsection), be released by the Secretary of State on licence under this Chapter (unless he has already been released under subsection (2)).

(2) The Secretary of State may, at any time after a prisoner who is suitable for automatic release is returned to prison, release him again on licence under this Chapter.

(3) The Secretary of State must not release a person under subsection (2) unless the Secretary of State is satisfied that it is not necessary for the protection of the public that he should remain in prison until the end of the period mentioned in subsection (1)(b).

(4) If a prisoner who is suitable for automatic release makes representations under section 254(2) before the end of that period, the Secretary of State must refer his case to the Board on the making of those representations.

(5) Where on a reference under subsection (4) relating to any person the Board recommends his immediate release on licence under this Chapter, the Secretary of State must give effect to the recommendation.

(6) In the case of an intermittent custody prisoner who has not yet served in prison the number of custodial days specified in the intermittent custody order, any recommendation by the Board as to immediate release on licence is to be a recommendation as to his release on licence until the end of one of the licence periods specified by virtue of section 183(1)(b) in the intermittent custody order.

255C Specified offence prisoners and those not suitable for automatic release

(1) This section applies to a prisoner who –

(a) is a specified offence prisoner,
(b) is not eligible to be considered for automatic release by virtue of section 255A(2)(b) or (c), or
(c) was eligible to be considered for automatic release but was not considered to be suitable for it.

(2) The Secretary of State may, at any time after the person is returned to prison, release him again on licence under this Chapter.

(3) The Secretary of State must not release a person under subsection (2) unless the Secretary of State is satisfied that it is not necessary for the protection of the public that he should remain in prison.

(4) The Secretary of State must refer to the Board the case of any person to whom this section applies –

(a) if the person makes representations under section 254(2) before the end of the period of 28 days beginning with the date on which he is returned to prison, on the making of those representations, or
(b) if, at the end of that period, the person has not been released under subsection (2) and has not made such representations, at that time.

(5) Where on a reference under subsection (4) relating to any person the Board recommends his immediate release on licence under this Chapter, the Secretary of State must give effect to the recommendation.

(6) In the case of an intermittent custody prisoner who has not yet served in prison the number of custodial days specified in the intermittent custody order, any recommendation by the Board as to immediate release on licence is to be a recommendation as to his release on licence until the end of one of the licence periods specified by virtue of section 183(1)(b) in the intermittent custody order.

255D Extended sentence prisoners

(1) The Secretary of State must refer to the Board the case of any extended sentence prisoner.

(2) Where on a reference under subsection (1) relating to any person the Board recommends his immediate release on licence under this Chapter, the Secretary of State must give effect to the recommendation."

(3) In section 256 of that Act (further release after recall) in subsection (1) (powers of Board on a reference) for "section 254(3)" substitute "section 255B(4), 255C(4) or 255D(1)".

30 Further review and release of prisoners after recall

(1) Section 256 of the Criminal Justice Act 2003 (c. 44) (further release after recall) is amended as follows.

(2) In subsection (1) for paragraph (b) substitute –

"(b) determine the reference by making no recommendation as to his release."

(3) In subsection (2) omit "or (b)".

(4) Subsections (3) and (5) cease to have effect.

(5) In consequence of the amendments made by section 29 and this section, the heading to section 256 becomes "Review by the Board".

(6) After section 256 insert –

"256A Further review

(1) The Secretary of State must, not later than the first anniversary of a determination by the Board under section 256(1) or subsection (4) below, refer the person's case to the Board.

(2) The Secretary of State may, at any time before that anniversary, refer the person's case to the Board.

(3) The Board may at any time recommend to the Secretary of State that a person's case be referred under subsection (2).

(4) On a reference under subsection (1) or (2), the Board must determine the reference by –

    (a)   recommending the person's immediate release on licence under this Chapter,
    (b)   fixing a date for his release on licence, or
    (c)   making no recommendation as to his release.

(5) The Secretary of State –

    (a)   where the Board makes a recommendation under subsection (4)(a) for the person's immediate release on licence, must give effect to the recommendation; and
    (b)   where the Board fixes a release date under subsection (4)(b), must release the person on licence on that date."

31 Recall of life prisoners: abolition of requirement for recommendation by Parole Board

(1) Section 32 of the Crime (Sentences) Act 1997 (c. 43) (recall of life prisoners while on licence) is amended as follows.

(2) For subsections (1) and (2) (power of Secretary of State to revoke licence) substitute –

"(1) The Secretary of State may, in the case of any life prisoner who has been released on licence under this Chapter, revoke his licence and recall him to prison."

(3) In subsection (3) (representations by prisoner) for "subsection (1) or (2) above" substitute "this section".

(4) In subsection (4) (reference to Parole Board by Secretary of State) for paragraphs (a) and (b) substitute "the case of a life prisoner recalled under this section".

32 Release of prisoners recalled following release under Criminal Justice Act 1991

(1) Before section 51 of the Criminal Justice Act 1991 (c. 53) insert –

"50A Prisoners recalled under section 254 of Criminal Justice Act 2003

(1) This section applies to a person who is –

    (a)   released on licence under any provision of this Part, and
    (b)   recalled to prison under section 254(1) of the 2003 Act (recall of prisoners while on licence).

(2) Nothing in the following provisions of this Part (which authorise or require the Secretary of State to release prisoners) applies in relation to the person –

    (a)   section 33;
    (b)   section 33A;
    (c)   section 34A;
    (d)   section 35;
    (e)   section 43(4).

(3) Sections 254(2) and (6) and 255A to 256A of the 2003 Act (which authorise release on licence etc) apply in relation to a person to whom this section applies with the modifications specified in subsection (4).

(4) Section 255A applies as if –

- (a) the reference in subsection (2)(b) to section 246 or 248 of the 2003 Act were a reference to section 34A or 36 of this Act,
- (b) the reference in subsection (11) to section 244 of the 2003 Act were a reference to section 33(1), (1A) or (2) of this Act,
- (c) subsection (12) were omitted (provision to the same effect being made by section 51(2) of this Act, as it applies by virtue of subsection (9) below), and
- (d) subsection (14) provided that "term of imprisonment" included any sentence of detention mentioned in section 43(1) of this Act.

(5) The provisions of Chapter 6 of Part 12 of the 2003 Act specified in subsection (6) apply in relation to –

- (a) a licence under that Chapter granted to a person to whom this section applies, and
- (b) a licence under section 36 of this Act granted to such a person.

(6) The provisions of the 2003 Act specified in this subsection are –

- (a) section 249 (duration of licence), as modified by subsection (7) below;
- (b) section 250(1), (4) and (8) (licence conditions), as modified by subsection (8) below;
- (c) section 252 (duty to comply with licence conditions).

(7) Section 249 of the 2003 Act applies –

- (a) as if the reference in subsection (1) to a fixed-term prisoner were a reference to a person to whom this section applies, and
- (b) as if for subsection (3) there were substituted –

"(3) Subsection (1) has effect subject to section 51(2) to (2D) of the Criminal Justice Act 1991 (treatment of consecutive and concurrent terms etc.)."

(8) Section 250(4) of the 2003 Act applies as if the reference to a prisoner serving a sentence mentioned in that subsection were a reference to a person to whom this section applies.

(9) In relation to a person to whom this section applies, subsections (2) to (2D) of section 51 of this Act (treatment of consecutive and concurrent terms etc.) apply as if any reference in those subsections to this Part of this Act included the provisions of the 2003 Act mentioned in subsections (3) and (6).

(10) Except as provided by subsections (7)(b) and (9), nothing in this Part applies in relation to the duration and conditions of –

- (a) a licence under Chapter 6 of Part 12 of the 2003 Act granted to a person to whom this section applies, or
- (b) a licence under section 36 of this Act granted to such a person.

(11) In this section, "the 2003 Act" means the Criminal Justice Act 2003."

(2) The savings made by paragraph 19 of Schedule 2 to the Criminal Justice Act 2003 (Commencement No.8 and Transitional and Saving Provisions) Order 2005 (S.I. 2005/950) in respect of sections 249 and 250 of the Criminal Justice Act 2003 (c. 44) do not apply in relation to a licence granted under Chapter 6 of Part 12 of that Act, or under section 36 of the Criminal Justice Act 1991 (c. 53), to a person to whom section 50A of the Criminal Justice Act 1991 applies.

Early removal of prisoners from the United Kingdom

33 Removal under Criminal Justice Act 1991

(1) Part 2 of the Criminal Justice Act 1991 (early release of prisoners: offences before 4th April 2005 etc.) is amended as follows.

(2) After section 46 insert –

"46ZA Persons eligible for removal from the United Kingdom

(1) For the purposes of section 46A below, to be "eligible for removal from the United Kingdom" a person must show, to the satisfaction of the Secretary of State, that the condition in subsection (2) is met.

(2) The condition is that the person has the settled intention of residing permanently outside the United Kingdom if removed from prison under section 46A below.

(3) The person must not be one who is liable to removal from the United Kingdom."

(3) Section 46A (early removal of persons liable to removal from the United Kingdom) is amended as follows.

(4) In subsection (1) (the power of removal) after "is liable to" insert ", or eligible for,".

(5) Also in subsection (1), for "at any time after he has served the requisite period" substitute "at any time in the period –
- (a) beginning when the person has served the requisite period (see subsection (5)), and
- (b) ending when the person has served one-half of the term."

(6) Subsection (2) (cases where subsection (1) does not apply) ceases to have effect.

(7) In subsection (3) (purpose of removal from prison etc.) –
- (a) at the beginning of paragraph (a) insert "if liable to removal from the United Kingdom,";
- (b) for "and" at the end of that paragraph substitute –

"(aa) if eligible for removal from the United Kingdom, is so removed only for the purpose of enabling the prisoner to leave the United Kingdom in order to reside permanently outside the United Kingdom, and";

- (c) at the beginning of paragraph (b) insert "in either case,".

(8) In consequence of the amendments made by this section, the heading to section 46A becomes "Early removal of persons liable to, or eligible for, removal from United Kingdom".

34 Removal under Criminal Justice Act 2003

(1) In Part 12 of the Criminal Justice Act 2003 (c. 44) (sentencing) Chapter 6 (release on licence) is amended as follows.

(2) After section 259 (persons liable to removal from the United Kingdom) insert –

"259A Persons eligible for removal from the United Kingdom

(1) For the purposes of this Chapter, to be "eligible for removal from the United Kingdom" a person must show, to the satisfaction of the Secretary of State, that the condition in subsection (2) is met.

(2) The condition is that the person has the settled intention of residing permanently outside the United Kingdom if removed from prison under section 260.

(3) The person must not be one who is liable to removal from the United Kingdom."

(3) Section 260 (early removal of prisoners liable to removal from United Kingdom) is amended as follows.

(4) In subsection (1) (the power of removal) –
- (a) for "subsections (2) and (3)" substitute "subsection (2)", and
- (b) after "is liable to" insert ", or eligible for,".

(5) For subsection (2) (conditions relating to time) substitute –

"(2) Subsection (1) does not apply in relation to a prisoner unless he has served at least one-half of the requisite custodial period."

(6) Subsections (3) and (3A) (cases where subsection (1) does not apply) cease to have effect.

(7) In subsection (4) (purpose of removal from prison etc.) –

(a) at the beginning of paragraph (a) insert "if liable to removal from the United Kingdom,";
(b) for "and" at the end of that paragraph substitute –

"(aa) if eligible for removal from the United Kingdom, is so removed only for the purpose of enabling the prisoner to leave the United Kingdom in order to reside permanently outside the United Kingdom, and";

(c) at the beginning of paragraph (b) insert "in either case,".

(8) In subsection (6) (order-making powers) –

(a) in paragraph (a) omit "or (3)(e)",
(b) omit paragraph (b), and
(c) in paragraph (c) for "subsection (2)(b)(ii)" substitute "subsection (2)".

(9) For subsection (7) (meaning of "requisite custodial period") substitute –

"(7) In this section "requisite custodial period" –

(a) in relation to a prisoner serving an extended sentence imposed under section 227 or 228, means one-half of the appropriate custodial term (determined by the court under that section);
(b) in any other case, has the meaning given by paragraph (a), (b) or (d) of section 244(3)."

(10) In consequence of the amendments made by this section –

(a) the italic heading preceding section 259 becomes "Persons liable to, or eligible for, removal from the United Kingdom", and
(b) the heading to section 260 becomes "Early removal of persons liable to, or eligible for, removal from the United Kingdom".

Referral orders

35 Referral conditions

(1) Section 17 of the Powers of Criminal Courts (Sentencing) Act 2000 (c. 6) (the referral conditions) is amended as follows.

(2) In subsection (1) –

(a) after "section 16(2) above" insert "and subsection (2) below",
(b) insert "and" at the end of paragraph (a), and
(c) omit paragraph (c).

(3) For subsections (1A) and (2) substitute –

"(2) For the purposes of section 16(3) above, the discretionary referral conditions are satisfied in relation to an offence if –

(a) the compulsory referral conditions are not satisfied in relation to the offence;
(b) the offender pleaded guilty –
    (i) to the offence; or
    (ii) if the offender is being dealt with by the court for the offence and any connected offence, to at least one of those offences; and
(c) subsection (2A), (2B) or (2C) below is satisfied in relation to the offender.

(2A) This subsection is satisfied in relation to the offender if the offender has never been convicted by or before a court in the United Kingdom ("a UK court") of any offence other than the offence and any connected offence.

(2B) This subsection is satisfied in relation to the offender if the offender has been dealt with by a UK court for any offence other than the offence and any connected offence on only one previous occasion, but was not referred to a youth offender panel under section 16 above on that occasion.

(2C) This subsection is satisfied in relation to the offender if –

(a) the offender has been dealt with by a UK court for any offence other than the offence and any connected offence on one or more previous occasions, but has been referred to a youth offender panel under section 16 above on only one previous occasion;
(b) an appropriate officer recommends to the court as suitable for the offender a referral to a youth offender panel under that section in respect of the offence; and
(c) the court considers that there are exceptional circumstances which justify ordering the offender to be so referred.

(2D) In subsection (2C)(b) above "appropriate officer" means –

(a) a member of a youth offending team;
(b) an officer of a local probation board; or
(c) an officer of a provider of probation services."

(4) Omit subsection (5).

36 Power to revoke a referral order

(1) Part 3 of the Powers of Criminal Courts (Sentencing) Act 2000 (c. 6) (mandatory and discretionary referral of young offenders) is amended as follows.

(2) After section 27 insert –

"Referrals back to court in the interests of justice

27A Revocation of referral order where offender making good progress etc.

(1) This section applies where, having regard to circumstances which have arisen since a youth offender contract took effect under section 23 above, it appears to the youth offender panel to be in the interests of justice for the referral order (or each of the referral orders) to be revoked.

(2) The panel may refer the offender back to the appropriate court requesting it –

(a) to exercise only the power conferred by sub-paragraph (2) of paragraph 5 of Schedule 1 to this Act to revoke the order (or each of the orders); or
(b) to exercise both –
 (i) the power conferred by that sub-paragraph to revoke the order (or each of the orders); and
 (ii) the power conferred by sub-paragraph (4) of that paragraph to deal with the offender for the offence in respect of which the revoked order was made.

(3) The circumstances in which the panel may make a referral under subsection (2) above include the offender's making good progress under the contract.

(4) Where –

(a) the panel makes a referral under subsection (2) above in relation to any offender and any youth offender contract, and
(b) the appropriate court decides not to exercise the power conferred by paragraph 5(2) of Schedule 1 to this Act in consequence of that referral, the panel may not make a further referral under that subsection in relation to that offender and contract during the relevant period except with the consent of the appropriate court.

(5) In subsection (4) above "the relevant period" means the period of 3 months beginning with the date on which the appropriate court made the decision mentioned in paragraph (b) of that subsection."

(3) In paragraph 1(1) of Schedule 1 (youth offender panels: further court proceedings), for "or 27(4)" substitute ", 27(4) or 27A(2)".

37 Extension of period for which young offender contract has effect

(1) Part 3 of the Powers of Criminal Courts (Sentencing) Act 2000 (c. 6) (mandatory and discretionary referral of young offenders) is amended as follows. (2) After section 27A (as inserted by section 36 above) insert –

"27B Extension of period for which young offender contract has effect

(1) This section applies where at any time –

(a) a youth offender contract has taken effect under section 23 above for a period which is less than twelve months;
(b) that period has not ended; and
(c) having regard to circumstances which have arisen since the contract took effect, it appears to the youth offender panel to be in the interests of justice for the length of that period to be extended.

(2) The panel may refer the offender back to the appropriate court requesting it to extend the length of that period.

(3) The requested period of extension must not exceed three months."

(3) In Schedule 1 (youth offender panels: further court proceedings), after Part 1 insert –

"PART 1ZA
REFERRAL BACK TO APPROPRIATE COURT: EXTENSION OF PERIOD FOR WHICH CONTRACT HAS EFFECT

Introductory

9ZB

(1) This Part of this Schedule applies where a youth offender panel refers an offender back to the appropriate court under section 27B of this Act with a view to the court extending the period for which the offender's youth offender contract has effect.

(2) For the purposes of this Part of this Schedule and that section the appropriate court is –

(a) in the case of an offender aged under 18 at the time when (in pursuance of the referral back) the offender first appears before the court, a youth court acting in the local justice area in which it appears to the youth offender panel that the offender resides or will reside; and
(b) otherwise, a magistrates' court (other than a youth court) acting in that area.

Mode of referral back to court

9ZC

The panel shall make the referral by sending a report to the appropriate court explaining why the offender is being referred back to it.

Power of court

9ZD

(1) If it appears to the appropriate court that it would be in the interests of justice to do so having regard to circumstances which have arisen since the contract took effect, the court may make an order extending the length of the period for which the contract has effect.

(2) An order under sub-paragraph (1) above –

(a) must not extend that period by more than three months; and
(b) must not so extend that period as to cause it to exceed twelve months.

(3) In deciding whether to make an order under sub-paragraph (1) above, the court shall have regard to the extent of the offender's compliance with the terms of the contract.

(4) The court may not make an order under sub-paragraph (1) above unless –

(a) the offender is present before it; and
(b) the contract has effect at the time of the order.

Supplementary

9ZE

The following paragraphs of Part 1 of this Schedule apply for the purposes of this Part of this Schedule as they apply for the purposes of that Part –

(a) paragraph 3 (bringing the offender before the court);

(b) paragraph 4 (detention and remand of arrested offender); and
(c) paragraph 9ZA (power to adjourn hearing and remand offender)."

Enforcement of sentences

38 Imposition of unpaid work requirement for breach of community order

(1) Part 2 of Schedule 8 to the Criminal Justice Act 2003 (c. 44) (breach of community order) is amended as follows.

(2) In paragraph 9 (powers of magistrates' court) after sub-paragraph (3) insert –

"(3A) Where –
 (a) the court is dealing with the offender under sub-paragraph (1)(a), and
 (b) the community order does not contain an unpaid work requirement, section 199(2)(a) applies in relation to the inclusion of such a requirement as if for "40" there were substituted "20"."

(3) In paragraph 10 (powers of Crown Court) after sub-paragraph (3) insert –

"(3A) Where –
 (a) the court is dealing with the offender under sub-paragraph (1)(a), and
 (b) the community order does not contain an unpaid work requirement, section 199(2)(a) applies in relation to the inclusion of such a requirement as if for "40" there were substituted "20"."

39 Youth default orders

(1) Subsection (2) applies in any case where, in respect of a person aged under 18, a magistrates' court would, but for section 89 of the Powers of Criminal Courts (Sentencing) Act 2000 (c. 6) (restrictions on custodial sentences), have power to issue a warrant of commitment for default in paying a sum adjudged to be paid by a conviction (other than a sum ordered to be paid under section 6 of the Proceeds of Crime Act 2002 (c. 29)).

(2) The magistrates' court may, instead of proceeding under section 81 of the Magistrates' Courts Act 1980 (enforcement of fines imposed on young offender), order the person in default to comply with –

(a) in the case of a person aged 16 or 17, an unpaid work requirement (see paragraph 10 of Schedule 1),
(b) an attendance centre requirement (see paragraph 12 of that Schedule), or
(c) a curfew requirement (see paragraph 14 of that Schedule).

(3) In this section (and Schedule 7) "youth default order" means an order under subsection (2).

(4) Section 1(2) and paragraph 2 of Schedule 1 (power or requirement to impose electronic monitoring requirement) have effect in relation to a youth default order as they have effect in relation to a youth rehabilitation order.

(5) Where a magistrates' court has power to make a youth default order, it may, if it thinks it expedient to do so, postpone the making of the order until such time and on such conditions (if any) as it thinks just.

(6) The following provisions have effect in relation to youth default orders as they have effect in relation to youth rehabilitation orders, but subject to the modifications contained in Schedule 7 –

(a) sections 4, 5 and 7,
(b) paragraphs 1, 10, 12, 14, 26, 27, 29, 33 and 34 of Schedule 1 (youth rehabilitation orders: further provisions),
(c) Schedule 2 (breach, revocation or amendment of youth rehabilitation orders), and
(d) Schedule 3 (transfer of youth rehabilitation orders to Northern Ireland).

(7) Where a youth default order has been made for default in paying any sum –

(a) on payment of the whole sum to any person authorised to receive it, the order ceases to have effect, and

(b) on payment of a part of the sum to any such person, the total number of hours or days to which the order relates is to be taken to be reduced by a proportion corresponding to that which the part paid bears to the whole sum.

(8) In calculating any reduction required by subsection (7)(b), any fraction of a day or hour is to be disregarded.

40 Power to impose attendance centre requirement on fine defaulter

(1) Section 300 of the Criminal Justice Act 2003 (c. 44) (power to impose unpaid work requirement or curfew requirement on fine defaulter) is amended as follows.

(2) In the heading for "or curfew requirement" substitute "curfew requirement or attendance centre requirement".

(3) In subsection (2), at the end of paragraph (b) insert ", or

(c) in a case where the person is aged under 25, an attendance centre requirement (as defined by section 214)".

41 Disclosure of information for enforcing fines

(1) Part 3 of Schedule 5 to the Courts Act 2003 (c. 39) (attachment of earnings orders and applications for benefit deductions) is amended as follows.

(2) After paragraph 9 insert –

"Disclosure of information in connection with application for benefit deductions

9A

(1) The designated officer for a magistrates' court may make an information request to the Secretary of State for the purpose of facilitating the making of a decision by the court as to whether it is practicable or appropriate to make an application for benefit deductions in respect of P.

(2) An information request is a request for the disclosure of some or all of the following information –

(a) P's full name;
(b) P's address (or any of P's addresses);
(c) P's date of birth;
(d) P's national insurance number;
(e) P's benefit status.

(3) On receiving an information request, the Secretary of State may disclose the information requested to –

(a) the officer who made the request, or
(b) a justices' clerk specified in the request.

Restrictions on disclosure

9B

(1) A person to whom information is disclosed under paragraph 9A(3), or this sub-paragraph, may disclose the information to any person to whom its disclosure is necessary or expedient in connection with facilitating the making of a decision by the court as to whether it is practicable or appropriate to make an application for benefit deductions in respect of P.

(2) A person to whom such information is disclosed commits an offence if the person –

(a) discloses or uses the information, and
(b) the disclosure is not authorised by sub-paragraph (1) or (as the case may be) the use is not for the purpose of facilitating the making of such a decision as is mentioned in that sub-paragraph.

(3) But it is not an offence under sub-paragraph (2) –

(a) to disclose any information in accordance with any enactment or order of a court or for the purposes of any proceedings before a court; or
(b) to disclose any information which has previously been lawfully disclosed to the public.

(4) It is a defence for a person charged with an offence under sub-paragraph (2) to prove that the person reasonably believed that the disclosure or use was lawful.

(5) A person guilty of an offence under sub-paragraph (2) is liable on summary conviction to a fine not exceeding level 4 on the standard scale.

Paragraphs 9A and 9B: supplementary

9C

(1) This paragraph applies for the purposes of paragraphs 9A and 9B.

(2) "Benefit status", in relation to P, means whether or not P is in receipt of any prescribed benefit or benefits and, if so (in the case of each benefit) –

(a) which benefit it is,
(b) where it is already subject to deductions under any enactment, the nature of the deductions concerned, and
(c) the amount received by P by way of the benefit, after allowing for any such deductions.

(3) "Information" means information held in any form.

(4) "Prescribed" means prescribed by regulations made by the Lord Chancellor.

(5) Nothing in paragraph 9A or 9B authorises the making of a disclosure which contravenes the Data Protection Act 1998."

PART 3
APPEALS

Appeals by defendant

42 Power to dismiss certain appeals following references by the CCRC: England and Wales

After section 16B of the Criminal Appeal Act 1968 (c. 19) insert –

"Appeals following references by the CCRC

16C Power to dismiss certain appeals following references by the CCRC

(1) This section applies where there is an appeal under this Part following a reference by the Criminal Cases Review Commission under section 9(1)(a), (5) or (6) of the Criminal Appeal Act 1995 or section 1(1) of the Criminal Cases Review (Insanity) Act 1999.

(2) Notwithstanding anything in section 2, 13 or 16 of this Act, the Court of Appeal may dismiss the appeal if –

(a) the only ground for allowing it would be that there has been a development in the law since the date of the conviction, verdict or finding that is the subject of the appeal, and
(b) the condition in subsection (3) is met.

(3) The condition in this subsection is that if –

(a) the reference had not been made, but
(b) the appellant had made (and had been entitled to make) an application for an extension of time within which to seek leave to appeal on the ground of the development in the law, the Court would not think it appropriate to grant the application by exercising the power conferred by section 18(3)."

43 Power to dismiss certain appeals following references by the CCRC: Northern Ireland

After section 13A of the Criminal Appeal (Northern Ireland) Act 1980 (c. 47) insert –

"Appeals following references by the CCRC

13B Power to dismiss certain appeals following references by the CCRC

(1) This section applies where there is an appeal under this Part following a reference by the Criminal Cases Review Commission under section 10(1)(a), (6) or (7) of the Criminal Appeal Act 1995 or section 1(1) of the Criminal Cases Review (Insanity) Act 1999.

(2) Notwithstanding anything in section 2, 12 or 13A of this Act, the Court of Appeal may dismiss the appeal if –

(a) the only ground for allowing it would be that there has been a development in the law since the date of the conviction, verdict or finding that is the subject of the appeal, and
(b) the condition in subsection (3) is met.

(3) The condition in this subsection is that if –

(a) the reference had not been made, but
(b) the appellant had made (and had been entitled to make) an application for an extension of time within which to seek leave to appeal on the ground of the development in the law, the Court would not think it appropriate to grant the application by exercising the power conferred by section 16(2)."

Appeals by prosecution

44 Determination of prosecution appeals: England and Wales

In section 61 of the Criminal Justice Act 2003 (c. 44) (determination of prosecution appeal by Court of Appeal) for subsection (5) substitute –

"(5) But the Court of Appeal may not make an order under subsection (4)(c) in respect of an offence unless it considers that the defendant could not receive a fair trial if an order were made under subsection (4)(a) or (b)."

45 Determination of prosecution appeals: Northern Ireland

In Article 20 of the Criminal Justice (Northern Ireland) Order 2004 (S.I. 2004/ 1500 (N.I.9)) (determination of prosecution appeal by Court of Appeal) for paragraph (5) substitute –

"(5) But the Court of Appeal may not make an order under paragraph (4)(c) in respect of an offence unless it considers that the defendant could not receive a fair trial if an order were made under paragraph (4)(a) or (b)."

Miscellaneous

46 Review of sentence on reference by Attorney General

(1) Section 36 of the Criminal Justice Act 1988 (c. 33) (reviews of sentencing) is amended as follows.

(2) For subsection (3A) substitute –

"(3A) Where a reference under this section relates to a case in which the judge made an order specified in subsection (3B), the Court of Appeal shall not, in deciding what sentence is appropriate for the case, make any allowance for the fact that the person to whom it relates is being sentenced for a second time.

(3B) The orders specified in this subsection are –

(a) an order under section 269(2) of the Criminal Justice Act 2003 (determination of minimum term in relation to mandatory life sentence);
(b) an order under section 82A(2) of the Powers of Criminal Courts (Sentencing) Act 2000 (determination of minimum term in relation to discretionary life sentences and certain other sentences)."

(3) In subsection (9) after paragraph (b) insert ", and

(c) the reference in subsection (3A) to an order specified in subsection (3B) shall be construed as a reference to an order under Article 5(1) of the Life Sentences (Northern Ireland) Order 2001."

47 Further amendments relating to appeals in criminal cases

Schedule 8 amends the Criminal Appeal Act 1968 (c. 19), the Criminal Appeal (Northern Ireland) Act 1980 (c. 47) and other Acts relating to appeals in criminal cases.

PART 4
OTHER CRIMINAL JUSTICE PROVISIONS

Alternatives to prosecution

48 Alternatives to prosecution for offenders under 18

(1) Schedule 9 amends the Crime and Disorder Act 1998 (c. 37) –

  (a) to make provision for the giving of youth conditional cautions to children and young persons, and
  (b) to make minor amendments relating to reprimands and warnings under section 65 of that Act.

(2) The Secretary of State may by order amend the Crime and Disorder Act 1998 (c. 37), as amended by Schedule 9, so as to vary the provision made by it for the giving of youth conditional cautions to children and young persons under the age of 16 (including doing so by adding or omitting any provision).

49 Protection for spent cautions under Rehabilitation of Offenders Act 1974

(1) Schedule 10 amends the Rehabilitation of Offenders Act 1974 (c. 53) so as to provide for the protection of spent cautions.

(2) The provisions of Schedule 10 (and this section) extend only to England and Wales.

50 Criminal conviction certificates and criminal record certificates

(1) Part 5 of the Police Act 1997 (c. 50) (certificates of criminal records) is amended as follows.

(2) In section 112 (criminal conviction certificates) –

  (a) in the definition of "central records", after "convictions" insert "and conditional cautions";
  (b) after that definition insert –

  ""conditional caution" means a caution given under section 22 of the Criminal Justice Act 2003 (c. 44) or section 66A of the Crime and Disorder Act 1998, other than one that is spent for the purposes of Schedule 2 to the Rehabilitation of Offenders Act 1974."

(3) In section 113A(6) (criminal record certificates) –

  (a) in the definition of "exempted question", after "a question" insert
      "which –
      "(a)   so far as it applies to convictions, is a question";
  (b) in that definition, at the end insert "; and –
      "(b)   so far as it applies to cautions, is a question to which paragraph 3(3) or (4) of Schedule 2 to that Act has been excluded by an order of the Secretary of State under paragraph 4 of that Schedule;";
  (c) in the definition of "relevant matter", after "caution" insert ", including a caution that is spent for the purposes of Schedule 2 to that Act".

(4) This section extends to England and Wales only.

Bail

51 Bail conditions: electronic monitoring

Schedule 11 makes provision in connection with the electronic monitoring of persons released on bail subject to conditions.

52 Bail for summary offences and certain other offences to be tried summarily

Schedule 12 –

(a) imposes a duty on a magistrates' court considering whether to withhold or grant bail in relation to a person under 18 accused of an offence mentioned in Schedule 2 to the Magistrates' Courts Act 1980 (c. 43) (offences for which the value involved is relevant to the mode of trial) to consider the value involved in the offence; and

(b) amends Schedule 1 to the Bail Act 1976 (persons entitled to bail: supplementary provisions).

Proceedings in magistrates' courts

53 Allocation of offences triable either way etc.

Schedule 13 amends Schedule 3 to the Criminal Justice Act 2003 (c. 44) (which makes provision in relation to the allocation and other treatment of offences triable either way, and the sending of cases to the Crown Court).

54 Trial or sentencing in absence of accused in magistrates' courts

(1) Section 11 of the Magistrates' Courts Act 1980 (non-appearance of accused) is amended as follows.

(2) In subsection (1), for "the court may proceed in his absence" substitute " –

(a) if the accused is under 18 years of age, the court may proceed in his absence; and
(b) if the accused has attained the age of 18 years, the court shall proceed in his absence unless it appears to the court to be contrary to the interests of justice to do so. This is subject to subsections (2), (2A), (3) and (4)."

(3) After subsection (2) insert –

"(2A) The court shall not proceed in the absence of the accused if it considers that there is an acceptable reason for his failure to appear."

(4) In each of subsections (3) and (4), for "A magistrates' court" substitute "In proceedings to which this subsection applies, the court."

(5) After subsection (3) insert –

"(3A) But where a sentence or order of a kind mentioned in subsection (3) is imposed or given in the absence of the offender, the offender must be brought before the court before being taken to a prison or other institution to begin serving his sentence (and the sentence or order is not to be regarded as taking effect until he is brought before the court)."

(6) After subsection (4) insert –

"(5) Subsections (3) and (4) apply to –

(a) proceedings instituted by an information, where a summons has been issued; and
(b) proceedings instituted by a written charge.

(6) Nothing in this section requires the court to enquire into the reasons for the accused's failure to appear before deciding whether to proceed in his absence.

(7) The court shall state in open court its reasons for not proceeding under this section in the absence of an accused who has attained the age of 18 years; and the court shall cause those reasons to be entered in its register of proceedings."

(7) Section 13(5) of that Act (non-appearance of accused: issue of warrant) ceases to have effect.

55 Extension of powers of non-legal staff

(1) Section 7A of the Prosecution of Offences Act 1985 (c. 23) (powers of non-legal staff) is amended as follows.

(2) In subsection (2) (powers of designated non-legal staff) –

(a) in paragraph (a)(ii), after "trials" insert "of offences triable either way or offences which are punishable with imprisonment in the case of persons aged 21 or over";
(b) after paragraph (a)(ii) insert –
"(iii) the conduct of applications or other proceedings relating to preventative civil orders;
(iv) the conduct of proceedings (other than criminal proceedings) in, or in connection with, the discharge of functions assigned to the Director under section 3(2)(g) above.";
(c) for paragraph (b) substitute –
"(b) any powers of a Crown Prosecutor that do not involve the exercise of such rights of audience as are mentioned in paragraph (a) above but are exercisable in relation to the conduct of –
(i) criminal proceedings in magistrates' courts, or
(ii) applications or proceedings falling within paragraph (a)(iii) or (iv)."

(3) For subsection (5) (interpretation) substitute –

"(5) In this section –

"bail in criminal proceedings" has the same meaning as in the Bail Act 1976 (see section 1 of that Act);
"preventative civil orders" means –
(a) orders within section 3(2)(fa) to (fe) above;
(b) orders under section 5 or 5A of the Protection from Harassment Act 1997 (restraining orders); or
(c) orders under section 8 of the Crime and Disorder Act 1998 (parenting orders).

(5A) For the purposes of this section a trial begins with the opening of the prosecution case after the entry of a plea of not guilty and ends with the conviction or acquittal of the accused."

(4) Omit subsection (6) (powers not applicable to offences triable only on indictment etc.).

(5) After subsection (7) insert –

"(8) As from 1 May 2011 nothing in this section confers on persons designated under this section –
(a) any rights of audience, or
(b) any right to conduct litigation, for the purposes of Part 3 of the Legal Services Act 2007 (reserved legal activities).

(9) As from that date the following provisions of that Act accordingly do not apply to persons designated under this section –
(a) paragraph 1(3) of Schedule 3 (exemption for persons with statutory rights of audience), and
(b) paragraph 2(3) of that Schedule (exemption for persons with statutory right to conduct litigation).

(10) The Attorney General may by order make such modifications in the application of any enactment (including this section) in relation to persons designated under this section as the Attorney General considers appropriate in consequence of, or in connection with, the matters provided for by subsections (8) and (9).

(11) The Attorney General may also by order amend subsection (2)(a)(ii) so as to omit the words "or offences which are punishable with imprisonment in the case of persons aged 21 or over".

(12) The power to make an order under subsection (10) or (11) is exercisable by statutory instrument, but a statutory instrument containing such an order may not be made unless a draft of the instrument has been laid before, and approved by a resolution of, each House of Parliament."

(6) In section 15 of that Act (interpretation of Part 1) in subsection (4) (provisions for the purposes of which binding over proceedings are to be taken to be criminal proceedings) for "and 7(1)" substitute ", 7(1) and 7A".

Criminal legal aid

56 Provisional grant of right to representation

(1) Part 1 of the Access to Justice Act 1999 (c. 22) is amended as follows.

(2) In section 14(1) (representation) –

(a) after "criminal proceedings" insert "and about the provisional grant of a right to representation in prescribed circumstances";
(b) after "granted" insert ", or provisionally granted,".

(3) In section 15(1) (selection of representative) after "granted" insert ", or provisionally granted,".

(4) In section 25(9) (orders, regulations and directions subject to affirmative resolution procedure) for "paragraph 2A" substitute "paragraph 1A, 2A,".

(5) In section 26 (interpretation) after the definition of "representation" insert –

"and, for the purposes of the definition of "representation", "proceedings" includes, in the context of a provisional grant of a right to representation, proceedings that may result from the investigation concerned."

(6) After paragraph 1 of Schedule 3 (individuals to whom right may be granted) insert –

"Individuals to whom right may be provisionally granted

1A

(1) Regulations may provide that, in prescribed circumstances, and subject to any prescribed conditions, a right to representation may be provisionally granted to an individual where –

(a) the individual is involved in an investigation which may result in criminal proceedings, and
(b) the right is so granted for the purposes of criminal proceedings that may result from the investigation.

(2) Regulations under sub-paragraph (1) may, in particular, make provision about –

(a) the stage in an investigation at which a right to representation may be provisionally granted;
(b) the circumstances in which a right which has been so granted –
 (i) is to become, or be treated as if it were, a right to representation under paragraph 1, or
 (ii) is to be, or may be, withdrawn."

(7) In paragraph 2A of Schedule 3 (grant of right by Commission) at the end of sub-paragraph (1)(b) insert –

"(c) provide that any provisional grant of a right to representation, or any withdrawal of a right so granted, in accordance with regulations under paragraph 1A is to be made by the Commission."

(8) In paragraph 3A(1) of Schedule 3 (form of the grant of a right to representation) after "grant" insert ", or provisional grant,".

(9) In paragraph 3B of Schedule 3 (financial eligibility) –

(a) in sub-paragraph (1) –
 (i) after "grant" insert ", or provisionally grant,",
 (ii) after "granted" insert ", or provisionally granted,";
(b) in sub-paragraph (2)(a), after "granted" insert ", or provisionally granted,".

(10) In paragraph 4 of Schedule 3 (appeals) at the end insert –

"This paragraph does not apply in relation to any right to representation granted in accordance with paragraph 1A."

(11) In paragraph 5 of Schedule 3 (criteria for grant of right) –

(a) in sub-paragraph (1), after "grant" insert ", or provisionally grant,";
(b) after sub-paragraph (2) insert –

"(2A) For the purposes of sub-paragraph (2), "proceedings" includes, in the context of a provisional grant of a right to representation, proceedings that may result from the investigation in which the individual is involved.";

(c) in sub-paragraph (4), after "grant" insert ", or provisional grant,".

57 Disclosure of information to enable assessment of financial eligibility

(1) The Access to Justice Act 1999 (c. 22) is amended as follows.

(2) In section 25(9) (orders, regulations and directions subject to affirmative resolution procedure), for "or 4" substitute "4 or 6".

(3) In Schedule 3 (criminal defence service: right to representation), after paragraph 5 insert –

"Information requests

6

(1) The relevant authority may make an information request to –

    (a)   the Secretary of State, or
    (b)   the Commissioners,

for the purpose of facilitating the making of a decision by the authority about the application of paragraph 3B(1) or (2), or regulations under paragraph 3B(3), in relation to an individual.

(2) An information request made to the Secretary of State is a request for the disclosure of some or all of the following information –

    (a)   the individual's full name;
    (b)   the individual's address;
    (c)   the individual's date of birth;
    (d)   the individual's national insurance number;
    (e)   the individual's benefit status;
    (f)   information of any description specified in regulations.

(3) An information request made to the Commissioners is a request for the disclosure of some or all of the following information –

    (a)   whether or not the individual is employed;
    (b)   the name and address of the employer (if the individual is employed);
    (c)   the individual's national insurance number;
    (d)   information of any description specified in regulations made with the agreement of the Commissioners.

(4) The information that may be specified under subsection (3)(d) includes, in particular, information relating to the individual's income (as defined in the regulations) for a period so specified.

(5) On receiving an information request, the Secretary of State or (as the case may be) the Commissioners may disclose the information requested to the relevant authority.

Restrictions on disclosure

7

(1) A person to whom information is disclosed under paragraph 6(5), or this sub-paragraph, may disclose the information to any person to whom its disclosure is necessary or expedient in connection with facilitating the making of a decision by the relevant authority about the application of paragraph 3B(1) or (2), or regulations under paragraph 3B(3), in relation to an individual.

(2) A person to whom such information is disclosed commits an offence if the person –

    (a)   discloses or uses the information, and
    (b)   the disclosure is not authorised by sub-paragraph (1) or (as the case may be) the use is not for the purpose of facilitating the making of such a decision as is mentioned in that sub-paragraph.

(3) But it is not an offence under sub-paragraph (2) –

    (a)   to disclose any information in accordance with any enactment or order of a court or for the purposes of any proceedings before a court; or
    (b)   to disclose any information which has previously been lawfully disclosed to the public.

(4) It is a defence for a person charged with an offence under sub-paragraph (2) to prove that the person reasonably believed that the disclosure or use was lawful.

(5) A person guilty of an offence under sub-paragraph (2) is liable –

 (a) on conviction on indictment, to imprisonment for a term not exceeding 2 years or a fine or both;
 (b) on summary conviction, to imprisonment for a term not exceeding 12 months or a fine not exceeding the statutory maximum or both.

(6) In sub-paragraph (5)(b) the reference to 12 months is to be read as a reference to 6 months in relation to an offence committed before the commencement of section 154(1) of the Criminal Justice Act 2003.

(7) Nothing in section 20 applies in relation to the disclosure of information to which sub-paragraph (1) applies.

Paragraphs 6 and 7: supplementary

8

(1) This paragraph applies for the purposes of paragraphs 6 and 7.

(2) "Benefit status", in relation to an individual, means whether or not the individual is in direct or indirect receipt of any prescribed benefit or benefits and, if so (in the case of each benefit) –

 (a) which benefit the individual is so receiving, and
 (b) (in prescribed cases) the amount the individual is so receiving by way of the benefit.

(3) "The Commissioners" means the Commissioners for Her Majesty's Revenue and Customs.

(4) "Information" means information held in any form.

(5) Nothing in paragraph 6 or 7 authorises the making of a disclosure which contravenes the Data Protection Act 1998."

58 Pilot schemes

(1) The Access to Justice Act 1999 (c. 22) is amended as follows.

(2) In section 17A (contribution orders) omit subsection (5) (piloting of regulations).

(3) After section 18 insert –

"**18A Pilot schemes**

(1) This section applies to the following instruments –

 (a) any order under section 14 or paragraph 5 of Schedule 3;
 (b) any regulations under section 12, 13, 15, 17 or 17A or any of paragraphs 1A to 5 of Schedule 3, and
 (c) any regulations under section 22(5) having effect in relation to the Criminal Defence Service.

(2) Any instrument to which this section applies may be made so as to have effect for a specified period not exceeding 12 months.

(3) But if the Lord Chancellor thinks that it is necessary or expedient for either of the purposes in subsection (4), the period specified in the instrument –

 (a) may in the first instance be a period not exceeding 18 months;
 (b) may be varied so as to become a period not exceeding 18 months.

(4) The purposes are –

 (a) ensuring the effective operation of the instrument;
 (b) co-ordinating the operation of the instrument with the operation of any other provision made under an enactment relating to any aspect of the criminal justice system.

(5) The period for the time being specified in an instrument to which this section applies may also be varied so that the instrument has effect for such further period as the Lord Chancellor thinks necessary for the purpose of securing that it remains in operation until the coming into force of any order or regulations made under the same provision of this Act that will have effect –

(a) generally, or
(b) for purposes wider than those for which the instrument has effect.

(6) In the following provisions of this section "pilot scheme" means any instrument which, in accordance with subsections (2) to (5), is to have effect for a limited period.

(7) A pilot scheme may provide that its provisions are to apply only in relation to –

(a) one or more specified areas or localities;
(b) one or more specified descriptions of court;
(c) one or more specified offences or descriptions of offence;
(d) one or more specified classes of person;
(e) persons selected –
 (i) by reference to specified criteria; or
 (ii) on a sampling basis.

(8) A pilot scheme may make consequential or transitional provision with respect to the cessation of the scheme on the expiry of the specified period (or that period as varied under subsection (3)(b) or (5)).

(9) A pilot scheme may be replaced by a further pilot scheme making the same or similar provision."

(4) In section 25 (regulations, orders and directions) after subsection (9A) insert—

"(9B) No order or regulations which, by virtue of section 18A, is or are to have effect for a limited period shall be made unless a draft of the order or regulations has been laid before, and approved by a resolution of, each House of Parliament."

Miscellaneous

59 SFO's pre-investigation powers in relation to bribery and corruption: foreign officers etc.

(1) The Criminal Justice Act 1987 (c. 38) is amended as follows.

(2) After section 2 insert –

"**2A Director's pre-investigation powers in relation to bribery and corruption: foreign officers etc**

(1) The powers of the Director under section 2 are also exercisable for the purpose of enabling him to determine whether to start an investigation under section 1 in a case where it appears to him that conduct to which this section applies may have taken place.

(2) But –

(a) the power under subsection (2) of section 2 is so exercisable only if it appears to the Director that for the purpose of enabling him to make that determination it is expedient to require any person appearing to him to have relevant information to do as mentioned in that subsection, and
(b) the power under subsection (3) of that section is so exercisable only if it appears to the Director that for that purpose it is expedient to require any person to do as mentioned in that subsection.

(3) Accordingly, where the powers of the Director under section 2 are exercisable in accordance with subsections (1) and (2) above –

(a) the reference in subsection (2) of that section to the person under investigation or any other person whom the Director has reason to believe has relevant information is to be read as a reference to any such person as is mentioned in subsection (2)(a) above,
(b) the reference in subsection (3) of that section to the person under investigation or any other person is to be read as a reference to any such person as is mentioned in subsection (2)(b) above, and
(c) any reference in subsection (2), (3) or (4) of that section to the investigation is to be read as a reference to the making of any such determination as is mentioned in subsection (1) above.

(4) Any reference in section 2(16) to the carrying out of an investigation by the Serious Fraud Office into serious or complex fraud includes a reference to the making of any such determination as is mentioned in subsection (1) above.

(5) This section applies to any conduct which, as a result of section 108 of the Anti-terrorism, Crime and Security Act 2001 (bribery and corruption: foreign officers etc), constitutes a corruption offence (wherever committed).

(6) The following are corruption offences for the purposes of this section— (a) any common law offence of bribery;

> (b) the offences under section 1 of the Public Bodies Corrupt Practices Act 1889 (corruption in office); and
> (c) the offences under section 1 of the Prevention of Corruption Act 1906 (corrupt transactions with agents)."

(3) In section 17 (extent) –

(a) in subsection (2) (provisions of Act extending to Scotland), for "section 2" substitute "sections 2 and 2A"; and
(b) in subsection (3) (provisions of Act extending to Northern Ireland), after "sections 2" insert ", 2A".

60 Contents of an accused's defence statement

(1) In section 6A(1) of the Criminal Procedure and Investigations Act 1996 (c. 25) (contents of defence statement), after "prosecution," in paragraph (c) insert –

> "(ca) setting out particulars of the matters of fact on which he intends to rely for the purposes of his defence,".

(2) In section 11(2)(f)(ii) of that Act (faults in disclosure by accused), after "matter" insert "(or any particular of any matter of fact)".

61 Compensation for miscarriages of justice

(1) The Criminal Justice Act 1988 (c. 33) has effect subject to the following amendments.

(2) Section 133 (compensation for miscarriages of justice) is amended as follows.

> (3) At the end of subsection (2) (compensation only payable if application for compensation is made) insert "before the end of the period of 2 years beginning with the date on which the conviction of the person concerned is reversed or he is pardoned.
>
> (2A) But the Secretary of State may direct that an application for compensation made after the end of that period is to be treated as if it had been made within that period if the Secretary of State considers that there are exceptional circumstances which justify doing so."

(4) For subsection (4A) substitute –

> "(4A) Section 133A applies in relation to the assessment of the amount of the compensation."

(5) After subsection (5) (meaning of "reversed" in relation to a conviction) insert –

> "(5A) But in a case where –
>
> (a) a person's conviction for an offence is quashed on an appeal out of time, and
> (b) the person is to be subject to a retrial, the conviction is not to be treated for the purposes of this section as "reversed" unless and until the person is acquitted of all offences at the retrial or the prosecution indicates that it has decided not to proceed with the retrial.
>
> (5B) In subsection (5A) above any reference to a retrial includes a reference to proceedings held following the remission of a matter to a magistrates' court by the Crown Court under section 48(2)(b) of the Supreme Court Act 1981."

> (6) In subsection (6) (meaning of suffering punishment as a result of conviction) after "this section" insert "and section 133A".

(7) After section 133 insert –

"**133A Miscarriages of justice: amount of compensation**

(1) This section applies where an assessor is required to assess the amount of compensation payable to or in respect of a person under section 133 for a miscarriage of justice.

(2) In assessing so much of any compensation payable under section 133 as is attributable to suffering, harm to reputation or similar damage, the assessor must have regard in particular to –

  (a) the seriousness of the offence of which the person was convicted and the severity of the punishment suffered as a result of the conviction, and
  (b) the conduct of the investigation and prosecution of the offence.

(3) The assessor may make from the total amount of compensation that the assessor would otherwise have assessed as payable under section 133 any deduction or deductions that the assessor considers appropriate by reason of either or both of the following –

  (a) any conduct of the person appearing to the assessor to have directly or indirectly caused, or contributed to, the conviction concerned; and
  (b) any other convictions of the person and any punishment suffered as a result of them.

(4) If, having had regard to any matters falling within subsection (3)(a) or

  (b) the assessor considers that there are exceptional circumstances which justify doing so, the assessor may determine that the amount of compensation payable under section 133 is to be a nominal amount only.

(5) The total amount of compensation payable to or in respect of a person under section 133 for a particular miscarriage of justice must not exceed the overall compensation limit. That limit is –

  (a) £1 million in a case to which section 133B applies, and
  (b) £500,000 in any other case.

(6) The total amount of compensation payable under section 133 for a person's loss of earnings or earnings capacity in respect of any one year must not exceed the earnings compensation limit. That limit is an amount equal to 1.5 times the median annual gross earnings according to the latest figures published by the Office of National Statistics at the time of the assessment.

(7) The Secretary of State may by order made by statutory instrument amend subsection (5) or (6) so as to alter any amount for the time being specified as the overall compensation limit or the earnings compensation limit.

(8) No order may be made under subsection (7) unless a draft of the order has been laid before and approved by a resolution of each House of Parliament.

133B Cases where person has been detained for at least 10 years

(1) For the purposes of section 133A(5) this section applies to any case where the person concerned ("P") has been in qualifying detention for a period (or total period) of at least 10 years by the time when –

  (a) the conviction is reversed, or
  (b) the pardon is given, as mentioned in section 133(1).

(2) P was "in qualifying detention" at any time when P was detained in a prison, a hospital or at any other place, if P was so detained –

  (a) by virtue of a sentence passed in respect of the relevant offence,
  (b) under mental health legislation by reason of P's conviction of that offence (disregarding any conditions other than the fact of the conviction that had to be fulfilled in order for P to be so detained), or
  (c) as a result of P's having been remanded in custody in connection with the relevant offence or with any other offence the charge for which was founded on the same facts or evidence as that for the relevant offence.

(3) In calculating the period (or total period) during which P has been in qualifying detention as mentioned in subsection (1), no account is to be taken of any period of time during which P was both –

  (a) in qualifying detention, and
  (b) in excluded concurrent detention.

(4) P was "in excluded concurrent detention" at any time when P was detained in a prison, a hospital or at any other place, if P was so detained –

(a) during the term of a sentence passed in respect of an offence other than the relevant offence,
(b) under mental health legislation by reason of P's conviction of any such other offence (disregarding any conditions other than the fact of the conviction that had to be fulfilled in order for P to be so detained), or
(c) as a result of P's having been remanded in custody in connection with an offence for which P was subsequently convicted other than –
  (i) the relevant offence, or
  (ii) any other offence the charge for which was founded on the same facts or evidence as that for the relevant offence.

(5) But P was not "in excluded concurrent detention" at any time by virtue of subsection (4)(a), (b) or (c) if P's conviction of the other offence mentioned in that provision was quashed on appeal, or a pardon was given in respect of it.

(6) In this section –

"mental health legislation" means –
(a) Part 3 of the Mental Health Act 1983,
(b) Part 3 of the Mental Health (Northern Ireland) Order 1986, or
(c) the provisions of any earlier enactment corresponding to Part 3 of that Act or Part 3 of that Order; "the relevant offence" means the offence in respect of which the conviction is quashed or the pardon is given (but see subsection (7));

"remanded in custody" is to be read in accordance with subsections (8) and (9); "reversed" has the same meaning as in section 133 of this Act.

(7) If, as a result of the miscarriage of justice –

(a) two or more convictions are reversed, or
(b) a pardon is given in respect of two or more offences, "the relevant offence" means any of the offences concerned.

(8) In relation to England and Wales, "remanded in custody" has the meaning given by section 242(2) of the Criminal Justice Act 2003, but that subsection applies for the purposes of this section as if any reference there to a provision of the Mental Health Act 1983 included a reference to any corresponding provision of any earlier enactment.

(9) In relation to Northern Ireland, "remanded in custody" means –

(a) remanded in or committed to custody by an order of a court, or
(b) remanded, admitted or removed to hospital under Article 42, 43, 45 or 54 of the Mental Health (Northern Ireland) Order 1986 or under any corresponding provision of any earlier enactment."

(8) In section 172 (extent) in subsection (3) (provisions extending to Northern Ireland as well as England and Wales) for "section 133" substitute "sections 133 to 133B".

(9) This section extends to England and Wales and Northern Ireland.

62 Annual report on Criminal Justice (Terrorism and Conspiracy) Act 1998

(1) Section 8 of the Criminal Justice (Terrorism and Conspiracy) Act 1998 (c. 40) (requirement for annual report on working of the Act) ceases to have effect.

(2) The following provisions, namely –

(a) subsection (1), and
(b) the repeal of section 8 of that Act in Part 4 of Schedule 28, extend to England and Wales and Northern Ireland.

PART 5
CRIMINAL LAW

Pornography etc.

63 Possession of extreme pornographic images

(1) It is an offence for a person to be in possession of an extreme pornographic image.

(2) An "extreme pornographic image" is an image which is both –

- (a) pornographic, and
- (b) an extreme image.

(3) An image is "pornographic" if it is of such a nature that it must reasonably be assumed to have been produced solely or principally for the purpose of sexual arousal.

(4) Where (as found in the person's possession) an image forms part of a series of images, the question whether the image is of such a nature as is mentioned in subsection (3) is to be determined by reference to –

- (a) the image itself, and
- (b) (if the series of images is such as to be capable of providing a context for the image) the context in which it occurs in the series of images.

(5) So, for example, where –

- (a) an image forms an integral part of a narrative constituted by a series of images, and
- (b) having regard to those images as a whole, they are not of such a nature that they must reasonably be assumed to have been produced solely or principally for the purpose of sexual arousal, the image may, by virtue of being part of that narrative, be found not to be pornographic, even though it might have been found to be pornographic if taken by itself.

(6) An "extreme image" is an image which –

- (a) falls within subsection (7), and
- (b) is grossly offensive, disgusting or otherwise of an obscene character.

(7) An image falls within this subsection if it portrays, in an explicit and realistic way, any of the following –

- (a) an act which threatens a person's life,
- (b) an act which results, or is likely to result, in serious injury to a person's anus, breasts or genitals,
- (c) an act which involves sexual interference with a human corpse, or
- (d) a person performing an act of intercourse or oral sex with an animal (whether dead or alive), and a reasonable person looking at the image would think that any such person or animal was real.

(8) In this section "image" means –

- (a) a moving or still image (produced by any means); or
- (b) data (stored by any means) which is capable of conversion into an image within paragraph (a).

(9) In this section references to a part of the body include references to a part surgically constructed (in particular through gender reassignment surgery).

(10) Proceedings for an offence under this section may not be instituted –

- (a) in England and Wales, except by or with the consent of the Director of Public Prosecutions; or
- (b) in Northern Ireland, except by or with the consent of the Director of Public Prosecutions for Northern Ireland.

64 Exclusion of classified films etc.

(1) Section 63 does not apply to excluded images.

(2) An "excluded image" is an image which forms part of a series of images contained in a recording of the whole or part of a classified work.

(3) But such an image is not an "excluded image" if –

(a) it is contained in a recording of an extract from a classified work, and
(b) it is of such a nature that it must reasonably be assumed to have been extracted (whether with or without other images) solely or principally for the purpose of sexual arousal.

(4) Where an extracted image is one of a series of images contained in the recording, the question whether the image is of such a nature as is mentioned in subsection (3)(b) is to be determined by reference to –

(a) the image itself, and
(b) (if the series of images is such as to be capable of providing a context for the image) the context in which it occurs in the series of images; and section 63(5) applies in connection with determining that question as it applies in connection with determining whether an image is pornographic.

(5) In determining for the purposes of this section whether a recording is a recording of the whole or part of a classified work, any alteration attributable to –

(a) a defect caused for technical reasons or by inadvertence on the part of any person, or
(b) the inclusion in the recording of any extraneous material (such as advertisements), is to be disregarded.

(6) Nothing in this section is to be taken as affecting any duty of a designated authority to have regard to section 63 (along with other enactments creating criminal offences) in determining whether a video work is suitable for a classification certificate to be issued in respect of it.

(7) In this section –

"classified work" means (subject to subsection (8)) a video work in respect of which a classification certificate has been issued by a designated authority (whether before or after the commencement of this section);
"classification certificate" and "video work" have the same meanings as in the Video Recordings Act 1984 (c. 39);
"designated authority" means an authority which has been designated by the Secretary of State under section 4 of that Act;
"extract" includes an extract consisting of a single image;
"image" and "pornographic" have the same meanings as in section 63;
"recording" means any disc, tape or other device capable of storing data electronically and from which images may be produced (by any means).

(8) Section 22(3) of the Video Recordings Act 1984 (effect of alterations) applies for the purposes of this section as it applies for the purposes of that Act.

65 Defences: general

(1) Where a person is charged with an offence under section 63, it is a defence for the person to prove any of the matters mentioned in subsection (2).

(2) The matters are –

(a) that the person had a legitimate reason for being in possession of the image concerned;
(b) that the person had not seen the image concerned and did not know, nor had any cause to suspect, it to be an extreme pornographic image;
(c) that the person –
(i) was sent the image concerned without any prior request having been made by or on behalf of the person, and

(ii) did not keep it for an unreasonable time.

(3) In this section "extreme pornographic image" and "image" have the same meanings as in section 63.

66 Defence: participation in consensual acts

(1) This section applies where –

- (a) a person ("D") is charged with an offence under section 63, and
- (b) the offence relates to an image that portrays an act or acts within paragraphs (a) to (c) (but none within paragraph (d)) of subsection (7) of that section.

(2) It is a defence for D to prove –

- (a) that D directly participated in the act or any of the acts portrayed, and
- (b) that the act or acts did not involve the infliction of any non-consensual harm on any person, and
- (c) if the image portrays an act within section 63(7)(c), that what is portrayed as a human corpse was not in fact a corpse.

(3) For the purposes of this section harm inflicted on a person is "non-consensual" harm if –

- (a) the harm is of such a nature that the person cannot, in law, consent to it being inflicted on himself or herself; or
- (b) where the person can, in law, consent to it being so inflicted, the person does not in fact consent to it being so inflicted.

67 Penalties etc. for possession of extreme pornographic images

(1) This section has effect where a person is guilty of an offence under section 63.

(2) Except where subsection (3) applies to the offence, the offender is liable –

- (a) on summary conviction, to imprisonment for a term not exceeding the relevant period or a fine not exceeding the statutory maximum or both;
- (b) on conviction on indictment, to imprisonment for a term not exceeding 3 years or a fine or both.

(3) If the offence relates to an image that does not portray any act within section 63(7)(a) or (b), the offender is liable –

- (a) on summary conviction, to imprisonment for a term not exceeding the relevant period or a fine not exceeding the statutory maximum or both;
- (b) on conviction on indictment, to imprisonment for a term not exceeding 2 years or a fine or both.

(4) In subsection (2)(a) or (3)(a) "the relevant period" means –

- (a) in relation to England and Wales, 12 months;
- (b) in relation to Northern Ireland, 6 months.

68 Special rules relating to providers of information society services

Schedule 14 makes special provision in connection with the operation of section 63 in relation to persons providing information society services within the meaning of that Schedule.

69 Indecent photographs of children: England and Wales

(1) The Protection of Children Act 1978 (c. 37) is amended as follows.

(2) In section 1B(1)(b) (exception for members of the Security Service) –

- (a) after "Security Service" insert "or the Secret Intelligence Service";

(b) for "the Service" substitute "that Service".

(3) After section 7(4) (meaning of photograph), insert –

"(4A) References to a photograph also include –

(a) a tracing or other image, whether made by electronic or other means (of whatever nature) –
   (i) which is not itself a photograph or pseudo-photograph, but
   (ii) which is derived from the whole or part of a photograph or pseudo-photograph (or a combination of either or both); and
(b) data stored on a computer disc or by other electronic means which is capable of conversion into an image within paragraph (a); and subsection (8) applies in relation to such an image as it applies in relation to a pseudo-photograph."

(4) In section 7(9)(b) (meaning of indecent pseudo-photograph), for "a pseudo-photograph" substitute "an indecent pseudo-photograph".

70 Indecent photographs of children: Northern Ireland

(1) The Protection of Children (Northern Ireland) Order 1978 (S.I. 1978/1047 (N.I. 17)) is amended as follows.

(2) In Article 2(2) (interpretation) in paragraph (b) of the definition of "indecent pseudo-photograph", for "a pseudo-photograph" substitute "an indecent pseudo-photograph".

(3) After Article 2(2) insert –

"(2A) In this Order, references to a photograph also include –

(a) a tracing or other image, whether made by electronic or other means (of whatever nature) –
   (i) which is not itself a photograph or pseudo-photograph, but
   (ii) which is derived from the whole or part of a photograph or pseudo-photograph (or a combination of either or both); and
(b) data stored on a computer disc or by other electronic means which is capable of conversion into an image within paragraph (a);

and paragraph (3)(c) applies in relation to such an image as it applies in relation to a pseudo-photograph."

(4) In article 3A(1)(b) (exception for members of the Security Service) –

(a) after "Security Service" insert "or the Secret Intelligence Service";
(b) for "the Service" substitute "that Service".

71 Maximum penalty for publication etc. of obscene articles

In section 2(1)(b) of the Obscene Publications Act 1959 (c. 66) (maximum penalty on indictment for publication etc. of obscene articles) for "three years" substitute "five years".

Sexual offences

72 Offences committed outside the United Kingdom

(1) For section 72 of the Sexual Offences Act 2003 (c. 42) substitute –

"**72 Offences outside the United Kingdom**

(1) If –

(a) a United Kingdom national does an act in a country outside the United Kingdom, and
(b) the act, if done in England and Wales or Northern Ireland, would constitute a sexual offence to which this section applies, the United Kingdom national is guilty in that part of the United Kingdom of that sexual offence.

(2) If –

(a) a United Kingdom resident does an act in a country outside the United Kingdom,
(b) the act constitutes an offence under the law in force in that country, and

(c) the act, if done in England and Wales or Northern Ireland, would constitute a sexual offence to which this section applies, the United Kingdom resident is guilty in that part of the United Kingdom of that sexual offence.

(3) If –

(a) a person does an act in a country outside the United Kingdom at a time when the person was not a United Kingdom national or a United Kingdom resident,
(b) the act constituted an offence under the law in force in that country,
(c) the act, if done in England and Wales or Northern Ireland, would have constituted a sexual offence to which this section applies, and
(d) the person meets the residence or nationality condition at the relevant time, proceedings may be brought against the person in that part of the United Kingdom for that sexual offence as if the person had done the act there.

(4) The person meets the residence or nationality condition at the relevant time if the person is a United Kingdom national or a United Kingdom resident at the time when the proceedings are brought.

(5) An act punishable under the law in force in any country constitutes an offence under that law for the purposes of subsections (2) and (3) however it is described in that law.

(6) The condition in subsection (2)(b) or (3)(b) is to be taken to be met unless, not later than rules of court may provide, the defendant serves on the prosecution a notice –

(a) stating that, on the facts as alleged with respect to the act in question, the condition is not in the defendant's opinion met,
(b) showing the grounds for that opinion, and
(c) requiring the prosecution to prove that it is met.

(7) But the court, if it thinks fit, may permit the defendant to require the prosecution to prove that the condition is met without service of a notice under subsection (6).

(8) In the Crown Court the question whether the condition is met is to be decided by the judge alone.

(9) In this section –

"country" includes territory;
"United Kingdom national" means an individual who is –
(a) a British citizen, a British overseas territories citizen, a British National (Overseas) or a British Overseas citizen;
(b) a person who under the British Nationality Act 1981 is a British subject; or
(c) a British protected person within the meaning of that Act;

"United Kingdom resident" means an individual who is resident in the United Kingdom.

(10) Schedule 2 lists the sexual offences to which this section applies."

(2) Schedule 2 to that Act (list of sexual offences to which section 72 applies) is amended as follows.

(3) In paragraph 1 (offences under the law of England and Wales) –

(a) for paragraphs (a) and (b) substitute –
"(a) an offence under any of sections 5 to 19, 25 and 26 and 47 to 50;
(b) an offence under any of sections 1 to 4, 30 to 41 and 61 where the victim of the offence was under 18 at the time of the offence;";
(b) in paragraph (c), for "16" substitute "18"; and
(c) in paragraph (d), omit "in relation to a photograph or pseudophotograph showing a child under 16".

(4) In paragraph 2 (offences under the law of Northern Ireland) –

(a) in sub-paragraph (1)(c)(iv), for "17" substitute "18"; and
(b) in sub-paragraph (2), for "17" substitute "18".

73 Grooming and adoption

Schedule 15 –

(a) amends section 15 of the Sexual Offences Act 2003 (c. 42) (meeting a child following sexual grooming etc.),
(b) amends that Act in relation to adoption, and
(c) amends the Adoption Act 1976 (c. 36) in relation to offences under sections 64 and 65 of the Sexual Offences Act 2003.

Hatred on the grounds of sexual orientation

74 Hatred on the grounds of sexual orientation

Schedule 16 –

(a) amends Part 3A of the Public Order Act 1986 (c. 64) (hatred against persons on religious grounds) to make provision about hatred against a group of persons defined by reference to sexual orientation, and
(b) makes minor amendments of that Part.

Offences relating to nuclear material and nuclear facilities

75 Offences relating to the physical protection of nuclear material and nuclear facilities

(1) Part 1 of Schedule 17 amends the Nuclear Material (Offences) Act 1983 (c. 18) to create –

(a) further offences relating to the physical protection of nuclear material, and
(b) offences relating to the physical protection of nuclear facilities, and makes other amendments to that Act.

(2) Part 2 of that Schedule makes related amendments to the Customs and Excise Management Act 1979 (c. 2).

Self-defence etc.

76 Reasonable force for purposes of self-defence etc.

(1) This section applies where in proceedings for an offence –

(a) an issue arises as to whether a person charged with the offence ("D") is entitled to rely on a defence within subsection (2), and
(b) the question arises whether the degree of force used by D against a person ("V") was reasonable in the circumstances.

(2) The defences are –

(a) the common law defence of self-defence; and
(b) the defences provided by section 3(1) of the Criminal Law Act 1967 (c. 58) or section 3(1) of the Criminal Law Act (Northern Ireland) 1967 (c. 18 (N.I.)) (use of force in prevention of crime or making arrest).

(3) The question whether the degree of force used by D was reasonable in the circumstances is to be decided by reference to the circumstances as D believed them to be, and subsections (4) to (8) also apply in connection with deciding that question.

(4) If D claims to have held a particular belief as regards the existence of any circumstances –

(a) the reasonableness or otherwise of that belief is relevant to the question whether D genuinely held it; but
(b) if it is determined that D did genuinely hold it, D is entitled to rely on it for the purposes of subsection (3), whether or not –
   (i) it was mistaken, or
   (ii) (if it was mistaken) the mistake was a reasonable one to have made.

(5) But subsection (4)(b) does not enable D to rely on any mistaken belief attributable to intoxication that was voluntarily induced.

(6) The degree of force used by D is not to be regarded as having been reasonable in the circumstances as D believed them to be if it was disproportionate in those circumstances.

(7) In deciding the question mentioned in subsection (3) the following considerations are to be taken into account (so far as relevant in the circumstances of the case) –

(a) that a person acting for a legitimate purpose may not be able to weigh to a nicety the exact measure of any necessary action; and
(b) that evidence of a person's having only done what the person honestly and instinctively thought was necessary for a legitimate purpose constitutes strong evidence that only reasonable action was taken by that person for that purpose.

(8) Subsection (7) is not to be read as preventing other matters from being taken into account where they are relevant to deciding the question mentioned in subsection (3).

(9) This section is intended to clarify the operation of the existing defences mentioned in subsection (2).

(10) In this section –

(a) "legitimate purpose" means –
  (i) the purpose of self-defence under the common law, or
  (ii) the prevention of crime or effecting or assisting in the lawful arrest of persons mentioned in the provisions referred to in subsection (2)(b);
(b) references to self-defence include acting in defence of another person; and
(c) references to the degree of force used are to the type and amount of force used.

Unlawfully obtaining etc. personal data

77 Power to alter penalty for unlawfully obtaining etc. personal data

(1) The Secretary of State may by order provide for a person who is guilty of an offence under section 55 of the Data Protection Act 1998 (c. 29) (unlawful obtaining etc. of personal data) to be liable –

(a) on summary conviction, to imprisonment for a term not exceeding the specified period or to a fine not exceeding the statutory maximum or to both,
(b) on conviction on indictment, to imprisonment for a term not exceeding the specified period or to a fine or to both.

(2) In subsection (1)(a) and (b) "specified period" means a period provided for by the order but the period must not exceed –

(a) in the case of summary conviction, 12 months (or, in Northern Ireland, 6 months), and
(b) in the case of conviction on indictment, two years.

(3) The Secretary of State must ensure that any specified period for England and Wales which, in the case of summary conviction, exceeds 6 months is to be read as a reference to 6 months so far as it relates to an offence committed before the commencement of section 282(1) of the Criminal Justice Act 2003 (c. 44) (increase in sentencing powers of magistrates' courts from 6 to 12 months for certain offences triable either way).

(4) Before making an order under this section, the Secretary of State must consult –

(a) the Information Commissioner,
(b) such media organisations as the Secretary of State considers appropriate, and
(c) such other persons as the Secretary of State considers appropriate.

(5) An order under this section may, in particular, amend the Data Protection Act 1998.

78 New defence for purposes of journalism and other special purposes

In section 55(2) of the Data Protection Act 1998 (c. 29) (defences against offence of unlawfully obtaining etc. personal data) after "it," at the end of paragraph (c) insert –

"(ca) that he acted –
    (i) for the special purposes,
    (ii) with a view to the publication by any person of any journalistic, literary or artistic material, and
    (iii) in the reasonable belief that in the particular circumstances the obtaining, disclosing or procuring was justified as being in the public interest,".

Blasphemy

79 Abolition of common law offences of blasphemy and blasphemous libel

(1) The offences of blasphemy and blasphemous libel under the common law of England and Wales are abolished.

(2) In section 1 of the Criminal Libel Act 1819 (60 Geo. 3 & 1 Geo. 4 c. 8) (orders for seizure of copies of blasphemous or seditious libel) the words "any blasphemous libel, or" are omitted.

(3) In sections 3 and 4 of the Law of Libel Amendment Act 1888 (c. 64) (privileged matters) the words "blasphemous or" are omitted.

(4) Subsections (2) and (3) (and the related repeals in Schedule 28) extend to England and Wales only.

PART 6
INTERNATIONAL CO-OPERATION IN RELATION TO CRIMINAL JUSTICE MATTERS

Recognition of financial penalties: requests to other member States

80 Requests to other member States: England and Wales

(1) In Schedule 5 to the Courts Act 2003 (c. 39) (collection of fines and other sums imposed on conviction) in paragraph 38 (the range of further steps available against defaulters) –

(a) after sub-paragraph (1)(e) insert –
"(f) subject to sub-paragraph (4), issuing a certificate requesting enforcement under the Framework Decision on financial penalties;", and
(b) after sub-paragraph (3) insert –

"(4) A certificate requesting enforcement under the Framework Decision on financial penalties may only be issued where –

(a) the sum due is a financial penalty within the meaning of section 80 of the Criminal Justice and Immigration Act 2008, and
(b) it appears to the fines officer or the court that P is normally resident, or has property or income, in a member State other than the United Kingdom.

(5) In this paragraph, references to a certificate requesting enforcement under the Framework Decision on financial penalties are to be construed in accordance with section 92(3) of the Criminal Justice and Immigration Act 2008."

(2) The designated officer for a magistrates' court may issue a certificate requesting enforcement under the Framework Decision on financial penalties where –

(a) a person is required to pay a financial penalty,
(b) the penalty is not paid in full within the time allowed for payment,
(c) there is no appeal outstanding in relation to the penalty,
(d) Schedule 5 to the Courts Act 2003 (c. 39) does not apply in relation to the enforcement of the penalty, and
(e) it appears to the designated officer that the person is normally resident in, or has property or income in, a member State other than the United Kingdom.

(3) For the purposes of subsection (2)(c), there is no appeal outstanding in relation to a financial penalty if –

(a) no appeal has been brought in relation to the imposition of the financial penalty within the time allowed for making such an appeal, or

(b) such an appeal has been brought but the proceedings on appeal have been concluded.

(4) Where the person required to pay the financial penalty is a body corporate, subsection (2)(e) applies as if the reference to the person being normally resident in a member State other than the United Kingdom were a reference to the person having its registered office in a member State other than the United Kingdom.

(5) In this section, "financial penalty" means –

(a) a fine imposed by a court in England and Wales on a person's conviction of an offence;
(b) any sum payable under a compensation order (within the meaning of section 130(1) of the Powers of Criminal Courts (Sentencing) Act 2000 (c. 6));
(c) a surcharge under section 161A of the Criminal Justice Act 2003 (c. 44);
(d) any sum payable under any such order as is mentioned in paragraphs 1 to 9 of Schedule 9 to the Administration of Justice Act 1970 (c. 31) (orders for payment of costs);
(e) any sum payable by virtue of section 137(1) or (1A) of the Powers of Criminal Courts (Sentencing) Act 2000 (orders requiring parents to pay fines etc.);
(f) any fine or other sum mentioned in section 82(4)(b)(i) to (iv), or any fine imposed by a court in Scotland, which is enforceable in a local justice area in England and Wales by virtue of section 91 of the Magistrates' Courts Act 1980 (c. 43);
(g) any other financial penalty, within the meaning of the Framework Decision on financial penalties, specified in an order made by the Lord Chancellor.

81 Procedure on issue of certificate: England and Wales

(1) This section applies where –

(a) a magistrates' court or a fines officer has, under paragraph 39(3)(b) or 40 of Schedule 5 to the Courts Act 2003 (c. 39), issued a certificate requesting enforcement under the Framework Decision on financial penalties, or
(b) the designated officer for a magistrates' court has issued such a certificate under section 80(2) of this Act.

(2) The fines officer (in the case of a certificate issued by the officer) or the designated officer for the magistrates' court (in any other case) must give the Lord Chancellor the certificate, together with a certified copy of the decision requiring payment of the financial penalty.

(3) On receipt of the documents mentioned in subsection (2), the Lord Chancellor must give those documents to the central authority or competent authority of the member State in which the person required to pay the penalty appears to be normally resident or (as the case may be) to have property or income.

(4) Where a certified copy of the decision is given to the central authority or competent authority of a member State in accordance with subsection (3), no further steps to enforce the decision may be taken in England and Wales except in accordance with provision made by order by the Lord Chancellor.

(5) Where the person required to pay the financial penalty is a body corporate, subsection (3) applies as if the reference to the member State in which the person appears to be normally resident were a reference to the member State in which the person appears to have its registered office.

82 Requests to other member States: Northern Ireland

(1) A designated officer of the Northern Ireland Court Service may issue a certificate requesting enforcement under the Framework Decision on financial penalties where –

(a) a person is required to pay a financial penalty,
(b) the penalty is not paid in full within the time allowed for payment,
(c) there is no appeal outstanding in relation to the penalty, and
(d) it appears to the designated officer that the person is normally resident in, or has property or income in, a member State other than the United Kingdom.

(2) For the purposes of subsection (1)(c), there is no appeal outstanding in relation to a financial penalty if –

  (a) no appeal has been brought in relation to the imposition of the financial penalty within the time allowed for making such an appeal, or
  (b) such an appeal has been brought but the proceedings on appeal have been concluded.

(3) Where the person required to pay the financial penalty is a body corporate, subsection (1)(d) applies as if the reference to the person being normally resident in a member State other than the United Kingdom were a reference to the person having its registered office in a member State other than the United Kingdom.

(4) In this section –

  (a) "designated officer of the Northern Ireland Court Service" means a member of the staff of the Northern Ireland Court Service designated by the Lord Chancellor for the purposes of this section;
  (b) "financial penalty" means –
    (i) a fine imposed by a court in Northern Ireland on a person's conviction of an offence;
    (ii) any sum payable under a compensation order (within the meaning of Article 14 of the Criminal Justice (Northern Ireland) Order 1994 (S.I.1994/2795 (N.I.15));
    (iii) any sum payable under an order made under section 2(1), 4(1) or 5(1) of the Costs in Criminal Cases Act (Northern Ireland) 1968 (N.I. 10) or section 41(1) of the Criminal Appeal (Northern Ireland) Act 1980 (c. 47);
    (iv) any sum payable by virtue of Article 35 of the Criminal Justice (Children) (Northern Ireland) Order 1998 (S.I. 1998/1504 (N.I. 9) (orders requiring parents to pay fines etc.);
    (v) any fine or other sum mentioned in section 80(5)(a) to (e), or any fine imposed by a court in Scotland, which is enforceable in a petty sessions district in Northern Ireland by virtue of Article 96 of the Magistrates' Courts (Northern Ireland) Order 1981 (S.I. 1981/1675 (N.I.26));
    (vi) any other financial penalty, within the meaning of the Framework Decision on financial penalties, specified in an order made by the Lord Chancellor.

83 Procedure on issue of certificate: Northern Ireland

(1) This section applies where a designated officer has issued a certificate under section 82(1).

(2) The designated officer must give the Lord Chancellor the certificate, together with a certified copy of the decision requiring payment of the financial penalty.

(3) On receipt of the documents mentioned in subsection (2), the Lord Chancellor must give those documents to the central authority or competent authority of the member State in which the person required to pay the penalty appears to be normally resident or (as the case may be) to have property or income.

(4) Where a certified copy of the decision is given to the central authority or competent authority of a member State in accordance with subsection (3), no further steps to enforce the decision may be taken in Northern Ireland except in accordance with provision made by order by the Lord Chancellor.

(5) Where the person required to pay the financial penalty is a body corporate, subsection (3) applies as if the reference to the member State in which the person appears to be normally resident were a reference to the member State in which the person appears to have its registered office.

Recognition of financial penalties: requests from other member States

84 Requests from other member States: England and Wales

(1) This section applies where –

(a) the competent authority or central authority of a member State other than the United Kingdom gives the Lord Chancellor –
 (i) a certificate requesting enforcement under the Framework Decision on financial penalties, and
 (ii) the decision, or a certified copy of the decision, requiring payment of the financial penalty to which the certificate relates, and
(b) the financial penalty is suitable for enforcement in England and Wales (see section 91(1)).

(2) If the certificate states that the person required to pay the financial penalty is normally resident in England and Wales, the Lord Chancellor must give the documents mentioned in subsection (1)(a) to the designated officer for the local justice area in which it appears that the person is normally resident.

(3) Otherwise, the Lord Chancellor must give the documents mentioned in subsection (1)(a) to the designated officer for such local justice area as appears appropriate.

(4) Where the Lord Chancellor acts under subsection (2) or (3), the Lord Chancellor must also give the designated officer a notice –

(a) stating whether the Lord Chancellor thinks that any of the grounds for refusal apply (see section 91(2)), and
(b) giving reasons for that opinion.

(5) Where the person required to pay the financial penalty is a body corporate, subsection (2) applies as if the reference to the local justice area in which it appears that the person is normally resident were a reference to the local justice area in which it appears that the person has its registered office.

(6) Where –

(a) the competent authority or central authority of a member State other than the United Kingdom gives the central authority for Scotland the documents mentioned in subsection (1)(a), and
(b) without taking any action to enforce the financial penalty in Scotland, the central authority for Scotland gives the documents to the Lord Chancellor, this section applies as if the competent authority or central authority of the other member State gave the documents to the Lord Chancellor.

85 Procedure on receipt of certificate by designated officer

(1) This section applies where the Lord Chancellor gives the designated officer for a local justice area –

(a) a certificate requesting enforcement under the Framework Decision on financial penalties,
(b) the decision, or a certified copy of the decision, requiring payment of the financial penalty to which the certificate relates, and
(c) a notice under section 84(4).

(2) The designated officer must refer the matter to a magistrates' court acting for that area.

(3) The magistrates' court must decide whether it is satisfied that any of the grounds for refusal apply (see section 91(2)).

(4) The designated officer must inform the Lord Chancellor of the decision of the magistrates' court.

(5) Subsection (6) applies unless the magistrates' court is satisfied that one or more of the grounds for refusal apply.

(6) The enactments specified in subsection (7) apply in relation to the financial penalty as if it were a sum adjudged to be paid by a conviction of the magistrates' court on the date when the court made the decision mentioned in subsection (4).

(7) The enactments specified in this subsection are –

(a) Part 3 of the Magistrates' Courts Act 1980 (c. 43) (satisfaction and enforcement);
(b) Schedules 5 and 6 to the Courts Act 2003 (c. 39) (collection of fines etc. and discharge of fines etc. by unpaid work);
(c) any subordinate legislation (within the meaning of the Interpretation Act 1978 (c. 30)) made under the enactments specified in paragraphs (a) and (b).

(8) If the certificate requesting enforcement under the Framework Decision on financial penalties states that part of the financial penalty has been paid, the reference in subsection (6) to the financial penalty is to be read as a reference to such part of the penalty as remains unpaid.

86 Modification of Magistrates' Courts Act 1980

(1) Section 90 of the Magistrates' Courts Act 1980 is modified as follows in its application to financial penalties by virtue of section 85(6) of this Act.

(2) Subsection (1) applies as if for the words from "he is residing" to the end of that subsection there were substituted "he is residing, or has property or a source of income, in any petty sessions district in Northern Ireland –

(a) the court or the fines officer (as the case may be) may order that payment of the sum shall be enforceable in that petty sessions district, and
(b) if such an order is made, the court or the fines officer must notify the Lord Chancellor."

87 Requests from other member States: Northern Ireland

(1) This section applies where –

(a) the competent authority or central authority of a member State other than the United Kingdom gives the Lord Chancellor –
(i) a certificate requesting enforcement under the Framework Decision on financial penalties, and
(ii) the decision, or a certified copy of the decision, requiring payment of the financial penalty to which the certificate relates, and
(b) the financial penalty is suitable for enforcement in Northern Ireland (see section 91(1)).

(2) If the certificate states that the person required to pay the financial penalty is normally resident in Northern Ireland, the Lord Chancellor must give the documents mentioned in subsection (1)(a) to the clerk of petty sessions for the petty sessions district in which it appears that the person is normally resident.

(3) Otherwise, the Lord Chancellor must give the documents mentioned in subsection (1)(a) to the clerk of petty sessions for such petty sessions district as appears appropriate.

(4) Where the Lord Chancellor acts under subsection (2) or (3), the Lord Chancellor must also give the clerk of petty sessions a notice –

(a) stating whether the Lord Chancellor thinks that any of the grounds for refusal apply (see section 91(2)), and
(b) giving reasons for that opinion.

(5) Where the person required to pay the financial penalty is a body corporate, subsection (2) applies as if the reference to the petty sessions district in which it appears that the person is normally resident were a reference to the petty sessions district in which it appears that the person has its registered office.

(6) Where –

(a) the competent authority or central authority of a member State other than the United Kingdom gives the central authority for Scotland the documents mentioned in subsection (1)(a), and
(b) without taking any action to enforce the financial penalty in Scotland, the central authority for Scotland gives the documents to the Lord Chancellor, this section applies as if the competent authority or central authority of the other member State gave the documents to the Lord Chancellor.

88 Procedure on receipt of certificate by clerk of petty sessions

(1) This section applies where the Lord Chancellor gives the clerk of petty sessions for a petty sessions district –

(a) a certificate requesting enforcement under the Framework Decision on financial penalties,
(b) the decision, or a certified copy of the decision, requiring payment of the financial penalty to which the certificate relates, and
(c) a notice under section 87(4).

(2) The clerk must refer the matter to a magistrates' court acting for the petty sessions district.

(3) The magistrates' court must decide whether it is satisfied that any of the grounds for refusal apply (see section 91(2)).

(4) The clerk must inform the Lord Chancellor of the decision of the magistrates' court.

(5) Subsection (6) applies unless the magistrates' court is satisfied that one or more of the grounds for refusal apply.

(6) Part 9 of the Magistrates' Courts (Northern Ireland) Order 1981 (S.I. 1981/1675 (N.I.26)), and any instrument made under that Part, apply in relation to the financial penalty as if it were a sum adjudged to be paid by a conviction of the magistrates' court on the date when the court made the decision mentioned in subsection (4).

(7) If the certificate requesting enforcement under the Framework Decision on financial penalties states that part of the financial penalty has been paid, the reference in subsection (6) to the financial penalty is to be read as a reference to such part of the penalty as remains unpaid.

89 Modification of Magistrates' Courts (Northern Ireland) Order 1981

(1) Part 9 of the Magistrates' Courts (Northern Ireland) Order 1981 is modified as follows in its application to financial penalties by virtue of section 88(6) of this Act.

(2) Article 92 applies in relation to any financial penalty for an amount exceeding £20,000 as if for paragraph (5) there were substituted –

> "(5) The period for which a person may be committed to prison under this Article in default of payment or levy of any sum or part of such sum shall not exceed the maximum period which the Crown Court could have fixed under section 35(1)(c) of the Criminal Justice Act (Northern Ireland) 1945 had the financial penalty been a fine imposed by the Crown Court."

(3) For the purposes of subsection (2), if the amount of a financial penalty is specified in a currency other than sterling, that amount must be converted to sterling by reference to the London closing exchange rate on the relevant date.

(4) In subsection (3), the "relevant date" means the date on which the decision imposing the financial penalty was made.

(5) Article 95 applies as if for the words from "he is residing" in paragraph (1) to the end of that paragraph there were substituted "he is residing, or has property or a source of income, in any local justice area in England and Wales –

(a) the court may order that payment of the sum shall be enforceable in that local justice area, and

(b) if such an order is made, the court must notify the Lord Chancellor."

90 Transfer of certificates to central authority for Scotland

(1) This section applies where –

(a) the competent authority or central authority of a member State other than the United Kingdom gives the Lord Chancellor –
 (i) a certificate requesting enforcement under the Framework Decision on financial penalties, and
 (ii) the decision, or a certified copy of the decision, requiring payment of the financial penalty to which the certificate relates, but
(b) the Lord Chancellor is not required by section 84 or 87 to give the documents to a designated officer for a local justice area in England and Wales or to a clerk of petty sessions for a petty sessions district in Northern Ireland.

(2) If the certificate states that the person is normally resident or has property or a source of income in Scotland, the Lord Chancellor must give the documents to the central authority for Scotland.

Recognition of financial penalties: miscellaneous

91 Recognition of financial penalties: general

(1) Schedule 18 specifies when a financial penalty is suitable for enforcement in England and Wales for the purposes of section 84(1) and when a financial penalty is suitable for enforcement in Northern Ireland for the purposes of section 87(1).

(2) Schedule 19 specifies the grounds for refusal for the purposes of sections 84(4)(a), 85(3) and (5), 87(4)(a) and 88(3) and (5).

(3) The Lord Chancellor may by order make further provision for or in connection with giving effect to the Framework Decision on financial penalties.

(4) An order under section 81(4), 83(4) or subsection (3) of this section may in particular modify, amend, repeal or revoke any provision of –

(a) any Act (including this Act and any Act passed in the same Session as this Act);
(b) subordinate legislation (within the meaning of the Interpretation Act 1978 (c. 30)) made before the passing of this Act;
(c) Northern Ireland legislation passed, or made, before the passing of this Act;
(d) any instrument made, before the passing of this Act, under Northern Ireland legislation.

92 Interpretation of sections 80 to 91 etc.

(1) In sections 80 to 91 and Schedules 18 and 19 –

"central authority", in relation to a member State other than the United Kingdom, means an authority designated by the State as a central authority for the purposes of the Framework Decision on financial penalties;
"central authority for Scotland" means the person or body which, by virtue of an order under section 56 of the Criminal Proceedings etc. (Reform) (Scotland) Act 2007 (asp 6) (recognition of EU financial penalties), acts as the central authority in relation to Scotland for the purposes of the Framework Decision;
"competent authority", in relation to a member State, means an authority designated by the State as a competent authority for the purposes of that Decision;
"the Framework Decision on financial penalties" means the Framework Decision of the Council of the European Union made on 24 February 2005 on the application of the principle of mutual recognition to financial penalties (2005/214/JHA).

(2) In sections 84 to 91 and Schedules 18 and 19 –

"decision" has the meaning given by Article 1 of the Framework Decision on financial penalties (except in sections 85(4) and 88(4));

"financial penalty" has the meaning given by that Article.

(3) References in sections 80 to 91 to a certificate requesting enforcement under the Framework Decision on financial penalties are references to such a certificate as is provided for by Article 4 of that Decision.

Repatriation of prisoners

93 Delivery of prisoner to place abroad for purposes of transfer out of the United Kingdom

In section 2(1) of the Repatriation of Prisoners Act 1984 (c. 47) (transfer out of the UK), for subsection (1) substitute –

"(1) The effect of a warrant under section 1 providing for the transfer of the prisoner out of the United Kingdom shall be to authorise –

(a) the taking of the prisoner to any place in any part of the United Kingdom, his delivery at a place of departure from the United Kingdom into the custody of an appropriate person and his removal by that person from the United Kingdom to a place outside the United Kingdom; or

(b) the taking of the prisoner to any place in any part of the United Kingdom, his removal from the United Kingdom and his delivery, at the place of arrival from the United Kingdom, into the custody of an appropriate person.

(1A) In subsection (1) "appropriate person" means a person representing the appropriate authority of the country or territory to which the prisoner is to be transferred."

94 Issue of warrant transferring responsibility for detention and release of an offender to or from the relevant Minister

After section 4 of the Repatriation of Prisoners Act 1984 (transfer into the United Kingdom) insert –

"Transfer of responsibility for detention and release of offender present outside the country or territory in which he is required to be detained

4A Issue of warrant transferring responsibility for detention and release of offender

(1) This section enables responsibility for the detention and release of a person to whom subsection (2) or (3) applies to be transferred between the relevant Minister in the United Kingdom and the appropriate authority in a country or territory outside the British Islands.

(2) A person falls within this subsection if that person –

(a) is a person to whom section 1(7) applies by virtue of –
 (i) an order made in the course of the exercise by a court or tribunal in any part of the United Kingdom of its criminal jurisdiction; or
 (ii) any of the provisions of this Act or any similar provisions of the law of any part of the United Kingdom; and
(b) is present in a country or territory outside the British Islands.

(3) A person falls within this subsection if that person –

(a) is a person to whom section 1(7) applies by virtue of –
 (i) an order made in the course of the exercise by a court or tribunal in a country or territory outside the British Islands of its criminal jurisdiction; or
 (ii) any provisions of the law of such a country or territory which are similar to any of the provisions of this Act; and
(b) is present in the United Kingdom.

(4) Terms used in subsection (2)(a) and (3)(a) have the same meaning as in section 1(7).

(5) Subject to the following provisions of this section, where –

- (a) the United Kingdom is a party to international arrangements providing for the transfer between the United Kingdom and a country or territory outside the British Islands of responsibility for the detention and release of persons to whom subsection (2) or (3) applies,
- (b) the relevant Minister and the appropriate authority of that country or territory have each agreed to the transfer under those arrangements of responsibility for the detention and release of a particular person to whom subsection (2) or (3) applies (in this Act referred to as "the relevant person"), and
- (c) in a case in which the terms of those arrangements provide for the transfer of responsibility to take place only with the relevant person's consent, that consent has been given, the relevant Minister shall issue a warrant providing for the transfer of responsibility for the detention and release of the relevant person from that Minister (where subsection (2) applies) or to that Minister (where subsection (3) applies).

(6) The relevant Minister shall not issue a warrant under this section providing for the transfer of responsibility for the detention and release of a person to the relevant Minister unless –

- (a) that person is a British citizen;
- (b) the transfer appears to the relevant Minister to be appropriate having regard to any close ties which that person has with the United Kingdom.

(7) The relevant Minister shall not issue a warrant under this section where, after the duty in subsection (5) has arisen, circumstances arise or are brought to his attention which in his opinion make it inappropriate that the transfer of responsibility should take place.

(8) The relevant Minister shall not issue a warrant under this section (other than one superseding an earlier warrant) unless he is satisfied that all reasonable steps have been taken to inform the relevant person in writing in his own language –

- (a) of the substance, so far as relevant to the case, of the international arrangements in accordance with which it is proposed to transfer responsibility for his detention and release;
- (b) of the effect in relation to the relevant person of the warrant which it is proposed to issue under this section;
- (c) in the case of a person to whom subsection (2) applies, of the effect in relation to his case of so much of the law of the country or territory concerned as has effect with respect to transfers under those arrangements of responsibility for his detention and release;
- (d) in the case of a person to whom subsection (3) applies, of the effect in relation to his case of the law relating to his detention under that warrant and subsequent release (including the effect of any enactment or instrument under which he may be released earlier than provided for by the terms of the warrant); and
- (e) of the powers of the relevant Minister under section 6; and the relevant Minister shall not issue a warrant superseding an earlier warrant under this section unless the requirements of this subsection were fulfilled in relation to the earlier warrant.

(9) A consent given for the purposes of subsection (5)(c) shall not be capable of being withdrawn after a warrant under this section has been issued in respect of the relevant person; and, accordingly, a purported withdrawal of that consent after that time shall not affect the validity of the warrant, or of any provision which by virtue of section 6 subsequently supersedes provisions of that warrant, or of any direction given in relation to the prisoner under section 4B(3).

(10) In this section "relevant Minister" means –

- (a) the Scottish Ministers in a case where the person who is the subject of the proposed transfer of responsibility is –
  - (i) a person to whom subsection (2) applies who is for the time being required to be detained at a place in Scotland; or
  - (ii) a person to whom subsection (3) applies, if it is proposed that he will be detained at a place in Scotland;
- (b) the Secretary of State, in any other case.

4B Transfer of responsibility from the United Kingdom

(1) The effect of a warrant under section 4A relating to a person to whom subsection (2) of that section applies shall be to transfer responsibility for the detention and release of that person from the relevant Minister (as defined in section 4A(10)) to the appropriate authority of the country or territory in which he is present.

(2) Subject to subsections (3) to (6), the order by virtue of which the relevant person is required to be detained at the time such a warrant is issued in respect of him shall continue to have effect after the transfer of responsibility so as to apply to him if he comes to be in the United Kingdom at any time when under that order he is to be, or may be, detained.

(3) If, at any time after the transfer of responsibility, it appears to the relevant Minister appropriate to do so in order that effect may be given to the international arrangements in accordance with which the transfer took place, the relevant Minister may give a direction –

(a) varying the order referred to in subsection (2); or
(b) providing for the order to cease to have effect.

(4) In subsection (3) "relevant Minister" means –

(a) the Scottish Ministers, where Scotland is the part of the United Kingdom in which the order referred to in subsection (2) has effect; and
(b) the Secretary of State in any other case.

(5) The power by direction under subsection (3) to vary the order referred to in subsection (2) includes power by direction –

(a) to provide for how any period during which the detention and release of the relevant person is, by virtue of a warrant under section 4A, the responsibility of a country or territory outside the United Kingdom is to be treated for the purposes of the order; and
(b) to provide for the relevant person to be treated as having been released or discharged as mentioned in any paragraph of section 2(4)(b).

(6) Except in relation to any period during which a restriction order is in force in respect of the relevant person, subsection (2) shall not apply in relation to a hospital order; and, accordingly, a hospital order shall cease to have effect in relation to that person –

(a) at the time of the transfer of responsibility, if no restriction order is in force in respect of him at that time; and
(b) if at that time a restriction order is in force in respect of him, as soon after the transfer of responsibility as the restriction order ceases to have effect.

(7) In subsection (6) "hospital order" and "restriction order" have the same meaning as in section 2(6).

(8) References in this section to the order by virtue of which a person is required to be detained at the time a warrant under section 4A is issued in respect of him include references to any order by virtue of which he is required to be detained after the order by virtue of which he is required to be detained at that time ceases to have effect.

4C Transfer of responsibility to the United Kingdom

(1) The effect of a warrant under section 4A relating to a person to whom subsection (3) of that section applies shall be to transfer responsibility for the detention and release of that person to the relevant Minister (as defined in section 4A(10)) and to authorise –

(a) the taking of that person in custody to such place in any part of the United Kingdom as may be specified in the warrant, being a place at which effect may be given to the provisions contained in the warrant by virtue of paragraph (b); and
(b) the detention of that person in any part of the United Kingdom in accordance with such provisions as may be contained in the warrant, being provisions appearing to the relevant Minister to be appropriate for giving effect to the international arrangements in accordance with which responsibility for that person is transferred.

(2) A provision shall not be contained by virtue of subsection (1)(b) in a warrant under section 4A unless it satisfies the following two conditions, that is to say –

(a) it is a provision with respect to the detention of a person in a prison, a hospital or any other institution; and
(b) it is a provision which at the time the warrant is issued may be contained in an order made either –
 (i) in the course of the exercise of its criminal jurisdiction by a court in the part of the United Kingdom in which the person is to be detained; or
 (ii) otherwise than by a court but for the purpose of giving effect to an order made as mentioned in sub-paragraph (i).

(3) Section 3(3) applies for determining for the purposes of paragraph (b) of subsection (1) above what provisions are appropriate for giving effect to the international arrangements mentioned in that paragraph in a relevant person's case as it applies for the purposes of section 3(1)(c) in the case of a prisoner who is to be transferred into the United Kingdom.

(4) Subject to subsection (6) and Part 2 of the Schedule to this Act, a provision contained by virtue of subsection (1)(b) in a warrant under section 4A shall for all purposes have the same effect as the same provision contained in an order made as mentioned in sub-paragraph (i) or, as the case may be, sub-paragraph (ii) of subsection (2)(b).

(5) A provision contained by virtue of subsection (1)(b) in a warrant under section 4A shall take effect with the delivery of the relevant person to the place specified in the warrant for the purposes of subsection (1)(a).

(6) Subsection (4) shall not confer any right of appeal on the relevant person against provisions contained by virtue of subsection (1)(b) in a warrant under this section.

(7) Part 2 of the Schedule to this Act shall have effect with respect to the operation of certain enactments in relation to provisions contained by virtue of subsection (1)(b) in a warrant under section 4A.

(8) For the purposes of determining whether at any particular time any such order as is mentioned in subsection (2)(b) could have been made as so mentioned, there shall be disregarded both –

(a) any requirement that certain conditions must be satisfied before the order is made; and
(b) any restriction on the minimum period in respect of which the order may be made."

95 Powers to arrest and detain persons believed to fall within section 4A(3) of Repatriation of Prisoners Act 1984

After section 4C of the Repatriation of Prisoners Act 1984 (c. 47) (as inserted by section 94) insert –

"Persons believed to fall within section 4A(3): powers of arrest and detention

4D Arrest and detention with a view to establishing whether a person falls within section 4A(3) etc.

(1) The Secretary of State or the Scottish Ministers may issue a certificate stating that the issuing authority –

(a) considers that there are reasonable grounds for believing that a person in the United Kingdom is a person falling within section 4A(3), and
(b) has requested written confirmation from the country or territory concerned of the details of that person's case.

(2) The issuing authority may send the certificate (with any other documents appearing to the authority to be relevant) to the appropriate judge with a view to obtaining the issue of a warrant under subsection (3).

(3) The appropriate judge may, on receiving the certificate, issue a warrant for the arrest of the person concerned if the judge is satisfied that there are reasonable grounds for believing that the person falls within section 4A(3).

(4) The warrant may be executed anywhere in the United Kingdom by any designated person (and it is immaterial whether or not he is in possession of the warrant or a copy of it).

(5) A person arrested under this section shall, as soon as is practicable –

(a) be given a copy of the warrant for his arrest; and
(b) be brought before the appropriate judge.

(6) The appropriate judge may order that a person before him who is the subject of a certificate under this section is to be detained from the time the order is made until the end of the period of seven days beginning with the day after that on which the order is made.

(7) The purpose of an order under subsection (6) is to secure the detention of the person concerned while –

(a) written confirmation is obtained from a representative of the country or territory concerned of the details of his case;
(b) it is established whether he is a person falling within section 4A(3); and
(c) any application for an order under section 4E(6) is made in respect of him.

(8) Subject to subsection (9), a person detained under such an order may be released at any time during the period mentioned in subsection (6) and shall be released at the end of that period (if not released sooner).

(9) Subsection (8) ceases to apply to the detained person if, during that period, an order under section 4E is made in respect of him.

(10) It is immaterial for the purposes of subsection (6) whether or not the person concerned has previously been arrested under this section.

4E Arrest and detention with a view to determining whether to issue a warrant under section 4A

(1) The Secretary of State or the Scottish Ministers may issue a certificate stating that the issuing authority –

(a) considers that a person in the United Kingdom is a person falling within section 4A(3), and
(b) has received written confirmation from a representative of the country or territory concerned of the details of that person's case; and it is immaterial for the purposes of this section whether or not the person concerned has been previously arrested or detained under section 4D.

(2) The issuing authority may send the certificate (with a copy of the written confirmation mentioned in subsection (1)(b) and any other documents appearing to that authority to be relevant) to the appropriate judge with a view to obtaining the issue of a warrant under subsection (3).

(3) The appropriate judge may, on receiving the certificate, issue a warrant for the arrest of the person concerned if the judge is satisfied that there are reasonable grounds for believing that the person falls within section 4A(3).

(4) The warrant may be executed anywhere in the United Kingdom by any designated person (and it is immaterial whether or not that person is in possession of the warrant or a copy of it).

(5) A person arrested under this section shall, as soon as is practicable –

(a) be given a copy of the warrant for his arrest; and
(b) be brought before the appropriate judge.

(6) The appropriate judge may, on the application of the Secretary of State or the Scottish Ministers, order that a person before the judge who –

(a) is the subject of a certificate under this section, and
(b) the judge is satisfied is a person falling within section 4A(3), shall be detained from the time the order is made until the end of the period of fourteen days beginning with the day after that on which the order is made.

(7) The purpose of an order under subsection (6) is to secure the detention of the person concerned until –

(a) it is determined whether to issue a warrant under section 4A; and
(b) if so determined, such a warrant is issued.

(8) Subject to subsection (9), a person detained under such an order may be released at any time during the period mentioned in subsection (6) and shall be released at the end of that period (if not released sooner).

(9) Subsection (8) ceases to apply to the detained person if, during that period, a warrant under section 4A is issued in respect of him.

(10) It is immaterial for the purposes of subsection (6) whether or not the person concerned has previously been arrested or detained under section 4D or arrested under this section.

4F Sections 4D and 4E: supplementary provisions

(1) This section has effect for the purposes of sections 4D and 4E.

(2) A "designated person" is a person designated by the Secretary of State or the Scottish Ministers.

(3) The appropriate judge is –

  (a) in England and Wales, any District Judge (Magistrates' Courts) who is designated for those purposes by the Lord Chief Justice after consulting the Lord Chancellor;
  (b) in Scotland, the sheriff of Lothian and Borders; and
  (c) in Northern Ireland, any county court judge or resident magistrate who is designated for those purposes by the Lord Chief Justice of Northern Ireland after consulting the Lord Chancellor.

(4) A designation under subsection (2) or (3)(a) or (c) may be made –

  (a) for the purposes of section 4D or 4E (or both); and
  (b) for all cases or only for cases (or cases of a description) specified in the designation.

(5) A designated person shall have all the powers, authority, protection and privileges of a constable in any part of the United Kingdom in which a person who may be arrested under section 4D or 4E is for the time being."

96 Amendments relating to Scotland

(1) The amendments of section 1 of the Repatriation of Prisoners Act 1984 (c. 47) made by section 44(2) and (3) of the Police and Justice Act 2006 (c. 48) (which amend the requirement for the prisoner's consent to any transfer to or from the United Kingdom) apply in relation to cases in which the relevant Minister for the purposes of section 1 is the Scottish Ministers as they apply in other cases.

(2) In section 2(6) of the Repatriation of Prisoners Act 1984 (transfer out of the United Kingdom) in the definition of "hospital order", after "1986" insert "or a compulsion order under section 57A of the Criminal Procedure (Scotland) Act 1995".

(3) In section 8(1) (interpretation etc.), before the definition of "international arrangements" insert –

  ""enactment" includes an enactment comprised in, or in an instrument under, an Act of the Scottish Parliament;".

Mutual legal assistance in revenue matters

97 Power to transfer functions under Crime (International Co-operation) Act 2003 in relation to direct taxation

(1) In section 27(1) of the Crime (International Co-operation) Act 2003 (c. 32) (exercise of powers by others) –

  (a) in paragraph (a), for "Commissioners of Customs and Excise" substitute "Commissioners for Revenue and Customs"; and
  (b) in paragraph (b), for "a customs officer" substitute "an officer of Revenue and Customs".

(2) Paragraph 14 of Schedule 2 to the Commissioners for Revenue and Customs Act 2005 (c. 11) (power under section 27(1) not applicable to former inland revenue matters etc.) ceases to have effect.

PART 7
VIOLENT OFFENDER ORDERS

Violent offender orders

98 Violent offender orders

(1) A violent offender order is an order made in respect of a qualifying offender which –

(a) contains such prohibitions, restrictions or conditions authorised by section 102 as the court making the order considers necessary for the purpose of protecting the public from the risk of serious violent harm caused by the offender, and
(b) has effect for such period of not less than 2, nor more than 5, years as is specified in the order (unless renewed or discharged under section 103).

(2) For the purposes of this Part any reference to protecting the public from the risk of serious violent harm caused by a person is a reference to protecting –

(a) the public in the United Kingdom, or
(b) any particular members of the public in the United Kingdom, from a current risk of serious physical or psychological harm caused by that person committing one or more specified offences.

(3) In this Part "specified offence" means –

(a) manslaughter;
(b) an offence under section 4 of the Offences against the Person Act 1861 (c. 100) (soliciting murder);
(c) an offence under section 18 of that Act (wounding with intent to cause grievous bodily harm);
(d) an offence under section 20 of that Act (malicious wounding);
(e) attempting to commit murder or conspiracy to commit murder; or
(f) a relevant service offence.

(4) The following are relevant service offences –

(a) any offence under –
　(i) section 70 of the Army Act 1955 (3 & 4 Eliz. 2 c. 18),
　(ii) section 70 of the Air Force Act 1955 (3 & 4 Eliz. 2 c. 19), or
　(iii) section 42 of the Naval Discipline Act 1957 (c. 53), of which the corresponding civil offence (within the meaning of the section in question) is an offence within any of paragraphs (a) to (e) of subsection (3) above; and
(b) any offence under section 42 of the Armed Forces Act 2006 (c. 52) as respects which the corresponding offence under the law of England and Wales (within the meaning of that section) is an offence within any of those paragraphs.

(5) Section 48 of the Armed Forces Act 2006 (c. 52) (attempts, conspiracy etc.) applies for the purposes of subsection (4)(b) as if the reference in subsection (3)(b) of that section to any of the following provisions of that Act were a reference to subsection (4)(b).

99 Qualifying offenders

(1) In this Part "qualifying offender" means a person aged 18 or over who is within subsection (2) or (4).

(2) A person is within this subsection if (whether before or after the commencement of this Part) –

(a) the person has been convicted of a specified offence and either –
　(i) a custodial sentence of at least 12 months was imposed for the offence, or
　(ii) a hospital order was made in respect of it (with or without a restriction order),
(b) the person has been found not guilty of a specified offence by reason of insanity and subsection (3) applies, or
(c) the person has been found to be under a disability and to have done the act charged in respect of a specified offence and subsection (3) applies.

(3) This subsection applies in the case of a person within (2)(b) or (2)(c) if the court made in respect of the offence –

(a) a hospital order (with or without a restriction order), or
(b) a supervision order.

(4) A person is within this subsection if, under the law in force in a country outside England and Wales (and whether before or after the commencement of this Part) –

    (a)   the person has been convicted of a relevant offence and either –

        (i)   a sentence of imprisonment or other detention for at least 12 months was imposed for the offence, or

        (ii)   an order equivalent to that mentioned in subsection (3)(a) was made in respect of it,

    (b)   a court exercising jurisdiction under that law has made in respect of a relevant offence a finding equivalent to a finding that the person was not guilty by reason of insanity, and has made in respect of the offence an order equivalent to one mentioned in subsection (3), or

    (c)   such a court has, in respect of a relevant offence, made a finding equivalent to a finding that the person was under a disability and did the act charged in respect of the offence, and has made in respect of the offence an order equivalent to one mentioned in subsection (3).

(5) In subsection (4) "relevant offence" means an act which –

    (a)   constituted an offence under the law in force in the country concerned, and

    (b)   would have constituted a specified offence if it had been done in England and Wales.

(6) An act punishable under the law in force in a country outside England and Wales constitutes an offence under that law for the purposes of subsection (5) however it is described in that law.

(7) Subject to subsection (8), on an application under section 100 the condition in subsection (5)(b) (where relevant) is to be taken as met in relation to the person to whom the application relates ("P") unless, not later than rules of court may provide, P serves on the applicant a notice –

    (a)   denying that, on the facts as alleged with respect to the act in question, the condition is met,

    (b)   giving the reasons for denying that it is met, and

    (c)   requiring the applicant to prove that it is met.

(8) If the court thinks fit, it may permit P to require the applicant to prove that the condition is met even though no notice has been served under subsection (7).

100   Applications for violent offender orders

(1) A chief officer of police may by complaint to a magistrates' court apply for a violent offender order to be made in respect of a person –

    (a)   who resides in the chief officer's police area, or

    (b)   who the chief officer believes is in, or is intending to come to, that area, if it appears to the chief officer that the conditions in subsection (2) are met.

(2) The conditions are –

    (a)   that the person is a qualifying offender, and

    (b)   that the person has, since the appropriate date, acted in such a way as to give reasonable cause to believe that it is necessary for a violent offender order to be made in respect of the person.

(3) An application under this section may be made to any magistrates' court whose commission area includes –

    (a)   any part of the applicant's police area, or

    (b)   any place where it is alleged that the person acted in such a way as is mentioned in subsection (2)(b).

(4) The Secretary of State may by order make provision –

    (a)   for applications under this section to be made by such persons or bodies as are specified or described in the order;

(b) specifying cases or circumstances in which applications may be so made;
(c) for provisions of this Part to apply, in relation to the making of applications (or cases where applications are made) by any such persons or bodies, with such modifications as are specified in relation to them in the order.

(5) In this Part "the appropriate date" means the date (or, as the case may be, the first date) on which the person became a person within any of paragraphs (a) to (c) of section 99(2) or (4), whether that date fell before or after the commencement of this Part.

101 Making of violent offender orders

(1) This section applies where an application is made to a magistrates' court under section 100 in respect of a person ("P").

(2) After hearing –
   (a) the applicant, and
   (b) P, if P wishes to be heard, the court may make a violent offender order in respect of P if it is satisfied that the conditions in subsection (3) are met.

(3) The conditions are –
   (a) that P is a qualifying offender, and
   (b) that P has, since the appropriate date, acted in such a way as to make it necessary to make a violent offender order for the purpose of protecting the public from the risk of serious violent harm caused by P.

(4) When deciding whether it is necessary to make such an order for that purpose, the court must have regard to whether P would, at any time when such an order would be in force, be subject under any other enactment to any measures that would operate to protect the public from the risk of such harm.

(5) A violent offender order may not be made so as to come into force at any time when P –
   (a) is subject to a custodial sentence imposed in respect of any offence,
   (b) is on licence for part of the term of such a sentence, or
   (c) is subject to a hospital order or a supervision order made in respect of any offence.

(6) But such an order may be applied for, and made, at such a time.

102 Provisions that orders may contain

(1) A violent offender order may contain prohibitions, restrictions or conditions preventing the offender –
   (a) from going to any specified premises or any other specified place (whether at all, or at or between any specified time or times);
   (b) from attending any specified event;
   (c) from having any, or any specified description of, contact with any specified individual.

(2) Any of the prohibitions, restrictions or conditions contained in a violent offender order may relate to conduct in Scotland or Northern Ireland (as well as to conduct in England or Wales).

(3) The Secretary of State may by order amend subsection (1).

(4) In this section "specified" means specified in the violent offender order concerned.

103 Variation, renewal or discharge of violent offender orders

(1) A person within subsection (2) may by complaint apply to the appropriate magistrates' court –
   (a) for an order varying or discharging a violent offender order;
   (b) for an order (a "renewal order") renewing a violent offender order for such period of not more than 5 years as is specified in the renewal order.

(2) The persons are –

(a) the offender,
(b) the chief officer of police who applied for the order,
(c) (if different) the chief officer of police for the area in which the offender resides, and
(d) (if different) a chief officer of police who believes that the offender is in, or is intending to come to, his police area.

(3) The "appropriate magistrates' court" means the magistrates' court that made the order or (if different) –

(a) a magistrates' court for the area in which the offender resides, or
(b) where the application under this section is made by a chief officer of police, any magistrates' court whose commission area includes any part of the chief officer's police area.

(4) On an application under this section the appropriate magistrates' court may, after hearing –

(a) the applicant, and
(b) any other persons mentioned in subsection (2) who wish to be heard, make such order varying, renewing or discharging the violent offender order as the court considers appropriate. But this is subject to subsections (5) to (7).

(5) A violent offender order may only be –

(a) renewed, or
(b) varied so as to impose additional prohibitions, restrictions or conditions on the offender, if the court considers that it is necessary to do so for the purpose of protecting the public from the risk of serious violent harm caused by the offender (and any renewed or varied order may contain only such prohibitions, restrictions or conditions as the court considers necessary for this purpose).

(6) References in subsection (5) to prohibitions, restrictions or conditions are to prohibitions, restrictions or conditions authorised by section 102.

(7) The court may not discharge the violent offender order before the end of the period of 2 years beginning with the date on which it comes into force under section 101 unless consent to its discharge is given by the offender and –

(a) where the application under this section is made by a chief officer of police, by that chief officer, or
(b) where the application is made by the offender, by the chief officer of police for the area in which the offender resides.

104 Interim violent offender orders

(1) This section applies where an application under section 100 ("the main application") has not yet been determined.

(2) An application for an order under this section ("an interim violent offender order") may be made –

(a) by the complaint by which the main application is made, or
(b) if the main application has already been made to a court, by means of a further complaint made to that court by the person making the main application.

(3) If it appears to the court –

(a) that the person to whom the main application relates ("P") is a qualifying offender,
(b) that, if the court were determining that application, it would be likely to make a violent offender order in respect of P, and
(c) that it is desirable to act before that application is determined, with a view to securing the immediate protection of the public from the risk of serious violent harm caused by P, the court may make an interim violent offender order in respect of P that contains such

prohibitions, restrictions or conditions as it considers necessary for the purpose of protecting the public from the risk of such harm.

(4) The reference in subsection (3) to prohibitions, restrictions or conditions is to prohibitions, restrictions or conditions authorised by section 102 in the case of a violent offender order.

(5) But an interim violent offender order may not be made so as to come into force at any time when the person –

- (a) is subject to a custodial sentence for any offence,
- (b) is on licence for part of the term of such a sentence, or
- (c) is subject to a hospital order or a supervision order made in respect of any offence.

(6) An interim violent offender order –

- (a) has effect only for such period as is specified in the order, and
- (b) ceases to have effect (if it has not already done so) at the appropriate time.

(7) "The appropriate time" means –

- (a) if the court grants the main application, the time when a violent offender order made in pursuance of it comes into force;
- (b) if the court decides not to grant the main application or it is withdrawn, the time when the court so decides or the application is withdrawn.

(8) Section 103 applies in relation to the variation or discharge of an interim violent offender order as it applies in relation to the variation or discharge of a violent offender order, but with the omission of subsection (7).

105 Notice of applications

(1) This section applies to –

- (a) any application under section 100 for a violent offender order,
- (b) any application under section 104 for an interim violent offender order, and
- (c) any application under section 103 for the variation, discharge or renewal of a violent offender order, or for the variation or discharge of an interim violent offender order.

(2) A magistrates' court may not begin hearing such an application unless it is satisfied that the relevant person has been given notice of –

- (a) the application, and
- (b) the time and place of the hearing, a reasonable time before the hearing.

(3) In this section "the relevant person" means –

- (a) the person to whom the application mentioned in subsection (1)(a) or (b)relates, or
- (b) the person in respect of whom the order mentioned in subsection (1)(c) has been made,

as the case may be.

106 Appeals

(1) A person in respect of whom –

- (a) a violent offender order, or
- (b) an interim violent offender order, has been made may appeal to the Crown Court against the making of the order.

(2) Such a person may also appeal to the Crown Court against –

- (a) the making of an order under section 103, or
- (b) any refusal to make such an order.

(3) On an appeal under this section, the Crown Court –

(a) may make such orders as may be necessary to give effect to its determination of the appeal; and
(b) may also make such incidental or consequential orders as appear to it to be just.

(4) For the purposes of section 103(3) an order made by the Crown Court on an appeal made by virtue of subsection (1) or (2) is to be treated as if made by the court from which the appeal was brought.

Notification requirements

107 Offenders subject to notification requirements

(1) References in this Part to an offender subject to notification requirements are references to an offender who is for the time being subject to –

(a) a violent offender order, or
(b) an interim violent offender order, which is in force under this Part.

(2) Subsection (1) has effect subject to section 110(7) (which excludes from section 110 an offender subject to an interim violent offender order).

108 Notification requirements: initial notification

(1) An offender subject to notification requirements must notify the required information to the police within the period of 3 days beginning with the date on which –

(a) the violent offender order, or
(b) the interim violent offender order,

comes into force in relation to the offender ("the relevant date").

(2) The "required information" is the following information about the offender –

(a) date of birth;
(b) national insurance number;
(c) name on the relevant date or, if the offender used two or more names on that date, each of those names;
(d) home address on the relevant date;
(e) name on the date on which the notification is given or, if the offender used two or more names on that date, each of those names;
(f) home address on the date on which the notification is given;
(g) the address of any other premises in the United Kingdom at which on that date the offender regularly resides or stays;
(h) any prescribed information.

(3) In subsection (2)(h) "prescribed" means prescribed by regulations made by the Secretary of State.

(4) When determining the period of 3 days mentioned in subsection (1), there is to be disregarded any time when the offender is –

(a) remanded in or committed to custody by an order of a court or kept in service custody;
(b) serving a sentence of imprisonment or a term of service detention;
(c) detained in a hospital; or
(d) outside the United Kingdom.

(5) In this Part "home address" means in relation to the offender –

(a) the address of the offender's sole or main residence in the United Kingdom, or
(b) if the offender has no such residence, the address or location of a place in the United Kingdom where the offender can regularly be found or, if there is more than one such place, such one of them as the offender selects.

109 Notification requirements: changes

(1) An offender subject to notification requirements must notify to the police –

- (a) the required new information, and
- (b) the information mentioned in section 108(2), within the period of 3 days beginning with the date on which any notifiable event occurs.

(2) A "notifiable event" means –

- (a) the use by the offender of a name which has not been notified to the police under section 108 or this section;
- (b) any change of the offender's home address;
- (c) the expiry of any qualifying period during which the offender has resided or stayed at any premises in the United Kingdom the address of which has not been notified to the police under section 108 or this section,
- (d) any prescribed change of circumstances, or
- (e) the release of the offender from custody pursuant to an order of a court or from imprisonment, service detention or detention in a hospital.

(3) The "required new information" is –

- (a) the name referred to in subsection (2)(a),
- (b) the new home address (see subsection (2)(b)),
- (c) the address of the premises referred to in subsection (2)(c),
- (d) the prescribed details, or
- (e) the fact that the offender has been released as mentioned in subsection (2)(e), as the case may be.

(4) A notification under subsection (1) may be given before the notifiable event occurs, but in that case the offender must also specify the date when the event is expected to occur.

(5) If a notification is given in accordance with subsection (4) and the event to which it relates occurs more than 2 days before the date specified, the notification does not affect the duty imposed by subsection (1).

(6) If a notification is given in accordance with subsection (4) and the event to which it relates has not occurred by the end of the period of 3 days beginning with the date specified –

- (a) the notification does not affect the duty imposed by subsection (1), and
- (b) the offender must, within the period of 6 days beginning with the date specified, notify to the police the fact that the event did not occur within the period of 3 days beginning with the date specified.

(7) Section 108(4) applies to the determination of –

- (a) any period of 3 days for the purposes of subsection (1), or
- (b) any period of 6 days for the purposes of subsection (6), as it applies to the determination of the period of 3 days mentioned in section 108(1).

(8) In this section –

- (a) "prescribed change of circumstances" means any change –
  - (i) occurring in relation to any matter in respect of which information is required to be notified by virtue of section 108(2)(h), and
  - (ii) of a description prescribed by regulations made by the Secretary of State;
- (b) "the prescribed details", in relation to a prescribed change of circumstances, means such details of the change as may be so prescribed.

(9) In this section "qualifying period" means –

- (a) a period of 7 days, or
- (b) two or more periods, in any period of 12 months, which taken together amount to 7 days.

110 Notification requirements: periodic notification

(1) An offender subject to notification requirements must, within the applicable period after each notification date, notify to the police the information mentioned in section 108(2), unless the offender has already given a notification under section 109(1) within that period.

(2) A "notification date" means, in relation to the offender, the date of any notification given by the offender under section 108(1) or 109(1) or subsection (1) above.

(3) Where the applicable period would (apart from this subsection) end while subsection (4) applies, that period is to be treated as continuing until the end of the period of 3 days beginning with the date on which subsection (4) first ceases to apply.

(4) This subsection applies if the offender is –

- (a) remanded in or committed to custody by an order of a court or kept in service custody,
- (b) serving a sentence of imprisonment or a term of service detention,
- (c) detained in a hospital, or
- (d) outside the United Kingdom.

(5) In this section "the applicable period" means –

- (a) in any case where subsection (6) applies, such period as may be prescribed by regulations made by the Secretary of State, and
- (b) in any other case, the period of one year.

(6) This subsection applies if the last home address notified by the offender under section 108(1) or 109(1) or subsection (1) above was the address or location of such a place as is mentioned in section 108(5)(b).

(7) Nothing in this section applies to an offender who is subject to an interim violent offender order.

111 Notification requirements: travel outside United Kingdom

(1) The Secretary of State may by regulations make provision with respect to offenders subject to notification requirements, or any description of such offenders –

- (a) requiring such persons, before they leave the United Kingdom, to give in accordance with the regulations a notification under subsection (2);
- (b) requiring such persons, if they subsequently return to the United Kingdom, to give in accordance with the regulations a notification under subsection (3).

(2) A notification under this subsection must disclose –

- (a) the date on which the offender proposes to leave the United Kingdom;
- (b) the country (or, if there is more than one, the first country) to which the offender proposes to travel and the proposed point of arrival (determined in accordance with the regulations) in that country;
- (c) any other information prescribed by the regulations which the offender holds about the offender's departure from or return to the United Kingdom, or about the offender's movements while outside the United Kingdom.

(3) A notification under this subsection must disclose any information prescribed by the regulations about the offender's return to the United Kingdom.

112 Method of notification and related matters

(1) An offender gives a notification to the police under section 108(1), 109(1) or 110(1) by –

- (a) attending at any police station in the offender's local police area, and
- (b) giving an oral notification to any police officer, or to any person authorised for the purpose by the officer in charge of the station.

(2) An offender giving a notification under section 109(1) –

- (a) in relation to a prospective change of home address, or
- (b) in relation to such premises as are mentioned in section 109(2)(c), may also give the notification at a police station that would fall within subsection (1)(a) above if the change of home address had already occurred or (as the case may be) the premises in question were the offender's home address.

(3) Any notification given in accordance with this section must be acknowledged; and the acknowledgement must be –

- (a) in writing, and
- (b) in such form as the Secretary of State may direct.

(4) Where a notification is given under section 108(1), 109(1) or 110(1), the offender must, if requested to do so by the police officer or other person mentioned in subsection (1)(b) above, allow that officer or person to –

- (a) take the offender's fingerprints,
- (b) photograph any part of the offender, or
- (c) do both of those things, in order to verify the offender's identity.

(5) In this section –

"local police area", in relation to the offender, means –
- (a) the police area in England and Wales in which the home address is situated,
- (b) in the absence of a home address in England and Wales, the police area in England and Wales in which the home address last notified is situated, or
- (c) in the absence of such a home address and any such notification, the police area in which the court that made the violent offender order (or, as the case may be, the interim violent offender order) is situated; "photograph" includes any process by means of which an image may be produced.

Supplementary

113 Offences

(1) If a person fails, without reasonable excuse, to comply with any prohibition, restriction or condition contained in –

- (a) a violent offender order, or
- (b) an interim violent offender order, the person commits an offence.

(2) If a person fails, without reasonable excuse, to comply with –

- (a) section 108(1), 109(1) or (6)(b), 110(1) or 112(4), or
- (b) any requirement imposed by regulations made under section 111(1), the person commits an offence.

(3) If a person notifies to the police, in purported compliance with –

- (a) section 108(1), 109(1) or 110(1), or
- (b) any requirement imposed by regulations made under section 111(1), any information which the person knows to be false, the person commits an offence.

(4) As regards an offence under subsection (2), so far as it relates to noncompliance with –

- (a) section 108(1), 109(1) or 110(1), or
- (b) any requirement imposed by regulations made under section 111(1),

a person commits such an offence on the first day on which the person first fails, without reasonable excuse, to comply with the provision mentioned in paragraph (a) or (as the case may be) the requirement mentioned in paragraph (b), and continues to commit it throughout any period during which the failure continues.

(5) But a person must not be prosecuted under subsection (2) more than once in respect of the same failure.

(6) A person guilty of an offence under this section is liable –

(a) on summary conviction, to imprisonment for a term not exceeding the relevant period or a fine not exceeding the statutory maximum or both;
(b) on conviction on indictment, to imprisonment for a term not exceeding 5 years or a fine or both.

(7) In subsection (6)(a) "the relevant period" means –

(a) in relation to England and Wales and Scotland, 12 months;
(b) in relation to Northern Ireland, 6 months.

(8) Proceedings for an offence under this section may be commenced in any court having jurisdiction in any place where the person charged with the offence resides or is found.

114 Supply of information to Secretary of State etc.

(1) This section applies to information notified to the police under section 108(1), 109(1) or 110(1).

(2) A chief officer of police may, for the purposes of the prevention, detection, investigation or prosecution of offences under this Part, supply information to which this section applies to –

(a) the Secretary of State, or
(b) a person providing services to the Secretary of State in connection with a relevant function, for use for the purpose of verifying the information.

(3) In relation to information supplied to any person under subsection (2), the reference to verifying the information is a reference to –

(a) checking its accuracy by comparing it with information held –
    (i) where the person is the Secretary of State, by that person in connection with the exercise of a relevant function, or
    (ii) where the person is within subsection (2)(b), by that person in connection with the provision of services as mentioned there, and
(b) compiling a report of that comparison.

(4) Subject to subsection (5), the supply of information under this section is to be taken not to breach any restriction on the disclosure of information (however arising).

(5) This section does not authorise the doing of anything that contravenes the Data Protection Act 1998 (c. 29).

(6) This section does not affect any power to supply information that exists apart from this section.

(7) In this section "relevant function" means –

(a) a function relating to social security, child support, employment or training,
(b) a function relating to passports, or
(c) a function under Part 3 of the Road Traffic Act 1988 (c. 52).

115 Supply of information by Secretary of State etc.

(1) A report compiled under section 114 may be supplied to a chief officer of police by –

(a) the Secretary of State, or
(b) a person within section 114(2)(b).

(2) Such a report may contain any information held –

(a) by the Secretary of State in connection with the exercise of a relevant function, or

(b) by a person within section 114(2)(b) in connection with the provision of services as mentioned there.

(3) Where such a report contains information within subsection (2), the chief officer to whom it is supplied –

(a) may retain the information, whether or not used for the purposes of the prevention, detection, investigation or prosecution of offences under this Part, and
(b) may use the information for any purpose related to the prevention, detection, investigation or prosecution of offences (whether or not under this Part), but for no other purpose.

(4) Subsections (4) to (7) of section 114 apply in relation to this section as they apply in relation to section 114.

116 Information about release or transfer

(1) This section applies to an offender subject to notification requirements who is –

(a) serving a sentence of imprisonment or a term of service detention, or (b) detained in a hospital.

(2) The Secretary of State may by regulations make provision requiring the person who is responsible for such an offender to give notice to specified persons –

(a) of the fact that that person has become responsible for the offender; and
(b) of any occasion when –
   (i) the offender is released, or
   (ii) a different person is to become responsible for the offender.

(3) In subsection (2) "specified persons" means persons specified, or of a description specified, in the regulations.

(4) The regulations may make provision for determining who is to be taken for the purposes of this section as being responsible for an offender.

117 Interpretation of Part 7

(1) In this Part –

"the appropriate date" has the meaning given by section 100(5); "country" includes territory; "custodial sentence" means –
   (a) a sentence of imprisonment, any other sentence or order mentioned in section 76(1) of the Powers of Criminal Courts (Sentencing) Act 2000 (c. 6) (as in force at any time after the passing of this Act) or any corresponding sentence or order imposed or made under any earlier enactment, or
   (b) a relevant service sentence (see subsection (2) below); "home address" has the meaning given by section 108(5);

"hospital order" means –
   (a) an order under section 37 of the Mental Health Act 1983 (c. 20) or section 60 of the Mental Health Act 1959 (c. 72), or
   (b) any other order providing for the admission of a person to hospital following a finding of the kind mentioned in section 99(2)(b) or (c) of this Act;

"interim violent offender order" means an order made under section 104;
"kept in service custody" means kept in service custody by virtue of an order under section 105(2) of the Armed Forces Act 2006 (c. 52);
"the offender", in relation to a violent offender order or an interim violent offender order, means the person in respect of whom the order is made;
"qualifying offender" has the meaning given by section 99(1);
"restriction order" means an order under section 41 of the Mental Health Act 1983 or section 65 of the Mental Health Act 1959;

"service detention" has the meaning given by section 374 of the Armed Forces Act 2006;
"specified offence" has the meaning given by section 98(3);
"supervision order" means –

(a) a supervision order within the meaning of Schedule 1A to the Criminal Procedure (Insanity) Act 1964 (c. 84), or
(b) a supervision and treatment order within the meaning of Schedule 2 to that Act;

"violent offender order" has the meaning given by section 98(1).

(2) The following are relevant service sentences –

(a) a sentence of imprisonment passed under the Army Act 1955 (3 & 4 Eliz. 2 c. 18), the Air Force Act 1955 (3 & 4 Eliz. 2 c. 19) or the Naval Discipline Act 1957 (c. 53);
(b) a sentence of custody for life, or detention, under section 71A of either of those Acts of 1955 or section 43A of that Act of 1957;
(c) a sentence under a custodial order within the meaning of –
    (i) section 71AA of, or paragraph 10 of Schedule 5A to, either of those Acts of 1955, or
    (ii) section 43AA of, or paragraph 10 of Schedule 4A to, that Act of 1957;
(d) a custodial sentence within the meaning of the Armed Forces Act 2006 (c. 52) (see section 374 of that Act).

(3) References in this Part to protecting the public from the risk of serious violent harm caused by a person are to be read in accordance with section 98(2).

(4) References in this Part to a finding of the kind mentioned in section 99(2)(b) or (c) or (4)(b) or (c) include references to a case where a decision on appeal is to the effect that there should have been such a finding in the proceedings concerned.

(5) References in this Part to an offender subject to notification requirements are to be read in accordance with section 107.

(6) The following expressions have the same meanings as in Part 2 of the Sexual Offences Act 2003 (c. 42) (notifications and orders) –

"detained in a hospital" (see sections 133 and 135 of that Act);
"sentence of imprisonment" (see section 131 of that Act);

and references to a person having been found to be under a disability and to have done the act charged are to be read in accordance with section 135 of that Act.

PART 8
ANTI-SOCIAL BEHAVIOUR

Premises closure orders

118 Closure orders: premises associated with persistent disorder or nuisance

Schedule 20 inserts a new Part 1A into the Anti-social Behaviour Act 2003 (c. 38) which makes provision about the issue of closure notices and the making of closure orders in respect of premises associated with persistent disorder or nuisance.

Nuisance or disturbance on hospital premises

119 Offence of causing nuisance or disturbance on NHS premises

(1) A person commits an offence if –

(a) the person causes, without reasonable excuse and while on NHS premises, a nuisance or disturbance to an NHS staff member who is working there or is otherwise there in connection with work,
(b) the person refuses, without reasonable excuse, to leave the NHS premises when asked to do so by a constable or an NHS staff member, and

(c) the person is not on the NHS premises for the purpose of obtaining medical advice, treatment or care for himself or herself.

(2) A person who commits an offence under this section is liable on summary conviction to a fine not exceeding level 3 on the standard scale.

(3) For the purposes of this section –

  (a) a person ceases to be on NHS premises for the purpose of obtaining medical advice, treatment or care for himself or herself once the person has received the advice, treatment or care, and
  (b) a person is not on NHS premises for the purpose of obtaining medical advice, treatment or care for himself or herself if the person has been refused the advice, treatment or care during the last 8 hours.

(4) In this section –

"English NHS premises" means –
  (a) any hospital vested in, or managed by, a relevant English NHS body,
  (b) any building or other structure, or vehicle, associated with the hospital and situated on hospital grounds (whether or not vested in, or managed by, a relevant English NHS body), and
  (c) the hospital grounds,

"hospital grounds" means land in the vicinity of a hospital and associated with it,

"NHS premises" means English NHS premises or Welsh NHS premises,

"NHS staff member" means a person employed by a relevant English NHS body, or a relevant Welsh NHS body, or otherwise working for such a body (whether as or on behalf of a contractor, as a volunteer or otherwise),

"relevant English NHS body" means –
  (a) a National Health Service trust (see section 25 of the National Health Service Act 2006 (c. 41)), all or most of whose hospitals, establishments and facilities are situated in England,
  (b) a Primary Care Trust (see section 18 of that Act), or
  (c) an NHS foundation trust (see section 30 of that Act),

"relevant Welsh NHS body" means –
  (a) a National Health Service trust (see section 18 of the National Health Service (Wales) Act 2006 (c. 42)), all or most of whose hospitals, establishments and facilities are situated in Wales, or
  (b) a Local Health Board (see section 11 of that Act),

"vehicle" includes an air ambulance,

"Welsh NHS premises" means –
  (a) any hospital vested in, or managed by, a relevant Welsh NHS body,
  (b) any building or other structure, or vehicle, associated with the hospital and situated on hospital grounds (whether or not vested in, or managed by, a relevant Welsh NHS body), and
  (c) the hospital grounds.

120 Power to remove person causing nuisance or disturbance

(1) If a constable reasonably suspects that a person is committing or has committed an offence under section 119, the constable may remove the person from the NHS premises concerned.

(2) If an authorised officer reasonably suspects that a person is committing or has committed an offence under section 119, the authorised officer may –

  (a) remove the person from the NHS premises concerned, or
  (b) authorise an appropriate NHS staff member to do so.

(3) Any person removing another person from NHS premises under this section may use reasonable force (if necessary).

(4) An authorised officer cannot remove a person under this section or authorise another person to do so if the authorised officer has reason to believe that –

- (a) the person to be removed requires medical advice, treatment or care for himself or herself, or
- (b) the removal of the person would endanger the person's physical or mental health.

(5) In this section –

"appropriate NHS staff member" –
- (a) in relation to English NHS premises, means an English NHS staff member, and
- (b) in relation to Welsh NHS premises, means a Welsh NHS staff member,

"authorised officer" –
- (a) in relation to English NHS premises, means any English NHS staff member authorised by a relevant English NHS body to exercise the powers which are conferred by this section on an authorised officer in respect of English NHS premises, and
- (b) in relation to Welsh NHS premises, means any Welsh NHS staff member authorised by a relevant Welsh NHS body to exercise the powers which are conferred by this section on an authorised officer in respect of Welsh NHS premises,

"English NHS staff member" means a person employed by a relevant English NHS body or otherwise working for it (whether as or on behalf of a contractor, as a volunteer or otherwise),

"Welsh NHS staff member" means a person employed by a relevant Welsh NHS body or otherwise working for it (whether as or on behalf of a contractor, as a volunteer or otherwise).

(6) Terms defined in section 119 have the same meaning in this section as in that section.

121 Guidance about the power to remove etc.

(1) The appropriate national authority may from time to time prepare and publish guidance to relevant NHS bodies and authorised officers about the powers in section 120.

(2) Such guidance may, in particular, relate to –

- (a) the authorisation by relevant NHS bodies of authorised officers,
- (b) the authorisation by authorised officers of appropriate NHS staff members to remove persons under section 120,
- (c) training requirements for authorised officers and persons authorised by them to remove persons under section 120,
- (d) matters that may be relevant to a consideration by authorised officers for the purposes of section 120 of whether offences are being, or have been, committed under section 119,
- (e) matters to be taken into account by authorised officers in deciding whether there is reason to believe that a person requires medical advice, treatment or care for himself or herself or that the removal of a person would endanger the person's physical or mental health,
- (f) the procedure to be followed by authorised officers or persons authorised by them before using the power of removal in section 120,
- (g) the degree of force that it may be appropriate for authorised officers or persons authorised by them to use in particular circumstances,
- (h) arrangements for ensuring that persons on NHS premises are aware of the offence in section 119 and the powers of removal in section 120, or
- (i) the keeping of records.

(3) Before publishing guidance under this section, the appropriate national authority must consult such persons as the authority considers appropriate.

(4) A relevant NHS body and an authorised officer must, when exercising functions under, or in connection with, section 120, have regard to any guidance published by the appropriate national authority under this section.

(5) In this section –

"appropriate national authority" –
- (a) in relation to a relevant English NHS body and authorised officers in respect of English NHS premises, means the Secretary of State, and
- (b) in relation to a relevant Welsh NHS body and authorised officers in respect of Welsh NHS premises, means the Welsh Ministers,

"appropriate NHS staff member" and "authorised officer" have the same meaning as in section 120,

"relevant NHS body" means a relevant English NHS body or a relevant Welsh NHS body.

(6) Terms defined in section 119 have the same meaning in this section as in that section.

122 Nuisance or disturbance on HSS premises

Schedule 21 makes provision for Northern Ireland corresponding to the provision made for England and Wales by sections 119 to 121.

Anti-social behaviour orders etc. in respect of children and young persons

123 Review of anti-social behaviour orders etc.

(1) In Part 1 of the Crime and Disorder Act 1998 (c. 37) (prevention of crime and disorder) after section 1I insert –

"**1J Review of orders under sections 1, 1B and 1C**

(1) This section applies where –
- (a) an anti-social behaviour order,
- (b) an order under section 1B, or
- (c) an order under section 1C, has been made in respect of a person under the age of 17.

(2) If –
- (a) the person subject to the order will be under the age of 18 at the end of a period specified in subsection (3) (a "review period"), and
- (b) the term of the order runs until the end of that period or beyond, then before the end of that period a review of the operation of the order shall be carried out.

(3) The review periods are –
- (a) the period of 12 months beginning with –
  - (i) the day on which the order was made, or
  - (ii) if during that period there is a supplemental order (or more than one), the date of the supplemental order (or the last of them);
- (b) a period of 12 months beginning with –
  - (i) the day after the end of the previous review period, or
  - (ii) if during that period there is a supplemental order (or more than one), the date of the supplemental order (or the last of them).

(4) In subsection (3) "supplemental order" means –
- (a) a further order varying the order in question;
- (b) an individual support order made in relation to the order in question on an application under section 1AA(1A).

(5) Subsection (2) does not apply in relation to any review period if the order is discharged before the end of that period.

(6) A review under this section shall include consideration of –

(a) the extent to which the person subject to the order has complied with it;
(b) the adequacy of any support available to the person to help him comply with it;
(c) any matters relevant to the question whether an application should be made for the order to be varied or discharged.

(7) Those carrying out or participating in a review under this section shall have regard to any guidance issued by the Secretary of State when considering –

(a) how the review should be carried out;
(b) what particular matters should be dealt with by the review;
(c) what action (if any) it would be appropriate to take in consequence of the findings of the review.

1K Responsibility for, and participation in, reviews under section 1J

(1) A review under section 1J of an anti-social behaviour order or an order under section 1B shall be carried out by the relevant authority that applied for the order.

(2) A review under section 1J of an order under section 1C shall be carried out –

(a) (except where paragraph (b) applies) by the appropriate chief officer of police;
(b) where a relevant authority is specified under section 1C(9ZA), by that authority.

(3) A local authority, in carrying out a review under section 1J, shall act in co-operation with the appropriate chief officer of police; and it shall be the duty of that chief officer to co-operate in the carrying out of the review.

(4) The chief officer of police of a police force, in carrying out a review under section 1J, shall act in co-operation with the appropriate local authority; and it shall be the duty of that local authority to co-operate in the carrying out of the review.

(5) A relevant authority other than a local authority or chief officer of police, in carrying out a review under section 1J, shall act in cooperation with –

(a) the appropriate local authority, and
(b) the appropriate chief officer of police; and it shall be the duty of that local authority and that chief officer to co-operate in the carrying out of the review.

(6) A chief officer of police or other relevant authority carrying out a review under section 1J may invite the participation in the review of a person or body not required by subsection (3), (4) or (5) to co-operate in the carrying out of the review.

(7) In this section –

"the appropriate chief officer of police" means the chief officer of police of the police force maintained for the police area in which the person subject to the order resides or appears to reside;
"the appropriate local authority" means the council for the local government area (within the meaning given in section 1(12)) in which the person subject to the order resides or appears to reside."

(2) In section 1(1A) of that Act (meaning of "relevant authority") for "1CA, 1E and 1F" substitute "1C, 1CA, 1E, IF and 1K".

(3) In section 1C of that Act (orders on conviction in criminal proceedings) after section (9) insert –

"(9ZA) An order under this section made in respect of a person under the age of 17, or an order varying such an order, may specify a relevant authority (other than the chief officer of police mentioned in section 1K(2)(a)) as being responsible for carrying out a review under section 1J of the operation of the order."

124 Individual support orders

(1) In section 1AA of the Crime and Disorder Act 1998 (c. 37) (individual support orders) for subsection (1) and the words in subsection (2) before paragraph (a) substitute –

"(1) This section applies where a court makes an anti-social behaviour order in respect of a defendant who is a child or young person when that order is made.

(1A) This section also applies where –

(a) an anti-social behaviour order has previously been made in respect of such a defendant;
(b) an application is made by complaint to the court which made that order, by the relevant authority which applied for it, for an order under this section; and (c) at the time of the hearing of the application –
  (i) the defendant is still a child or young person, and
  (ii) the anti-social behaviour order is still in force.

(1B) The court must consider whether the individual support conditions are fulfilled and, if satisfied that they are, must make an individual support order.

(2) An individual support order is an order which—".

(2) In subsection (3)(a) of that section, for the words after "the kind of behaviour which led to" substitute "the making of –
  (i) the anti-social behaviour order, or
  (ii) an order varying that order (in a case where the variation is made as a result of further anti-social behaviour by the defendant);".

(3) In subsection (5) of that section, for "which led to the making of the anti-social behaviour order" substitute "mentioned in subsection (3)(a) above".

(4) In section 1(1A) of that Act (meaning of "relevant authority") after "and sections" insert "1AA,".

(5) In section 1AB of that Act (which makes further provision about individual support orders) after subsection (5) insert –

"(5A) The period specified as the term of an individual support order made on an application under section 1AA(1A) above must not be longer than the remaining part of the term of the anti-social behaviour order as a result of which it is made."

(6) In section 1B of that Act (orders in county court proceedings) after subsection (7) insert –

"(8) Sections 1AA and 1AB apply in relation to orders under this section, with any necessary modifications, as they apply in relation to antisocial behaviour orders.

(9) In their application by virtue of subsection (8), sections 1AA(1A)(b) and 1AB(6) have effect as if the words "by complaint" were omitted."

(7) In section 1C of that Act (orders on conviction in criminal proceedings) after subsection (9A) insert –

"(9AA) Sections 1AA and 1AB apply in relation to orders under this section, with any necessary modifications, as they apply in relation to antisocial behaviour orders.

(9AB) In their application by virtue of subsection (9AA), sections 1AA(1A)(b) and 1AB(6) have effect as if the words "by complaint" were omitted.

(9AC) In its application by virtue of subsection (9AA), section 1AA(1A)(b) has effect as if the reference to the relevant authority which applied for the anti-social behaviour order were a reference to the chief officer of police, or other relevant authority, responsible under section 1K(2)(a) or (b) for carrying out a review of the order under this section."

Parenting contracts and parenting orders

125 Parenting contracts and parenting orders: local authorities

(1) Part 3 of the Anti-social Behaviour Act 2003 (c. 38) (parental responsibilities) is amended as follows.

(2) In section 29(1) (interpretation) in the definition of "local authority" for paragraphs (b) and (c) substitute –

"(aa) a district council in England;".

(3) In section 26B (parenting orders: registered social landlords) –

(a) in subsection (8), after "the local authority" insert "(or, if subsection (8A) applies, each local authority)";
(b) after that subsection insert –

"(8A) This subsection applies if the place where the child or young person resides or appears to reside is within the area of a county council and within the area of a district council.";

(c) in subsection (10)(a), after "the local authority" insert "(or authorities)".

(4) In section 27 (parenting orders: supplemental) for subsection (3A) substitute –

"(3A) Proceedings for an offence under section 9(7) of the 1998 Act (parenting orders: breach of requirement etc.) as applied by subsection (3)(b) above may be brought by any of the following local authorities –

(a) the local authority that applied for the order, if the child or young person, or the person alleged to be in breach, resides or appears to reside in that authority's area;
(b) the local authority of the child or young person, if that child or young person does not reside or appear to reside in the area of the local authority that applied for the order;
(c) the local authority of the person alleged to be in breach, if that person does not reside or appear to reside in the area of the local authority that applied for the order.

(3B) For the purposes of subsection (3A)(b) and (c) –

(a) an individual's local authority is the local authority in whose area the individual resides or appears to reside; but
(b) if the place where an individual resides or appears to reside is within the area of a county council and within the area of a district council, a reference to that individual's local authority is to be read as a reference to either of those authorities."

PART 9
POLICING

Misconduct procedures etc.

126 Police misconduct and performance procedures

(1) Part 1 of Schedule 22 –

(a) amends the Police Act 1996 (c. 16) to make provision for or in connection with disciplinary and other proceedings in respect of the conduct and performance of members of police forces and special constables, and
(b) makes other minor amendments to that Act.

(2) Part 2 of that Schedule makes equivalent amendments to the Ministry of Defence Police Act 1987 (c. 4) for the purposes of the Ministry of Defence Police.

(3) Part 3 of that Schedule makes equivalent amendments to the Railways and Transport Safety Act 2003 (c. 20) for the purposes of the British Transport Police.

127 Investigation of complaints of police misconduct etc.

Schedule 23 amends the Police Reform Act 2002 (c. 30) to make further provision about the investigation of complaints of police misconduct and other matters.

Financial assistance

128 Financial assistance under section 57 of Police Act 1996

(1) After section 57(1) of the Police Act 1996 (common services: power for Secretary of State to provide and maintain etc. organisations, facilities and services which promote the efficiency or effectiveness of police) insert –

"(1A) The power conferred by subsection (1) includes power to give financial assistance to any person in connection with the provision or maintenance of such organisations, facilities and services as are mentioned in that subsection.

(1B) Financial assistance under subsection (1) –

(a) may, in particular, be given in the form of a grant, loan or guarantee or investment in a body corporate; and
(b) may be given subject to terms and conditions determined by the Secretary of State; but any financial assistance under that subsection other than a grant requires the consent of the Treasury.

(1C) Terms and conditions imposed under subsection (1B)(b) may include terms and conditions as to repayment with or without interest.

(1D) Any sums received by the Secretary of State by virtue of terms and conditions imposed under that subsection are to be paid into the Consolidated Fund."

(2) Any loan made by the Secretary of State by virtue of section 57 of the Police Act 1996 (c. 16) and outstanding on the day on which this Act is passed is to be treated as if it were a loan made in accordance with that section as amended by subsection (1) above.

Inspection

129 Inspection of police authorities

In section 54 of the Police Act 1996 (c. 16) (appointment and functions of inspectors of constabulary) for subsection (2A) substitute –

"(2A) The inspectors of constabulary may carry out an inspection of, and report to the Secretary of State on, a police authority's performance of its functions or of any particular function or functions (including in particular its compliance with the requirements of Part 1 of the Local Government Act 1999 (best value))."

PART 10
SPECIAL IMMIGRATION STATUS

130 Designation

(1) The Secretary of State may designate a person who satisfies Condition 1 or 2 (subject to subsections (4) and (5)).

(2) Condition 1 is that the person –

(a) is a foreign criminal within the meaning of section 131, and
(b) is liable to deportation, but cannot be removed from the United Kingdom because of section 6 of the Human Rights Act 1998 (c. 42) (public authority not to act contrary to Convention).

(3) Condition 2 is that the person is a member of the family of a person who satisfies Condition 1.

(4) A person who has the right of abode in the United Kingdom may not be designated.

(5) The Secretary of State may not designate a person if the Secretary of State thinks that an effect of designation would breach –

(a) the United Kingdom's obligations under the Refugee Convention, or
(b) the person's rights under the Community treaties.

131 "Foreign criminal"

(1) For the purposes of section 130 "foreign criminal" means a person who –

(a) is not a British citizen, and
(b) satisfies any of the following Conditions.

(2) Condition 1 is that section 72(2)(a) and (b) or (3)(a) to (c) of the Nationality, Immigration and Asylum Act 2002 (c. 41) applies to the person (Article 33(2) of the Refugee Convention: imprisonment for at least two years).

(3) Condition 2 is that –

(a) section 72(4)(a) or (b) of that Act applies to the person (person convicted of specified offence), and
(b) the person has been sentenced to a period of imprisonment.

(4) Condition 3 is that Article 1F of the Refugee Convention applies to the person (exclusions for criminals etc.).

(5) Section 72(6) of that Act (rebuttal of presumption under section 72(2) to (4)) has no effect in relation to Condition 1 or 2.

(6) Section 72(7) of that Act (non-application pending appeal) has no effect in relation to Condition 1 or 2.

132 Effect of designation

(1) A designated person does not have leave to enter or remain in the United Kingdom.

(2) For the purposes of a provision of the Immigration Acts and any other enactment which concerns or refers to immigration or nationality (including any provision which applies or refers to a provision of the Immigration Acts or any other enactment about immigration or nationality) a designated person –

(a) is a person subject to immigration control,
(b) is not to be treated as an asylum-seeker or a former asylum-seeker, and
(c) is not in the United Kingdom in breach of the immigration laws.

(3) Despite subsection (2)(c), time spent in the United Kingdom as a designated person may not be relied on by a person for the purpose of an enactment about nationality.

(4) A designated person –

(a) shall not be deemed to have been given leave in accordance with paragraph 6 of Schedule 2 to the Immigration Act 1971 (c. 77) (notice of leave or refusal), and
(b) may not be granted temporary admission to the United Kingdom under paragraph 21 of that Schedule.

(5) Sections 134 and 135 make provision about support for designated persons and their dependants.

133 Conditions

(1) The Secretary of State or an immigration officer may by notice in writing impose a condition on a designated person.

(2) A condition may relate to –

(a) residence,
(b) employment or occupation, or
(c) reporting to the police, the Secretary of State or an immigration officer.

(3) Section 36 of the Asylum and Immigration (Treatment of Claimants, etc.) Act 2004 (c. 19) (electronic monitoring) shall apply in relation to conditions imposed under this section as it applies to restrictions imposed under paragraph 21 of Schedule 2 to the Immigration Act 1971 (with a reference to the Immigration Acts being treated as including a reference to this section).

(4) Section 69 of the Nationality, Immigration and Asylum Act 2002 (c. 41) (reporting restrictions: travel expenses) shall apply in relation to conditions imposed under subsection (2)(c) above as it applies to restrictions imposed under paragraph 21 of Schedule 2 to the Immigration Act 1971.

(5) A person who without reasonable excuse fails to comply with a condition imposed under this section commits an offence.

(6) A person who is guilty of an offence under subsection (5) shall be liable on summary conviction to –

(a) a fine not exceeding level 5 on the standard scale,
(b) imprisonment for a period not exceeding 51 weeks, or
(c) both.

(7) A provision of the Immigration Act 1971 (c. 77) which applies in relation to an offence under any provision of section 24(1) of that Act (illegal entry etc.) shall also apply in relation to the offence under subsection (5) above.

(8) In the application of this section to Scotland or Northern Ireland the reference in subsection (6)(b) to 51 weeks shall be treated as a reference to six months.

134 Support

(1) Part VI of the Immigration and Asylum Act 1999 (c. 33) (support for asylumseekers) shall apply in relation to designated persons and their dependants as it applies in relation to asylum-seekers and their dependants.

(2) But the following provisions of that Part shall not apply –

(a) section 96 (kinds of support),
(b) section 97(1)(b) (desirability of providing accommodation in wellsupplied area),
(c) section 100 (duty to co-operate in providing accommodation),
(d) section 101 (reception zones),
(e) section 108 (failure of sponsor to maintain),
(f) section 111 (grants to voluntary organisations), and
(g) section 113 (recovery of expenditure from sponsor).

(3) Support may be provided under section 95 of the 1999 Act as applied by this section –

(a) by providing accommodation appearing to the Secretary of State to be adequate for a person's needs;
(b) by providing what appear to the Secretary of State to be essential living needs;
(c) in other ways which the Secretary of State thinks necessary to reflect exceptional circumstances of a particular case.

(4) Support by virtue of subsection (3) may not be provided wholly or mainly by way of cash unless the Secretary of State thinks it appropriate because of exceptional circumstances.

(5) Section 4 of the 1999 Act (accommodation) shall not apply in relation to designated persons.

(6) A designated person shall not be treated –

(a) as a person subject to immigration control, for the purposes of section 119(1)(b) of the 1999 Act (homelessness: Scotland and Northern Ireland), or
(b) as a person from abroad who is not eligible for housing assistance, for the purposes of section 185(4) of the Housing Act 1996 (c. 52) (housing assistance).

135 Support: supplemental

(1) A reference in an enactment to Part VI of the 1999 Act or to a provision of that Part includes a reference to that Part or provision as applied by section 134 above; and for that purpose –

(a) a reference to section 96 shall be treated as including a reference to section 134(3) above,

(b) a reference to a provision of section 96 shall be treated as including a reference to the corresponding provision of section 134(3), and
(c) a reference to asylum-seekers shall be treated as including a reference to designated persons.

(2) A provision of Part VI of the 1999 Act which requires or permits the Secretary of State to have regard to the temporary nature of support shall be treated, in the application of Part VI by virtue of section 134 above, as requiring the Secretary of State to have regard to the nature and circumstances of support by virtue of that section.

(3) Rules under section 104 of the 1999 Act (appeals) shall have effect for the purposes of Part VI of that Act as it applies by virtue of section 134 above.

(4) Any other instrument under Part VI of the 1999 Act –

(a) may make provision in respect of that Part as it applies by virtue of section 134 above, as it applies otherwise than by virtue of that section, or both, and
(b) may make different provision for that Part as it applies by virtue of section 134 above and as it applies otherwise than by virtue of that section.

(5) In the application of paragraph 9 of Schedule 8 to the 1999 Act (regulations: notice to quit accommodation) the reference in paragraph (2)(b) to the determination of a claim for asylum shall be treated as a reference to ceasing to be a designated person.

(6) The Secretary of State may by order repeal, modify or disapply (to any extent) section 134(4).

(7) An order under section 10 of the Human Rights Act 1998 (c. 42) (power to remedy incompatibility) which amends a provision mentioned in subsection (6) of section 134 above may amend or repeal that subsection.

136 End of designation

(1) Designation lapses if the designated person –

(a) is granted leave to enter or remain in the United Kingdom,
(b) is notified by the Secretary of State or an immigration officer of a right of residence in the United Kingdom by virtue of the Community treaties,
(c) leaves the United Kingdom, or
(d) is made the subject of a deportation order under section 5 of the Immigration Act 1971 (c. 77).

(2) After designation lapses support may not be provided by virtue of section 134, subject to the following exceptions.

(3) Exception 1 is that, if designation lapses under subsection (1)(a) or (b), support may be provided in respect of a period which –

(a) begins when the designation lapses, and
(b) ends on a date determined in accordance with an order of the Secretary of State.

(4) Exception 2 is that, if designation lapses under subsection (1)(d), support may be provided in respect of –

(a) any period during which an appeal against the deportation order may be brought (ignoring any possibility of an appeal out of time with permission),
(b) any period during which an appeal against the deportation order is pending, and
(c) after an appeal ceases to be pending, such period as the Secretary of State may specify by order.

137 Interpretation: general

(1) This section applies to sections 130 to 136.

(2) A reference to a designated person is a reference to a person designated under section 130.

(3) "Family" shall be construed in accordance with section 5(4) of the Immigration Act 1971 (c. 77) (deportation: definition of "family").

(4) "Right of abode in the United Kingdom" has the meaning given by section 2 of that Act.

(5) "The Refugee Convention" means the Convention relating to the Status of Refugees done at Geneva on 28th July 1951 and its Protocol.

(6) "Period of imprisonment" shall be construed in accordance with section 72(11)(b)(i) and (ii) of the Nationality, Immigration and Asylum Act 2002 (c. 41).

(7) A voucher is not cash.

(8) A reference to a pending appeal has the meaning given by section 104(1) of that Act.

(9) A reference in an enactment to the Immigration Acts includes a reference to sections 130 to 136.

PART 11
MISCELLANEOUS

Industrial action by prison officers

138 Amendment of section 127 of Criminal Justice and Public Order Act 1994

(1) Section 127 of the Criminal Justice and Public Order Act 1994 (c. 33) (inducements to prison officers to withhold services or breach discipline) is amended as follows.

(2) In subsection (1), for paragraph (a) substitute –

"(a) to take (or continue to take) any industrial action;".

(3) After subsection (1) insert –

"(1A) In subsection (1) "industrial action" means –

(a) the withholding of services as a prison officer; or
(b) any action that would be likely to put at risk the safety of any person (whether a prisoner, a person working at or visiting a prison, a person working with prisoners or a member of the public)."

(4) In subsection (4), after paragraph (a) insert –

"(aa) holds any post, other than as a chaplain or assistant chaplain, to which he has been appointed for the purposes of section 7 of the Prison Act 1952 (appointment of prison staff),".

(5) In subsection (4), after paragraph (aa) (inserted by subsection (4) above) insert –

"(b) holds any post, otherwise than as a medical officer, to which he has been appointed for the purposes of section 3(1A) of the Prisons (Scotland) Act 1989;".

139 Power to suspend the operation of section 127 of Criminal Justice and Public Order Act 1994

After section 127 of the Criminal Justice and Public Order Act 1994 (c. 33) insert –

"**127A Power to suspend the operation of section 127**

(1) The Secretary of State may make orders suspending, or later reviving, the operation of section 127.

(2) An order under this section may make different provision in relation to different descriptions of prison officer.

(3) The power to make orders under this section is exercisable by statutory instrument.

(4) A statutory instrument containing an order under this section may not be made unless a draft of the instrument has been laid before, and approved by resolution of, each House of Parliament."

Sex offenders

140 Disclosure of information about convictions etc. of child sex offenders to members of the public

(1) After section 327 of the Criminal Justice Act 2003 (c. 44) insert –

"327A Disclosure of information about convictions etc. of child sex offenders to members of the public

(1) The responsible authority for each area must, in the course of discharging its functions under arrangements established by it under section 325, consider whether to disclose information in its possession about the relevant previous convictions of any child sex offender managed by it to any particular member of the public.

(2) In the case mentioned in subsection (3) there is a presumption that the responsible authority should disclose information in its possession about the relevant previous convictions of the offender to the particular member of the public.

(3) The case is where the responsible authority for the area has reasonable cause to believe that –

(a) a child sex offender managed by it poses a risk in that or any other area of causing serious harm to any particular child or children or to children of any particular description, and

(b) the disclosure of information about the relevant previous convictions of the offender to the particular member of the public is necessary for the purpose of protecting the particular child or children, or the children of that description, from serious harm caused by the offender.

(4) The presumption under subsection (2) arises whether or not the person to whom the information is disclosed requests the disclosure.

(5) Where the responsible authority makes a disclosure under this section –

(a) it may disclose such information about the relevant previous convictions of the offender as it considers appropriate to disclose to the member of the public concerned, and

(b) it may impose conditions for preventing the member of the public concerned from disclosing the information to any other person.

(6) Any disclosure under this section must be made as soon as is reasonably practicable having regard to all the circumstances.

(7) The responsible authority for each area must compile and maintain a record about the decisions it makes in relation to the discharge of its functions under this section.

(8) The record must include the following information –

(a) the reasons for making a decision to disclose information under this section,
(b) the reasons for making a decision not to disclose information under this section, and
(c) the information which is disclosed under this section, any conditions imposed in relation to its further disclosure and the name and address of the person to whom it is disclosed.

(9) Nothing in this section requires or authorises the making of a disclosure which contravenes the Data Protection Act 1998.

(10) This section is not to be taken as affecting any power of any person to disclose any information about a child sex offender.

327B Section 327A: interpretation

(1) This section applies for the purposes of section 327A.

(2) "Child" means a person under 18.

(3) "Child sex offence" means an offence listed in Schedule 34A, whenever committed.

(4) "Child sex offender" means any person who –

(a) has been convicted of such an offence,
(b) has been found not guilty of such an offence by reason of insanity,
(c) has been found to be under a disability and to have done the act charged against the person in respect of such an offence, or

(d) has been cautioned in respect of such an offence.

(5) In relation to a responsible authority, references to information about the relevant previous convictions of a child sex offender are references to information about –

    (a) convictions, findings and cautions mentioned in subsection (4)(a) to (d) which relate to the offender, and

    (b) anything under the law of any country or territory outside England and Wales which in the opinion of the responsible authority corresponds to any conviction, finding or caution within paragraph (a) (however described).

(6) References to serious harm caused by a child sex offender are references to serious physical or psychological harm caused by the offender committing any offence listed in any paragraph of Schedule 34A other than paragraphs 1 to 6 (offences under provisions repealed by Sexual Offences Act 2003).

(7) A responsible authority for any area manages a child sex offender if the offender is a person who poses risks in that area which fall to be managed by the authority under the arrangements established by it under section 325.

(8) For the purposes of this section the provisions of section 4 of, and paragraph 3 of Schedule 2 to, the Rehabilitation of Offenders Act 1974 (protection for spent convictions and cautions) are to be disregarded.

(9) In this section "cautioned", in relation to any person and any offence, means –

    (a) cautioned after the person has admitted the offence, or

    (b) reprimanded or warned within the meaning given by section 65 of the Crime and Disorder Act 1998.

(10) Section 135(1), (2)(a) and (c) and (3) of the Sexual Offences Act 2003 (mentally disordered offenders) apply for the purposes of this section as they apply for the purposes of Part 2 of that Act."

(2) After Schedule 34 to that Act insert the Schedule 34A set out in Schedule 24 to this Act.

141 Sexual offences prevention orders: relevant sexual offences

(1) In section 106 of the Sexual Offences Act 2003 (c. 42) (supplemental provisions about sexual offences prevention orders), at the end insert –

"(13) Subsection (14) applies for the purposes of section 104 and this section in their application in relation to England and Wales or Northern Ireland.

(14) In construing any reference to an offence listed in Schedule 3, any condition subject to which an offence is so listed that relates –

    (a) to the way in which the defendant is dealt with in respect of an offence so listed or a relevant finding (as defined by section 132(9)), or

    (b) to the age of any person, is to be disregarded."

(2) This section extends to England and Wales and Northern Ireland only.

142 Notification requirements: prescribed information

(1) In section 83 of the Sexual Offences Act 2003 (c. 42) (notification requirements: initial notification) –

    (a) at the end of subsection (5) insert –

        "(h) any prescribed information."; and

    (b) after that subsection insert –

        "(5A) In subsection (5)(h) "prescribed" means prescribed by regulations made by the Secretary of State."

(2) Section 84 of that Act (notification requirements: changes) is amended as follows.

(3) In subsection (1) –

(a) after "1997," in paragraph (c) insert –

"(ca) any prescribed change of circumstances,"; and

(b) after "the address of those premises" insert ", the prescribed details".

(4) In subsection (2) after "home address" insert "or the prescribed change of circumstances".

(5) After subsection (5) insert –

"(5A) In this section –

(a) "prescribed change of circumstances" means any change –
 (i) occurring in relation to any matter in respect of which information is required to be notified by virtue of section 83(5)(h), and
 (ii) of a description prescribed by regulations made by the Secretary of State;
(b) "the prescribed details", in relation to a prescribed change of circumstances, means such details of the change as may be so prescribed."

(6) Section 85 of that Act (notification requirements: periodic notification) is amended as follows.

(7) In subsection (1), for "the period of one year" substitute "the applicable period".

(8) In subsection (3), for "the period referred to in subsection (1)" substitute "the applicable period".

(9) After subsection (4) insert –

"(5) In this section, "the applicable period" means –

(a) in any case where subsection (6) applies to the relevant offender, such period as may be prescribed by regulations made by the Secretary of State, and
(b) in any other case, the period of one year.

(6) This subsection applies to the relevant offender if the last home address notified by him under section 83(1) or 84(1) or subsection (1) was the address or location of such a place as is mentioned in section 83(7)(b)."

(10) In section 138(2) of that Act (orders and regulations subject to the affirmative resolution procedure), for "86 or 130" substitute "any of sections 83 to 86 or section 130".

(11) This section extends to England and Wales and Northern Ireland only.

Persistent sales of tobacco to persons under 18

143 Persistent sales of tobacco to persons under 18

(1) The Children and Young Persons Act 1933 (c. 12) is amended as follows.

(2) After section 12 insert –

"Persistent sales of tobacco to persons under 18

12A Restricted premises orders

(1) This section applies where a person ("the offender") is convicted of a tobacco offence ("the relevant offence").

(2) The person who brought the proceedings for the relevant offence may by complaint to a magistrates' court apply for a restricted premises order to be made in respect of the premises in relation to which that offence was committed ("the relevant premises").

(3) A restricted premises order is an order prohibiting the sale on the premises to which it relates of any tobacco or cigarette papers to any person.

(4) The prohibition applies to sales whether made –

(a) by the offender or any other person, or
(b) by means of any machine kept on the premises or any other means.

(5) The order has effect for the period specified in the order, but that period may not exceed one year.

(6) The applicant must, after making reasonable enquiries, give notice of the application to every person appearing to the applicant to be a person affected by it.

(7) The court may make the order if (and only if) it is satisfied that –

    (a)   on at least 2 occasions within the period of 2 years ending with the date on which the relevant offence was committed, the offender has committed other tobacco offences in relation to the relevant premises, and

    (b)   the applicant has complied with subsection (6).

(8) Persons affected by the application may make representations to the court as to why the order should not be made.

(9) If –

    (a)   a person affected by an application for a restricted premises order was not given notice under subsection (6), and

    (b)   consequently the person had no opportunity to make representations to the court as to why the order should not be made, the person may by complaint apply to the court for an order varying or discharging it.

(10) On an application under subsection (9) the court may, after hearing –

    (a)   that person, and

    (b)   the applicant for the restricted premises order, make such order varying or discharging the restricted premises order as it considers appropriate.

(11) For the purposes of this section the persons affected by an application for a restricted premises order in respect of any premises are –

    (a)   the occupier of the premises, and

    (b)   any other person who has an interest in the premises.

12B   Restricted sale orders

(1) This section applies where a person ("the offender") is convicted of a tobacco offence ("the relevant offence").

(2) The person who brought the proceedings for the relevant offence may by complaint to a magistrates' court apply for a restricted sale order to be made in respect of the offender.

(3) A restricted sale order is an order prohibiting the person to whom it relates –

    (a)   from selling any tobacco or cigarette papers to any person,

    (b)   from having any management functions in respect of any premises in so far as those functions relate to the sale on the premises of tobacco or cigarette papers to any person,

    (c)   from keeping any cigarette machine on any premises for the purpose of selling tobacco or permitting any cigarette machine to be kept on any premises by any other person for that purpose, and

    (d)   from having any management functions in respect of any premises in so far as those functions relate to any cigarette machine kept on the premises for the purpose of selling tobacco.

(4) The order has effect for the period specified in the order, but that period may not exceed one year.

(5) The court may make the order if (and only if) it is satisfied that, on at least 2 occasions within the period of 2 years ending with the date on which the relevant offence was committed, the offender has committed other tobacco offences.

(6) In this section any reference to a cigarette machine is a reference to an automatic machine for the sale of tobacco.

12C   Enforcement

(1) If –

    (a)   a person sells on any premises any tobacco or cigarette papers in contravention of a restricted premises order, and

    (b)   the person knew, or ought reasonably to have known, that the sale was in contravention of the order, the person commits an offence.

(2) If a person fails to comply with a restricted sale order, the person commits an offence.

(3) It is a defence for a person charged with an offence under subsection (2) to prove that the person took all reasonable precautions and exercised all due diligence to avoid the commission of the offence.

(4) A person guilty of an offence under this section is liable, on summary conviction, to a fine not exceeding £20,000.

(5) A restricted premises order is a local land charge and in respect of that charge the applicant for the order is the originating authority for the purposes of the Local Land Charges Act 1975.

12D Interpretation

(1) In sections 12A and 12B a "tobacco offence" means –

    (a) an offence committed under section 7(1) on any premises (which are accordingly "the premises in relation to which the offence is committed"), or

    (b) an offence committed under section 7(2) in respect of an order relating to any machine kept on any premises (which are accordingly "the premises in relation to which the offence is committed").

(2) In sections 12A to 12C the expressions "tobacco" and "cigarette" have the same meaning as in section 7.

(3) In sections 12A and 12B "notice" means notice in writing."

(3) In section 102(1) (appeals to the Crown Court), after paragraph (e) insert –

"(f) in the case of a restricted premises order under section 12A or a restricted sale order under section 12B, by any person aggrieved."

Penalties for serious contraventions of data protection principles

144 Power to require data controllers to pay monetary penalty

(1) After section 55 of the Data Protection Act 1998 (c. 29) insert –

"Monetary penalties

55A Power of Commissioner to impose monetary penalty

(1) The Commissioner may serve a data controller with a monetary penalty notice if the Commissioner is satisfied that –

    (a) there has been a serious contravention of section 4(4) by the data controller,

    (b) the contravention was of a kind likely to cause substantial damage or substantial distress, and

    (c) subsection (2) or (3) applies.

(2) This subsection applies if the contravention was deliberate.

(3) This subsection applies if the data controller –

    (a) knew or ought to have known –

        (i) that there was a risk that the contravention would occur, and

        (ii) that such a contravention would be of a kind likely to cause substantial damage or substantial distress, but

    (b) failed to take reasonable steps to prevent the contravention.

(4) A monetary penalty notice is a notice requiring the data controller to pay to the Commissioner a monetary penalty of an amount determined by the Commissioner and specified in the notice.

(5) The amount determined by the Commissioner must not exceed the prescribed amount.

(6) The monetary penalty must be paid to the Commissioner within the period specified in the notice.

(7) The notice must contain such information as may be prescribed.

(8) Any sum received by the Commissioner by virtue of this section must be paid into the Consolidated Fund.

(9) In this section –

"data controller" does not include the Crown Estate Commissioners or a person who is a data controller by virtue of section 63(3);
"prescribed" means prescribed by regulations made by the Secretary of State.

55B Monetary penalty notices: procedural rights

(1) Before serving a monetary penalty notice, the Commissioner must serve the data controller with a notice of intent.

(2) A notice of intent is a notice that the Commissioner proposes to serve a monetary penalty notice.

(3) A notice of intent must –

(a)   inform the data controller that he may make written representations in relation to the Commissioner's proposal within a period specified in the notice, and
(b)   contain such other information as may be prescribed.

(4) The Commissioner may not serve a monetary penalty notice until the time within which the data controller may make representations has expired.

(5) A person on whom a monetary penalty notice is served may appeal to the Tribunal against –

(a)   the issue of the monetary penalty notice;
(b)   the amount of the penalty specified in the notice.

(6) In this section, "prescribed" means prescribed by regulations made by the Secretary of State.

55C Guidance about monetary penalty notices

(1) The Commissioner must prepare and issue guidance on how he proposes to exercise his functions under sections 55A and 55B.

(2) The guidance must, in particular, deal with –

(a)   the circumstances in which he would consider it appropriate to issue a monetary penalty notice, and
(b)   how he will determine the amount of the penalty.

(3) The Commissioner may alter or replace the guidance.

(4) If the guidance is altered or replaced, the Commissioner must issue the altered or replacement guidance.

(5) The Commissioner may not issue guidance under this section without the approval of the Secretary of State.

(6) The Commissioner must lay any guidance issued under this section before each House of Parliament.

(7) The Commissioner must arrange for the publication of any guidance issued under this section in such form and manner as he considers appropriate.

(8) In subsections (5) to (7), "guidance" includes altered or replacement guidance.

55D Monetary penalty notices: enforcement

(1) This section applies in relation to any penalty payable to the Commissioner by virtue of section 55A.

(2) In England and Wales, the penalty is recoverable –

(a)   if a county court so orders, as if it were payable under an order of that court;
(b)   if the High Court so orders, as if it were payable under an order of that court.

(3) In Scotland, the penalty may be enforced in the same manner as an extract registered decree arbitral bearing a warrant for execution issued by the sheriff court of any sheriffdom in Scotland.

(4) In Northern Ireland, the penalty is recoverable –

(a)   if a county court so orders, as if it were payable under an order of that court;

(b) if the High Court so orders, as if it were payable under an order of that court.

55E Notices under sections 55A and 55B: supplemental

(1) The Secretary of State may by order make further provision in connection with monetary penalty notices and notices of intent.

(2) An order under this section may in particular –

- (a) provide that a monetary penalty notice may not be served on a data controller with respect to the processing of personal data for the special purposes except in circumstances specified in the order;
- (b) make provision for the cancellation or variation of monetary penalty notices;
- (c) confer rights of appeal to the Tribunal against decisions of the Commissioner in relation to the cancellation or variation of such notices;
- (d) make provision for the proceedings of the Tribunal in respect of appeals under section 55B(5) or appeals made by virtue of paragraph (c);
- (e) make provision for the determination of such appeals;
- (f) confer rights of appeal against any decision of the Tribunal in relation to monetary penalty notices or their cancellation or variation.

(3) An order under this section may apply any provision of this Act with such modifications as may be specified in the order.

(4) An order under this section may amend this Act."

(2) In section 67 of that Act (orders, regulations, rules) –

(a) in subsection (4) insert at the appropriate place –

"section 55E(1),"; and

(b) in subsection (5) after paragraph (c) insert –
"(ca) regulations under section 55A(5) or (7) or 55B(3)(b),".

Armed forces legislation

145 Amendments to armed forces legislation

Schedule 25 contains –

- (a) amendments to armed forces legislation (which make provision for service courts etc. corresponding to other provisions of this Act); and
- (b) transitional provision relating to certain of those amendments.

Automatic deportation of criminals

146 Convention against human trafficking

After section 33(6) of the UK Borders Act 2007 (automatic deportation: exceptions) insert –

"(6A) Exception 6 is where the Secretary of State thinks that the application of section 32(4) and (5) would contravene the United Kingdom's obligations under the Council of Europe Convention on Action against Trafficking in Human Beings (done at Warsaw on 16th May 2005)."

PART 12
GENERAL

147 Orders, rules and regulations

(1) Orders, rules or regulations made by the Secretary of State or the Lord Chancellor under this Act are to be made by statutory instrument.

(2) Any such orders or regulations –

- (a) may make provision generally or only for specified cases or circumstances;
- (b) may make different provision for different cases, circumstances or areas;

(c) may make incidental, supplementary, consequential, transitional, transitory or saving provision.

(3) Subject to subsection (4), a statutory instrument containing any order or regulations under this Act is subject to annulment in pursuance of a resolution of either House of Parliament.

(4) Subsection (3) does not apply to –

- (a) a statutory instrument containing an order under section 153,
- (b) a statutory instrument containing an order under paragraph 26(5) of Schedule 1,
- (c) a statutory instrument containing an Order in Council under paragraph 9 of Schedule 17, or
- (d) a statutory instrument to which subsection (5) applies.

(5) A statutory instrument containing (whether alone or with other provision) –

- (a) an order under section 4(3),
- (b) an order under section 48(2),
- (c) an order under section 77,
- (d) an order under section 81(4), 83(4) or 91(3) which amends or repeals any provision of an Act,
- (e) an order under section 102,
- (f) regulations under any of sections 108 to 111,
- (g) an order under section 135(6),
- (h) an order under section 148(3) which amends or repeals any provision of an Act,
- (i) an order under paragraph 27 or 35 of Schedule 1,
- (j) an order under paragraph 25 of Schedule 2,
- (k) rules under paragraph 2(4)(a) of Schedule 6, or
- (l) an order under paragraph 6 of Schedule 7,

may not be made unless a draft of the instrument has been laid before, and approved by a resolution of, each House of Parliament.

(6) An order under section 153(5)(b) is to be made by statutory instrument.

(7) An order under section 153(6) is to be made by statutory rule for the purposes of the Statutory Rules (Northern Ireland) Order 1979 (S.I. 1979/1573 (N.I. 12)).

148 Consequential etc. amendments and transitional and saving provision

(1) Schedule 26 contains minor and consequential amendments.

(2) Schedule 27 contains transitory, transitional and saving provisions.

(3) The Secretary of State may by order make –

- (a) such supplementary, incidental or consequential provision, or
- (b) such transitory, transitional or saving provision, as the Secretary of State considers appropriate for the general purposes, or any particular purposes, of this Act, or in consequence of, or for giving full effect to, any provision made by this Act.

(4) An order under subsection (3) may, in particular –

- (a) provide for any amendment or other provision made by this Act which comes into force before any other provision (whether made by this or any other Act or by any subordinate legislation) has come into force to have effect, until that other provision has come into force, with specified modifications, and
- (b) amend, repeal or revoke any provision of –
  - (i) any Act (including this Act and any Act passed in the same Session as this Act);
  - (ii) subordinate legislation made before the passing of this Act;
  - (iii) Northern Ireland legislation passed, or made, before the passing of this Act; and
  - (iv) any instrument made, before the passing of this Act, under Northern Ireland legislation.

(5) Nothing in this section limits the power under section 153(8) to include provision for transitory, transitional or saving purposes in an order under that section.

(6) The amendments that may be made by virtue of subsection (4)(b) are in addition to those made by or which may be made under any other provision of this Act.

(7) In this section "subordinate legislation" has the same meaning as in the Interpretation Act 1978 (c. 30).

(8) Her Majesty may by Order in Council extend any provision made by virtue of subsection (4)(b), with such modifications as may appear to Her Majesty to be appropriate, to the Isle of Man or any British overseas territory.

(9) The power under subsection (8) includes power to make supplementary, incidental, consequential, transitory, transitional or saving provision.

(10) Subsection (8) does not apply in relation to amendments of the Armed Forces Act 2006 (c. 52).

149 Repeals and revocations

Schedule 28 contains repeals and revocations, including repeals of spent enactments.

150 Financial provisions

There is to be paid out of money provided by Parliament –

(a) any expenditure incurred by virtue of this Act by a Minister of the Crown; and
(b) any increase attributable to this Act in the sums payable under any other Act out of money so provided.

151 Effect of amendments to criminal justice provisions applied for purposes of service law

(1) In this section "relevant criminal justice provisions" means provisions of, or made under, an Act which –

(a) relate to criminal justice; and
(b) have been applied (with or without modifications) for any purposes of service law by any provision of, or made under, any Act.

(2) Unless the contrary intention appears, any amendment by this Act of relevant criminal justice provisions also amends those provisions as so applied.

(3) Subsection (2) does not apply to any amendments made by Part 1.

(4) In this section "service law" means –

(a) the system of service law established by the Armed Forces Act 2006 (c. 52); or
(b) any of the systems of service law superseded by that Act (namely, military law, air force law and the Naval Discipline Act 1957 (c. 53)).

152 Extent

(1) Subject as follows and to any other provision of this Act, this Act extends to England and Wales only.

(2) The following provisions of this Act extend to England and Wales, Scotland and Northern Ireland –

(a) section 77;
(b) section 96;
(c) section 113 (together with such of the other provisions of Part 7 as relate to the commission of offences under that section);
(d) Part 10;

(e) this Part (subject to subsection (5)).

(3) The following provisions of this Act extend to England and Wales and Northern Ireland –

- (a) section 3 and Schedule 3;
- (b) section 39(3) and (6)(d) and paragraph 7 of Schedule 7;
- (c) sections 63 to 68 and Schedule 14;
- (d) section 76;
- (e) section 85(6) and (7) (so far as relating to any provision of Part 3 of the Magistrates' Courts Act 1980 which extends to Northern Ireland);
- (f) sections 86 and 90 to 92 and Schedules 18 and 19.

(4) The following provisions of this Act extend to Northern Ireland only –

- (a) sections 82 and 83;
- (b) sections 87 to 89;
- (c) section 122 and Schedule 21.

(5) Except as otherwise provided by this Act, an amendment, repeal or revocation of any enactment by any provision of this Act extends to the part or parts of the United Kingdom to which the enactment extends.

(6) The following amendments and repeals also extend to the Channel Islands and the Isle of Man –

- (a) the amendments of sections 26 and 70(1) of the Children and Young Persons Act 1969 (c. 54) (transfers between England or Wales and the Channel Islands or Isle of Man) made by Schedule 4, and
- (b) the repeals in Part 1 of Schedule 28 relating to those amendments.

(7) In section 7(2) of the Nuclear Material (Offences) Act 1983 (c. 18) (application to Channel Islands, Isle of Man, etc.) the reference to that Act includes a reference to that Act as amended by Schedule 17.

(8) In section 9(4) of the Repatriation of Prisoners Act 1984 (c. 47) (power to extend provisions of that Act to the Channel Islands etc.) the reference to that Act includes a reference to that Act as amended by any provision of this Act.

(9) In section 384 of the Armed Forces Act 2006 (c. 52) (extent to Channel Islands, Isle of Man, etc.) any reference to that Act includes a reference to –

- (a) that Act as amended by or under any provision of this Act,
- (b) section 151, and
- (c) paragraph 34 of Schedule 25.

(10) Nothing in this section restricts the operation of section 76 and paragraph 27 of Schedule 27 in their application in relation to service offences (within the meaning of that paragraph).

153 Commencement

(1) The following provisions of this Act come into force on the day on which this Act is passed –

- (a) section 53, Schedule 13, paragraph 77 of Schedule 26 and the repeals in Part 4 of Schedule 28 relating to –
  - (i) paragraphs 13 and 22 of Schedule 3 to the Criminal Justice Act 2003 (c. 44), and
  - (ii) Part 4 of Schedule 37 to that Act;
- (b) section 77;
- (c) section 128;
- (d) sections 138(1) to (4) and 139;
- (e) section 147;
- (f) section 148(3) to (7);
- (g) sections 150 and 152;
- (h) this section;

(i) section 154;
(j) paragraphs 6(3) and 12 to 16 of Schedule 16 and the repeals in Part 5 of Schedule 28 relating to Part 3A of the Public Order Act 1986 (c. 64);
(k) paragraphs 35 to 39 of Schedule 26.

(2) The following provisions of this Act come into force at the end of the period of 2 months beginning with the day on which it is passed –

(a) section 62 and the related repeal in Part 4 of Schedule 28;
(b) section 69 and paragraph 24 of Schedule 26;
(c) section 70 and paragraph 25 of Schedule 26;
(d) section 79 and the related repeals in Part 5 of Schedule 28;
(e) paragraphs 2 to 7 of Schedule 15;
(f) paragraph 24 of Schedule 27.

(3) Where any particular provision or provisions of a Schedule come into force in accordance with subsection (1) or (2), the section introducing the Schedule also comes into force in accordance with that subsection so far as relating to the particular provision or provisions.

(4) The following provisions come into force on such day as the Lord Chancellor may by order appoint –

(a) section 19;
(b) section 41;
(c) sections 56 to 58;
(d) sections 80 to 92 and Schedules 18 and 19;
(e) paragraph 29 of Schedule 27.

(5) Sections 119 to 121 come into force –

(a) in relation to English NHS premises, on such day as the Secretary of State may by order appoint, and
(b) in relation to Welsh NHS premises, on such day as the Welsh Ministers may by order appoint.

(6) Section 122 and Schedule 21 come into force on such day as the Department of Health, Social Services and Public Safety may by order appoint.

(7) The other provisions of this Act come into force on such day as the Secretary of State may by order appoint.

(8) An order under any of subsections (4) to (7) may –

(a) appoint different days for different purposes and in relation to different areas;
(b) make such provision as the person making the order considers necessary or expedient for transitory, transitional or saving purposes in connection with the coming into force of any provision falling within that subsection.

154 Short title

This Act may be cited as the Criminal Justice and Immigration Act 2008.

Schedule 1

Section 1

Further Provisions About Youth Rehabilitation Orders

PART 1
PROVISIONS TO BE INCLUDED IN YOUTH REHABILITATION ORDERS

1 Imposition of requirements

Subsection (1) of section 1 has effect subject to the following provisions of Part 2 of this Schedule which relate to particular requirements –

(a) paragraph 8(3) and (4) (activity requirement),
(b) paragraph 10(3) (unpaid work requirement),
(c) paragraph 11(3) and (4) (programme requirement),
(d) paragraph 12(3) (attendance centre requirement),
(e) paragraph 13(2) (prohibited activity requirement),
(f) paragraph 16(2), (4) and (7) (residence requirement),
(g) paragraphs 17(3) and (4) and 19 (local authority residence requirement),
(h) paragraph 20(3) (mental health treatment requirement),
(i) paragraph 22(2) and (4) (drug treatment requirement),
(j) paragraph 23(3) (drug testing requirement),
(k) paragraph 24(2) and (4) (intoxicating substance treatment requirement), and
(l) paragraph 25(4) (education requirement).

2 Electronic monitoring requirement

(1) Sub-paragraph (2) applies to a youth rehabilitation order which –

(a) imposes a curfew requirement (whether by virtue of paragraph 3(4)(b) or otherwise), or
(b) imposes an exclusion requirement.

(2) The order must also impose an electronic monitoring requirement unless –

(a) in the particular circumstances of the case, the court considers it inappropriate for the order to do so, or
(b) the court is prevented by paragraph 26(3) or (6) from including such a requirement in the order.

(3) Subsection (2)(a) of section 1 has effect subject to paragraph 26(3) and (6).

3 Youth rehabilitation order with intensive supervision and surveillance

(1) This paragraph applies where paragraphs (a) to (c) of section 1(4) are satisfied.

(2) The court, if it makes a youth rehabilitation order which imposes an activity requirement, may specify in relation to that requirement a number of days which is more than 90 but not more than 180.

(3) Such an activity requirement is referred to in this Part of this Act as "an extended activity requirement".

(4) A youth rehabilitation order which imposes an extended activity requirement must also impose –

(a) a supervision requirement, and
(b) a curfew requirement (and, accordingly, if so required by paragraph 2, an electronic monitoring requirement).

(5) A youth rehabilitation order which imposes an extended activity requirement (and other requirements in accordance with sub-paragraph (4)) is referred to in this Part of this Act as "a youth rehabilitation order with intensive supervision and surveillance" (whether or not it also imposes any other requirement mentioned in section 1(1)).

4 Youth rehabilitation order with fostering

(1) This paragraph applies where paragraphs (a) to (c) of section 1(4) are satisfied.

(2) If the court is satisfied –

- (a) that the behaviour which constituted the offence was due to a significant extent to the circumstances in which the offender was living, and
- (b) that the imposition of a fostering requirement (see paragraph 18) would assist in the offender's rehabilitation, it may make a youth rehabilitation order in accordance with section 1 which imposes a fostering requirement.

(3) But a court may not impose a fostering requirement unless –

- (a) it has consulted the offender's parents or guardians (unless it is impracticable to do so), and
- (b) it has consulted the local authority which is to place the offender with a local authority foster parent.

(4) A youth rehabilitation order which imposes a fostering requirement must also impose a supervision requirement.

(5) This paragraph has effect subject to paragraphs 18(7) and 19 (pre-conditions to imposing fostering requirement).

(6) A youth rehabilitation order which imposes a fostering requirement is referred to in this Part of this Act as "a youth rehabilitation order with fostering" (whatever other requirements mentioned in section 1(1) or (2) it imposes).

5 Intensive supervision and surveillance and fostering: further provisions

(1) A youth rehabilitation order with intensive supervision and surveillance may not impose a fostering requirement.

(2) Nothing in –

- (a) section 1(4)(b), or
- (b) section 148(1) or (2)(b) of the Criminal Justice Act 2003 (c. 44) (restrictions on imposing community sentences), prevents a court from making a youth rehabilitation order with intensive supervision and surveillance in respect of an offender if the offender fails to comply with an order under section 161(2) of the Criminal Justice Act 2003 (pre-sentence drug testing).

PART 2
REQUIREMENTS

6 Activity requirement

(1) In this Part of this Act "activity requirement", in relation to a youth rehabilitation order, means a requirement that the offender must do any or all of the following –

- (a) participate, on such number of days as may be specified in the order, in activities at a place, or places, so specified;
- (b) participate in an activity, or activities, specified in the order on such number of days as may be so specified;
- (c) participate in one or more residential exercises for a continuous period or periods comprising such number or numbers of days as may be specified in the order;

(d) in accordance with paragraph 7, engage in activities in accordance with instructions of the responsible officer on such number of days as may be specified in the order.

(2) Subject to paragraph 3(2), the number of days specified in the order under sub-paragraph (1) must not, in aggregate, be more than 90.

(3) A requirement such as is mentioned in sub-paragraph (1)(a) or (b) operates to require the offender, in accordance with instructions given by the responsible officer, on the number of days specified in the order in relation to the requirement –

- (a) in the case of a requirement such as is mentioned in sub-paragraph (1)(a), to present himself or herself at a place specified in the order to a person of a description so specified, or
- (b) in the case of a requirement such as is mentioned in sub-paragraph (1)(b), to participate in an activity specified in the order, and, on each such day, to comply with instructions given by, or under the authority of, the person in charge of the place or the activity (as the case may be).

(4) Where the order requires the offender to participate in a residential exercise, it must specify, in relation to the exercise –

- (a) a place, or
- (b) an activity.

(5) A requirement to participate in a residential exercise operates to require the offender, in accordance with instructions given by the responsible officer –

- (a) if a place is specified under sub-paragraph (4)(a) –
  - (i) to present himself or herself at the beginning of the period specified in the order in relation to the exercise, at the place so specified to a person of a description specified in the instructions, and
  - (ii) to reside there for that period,
- (b) if an activity is specified under sub-paragraph (4)(b), to participate, for the period specified in the order in relation to the exercise, in the activity so specified,

and, during that period, to comply with instructions given by, or under the authority of, the person in charge of the place or the activity (as the case may be).

7 Activity requirement: instructions of responsible officer under paragraph 6(1)(d)

(1) Subject to sub-paragraph (3), instructions under paragraph 6(1)(d) relating to any day must require the offender to do either of the following –

- (a) present himself or herself to a person or persons of a description specified in the instructions at a place so specified;
- (b) participate in an activity specified in the instructions.

(2) Any such instructions operate to require the offender, on that day or while participating in that activity, to comply with instructions given by, or under the authority of, the person in charge of the place or, as the case may be, the activity.

(3) If the order so provides, instructions under paragraph 6(1)(d) may require the offender to participate in a residential exercise for a period comprising not more than 7 days, and, for that purpose –

- (a) to present himself or herself at the beginning of that period to a person of a description specified in the instructions at a place so specified and to reside there for that period, or
- (b) to participate for that period in an activity specified in the instructions.

(4) Instructions such as are mentioned in sub-paragraph (3) –

- (a) may not be given except with the consent of a parent or guardian of the offender, and

(b) operate to require the offender, during the period specified under that sub-paragraph, to comply with instructions given by, or under the authority of, the person in charge of the place or activity specified under sub-paragraph (3)(a) or (b) (as the case may be).

8 Activity requirement: further provisions

(1) Instructions given by, or under the authority of, a person in charge of any place under any of the following provisions –

- (a) paragraph 6(3),
- (b) paragraph 6(5),
- (c) paragraph 7(2), or
- (d) paragraph 7(4)(b),

may require the offender to engage in activities otherwise than at that place.

(2) An activity specified –

- (a) in an order under paragraph 6(1)(b), or
- (b) in instructions given under paragraph 6(1)(d),

may consist of or include an activity whose purpose is that of reparation, such as an activity involving contact between an offender and persons affected by the offences in respect of which the order was made.

(3) A court may not include an activity requirement in a youth rehabilitation order unless –

- (a) it has consulted a member of a youth offending team, an officer of a local probation board or an officer of a provider of probation services,
- (b) it is satisfied that it is feasible to secure compliance with the requirement, and
- (c) it is satisfied that provision for the offender to participate in the activities proposed to be specified in the order can be made under the arrangements for persons to participate in such activities which exist in the local justice area in which the offender resides or is to reside.

(4) A court may not include an activity requirement in a youth rehabilitation order if compliance with that requirement would involve the co-operation of a person other than the offender and the responsible officer, unless that other person consents to its inclusion.

9 Supervision requirement

In this Part of this Act "supervision requirement", in relation to a youth rehabilitation order, means a requirement that, during the period for which the order remains in force, the offender must attend appointments with the responsible officer or another person determined by the responsible officer, at such times and places as may be determined by the responsible officer.

10 Unpaid work requirement

(1) In this Part of this Act "unpaid work requirement", in relation to a youth rehabilitation order, means a requirement that the offender must perform unpaid work in accordance with this paragraph.

(2) The number of hours which a person may be required to work under an unpaid work requirement must be specified in the youth rehabilitation order and must be, in aggregate –

- (a) not less than 40, and
- (b) not more than 240.

(3) A court may not impose an unpaid work requirement in respect of an offender unless –

- (a) after hearing (if the court thinks necessary) an appropriate officer, the court is satisfied that the offender is a suitable person to perform work under such a requirement, and

(b) the court is satisfied that provision for the offender to work under such a requirement can be made under the arrangements for persons to perform work under such a requirement which exist in the local justice area in which the offender resides or is to reside.

(4) In sub-paragraph (3)(a) "an appropriate officer" means a member of a youth offending team, an officer of a local probation board or an officer of a provider of probation services.

(5) An offender in respect of whom an unpaid work requirement of a youth rehabilitation order is in force must perform for the number of hours specified in the order such work at such times as the responsible officer may specify in instructions.

(6) Subject to paragraph 17 of Schedule 2, the work required to be performed under an unpaid work requirement of a youth rehabilitation order must be performed during the period of 12 months beginning with the day on which the order takes effect.

(7) Unless revoked, a youth rehabilitation order imposing an unpaid work requirement remains in force until the offender has worked under it for the number of hours specified in it.

11 Programme requirement

(1) In this Part of this Act "programme requirement", in relation to a youth rehabilitation order, means a requirement that the offender must participate in a systematic set of activities ("a programme") specified in the order at a place or places so specified on such number of days as may be so specified.

(2) A programme requirement may require the offender to reside at any place specified in the order under sub-paragraph (1) for any period so specified if it is necessary for the offender to reside there for that period in order to participate in the programme.

(3) A court may not include a programme requirement in a youth rehabilitation order unless –

(a) the programme which the court proposes to specify in the order has been recommended to the court by –
 (i) a member of a youth offending team,
 (ii) an officer of a local probation board, or
 (iii) an officer of a provider of probation services,

as being suitable for the offender, and

(b) the court is satisfied that the programme is available at the place or places proposed to be specified.

(4) A court may not include a programme requirement in a youth rehabilitation order if compliance with that requirement would involve the co-operation of a person other than the offender and the offender's responsible officer, unless that other person consents to its inclusion.

(5) A requirement to participate in a programme operates to require the offender –

(a) in accordance with instructions given by the responsible officer to participate in the programme at the place or places specified in the order on the number of days so specified, and
(b) while at any of those places, to comply with instructions given by, or under the authority of, the person in charge of the programme.

12 Attendance centre requirement

(1) In this Part of this Act "attendance centre requirement", in relation to a youth rehabilitation order, means a requirement that the offender must attend at an attendance centre specified in the order for such number of hours as may be so specified.

(2) The aggregate number of hours for which the offender may be required to attend at an attendance centre –

(a) if the offender is aged 16 or over at the time of conviction, must be –
 (i) not less than 12, and
 (ii) not more than 36;
(b) if the offender is aged 14 or over but under 16 at the time of conviction, must be –
 (i) not less than 12, and
 (ii) not more than 24;
(c) if the offender is aged under 14 at the time of conviction, must not be more than 12.

(3) A court may not include an attendance centre requirement in a youth rehabilitation order unless it –

(a) has been notified by the Secretary of State that –
 (i) an attendance centre is available for persons of the offender's description, and
 (ii) provision can be made at the centre for the offender, and
(b) is satisfied that the attendance centre proposed to be specified is reasonably accessible to the offender, having regard to the means of access available to the offender and any other circumstances.

(4) The first time at which the offender is required to attend at the attendance centre is a time notified to the offender by the responsible officer.

(5) The subsequent hours are to be fixed by the officer in charge of the centre –

(a) in accordance with arrangements made by the responsible officer, and
(b) having regard to the offender's circumstances.

(6) An offender may not be required under this paragraph to attend at an attendance centre –

(a) on more than one occasion on any day, or
(b) for more than three hours on any occasion.

(7) A requirement to attend at an attendance centre for any period on any occasion operates as a requirement –

(a) to attend at the centre at the beginning of the period, and
(b) during that period, to engage in occupation, or receive instruction, under the supervision of and in accordance with instructions given by, or under the authority of, the officer in charge of the centre, whether at the centre or elsewhere.

13 Prohibited activity requirement

(1) In this Part of this Act "prohibited activity requirement", in relation to a youth rehabilitation order, means a requirement that the offender must refrain from participating in activities specified in the order –

(a) on a day or days so specified, or
(b) during a period so specified.

(2) A court may not include a prohibited activity requirement in a youth rehabilitation order unless it has consulted –

(a) a member of a youth offending team,
(b) an officer of a local probation board, or
(c) an officer of a provider of probation services.

(3) The requirements that may by virtue of this paragraph be included in a youth rehabilitation order include a requirement that the offender does not possess, use or carry a firearm within the meaning of the Firearms Act 1968 (c. 27).

14 Curfew requirement

(1) In this Part of this Act "curfew requirement", in relation to a youth rehabilitation order, means a requirement that the offender must remain, for periods specified in the order, at a place so specified.

(2) A youth rehabilitation order imposing a curfew requirement may specify different places or different periods for different days, but may not specify periods which amount to less than 2 hours or more than 12 hours in any day.

(3) A youth rehabilitation order imposing a curfew requirement may not specify periods which fall outside the period of 6 months beginning with the day on which the requirement first takes effect.

(4) Before making a youth rehabilitation order imposing a curfew requirement, the court must obtain and consider information about the place proposed to be specified in the order (including information as to the attitude of persons likely to be affected by the enforced presence there of the offender).

15 Exclusion requirement

(1) In this Part of this Act "exclusion requirement", in relation to a youth rehabilitation order, means a provision prohibiting the offender from entering a place specified in the order for a period so specified.

(2) The period specified must not be more than 3 months.

(3) An exclusion requirement –
- (a) may provide for the prohibition to operate only during the periods specified in the order, and
- (b) may specify different places for different periods or days.

(4) In this paragraph "place" includes an area.

16 Residence requirement

(1) In this Part of this Act, "residence requirement", in relation to a youth rehabilitation order, means a requirement that, during the period specified in the order, the offender must reside –
- (a) with an individual specified in the order, or
- (b) at a place specified in the order.

(2) A court may not by virtue of sub-paragraph (1)(a) include in a youth rehabilitation order a requirement that the offender reside with an individual unless that individual has consented to the requirement.

(3) In this paragraph, a residence requirement falling within sub-paragraph (1)(b) is referred to as "a place of residence requirement".

(4) A court may not include a place of residence requirement in a youth rehabilitation order unless the offender was aged 16 or over at the time of conviction.

(5) If the order so provides, a place of residence requirement does not prohibit the offender from residing, with the prior approval of the responsible officer, at a place other than that specified in the order.

(6) Before making a youth rehabilitation order containing a place of residence requirement, the court must consider the home surroundings of the offender.

(7) A court may not specify a hostel or other institution as the place where an offender must reside for the purposes of a place of residence requirement except on the recommendation of –
- (a) a member of a youth offending team,
- (b) an officer of a local probation board,

(c) an officer of a provider of probation services, or
(d) a social worker of a local authority.

17 Local authority residence requirement

(1) In this Part of this Act, "local authority residence requirement", in relation to a youth rehabilitation order, means a requirement that, during the period specified in the order, the offender must reside in accommodation provided by or on behalf of a local authority specified in the order for the purposes of the requirement.

(2) A youth rehabilitation order which imposes a local authority residence requirement may also stipulate that the offender is not to reside with a person specified in the order.

(3) A court may not include a local authority residence requirement in a youth rehabilitation order made in respect of an offence unless it is satisfied –

(a) that the behaviour which constituted the offence was due to a significant extent to the circumstances in which the offender was living, and
(b) that the imposition of that requirement will assist in the offender's rehabilitation.

(4) A court may not include a local authority residence requirement in a youth rehabilitation order unless it has consulted –

(a) a parent or guardian of the offender (unless it is impracticable to consult such a person), and
(b) the local authority which is to receive the offender.

(5) A youth rehabilitation order which imposes a local authority residence requirement must specify, as the local authority which is to receive the offender, the local authority in whose area the offender resides or is to reside.

(6) Any period specified in a youth rehabilitation order as a period for which the offender must reside in accommodation provided by or on behalf of a local authority must –

(a) not be longer than 6 months, and
(b) not include any period after the offender has reached the age of 18.

18 Fostering requirement

(1) In this Part of this Act "fostering requirement", in relation to a youth rehabilitation order, means a requirement that, for a period specified in the order, the offender must reside with a local authority foster parent.

(2) A period specified in a youth rehabilitation order as a period for which the offender must reside with a local authority foster parent must –

(a) end no later than the end of the period of 12 months beginning with the date on which the requirement first has effect (but subject to paragraphs 6(9), 8(9) and 16(2) of Schedule 2), and
(b) not include any period after the offender has reached the age of 18.

(3) A youth rehabilitation order which imposes a fostering requirement must specify the local authority which is to place the offender with a local authority foster parent under section 23(2)(a) of the Children Act 1989 (c. 41).

(4) The authority so specified must be the local authority in whose area the offender resides or is to reside.

(5) If at any time during the period specified under sub-paragraph (1), the responsible officer notifies the offender –

(a) that no suitable local authority foster parent is available, and
(b) that the responsible officer has applied or proposes to apply under Part 3 or 4 of Schedule 2 for the revocation or amendment of the order, the fostering requirement is,

until the determination of the application, to be taken to require the offender to reside in accommodation provided by or on behalf of a local authority.

(6) This paragraph does not affect the power of a local authority to place with a local authority foster parent an offender in respect of whom a local authority residence requirement is imposed.

(7) A court may not include a fostering requirement in a youth rehabilitation order unless the court has been notified by the Secretary of State that arrangements for implementing such a requirement are available in the area of the local authority which is to place the offender with a local authority foster parent.

(8) In this paragraph, "local authority foster parent" has the same meaning as it has in the Children Act 1989.

19 Pre-conditions to imposing local authority residence requirement or fostering requirement

(1) A court may not include a local authority residence requirement or a fostering requirement in a youth rehabilitation order in respect of an offender unless –

- (a) the offender was legally represented at the relevant time in court, or
- (b) either of the conditions in sub-paragraph (2) is satisfied.

(2) Those conditions are –

- (a) that the offender was granted a right to representation funded by the Legal Services Commission as part of the Criminal Defence Service for the purposes of the proceedings but the right was withdrawn because of the offender's conduct, or
- (b) that the offender has been informed of the right to apply for such representation for the purposes of the proceedings and has had the opportunity to do so, but nevertheless refused or failed to apply.

(3) In this paragraph –

"the proceedings" means –
- (a) the whole proceedings, or
- (b) the part of the proceedings relating to the imposition of the local authority residence requirement or the fostering requirement;

"the relevant time" means the time when the court is considering whether to impose that requirement.

20 Mental health treatment requirement

(1) In this Part of this Act "mental health treatment requirement", in relation to a youth rehabilitation order, means a requirement that the offender must submit, during a period or periods specified in the order, to treatment by or under the direction of a registered medical practitioner or a chartered psychologist (or both, for different periods) with a view to the improvement of the offender's mental condition.

(2) The treatment required during a period specified under sub-paragraph (1) must be such one of the following kinds of treatment as may be specified in the youth rehabilitation order –

- (a) treatment as a resident patient in an independent hospital or care home within the meaning of the Care Standards Act 2000 (c. 14) or a hospital within the meaning of the Mental Health Act 1983 (c. 20), but not in hospital premises where high security psychiatric services within the meaning of that Act are provided;
- (b) treatment as a non-resident patient at such institution or place as may be specified in the order;
- (c) treatment by or under the direction of such registered medical practitioner or chartered psychologist (or both) as may be so specified;

but the order must not otherwise specify the nature of the treatment.

(3) A court may not include a mental health treatment requirement in a youth rehabilitation order unless –

    (a)   the court is satisfied, on the evidence of a registered medical practitioner approved for the purposes of section 12 of the Mental Health Act 1983 (c. 20), that the mental condition of the offender –
        (i)   is such as requires and may be susceptible to treatment, but
        (ii)   is not such as to warrant the making of a hospital order or guardianship order within the meaning of that Act,
    (b)   the court is also satisfied that arrangements have been or can be made for the treatment intended to be specified in the order (including, where the offender is to be required to submit to treatment as a resident patient, arrangements for the reception of the offender), and
    (c)   the offender has expressed willingness to comply with the requirement.

(4) While the offender is under treatment as a resident patient in pursuance of a mental health treatment requirement of a youth rehabilitation order, the responsible officer is to carry out the supervision of the offender to such extent only as may be necessary for the purpose of the revocation or amendment of the order.

(5) Subsections (2) and (3) of section 54 of the Mental Health Act 1983 have effect with respect to proof of an offender's mental condition for the purposes of sub-paragraph (3)(a) as they have effect with respect to proof of an offender's mental condition for the purposes of section 37(2)(a) of that Act.

(6) In this paragraph and paragraph 21, "chartered psychologist" means a person for the time being listed in the British Psychological Society's Register of Chartered Psychologists.

21 Mental health treatment at place other than that specified in order

(1) Where the registered medical practitioner or chartered psychologist by whom or under whose direction an offender is being treated in pursuance of a mental health treatment requirement is of the opinion that part of the treatment can be better or more conveniently given in or at an institution or place which –

    (a)   is not specified in the youth rehabilitation order, and
    (b)   is one in or at which the treatment of the offender will be given by or under the direction of a registered medical practitioner or chartered psychologist, the medical practitioner or psychologist may make arrangements for the offender to be treated accordingly.

(2) Such arrangements as are mentioned in sub-paragraph (1) may only be made if the offender has expressed willingness for the treatment to be given as mentioned in that sub-paragraph.

(3) Such arrangements as are mentioned in sub-paragraph (1) may provide for part of the treatment to be provided to the offender as a resident patient in an institution or place notwithstanding that the institution or place is not one which could have been specified for that purpose in the youth rehabilitation order.

(4) Where any such arrangements as are mentioned in sub-paragraph (1) are made for the treatment of an offender –

    (a)   the registered medical practitioner or chartered psychologist by whom the arrangements are made must give notice in writing to the offender's responsible officer, specifying the institution or place in or at which the treatment is to be carried out, and
    (b)   the treatment provided for by the arrangements is deemed to be treatment to which the offender is required to submit in pursuance of the youth rehabilitation order.

22 Drug treatment requirement

(1) In this Part of this Act, "drug treatment requirement", in relation to a youth rehabilitation order, means a requirement that the offender must submit, during a period or periods specified in the order, to treatment, by or under the direction of a person so specified having the necessary

qualifications or experience ("the treatment provider"), with a view to the reduction or elimination of the offender's dependency on, or propensity to misuse, drugs.

(2) A court may not include a drug treatment requirement in a youth rehabilitation order unless it is satisfied –

(a) that the offender is dependent on, or has a propensity to misuse, drugs, and
(b) that the offender's dependency or propensity is such as requires and may be susceptible to treatment.

(3) The treatment required during a period specified under sub-paragraph (1) must be such one of the following kinds of treatment as may be specified in the youth rehabilitation order –

(a) treatment as a resident in such institution or place as may be specified in the order, or
(b) treatment as a non-resident at such institution or place, and at such intervals, as may be so specified, but the order must not otherwise specify the nature of the treatment.

(4) A court may not include a drug treatment requirement in a youth rehabilitation order unless –

(a) the court has been notified by the Secretary of State that arrangements for implementing drug treatment requirements are in force in the local justice area in which the offender resides or is to reside,
(b) the court is satisfied that arrangements have been or can be made for the treatment intended to be specified in the order (including, where the offender is to be required to submit to treatment as a resident, arrangements for the reception of the offender),
(c) the requirement has been recommended to the court as suitable for the offender by a member of a youth offending team, an officer of a local probation board or an officer of a provider of probation services, and
(d) the offender has expressed willingness to comply with the requirement.

(5) In this paragraph "drug" means a controlled drug as defined by section 2 of the Misuse of Drugs Act 1971 (c. 38).

23 Drug testing requirement

(1) In this Part of this Act, "drug testing requirement", in relation to a youth rehabilitation order, means a requirement that, for the purpose of ascertaining whether there is any drug in the offender's body during any treatment period, the offender must, during that period, provide samples in accordance with instructions given by the responsible officer or the treatment provider.

(2) In sub-paragraph (1) –

"drug" has the same meaning as in paragraph 22,
"treatment period" means a period specified in the youth rehabilitation order as a period during which the offender must submit to treatment as mentioned in sub-paragraph (1) of that paragraph, and
"the treatment provider" has the meaning given by that sub-paragraph.

(3) A court may not include a drug testing requirement in a youth rehabilitation order unless –

(a) the court has been notified by the Secretary of State that arrangements for implementing drug testing requirements are in force in the local justice area in which the offender resides or is to reside,
(b) the order also imposes a drug treatment requirement, and
(c) the offender has expressed willingness to comply with the requirement.

(4) A youth rehabilitation order which imposes a drug testing requirement –

(a) must specify for each month the minimum number of occasions on which samples are to be provided, and
(b) may specify –
(i) times at which and circumstances in which the responsible officer or treatment provider may require samples to be provided, and

(ii) descriptions of the samples which may be so required.

(5) A youth rehabilitation order which imposes a drug testing requirement must provide for the results of tests carried out otherwise than by the responsible officer on samples provided by the offender in pursuance of the requirement to be communicated to the responsible officer.

24 Intoxicating substance treatment requirement

(1) In this Part of this Act, "intoxicating substance treatment requirement", in relation to a youth rehabilitation order, means a requirement that the offender must submit, during a period or periods specified in the order, to treatment, by or under the direction of a person so specified having the necessary qualifications or experience, with a view to the reduction or elimination of the offender's dependency on or propensity to misuse intoxicating substances.

(2) A court may not include an intoxicating substance treatment requirement in a youth rehabilitation order unless it is satisfied –

(a) that the offender is dependent on, or has a propensity to misuse, intoxicating substances, and
(b) that the offender's dependency or propensity is such as requires and may be susceptible to treatment.

(3) The treatment required during a period specified under sub-paragraph (1) must be such one of the following kinds of treatment as may be specified in the youth rehabilitation order –

(a) treatment as a resident in such institution or place as may be specified in the order, or
(b) treatment as a non-resident at such institution or place, and at such intervals, as may be so specified, but the order must not otherwise specify the nature of the treatment.

(4) A court may not include an intoxicating substance treatment requirement in a youth rehabilitation order unless –

(a) the court is satisfied that arrangements have been or can be made for the treatment intended to be specified in the order (including, where the offender is to be required to submit to treatment as a resident, arrangements for the reception of the offender),
(b) the requirement has been recommended to the court as suitable for the offender by a member of a youth offending team, an officer of a local probation board or an officer of a provider of probation services, and
(c) the offender has expressed willingness to comply with the requirement.

(5) In this paragraph "intoxicating substance" means –

(a) alcohol, or
(b) any other substance or product (other than a drug) which is, or the fumes of which are, capable of being inhaled or otherwise used for the purpose of causing intoxication.

(6) In sub-paragraph (5)(b) "drug" means a controlled drug as defined by section 2 of the Misuse of Drugs Act 1971 (c. 38).

25 Education requirement

(1) In this Part of this Act "education requirement", in relation to a youth rehabilitation order, means a requirement that the offender must comply, during a period or periods specified in the order, with approved education arrangements.

(2) For this purpose, "approved education arrangements" means arrangements for the offender's education –

(a) made for the time being by the offender's parent or guardian, and
(b) approved by the local education authority specified in the order.

(3) The local education authority so specified must be the local education authority for the area in which the offender resides or is to reside.

(4) A court may not include an education requirement in a youth rehabilitation order unless –

  (a) it has consulted the local education authority proposed to be specified in the order with regard to the proposal to include the requirement, and
  (b) it is satisfied –
     (i) that, in the view of that local education authority, arrangements exist for the offender to receive efficient fulltime education suitable to the offender's age, ability, aptitude and special educational needs (if any), and
     (ii) that, having regard to the circumstances of the case, the inclusion of the education requirement is necessary for securing the good conduct of the offender or for preventing the commission of further offences.

(5) Any period specified in a youth rehabilitation order as a period during which an offender must comply with approved education arrangements must not include any period after the offender has ceased to be of compulsory school age.

(6) In this paragraph, "local education authority" and "parent" have the same meanings as in the Education Act 1996 (c. 56).

26 Electronic monitoring requirement

(1) In this Part of this Act "electronic monitoring requirement", in relation to a youth rehabilitation order, means a requirement for securing the electronic monitoring of the offender's compliance with other requirements imposed by the order during a period specified in the order or determined by the responsible officer in accordance with the order.

(2) Where an electronic monitoring requirement is required to take effect during a period determined by the responsible officer in accordance with the youth rehabilitation order, the responsible officer must, before the beginning of that period, notify –

  (a) the offender,
  (b) the person responsible for the monitoring, and
  (c) any person falling within sub-paragraph (3)(b), of the time when the period is to begin.

(3) Where –

  (a) it is proposed to include an electronic monitoring requirement in a youth rehabilitation order, but
  (b) there is a person (other than the offender) without whose cooperation it will not be practicable to secure that the monitoring takes place, the requirement may not be included in the order without that person's consent.

(4) A youth rehabilitation order which imposes an electronic monitoring requirement must include provision for making a person responsible for the monitoring.

(5) The person who is made responsible for the monitoring must be of a description specified in an order made by the Secretary of State.

(6) A court may not include an electronic monitoring requirement in a youth rehabilitation order unless the court –

  (a) has been notified by the Secretary of State that arrangements for electronic monitoring of offenders are available –
     (i) in the local justice area proposed to be specified in the order, and
     (ii) for each requirement mentioned in the first column of the Table in sub-paragraph (7) which the court proposes to include in the order, in the area in which the relevant place is situated, and
  (b) is satisfied that the necessary provision can be made under the arrangements currently available.

(7) For the purposes of sub-paragraph (6), "relevant place", in relation to a requirement mentioned in the first column of the following Table which the court proposes to include in the order, means the place mentioned in relation to it in the second column of the Table.

Proposed requirement of youth rehabilitation order	Relevant place
Curfew requirement.	The place which the court proposes to specify in the order for the purposes of that requirement
Exclusion requirement	The place (within the meaning of paragraph 15) which the court proposes to specify in the order.
Attendance centre requirement.	The attendance centre which the court proposes to specify in the order.

27 Power to amend limits

(1) The Secretary of State may by order amend –

(a) paragraph 10(2) (unpaid work requirement), or
(b) paragraph 14(2) (curfew requirement), by substituting, for the maximum number of hours for the time being specified in that provision, such other number of hours as may be specified in the order.

(2) The Secretary of State may by order amend any of the provisions mentioned in sub-paragraph (3) by substituting, for any period for the time being specified in the provision, such other period as may be specified in the order.

(3) Those provisions are –

(a) paragraph 14(3) (curfew requirement);
(b) paragraph 15(2) (exclusion requirement);
(c) paragraph 17(6) (local authority residence requirement);
(d) paragraph 18(2) (fostering requirement).

(4) An order under this paragraph which amends paragraph 18(2) may also make consequential amendments of paragraphs 6(9), 8(9) and 16(2) of Schedule 2.

PART 3
PROVISIONS APPLYING WHERE COURT PROPOSES TO MAKE YOUTH REHABILITATION ORDER

28 Family circumstances

Before making a youth rehabilitation order, the court must obtain and consider information about the offender's family circumstances and the likely effect of such an order on those circumstances.

29 Compatibility of requirements, requirement to avoid conflict with religious beliefs, etc.

(1) Before making –

(a) a youth rehabilitation order imposing two or more requirements, or
(b) two or more youth rehabilitation orders in respect of associated offences,

the court must consider whether, in the circumstances of the case, the requirements to be imposed by the order or orders are compatible with each other.

(2) Sub-paragraph (1) is subject to paragraphs 2, 3(4) and 4(4).

(3) The court must ensure, as far as practicable, that any requirement imposed by a youth rehabilitation order is such as to avoid –

(a) any conflict with the offender's religious beliefs,
(b) any interference with the times, if any, at which the offender normally works or attends school or any other educational establishment, and
(c) any conflict with the requirements of any other youth rehabilitation order to which the offender may be subject.

(4) The Secretary of State may by order provide that sub-paragraph (3) is to have effect with such additional restrictions as may be specified in the order.

30 Date of taking effect and other existing orders

(1) Subject to sub-paragraph (2), a youth rehabilitation order takes effect on the day after the day on which the order is made.

(2) If a detention and training order is in force in respect of an offender, a court making a youth rehabilitation order in respect of the offender may order that it is to take effect instead –

(a) when the period of supervision begins in relation to the detention and training order in accordance with section 103(1)(a) of the Powers of Criminal Courts (Sentencing) Act 2000 (c. 6), or
(b) on the expiry of the term of the detention and training order.

(3) In sub-paragraph (2) –

(a) the references to a detention and training order include an order made under section 211 of the Armed Forces Act 2006 (c. 52) (detention and training orders made by service courts); and
(b) the reference to section 103(1)(a) of the Powers of Criminal Courts (Sentencing) Act 2000 includes that provision as applied by section 213(1) of the Armed Forces Act 2006.

(4) A court must not make a youth rehabilitation order in respect of an offender at a time when –

(a) another youth rehabilitation order, or
(b) a reparation order made under section 73(1) of the Powers of Criminal Courts (Sentencing) Act 2000 (c. 6), is in force in respect of the offender, unless when it makes the order it revokes the earlier order.

(5) Where the earlier order is revoked under sub-paragraph (4), paragraph 24 of Schedule 2 (provision of copies of orders) applies to the revocation as it applies to the revocation of a youth rehabilitation order.

31 Concurrent and consecutive orders

(1) This paragraph applies where the court is dealing with an offender who has been convicted of two or more associated offences.

(2) If, in respect of one of the offences, the court makes an order of any of the following kinds –

(a) a youth rehabilitation order with intensive supervision and surveillance,
(b) a youth rehabilitation order with fostering, or
(c) any other youth rehabilitation order,

it may not make an order of any other of those kinds in respect of the other offence, or any of the other offences.

(3) If the court makes two or more youth rehabilitation orders with intensive supervision and surveillance, or with fostering, both or all of the orders must take effect at the same time (in accordance with paragraph 30(1) or (2)).

(4) Where the court includes requirements of the same kind in two or more youth rehabilitation orders, it must direct, in relation to each requirement of that kind, whether –

(a) it is to be concurrent with the other requirement or requirements of that kind, or any of them, or
(b) it and the other requirement or requirements of that kind, or any of them, are to be consecutive.

(5) But the court may not direct that two or more fostering requirements are to be consecutive.

(6) Where the court directs that two or more requirements of the same kind are to be consecutive –

(a) the number of hours, days or months specified in relation to one of them is additional to the number of hours, days, or months specified in relation to the other or others, but
(b) the aggregate number of hours, days or months specified in relation to both or all of them must not exceed the maximum number which may be specified in relation to any one of them.

(7) For the purposes of sub-paragraphs (4) and (6), requirements are of the same kind if they fall within the same paragraph of Part 2 of this Schedule.

PART 4
PROVISIONS APPLYING WHERE COURT MAKES YOUTH REHABILITATION ORDER ETC.

32 Date for compliance with requirements to be specified in order

(1) A youth rehabilitation order must specify a date, not more than 3 years after the date on which the order takes effect, by which all the requirements in it must have been complied with.

(2) A youth rehabilitation order which imposes two or more different requirements falling within Part 2 of this Schedule may also specify an earlier date or dates in relation to compliance with any one or more of them.

(3) In the case of a youth rehabilitation order with intensive supervision and surveillance, the date specified for the purposes of sub-paragraph (1) must not be earlier than 6 months after the date on which the order takes effect.

33 Local justice area to be specified in order

A youth rehabilitation order must specify the local justice area in which the offender resides or will reside.

34 Provision of copies of orders

(1) The court by which any youth rehabilitation order is made must forthwith provide copies of the order –

(a) to the offender,
(b) if the offender is aged under 14, to the offender's parent or guardian, and
(c) to a member of a youth offending team assigned to the court, to an officer of a local probation board assigned to the court or to an officer of a provider of probation services.

(2) Sub-paragraph (3) applies where a youth rehabilitation order –

(a) is made by the Crown Court, or
(b) is made by a magistrates' court which does not act in the local justice area specified in the order.

(3) The court making the order must –

(a) provide to the magistrates' court acting in the local justice area specified in the order –
(i) a copy of the order, and

(ii) such documents and information relating to the case as it considers likely to be of assistance to a court acting in that area in the exercise of its functions in relation to the order, and
(b) provide a copy of the order to the local probation board acting for that area or (as the case may be) a provider of probation services operating in that area.

(4) Where a youth rehabilitation order imposes any requirement specified in the first column of the following Table, the court by which the order is made must also forthwith provide the person specified in relation to that requirement in the second column of that Table with a copy of so much of the order as relates to that requirement.

Requirement	Person to whom copy of requirement is to be given
An activity requirement specifying a place under paragraph 6(1)(a)	The person in charge of that place.
An activity requirement specifying an activity under paragraph 6(1)(b)	The person in charge of that activity.
An activity requirement specifying a residential exercise under paragraph 6(1)(c)	The person in charge of the place or activity specified under paragraph 6(4) in relation to that residential exercise.
An attendance centre requirement.	The officer in charge of the attendance centre specified under paragraph 12(1).
An exclusion requirement imposed for the purpose (or partly for the purpose) of protecting a person from being approached by the offender.	The person intended to be protected.
A residence requirement requiring residence with an individual.	The individual specified under paragraph 16(1)(a)
A place of residence requirement (within the meaning of paragraph 16) relating to residence in an institution	The person in charge of the institution.
A local authority residence requirement.	The local authority specified under paragraph 17(1).
A mental health treatment requirement.	The person in charge of the institution or place specified under sub-paragraph (2)(a) or (b) of paragraph 20, or the person specified under sub-paragraph (2)(c) of that paragraph.
A drug treatment requirement	The treatment provider specified under paragraph 22(1).
A drug testing requirement.	The treatment provider specified under paragraph 22(1).
An intoxicating substance treatment requirement	The person specified under paragraph 24(1).
An education requirement.	The local education authority specified under paragraph 25(2).
An electronic monitoring requirement.	Any person who by virtue of paragraph 26(4) will be responsible for the electronic monitoring Any person without whose consent the requirement could not have been included in the order

35 Power to provide for court review of orders

(1) The Secretary of State may by order –

(a) enable or require a court making a youth rehabilitation order to provide for the order to be reviewed periodically by that or another court,
(b) enable a court to amend a youth rehabilitation order so as to include or remove a provision for review by a court, and
(c) make provision as to the timing and conduct of reviews and as to the powers of the court on a review.

(2) An order under this paragraph may, in particular, make provision in relation to youth rehabilitation orders corresponding to any provision made by sections 191 and 192 of the Criminal Justice Act 2003 (c. 44) (reviews of suspended sentence orders) in relation to suspended sentence orders.

(3) An order under this paragraph may repeal or amend any provision of –

(a) this Part of this Act, or
(b) Chapter 1 of Part 12 of the Criminal Justice Act 2003 (general provisions about sentencing).

36 Order made by Crown Court: direction in relation to further proceedings

(1) Where the Crown Court makes a youth rehabilitation order, it may include in the order a direction that further proceedings relating to the order be in a youth court or other magistrates' court (subject to paragraph 7 of Schedule 2).

(2) In sub-paragraph (1), "further proceedings", in relation to a youth rehabilitation order, means proceedings –

(a) for any failure to comply with the order within the meaning given by paragraph 1(2)(b) of Schedule 2, or
(b) on any application for amendment or revocation of the order under Part 3 or 4 of that Schedule.

Schedule 2

Section 2

Breach, Revocation Or Amendment Of Youth Rehabilitation Orders

PART 1
PRELIMINARY

1 Interpretation

(1) In this Schedule, "the offender", in relation to a youth rehabilitation order, means the person in respect of whom the order is made.

(2) In this Schedule –

(a) any reference (however expressed) to an offender's compliance with a youth rehabilitation order is a reference to the offender's compliance with –
 (i) the requirement or requirements imposed by the order, and (ii) if the order imposes an attendance centre requirement, rules made under section 222(1)(d) or (e) of the Criminal Justice Act 2003 (c. 44) ("attendance centre rules"), and
(b) any reference (however expressed) to the offender's failure to comply with the order is a reference to any failure of the offender to comply –
 (i) with a requirement imposed by the order, or
 (ii) if the order imposes an attendance centre requirement, with attendance centre rules.

(3) For the purposes of this Schedule –

(a) a requirement falling within any paragraph of Part 2 of Schedule 1 is of the same kind as any other requirement falling within that paragraph, and
(b) an electronic monitoring requirement is a requirement of the same kind as any requirement falling within Part 2 of Schedule 1 to which it relates.

2 Orders made on appeal

Where a youth rehabilitation order has been made on appeal, for the purposes of this Schedule it is to be treated –

(a) if it was made on an appeal from a magistrates' court, as having been made by a magistrates' court;
(b) if it was made on an appeal brought from the Crown Court or from the criminal division of the Court of Appeal, as having been made by the Crown Court.

PART 2
BREACH OF REQUIREMENT OF ORDER

3 Duty to give warning

(1) If the responsible officer is of the opinion that the offender has failed without reasonable excuse to comply with a youth rehabilitation order, the responsible officer must give the offender a warning under this paragraph unless under paragraph 4(1) or (3) the responsible officer causes an information to be laid before a justice of the peace in respect of the failure.

(2) A warning under this paragraph must –

(a) describe the circumstances of the failure,
(b) state that the failure is unacceptable, and
(c) state that the offender will be liable to be brought before a court –
 (i) in a case where the warning is given during the warned period relating to a previous warning under this paragraph, if during that period the offender again fails to comply with the order, or
 (ii) in any other case, if during the warned period relating to the warning, the offender fails on more than one occasion to comply with the order.

(3) The responsible officer must, as soon as practicable after the warning has been given, record that fact.

(4) In this paragraph, "warned period", in relation to a warning under this paragraph, means the period of 12 months beginning with the date on which the warning was given.

4 Breach of order

(1) If the responsible officer –

(a) has given a warning ("the first warning") under paragraph 3 to the offender in respect of a youth rehabilitation order,
(b) during the warned period relating to the first warning, has given another warning under that paragraph to the offender in respect of a failure to comply with the order, and
(c) is of the opinion that, during the warned period relating to the first warning, the offender has again failed without reasonable excuse to comply with the order, the responsible officer must cause an information to be laid before a justice of the peace in respect of the failure mentioned in paragraph (c).

(2) But sub-paragraph (1) does not apply if the responsible officer is of the opinion that there are exceptional circumstances which justify not causing an information to be so laid.

(3) If –

(a) the responsible officer is of the opinion that the offender has failed without reasonable excuse to comply with a youth rehabilitation order, and
(b) sub-paragraph (1) does not apply (in a case not within sub-paragraph (2)), the responsible officer may cause an information to be laid before a justice of the peace in respect of that failure.

(4) In this paragraph, "warned period" has the same meaning as in paragraph 3.

5 Issue of summons or warrant by justice of the peace

(1) If at any time while a youth rehabilitation order is in force it appears on information to a justice of the peace that an offender has failed to comply with a youth rehabilitation order, the justice may –

(a) issue a summons requiring the offender to appear at the place and time specified in it, or
(b) if the information is in writing and on oath, issue a warrant for the offender's arrest.

(2) Any summons or warrant issued under this paragraph must direct the offender to appear or be brought –

(a) if the youth rehabilitation order was made by the Crown Court and does not include a direction under paragraph 36 of Schedule 1, before the Crown Court, and
(b) in any other case, before the appropriate court.

(3) In sub-paragraph (2), "appropriate court" means –

(a) if the offender is aged under 18, a youth court acting in the relevant local justice area, and
(b) if the offender is aged 18 or over, a magistrates' court (other than a youth court) acting in that local justice area.

(4) In sub-paragraph (3), "relevant local justice area" means –

(a) the local justice area in which the offender resides, or
(b) if it is not known where the offender resides, the local justice area specified in the youth rehabilitation order.

(5) Sub-paragraphs (6) and (7) apply where the offender does not appear in answer to a summons issued under this paragraph.

(6) If the summons required the offender to appear before the Crown Court, the Crown Court may –

(a) unless the summons was issued under this sub-paragraph, issue a further summons requiring the offender to appear at the place and time specified in it, or
(b) in any case, issue a warrant for the arrest of the offender.

(7) If the summons required the offender to appear before a magistrates' court, the magistrates' court may issue a warrant for the arrest of the offender.

6 Powers of magistrates' court

(1) This paragraph applies where –

(a) an offender appears or is brought before a youth court or other magistrates' court under paragraph 5, and
(b) it is proved to the satisfaction of the court that the offender has failed without reasonable excuse to comply with the youth rehabilitation order.

(2) The court may deal with the offender in respect of that failure in any one of the following ways –

(a) by ordering the offender to pay a fine of an amount not exceeding –
    (i) £250, if the offender is aged under 14, or

(ii) £1,000, in any other case;
(b) by amending the terms of the youth rehabilitation order so as to impose any requirement which could have been included in the order when it was made –
(i) in addition to, or
(ii) in substitution for,
any requirement or requirements already imposed by the order;
(c) by dealing with the offender, for the offence in respect of which the order was made, in any way in which the court could have dealt with the offender for that offence (had the offender been before that court to be dealt with for it).

(3) Sub-paragraph (2)(b) is subject to sub-paragraphs (6) to (9).

(4) In dealing with the offender under sub-paragraph (2), the court must take into account the extent to which the offender has complied with the youth rehabilitation order.

(5) A fine imposed under sub-paragraph (2)(a) is to be treated, for the purposes of any enactment, as being a sum adjudged to be paid by a conviction.

(6) Any requirement imposed under sub-paragraph (2)(b) must be capable of being complied with before the date specified under paragraph 32(1) of Schedule 1.

(7) Where –
(a) the court is dealing with the offender under sub-paragraph (2)(b), and
(b) the youth rehabilitation order does not contain an unpaid work requirement,

paragraph 10(2) of Schedule 1 applies in relation to the inclusion of such a requirement as if for "40" there were substituted "20".

(8) The court may not under sub-paragraph (2)(b) impose –
(a) an extended activity requirement, or
(b) a fostering requirement, if the order does not already impose such a requirement.

(9) Where –
(a) the order imposes a fostering requirement (the "original requirement"), and
(b) under sub-paragraph (2)(b) the court proposes to substitute a new fostering requirement ("the substitute requirement") for the original requirement,

paragraph 18(2) of Schedule 1 applies in relation to the substitute requirement as if the reference to the period of 12 months beginning with the date on which the original requirement first had effect were a reference to the period of 18 months beginning with that date.

(10) Where –
(a) the court deals with the offender under sub-paragraph (2)(b), and
(b) it would not otherwise have the power to amend the youth rehabilitation order under paragraph 13 (amendment by reason of change of residence), that paragraph has effect as if references in it to the appropriate court were references to the court which is dealing with the offender.

(11) Where the court deals with the offender under sub-paragraph (2)(c), it must revoke the youth rehabilitation order if it is still in force.

(12) Sub-paragraphs (13) to (15) apply where –
(a) the court is dealing with the offender under sub-paragraph (2)(c), and
(b) the offender has wilfully and persistently failed to comply with a youth rehabilitation order.

(13) The court may impose a youth rehabilitation order with intensive supervision and surveillance notwithstanding anything in section 1(4)(a) or (b).

(14) If –

(a) the order is a youth rehabilitation order with intensive supervision and surveillance, and
(b) the offence mentioned in sub-paragraph (2)(c) was punishable with imprisonment, the court may impose a custodial sentence notwithstanding anything in section 152(2) of the Criminal Justice Act 2003 (c. 44) (general restrictions on imposing discretionary custodial sentences).

(15) If –

(a) the order is a youth rehabilitation order with intensive supervision and surveillance which was imposed by virtue of sub-paragraph (13) or paragraph 8(12), and
(b) the offence mentioned in sub-paragraph (2)(c) was not punishable with imprisonment, for the purposes of dealing with the offender under sub-paragraph (2)(c), the court is to be taken to have had power to deal with the offender for that offence by making a detention and training order for a term not exceeding 4 months.

(16) An offender may appeal to the Crown Court against a sentence imposed under sub-paragraph (2)(c).

7 Power of magistrates' court to refer offender to Crown Court

(1) Sub-paragraph (2) applies if –

(a) the youth rehabilitation order was made by the Crown Court and contains a direction under paragraph 36 of Schedule 1, and
(b) a youth court or other magistrates' court would (apart from that sub-paragraph) be required, or has the power, to deal with the offender in one of the ways mentioned in paragraph 6(2).

(2) The court may instead –

(a) commit the offender in custody, or
(b) release the offender on bail, until the offender can be brought or appear before the Crown Court.

(3) Where a court deals with the offender's case under sub-paragraph (2) it must send to the Crown Court –

(a) a certificate signed by a justice of the peace certifying that the offender has failed to comply with the youth rehabilitation order in the respect specified in the certificate, and
(b) such other particulars of the case as may be desirable; and a certificate purporting to be so signed is admissible as evidence of the failure before the Crown Court.

8 Powers of Crown Court

(1) This paragraph applies where –

(a) an offender appears or is brought before the Crown Court under paragraph 5 or by virtue of paragraph 7(2), and
(b) it is proved to the satisfaction of that court that the offender has failed without reasonable excuse to comply with the youth rehabilitation order.

(2) The Crown Court may deal with the offender in respect of that failure in any one of the following ways –

(a) by ordering the offender to pay a fine of an amount not exceeding –
   (i) £250, if the offender is aged under 14, or
   (ii) £1,000, in any other case;
(b) by amending the terms of the youth rehabilitation order so as to impose any requirement which could have been included in the order when it was made –
   (i) in addition to, or
   (ii) in substitution for,
   any requirement or requirements already imposed by the order;

(c) by dealing with the offender, for the offence in respect of which the order was made, in any way in which the Crown Court could have dealt with the offender for that offence.

(3) Sub-paragraph (2)(b) is subject to sub-paragraphs (6) to (9).

(4) In dealing with the offender under sub-paragraph (2), the Crown Court must take into account the extent to which the offender has complied with the youth rehabilitation order.

(5) A fine imposed under sub-paragraph (2)(a) is to be treated, for the purposes of any enactment, as being a sum adjudged to be paid by a conviction.

(6) Any requirement imposed under sub-paragraph (2)(b) must be capable of being complied with before the date specified under paragraph 32(1) of Schedule 1.

(7) Where –
- (a) the court is dealing with the offender under sub-paragraph (2)(b), and
- (b) the youth rehabilitation order does not contain an unpaid work requirement, paragraph 10(2) of Schedule 1 applies in relation to the inclusion of such a requirement as if for "40" there were substituted "20".

(8) The court may not under sub-paragraph (2)(b) impose –
- (a) an extended activity requirement, or
- (b) a fostering requirement,

if the order does not already impose such a requirement.

(9) Where –
- (a) the order imposes a fostering requirement (the "original requirement"), and
- (b) under sub-paragraph (2)(b) the court proposes to substitute a new fostering requirement ("the substitute requirement") for the original requirement,

paragraph 18(2) of Schedule 1 applies in relation to the substitute requirement as if the reference to the period of 12 months beginning with the date on which the original requirement first had effect were a reference to the period of 18 months beginning with that date.

(10) Where the Crown Court deals with an offender under sub-paragraph (2)(c), it must revoke the youth rehabilitation order if it is still in force.

(11) Sub-paragraphs (12) to (14) apply where –
- (a) an offender has wilfully and persistently failed to comply with a youth rehabilitation order; and
- (b) the Crown Court is dealing with the offender under sub-paragraph (2)(c).

(12) The court may impose a youth rehabilitation order with intensive supervision and surveillance notwithstanding anything in section 1(4)(a) or (b).

(13) If –
- (a) the order is a youth rehabilitation order with intensive supervision and surveillance, and
- (b) the offence mentioned in sub-paragraph (2)(c) was punishable with imprisonment,

the court may impose a custodial sentence notwithstanding anything in section 152(2) of the Criminal Justice Act 2003 (c. 44) (general restrictions on imposing discretionary custodial sentences).

(14) If –
- (a) the order is a youth rehabilitation order with intensive supervision and surveillance which was imposed by virtue of paragraph 6(13) or sub-paragraph (12), and
- (b) the offence mentioned in sub-paragraph (2)(c) was not punishable with imprisonment, for the purposes of dealing with the offender under sub-paragraph (2)(c), the Crown

Court is to be taken to have had power to deal with the offender for that offence by making a detention and training order for a term not exceeding 4 months.

(15) In proceedings before the Crown Court under this paragraph any question whether the offender has failed to comply with the youth rehabilitation order is to be determined by the court and not by the verdict of a jury.

9 Restriction of powers in paragraphs 6 and 8 where treatment required

(1) Sub-paragraph (2) applies where a youth rehabilitation order imposes any of the following requirements in respect of an offender –

    (a)   a mental health treatment requirement;
    (b)   a drug treatment requirement;
    (c)   an intoxicating substance treatment requirement.

(2) The offender is not to be treated for the purposes of paragraph 6 or 8 as having failed to comply with the order on the ground only that the offender had refused to undergo any surgical, electrical or other treatment required by that requirement if, in the opinion of the court, the refusal was reasonable having regard to all the circumstances.

10 Power to amend amounts of fines

(1) The Secretary of State may by order amend any sum for the time being specified in paragraph 6(2)(a)(i) or (ii) or 8(2)(a)(i) or (ii).

(2) The power conferred by sub-paragraph (1) may be exercised only if it appears to the Secretary of State that there has been a change in the value of money since the relevant date which justifies the change.

(3) In sub-paragraph (2), "the relevant date" means –

    (a)   if the sum specified in paragraph 6(2)(a)(i) or (ii) or 8(2)(a)(i) or (ii) (as the case may be) has been substituted by an order under sub-paragraph (1), the date on which the sum was last so substituted;
    (b)   otherwise, the date on which this Act was passed.

(4) An order under sub-paragraph (1) (a "fine amendment order") must not have effect in relation to any youth rehabilitation order made in respect of an offence committed before the fine amendment order comes into force.

PART 3
REVOCATION OF ORDER

11 Revocation of order with or without re-sentencing: powers of appropriate court

(1) This paragraph applies where –

    (a)   a youth rehabilitation order is in force in respect of any offender,
    (b)   the order –
        (i)   was made by a youth court or other magistrates' court, or
        (ii)   was made by the Crown Court and contains a direction under paragraph 36 of Schedule 1, and
    (c)   the offender or the responsible officer makes an application to the appropriate court under this sub-paragraph.

(2) If it appears to the appropriate court to be in the interests of justice to do so, having regard to circumstances which have arisen since the order was made, the appropriate court may –

    (a)   revoke the order, or
    (b)   both –
        (i)   revoke the order, and

(ii) deal with the offender, for the offence in respect of which the order was made, in any way in which the appropriate court could have dealt with the offender for that offence (had the offender been before that court to be dealt with for it).

(3) The circumstances in which a youth rehabilitation order may be revoked under sub-paragraph (2) include the offender's making good progress or responding satisfactorily to supervision or treatment (as the case requires).

(4) In dealing with an offender under sub-paragraph (2)(b), the appropriate court must take into account the extent to which the offender has complied with the requirements of the youth rehabilitation order.

(5) A person sentenced under sub-paragraph (2)(b) for an offence may appeal to the Crown Court against the sentence.

(6) No application may be made by the offender under sub-paragraph (1) while an appeal against the youth rehabilitation order is pending.

(7) If an application under sub-paragraph (1) relating to a youth rehabilitation order is dismissed, then during the period of three months beginning with the date on which it was dismissed no further such application may be made in relation to the order by any person except with the consent of the appropriate court.

(8) In this paragraph, "the appropriate court" means –

(a) if the offender is aged under 18 when the application under sub-paragraph (1) was made, a youth court acting in the local justice area specified in the youth rehabilitation order, and
(b) if the offender is aged 18 or over at that time, a magistrates' court (other than a youth court) acting in that local justice area.

12 Revocation of order with or without re-sentencing: powers of Crown Court

(1) This paragraph applies where –

(a) a youth rehabilitation order is in force in respect of an offender,
(b) the order –
(i) was made by the Crown Court, and
(ii) does not contain a direction under paragraph 36 of Schedule 1, and
(c) the offender or the responsible officer makes an application to the Crown Court under this sub-paragraph.

(2) If it appears to the Crown Court to be in the interests of justice to do so, having regard to circumstances which have arisen since the youth rehabilitation order was made, the Crown Court may –

(a) revoke the order, or
(b) both –
(i) revoke the order, and
(ii) deal with the offender, for the offence in respect of which the order was made, in any way in which the Crown Court could have dealt with the offender for that offence.

(3) The circumstances in which a youth rehabilitation order may be revoked under sub-paragraph (2) include the offender's making good progress or responding satisfactorily to supervision or treatment (as the case requires).

(4) In dealing with an offender under sub-paragraph (2)(b), the Crown Court must take into account the extent to which the offender has complied with the youth rehabilitation order.

(5) No application may be made by the offender under sub-paragraph (1) while an appeal against the youth rehabilitation order is pending.

(6) If an application under sub-paragraph (1) relating to a youth rehabilitation order is dismissed, then during the period of three months beginning with the date on which it was dismissed no further such application may be made in relation to the order by any person except with the consent of the Crown Court.

PART 4
AMENDMENT OF ORDER

13 Amendment by appropriate court

(1) This paragraph applies where –

    (a)   a youth rehabilitation order is in force in respect of an offender,
    (b)   the order –
        (i)   was made by a youth court or other magistrates' court, or
        (ii)   was made by the Crown Court and contains a direction under paragraph 36 of Schedule 1, and
    (c)   an application for the amendment of the order is made to the appropriate court by the offender or the responsible officer.

(2) If the appropriate court is satisfied that the offender proposes to reside, or is residing, in a local justice area ("the new local justice area") other than the local justice area for the time being specified in the order, the court –

    (a)   must, if the application under sub-paragraph (1)(c) was made by the responsible officer, or
    (b)   may, in any other case, amend the youth rehabilitation order by substituting the new local justice area for the area specified in the order.

(3) Sub-paragraph (2) is subject to paragraph 15.

(4) The appropriate court may by order amend the youth rehabilitation order –

    (a)   by cancelling any of the requirements of the order, or
    (b)   by replacing any of those requirements with a requirement of the same kind which could have been included in the order when it was made.

(5) Sub-paragraph (4) is subject to paragraph 16.

(6) In this paragraph, "the appropriate court" means –

    (a)   if the offender is aged under 18 when the application under sub-paragraph (1) was made, a youth court acting in the local justice area specified in the youth rehabilitation order, and
    (b)   if the offender is aged 18 or over at that time, a magistrates' court (other than a youth court) acting in that local justice area.

14 Amendment by Crown Court

(1) This paragraph applies where –

    (a)   a youth rehabilitation order is in force in respect of an offender,
    (b)   the order –
        (i)   was made by the Crown Court, and
        (ii)   does not contain a direction under paragraph 36 of Schedule 1, and
    (c)   an application for the amendment of the order is made to the Crown Court by the offender or the responsible officer.

(2) If the Crown Court is satisfied that the offender proposes to reside, or is residing, in a local justice area ("the new local justice area") other than the local justice area for the time being specified in the order, the court –

(a) must, if the application under sub-paragraph (1)(c) was made by the responsible officer, or
(b) may, in any other case,

amend the youth rehabilitation order by substituting the new local justice area for the area specified in the order.

(3) Sub-paragraph (2) is subject to paragraph 15.

(4) The Crown Court may by order amend the youth rehabilitation order –

(a) by cancelling any of the requirements of the order, or
(b) by replacing any of those requirements with a requirement of the same kind which could have been included in the order when it was made.

(5) Sub-paragraph (4) is subject to paragraph 16.

15 Exercise of powers under paragraph 13(2) or 14(2): further provisions

(1) In sub-paragraphs (2) and (3), "specific area requirement", in relation to a youth rehabilitation order, means a requirement contained in the order which, in the opinion of the court, cannot be complied with unless the offender continues to reside in the local justice area specified in the youth rehabilitation order.

(2) A court may not under paragraph 13(2) or 14(2) amend a youth rehabilitation order which contains specific area requirements unless, in accordance with paragraph 13(4) or, as the case may be, 14(4), it either –

(a) cancels those requirements, or
(b) substitutes for those requirements other requirements which can be complied with if the offender resides in the new local justice area mentioned in paragraph 13(2) or (as the case may be) 14(2).

(3) If –

(a) the application under paragraph 13(1)(c) or 14(1)(c) was made by the responsible officer, and
(b) the youth rehabilitation order contains specific area requirements, the court must, unless it considers it inappropriate to do so, so exercise its powers under paragraph 13(4) or, as the case may be, 14(4) that it is not prevented by sub-paragraph (2) from amending the order under paragraph 13(2) or, as the case may be, 14(2).

(4) The court may not under paragraph 13(2) or, as the case may be, 14(2) amend a youth rehabilitation order imposing a programme requirement unless the court is satisfied that a programme which –

(a) corresponds as nearly as practicable to the programme specified in the order for the purposes of that requirement, and
(b) is suitable for the offender,

is available in the new local justice area.

16 Exercise of powers under paragraph 13(4) or 14(4): further provisions

(1) Any requirement imposed under paragraph 13(4)(b) or 14(4)(b) must be capable of being complied with before the date specified under paragraph 32(1) of Schedule 1.

(2) Where –

(a) a youth rehabilitation order imposes a fostering requirement (the "original requirement"), and
(b) under paragraph 13(4)(b) or 14(4)(b) a court proposes to substitute a new fostering requirement ("the substitute requirement") for the original requirement,

paragraph 18(2) of Schedule 1 applies in relation to the substitute requirement as if the reference to the period of 12 months beginning with the date on which the original requirement first had effect were a reference to the period of 18 months beginning with that date.

(3) The court may not under paragraph 13(4) or 14(4) impose –

(a) a mental health treatment requirement,
(b) a drug treatment requirement, or
(c) a drug testing requirement,

unless the offender has expressed willingness to comply with the requirement.

(4) If an offender fails to express willingness to comply with a mental health treatment requirement, a drug treatment requirement or a drug testing requirement which the court proposes to impose under paragraph 13(4) or 14(4), the court may –

(a) revoke the youth rehabilitation order, and
(b) deal with the offender, for the offence in respect of which the order was made, in any way in which that court could have dealt with the offender for that offence (had the offender been before that court to be dealt with for it).

(5) In dealing with the offender under sub-paragraph (4)(b), the court must take into account the extent to which the offender has complied with the order.

17 Extension of unpaid work requirement

Where –

(a) a youth rehabilitation order imposing an unpaid work requirement is in force in respect of an offender, and
(b) on the application of the offender or the responsible officer, it appears to the appropriate court that it would be in the interests of justice to do so having regard to circumstances which have arisen since the order was made,

the court may, in relation to the order, extend the period of 12 months specified in paragraph 10(6) of Schedule 1.

PART 5
POWERS OF COURT IN RELATION TO ORDER FOLLOWING SUBSEQUENT CONVICTION

18 Powers of magistrates' court following subsequent conviction

(1) This paragraph applies where –

(a) a youth rehabilitation order is in force in respect of an offender, and
(b) the offender is convicted of an offence (the "further offence") by a youth court or other magistrates' court ("the convicting court").

(2) Sub-paragraphs (3) and (4) apply where –

(a) the youth rehabilitation order –
　(i) was made by a youth court or other magistrates' court, or (ii) was made by the Crown Court and contains a direction under paragraph 36 of Schedule 1, and
(b) the convicting court is dealing with the offender for the further offence.

(3) The convicting court may revoke the order.

(4) Where the convicting court revokes the order under sub-paragraph (3), it may deal with the offender, for the offence in respect of which the order was made, in any way in which it could have dealt with the offender for that offence (had the offender been before that court to be dealt with for the offence).

(5)   The convicting court may not exercise its powers under sub-paragraph (3) or (4) unless it considers that it would be in the interests of justice to do so, having regard to circumstances which have arisen since the youth rehabilitation order was made.

(6)   In dealing with an offender under sub-paragraph (4), the sentencing court must take into account the extent to which the offender has complied with the order.

(7)   A person sentenced under sub-paragraph (4) for an offence may appeal to the Crown Court against the sentence.

(8)   Sub-paragraph (9) applies where –

(a)   the youth rehabilitation order was made by the Crown Court and contains a direction under paragraph 36 of Schedule 1, and
(b)   the convicting court would, but for that sub-paragraph, deal with the offender for the further offence.

(9)   The convicting court may, instead of proceeding under sub-paragraph (3) –

(a)   commit the offender in custody, or
(b)   release the offender on bail,

until the offender can be brought before the Crown Court.

(10)   Sub-paragraph (11) applies if the youth rehabilitation order was made by the Crown court and does not contain a direction under paragraph 36 of Schedule 1.

(11)   The convicting court may –

(a)   commit the offender in custody, or
(b)   release the offender on bail, until the offender can be brought or appear before the Crown Court.

(12)   Where the convicting court deals with an offender's case under sub-paragraph (9) or (11), it must send to the Crown Court such particulars of the case as may be desirable.

19   Powers of Crown Court following subsequent conviction

(1)   This paragraph applies where –

(a)   a youth rehabilitation order is in force in respect of an offender, and
(b)   the offender –
   (i)   is convicted by the Crown Court of an offence, or
   (ii)   is brought or appears before the Crown Court by virtue of paragraph 18(9) or (11) or having been committed by the magistrates' court to the Crown Court for sentence.

(2)   The Crown Court may revoke the order.

(3)   Where the Crown Court revokes the order under sub-paragraph (2), the Crown Court may deal with the offender, for the offence in respect of which the order was made, in any way in which the court which made the order could have dealt with the offender for that offence.

(4)   The Crown Court must not exercise its powers under sub-paragraph (2) or (3) unless it considers that it would be in the interests of justice to do so, having regard to circumstances which have arisen since the youth rehabilitation order was made.

(5)   In dealing with an offender under sub-paragraph (3), the Crown Court must take into account the extent to which the offender has complied with the order.

(6)   If the offender is brought or appears before the Crown Court by virtue of paragraph 18(9) or (11), the Crown Court may deal with the offender for the further offence in any way which the convicting court could have dealt with the offender for that offence.

(7) In sub-paragraph (6), "further offence" and "the convicting court" have the same meanings as in paragraph 18.

PART 6
SUPPLEMENTARY

20 Appearance of offender before court

(1) Subject to sub-paragraph (2), where, otherwise than on the application of the offender, a court proposes to exercise its powers under Part 3, 4 or 5 of this Schedule, the court –

- (a) must summon the offender to appear before the court, and
- (b) if the offender does not appear in answer to the summons, may issue a warrant for the offender's arrest.

(2) Sub-paragraph (1) does not apply where a court proposes to make an order –

- (a) revoking a youth rehabilitation order,
- (b) cancelling, or reducing the duration of, a requirement of a youth rehabilitation order, or
- (c) substituting a new local justice area or place for one specified in a youth rehabilitation order.

21 Warrants

(1) Sub-paragraph (2) applies where an offender is arrested in pursuance of a warrant issued by virtue of this Schedule and cannot be brought immediately before the court before which the warrant directs the offender to be brought ("the relevant court").

(2) The person in whose custody the offender is –

- (a) may make arrangements for the offender's detention in a place of safety for a period of not more than 72 hours from the time of the arrest, and
- (b) must within that period bring the offender before a magistrates' court.

(3) In the case of a warrant issued by the Crown Court, section 81(5) of the Supreme Court Act 1981 (c. 54) (duty to bring person before magistrates' court) does not apply.

(4) A person who is detained under arrangements made under sub-paragraph (2)(a) is deemed to be in legal custody.

(5) In sub-paragraph (2)(a) "place of safety" has the same meaning as in the Children and Young Persons Act 1933.

(6) Sub-paragraphs (7) to (10) apply where, under sub-paragraph (2), the offender is brought before a court ("the alternative court") which is not the relevant court.

(7) If the relevant court is a magistrates' court –

- (a) the alternative court may –
  - (i) direct that the offender be released forthwith, or
  - (ii) remand the offender, and
- (b) for the purposes of paragraph (a), section 128 of the Magistrates' Courts Act 1980 (c. 43) (remand in custody or on bail) has effect as if the court referred to in subsections (1)(a), (3), (4)(a) and (5) were the relevant court.

(8) If the relevant court is the Crown Court, section 43A of that Act (functions of magistrates' court where a person in custody is brought before it with a view to appearance before the Crown Court) applies as if, in subsection (1) –

- (a) the words "issued by the Crown Court" were omitted, and
- (b) the reference to section 81(5) of the Supreme Court Act 1981 were a reference to sub-paragraph (2)(b).

(9) Any power to remand the offender in custody which is conferred by section 43A or 128 of the Magistrates' Courts Act 1980 is to be taken to be a power –

(a) if the offender is aged under 18, to remand the offender to accommodation provided by or on behalf of a local authority, and
(b) in any other case, to remand the offender to a prison.

(10) Where the court remands the offender to accommodation provided by or on behalf of a local authority, the court must designate, as the authority which is to receive the offender, the local authority for the area in which it appears to the court that the offender resides.

22 Adjournment of proceedings

(1) This paragraph applies to any hearing relating to an offender held by a youth court or other magistrates' court in any proceedings under this Schedule.

(2) The court may adjourn the hearing, and, where it does so, may –

(a) direct that the offender be released forthwith, or
(b) remand the offender.

(3) Where the court remands the offender under sub-paragraph (2) –

(a) it must fix the time and place at which the hearing is to be resumed, and
(b) that time and place must be the time and place at which the offender is required to appear or be brought before the court by virtue of the remand.

(4) Where the court adjourns the hearing under sub-paragraph (2) but does not remand the offender –

(a) it may fix the time and place at which the hearing is to be resumed, but
(b) if it does not do so, must not resume the hearing unless it is satisfied that the offender, the responsible officer and, if the offender is aged under 14, a parent or guardian of the offender have had adequate notice of the time and place of the resumed hearing.

(5) The powers of a magistrates' court under this paragraph may be exercised by a single justice of the peace, notwithstanding anything in the Magistrates' Courts Act 1980 (c. 43).

(6) This paragraph –

(a) applies to any hearing in any proceedings under this Schedule in place of section 10 of the Magistrates' Courts Act 1980 (adjournment of trial) where that section would otherwise apply, but
(b) is not to be taken to affect the application of that section to hearings of any other description.

23 Restrictions on imposition of intensive supervision and surveillance or fostering

Subsection (4), and the provisions mentioned in subsection (6), of section 1 apply in relation to a power conferred by paragraph 6(2)(b), 8(2)(b), 13(4)(b) or 14(4)(b) to impose a requirement as they apply in relation to any power conferred by section 1 or Part 1 of Schedule 1 to make a youth rehabilitation order which includes such a requirement.

24 Provision of copies of orders etc.

(1) Where a court makes an order under this Schedule revoking or amending a youth rehabilitation order, the proper officer of the court must forthwith –

(a) provide copies of the revoking or amending order to the offender and, if the offender is aged under 14, to the offender's parent or guardian,
(b) provide a copy of the revoking or amending order to the responsible officer,
(c) in the case of an amending order which substitutes a new local justice area, provide copies of the amending order to –

(i) the local probation board acting for that area or (as the case may be) a provider of probation services operating in that area, and
(ii) the magistrates' court acting in that area,
(d) in the case of an amending order which imposes or cancels a requirement specified in the first column of the Table in paragraph 34(4) of Schedule 1, provide a copy of so much of the amending order as relates to that requirement to the person specified in relation to that requirement in the second column of that Table,
(e) in the case of an order which revokes a requirement specified in the first column of that Table, provide a copy of the revoking order to the person specified in relation to that requirement in the second column of that Table, and
(f) if the court is a magistrates' court acting in a local justice area other than the area specified in the youth rehabilitation order, provide a copy of the revoking or amending order to a magistrates' court acting in the local justice area specified in the order.

(2) Where under sub-paragraph (1)(c) the proper officer of the court provides a copy of an amending order to a magistrates' court acting in a different area, the officer must also provide to that court such documents and information relating to the case as appear likely to be of assistance to a court acting in that area in the exercise of its functions in relation to the order.

(3) In this paragraph "proper officer" means –

(a) in relation to a magistrates' court, the designated officer for the court, and
(b) in relation to the Crown Court, the appropriate officer.

25 Power to amend maximum period of fostering requirement

The Secretary of State may by order amend paragraph 6(9), 8(9) or 16(2) by substituting, for –

(a) the period of 18 months specified in the provision, or
(b) any other period which may be so specified by virtue of a previous order under this paragraph, such other period as may be specified in the order.

Schedule 3

Section 3

Transfer Of Youth Rehabilitation Orders To Northern Ireland

PART 1
MAKING OR AMENDMENT OF A YOUTH REHABILITATION ORDER WHERE OFFENDER RESIDES OR PROPOSES TO RESIDE IN NORTHERN IRELAND

1 Making of youth rehabilitation order where offender resides or will reside in Northern Ireland

(1) This paragraph applies where a court considering the making of a youth rehabilitation order is satisfied that the offender –

(a) resides in Northern Ireland, or
(b) will reside there when the order takes effect.

(2) The court may not make a youth rehabilitation order in respect of the offender unless it appears to the court that –

(a) in the case of an order imposing a requirement mentioned in sub-paragraph (6), the conditions in sub-paragraphs (3), (4) and (5) are satisfied, or
(b) in any other case, that the conditions in sub-paragraphs (3) and (4) are satisfied.

(3) The condition in this sub-paragraph is satisfied if the number of hours, days or months in respect of which any requirement of the order is imposed is no greater than the number of hours,

days or months which may be imposed by a court in Northern Ireland in respect of a similar requirement in the order which the court proposes to specify as the corresponding order under paragraph 3(b).

(4) The condition in this sub-paragraph is satisfied if suitable arrangements for the offender's supervision can be made by the Probation Board for Northern Ireland or any other body designated by the Secretary of State by order.

(5) The condition in this sub-paragraph is satisfied in relation to an order imposing a requirement mentioned in sub-paragraph (6) if –

- (a) arrangements exist for persons to comply with such a requirement in the petty sessions district in Northern Ireland in which the offender resides, or will be residing when the order takes effect, and
- (b) provision can be made for the offender to comply with the requirement under those arrangements.

(6) The requirements referred to in sub-paragraphs (2)(a) and (5) are –

- (a) an activity requirement (including an extended activity requirement);
- (b) an unpaid work requirement;
- (c) a programme requirement;
- (d) an attendance centre requirement;
- (e) a mental health treatment requirement;
- (f) a drug treatment requirement;
- (g) a drug testing requirement;
- (h) an education requirement;
- (i) an electronic monitoring requirement.

(7) The court may not by virtue of this paragraph require a local authority residence requirement or a fostering requirement to be complied with in Northern Ireland.

2 Amendment of youth rehabilitation order where offender resides or proposes to reside in Northern Ireland

(1) This paragraph applies where the appropriate court for the purposes of paragraph 13(2) of Schedule 2 (amendment by reason of change of residence) or the Crown Court is satisfied that an offender in respect of whom a youth rehabilitation order is in force is residing or proposes to reside in Northern Ireland.

(2) The power of the court to amend the order under Part 4 of Schedule 2 includes power to amend it by requiring it to be complied with in Northern Ireland if it appears to the court that –

- (a) in the case of an order which once amended will impose a requirement mentioned in sub-paragraph (6), that the conditions in sub-paragraphs (3), (4) and (5) are satisfied, or
- (b) in any other case, that the conditions in sub-paragraphs (3) and (4) are satisfied.

(3) The condition in this sub-paragraph is satisfied if the number of hours, days or months in respect of which any requirement of the order is imposed is no greater than the number of hours, days or months which may be imposed by a court in Northern Ireland in respect of a similar requirement in the order which the court proposes to specify as the corresponding order under paragraph 3(b).

(4) The condition in this sub-paragraph is satisfied if suitable arrangements for the offender's supervision can be made by the Probation Board for Northern Ireland or any other body designated by the Secretary of State by order.

(5) The condition in this sub-paragraph is satisfied in relation to an order that will impose a requirement mentioned in sub-paragraph (6) if –

- (a) arrangements exist for persons to comply with such a requirement in the petty sessions district in Northern Ireland in which the offender resides, or will be residing when the amendment to the order takes effect, and

(b) provision can be made for the offender to comply with the requirement under those arrangements.

(6) The requirements referred to in sub-paragraphs (2)(a) and (5) are –

(a) an activity requirement (including an extended activity requirement);
(b) an unpaid work requirement;
(c) a programme requirement;
(d) an attendance centre requirement;
(e) a mental health treatment requirement;
(f) a drug treatment requirement;
(g) a drug testing requirement;
(h) an education requirement;
(i) an electronic monitoring requirement.

(7) The court may not by virtue of this paragraph require a local authority residence requirement or a fostering requirement to be complied with in Northern Ireland.

3 Further provisions regarding the making or amending of youth rehabilitation orders under paragraph 1 or 2

A youth rehabilitation order made or amended in accordance with paragraph 1 or 2 must –

(a) specify the petty sessions district in Northern Ireland in which the offender resides or will be residing when the order or amendment takes effect, and
(b) specify as the corresponding order for the purposes of this Schedule an order that may be made by a court in Northern Ireland, and paragraph 33 of Schedule 1 (local justice area to be specified in order) does not apply in relation to an order so made or amended.

4

(1) Before making or amending a youth rehabilitation order in accordance with paragraph 1 or 2, the court must explain to the offender in ordinary language –

(a) the requirements of the legislation in Northern Ireland relating to the order to be specified under paragraph 3(b),
(b) the powers of the home court under that legislation, as modified by Part 2 of this Schedule, and
(c) its own powers under Part 2 of this Schedule.

(2) The court which makes or amends the order must –

(a) provide the persons mentioned in sub-paragraph (3) with a copy of the order as made or amended, and
(b) provide the home court with such other documents and information relating to the case as it considers likely to be of assistance to that court; and sub-paragraphs (1) to (3) of paragraph 34 of Schedule 1 (provision of copies of orders) do not apply.

(3) The persons referred to in sub-paragraph (2)(a) are –

(a) the offender,
(b) where the offender is aged under 14 –
 (i) the offender's parent or guardian, or
 (ii) if an authority in Northern Ireland has parental responsibility for, and is looking after, the offender, the authority,
(c) the body which is to make suitable arrangements for the offender's supervision under the order, and
(d) the home court.

(4) In sub-paragraph (3)(b)(ii) –

(a) "authority" has the meaning given by Article 2 of the Children (Northern Ireland) Order 1995 (S.I. 1995/755 (N.I. 2)),

(b) references to an offender who is looked after by an authority are to be construed in accordance with Article 25 of that Order, and

(c) "parental responsibility" has the same meaning as in that Order.

(5) In this paragraph, "home court" has the meaning given by paragraph 8.

5 Modifications to Part 1

(1) Where a court is considering the making or amendment of a youth rehabilitation order by virtue of paragraph 1 or 2, Part 1 of this Act (youth rehabilitation orders) has effect subject to the following modifications.

(2) The following provisions of Schedule 1 are omitted –

(a) in paragraph 8(3)(a) (activity requirement: further provisions), the words "a member of a youth offending team or",

(b) paragraphs 8(3)(c), 10(3)(b) and 12(3)(a) (availability of arrangements in local area: activity requirement, unpaid work requirement and attendance centre requirement),

(c) paragraph 16(7) (residence requirement: restriction on requiring residence at hostel or institution), and

(d) paragraphs 18(7), 22(4)(a), 23(3)(a) and 26(6) and (7) (availability of arrangements in local area: fostering requirement, drug treatment and testing requirements and electronic monitoring requirement).

(3) In paragraph 12 of Schedule 1 (attendance centre requirement) any reference to an attendance centre has effect as a reference to an attendance centre as defined by Article 50(1) of the Criminal Justice (Children) (Northern Ireland) Order 1998 (S.I. 1998/1504 (N.I. 9)).

(4) In paragraph 20 of that Schedule (mental health treatment requirement), for sub-paragraph (2)(a) there is substituted –

"(a) treatment as a resident patient at such hospital as may be specified in the order, being a hospital within the meaning of the Health and Personal Social Services (Northern Ireland) Order 1972 (S.I. 1972/1265 (N.I. 14)), approved by the Department of Health, Social Services and Public Safety for the purposes of paragraph 4(3) of Schedule 1 to the Criminal Justice (Northern Ireland) Order 1996 (S.I. 1996/3160 (N.I. 24));".

(5) In paragraphs 25 (education requirement) and 34(4) (additional persons to whom court must give a copy of the order) of that Schedule, any reference to a local education authority (except in sub-paragraph (6) of paragraph 25) has effect as a reference to an Education and Library Board established under Article 3 of the Education and Libraries (Northern Ireland) Order 1986 (S.I. 1986/594 (N.I. 3)).

(6) In paragraph 26 of that Schedule (electronic monitoring requirements: common provisions) sub-paragraph (5) is omitted.

(7) Paragraph 36 of that Schedule has effect as if it required the Crown Court, where it makes a direction under that paragraph, to specify the youth court or other magistrates' court in England and Wales which is to be the relevant court in England or Wales for the purposes of Part 2 of this Schedule.

(8) Any reference to the responsible officer has effect as a reference to the person who is to be responsible for the offender's supervision under the order.

6 Meaning of "supervision"

In this Part of this Schedule "supervision", in relation to a youth rehabilitation order which a court is considering making or amending in accordance with paragraph 1 or 2, means the performance of supervisory, enforcement and other related functions conferred by the legislation which has effect in Northern Ireland relating to corresponding orders of the kind which the court proposes to specify under paragraph 3(b).

PART 2
PROVISIONS RELATING TO AN ORDER MADE OR AMENDED UNDER PART 1

7 Application of this Part

This Part of this Schedule applies where a youth rehabilitation order is made or amended in accordance with Part 1 of this Schedule.

8 Interpretation

In this Part of this Schedule, in relation to the youth rehabilitation order –

"corresponding order" means the order specified under paragraph 3(b);
"home court" means –
- (a) the court of summary jurisdiction acting for the petty sessions district in Northern Ireland in which the offender resides or proposes to reside, or
- (b) where the youth rehabilitation order was made or amended by the Crown Court and the Crown Court in Northern Ireland has not made a direction under paragraph 11, the Crown Court in Northern Ireland;

"supervision" means the performance of supervisory, enforcement and other related functions conferred by the legislation which has effect in Northern Ireland relating to the corresponding order;
"the relevant court in England or Wales" means –
- (a) the court in England and Wales which made or which last amended the order, or
- (b) if the order was made by the Crown Court and includes a direction under paragraph 36 of Schedule 1, such youth court or other magistrates' court as may be specified in the order;

"the relevant officer" means the person responsible for the offender's supervision under the order.

9 Effect of the youth rehabilitation order in Northern Ireland

(1) The youth rehabilitation order is to be treated in Northern Ireland as if it were a corresponding order and the legislation which has effect in Northern Ireland in relation to such orders applies accordingly.

(2) Sub-paragraph (1) is subject to paragraphs 12 to 16.

10 Duty of offender to keep in touch with relevant officer

In section 5(5) (duty of offender to keep in touch with responsible officer), references to the responsible officer are to be read as references to the relevant officer.

11 Direction by Crown Court in Northern Ireland that proceedings in Northern Ireland be before a court of summary jurisdiction

Where the youth rehabilitation order was made or amended by the Crown Court, the Crown Court in Northern Ireland may direct that any proceedings in Northern Ireland in relation to the order be before the court of summary jurisdiction acting for the petty sessions district in which the offender resides or proposes to reside.

12 Powers of the home court in respect of the youth rehabilitation order

The home court may exercise in relation to the youth rehabilitation order any power which it could exercise in relation to a corresponding order made by a court in Northern Ireland, by virtue of the legislation relating to such orders which has effect there, except the following –

(a) any power to discharge or revoke the order (other than a power to revoke the order where the offender has been convicted of a further offence and the court has imposed a custodial sentence),
(b) any power to deal with the offender for the offence in respect of which the order was made, and
(c) in the case of a youth rehabilitation order imposing a curfew requirement, any power to vary the order by substituting for the period specified in it any longer period than the court which made the order could have specified.

13

(1) The home court may require the offender to appear before the relevant court in England or Wales if sub-paragraph (2) or (3) applies.

(2) This sub-paragraph applies where it appears to the home court upon a complaint being made to a lay magistrate acting for the petty sessions district for the time being specified in the order that the offender has failed to comply with one or more requirements of the order.

(3) This sub-paragraph applies where it appears to the home court, on the application of the offender or the relevant officer, that it would be in the interests of justice for a power conferred by any of paragraphs 11 to 14 of Schedule 2 to be exercised.

14

Where an offender is required by virtue of paragraph 13 to appear before the relevant court in England or Wales –

(a) the home court must send to that court a certificate certifying that the offender has failed to comply with such of the requirements of the order as may be specified in the certificate, together with such other particulars of the case as may be desirable, and
(b) a certificate purporting to be signed by the clerk of the home court (or, if the home court is the Crown Court in Northern Ireland, by the chief clerk) is admissible as evidence of the failure before the relevant court in England or Wales.

15 Powers of court in England or Wales before which the offender is required to appear

Where an offender is required by virtue of paragraph 13 to appear before the relevant court in England or Wales, that court may –

(a) issue a warrant for the offender's arrest, and
(b) exercise any power which it could exercise in respect of the youth rehabilitation order if the offender resided in England or Wales, and any enactment relating to the exercise of such powers has effect accordingly, and with any reference to the responsible officer being read as a reference to the relevant officer.

16

(1) Paragraph 15(b) does not enable the relevant court in England or Wales to amend the youth rehabilitation order unless it appears to the court that the conditions in paragraph 2(2)(a) and (b) are satisfied in relation to any requirement to be imposed.

(2) The preceding paragraphs of this Schedule have effect in relation to the amendment of the youth rehabilitation order by virtue of paragraph 15(b) as they have effect in relation to the amendment of such an order by virtue of paragraph 2(2).

17 Power to amend provisions of Schedule in consequence of changes to the law in Northern Ireland

(1) This paragraph applies where a change is made to the law in Northern Ireland adding further descriptions of orders to the kinds of orders which a court in that jurisdiction may impose in dealing with an offender aged under 18 at the time of conviction.

(2) The Secretary of State may by order make such amendments to any of the preceding provisions of this Schedule as appear expedient in consequence of the change.

Schedule 4

Section 6

Youth Rehabilitation Orders: Consequential And Related Amendments

PART 1
CONSEQUENTIAL AMENDMENTS

Children and Young Persons Act 1933 (c. 12)

1

The Children and Young Persons Act 1933 has effect subject to the following amendments.

2

(1) Section 34 (attendance at court of parent of child or young person charged with an offence, etc.) is amended as follows.

(2) In subsection (7), omit "section 163 of the Powers of Criminal Courts (Sentencing) Act 2000 or".

(3) After subsection (7A) insert –

"(7B) If it appears that at the time of his arrest a youth rehabilitation order, as defined in Part 1 of the Criminal Justice and Immigration Act 2008, is in force in respect of him, the responsible officer, as defined in section 4 of that Act, shall also be informed as described in subsection (3) above as soon as it is reasonably practicable to do so."

3

(1) Section 49 (restrictions on reports of proceedings in which children or young persons are concerned) is amended as follows.

(2) In subsection (2), for paragraphs (c) and (d) substitute –

"(c) proceedings in a magistrates' court under Schedule 2 to the Criminal Justice and Immigration Act 2008 (proceedings for breach, revocation or amendment of youth rehabilitation orders);

(d) proceedings on appeal from a magistrates' court arising out of any proceedings mentioned in paragraph (c) (including proceedings by way of case stated)."

(3) In subsection (4A), omit paragraph (d) (but not the word "or" immediately following it).

(4) In subsection (10), for the words from "Schedule 7" to "supervision orders)" substitute the words "Schedule 2 to the Criminal Justice and Immigration Act 2008 (proceedings for breach, revocation or amendment of youth rehabilitation orders)".

(5) In subsection (13), omit paragraph (c)(i).

Criminal Appeal Act 1968 (c. 19)

4

In section 10(2) of the Criminal Appeal Act 1968 (appeal against sentence in other cases dealt with at assizes or quarter sessions), for paragraph (b) substitute –

"(b) having been given a suspended sentence or made the subject of –
  (i) an order for conditional discharge,
  (ii) a youth rehabilitation order within the meaning of Part 1 of the Criminal Justice and Immigration Act 2008, or

(iii) a community order within the meaning of Part 12 of the Criminal Justice Act 2003, appears or is brought before the Crown Court to be further dealt with for the offence."

Firearms Act 1968 (c. 27)

5

The Firearms Act 1968 has effect subject to the following amendments.

6

In section 21(3ZA)(a) (possession of firearms by persons previously convicted of crime), after "2003", insert ", or a youth rehabilitation order within the meaning of Part 1 of the Criminal Justice and Immigration Act 2008,".

7

In section 52(1A)(a) (forfeiture and disposal of firearms; cancellation of certificate by convicting court), after "2003", insert ", or a youth rehabilitation order within the meaning of Part 1 of the Criminal Justice and Immigration Act 2008,".

Health Services and Public Health Act 1968 (c. 46)

8

The Health Services and Public Health Act 1968 has effect subject to the following amendments.

9

In section 64(3)(a) (financial assistance by the Secretary of State to certain voluntary organisations) –

(a) in paragraph (xxi) of the definition of "the relevant enactments", for "sections 63 to 66 and 92 of, and Schedules 6 and 7 to," substitute "section 92 of", and

(b) after that paragraph, insert –

"(xxii) Part 1 of the Criminal Justice and Immigration Act 2008;".

10

In section 65(3)(b) (financial and other assistance by local authorities to certain voluntary organisations), for paragraph (xxii) of the definition of "relevant enactments" substitute –

"(xxii) Part 1 of the Criminal Justice and Immigration Act 2008;".

Social Work (Scotland) Act 1968 (c. 49)

11

The Social Work (Scotland) Act 1968 has effect subject to the following amendments.

12

In section 86(3) (adjustments between authority providing accommodation etc, and authority of area of residence) after "supervision order" insert ", youth rehabilitation order".

13

In section 94(1) (interpretation) –

(a) for the definition of "probation order" substitute –

""probation order", in relation to an order imposed by a court in Northern Ireland, has the same meaning as in the Criminal Justice (Northern Ireland) Order 1996,",

(b) in the definition of "supervision order", omit "the Powers of Criminal Courts (Sentencing) Act 2000 or", and

(c) at the end insert –

""youth rehabilitation order" means an order made under section 1 of the Criminal Justice and Immigration Act 2008."

Children and Young Persons Act 1969 (c. 54)

14

The Children and Young Persons Act 1969 has effect subject to the following amendments.

15

Omit section 25 (transfers between England or Wales and Northern Ireland).

16

(1) Section 26 (transfers between England or Wales and the Channel Islands or Isle of Man) is amended as follows.

(2) In subsection (1)(c), for the words from "supervision order" to "2000" substitute "youth rehabilitation order imposing a local authority residence requirement".

(3) In subsection (2), for the words from "supervision order" to "2000" substitute "youth rehabilitation order imposing a local authority residence requirement".

17

(1) Section 32 (detention of absentees) is amended as follows.

(2) In subsection (1A) –

(a) in paragraph (a), for "paragraph 7(4) of Schedule 7 to the Powers of Criminal Courts (Sentencing) Act 2000" substitute "paragraph 21(2) of Schedule 2 to the Criminal Justice and Immigration Act 2008", and

(b) for paragraph (b) substitute –

"(b) from local authority accommodation –
  (i) in which he is required to live by virtue of a youth rehabilitation order imposing a local authority residence requirement (within the meaning of Part 1 of the Criminal Justice and Immigration Act 2008); or
  (ii) to which he has been remanded under paragraph 21 of Schedule 2 to that Act; or
  (iii) to which he has been remanded or committed under section 23(1) of this Act,".

(3) For subsection (1C) substitute –

"(1C) In this section "the responsible person" means, as the case may be –

(a) the person who made the arrangements under paragraph 21(2) of Schedule 2 to the Criminal Justice and Immigration Act 2008;
(b) the authority specified under paragraph 17(5) of Schedule 1 to that Act;
(c) the authority designated under paragraph 21(10) of Schedule 2 to that Act; or
(d) the authority designated under section 23 of this Act."

(4) After subsection (1C) insert –

"(1D) If a child or young person –

(a) is required to reside with a local authority foster parent by virtue of a youth rehabilitation order with fostering, and
(b) is absent, without the consent of the responsible officer (within the meaning of Part 1 of the Criminal Justice and Immigration Act 2008), from the place in which he is required to reside,

he may be arrested by a constable anywhere in the United Kingdom without a warrant.

(1E) A person so arrested shall be conducted to –

(a) the place where he is required to reside, or
(b) such other place as the local authority specified under paragraph 18(3) of Schedule 1 to the Criminal Justice and Immigration Act 2008 may direct, at that local authority's expense."

(5) In subsection (2), for "or (1A)" substitute ", (1A) or (1D)".

(6) In subsection (2A), for the words from "mentioned in subsection" to "this section is in premises" substitute "mentioned in subsection (1), (1A)(a) or (b)(i) or (ii) or (1D) of this section is in premises".

(7) In subsection (2B) –

(a) after "subsection (1A)" insert "or (1D)", and
(b) at the end insert "or the responsible officer, as the case may be."

(8) In subsection (3), for "or (1A)" substitute ", (1A) or (1D)".

(9) In subsection (4), after "(1A)" insert ", (1D)".

18

In section 70(1) (interpretation) –

(a) omit the definition of "supervision order",
(b) after the definition of "local authority accommodation" insert –

""local authority residence requirement" has the same meaning as in Part 1 of the Criminal Justice and Immigration Act 2008;", and

(c) after the definition of "youth offending team" insert –

""youth rehabilitation order" and "youth rehabilitation order with fostering" have the same meanings as in Part 1 of the Criminal Justice and Immigration Act 2008 (see section 1 of that Act);".

19

In section 73(4)(a) (provisions of section 32 extending to Scotland) for "to (1C)" substitute "to (1E)".

Rehabilitation of Offenders Act 1974 (c. 53)

20

The Rehabilitation of Offenders Act 1974 has effect subject to the following amendments.

21

In section 5(5) (rehabilitation periods for particular sentences) after paragraph (d) insert –

"(da) a youth rehabilitation order under Part 1 of the Criminal Justice and Immigration Act 2008;".

22

In section 7(2) (limitations on rehabilitation under Act, etc.) for paragraph (d) substitute –

"(d) in any proceedings relating to the variation or discharge of a youth rehabilitation order under Part 1 of the Criminal Justice and Immigration Act 2008, or on appeal from any such proceedings;".

Bail Act 1976 (c. 63)

23

In section 4(3) of the Bail Act 1976 (general right to bail of accused persons and others) –

(a) omit the words "to be dealt with", and

(b) for paragraph (a), substitute –

"(a) Schedule 2 to the Criminal Justice and Immigration Act 2008 (breach, revocation or amendment of youth rehabilitation orders), or".

Magistrates' Courts Act 1980 (c. 43)

24

In Schedule 6A to the Magistrates' Courts Act 1980 (fines that may be altered under section 143), omit the entries relating to Schedules 3, 5 and 7 to the Powers of Criminal Courts (Sentencing) Act 2000 (c. 6).

Contempt of Court Act 1981 (c. 49)

25

In section 14 of the Contempt of Court Act 1981 (proceedings in England and Wales), omit the subsection (2A) inserted by the Criminal Justice Act 1982 (c. 48).

Criminal Justice Act 1982

26

Part 3 of Schedule 13 to the Criminal Justice Act 1982 (reciprocal arrangements for transfer of community service orders from Northern Ireland) has effect subject to the following amendments.

27

(1) Paragraph 7 (transfer to England and Wales) is amended as follows.

(2) In sub-paragraph (1), in Article 13(4)(b) inserted by that provision, for "such orders" substitute "an unpaid work requirement of a community order under section 177 of the Criminal Justice Act 2003 or youth rehabilitation order under section 1 of the Criminal Justice and Immigration Act 2008".

(3) In sub-paragraph (2)(b) –

(a) after "a community order" insert "or a youth rehabilitation order", and
(b) omit "(within the meaning of Part 12 of the Criminal Justice Act 2003)".

(4) In sub-paragraph (3) –

(a) for "A community service order" substitute "An adult community service order", and
(b) in paragraph (b) –
   (i) omit "within the meaning of Part 12 of the Criminal Justice Act 2003", and
   (ii) for "by that Part of that Act" substitute "by Part 12 of the Criminal Justice Act 2003".

(5) After sub-paragraph (3) insert –

"(4) A youth community service order made or amended in accordance with this paragraph shall –

(a) specify the local justice area in England or Wales in which the offender resides or will be residing when the order or the amendment comes into force; and
(b) require –
   (i) the local probation board for that area established under section 4 of the Criminal Justice and Court Services Act 2000 or (as the case may be) a provider of probation services operating in that area, or
   (ii) a youth offending team established under section 39 of the Crime and Disorder Act 1998 by a local authority for the area in which the offender resides or will be residing when the order or amendment comes into force,

to appoint a person who will discharge in respect of the order the functions in respect of youth rehabilitation orders conferred on responsible officers by Part 1 of the Criminal Justice and Immigration Act 2008.

(5) The person appointed under sub-paragraph (4)(b) must be –
- (a) where the appointment is made by a local probation board, an officer of that board;
- (b) where the appointment is made by a provider of probation services, an officer of that provider;
- (c) where the appointment is made by a youth offending team, a member of that team."

28

(1) Paragraph 9 (general provision) is amended as follows.

(2) In sub-paragraph (3) –
- (a) in paragraph (a) –
    - (i) for "a community service order" substitute "an adult community service order";
    - (ii) omit "under section 177 of the Criminal Justice Act 2003";
    - (iii) for "of that Act" substitute "of the Criminal Justice Act 2003", and
- (b) before "and" at the end of that paragraph insert –

"(aa) a youth community service order made or amended in the circumstances specified in paragraph 7 above shall be treated as if it were a youth rehabilitation order made in England and Wales and the provisions of Part 1 of the Criminal Justice and Immigration Act 2008 shall apply accordingly;".

(3) In sub-paragraph (4)(a) –
- (a) after "community orders" insert "or youth rehabilitation orders", and
- (b) omit "(within the meaning of Part 12 of the Criminal Justice Act 2003)".

(4) In sub-paragraph (5) –
- (a) after "community order" insert "or youth rehabilitation order", and
- (b) omit "(within the meaning of Part 12 of the Criminal Justice Act 2003)".

(5) In sub-paragraph (6) –
- (a) after "community orders" insert "or youth rehabilitation orders",
- (b) omit "(within the meaning of Part 12 of the Criminal Justice Act 2003)", and
- (c) in paragraph (b)(i), after "2003" insert "or, as the case may be, Part 1 of the Criminal Justice and Immigration Act 2008".

29

After that paragraph insert –

10 "Community service orders relating to persons residing in England and Wales: interpretation

In paragraphs 7 and 9 above –

"adult community service order" means a community service order made in respect of an offender who was aged at least 18 when convicted of the offence in respect of which the order is made;
"community order" means an order made under section 177 of the Criminal Justice Act 2003;
"youth community service order" means a community service order made in respect of an offender who was aged under 18 when convicted of the offence in respect of which the order is made;
"youth rehabilitation order" means an order made under section 1 of the Criminal Justice and Immigration Act 2008."

Mental Health Act 1983 (c. 20)

30

In section 37(8) of the Mental Health Act 1983 (powers of courts to order hospital admission or guardianship) –

(a) in paragraph (a), after "Criminal Justice Act 2003)" insert "or a youth rehabilitation order (within the meaning of Part 1 of the Criminal Justice and Immigration Act 2008)", and
(b) in paragraph (c), omit the words "a supervision order (within the meaning of that Act) or".

Child Abduction Act 1984 (c. 37)

31

In paragraph 2(1) of the Schedule to the Child Abduction Act 1984 (modifications of section 1 for children in certain cases) –

(a) in paragraph (a), for "paragraph 7(4) of Schedule 7 to the Powers of Criminal Courts (Sentencing) Act 2000" substitute "paragraph 21(2) of Schedule 2 to the Criminal Justice and Immigration Act 2008", and
(b) in paragraph (b), after "1969" insert "or paragraph 21 of Schedule 2 to the Criminal Justice and Immigration Act 2008".

Prosecution of Offences Act 1985 (c. 23)

32

(1) Section 19 of the Prosecution of Offences Act 1985 (provision for orders as to costs in other circumstances) is amended as follows.

(2) In subsection (3B)(b)(i), for the words from "in a community order" to "that Act" substitute "a mental health treatment requirement in a community order or youth rehabilitation order".

(3) After subsection (3B) insert –

"(3C) For the purposes of subsection (3B)(b)(i) –

"community order" has the same meaning as in Part 12 of the Criminal Justice Act 2003;
"mental health treatment requirement" means –
(a) in relation to a community order, a mental health treatment requirement under section 207 of the Criminal Justice Act 2003, and
(b) in relation to a youth rehabilitation order, a mental health treatment requirement under paragraph 20 of Schedule 1 to the Criminal Justice and Immigration Act 2008;

"youth rehabilitation order" has the same meaning as in Part 1 of the Criminal Justice and Immigration Act 2008."

Children Act 1989 (c. 41)

33

The Children Act 1989 has effect subject to the following amendments.

34

(1) Section 21 (provision of accommodation for children in police protection or detention or on remand, etc.) is amended as follows.

(2) In subsection (2)(c) –

(a) in sub-paragraph (i), omit "paragraph 7(5) of Schedule 7 to the Powers of Criminal Courts (Sentencing) Act 2000 or" and "or" at the end of that sub-paragraph, and
(b) for sub-paragraph (ii), substitute –
"(ii) remanded to accommodation provided by or on behalf of a local authority by virtue of paragraph 21 of Schedule 2 to the Criminal Justice and Immigration Act 2008 (breach etc. of youth rehabilitation orders); or
(iii) the subject of a youth rehabilitation order imposing a local authority residence requirement or a youth rehabilitation order with fostering,".

(3) After subsection (2) insert –

> (2A) In subsection (2)(c)(iii), the following terms have the same meanings as in Part 1 of the Criminal Justice and Immigration Act 2008 (see section 7 of that Act) –
>
> > "local authority residence requirement";
> > "youth rehabilitation order";
> > "youth rehabilitation order with fostering"."

35

In section 31(7)(b) (care and supervision orders), for sub-paragraph (ii) substitute –

> > "(ii) a youth rehabilitation order within the meaning of Part 1 of the Criminal Justice and Immigration Act 2008; or".

36

In section 105(6) (interpretation) –

(a) in paragraph (b), omit from the words "or an" to the end of the paragraph, and
(b) after that paragraph insert –
> > "(ba) in accordance with the requirements of a youth rehabilitation order under Part 1 of the Criminal Justice and Immigration Act 2008; or"

37

(1) Part 3 of Schedule 3 (education supervision orders) is amended as follows.

(2) In paragraph 13(2), for paragraph (c) substitute –

> > "(c) a youth rehabilitation order made under Part 1 of the Criminal Justice and Immigration Act 2008 with respect to the child, while the education supervision order is in force, may not include an education requirement (within the meaning of that Part);".

(3) In paragraph 14 –

(a) in sub-paragraph (1), for "order under section 63(1) of the Powers of Criminal Courts (Sentencing) Act 2000" substitute "youth rehabilitation order (within the meaning of Part 1 of the Criminal Justice and Immigration Act 2008)", and
(b) in sub-paragraph (2), after "direction" (in the second place it occurs) insert "or instruction". 38 In paragraph 3 of Schedule 8 (privately fostered children) for paragraph (a) substitute –
> > "(a) a youth rehabilitation order made under section 1 of the Criminal Justice and Immigration Act 2008;".

Criminal Justice Act 1991 (c. 53)

39

Part 3 of Schedule 3 to the Criminal Justice Act 1991 (transfer of probation orders from Northern Ireland to England and Wales) has effect subject to the following amendments.

40

(1) Paragraph 10 is amended as follows.

(2) In sub-paragraph (2)(b), for the words from "the local probation board" to the end substitute " –

> > (i) the local probation board for the area which contains the local justice area in which he resides or will reside or (as the case may be) a provider of probation services operating in the local justice area in which he resides or will reside, or
> > (ii) a youth offending team established by a local authority for the area in which he resides or will reside,", and

(3) In sub-paragraph (3)(a), for the words from "an officer of a local probation board" to the end substitute " –

(i) an officer of a local probation board assigned to the local justice area in England and Wales in which the offender resides or will be residing when the order or amendment comes into force or (as the case may be) an officer of a provider of probation services acting in the local justice area in which the offender resides or will then be residing, or

(ii) a member of a youth offending team established by a local authority for the area in England and Wales in which the offender resides or will then be residing;".

41

(1) Paragraph 11 is amended as follows.

(2) In sub-paragraph (2) –

    (a) for "a probation order" substitute "an adult probation order",

    (b) in paragraph (a), omit "under section 177 of the Criminal Justice Act 2003", and

    (c) in paragraph (b), for "of that Act" substitute "of the Criminal Justice Act 2003".

(3) After that sub-paragraph insert –

"(2A) Where a youth probation order is made or amended in any of the circumstances specified in paragraph 10 above then, subject to the following provisions of this paragraph –

    (a) the order shall be treated as if it were a youth rehabilitation order made in England and Wales, and

    (b) the provisions of Part 1 of the Criminal Justice and Immigration Act 2008 shall apply accordingly."

(4) In sub-paragraph (3) –

    (a) for paragraph (a) substitute –
"(a) the requirements of the legislation relating to community orders or, as the case may be, youth rehabilitation orders;";

    (b) in paragraph (b), for "Schedule 8 to that Act" substitute "that legislation".

(5) In sub-paragraph (4) –

    (a) after "a community order" insert "or, as the case may be, a youth rehabilitation order",

    (b) omit "under section 177 of the Criminal Justice Act 2003", and

    (c) for "to that Act" substitute "to the Criminal Justice Act 2003 or by paragraph 6(2)(c) or 11(2) of Schedule 2 to the Criminal Justice and Immigration Act 2008".

(6) In sub-paragraph (5) –

    (a) after "2003" insert "or, as the case may be, Part 1 of the Criminal Justice and Immigration Act 2008",

    (b) for "(2) above" substitute "(2) or (2A) (as the case may be)", and

    (c) in paragraph (b) for the words from "of the" to "board" substitute
"of –
(i) the offender, or
(ii) the officer of a local probation board, officer of a provider of probation services or member of a youth offending team (as the case may be),".

(7) In sub-paragraph (8) –

    (a) after "In this paragraph" insert –

""adult probation order" means a probation order made in respect of an offender who was aged at least 18 when convicted of the offence in respect of which the order is made;
"community order" means an order made under section 177 of the Criminal Justice Act 2003;";

    (b) at the end insert –

""youth probation order" means a probation order made in respect of an offender who was aged under 18 when convicted of the offence in respect of which the order is made;
"youth rehabilitation order" means an order made under section 1 of the Criminal Justice and Immigration Act 2008."

Criminal Justice and Public Order Act 1994 (c. 33)

42

In section 136 of the Criminal Justice and Public Order Act 1994 (crossborder enforcement: execution of warrants), in subsection (7A), after "youth offender panel)" insert "or under Schedule 2 to the Criminal Justice and Immigration Act 2008 (youth rehabilitation orders: breach etc.)".

Criminal Procedure (Scotland) Act 1995 (c. 46)

43

The Criminal Procedure (Scotland) Act 1995 has effect subject to the following amendments.

44

(1) Section 234 (probation orders: persons residing in England and Wales) is amended as follows.

(2) In subsection (2), at the end insert "(in any case where the offender has attained the age of 18 years) or under section 1 of the Criminal Justice and Immigration Act 2008 (in any other case)".

(3) In subsection (4) –

- (a) in paragraph (a), for "and section 207(2) of the Criminal Justice Act 2003" substitute ", section 207(2) of the Criminal Justice Act 2003 and paragraph 20(2) of Schedule 1 to the Criminal Justice and Immigration Act 2008",
- (b) in paragraph (a), for "or, as the case may be, community orders under Part 12 of that Act" substitute ", community orders under Part 12 of the Criminal Justice Act 2003 or, as the case may be, youth rehabilitation orders under Part 1 of the Criminal Justice and Immigration Act 2008",
- (c) in paragraph (a), for "and section 207 of the Criminal Justice Act 2003" substitute ", section 207 of the Criminal Justice Act 2003 and paragraph 20 of Schedule 1 to the Criminal Justice and Immigration Act 2008",
- (d) in paragraph (b), after "2003" insert "or (as the case may be) paragraphs 20(4) and 21(1) to (3) of Schedule 1 to the Criminal Justice and Immigration Act 2008", and
- (e) in paragraph (b), at the end insert "or that paragraph".

(4) In subsection (4A) at the end insert "(in any case where the offender has attained the age of 18 years) or in a youth rehabilitation order made under section 1 of the Criminal Justice and Immigration Act 2008 (in any other case)".

(5) In subsection (5) for the words from "subject to subsection (6)" to the end substitute "subject to subsections (6) and (6A) below –

- (a) Schedule 8 to the Criminal Justice Act 2003 shall apply as if it were a community order made by a magistrates' court under section 177 of that Act and imposing the requirements specified under subsection (4A) above (in any case where the offender has attained the age of 18 years); and
- (b) Schedule 2 to the Criminal Justice and Immigration Act 2008 shall apply as if it were a youth rehabilitation order made by a magistrates' court under section 1 of that Act and imposing the requirements specified under that subsection (in any other case)."

(6) After subsection (6) insert –

"(6A) In its application to a probation order made or amended under this section, Schedule 2 to the Criminal Justice and Immigration Act 2008 has effect subject to the following modifications –

- (a) any reference to the responsible officer has effect as a reference to the person appointed or assigned under subsection (1)(a) above,
- (b) in paragraph 6, sub-paragraph (2)(c) is omitted and, in sub-paragraph (16), the reference to the Crown Court has effect as a reference to a court in Scotland, and
- (c) Parts 3 and 5 are omitted."

45

(1) Section 242 (community service orders: persons residing in England and Wales) is amended as follows.

(2) In subsection (1)(a) –

(a) in sub-paragraph (ii), after "Part 12 of the Criminal Justice Act 2003)" insert ", in any case where the offender has attained the age of 18 years, or an unpaid work requirement imposed by a youth rehabilitation order (within the meaning of Part 1 of the Criminal Justice and Immigration Act 2008), in any other case", and
(b) in sub-paragraph (iii), after "section 177 of the Criminal Justice Act 2003" insert "or, as the case may be, imposed by youth rehabilitation orders made under section 1 of the Criminal Justice and Immigration Act 2008".

(3) In subsection (2)(b) –

(a) after "that court" insert ", in any case where the offender has attained the age of 18 years," and
(b) after "2003" insert "or it appears to that court, in any other case, that provision can be made for the offender to perform work under the order under the arrangements which exist in that area for persons to perform work under unpaid work requirements imposed by youth rehabilitation orders made under section 1 of the Criminal Justice and Immigration Act 2008".

(4) In subsection (3)(b) –

(a) after "the board" insert "or (as the case may be) require a provider of probation services to appoint an officer of the provider,",
(b) after "the order" insert " –
(a)", and
(c) at the end insert "; or
(b) the functions conferred on responsible officers by Part 1 of the Criminal Justice and Immigration Act 2008 in respect of unpaid work requirements imposed by youth rehabilitation orders (within the meaning of that Part) as the case may be."

46

(1) Section 244 (community service orders: general provisions relating to persons residing in England and Wales or Northern Ireland) is amended as follows.

(2) In subsection (3)(a) –

(a) after "2003)" insert "or, as the case may be, a youth rehabilitation order (within the meaning of Part 1 of the Criminal Justice and Immigration Act 2008)", and
(b) after "such community orders" insert "or youth rehabilitation orders".

(3) In subsection (4)(a) –

(a) for "or, as the case may be, community orders" substitute ", community orders", and
(b) after "2003)" insert "or, as the case may be, youth rehabilitation orders (within the meaning of Part 1 of the Criminal Justice and Immigration Act 2008)".

(4) In subsection (5) –

(a) for "or, as the case may be, a community order" substitute ", a community order", and
(b) after "2003)" insert "or, as the case may be, a youth rehabilitation order (within the meaning of Part 1 of the Criminal Justice and Immigration Act 2008)".

(5) In subsection (6) –

(a) for "or, as the case may be, community orders" substitute ", community orders",

(b) after "within the meaning of Part 12 of the Criminal Justice Act 2003)" insert "or, as the case may be, youth rehabilitation orders (within the meaning of Part 1 of the Criminal Justice and Immigration Act 2008)", and
(c) after "the responsible officer under Part 12 of the Criminal Justice Act 2003" insert "or, as the case may be, under Part 1 of the Criminal Justice and Immigration Act 2008".

Education Act 1996 (c. 56)

47

In section 562(2)(b) of the Education Act 1996 (Act not to apply to persons detained under order of a court), for "community order under section 177 of the Criminal Justice Act 2003" substitute "youth rehabilitation order under section 1 of the Criminal Justice and Immigration Act 2008".

Crime and Disorder Act 1998 (c. 37)

48

The Crime and Disorder Act 1998 has effect subject to the following amendments.

49

In section 38(4) (local provision of youth justice services) –

(a) in paragraph (f), for ", reparation orders and action plan orders" substitute "and reparation orders",
(b) after paragraph (f) insert –
   "(fa) the provision of persons to act as responsible officers in relation to youth rehabilitation orders (within the meaning of Part 1 of the Criminal Justice and Immigration Act 2008);
   (fb) the supervision of children and young persons sentenced to a youth rehabilitation order under thatPart which includes a supervision requirement (within the meaning of that Part);",
(c) omit paragraph (g), and
(d) in paragraph (h), omit "or a supervision order".

50

In Schedule 8 (minor and consequential amendments), in paragraph 13(2), for "that section" substitute "section 10 of that Act".

Powers of Criminal Courts (Sentencing) Act 2000 (c. 6)

51

The Powers of Criminal Courts (Sentencing) Act 2000 has effect subject to the following amendments.

52

In section 19(4)(a) (making of referral orders: effect on court's other sentencing powers), for "community sentence" substitute "sentence which consists of or includes a youth rehabilitation order".

53

In section 73 (reparation orders) –

(a) for subsection (4)(b) substitute –
   "(b) to make in respect of him a youth rehabilitation order or a referral order."
(b) after subsection (4) insert –

   "(4A) The court shall not make a reparation order in respect of the offender at a time when a youth rehabilitation order is in force in respect of him unless when it makes the reparation order it revokes the youth rehabilitation order.

(4B) Where a youth rehabilitation order is revoked under subsection (4A), paragraph 24 of Schedule 2 to the Criminal Justice and Immigration Act 2008 (breach, revocation or amendment of youth rehabilitation order) applies to the revocation."

54

In section 74(3)(a) (requirements and provisions of reparation order, and obligations of person subject to it), omit "or with the requirements of any community order or any youth community order to which he may be subject".

55

In section 75 (breach, revocation and amendment of reparation orders) omit "action plan orders and" and "so far as relating to reparation orders".

56

In section 91(3) (offenders under 18 convicted of certain serious offences: power to detain for specified period), for "a community sentence" substitute "a youth rehabilitation order".

57

In section 137(2) (power to order parent or guardian to pay fine, costs, compensation or surcharge) –

    (a)   after "under—" insert –
        "(za)   paragraph 6(2)(a) or 8(2)(a) of Schedule 2 to the Criminal Justice and Immigration Act 2008 (breach of youth rehabilitation order),", and
    (b)   omit paragraphs (a) to (c), and
    (c)   in paragraph (d) omit "action plan order or".

58

In section 150(2) (binding over of parent or guardian), for "a community sentence on the offender" substitute "on the offender a sentence which consists of or includes a youth rehabilitation order".

59

In section 159 (execution of process between England and Wales and Scotland) –

    (a)   after "Schedule 1 to this Act," insert "or",
    (b)   omit "paragraph 3(1), 10(6) or 18(1) of Schedule 3 to this Act,",
    (c)   omit "paragraph 1(1) of Schedule 5 to this Act", and
    (d)   omit "paragraph 7(2) of Schedule 7 to this Act, or".

60

(1)   Section 160 (rules and orders) is amended as follows.

(2)   Omit subsection (2).

(3)   In subsection (3)(a) –

    (a)   omit "40(2)(a)," and
    (b)   for "103(2) or paragraph 1(1A) of Schedule 3," substitute "or 103(2)".

(4)   Omit subsection (5).

61

In section 163 (general definitions) –

(a) omit the definitions of "action plan order", "affected person", "attendance centre", "attendance centre order", "community sentence", "curfew order", "exclusion order", "supervision order", "supervisor" and "youth community order",
(b) in the definition of "responsible officer", omit paragraphs (a), (aa) and (f), and
(c) at the end add –

""youth rehabilitation order" has the meaning given by section 1(1) of the Criminal Justice and Immigration Act 2008."

62

(1) Schedule 8 (breach, revocation and amendment of action plan orders and reparation orders) is amended as follows.

(2) In the heading to the Schedule omit "action plan orders and".

(3) In the cross-heading before paragraph 2, omit "action plan order or".

(4) In paragraph 2 –

(a) in sub-paragraph (1), for "an action plan order or" substitute "a",
(b) in sub-paragraph (2) –
  (i) in paragraph (a), omit sub-paragraphs (ii) and (iii), and
  (ii) in each of paragraphs (b) and (c), omit "action plan order or",
(c) in each of sub-paragraphs (5) and (7), omit "action plan order or", and
(d) in sub-paragraph (8), omit "or action plan order" in both places where it occurs.

(5) Omit paragraphs 3 and 4.

(6) In the cross-heading before paragraph 5, omit "action plan order or".

(7) In paragraph 5 –

(a) in sub-paragraph (1), for "an action plan order or" substitute "a" and, in paragraph (a), omit "action plan order or", and
(b) in sub-paragraph (3), for "an action plan order or" substitute "a".

(8) In paragraph 6(9), in each of paragraphs (a), (b) and (c), omit "action plan order or".

(9) In paragraph 7(b), for "an action plan order or" substitute "a".

63

In Schedule 10 (transitory modifications), omit paragraphs 4 to 6 and 12 to 15.

64

In Schedule 11 (transitional provisions) –

(a) in paragraph 4, omit –
  (i) paragraph (a) of sub-paragraph (1),
  (ii) sub-paragraph (2), and
  (iii) sub-paragraph (3), and
(b) omit paragraph 5.

Child Support, Pensions and Social Security Act 2000 (c. 19)

65

The Child Support, Pensions and Social Security Act 2000 has effect subject to the following amendments.

66

(1) Section 62 (loss of benefit for breach of community order) is amended as follows.

(2) In the definition of "relevant community order" in subsection (8) –

(a) after "2003;" in paragraph (a) insert –

"(aa) a youth rehabilitation order made under section 1 of the Criminal Justice and Immigration Act 2008;", and

(b) in paragraph (b) for "such an order" substitute "an order specified in paragraph (a) or (aa)".

(3) In subsection (11)(c)(ii) for "and (b)" substitute "to (b)".

67

(1) Section 64 (information provision) is amended as follows.

(2) In subsection (6)(a) after "2003)" insert ", youth rehabilitation orders (as defined by section 1 of the Criminal Justice and Immigration Act 2008)".

(3) In subsection (7) after paragraph (b) insert –

"(ba) a responsible officer within the meaning of Part 1 of the Criminal Justice and Immigration Act 2008;".

Criminal Justice and Court Services Act 2000 (c. 43)

68

The Criminal Justice and Court Services Act 2000 has effect subject to the following amendments.

69

In section 1(2)(a) (purposes of Chapter), after "2003)" insert ", youth rehabilitation orders (as defined by section 1 of the Criminal Justice and Immigration Act 2008)".

70

In section 70 (interpretation, etc.) omit subsection (5).

Criminal Justice Act 2003 (c. 44)

71

Part 12 of the Criminal Justice Act 2003 (sentencing) has effect subject to the following amendments.

72

(1) Section 147 (meaning of "community sentence" etc.) is amended as follows.

(2) In subsection (1) –

(a) omit paragraph (b), and
(b) after that paragraph insert –

"(c) a youth rehabilitation order."

(3) Omit subsection (2).

73

(1) Section 148 (restrictions on imposing community sentences) is amended as follows.

(2) In subsection (2) –

(a) omit "which consists of or includes a community order", and
(b) in paragraph (a), after "community order" insert ", or, as the case may be, youth rehabilitation order, comprised in the sentence".

(3) After that subsection insert –

"(2A) Subsection (2) is subject to paragraph 3(4) of Schedule 1 to the Criminal Justice and Immigration Act 2008 (youth rehabilitation order with intensive supervision and surveillance)."

(4) Omit subsection (3).

74

In section 149(1) (passing of community sentence on offender remanded in custody) for "youth community order" substitute "youth rehabilitation order".

75

In section 150 (community sentence not available where sentence fixed by law etc.) for "youth community order" substitute "youth rehabilitation order".

76

(1) Section 151 (community order for persistent offender previously fined) is amended as follows.

(2) In the title, after "community order" insert "or youth rehabilitation order".

(3) In subsections (1)(a) and (1A)(a), for "16" substitute "18".

(4) After subsection (2) insert –

"(2A) Subsection (2B) applies where –
(a) a person aged 16 or 17 is convicted of an offence ("the current offence");
(b) on three or more previous occasions the offender has, on conviction by a court in the United Kingdom of any offence committed by him after attaining the age of 16, had passed on him a sentence consisting only of a fine; and
(c) despite the effect of section 143(2), the court would not (apart from this section) regard the current offence, or the combination of the current offence and one or more offences associated with it, as being serious enough to warrant a youth rehabilitation order.

(2B) The court may make a youth rehabilitation order in respect of the current offence instead of imposing a fine if it considers that, having regard to all the circumstances including the matters mentioned in subsection (3), it would be in the interests of justice to make such an order."

(5) In subsection (3) –
(a) after "(2)" insert "and (2B)"; and
(b) in paragraph (a) for "or (1A)(b)" substitute "(1A)(b) or (2A)(b)".

(6) In subsections (4), (5) and (6), for "and (1A)(b)" substitute "(1A)(b) and (2A)(b)".

(7) In section 166 (savings for powers to mitigate etc.), in subsection (1)(a) after "151(2)" insert "or (2B)".

77

(1) Section 156 (pre-sentence reports and other requirements) is amended as follows.

(2) In subsection (1) –
(a) for ", (2)(b) or (3)(b)" substitute "or (2)(b),", and
(b) after "153(2)," insert "or in section 1(4)(b) or (c) of the Criminal Justice and Immigration Act 2008 (youth rehabilitation orders with intensive supervision and surveillance or fostering),".

(3) In subsection (2) omit "or (3)(a)".

(4) In subsection (3)(b) –

(a) for ", (2)(b) or (3)(b)" substitute "or (2)(b), or in section 1(4)(b) or (c) of the Criminal Justice and Immigration Act 2008,", and
(b) after "community order" insert "or youth rehabilitation order".

78

In section 161 (pre-sentence drug testing) –

(a) in subsection (1), omit "aged 14 or over", and
(b) omit subsection (7).

79

(1) Section 166 (savings for powers to mitigate sentences and deal appropriately with mentally disordered offenders) is amended as follows.

(2) In subsection (1), after paragraph (d) add –

"(e) paragraph 3 of Schedule 1 to the Criminal Justice and Immigration Act 2008 (youth rehabilitation order with intensive supervision and surveillance), or

(f) paragraph 4 of Schedule 1 to that Act (youth rehabilitation order with fostering),".

(3) In subsections (3) and (5), for "(d)" substitute "(f)".

80

(1) Section 174 (duty to give reasons for, and explain effect of, sentence) is amended as follows.

(2) In subsection (2) –

(a) in paragraph (b), after "that section" insert "or any other statutory provision",
(b) in paragraph (c), after "community sentence" insert ", other than one consisting of or including a youth rehabilitation order with intensive supervision and surveillance or fostering,", and (c) after paragraph (c) insert –
"(ca) where the sentence consists of or includes a youth rehabilitation order with intensive supervision and surveillance and the case does not fall within paragraph 5(2) of Schedule 1 to the Criminal Justice and Immigration Act 2008, state that it is of the opinion that section 1(4)(a) to (c) of that Act and section 148(1) of this Act apply and why it is of that opinion,
(cb) where the sentence consists of or includes a youth rehabilitation order with fostering, state that it is of the opinion that section 1(4)(a) to (c) of the Criminal Justice and Immigration Act 2008 and section 148(1) of this Act apply and why it is of that opinion,".

(3) After subsection (4) insert –

"(4A) Subsection (4B) applies where –

(a) a court passes a custodial sentence in respect of an offence on an offender who is aged under 18, and
(b) the circumstances are such that the court must, in complying with subsection (1)(a), make the statement referred to in subsection (2)(b).

(4B) That statement must include –

(a) a statement by the court that it is of the opinion that a sentence consisting of or including a youth rehabilitation order with intensive supervision and surveillance or fostering cannot be justified for the offence, and
(b) a statement by the court why it is of that opinion."

81

In section 176 (interpretation of Chapter 1) –

(a) omit the definition of "youth community order", and

(b) at the end add –

""youth rehabilitation order" has the meaning given by section 1(1) of the Criminal Justice and Immigration Act 2008;
"youth rehabilitation order with fostering" has the meaning given by paragraph 4 of Schedule 1 to that Act;
"youth rehabilitation order with intensive supervision and surveillance" has the meaning given by paragraph 3 of Schedule 1 to that Act."

82

In section 177(1) (community orders) for "16" substitute "18".

83

In section 197(1)(b) (meaning of "the responsible officer"), omit "the offender is aged 18 or over and".

84

In section 199 (unpaid work requirement) –

(a) in subsection (3), for "appropriate officer" substitute "officer of a local probation board or an officer of a provider of probation services", and
(b) omit subsection (4).

85

In section 201 (activity requirement), in subsection (3)(a), for sub-paragraphs (i) and (ii) (but not the "and" immediately following sub-paragraph (ii)) substitute "an officer of a local probation board or an officer of a provider of probation services".

86

In section 202 (programme requirement), in subsection (4)(a), for sub-paragraphs (i) and (ii) (but not the "and" immediately following sub-paragraph (ii)) substitute "by an officer of a local probation board or an officer of a provider of probation services".

87

In section 203(2), for paragraphs (a) and (b) substitute "an officer of a local probation board or an officer of a provider of probation services".

88

In section 209(2)(c) (drug rehabilitation requirement), for sub-paragraphs (i) and (ii) substitute "by an officer of a local probation board or an officer of a provider of probation services, and".

89

In section 211 (periodic review of drug rehabilitation requirement), omit subsection (5).

90

In section 214 (attendance centre requirement), after subsection (6) add –

"(7) A requirement to attend at an attendance centre for any period on any occasion operates as a requirement, during that period, to engage in occupation, or receive instruction, under the supervision of and in accordance with instructions given by, or under the authority of, the officer in charge of the centre, whether at the centre or elsewhere."

91

In section 217(1)(b) (requirement to avoid conflict with religious beliefs etc.), for "school or any other" substitute "any".

92

In section 221(2) (provision of attendance centres) –

(a) omit "or" at the end of paragraph (a),
(b) after that paragraph insert –

"(aa) attendance centre requirements of youth rehabilitation orders, within the meaning of Part 1 of the Criminal Justice and Immigration Act 2008,", and

(c) omit paragraph (b).

93

In section 222(1)(e) (rules), after "attendance centre requirements" insert ", or to attendance centre requirements imposed by youth rehabilitation orders under Part 1 of the Criminal Justice and Immigration Act 2008,".

94

Omit section 279 (drug treatment and testing requirement in action plan order or supervision order).

95

In section 330(5)(a) (orders subject to the affirmative resolution procedure), omit the entry relating to section 161(7).

96

In Schedule 8 (breach, revocation or amendment of community order), omit paragraphs 12, 15 and 17(5) (powers of magistrates' court in case of offender reaching 18).

97

Omit Schedule 24 (drug treatment and testing requirement in action plan order or supervision order).

Violent Crime Reduction Act 2006 (c. 38)

98

In section 47 of the Violent Crime Reduction Act 2006 (power to search persons in attendance centres for weapons), in the definition of "relevant person" in subsection (11), for paragraph (b) substitute –

"(b) a youth rehabilitation order under Part 1 of the Criminal Justice and Immigration Act 2008;".

Offender Management Act 2007 (c. 21)

99

In section 1(4) of the Offender Management Act 2007 (meaning of "the probation purposes"), in the definition of "community order" –

(a) after paragraph (a) insert –

"(aa) a youth rehabilitation order within the meaning of Part 1 of the Criminal Justice and

Immigration Act 2008 (see section 1 of that Act);", and

(b) after paragraph (b) insert –

"(c) a youth community order within the meaning of that Act (as it applies to offences committed before section 1 of the Criminal Justice and Immigration Act 2008 comes into force)".

PART 2
RELATED AMENDMENTS

Children and Young Persons Act 1933 (c. 12)

100

In section 49 of the Children and Young Persons Act 1933 (restrictions on reports of proceedings in which children or young persons are concerned), in subsection (13)(g)(ii), for "the Powers of Criminal Courts (Sentencing) Act 2000" substitute "Part 1 or 2 of Schedule 15 to the Criminal Justice Act 2003".

Children and Young Persons Act 1969 (c. 54)

101

(1) Section 32 of the Children and Young Persons Act 1969 (detention of absentees) is amended as follows.

(2) In subsection (1A) –

(a) in paragraph (a), after "under" insert "paragraph 4(1)(a) of Schedule 1 or paragraph 6(4)(a) of Schedule 8 to the Powers of Criminal Courts (Sentencing) Act 2000 or",

(b) in paragraph (b) (as substituted by paragraph 17(2)(b) of this Schedule), in sub-paragraph (ii), after "under" insert "paragraph 4 of Schedule 1 or paragraph 6 of Schedule 8 to the Powers of Criminal Courts (Sentencing) Act 2000 or".

(3) In subsection (1C) (as substituted by paragraph 17(3) of this Schedule) –

(a) in paragraph (a), after "under" insert "paragraph 4(1)(a) of Schedule 1 or paragraph 6(4)(a) of Schedule 8 to the Powers of Criminal Courts (Sentencing) Act 2000 or", and

(b) in paragraph (c), after "under" insert "paragraph 4(6) of Schedule 1 or paragraph 6(8) of Schedule 8 to the Powers of Criminal Courts (Sentencing) Act 2000 or".

Bail Act 1976 (c. 63)

102

In section 4(3) of the Bail Act 1976 (general right to bail of accused persons and others), before paragraph (a) (as substituted by paragraph 23(b) of this Schedule) insert –

"(za) Schedule 1 to the Powers of Criminal Courts (Sentencing) Act 2000 (referral orders: referral back to appropriate court),

(zb) Schedule 8 to that Act (breach of reparation order),".

Magistrates' Courts Act 1980 (c. 43)

103

In Schedule 6A to the Magistrates' Courts Act 1980 (fines that may be altered under section 143), at the end insert –

| 'In Schedule 8, paragraph 2(2)(a)(i) (failure to comply with reparation order | £1,000'. |

Child Abduction Act 1984 (c. 37)

104

In paragraph 2(1) of the Schedule to the Child Abduction Act 1984 (modifications of section 1 for children in certain cases) –

(a) in paragraph (a), after "under" insert "paragraph 4(1)(a) of Schedule 1 or paragraph 6(4)(a) of Schedule 8 to the Powers of Criminal Courts (Sentencing) Act 2000 or", and

(b) in paragraph (b), before "or" (as inserted by paragraph 31(b) of this Schedule) insert ", paragraph 4 of Schedjule 1 or paragraph 6 of Schedule 8 to the Powers of Criminal Courts (Sentencing) Act 2000".

Children Act 1989 (c. 41)

105

In section 21(2)(c) of the Children Act 1989 (provision of accommodation for children in police protection or detention or on remand, etc.), after sub-paragraph (i) insert –

"(ia) remanded to accommodation provided by or on behalf of a local authority by virtue of paragraph 4 of Schedule 1 or paragraph 6 of Schedule 8 to the Powers of Criminal Courts (Sentencing) Act 2000 (breach etc. of referral orders and reparation orders);".

Powers of Criminal Courts (Sentencing) Act 2000 (c. 6)

106

The Powers of Criminal Courts (Sentencing) Act 2000 has effect subject to the following amendments.

107

In Schedule 1 (youth offender panels: further court proceedings), after paragraph 9 insert –

"Power to adjourn hearing and remand offender

9ZA

(1) This paragraph applies to any hearing relating to an offender held by a youth court or other magistrates' court in proceedings under this Part of this Schedule.

"In Schedule 8, paragraph 2(2)(a)(i) (failure to comply with reparation order) £1,000".

(2) The court may adjourn the hearing, and, where it does so, may –

(a) direct that the offender be released forthwith, or
(b) remand the offender.

(3) Where the court remands the offender under sub-paragraph (2) –

(a) it must fix the time and place at which the hearing is to be resumed, and
(b) that time and place must be the time and place at which the offender is required to appear or be brought before the court by virtue of the remand.

(4) Where the court adjourns the hearing under sub-paragraph (2) but does not remand the offender –

(a) it may fix the time and place at which the hearing is to be resumed, but
(b) if it does not do so, it must not resume the hearing unless it is satisfied that the persons mentioned in sub-paragraph (5) have had adequate notice of the time and place for the resumed hearing.

(5) The persons referred to in sub-paragraph (4)(b) are –

(a) the offender,
(b) if the offender is aged under 14, a parent or guardian of the offender, and
(c) a member of the youth offending team specified under section 18(1)(a) as responsible for implementing the order.

(6) If a local authority has parental responsibility for an offender who is in its care or provided with accommodation by it in the exercise of any social services functions, the reference in sub-paragraph (5)(b) to a parent or guardian of the offender is to be read as a reference to that authority.

(7) In sub-paragraph (6) –

"local authority" has the same meaning as it has in Part 1 of the Criminal Justice and Immigration Act 2008 by virtue of section 7 of that Act,
"parental responsibility" has the same meaning as it has in the Children Act 1989 by virtue of section 3 of that Act, and
"social services functions" has the same meaning as it has in the Local Authority Social Services Act 1970 by virtue of section 1A of that Act.

(8) The powers of a magistrates' court under this paragraph may be exercised by a single justice of the peace, notwithstanding anything in the Magistrates' Courts Act 1980.

(9) This paragraph –

(a) applies to any hearing in proceedings under this Part of this Schedule in place of section 10 of the Magistrates' Courts Act 1980 (adjournment of trial) where that section would otherwise apply, but
(b) is not to be taken to affect the application of that section to hearings of any other description."

108

(1) Schedule 8 (breach, revocation and amendment of action plan orders and reparation orders) is amended as follows.

(2) Omit paragraph 1 and the heading before that paragraph.

(3) In paragraph 2(1), for "the appropriate court," substitute –

"(a) a youth court acting in the local justice area in which the offender resides, or

(b) if it is not known where the offender resides, a youth court acting in the local justice area for the time being named in the order in pursuance of section 74(4) of this Act,".

(4) In paragraph 5 –

(a) in sub-paragraphs (1) and (3), for "appropriate court" substitute "relevant court", and
(b) at the end insert –

"(4) In this paragraph, "the relevant court" means –

(a) a youth court acting in the local justice area for the time being named in the order in pursuance of section 74(4) of this Act, or
(b) in the case of an application made both under this paragraph and under paragraph 2(1), the court mentioned in paragraph 2(1)."

(5) In paragraph 6 –

(a) in sub-paragraph (1), for "the appropriate court" substitute "a court",
(b) in sub-paragraph (4), for "the appropriate court" substitute "the court before which the warrant directs the offender to be brought ("the relevant court")",
(c) in sub-paragraph (5), for "the appropriate court" substitute "the relevant court", and
(d) in sub-paragraph (7), for "the appropriate court", in each place it occurs, substitute "the relevant court".

(6) After paragraph 6 insert –

"Power to adjourn hearing and remand offender

6A

(1) This paragraph applies to any hearing relating to an offender held by a youth court in any proceedings under this Schedule.

(2) The court may adjourn the hearing, and, where it does so, may –

(a) direct that the offender be released forthwith, or
(b) remand the offender.

(3) Where the court remands the offender under sub-paragraph (2) –

(a) it must fix the time and place at which the hearing is to be resumed, and
(b) that time and place must be the time and place at which the offender is required to appear or be brought before the court by virtue of the remand.

(4) Where the court adjourns the hearing under sub-paragraph (2) but does not remand the offender –

(a) it may fix the time and place at which the hearing is to be resumed, but
(b) if it does not do so, it must not resume the hearing unless it is satisfied that the persons mentioned in sub-paragraph (5) have had adequate notice of the time and place for the resumed hearing.

(5) The persons referred to in sub-paragraph (4)(b) are –

(a) the offender,
(b) if the offender is aged under 14, a parent or guardian of the offender, and
(c) the responsible officer.

(6) If a local authority has parental responsibility for an offender who is in its care or provided with accommodation by it in the exercise of any social services functions, the reference in sub-paragraph (5)(b) to a parent or guardian of the offender is to be read as a reference to that authority.

(7) In sub-paragraph (6) –

"local authority" has the same meaning as it has in Part 1 of the Criminal Justice and Immigration Act 2008 by virtue of section 7 of that Act,
"parental responsibility" has the same meaning as it has in the Children Act 1989 by virtue of section 3 of that Act, and
"social services functions" has the same meaning as it has in the Local Authority Social Services Act 1970 by virtue of section 1A of that Act.

(8) The powers of a youth court under this paragraph may be exercised by a single justice of the peace, notwithstanding anything in the Magistrates' Courts Act 1980.

(9) This paragraph –

(a) applies to any hearing in any proceedings under this Schedule in place of section 10 of the Magistrates' Courts Act 1980 (adjournment of trial) where that section would otherwise apply, but
(b) is not to be taken to affect the application of that section to hearings of any other description."

Criminal Justice Act 2003 (c. 44)

109

In Schedule 8 to the Criminal Justice Act 2003 (breach, revocation or amendment of community order), after paragraph 25 insert –

"25A

(1) This paragraph applies to any hearing relating to an offender held by a magistrates' court in any proceedings under this Schedule.

(2) The court may adjourn the hearing, and, where it does so, may –

(a) direct that the offender be released forthwith, or
(b) remand the offender.

(3) Where the court remands the offender under sub-paragraph (2) –

   (a) it must fix the time and place at which the hearing is to be resumed, and
   (b) that time and place must be the time and place at which the offender is required to appear or be brought before the court by virtue of the remand.

(4) Where the court adjourns the hearing under sub-paragraph (2) but does not remand the offender –

   (a) it may fix the time and place at which the hearing is to be resumed, but
   (b) if it does not do so, it must not resume the hearing unless it is satisfied that the offender and the responsible officer have had adequate notice of the time and place for the resumed hearing.

(5) The powers of a magistrates' court under this paragraph may be exercised by a single justice of the peace, notwithstanding anything in the Magistrates' Courts Act 1980.

(6) This paragraph –

   (a) applies to any hearing in any proceedings under this Schedule in place of section 10 of the Magistrates' Courts Act 1980 (adjournment of trial) where that section would otherwise apply, but
   (b) is not to be taken to affect the application of that section to hearings of any other description."

Schedule 5

Section 13(2)

Offences Specified For The Purposes Of Sections 225(3a) And 227(2a) Of Criminal Justice Act 2003

"Schedule 15a
Offences Specified For The Purposes Of Sections 225(3a) And 227(2a)

PART 1
OFFENCES UNDER THE LAW OF ENGLAND AND WALES

1

Murder.

2

Manslaughter.

3

An offence under section 4 of the Offences against the Person Act 1861 (c. 100) (soliciting murder).

4

An offence under section 18 of that Act (wounding with intent to cause grievous bodily harm).

5

An offence under section 1 of the Sexual Offences Act 1956 (c. 69) (rape).

6

An offence under section 5 of that Act (intercourse with a girl under 13).

7

An offence under section 16 of the Firearms Act 1968 (c. 27) (possession of firearm with intent to endanger life).

8

An offence under section 17(1) of that Act (use of a firearm to resist arrest).

9

An offence under section 18 of that Act (carrying a firearm with criminal intent).

10

An offence of robbery under section 8 of the Theft Act 1968 (c. 60) where, at some time during the commission of the offence, the offender had in his possession a firearm or an imitation firearm within the meaning of the Firearms Act 1968.

11

An offence under section 1 of the Sexual Offences Act 2003 (c. 42) (rape).

12

An offence under section 2 of that Act (assault by penetration).

13

An offence under section 4 of that Act (causing a person to engage in sexual activity without consent) if the offender was liable on conviction on indictment to imprisonment for life.

14

An offence under section 5 of that Act (rape of a child under 13).

15

An offence under section 6 of that Act (assault of a child under 13 by penetration).

16

An offence under section 8 of that Act (causing or inciting a child under 13 to engage in sexual activity) if the offender was liable on conviction on indictment to imprisonment for life.

17

An offence under section 30 of that Act (sexual activity with a person with a mental disorder impeding choice) if the offender was liable on conviction on indictment to imprisonment for life.

18

An offence under section 31 of that Act (causing or inciting a person with a mental disorder to engage in sexual activity) if the offender was liable on conviction on indictment to imprisonment for life.

19

An offence under section 34 of that Act (inducement, threat or deception to procure sexual activity with a person with a mental disorder) if the offender was liable on conviction on indictment to imprisonment for life.

20

An offence under section 35 of that Act (causing a person with a mental disorder to engage in or agree to engage in sexual activity by inducement etc.) if the offender was liable on conviction on indictment to imprisonment for life.

21

An offence under section 47 of that Act (paying for sexual services of a child) if the offender was liable on conviction on indictment to imprisonment for life.

22

An offence under section 62 of that Act (committing an offence with intent to commit a sexual offence) if the offender was liable on conviction on indictment to imprisonment for life.

23

(1) An attempt to commit an offence specified in the preceding paragraphs of this Part of this Schedule ("a listed offence").

(2) Conspiracy to commit a listed offence.

(3) Incitement to commit a listed offence.

(4) An offence under Part 2 of the Serious Crime Act 2007 in relation to which a listed offence is the offence (or one of the offences) which the person intended or believed would be committed.

(5) Aiding, abetting, counselling or procuring the commission of a listed offence.

PART 2
OFFENCES UNDER THE LAW OF SCOTLAND

24

Murder.

25

Culpable homicide.

26

Rape.

27

Assault where the assault –

(a) is aggravated because it caused severe injury or endangered the victim's life, or
(b) was carried out with intent to rape or ravish the victim.

28

Sodomy where the person against whom the offence was committed did not consent.

29

Lewd, indecent or libidinous behaviour or practices.

30

Robbery, where, at some time during the commission of the offence, the offender had in his possession a firearm or an imitation firearm within the meaning of the Firearms Act 1968 (c. 27).

31

An offence under section 16 of the Firearms Act 1968 (possession of firearm with intent to endanger life).

32

An offence under section 17(1) of that Act (use of a firearm to resist arrest).

33

An offence under section 18 of that Act (carrying a firearm with criminal intent).

34

An offence under section 5(1) of the Criminal Law (Consolidation) (Scotland) Act 1995 (c. 39) (unlawful intercourse with a girl under 13).

35

(1) An attempt to commit an offence specified in the preceding paragraphs of this Part of this Schedule ("a listed offence").

(2) Conspiracy to commit a listed offence.

(3) Incitement to commit a listed offence.

(4) Aiding, abetting, counselling or procuring the commission of a listed offence.

PART 3
OFFENCES UNDER THE LAW OF NORTHERN IRELAND

36

Murder.

37

Manslaughter.

38

Rape.

39

An offence under section 4 of the Offences against the Person Act 1861 (c. 100) (soliciting murder).

40

An offence under section 18 of that Act (wounding with intent to cause grievous bodily harm).

41

An offence under section 4 of the Criminal Law Amendment Act 1885 (c. 69) (intercourse with a girl under 14).

42

An offence of robbery under section 8 of the Theft Act (Northern Ireland) 1969 (c. 16) where, at some time during the commission of the offence, the offender had in his possession a firearm or an imitation firearm within the meaning of the Firearms (Northern Ireland) Order 2004 (S.I. 2004/702 (N.I.3)).

43

An offence under Article 17 of the Firearms (Northern Ireland) Order 1981 (S.I. 1981/155 (N.I.2)) (possession of firearm with intent to endanger life).

44

An offence under Article 18(1) of that Order (use of a firearm to resist arrest).

45

An offence under Article 19 of that Order (carrying a firearm with criminal intent).

46

An offence under Article 58 of the Firearms (Northern Ireland) Order 2004 (possession of firearm with intent to endanger life).

47

An offence under Article 59 of that Order (use of a firearm to resist arrest).

48

An offence under Article 60 of that Order (carrying a firearm with criminal intent).

49

An offence under section 47 of the Sexual Offences Act 2003 (paying for sexual services of a child) if the offender was liable on conviction on indictment to imprisonment for life.

50

(1) An attempt to commit an offence specified in the preceding paragraphs of this Part of this Schedule ("a listed offence").

(2) Conspiracy to commit a listed offence.

(3) Incitement to commit a listed offence.

(4) An offence under Part 2 of the Serious Crime Act 2007 in relation to which a listed offence is the offence (or one of the offences) which the person intended or believed would be committed.

(5) Aiding, abetting, counselling or procuring the commission of a listed offence.

PART 4
OFFENCES UNDER SERVICE LAW

51

An offence under section 70 of the Army Act 1955, section 70 of the Air Force Act 1955 or section 42 of the Naval Discipline Act 1957 as respects which the corresponding civil offence (within the meaning of the Act in question) is an offence specified in Part 1 of this Schedule.

52

(1) An offence under section 42 of the Armed Forces Act 2006 as respects which the corresponding offence under the law of England and Wales (within the meaning given by that section) is an offence specified in Part 1 of this Schedule.

(2) Section 48 of the Armed Forces Act 2006 (attempts, conspiracy etc.) applies for the purposes of this paragraph as if the reference in subsection (3)(b) of that section to any of the following provisions of that Act were a reference to this paragraph.

PART 5
INTERPRETATION

53

In this Schedule, "imprisonment for life" includes custody for life and detention for life."

Schedule 6

Section 23

Credit For Period Of Remand On Bail: Transitional Provisions

1

A period specified under paragraph 2 is to be treated as being a relevant period within the meaning of section 67 of the Criminal Justice Act 1967 (c. 80).

2

(1) This paragraph applies where –

    (a)   a court sentences an offender to a term of imprisonment for an offence that was committed before 4th April 2005,

    (b)   the offender was remanded on bail by a court in the course of or in connection with proceedings for the offence, or any related offence, after the coming into force of paragraph 1, and

    (c)   the offender's bail was subject to a qualifying curfew condition and an electronic monitoring condition ("the relevant conditions").

(2) Subject to sub-paragraph (4), the court must by order specify the credit period.

(3) The "credit period" is the number days represented by half of the sum of –

    (a)   the day on which the offender's bail was first subject to conditions that, had they applied throughout the day in question, would have been relevant conditions, and

    (b)   the number of other days on which the offender's bail was subject to those conditions (excluding the last day on which it was so subject), rounded up to the nearest whole number.

(4) Sub-paragraph (2) does not apply if and to the extent that –

    (a)   rules made by the Secretary of State so provide, or (b) it is in the opinion of the court just in all the circumstances not to give a direction under that subsection.

(5) Where as a result of paragraph (a) or (b) of sub-paragraph (4) the court does not specify the credit period under sub-paragraph (2), it may in accordance with either of those paragraphs by order specify a lesser period.

(6) Rules under sub-paragraph (4)(a) may, in particular, make provision in relation to –

    (a)   sentences of imprisonment for consecutive terms;

    (b)   sentences of imprisonment for terms which are wholly or partly concurrent;

    (c)   periods during which a person granted bail subject to the relevant conditions is also subject to electronic monitoring required by an order made by a court or the Secretary of State.

(7) In considering whether it is of the opinion mentioned in sub-paragraph (4)(b) the court must, in particular, take into account whether or not the offender has, at any time whilst on bail subject to the relevant conditions, broken either or both of them.

(8) Where the court specifies a period under sub-paragraph (2) or (5) it shall state in open court –

    (a)   the number of days on which the offender was subject to the relevant conditions, and

    (b)   the number of days in the period specified.

(9) Sub-paragraph (10) applies where the court –

    (a)   does not specify the credit period under sub-paragraph (2) but does specify a lesser period under sub-paragraph (5), or

    (b)   does not specify a period under either sub-paragraph (2) or (5).

(10) The court shall state in open court –

(a) that its decision is in accordance with rules made under paragraph (a) of sub-paragraph (4), or
(b) that it is of the opinion mentioned in paragraph (b) of that sub-paragraph and what the circumstances are.

(11) In this paragraph –

"electronic monitoring condition" means any electronic monitoring requirements imposed under section 3(6ZAA) of the Bail Act 1976 (c. 63) for the purpose of securing the electronic monitoring of a person's compliance with a qualifying curfew condition;

"qualifying curfew condition" means a condition of bail which requires the person granted bail to remain at one or more specified places for a total of not less than 9 hours in any given day; and

"related offence" means an offence, other than the offence for which the sentence is imposed ("offence A"), with which the offender was charged and the charge for which was founded on the same facts or evidence as offence A.

Schedule 7

Section 39(6)

Youth Default Orders: Modification Of Provisions Applying To Youth Rehabilitation Orders

1 General

Any reference to the offender is, in relation to a youth default order, to be read as a reference to the person in default; and any reference to the time when the offender is convicted is to be read as a reference to the time when the order is made.

2 Unpaid work requirement

(1) In its application to a youth default order, paragraph 10 of Schedule 1 (unpaid work requirement) is modified as follows.

(2) Sub-paragraph (2) has effect as if for paragraphs (a) and (b) there were substituted –

"(a) not less than 20, and
(b) in the case of an amount in default which is specified in the first column of the following Table, not more than the number of hours set out opposite that amount in the second column.

TABLE

Amount	Number of hours
An amount not exceeding £200	40
An amount exceeding £200 but not exceeding £500	60
An amount exceeding £500	100".

(3) Sub-paragraph (7) has effect as if after "Unless revoked" there were inserted "(or section 39(7)(a) applies)".

3 Attendance centre requirement

(1) In its application to a youth default order, paragraph 12 of Schedule 1 (attendance centre requirement) is modified as follows.

(2) Sub-paragraph (2) has effect as if –

    (a)   in paragraph (a), for the words following "conviction" there were substituted "must be, in the case of an amount in default which is specified in the first column of the following Table, not more than the number of hours set out opposite that amount in the second column.

TABLE

Amount	Number of hours
An amount not exceeding £250	8
An amount exceeding £250 but not exceeding £500	14

    (b)   in paragraph (b), for the words following "conviction" there were substituted "must be, in the case of an amount in default which is specified in the first column of the following Table, not more than the number of hours set out opposite that amount in the second column.

TABLE

Amount	Number of hours
An amount not exceeding £250	8
An amount exceeding £250 but not exceeding £500	14
An amount exceeding £500	24",

    (c)   in paragraph (c), for "must not be more than 12" there were substituted "must be, in the case of an amount in default which is specified in the first column of the following Table, not more than the number of hours set out opposite that amount in the second column.

TABLE

Amount	Number of hours
An amount not exceeding £250	8
An amount exceeding £250 but not exceeding £500	10
An amount exceeding £500	12"

4 Curfew requirement

(1) In its application to a youth default order, paragraph 14 of Schedule 1 (curfew requirement) is modified as follows.

(2) That paragraph has effect as if after sub-paragraph (2) there were inserted –

"(2A) In the case of an amount in default which is specified in the first column of the following Table, the number of days on which the person in default is subject to the curfew requirement must not exceed the number of days set out opposite that amount in the second column.

Amount	Number of days
An amount not exceeding £200	20
An amount exceeding £200 but not exceeding £500	30
An amount exceeding £500 but not exceeding £1,000	60
An amount exceeding £1,000 but not exceeding £2,000	90
An amount exceeding £2,000	180"

5 Enforcement, revocation and amendment of youth default order

(1) In its application to a youth default order, Schedule 2 (breach, revocation or amendment of youth rehabilitation orders) is modified as follows.

(2) Any reference to the offence in respect of which the youth rehabilitation order was made is to be read as a reference to the default in respect of which the youth default order was made.

(3) Accordingly, any power of the court to revoke a youth rehabilitation order and deal with the offender for the offence is to be taken to be a power to revoke the youth default order and deal with him in any way in which the court which made the youth default order could deal with him for his default in paying the sum in question.

(4) Paragraph 2 has effect as if for paragraphs (a) and (b) there were substituted "as having been made by a magistrates' court".

(5) The following provisions are omitted –

- (a) paragraph 6(2)(a) and (b)(i), (5) and (12) to (16),
- (b) paragraph 11(5),
- (c) paragraph 18(7), and
- (d) paragraph 19(3).

6 Power to alter amount of money or number of hours or days

The Secretary of State may by order amend paragraph 2, 3 or 4 by substituting for any reference to an amount of money or a number of hours or days there specified a reference to such other amount or number as may be specified in the order.

7 Transfer of youth default order to Northern Ireland

(1) In its application to a youth default order, Schedule 3 is modified as follows.

(2) Paragraph 9 has effect as if, after sub-paragraph (2) there were inserted –

"(3) Nothing in sub-paragraph (1) affects the application of section 39(7) to a youth default order made or amended in accordance with paragraph 1 or 2."

(3) Paragraph 12 has effect as if, after paragraph (b) there were inserted –

"(bb) any power to impose a fine on the offender".

Schedule 8

Section 47

Appeals In Criminal Cases

PART 1
AMENDMENTS OF CRIMINAL APPEAL ACT 1968

1

The Criminal Appeal Act 1968 (c. 19) has effect subject to the following amendments.

2 Time limit on grant of certificates of fitness for appeal

In section 1 (appeal against conviction), in subsection (2)(b) after "if" insert ", within 28 days from the date of the conviction,".

3

In section 11 (supplementary provisions as to appeal against sentence), in subsection (1A) –

(a) after "if" insert ", within 28 days from the date on which the sentence was passed,", and
(b) for "the sentence" substitute "it".

4

In section 12 (appeal against verdict of not guilty on ground of insanity), in subsection (1)(b) after "if" insert ", within 28 days from the date of the verdict,".

5

In section 15 (appeal against finding of disability), in subsection (2)(b) after "if" insert ", within 28 days from the date of the finding that the accused did the act or made the omission charged,".

6 Powers of Court to substitute different sentence

(1) Section 4 (sentence when appeal allowed on part of indictment) is amended as follows.

(2) For the heading substitute "Power to re-sentence where appellant remains convicted of related offences".

(3) For subsection (1) substitute –

"(1) This section applies where –

(a) two or more related sentences are passed,
(b) the Court of Appeal allow an appeal against conviction in respect of one or more of the offences for which the sentences were passed ("the related offences"), but
(c) the appellant remains convicted of one or more of those offences."

(4) In subsection (2) –

(a) for "in respect of any count on which the appellant remains convicted" substitute "in respect of any related offence of which the appellant remains convicted", and
(b) omit "for the offence of which he remains convicted on that count".

(5) In subsection (3) –

(a) for "on the indictment as a whole" substitute "(taken as a whole) for all the related offences of which he remains convicted", and
(b) for "for all offences of which he was convicted on the indictment" substitute "for all the related offences".

(6) After subsection (3) insert –

"(4) For the purposes of subsection (1)(a), two or more sentences are related if –
  (a) they are passed on the same day,
  (b) they are passed on different days but the court in passing any one of them states that it is treating that one together with the other or others as substantially one sentence, or
  (c) they are passed on different days but in respect of counts on the same indictment.

(5) Where –
  (a) two or more sentences are related to each other by virtue of subsection (4)(a) or (b), and
  (b) any one or more of those sentences is related to one or more other sentences by virtue of subsection (4)(c), all the sentences are to be treated as related for the purposes of subsection (1)(a)."

7 Interim hospital orders

The following provisions (which relate to the effect of interim hospital orders made by the Court of Appeal) are omitted –

(a) section 6(5) and the definition of interim hospital order in section 6(7),
(b) section 11(6),
(c) section 14(5) and the definition of interim hospital order in section 14(7), and
(d) section 16B(3).

8

Before section 31 (but after the cross-heading preceding it) insert –

"30A Effect of interim hospital orders

(1) This section applies where the Court of Appeal –
  (a) make an interim hospital order by virtue of any provision of this Part, or
  (b) renew an interim hospital order so made.

(2) The court below shall be treated for the purposes of section 38(7) of the Mental Health Act 1983 (absconding offenders) as the court that made the order."

9

In section 31 (powers of Court which are exercisable by single judge) after subsection (2) insert –

"(2ZA) The power of the Court of Appeal to renew an interim hospital order made by them by virtue of any provision of this Part may be exercised by a single judge in the same manner as it may be exercised by the Court."

10 Evidence

(1) Section 23 (evidence) is amended as follows.

(2) In subsection (1) after "an appeal" insert ", or an application for leave to appeal,".

(3) In that subsection, for paragraph (b) substitute –

"(b) order any witness to attend for examination and be examined before the Court (whether or not he was called in the proceedings from which the appeal lies); and".

(4) After subsection (1) insert –

"(1A) The power conferred by subsection (1)(a) may be exercised so as to require the production of any document, exhibit or other thing mentioned in that subsection to –
  (a) the Court;
  (b) the appellant;
  (c) the respondent."

(5) In subsection (4) after "an appeal" insert ", or an application for leave to appeal,".

(6) After subsection (5) insert –

"(6) In this section, "respondent" includes a person who will be a respondent if leave to appeal is granted."

11 Powers of single judge

(1) Section 31 (powers of Court of Appeal which are exercisable by single judge) is amended as follows.

(2) In the heading, omit "under Part 1".

(3) After subsection (2C) insert –

"(2D) The power of the Court of Appeal to grant leave to appeal under section 9(11) of the Criminal Justice Act 1987 may be exercised by a single judge in the same manner as it may be exercised by the Court.

(2E) The power of the Court of Appeal to grant leave to appeal under section 35(1) of the Criminal Procedure and Investigations Act 1996 may be exercised by a single judge in the same manner as it may be exercised by the Court."

12 Appeals against procedural directions

In section 31C (appeals against procedural directions), omit subsections (1) and (2).

13 Detention of defendant pending appeal to Supreme Court

(1) Section 37 (detention of defendant on appeal by Crown) is amended as follows.

(2) In subsection (2) for the words from "may make" to the end substitute "shall make –

    (a)   an order providing for his detention, or directing that he shall not be released except on bail (which may be granted by the Court as under section 36 above), so long as the appeal is pending, or

    (b)   an order that he be released without bail."

(3) After subsection (2) insert –

"(2A) The Court may make an order under subsection (2)(b) only if they think that it is in the interests of justice that the defendant should not be liable to be detained as a result of the decision of the Supreme Court on the appeal."

(4) In subsection (3) for "this section" substitute "subsection (2)(a)".

(5) In subsection (4) for "this section" (in each place where it occurs) substitute "subsection (2)(a)".

(6) In subsection (4A) for "this section" (in the first place where it occurs) substitute "subsection (2)(a)".

(7) For subsection (5) substitute –

"(5) The defendant shall not be liable to be detained again as a result of the decision of the Supreme Court on the appeal if –

    (a)   the Court of Appeal have made an order under subsection (2)(b), or

    (b)   the Court have made an order under subsection (2)(a) but the order has ceased to have effect by virtue of subsection (3) or the defendant has been released or discharged by virtue of subsection (4) or (4A)."

PART 2
AMENDMENTS OF CRIMINAL APPEAL (NORTHERN IRELAND) ACT 1980

14

The Criminal Appeal (Northern Ireland) Act 1980 (c. 47) has effect subject to the following amendments.

15 Time limit on grant of certificates of fitness for appeal

In section 1 (appeal against conviction), in paragraph (b) after "if" insert ", within 28 days from the date of the conviction,".

16

In section 12 (appeal against finding of not guilty on ground of insanity), in subsection (1)(b) after "if" insert ", within 28 days from the date of the finding,".

17

In section 13A (appeal against finding of unfitness to be tried), in subsection (2)(b) after "if" insert ", within 28 days from the date of the finding that the person did the act or made the omission charged,".

18 Powers of Court to substitute different sentence

(1) Section 4 (alteration of sentence on appeal against conviction) is amended as follows.

(2) For subsection (1) substitute –

"(1) Subsection (1A) applies where –

    (a)   two or more related sentences are passed,

    (b)   the Court of Appeal allows an appeal against conviction in respect of one or more of the offences for which the sentences were passed ("the related offences"), but

    (c)   the appellant remains convicted of one or more of those offences.

(1A) The Court may, in respect of any related offence of which the appellant remains convicted, pass such sentence, in substitution for the sentence passed thereon at the trial, as it thinks proper and is authorised by law."

(3) After subsection (2) insert –

"(3) For the purposes of subsection (1)(a), two or more sentences are related if –

    (a)   they are passed on the same day,

    (b)   they are passed on different days but the court in passing any one of them states that it is treating that one together with the other or others as substantially one sentence, or

    (c)   they are passed on different days but in respect of counts on the same indictment.

(4) Where –

    (a)   two or more sentences are related to each other by virtue of subsection (3)(a) or (b), and

    (b)   any one or more of those sentences is related to one or more other sentences by virtue of subsection (3)(c),

all the sentences are to be treated as related for the purposes of subsection (1)(a)."

19 Interim hospital orders

Section 10(6) (effect of interim hospital orders made by Court of Appeal) is omitted.

20

(1) For the cross-heading preceding section 30 substitute –

"Supplementary".

(2) Before section 30 (but after the cross-heading preceding it) insert –

"29A Effect of interim hospital orders

(1) This section applies where the Court of Appeal –

(a) makes an interim hospital order by virtue of any provision of this Part, or
(b) renews an interim hospital order so made.

(2) The Crown Court shall be treated for the purposes of Article 45(6) of the Mental Health Order (absconding offenders) as the court that made the order."

21

In section 45 (powers of Court which are exercisable by single judge) after subsection (3) insert –

"(3ZA) The power of the Court of Appeal to renew an interim hospital order made by it by virtue of any provision of this Act may be exercised by a single judge in the same manner as it may be exercised by the Court."

22 Evidence

(1) Section 25 (evidence) is amended as follows.

(2) In subsection (1) after "an appeal" insert ", or an application for leave to appeal,".

(3) In that subsection, for paragraph (b) substitute –

"(b) order any witness to attend and be examined before the Court (whether or not he was called at the trial); and".

(4) After subsection (1) insert –

"(1A) The power conferred by subsection (1)(a) may be exercised so as to require the production of any document, exhibit or other thing mentioned in that subsection to –

(a) the Court;
(b) the appellant;
(c) the respondent."

(5) After subsection (3) insert –

"(4) In this section, "respondent" includes a person who will be a respondent if leave to appeal is granted."

23

In section 26 (additional powers of Court), in subsection (1) after "an appeal" insert ", or an application for leave to appeal,".

24 Detention of defendant pending appeal to Supreme Court

(1) Section 36 (detention of defendant on appeal by Crown) is amended as follows.

(2) In subsection (1) for the words from "may make" to the end substitute "shall make –

(a) an order providing for his detention, or directing that he shall not be released except on bail (which may be granted by the Court as under section 35 above), so long as the appeal is pending, or
(b) an order that he be released without bail."

(3) After subsection (1) insert –

"(1A) The Court may make an order under subsection (1)(b) only if it thinks that it is in the interests of justice that the defendant should not be liable to be detained as a result of the decision of the Supreme Court on the appeal."

(4) In subsection (2) for "subsection (1)" substitute "subsection (1)(a)".

(5) In subsection (3) for "this section" (in each place where it occurs) substitute "subsection (1)(a)".

(6) In subsection (3A) for "this section" (in the first place where it occurs) substitute "subsection (1)(a)".

(7) For subsection (4) substitute –

"(4) The defendant shall not be liable to be detained again as a result of the decision of the Supreme Court on the appeal if –

(a) the Court of Appeal has made an order under subsection (1)(b), or
(b) the Court has made an order under subsection (1)(a) but the order has ceased to have effect by virtue of subsection (2) or the defendant has been released or discharged by virtue of subsection (3) or (3A)."

25 Powers of single judge

(1) Section 45 (powers of Court of Appeal which are exercisable by single judge) is amended as follows.

(2) After subsection (3C) insert –

"(3D) The power of the Court of Appeal to grant leave to appeal under Article 8(11) of the Criminal Justice (Serious Fraud) (Northern Ireland) Order 1988 may be exercised by a single judge in the same manner as it may be exercised by the Court."

PART 3
AMENDMENTS OF OTHER ACTS

26 Detention of defendant pending appeal from High Court to Supreme Court

(1) Section 5 of the Administration of Justice Act 1960 (c. 65) (power to order detention or admission to bail of defendant) is amended as follows.

(2) In subsection (1) for the words from "may make" to the end substitute "shall make –

(a) an order providing for the detention of the defendant, or directing that he shall not be released except on bail (which may be granted by the court as under section 4 above), so long as the appeal is pending, or
(b) an order that the defendant be released without bail."

(3) After subsection (1) insert –

"(1A) The court may make an order under subsection (1)(b) only if it thinks that it is in the interests of justice that the defendant should not be liable to be detained as a result of the decision of the Supreme Court on the appeal."

(4) In subsection (3) for "subsection (1)" substitute "subsection (1)(a)".

(5) In subsection (4) for "the said subsection (1)" substitute "the said subsection (1)(a)".

(6) In subsection (4A) for "the said subsection (1)" substitute "the said subsection (1)(a)".

(7) For subsection (5) substitute –

"(5) The defendant shall not be liable to be detained again as a result of the decision of the Supreme Court on the appeal if –

(a) the court has made an order under subsection (1)(b), or
(b) the court has made an order under subsection (1)(a) but the order has ceased to have effect by virtue of subsection (3) or the defendant has been released or discharged by virtue of subsection (4) or (4A)."

27 Variation of sentences by Crown Court

(1) Section 49 of the Judicature (Northern Ireland) Act 1978 (c. 23) (sentences imposed and other decisions made by Crown Court) is amended as follows.

(2) In subsection (2) –

    (a)   for "28 days" substitute "56 days", and

    (b)   omit the words from "or, where subsection (3) applies," to the end.

(3) After subsection (2) insert –

"(2A) The power conferred by subsection (1) may not be exercised in relation to any sentence or order if an appeal, or an application for leave to appeal, against that sentence or order has been determined."

(4) Subsection (3) is omitted.

28

(1) Section 155 of the Powers of Criminal Courts (Sentencing) Act 2000 (c. 6) (alteration of Crown Court sentence) is amended as follows.

(2) In subsection (1) –

    (a)   for "28 days" substitute "56 days", and

    (b)   omit the words from "or, where subsection (2) below applies," to the end.

(3) After subsection (1) insert –

"(1A) The power conferred by subsection (1) may not be exercised in relation to any sentence or order if an appeal, or an application for leave to appeal, against that sentence or order has been determined."

(4) Subsections (2) and (3) are omitted.

Schedule 9

Section 48

Alternatives To Prosecution For Persons Under 18

1

The Crime and Disorder Act 1998 (c. 37) has effect subject to the following amendments.

2

(1) Section 65 (reprimands and warnings) is amended as follows.

(2) In subsection (1) –

    (a)   for paragraph (b) substitute –
"(b) the constable considers that there is sufficient evidence to charge the offender with the offence;",

    (b)   in paragraph (d), after "an offence" insert "or given a youth conditional caution in respect of an offence", and

    (c)   for paragraph (e) substitute
"(e) the constable does not consider that the offender should be prosecuted or given a youth conditional caution."

(3) In subsection (3)(b) after "to be brought" insert "or a youth conditional caution to be given".

(4) In subsection (6), in paragraph (a)(i) after "to be brought" insert "or a youth conditional caution to be given".

(5) In subsection (7) for "In this section" substitute "In this Chapter".

(6) For subsection (8) (cautions not to be given to children or young persons) substitute –

"(8) No caution, other than a youth conditional caution, shall be given to a child or young person."

3

After section 66 insert –

"Young offenders: youth conditional cautions

66A Youth conditional cautions

(1) An authorised person may give a youth conditional caution to a child or young person ("the offender") if –

(a) the offender has not previously been convicted of an offence, and
(b) each of the five requirements in section 66B is satisfied.

(2) In this Chapter, "youth conditional caution" means a caution which is given in respect of an offence committed by the offender and which has conditions attached to it with which the offender must comply.

(3) The conditions which may be attached to such a caution are those which have one or more of the following objects –

(a) facilitating the rehabilitation of the offender;
(b) ensuring that the offender makes reparation for the offence;
(c) punishing the offender.

(4) The conditions that may be attached to a youth conditional caution include –

(a) (subject to section 66C) a condition that the offender pay a financial penalty;
(b) a condition that the offender attend at a specified place at specified times. "Specified" means specified by a relevant prosecutor.

(5) Conditions attached by virtue of subsection (4)(b) may not require the offender to attend for more than 20 hours in total, not including any attendance required by conditions attached for the purpose of facilitating the offender's rehabilitation.

(6) The Secretary of State may by order amend subsection (5) by substituting a different figure.

(7) In this section, "authorised person" means –

(a) a constable,
(b) an investigating officer, or
(c) a person authorised by a relevant prosecutor for the purposes of this section.

66B The five requirements

(1) The first requirement is that the authorised person has evidence that the offender has committed an offence.

(2) The second requirement is that a relevant prosecutor decides –

(a) that there is sufficient evidence to charge the offender with the offence, and
(b) that a youth conditional caution should be given to the offender in respect of the offence.

(3) The third requirement is that the offender admits to the authorised person that he committed the offence.

(4) The fourth requirement is that the authorised person explains the effect of the youth conditional caution to the offender and warns him that failure to comply with any of the conditions attached to the caution may result in his being prosecuted for the offence.

(5) If the offender is aged 16 or under, the explanation and warning mentioned in subsection (4) must be given in the presence of an appropriate adult.

(6) The fifth requirement is that the offender signs a document which contains –

(a) details of the offence,
(b) an admission by him that he committed the offence,
(c) his consent to being given the youth conditional caution, and
(d) the conditions attached to the caution.

66C Financial penalties

(1) A condition that the offender pay a financial penalty (a "financial penalty condition") may not be attached to a youth conditional caution given in respect of an offence unless the offence is one that is prescribed, or of a description prescribed, in an order made by the Secretary of State.

(2) An order under subsection (1) must prescribe, in respect of each offence or description of offence in the order, the maximum amount of the penalty that may be specified under subsection (5)(a).

(3) The amount that may be prescribed in respect of any offence must not exceed £100.

(4) The Secretary of State may by order amend subsection (3) by substituting a different figure.

(5) Where a financial penalty condition is attached to a youth conditional caution, a relevant prosecutor must also specify –

(a) the amount of the penalty, and
(b) the person to whom the financial penalty is to be paid and how it may be paid.

(6) To comply with the condition, the offender must pay the penalty in accordance with the provision specified under subsection (5)(b).

(7) Where a financial penalty is (in accordance with the provision specified under subsection (5)(b)) paid to a person other than a designated officer for a local justice area, the person to whom it is paid must give the payment to such an officer.

66D Variation of conditions

A relevant prosecutor may, with the consent of the offender, vary the conditions attached to a youth conditional caution by –

(a) modifying or omitting any of the conditions;
(b) adding a condition.

66E Failure to comply with conditions

(1) If the offender fails, without reasonable excuse, to comply with any of the conditions attached to the youth conditional caution, criminal proceedings may be instituted against the person for the offence in question.

(2) The document mentioned in section 66B(6) is to be admissible in such proceedings.

(3) Where such proceedings are instituted, the youth conditional caution is to cease to have effect.

(4) Section 24A(1) of the Criminal Justice Act 2003 ("the 2003 Act") applies in relation to the conditions attached to a youth conditional caution as it applies in relation to the conditions attached to a conditional caution (within the meaning of Part 3 of that Act).

(5) Sections 24A(2) to (9) and 24B of the 2003 Act apply in relation to a person who is arrested under section 24A(1) of that Act by virtue of subsection (4) above as they apply in relation to a person who is arrested under that section for failing to comply with any of the conditions attached to a conditional caution (within the meaning of Part 3 of that Act).

66F Restriction on sentencing powers where youth conditional caution given

Where a person who has been given a youth conditional caution is convicted of an offence committed within two years of the giving of the caution, the court by or before which the person is so convicted –

(a) may not make an order under section 12(1)(b) of the Powers of Criminal Courts (Sentencing) Act 2000 (conditional discharge) in respect of the offence unless it is of the opinion that there are exceptional circumstances relating to the offence or the offender which justify its doing so; and
(b) where it does make such an order, must state in open court that it is of that opinion and why it is.

66G Code of practice on youth conditional cautions

(1) The Secretary of State must prepare a code of practice in relation to youth conditional cautions.

(2) The code may, in particular, make provision as to –

(a) the circumstances in which youth conditional cautions may be given,
(b) the procedure to be followed in connection with the giving of such cautions,
(c) the conditions which may be attached to such cautions and the time for which they may have effect,
(d) the category of constable or investigating officer by whom such cautions may be given,
(e) the persons who may be authorised by a relevant prosecutor for the purposes of section 66A,
(f) the form which such cautions are to take and the manner in which they are to be given and recorded,
(g) the places where such cautions may be given,
(h) the provision which may be made by a relevant prosecutor under section 66C(5)(b),
(i) the monitoring of compliance with conditions attached to such cautions,
(j) the exercise of the power of arrest conferred by section 24A(1) of the Criminal Justice Act 2003 (c. 44) as it applies by virtue of section 66E(4),
(k) who is to decide how a person should be dealt with under section 24A(2) of that Act as it applies by virtue of section 66E(5).

(3) After preparing a draft of the code the Secretary of State –

(a) must publish the draft,
(b) must consider any representations made to him about the draft, and
(c) may amend the draft accordingly,

but he may not publish or amend the draft without the consent of the Attorney General.

(4) After the Secretary of State has proceeded under subsection (3) he must lay the code before each House of Parliament.

(5) When he has done so he may bring the code into force by order.

(6) The Secretary of State may from time to time revise a code of practice brought into force under this section.

(7) Subsections (3) to (6) are to apply (with appropriate modifications) to a revised code as they apply to an original code.

Interpretation of Chapter 1

66H Interpretation

In this Chapter –

(a) "appropriate adult" has the meaning given by section 65(7);
(b) "authorised person" has the meaning given by section 66A(7);
(c) "investigating officer" means an officer of Revenue and Customs, appointed in accordance with section 2(1) of the Commissioners for Revenue and Customs Act 2005, or a person designated as an investigating officer under section 38 of the Police Reform Act 2002 (c. 30);
(d) "the offender" has the meaning given by section 66A(1);
(e) "relevant prosecutor" means –
   (i) the Attorney General,
   (ii) the Director of the Serious Fraud Office,
   (iii) the Director of Revenue and Customs Prosecutions,
   (iv) the Director of Public Prosecutions,
   (v) the Secretary of State, or
   (vi) a person who is specified in an order made by the Secretary State as being a relevant prosecutor for the purposes of this Chapter;
(f) "youth conditional caution" has the meaning given by section 66A(2)."

4

(1) Section 114 (orders and regulations) is amended as follows.

(2) In subsection (2) (which specifies orders that are subject to annulment in pursuance of a resolution of either House of Parliament), for "or 10(6)" substitute "10(6), 66C(1) or 66H(e)(vi)".

(3) After subsection (2) insert –

"(2A) Subsection (2) also applies to a statutory instrument containing –

(a) an order under section 66C(4) unless the order makes provision of the kind mentioned in subsection (3A)(a) below, or
(b) an order under section 66G(5) other than the first such order."

(4) In subsection (3) (which specifies orders that may not be made unless a draft has been approved by a resolution of each House of Parliament) after "41(6)" insert ", 66A(6)".

(5) After subsection (3) insert –

"(3A) Subsection (3) also applies to –

(a) an order under section 66C(4) which makes provision increasing the figure in section 66C(3) by more than is necessary to reflect changes in the value of money, and
(b) the first order under section 66G(5)."

Schedule 10

Section 49

Protection For Spent Cautions Under Rehabilitation Of Offenders Act 1974

1 The Rehabilitation of Offenders Act 1974 (c. 53) is amended as follows.

2 In section 6(6) for "the Schedule" substitute "Schedule 1".

3 After section 8 (defamation actions) there is inserted –

"8A Protection afforded to spent cautions

(1) Schedule 2 to this Act (protection for spent cautions) shall have effect.

(2) In this Act "caution" means –

(a) a conditional caution, that is to say, a caution given under section 22 of the Criminal Justice Act 2003 (c. 44) (conditional cautions for adults) or under section 66A of the Crime and Disorder Act 1998 (c. 37) (conditional cautions for children and young persons);
(b) any other caution given to a person in England and Wales in respect of an offence which, at the time the caution is given, that person has admitted;
(c) a reprimand or warning given under section 65 of the Crime and Disorder Act 1998 (reprimands and warnings for persons aged under 18);
(d) anything corresponding to a caution, reprimand or warning falling within paragraphs (a) to (c) (however described) which is given to a person in respect of an offence under the law of a country outside England and Wales."

4

After section 9 (unauthorised disclosure of spent convictions) insert –

"9A Unauthorised disclosure of spent cautions

(1) In this section –

(a) "official record" means a record which –
   (i) contains information about persons given a caution for any offence or offences; and
   (ii) is kept for the purposes of its functions by any court, police force, Government department or other public authority in England and Wales;
(b) "caution information" means information imputing that a named or otherwise identifiable living person ("the named person") has committed, been charged with or prosecuted or cautioned for any offence which is the subject of a spent caution; and

(c) "relevant person" means any person who, in the course of his official duties (anywhere in the United Kingdom), has or at any time has had custody of or access to any official record or the information contained in it.

(2) Subject to the terms of any order made under subsection (5), a relevant person shall be guilty of an offence if, knowing or having reasonable cause to suspect that any caution information he has obtained in the course of his official duties is caution information, he discloses it, otherwise than in the course of those duties, to another person.

(3) In any proceedings for an offence under subsection (2) it shall be a defence for the defendant to show that the disclosure was made –

(a) to the named person or to another person at the express request of the named person;
(b) to a person whom he reasonably believed to be the named person or to another person at the express request of a person whom he reasonably believed to be the named person.

(4) Any person who obtains any caution information from any official record by means of any fraud, dishonesty or bribe shall be guilty of an offence.

(5) The Secretary of State may by order make such provision as appears to him to be appropriate for excepting the disclosure of caution information derived from an official record from the provisions of subsection (2) in such cases or classes of case as may be specified in the order.

(6) A person guilty of an offence under subsection (2) is liable on summary conviction to a fine not exceeding level 4 on the standard scale.

(7) A person guilty of an offence under subsection (4) is liable on summary conviction to a fine not exceeding level 5 on the standard scale, or to imprisonment for a term not exceeding 51 weeks, or to both.

(8) Proceedings for an offence under subsection (2) shall not be instituted except by or on behalf of the Director of Public Prosecutions."

5

The Schedule (service disciplinary proceedings) is re-numbered as Schedule 1.

6

After that Schedule insert –

"Schedule 2
Protection For Spent Cautions

1 Preliminary

(1) For the purposes of this Schedule a caution shall be regarded as a spent caution –

(a) in the case of a conditional caution (as defined in section 8A(2)(a)), at the end of the relevant period for the caution;
(b) in any other case, at the time the caution is given. (2) In sub-paragraph (1)(a) "the relevant period for the caution" means (subject to sub-paragraph (3)) the period of three months from the date on which the conditional caution was given.

(3) If the person concerned is subsequently prosecuted and convicted of the offence in respect of which a conditional caution was given –

(a) the relevant period for the caution shall end at the same time as the rehabilitation period for the offence; and (b) if the conviction occurs after the end of the period mentioned in sub-paragraph (1)(a), the caution shall be treated for the purposes of this Schedule as not having become spent in relation to any period before the end of the rehabilitation period for the offence.

2

(1) In this Schedule "ancillary circumstances", in relation to a caution, means any circumstances of the following –

(a) the offence which was the subject of the caution or the conduct constituting that offence;

(b) any process preliminary to the caution (including consideration by any person of how to deal with that offence and the procedure for giving the caution);

(c) any proceedings for that offence which take place before the caution is given (including anything which happens after that time for the purpose of bringing the proceedings to an end);

(d) any judicial review proceedings relating to the caution; (e) in the case of a warning under section 65 of the Crime and Disorder Act 1998 (c. 37), anything done in pursuance of or undergone in compliance with a requirement to participate in a rehabilitation programme under section 66(2) of that Act;

(f) in the case of a conditional caution, any conditions attached to the caution or anything done in pursuance of or undergone in compliance with those conditions.

(2) Where the caution relates to two or more offences, references in sub-paragraph (1) to the offence which was the subject of the caution include a reference to each of the offences concerned.

(3) In this Schedule "proceedings before a judicial authority" has the same meaning as in section 4.

3 Protection relating to spent cautions and ancillary circumstances

(1) A person who is given a caution for an offence shall, from the time the caution is spent, be treated for all purposes in law as a person who has not committed, been charged with or prosecuted for, or been given a caution for the offence; and notwithstanding the provisions of any other enactment or rule of law to the contrary –

(a) no evidence shall be admissible in any proceedings before a judicial authority exercising its jurisdiction or functions in England and Wales to prove that any such person has committed, been charged with or prosecuted for, or been given a caution for the offence; and

(b) a person shall not, in any such proceedings, be asked and, if asked, shall not be required to answer, any question relating to his past which cannot be answered without acknowledging or referring to a spent caution or any ancillary circumstances.

(2) Nothing in sub-paragraph (1) applies in relation to any proceedings for the offence which are not part of the ancillary circumstances relating to the caution.

(3) Where a question seeking information with respect to a person's previous cautions, offences, conduct or circumstances is put to him or to any other person otherwise than in proceedings before a judicial authority –

(a) the question shall be treated as not relating to spent cautions or to any ancillary circumstances, and the answer may be framed accordingly; and

(b) the person questioned shall not be subjected to any liability or otherwise prejudiced in law by reason of any failure to acknowledge or disclose a spent caution or any ancillary circumstances in his answer to the question.

(4) Any obligation imposed on any person by any rule of law or by the provisions of any agreement or arrangement to disclose any matters to any other person shall not extend to requiring him to disclose a spent caution or any ancillary circumstances (whether the caution is his own or another's).

(5) A caution which has become spent or any ancillary circumstances, or any failure to disclose such a caution or any such circumstances, shall not be a proper ground for dismissing or excluding a person from any office, profession, occupation or employment, or for prejudicing him in any way in any occupation or employment.

(6) This paragraph has effect subject to paragraphs 4 to 6.

4

The Secretary of State may by order –

(a) make provision for excluding or modifying the application of either or both of paragraphs (a) or (b) of paragraph 3(2) in relation to questions put in such circumstances as may be specified in the order;

(b) provide for exceptions from the provisions of sub-paragraphs (4) and (5) of paragraph 3, in such cases or classes of case, and in relation to cautions of such a description, as may be specified in the order.

5

Nothing in paragraph 3 affects –

(a) the operation of the caution in question; or
(b) the operation of any enactment by virtue of which, in consequence of any caution, a person is subject to any disqualification, disability, prohibition or other restriction or effect, the period of which extends beyond the rehabilitation period applicable to the caution.

6

(1) Section 7(2), (3) and (4) apply for the purposes of this Schedule as follows.

(2) Subsection (2) (apart from paragraphs (b) and (d)) applies to the determination of any issue, and the admission or requirement of any evidence, relating to a person's previous cautions or to ancillary circumstances as it applies to matters relating to a person's previous convictions and circumstances ancillary thereto.

(3) Subsection (3) applies to evidence of a person's previous cautions and ancillary circumstances as it applies to evidence of a person's convictions and the circumstances ancillary thereto; and for this purpose subsection (3) shall have effect as if –

(a) any reference to subsection (2) or (4) of section 7 were a reference to that subsection as applied by this paragraph; and
(b) the words "or proceedings to which section 8 below applies" were omitted.

(4) Subsection (4) applies for the purpose of excluding the application of paragraph 3(1); and for that purpose subsection (4) shall have effect as if the words "(other than proceedings to which section 8 below applies)" were omitted.

(5) References in the provisions applied by this paragraph to section 4(1) are to be read as references to paragraph 3(1)."

Schedule 11

Section 51

Electronic Monitoring Of Persons Released On Bail Subject To Conditions

1

The Bail Act 1976 (c. 63) has effect subject to the following amendments.

2

In section 3 (general provisions) for subsection (6ZAA) substitute –

"(6ZAA) The requirements which may be imposed under subsection (6) include electronic monitoring requirements. The imposition of electronic monitoring requirements is subject to section 3AA (in the case of a child or young person), section 3AB (in the case of other persons) and section 3AC (in all cases).

(6ZAB) In this section and sections 3AA to 3AC "electronic monitoring requirements" means requirements imposed for the purpose of securing the electronic monitoring of a person's compliance with any other requirement imposed on him as a condition of bail."

3

(1) Section 3AA (electronic monitoring of compliance with bail conditions) is amended as follows.

(2) In the heading to the section, for "Electronic monitoring of compliance with bail conditions" substitute "Conditions for the imposition of electronic monitoring requirements: children and young persons".

(3) For subsection (1) substitute –

"(1) A court may not impose electronic monitoring requirements on a child or young person unless each of the following conditions is met."

(4) For subsection (4) substitute –

"(4) The third condition is that the court is satisfied that the necessary provision for dealing with the person concerned can be made under arrangements for the electronic monitoring of persons released on bail that are currently available in each local justice area which is a relevant area.'"

(5) In subsection (5), for "such a requirement" substitute "electronic monitoring requirements".

(6) Subsections (6) to (10) and (12) (which are superseded by section 3AC) are omitted.

4

After section 3AA insert –

"3AB Conditions for the imposition of electronic monitoring requirements: other persons

(1) A court may not impose electronic monitoring requirements on a person who has attained the age of seventeen unless each of the following conditions is met.

(2) The first condition is that the court is satisfied that without the electronic monitoring requirements the person would not be granted bail.

(3) The second condition is that the court is satisfied that the necessary provision for dealing with the person concerned can be made under arrangements for the electronic monitoring of persons released on bail that are currently available in each local justice area which is a relevant area.

(4) If the person is aged seventeen, the third condition is that a youth offending team has informed the court that in its opinion the imposition of electronic monitoring requirements will be suitable in his case.

3AC Electronic monitoring: general provisions

(1) Where a court imposes electronic monitoring requirements as a condition of bail, the requirements must include provision for making a person responsible for the monitoring.

(2) A person may not be made responsible for the electronic monitoring of a person on bail unless he is of a description specified in an order made by the Secretary of State.

(3) The Secretary of State may make rules for regulating –

 (a) the electronic monitoring of persons on bail;
 (b) without prejudice to the generality of paragraph (a), the functions of persons made responsible for such monitoring.

(4) The rules may make different provision for different cases.

(5) Any power of the Secretary of State to make an order or rules under this section is exercisable by statutory instrument.

(6) A statutory instrument containing rules under this section shall be subject to annulment in pursuance of a resolution of either House of Parliament.

(7) For the purposes of section 3AA or 3AB a local justice area is a relevant area in relation to a proposed electronic monitoring requirement if the court considers that it will not be practicable to secure the electronic monitoring in question unless electronic monitoring arrangements are available in that area.

(8) Nothing in sections 3, 3AA or 3AB is to be taken to require the Secretary of State to ensure that arrangements are made for the electronic monitoring of persons released on bail."

Schedule 12

Section 52

Bail For Summary Offences And Certain Other Offences To Be Tried Summarily

1

The Bail Act 1976 (c. 63) is amended as follows.

2

In section 3(6D)(a) (condition to be imposed on person in relation to whom paragraph 6B(1)(a) to (c) of Part 1 of Schedule 1 to that Act apply), after "apply" insert "(including where P is a person to whom the provisions of Part 1A of Schedule 1 apply)".

3

After section 9 (offence of agreeing to indemnify sureties in criminal proceedings) insert –

> **"9A Bail decisions relating to persons aged under 18 who are accused of offences mentioned in Schedule 2 to the Magistrates' Courts Act 1980**
>
> (1) This section applies whenever –
>
> (a) a magistrates' court is considering whether to withhold or grant bail in relation to a person aged under 18 who is accused of a scheduled offence; and
>
> (b) the trial of that offence has not begun.
>
> (2) The court shall, before deciding whether to withhold or grant bail, consider whether, having regard to any representations made by the prosecutor or the accused person, the value involved does not exceed the relevant sum for the purposes of section 22.
>
> (3) The duty in subsection (2) does not apply in relation to an offence if –
>
> (a) a determination under subsection (4) has already been made in relation to that offence; or
>
> (b) the accused person is, in relation to any other offence of which he is accused which is not a scheduled offence, a person to whom Part 1 of Schedule 1 to this Act applies.
>
> (4) If where the duty in subsection (2) applies it appears to the court clear that, for the offence in question, the amount involved does not exceed the relevant sum, the court shall make a determination to that effect.
>
> (5) In this section –
>
> (a) "relevant sum" has the same meaning as in section 22(1) of the Magistrates' Courts Act 1980 (certain either way offences to be tried summarily if value involved is less than the relevant sum);
>
> (b) "scheduled offence" means an offence mentioned in Schedule 2 to that Act (offences for which the value involved is relevant to the mode of trial); and
>
> (c) "the value involved" is to be construed in accordance with section 22(10) to (12) of that Act."

4

Schedule 1 (persons entitled to bail: supplementary provisions) is amended as follows.

5

(1) Paragraph 1 (defendants to whom Part 1 applies) becomes sub-paragraph (1) of that paragraph.

(2) In that sub-paragraph at the beginning insert "Subject to sub-paragraph (2),".

(3) After that sub-paragraph insert –

"(2) But those provisions do not apply by virtue of sub-paragraph (1)(a) if the offence, or each of the offences punishable with imprisonment, is –

(a) a summary offence; or
(b) an offence mentioned in Schedule 2 to the Magistrates' Courts Act 1980 (offences for which the value involved is relevant to the mode of trial) in relation to which –
   (i) a determination has been made under section 22(2) of that Act (certain either way offences to be tried summarily if value involved is less than the relevant sum) that it is clear that the value does not exceed the relevant sum for the purposes of that section; or
   (ii) a determination has been made under section 9A(4) of this Act to the same effect."

6

After Part 1 insert –

"PART 1A
DEFENDANTS ACCUSED OR CONVICTED OF IMPRISONABLE OFFENCES TO WHICH PART 1 DOES NOT APPLY

1 Defendants to whom Part 1A applies

The following provisions of this Part apply to the defendant if –

(a) the offence or one of the offences of which he is accused or convicted is punishable with imprisonment, but
(b) Part 1 does not apply to him by virtue of paragraph 1(2) of that Part.

2 Exceptions to right to bail

The defendant need not be granted bail if –

(a) it appears to the court that, having been previously granted bail in criminal proceedings, he has failed to surrender to custody in accordance with his obligations under the grant of bail; and
(b) the court believes, in view of that failure, that the defendant, if released on bail (whether subject to conditions or not) would fail to surrender to custody.

3

The defendant need not be granted bail if –

(a) it appears to the court that the defendant was on bail in criminal proceedings on the date of the offence; and
(b) the court is satisfied that there are substantial grounds for believing that the defendant, if released on bail (whether subject to conditions or not) would commit an offence while on bail.

4

The defendant need not be granted bail if the court is satisfied that there are substantial grounds for believing that the defendant, if released on bail (whether subject to conditions or not), would commit an offence while on bail by engaging in conduct that would, or would be likely to, cause –

(a) physical or mental injury to any person other than the defendant; or
(b) any person other than the defendant to fear physical or mental injury.

5

The defendant need not be granted bail if the court is satisfied that the defendant should be kept in custody for his own protection or, if he is a child or young person, for his own welfare.

6

The defendant need not be granted bail if he is in custody in pursuance of a sentence of a court or a sentence imposed by an officer under the Armed Forces Act 2006.

7

The defendant need not be granted bail if –

(a) having been released on bail in or in connection with the proceedings for the offence, he has been arrested in pursuance of section 7 of this Act; and

(b) the court is satisfied that there are substantial grounds for believing that the defendant, if released on bail (whether subject to conditions or not) would fail to surrender to custody, commit an offence while on bail or interfere with witnesses or otherwise obstruct the course of justice (whether in relation to himself or any other person).

8

The defendant need not be granted bail where the court is satisfied that it has not been practicable to obtain sufficient information for the purpose of taking the decisions required by this Part of this Schedule for want of time since the institution of the proceedings against him.

9 Application of paragraphs 6A to 6C of Part 1

Paragraphs 6A to 6C of Part 1 (exception applicable to drug users in certain areas and related provisions) apply to a defendant to whom this Part applies as they apply to a defendant to whom that Part applies."

Schedule 13

Section 53

Allocation of cases triable either way etc.

1

Schedule 3 to the Criminal Justice Act 2003 (c. 44) (allocation of cases triable either way, and sending cases to the Crown Court etc.) has effect subject to the following amendments.

2

In paragraph 2, in the paragraph set out in sub-paragraph (2), after "committed" insert "for sentence".

3

In paragraph 6, for subsection (2)(c) of the section set out in that paragraph substitute –

"(c) that if he is tried summarily and is convicted by the court, he may be committed for sentence to the Crown Court under section 3 or (if applicable) section 3A of the Powers of Criminal Courts (Sentencing) Act 2000 if the court is of such opinion as is mentioned in subsection (2) of the applicable section."

4

In paragraph 8, in sub-paragraph (2)(a) for "trial on indictment" substitute "summary trial".

5

(1) Paragraph 9 is amended as follows.

(2) In sub-paragraph (3) after "(1A)" insert ", (1B)".

(3) After sub-paragraph (3) insert –

"(4) In subsection (3) for "the said Act of 2000" substitute "the Powers of Criminal Courts (Sentencing) Act 2000"."

6

Paragraph 13 is omitted.

7

Paragraph 22 is omitted.

8

Before paragraph 23 insert –

"**22A**

(1) Section 3 (committal for sentence on summary trial of offence triable either way) is amended as follows.

(2) In subsection (2) –

(a) in paragraph (a) for the words from "greater punishment" to the end of the paragraph substitute "the Crown Court should, in the court's opinion, have the power to deal with the offender in any way it could deal with him if he had been convicted on indictment", and

(b) omit paragraph (b) (and the word "or" immediately preceding it).

(3) In subsection (4), after "section" insert "17D or".

(4) In subsection (5), in paragraph (b) omit the words "paragraph (b) and"."

9

In paragraph 23, in subsection (5) of the first of the sections inserted by that paragraph (section 3A), for "a specified offence" substitute "an offender convicted of a specified offence".

10

In paragraph 24 after sub-paragraph (4) insert –

"(4A) In subsection (2) for "committed" substitute "sent"."

Schedule 14

Section 68

Special Rules Relating To Providers Of Information Society Services

1 Domestic service providers: extension of liability

(1) This paragraph applies where a service provider is established in England and Wales or Northern Ireland (a "domestic service provider").

(2) Section 63(1) applies to a domestic service provider who –

(a) is in possession of an extreme pornographic image in an EEA state other than the United Kingdom, and

(b) is in possession of it there in the course of providing information society services,

as well as to persons (of any description) who are in possession of such images in England and Wales or Northern Ireland.

(3) In the case of an offence under section 63, as it applies to a domestic service provider by virtue of sub-paragraph (2) –

(a) proceedings for the offence may be taken at any place in England and Wales or Northern Ireland, and
(b) the offence may for all incidental purposes be treated as having been committed at any such place.

(4) Nothing in this paragraph is to be read as affecting the operation of any of paragraphs 3 to 5.

2 Non-UK service providers: restriction on institution of proceedings

(1) This paragraph applies where a service provider is established in an EEA state other than the United Kingdom (a "non-UK service provider").

(2) Proceedings for an offence under section 63 may not be instituted against a non-UK service provider in respect of anything done in the course of the provision of information society services unless the derogation condition is satisfied.

(3) The derogation condition is satisfied where the institution of proceedings –

(a) is necessary for the purposes of the public interest objective;
(b) relates to an information society service that prejudices that objective or presents a serious and grave risk of prejudice to that objective; and
(c) is proportionate to that objective.

(4) "The public interest objective" means the pursuit of public policy.

3 Exceptions for mere conduits

(1) A service provider is not capable of being guilty of an offence under section 63 in respect of anything done in the course of providing so much of an information society service as consists in –

(a) the provision of access to a communication network, or
(b) the transmission in a communication network of information provided by a recipient of the service, if the condition in sub-paragraph (2) is satisfied.

(2) The condition is that the service provider does not –

(a) initiate the transmission,
(b) select the recipient of the transmission, or
(c) select or modify the information contained in the transmission.

(3) For the purposes of sub-paragraph (1) –

(a) the provision of access to a communication network, and
(b) the transmission of information in a communication network,

includes the automatic, intermediate and transient storage of the information transmitted so far as the storage is solely for the purpose of carrying out the transmission in the network.

(4) Sub-paragraph (3) does not apply if the information is stored for longer than is reasonably necessary for the transmission.

4 Exception for caching

(1) This paragraph applies where an information society service consists in the transmission in a communication network of information provided by a recipient of the service.

(2) The service provider is not capable of being guilty of an offence under section 63 in respect of the automatic, intermediate and temporary storage of information so provided, if –

(a) the storage of the information is solely for the purpose of making more efficient the onward transmission of the information to other recipients of the service at their request, and
(b) the condition in sub-paragraph (3) is satisfied.

(3) The condition is that the service provider –

 (a) does not modify the information,
 (b) complies with any conditions attached to having access to the information, and
 (c) (where sub-paragraph (4) applies) expeditiously removes the information or disables access to it.

(4) This sub-paragraph applies if the service provider obtains actual knowledge that –

 (a) the information at the initial source of the transmission has been removed from the network,
 (b) access to it has been disabled, or
 (c) a court or administrative authority has ordered the removal from the network of, or the disablement of access to, the information.

5 Exception for hosting

(1) A service provider is not capable of being guilty of an offence under section 63 in respect of anything done in the course of providing so much of an information society service as consists in the storage of information provided by a recipient of the service, if –

 (a) the service provider had no actual knowledge when the information was provided that it contained offending material, or
 (b) on obtaining actual knowledge that the information contained offending material, the service provider expeditiously removed the information or disabled access to it.

(2) "Offending material" means material the possession of which constitutes an offence under section 63.

(3) Sub-paragraph (1) does not apply if the recipient of the service is acting under the authority or control of the service provider.

6 Interpretation

(1) This paragraph applies for the purposes of this Schedule.

(2) "Extreme pornographic image" has the same meaning as in section 63.

(3) "Information society services" –

 (a) has the meaning given in Article 2(a) of the E-Commerce Directive (which refers to Article 1(2) of Directive 98/34/EC of the European Parliament and of the Council of 22 June 1998 laying down a procedure for the provision of information in the field of technical standards and regulations), and
 (b) is summarised in recital 17 of the E-Commerce Directive as covering "any service normally provided for remuneration, at a distance, by means of electronic equipment for the processing (including digital compression) and storage of data, and at the individual request of a recipient of a service";

and "the E-Commerce Directive" means Directive 2000/31/EC of the European Parliament and of the Council of 8 June 2000 on certain legal aspects of information society services, in particular electronic commerce, in the Internal Market (Directive on electronic commerce).

(4) "Recipient", in relation to a service, means any person who, for professional ends or otherwise, uses an information society service, in particular for the purposes of seeking information or making it accessible.

(5) "Service provider" means a person providing an information society service.

(6) For the purpose of construing references in this Schedule to a service provider who is established in a part of the United Kingdom or in some other EEA state –

 (a) a service provider is established in a particular part of the United Kingdom, or in a particular EEA state, if the service provider –

(i) effectively pursues an economic activity using a fixed establishment in that part of the United Kingdom, or that EEA state, for an indefinite period, and
(ii) is a national of an EEA state or a company or firm mentioned in Article 48 of the EEC Treaty;
(b) the presence or use in a particular place of equipment or other technical means of providing an information society service does not, of itself, constitute the establishment of a service provider;
(c) where it cannot be determined from which of a number of establishments a given information society service is provided, that service is to be regarded as provided from the establishment at the centre of the service provider's activities relating to that service.

Schedule 15

Section 73

Sexual Offences: Grooming And Adoption

1 Meeting a child following sexual grooming

In section 15(1) of the Sexual Offences Act 2003 (c. 42) (meeting a child following sexual grooming etc) for paragraphs (a) and (b) substitute –

"(a) A has met or communicated with another person (B) on at least two occasions and subsequently –
  (i) A intentionally meets B,
  (ii) A travels with the intention of meeting B in any part of the world or arranges to meet B in any part of the world, or
  (iii) B travels with the intention of meeting A in any part of the world,
(b) A intends to do anything to or in respect of B, during or after the meeting mentioned in paragraph (a)(i) to (iii) and in any part of the world, which if done will involve the commission by A of a relevant offence,".

2 Adoption

The Sexual Offences Act 2003 (c. 42) has effect subject to the following amendments.

3

In section 27(1)(b) (family relationships) after "but for" insert "section 39 of the Adoption Act 1976 or".

4

In section 29(1)(b) (sections 25 and 26: sexual relationships which pre-date family relationships) after "if" insert "section 39 of the Adoption Act 1976 or".

5

(1) Section 64 (sex with an adult relative: penetration) is amended as follows.

(2) In subsection (1) after "(A)" insert "(subject to subsection (3A))".

(3) In subsection (3) after "In subsection (2)—" insert –

"(za) "parent" includes an adoptive parent;
(zb) "child" includes an adopted person within the meaning of Chapter 4 of Part 1 of the Adoption and Children Act 2002;".

(4) After that subsection insert –

"(3A) Where subsection (1) applies in a case where A is related to B as B's child by virtue of subsection (3)(zb), A does not commit an offence under this section unless A is 18 or over."

(5) After subsection (5) insert –

"(6) Nothing in –
(a) section 47 of the Adoption Act 1976 (which disapplies the status provisions in section 39 of that Act for the purposes of this section in relation to adoptions before 30 December 2005), or
(b) section 74 of the Adoption and Children Act 2002 (which disapplies the status provisions in section 67 of that Act for those purposes in relation to adoptions on or after that date), is to be read as preventing the application of section 39 of the Adoption Act 1976 or section 67 of the Adoption and Children Act 2002 for the purposes of subsection (3)(za) and (zb) above."

6

(1) Section 65 (sex with an adult relative: consenting to penetration) is amended as follows.

(2) In subsection (1) after "(A)" insert "(subject to subsection (3A))".

(3) In subsection (3) after "In subsection (2)—" insert –

"(za) "parent" includes an adoptive parent;
(zb) "child" includes an adopted person within the meaning of Chapter 4 of Part 1 of the Adoption and Children Act 2002;".

(4) After that subsection insert –

"(3A) Where subsection (1) applies in a case where A is related to B as B's child by virtue of subsection (3)(zb), A does not commit an offence under this section unless A is 18 or over."

(5) After subsection (5) insert –

"(6) Nothing in –
(a) section 47 of the Adoption Act 1976 (which disapplies the status provisions in section 39 of that Act for the purposes of this section in relation to adoptions before 30 December 2005), or
(b) section 74 of the Adoption and Children Act 2002 (which disapplies the status provisions in section 67 of that Act for those purposes in relation to adoptions on or after that date), is to be read as preventing the application of section 39 of the Adoption Act 1976 or section 67 of the Adoption and Children Act 2002 for the purposes of subsection (3)(za) and (zb) above."

7

In section 47(1) of the Adoption Act 1976 (c. 36) (disapplication of section 39 (status conferred by adoption) for the purposes of miscellaneous enactments) for "sections 10 and 11 (incest) of the Sexual Offences Act 1956" substitute "or sections 64 and 65 of the Sexual Offences Act 2003 (sex with an adult relative)".

Schedule 16

Section 74

Hatred On The Grounds Of Sexual Orientation

1

Part 3A of the Public Order Act 1986 (c. 64) (hatred against persons on religious grounds) has effect subject to the following amendments.

2

In the heading for Part 3A at the end insert "OR GROUNDS OF SEXUAL ORIENTATION".

3

In the italic cross-heading before section 29A at the end insert "*and "hatred on the grounds of sexual orientation"*".

4

After that section insert –

> **"29AB Meaning of "hatred on the grounds of sexual orientation"**
>
> In this Part "hatred on the grounds of sexual orientation" means hatred against a group of persons defined by reference to sexual orientation (whether towards persons of the same sex, the opposite sex or both)."

5

In the italic cross-heading before section 29B at the end insert "*or hatred on the grounds of sexual orientation*".

6

(1) Section 29B (use of words or behaviour or display of written material) is amended as follows.

(2) In subsection (1), after "religious hatred" insert "or hatred on the grounds of sexual orientation".

(3) Omit subsection (3).

7

In section 29C(1) (publishing or distributing written material), after "religious hatred" insert "or hatred on the grounds of sexual orientation".

8

In section 29D(1) (public performance of play), after "religious hatred" insert "or hatred on the grounds of sexual orientation".

9

In section 29E(1) (distributing, showing or playing a recording), after "religious hatred" insert "or hatred on the grounds of sexual orientation".

10

In section 29F(1) (broadcasting or including programme in programme service), after "religious hatred" insert "or hatred on the grounds of sexual orientation".

11

In section 29G(1) (possession of inflammatory material), for "religious hatred to be stirred up thereby" substitute "thereby to stir up religious hatred or hatred on the grounds of sexual orientation".

12

(1) Section 29H (powers of entry and search) is amended as follows.

(2) In subsection (1), omit "in England and Wales".

(3) Omit subsection (2).

13

(1) Section 29I (power to order forfeiture) is amended as follows.

(2) In subsection (2) –

(a) in paragraph (a), omit "in the case of an order made in proceedings in England and Wales,"; and
(b) omit paragraph (b).

(3) Omit subsection (4).

14

After section 29J insert –

"29JA Protection of freedom of expression (sexual orientation)

In this Part, for the avoidance of doubt, the discussion or criticism of sexual conduct or practices or the urging of persons to refrain from or modify such conduct or practices shall not be taken of itself to be threatening or intended to stir up hatred."

15

In section 29K(1) (savings for reports of parliamentary or judicial proceedings), for "or in the Scottish Parliament" substitute ", in the Scottish Parliament or in the National Assembly for Wales".

16

(1) Section 29L (procedure and punishment) is amended as follows.

(2) In subsections (1) and (2), omit "in England and Wales".

(3) In subsection (3), in paragraph (b), for "six months" substitute "12 months".

(4) After that subsection insert –

"(4) In subsection (3)(b) the reference to 12 months shall be read as a reference to 6 months in relation to an offence committed before the commencement of section 154(1) of the Criminal Justice Act 2003."

17

In section 29N (interpretation), after the definition of "dwelling" insert –

""hatred on the grounds of sexual orientation" has the meaning given by section 29AB;".

Schedule 17

Section 75

Offences Relating To Nuclear Material And Nuclear Facilities

PART 1
AMENDMENTS OF NUCLEAR MATERIAL (OFFENCES) ACT 1983

1

The Nuclear Material (Offences) Act 1983 (c. 18) has effect subject to the following amendments.

2

(1) Section 1 (extended scope of certain offences) is amended as follows.

(2) In subsection (1)(b) (offences under certain enactments) for "section 78 of the Criminal Justice (Scotland) Act 1980" substitute "section 52 of the Criminal Law (Consolidation) (Scotland) Act 1995".

(3) After subsection (1) insert –

"(1A) If –

(a) a person, whatever his nationality, does outside the United Kingdom an act directed at a nuclear facility, or which interferes with the operation of such a facility,
(b) the act causes death, injury or damage resulting from the emission of ionising radiation or the release of radioactive material, and
(c) had he done that act in any part of the United Kingdom, it would have made him guilty of an offence mentioned in subsection (1)(a) or (b) above,

the person shall in any part of the United Kingdom be guilty of such of the offences mentioned in subsection (1)(a) and (b) as are offences of which the act would have made him guilty had he done it in that part of the United Kingdom."

(4) Omit subsection (2) (definition of "act").

3

After section 1 insert –

"1A Increase in penalties for offences committed in relation to nuclear material etc.

(1) If—

(a) a person is guilty of an offence to which subsection (2), (3) or (4) applies, and
(b) the penalty provided by this subsection would not otherwise apply, the person shall be liable, on conviction on indictment, to imprisonment for life.

(2) This subsection applies to an offence mentioned in section 1(1)(a) or (b) where the act making the person guilty of the offence was done in England and Wales or Northern Ireland and either –

(a) the act was done in relation to or by means of nuclear material, or
(b) the act –
    (i) was directed at a nuclear facility, or interfered with the operation of such a facility, and
    (ii) caused death, injury or damage resulting from the emission of ionising radiation or the release of radioactive material.

(3) This subsection applies to an offence mentioned in section 1(1)(c) or (d) where the act making the person guilty of the offence –

(a) was done in England and Wales or Northern Ireland, and
(b) was done in relation to or by means of nuclear material.

(4) This subsection applies to an offence mentioned in section 1(1)(a) to (d) where the offence is an offence in England and Wales or Northern Ireland by virtue of section 1(1) or (1A).

1B Offences relating to damage to environment

(1) If a person, whatever his nationality, in the United Kingdom or elsewhere contravenes subsection (2) or (3) he is guilty of an offence.

(2) A person contravenes this subsection if without lawful authority –

(a) he receives, holds or deals with nuclear material, and
(b) he does so either –
    (i) intending to cause, or for the purpose of enabling another to cause, damage to the environment by means of that material, or
    (ii) being reckless as to whether, as a result of his so receiving, holding or dealing with that material, damage would be caused to the environment by means of that material.

(3) A person contravenes this subsection if without lawful authority –

(a) he does an act directed at a nuclear facility, or which interferes with the operation of such a facility, and
(b) he does so either –
    (i) intending to cause, or for the purpose of enabling another to cause, damage to the environment by means of the emission of ionising radiation or the release of radioactive material, or

(ii) being reckless as to whether, as a result of his act, damage would be caused to the environment by means of such an emission or release.

(4) A person guilty of an offence under this section shall be liable, on conviction on indictment, to imprisonment for life.

1C Offences of importing or exporting etc. nuclear material: extended jurisdiction

(1) If a person, whatever his nationality, outside the United Kingdom contravenes subsection (2) below he shall be guilty of an offence.

(2) A person contravenes this subsection if he is knowingly concerned in –

(a) the unlawful export or shipment as stores of nuclear material from one country to another, or
(b) the unlawful import of nuclear material into one country from another.

(3) For the purposes of subsection (2) –

(a) the export or shipment as stores of nuclear material from a country, or
(b) the import of nuclear material into a country, is unlawful if it is contrary to any prohibition or restriction on the export, shipment as stores or import (as the case may be) of nuclear material having effect under or by virtue of the law of that country.

(4) A statement in a certificate issued by or on behalf of the government of a country outside the United Kingdom to the effect that a particular export, shipment as stores or import of nuclear material is contrary to such a prohibition or restriction having effect under or by virtue of the law of that country, shall be evidence (in Scotland, sufficient evidence) that the export, shipment or import was unlawful for the purposes of subsection (2).

(5) In any proceedings a document purporting to be a certificate of the kind mentioned in subsection (4) above shall be taken to be such a certificate unless the contrary is proved.

(6) A person guilty of an offence under this section shall be liable, on conviction on indictment, to imprisonment for a term not exceeding 14 years.

(7) In this section "country" includes territory.

1D Offences under section 1C: investigations and proceedings etc.

(1) Where the Commissioners for Her Majesty's Revenue and Customs investigate, or propose to investigate, any matter with a view to determining –

(a) whether there are grounds for believing that an offence under section 1C above has been committed, or
(b) whether a person should be prosecuted for such an offence, the matter is to be treated as an assigned matter within the meaning of CEMA 1979 (see section 1(1) of that Act).

(2) Section 138 of CEMA 1979 (provisions as to arrest of persons) applies to a person who has committed, or whom there are reasonable grounds to suspect of having committed, an offence under section 1C above as it applies to a person who has committed, or whom there are reasonable grounds to suspect of having committed, an offence for which he is liable to be arrested under the customs and excise Acts.

(3) Sections 145 to 148 and 150 to 155 of CEMA 1979 (provisions as to legal proceedings) apply in relation to an offence under section 1C above, and to the penalty and proceedings for the offence, as they apply in relation to offences, penalties and proceedings under the customs and excise Acts.

(4) In this section –

"CEMA 1979" means the Customs and Excise Management Act 1979;
"the customs and excise Acts", "shipment" and "stores" have the same meanings as in CEMA 1979 (see section 1(1) of that Act)."

4

For section 2 substitute –

"2 Offences involving preparatory acts and threats

(1) If a person, whatever his nationality, in the United Kingdom or elsewhere contravenes subsection (2), (3), (4) or (7) he shall be guilty of an offence.

(2) A person contravenes this subsection if without lawful authority –

    (a)   he receives, holds or deals with nuclear material, and
    (b)   he does so either –
        (i)   intending to cause, or for the purpose of enabling another to cause, relevant injury or damage by means of that material, or
        (ii)   being reckless as to whether, as a result of his so receiving, holding or dealing with that material, relevant injury or damage would be caused by means of that material.

(3) A person contravenes this subsection if without lawful authority –

    (a)   he does an act directed at a nuclear facility, or which interferes with the operation of such a facility, and
    (b)   he does so either –
        (i)   intending to cause, or for the purpose of enabling another to cause, relevant injury or damage by means of the emission of ionising radiation or the release of radioactive material, or
        (ii)   being reckless as to whether, as a result of his act, relevant injury or damage would be caused by means of such an emission or release.

(4) A person contravenes this subsection if he –

    (a)   makes a threat of a kind falling within subsection (5), and
    (b)   intends that the person to whom the threat is made shall fear that it will be carried out.

(5) A threat falls within this subsection if it is a threat that the person making it or any other person will cause any of the consequences set out in subsection (6) either –

    (a)   by means of nuclear material, or
    (b)   by means of the emission of ionising radiation or the release of radioactive material resulting from an act which is directed at a nuclear facility, or which interferes with the operation of such a facility.

(6) The consequences mentioned in subsection (5) are –

    (a)   relevant injury or damage, or
    (b)   damage to the environment.

(7) A person contravenes this subsection if, in order to compel a State, international organisation or person to do, or abstain from doing, any act, he threatens that he or any other person will obtain nuclear material by an act which, whether by virtue of section 1(1) above or otherwise, is an offence mentioned in section 1(1)(c) above.

(8) A person guilty of an offence under this section shall be liable, on conviction on indictment, to imprisonment for life.

(9) In this section references to relevant injury or damage are references to death or to injury or damage of a type which constitutes an element of any offence mentioned in section 1(1)(a) or (b) above.

2A Inchoate and secondary offences: extended jurisdiction

(1) If a person, whatever his nationality –

    (a)   does an act outside the United Kingdom, and
    (b)   his act, if done in any part of the United Kingdom, would constitute an offence falling within subsection (2), he shall be guilty in that part of the United Kingdom of the offence.

(2) The offences are –

    (a)   attempting to commit a nuclear offence;
    (b)   conspiring to commit a nuclear offence;
    (c)   inciting the commission of a nuclear offence;
    (d)   aiding, abetting, counselling or procuring the commission of a nuclear offence.

(3) In subsection (2) a "nuclear offence" means any of the following (wherever committed) –

(a) an offence mentioned in section 1(1)(a) to (d) above (other than a blackmail offence), the commission of which is (or would have been) in relation to or by means of nuclear material;
(b) an offence mentioned in section 1(1)(a) or (b) above, the commission of which involves (or would have involved) an act –
   (i) directed at a nuclear facility, or which interferes with the operation of such a facility, and
   (ii) which causes death, injury or damage resulting from the emission of ionising radiation or the release of radioactive material;
(c) an offence under section 1B, 1C or 2(1) and (2) or (3) above;
(d) an offence under section 50(2) or (3), 68(2) or 170(1) or (2) of the Customs and Excise Management Act 1979 the commission of which is (or would have been) in connection with a prohibition or restriction relating to the exportation, shipment as stores or importation of nuclear material;
(e) for the purposes of subsection (2)(b) to (d) –
   (i) a blackmail offence, the commission of which is in relation to or by means of nuclear material;
   (ii) an offence under section 2(1) and (4) or (7) above;
   (iii) an offence of attempting to commit an offence mentioned in paragraphs (a) to (d).

(4) In subsection (3) "a blackmail offence" means –

(a) an offence under section 21 of the Theft Act 1968,
(b) an offence under section 20 of the Theft Act (Northern Ireland) 1969, or
(c) an offence of extortion.

(5) In subsection (2)(c) the reference to incitement is –

(a) a reference to incitement under the law of Scotland, or
(b) in relation to any time before the coming into force of Part 2 of the Serious Crime Act 2007 (encouraging or assisting crime) in relation to England and Wales or Northern Ireland, a reference to incitement under the common law of England and Wales or (as the case may be) of Northern Ireland."

5

After section 3 (supplemental) insert –

"3A Application to activities of armed forces

(1) Nothing in this Act applies in relation to acts done by the armed forces of a country or territory –

(a) in the course of an armed conflict, or
(b) in the discharge of their functions.

(2) If in any proceedings a question arises whether an act done by the armed forces of a country or territory was an act falling within subsection (1), a certificate issued by or under the authority of the Secretary of State and stating that it was, or was not, such an act shall be conclusive of that question.

(3) In any proceedings a document purporting to be such a certificate as is mentioned in subsection (2) shall be taken to be such a certificate unless the contrary is proved."

6

(1) Section 6 (material to which the Act applies) is amended as follows.

(2) Before subsection (1) insert –

"(A1) This section applies for the purposes of this Act."

(3) In subsection (1), omit "in this Act".

(4) After subsection (1) insert –

"(1A) "A nuclear facility" means a facility (including associated buildings and equipment) used for peaceful purposes in which nuclear material is produced, processed, used, handled, stored or disposed of.

(1B) For the purposes of subsections (1) and (1A) –

(a) nuclear material is not used for peaceful purposes if it is used or retained for military purposes, and
(b) a facility is not used for peaceful purposes if it contains any nuclear material which is used or retained for military purposes."

(5) In subsection (2) (question whether or not nuclear material used for peaceful purposes to be determined conclusively by certificate of Secretary of State to that effect) after "material" insert "or facility".

(6) For subsection (5) substitute –

"(5) "Act" includes omission.

(6) "The Convention" means the Convention on the Physical Protection of Nuclear Material and Nuclear Facilities (formerly the Convention on the Physical Protection of Nuclear Material and renamed by virtue of the Amendment adopted at Vienna on 8th July 2005).

(7) "The environment" includes land, air and water and living organisms supported by any of those media.

(8) "Radioactive material" means nuclear material or any other radioactive substance which –

(a) contains nuclides that undergo spontaneous disintegration in a process accompanied by the emission of one or more types of ionising radiation, such as alpha radiation, beta radiation, neutron particles or gamma rays, and
(b) is capable, owing to its radiological or fissile properties, of –
 (i) causing bodily injury to a person,
 (ii) causing damage or destruction to property,
 (iii) endangering a person's life, or
 (iv) causing damage to the environment."

(7) For the sidenote, substitute "Interpretation".

7

In section 7 (application to the Channel Islands, Isle of Man etc.) in subsection (2), for "any colony" substitute "any British overseas territory".

PART 2
AMENDMENTS OF CUSTOMS AND EXCISE MANAGEMENT ACT 1979

8

(1) The Customs and Excise Management Act 1979 (c. 2) is amended as follows.

(2) In section 1 (interpretation) in subsection (1) insert at the appropriate place –

""nuclear material" has the same meaning as in the Nuclear Material (Offences) Act 1983 (see section 6 of that Act);".

(3) In section 50 (penalty for improper importation of goods) –

(a) in subsection (4) (penalty for offence) for "or (5B)" substitute ", (5B) or (5C)";
(b) after subsection (5B) insert –

"(5C) In the case of an offence under subsection (2) or (3) above in connection with a prohibition or restriction relating to the importation of nuclear material, subsection (4)(b) above shall have effect as if for the words "7 years" there were substituted the words "14 years"."

(4) In section 68 (offences in relation to exportation of prohibited or restricted goods) –

(a) in subsection (3) (penalty for offence) for "or (4A)" substitute ", (4A) or (4B)";
(b) after subsection (4A) insert –

"(4B) In the case of an offence under subsection (2) above in connection with a prohibition or restriction relating to the exportation or shipment as stores of nuclear material, subsection (3)(b) above shall have effect as if for the words "7 years" there were substituted the words "14 years"."

(5) In section 170 (penalty for fraudulent evasion of duty, etc.) –

(a) in subsection (3) (penalty for offence) for "or (4B)" substitute ", (4B) or (4C)";
(b) after subsection (4B) insert –

"(4C) In the case of an offence under subsection (1) or (2) above in connection with a prohibition or restriction relating to the importation, exportation or shipment as stores of nuclear material, subsection (3)(b) above shall have effect as if for the words "7 years" there were substituted the words "14 years"."

9

(1) Her Majesty may by Order in Council provide for any provisions of section 1, 50, 68 or 170 of the Customs and Excise Management Act 1979 (c. 2) as amended by paragraph 8 to extend, with or without modifications, to any of the Channel Islands or any British overseas territory.

(2) Section 147(2) applies in relation to an Order in Council under sub-paragraph (1) as it applies in relation to an order made by the Secretary of State.

Schedule 18

Section 91(1)

Penalties Suitable For Enforcement In England And Wales Or Northern Ireland

1 Person residing in England and Wales

The financial penalty is suitable for enforcement in England and Wales if the certificate states that the person required to pay the penalty is normally resident in England and Wales.

2 Person residing in Northern Ireland

The financial penalty is suitable for enforcement in Northern Ireland if the certificate states that the person required to pay the penalty is normally resident in Northern Ireland.

3 Person having property etc. in England and Wales

The financial penalty is suitable for enforcement in England and Wales if –

(a) the certificate states that the person required to pay the penalty has property or a source of income in England and Wales, and
(b) the certificate does not state –
    (i) that the person has property or a source of income in Northern Ireland or Scotland, or
    (ii) that the person is normally resident in the United Kingdom.

4 Person having property etc. in Northern Ireland

The financial penalty is suitable for enforcement in Northern Ireland if –

(a) the certificate states that the person required to pay the penalty has property or a source of income in Northern Ireland, and
(b) the certificate does not state –
    (i) that the person has property or a source of income in England and Wales or Scotland, or
    (ii) that the person is normally resident in the United Kingdom.

5 Person having property etc. in England and Wales and Northern Ireland

(1) This paragraph applies if –

(a) the certificate states that the person required to pay the financial penalty has property or a source of income in England and Wales,
(b) the certificate also states that the person has property or a source of income in Northern Ireland, and

(c) the certificate does not state –
　　(i) that the person has property or a source of income in Scotland, or
　　(ii) that the person is normally resident in the United Kingdom.

(2) The financial penalty is suitable for enforcement in England and Wales unless it is suitable for enforcement in Northern Ireland by virtue of sub-paragraph (3).

(3) The financial penalty is suitable for enforcement in Northern Ireland if the Lord Chancellor thinks that it is more appropriate for the penalty to be enforced in Northern Ireland than in England and Wales.

6 Person having property etc. in England and Wales and Scotland

(1) This paragraph applies if –

(a) the certificate states that the person required to pay the financial penalty has property or a source of income in England and Wales,
(b) the certificate also states that the person has property or a source of income in Scotland, and
(c) the certificate does not state –
　　(i) that the person has property or a source of income in Northern Ireland, or
　　(ii) that the person is normally resident in the United Kingdom.

(2) The financial penalty is suitable for enforcement in England and Wales unless sub-paragraph (3) applies.

(3) This sub-paragraph applies if –

(a) the Lord Chancellor was given the certificate by the competent authority or central authority of another member State (and not by the central authority for Scotland), and
(b) the Lord Chancellor thinks that it is more appropriate for the financial penalty to be enforced in Scotland than in England and Wales.

7 Person having property etc. in Northern Ireland and Scotland

(1) This paragraph applies if –

(a) the certificate states that the person required to pay the financial penalty has property or a source of income in Northern Ireland,
(b) the certificate also states that the person has property or a source of income in Scotland, and
(c) the certificate does not state –
　　(i) that the person has property or a source of income in England and Wales, or
　　(ii) that the person is normally resident in the United Kingdom.

(2) The financial penalty is suitable for enforcement in Northern Ireland unless sub-paragraph (3) applies.

(3) This sub-paragraph applies if –

(a) the Lord Chancellor was given the certificate by the competent authority or central authority of another member State (and not by the central authority for Scotland), and
(b) the Lord Chancellor thinks that it is more appropriate for the financial penalty to be enforced in Scotland than in Northern Ireland.

8 Person having property etc. in England and Wales, Scotland and Northern Ireland

(1) This paragraph applies if –

(a) the certificate states that the person required to pay the financial penalty has property or a source of income in Northern Ireland,
(b) the certificate also states that the person has property or a source of income in England and Wales and in Scotland, and

(c) the certificate does not state that the person is normally resident in the United Kingdom.

(2) The financial penalty is suitable for enforcement in England and Wales unless –

(a) the penalty is suitable for enforcement in Northern Ireland by virtue of sub-paragraph (3) or (4), or
(b) sub-paragraph (5) applies.

(3) The financial penalty is suitable for enforcement in Northern Ireland if –

(a) the Lord Chancellor was given the certificate by the competent authority or central authority of another member State (and not by the central authority for Scotland), and
(b) the Lord Chancellor thinks that it is more appropriate for the financial penalty to be enforced in Northern Ireland than in England and Wales or Scotland.

(4) The financial penalty is suitable for enforcement in Northern Ireland if –

(a) the Lord Chancellor was given the certificate by the central authority for Scotland, and
(b) the Lord Chancellor thinks that it is more appropriate for the financial penalty to be enforced in Northern Ireland than in England and Wales.

(5) This sub-paragraph applies if –

(a) the Lord Chancellor was given the certificate by the competent authority or central authority of another member State (and not by the central authority for Scotland), and
(b) the Lord Chancellor thinks that it is more appropriate for the financial penalty to be enforced in Scotland than in England and Wales or Northern Ireland.

9 Interpretation

Where the person required to pay the financial penalty is a body corporate, this Schedule applies as if –

(a) the reference in paragraph 1 to the person being normally resident in England and Wales were a reference to the person having its registered office in England and Wales,
(b) the reference in paragraph 2 to the person being normally resident in Northern Ireland were a reference to the person having its registered office in Northern Ireland, and
(c) any reference to the person being normally resident in the United Kingdom were a reference to the person having its registered office in the United Kingdom.

Schedule 19

Section 91(2)

Grounds For Refusal To Enforce Financial Penalties

PART 1
THE GROUNDS FOR REFUSAL

1

A penalty (of any kind) has been imposed on the liable person in respect of the conduct to which the certificate relates under the law of any part of the United Kingdom (whether or not the penalty has been enforced).

2

A penalty (of any kind) has been imposed on the liable person in respect of that conduct under the law of any member State, other than the United Kingdom and the issuing State, and that penalty has been enforced.

3

(1) The decision was made in respect of conduct –

(a) that is not specified in Part 2 of this Schedule, and
(b) would not constitute an offence under the law of the relevant part of the United Kingdom if it occurred in that part.

(2) In sub-paragraph (1), "the relevant part of the United Kingdom" means –

(a) in the application of this Schedule to England and Wales, England and Wales, and
(b) in the application of this Schedule to Northern Ireland, Northern Ireland.

4

(1) The decision was made in respect of conduct –

(a) that occurred outside the territory of the issuing State, and
(b) would not constitute an offence under the law of the relevant part of the United Kingdom if it occurred outside that part.

(2) In sub-paragraph (1), "the relevant part of the United Kingdom" has the same meaning as in paragraph 3(2).

5

The decision was made in respect of conduct by a person who was under the age of 10 when the conduct took place.

6

The certificate does not confirm that –

(a) if the proceedings in which the decision was made were conducted in writing, the liable person was informed of the right to contest the proceedings and of the time limits that applied to the exercise of that right;
(b) if those proceedings provided for a hearing to take place and the liable person did not attend, the liable person was informed of the proceedings or indicated an intention not to contest them.

7

(1) The financial penalty is for an amount less than 70 euros.

(2) For the purposes of sub-paragraph (1), if the amount of a financial penalty is specified in a currency other than the euro, that amount must be converted to euros by reference to the London closing exchange rate on the date the decision was made.

(3) The Lord Chancellor may by order substitute a different amount for the amount for the time being specified in sub-paragraph (1).

PART 2
EUROPEAN FRAMEWORK LIST (FINANCIAL PENALTIES)

8

Participation in a criminal organisation.

9

Terrorism.

10

Trafficking in human beings.

11

Sexual exploitation of children and child pornography.

12

Illicit trafficking in narcotic drugs and psychotropic substances.

13

Illicit trafficking in weapons, munitions and explosives.

14

Corruption.

15

Fraud, including that affecting the financial interests of the European Communities within the meaning of the Convention of 26 July 1995 on the protection of the European Communities' financial interests.

16

Laundering of the proceeds of crime.

17

Counterfeiting currency, including of the euro.

18

Computer-related crime.

19

Environmental crime, including illicit trafficking in endangered animal species and in endangered plant species and varieties.

20

Facilitation of unauthorised entry and residence.

21

Murder, grievous bodily injury.

22

Illicit trade in human organs and tissue.

23

Kidnapping, illegal restraint and hostage-taking.

24

Racism and xenophobia.

25

Organised or armed robbery.

26

Illicit trafficking in cultural goods, including antiques and works of art.

27

Swindling.

28

Racketeering and extortion.

29

Counterfeiting and piracy of products.

30

Forgery of administrative documents and trafficking therein.

31

Forgery of means of payment.

32

Illicit trafficking in hormonal substances and other growth promoters.

33

Illicit trafficking in nuclear or radioactive materials.

34

Trafficking in stolen vehicles.

35

Rape.

36

Arson.

37

Crimes within the jurisdiction of the International Criminal Court.

38

Unlawful seizure of aircraft or ships.

39

Sabotage.

40

Conduct which infringes road traffic regulations, including breaches of regulations pertaining to driving hours and rest periods and regulations on hazardous goods.

41

Smuggling of goods.

42

Infringement of intellectual property rights.

43

Threats and acts of violence against persons, including violence during sport events.

44

Criminal damage.

45

Theft.

46

Offences created by the issuing State and serving the purpose of implementing obligations arising from instruments adopted under the treaty establishing the European Community or under Title VI of the Treaty on European Union.

PART 3
INTERPRETATION

47

(1) In this Schedule –

    (a)   "conduct" includes any act or omission;
    (b)   "liable person" means the person required to pay the financial penalty to which the certificate relates.

(2) If the decision was made in respect of conduct by a person other than the liable person, the references in paragraph 6 to the liable person are to be read as references to that other person.

Schedule 20

Section 118

Closure Orders: Premises Associated With Persistent Disorder Or Nuisance

After Part 1 of the Anti-social Behaviour Act 2003 (c. 38) (premises where drugs used unlawfully) insert the following Part.

"PART 1A
PREMISES ASSOCIATED WITH PERSISTENT DISORDER OR NUISANCE

11A   Part 1A closure notice

(1) This section applies to premises if a police officer not below the rank of superintendent ("the authorising officer") or the local authority has reasonable grounds for believing –

- (a)   that at any time during the relevant period a person has engaged in anti-social behaviour on the premises, and
- (b)   that the use of the premises is associated with significant and persistent disorder or persistent serious nuisance to members of the public.

(2) The authorising officer may authorise the issue of a Part 1A closure notice in respect of the premises if the officer is satisfied –

- (a)   that the local authority has been consulted; and
- (b)   that reasonable steps have been taken to establish the identity of any person who lives on the premises or who has control of or responsibility for, or an interest in, the premises.

(3) The local authority may authorise the issue of a Part 1A closure notice in respect of the premises if it is satisfied –

- (a)   that the appropriate chief officer has been consulted; and
- (b)   that reasonable steps have been taken to establish the identity of any person who lives on the premises or who has control of or responsibility for, or an interest in, the premises.

(4) An authorisation under subsection (2) or (3) may be given orally or in writing, but if it is given orally the authorising officer or local authority (as the case may be) must confirm it in writing as soon as it is practicable.

(5) A Part 1A closure notice must –

- (a)   give notice that an application will be made under section 11B for the closure of the premises;
- (b)   state that access to the premises by any person other than a person who habitually resides in the premises or the owner of the premises is prohibited;
- (c)   specify the date and time when, and the place at which, the application will be heard;
- (d)   explain the effects of an order made in pursuance of section 11B;
- (e)   state that failure to comply with the notice amounts to an offence; and
- (f)   give information about relevant advice providers.

(6) A Part 1A closure notice must be served by –

- (a)   a constable if its issue was authorised by the authorising officer, or
- (b)   an employee of the local authority if its issue was authorised by the authority.

(7) Service is effected by –

- (a)   fixing a copy of the notice to at least one prominent place on the premises,
- (b)   fixing a copy of the notice to each normal means of access to the premises,
- (c)   fixing a copy of the notice to any outbuildings which appear to the server of the notice to be used with or as part of the premises,
- (d)   giving a copy of the notice to at least one person who appears to the server of the notice to have control of or responsibility for the premises, and
- (e)   giving a copy of the notice to the persons identified in pursuance of subsection (2)(b) or (3)(b) (as the case may be) and to any other person appearing to the server of the notice to be a person of a description mentioned in that provision.

(8) The Part 1A closure notice must also be served on any person who occupies any other part of the building or other structure in which the premises are situated if the server of the notice reasonably believes, at the time of serving the notice under subsection (7), that the person's access to the other part of the building or structure will be impeded if a Part 1A closure order is made under section 11B.

(9) A person acting under subsection (7) may enter any premises, using reasonable force if necessary, for the purposes of complying with subsection (7)(a).

(10) The Secretary of State may by regulations specify premises or descriptions of premises to which this section does not apply.

(11) In this section –

"information about relevant advice providers" means information about the names of, and means of contacting, persons and organisations in the area that provide advice about housing and legal matters;
"the relevant period" means the period of 3 months ending with the day on which the authorising officer or the local authority (as the case may be) considers whether to authorise the issue of a Part 1A closure notice in respect of the premises.

11B Part 1A closure order

(1) If a Part 1A closure notice has been issued under section 11A an application must be made under this section to a magistrates' court for the making of a Part 1A closure order.

(2) An application under subsection (1) must be made by –

(a) a constable if the issue of the Part 1A closure notice was authorised by the authorising officer, or
(b) the local authority if the issue of the Part 1A closure notice was authorised by the authority.

(3) The application must be heard by the magistrates' court not later than 48 hours after the notice was served in pursuance of section 11A(7)(a).

(4) The magistrates' court may make a Part 1A closure order if and only if it is satisfied that each of the following paragraphs applies –

(a) a person has engaged in anti-social behaviour on the premises in respect of which the Part 1A closure notice was issued;
(b) the use of the premises is associated with significant and persistent disorder or persistent serious nuisance to members of the public;
(c) the making of the order is necessary to prevent the occurrence of such disorder or nuisance for the period specified in the order.

(5) A Part 1A closure order is an order that the premises in respect of which the order is made are closed to all persons for such period (not exceeding 3 months) as is specified in the order.

(6) But the order may include such provision as the court thinks appropriate relating to access to any part of the building or structure of which the premises form part.

(7) The magistrates' court may adjourn the hearing on the application for a period of not more than 14 days to enable –

(a) the occupier of the premises,
(b) the person who has control of or responsibility for the premises, or
(c) any other person with an interest in the premises, to show why a Part 1A closure order should not be made.

(8) If the magistrates' court adjourns the hearing under subsection (7) it may order that the Part 1A closure notice continues in effect until the end of the period of the adjournment.

(9) A Part 1A closure order may be made in respect of the whole or any part of the premises in respect of which the Part 1A closure notice was issued.

11C Part 1A closure order: enforcement

(1) This section applies if a magistrates' court makes an order under section 11B.

(2) A relevant person may –

(a) enter the premises in respect of which the order is made;
(b) do anything reasonably necessary to secure the premises against entry by any person.

(3) A person acting under subsection (2) may use reasonable force.

(4) But a relevant person seeking to enter the premises for the purposes of subsection (2) must, if required to do so by or on behalf of the owner, occupier or other person in charge of the premises, produce evidence of his identity and authority before entering the premises.

(5) A relevant person may also enter the premises at any time while the order has effect for the purpose of carrying out essential maintenance of or repairs to the premises.

(6) In this section "a relevant person" –

(a) in relation to premises in respect of which a police Part 1A closure order has effect, means a constable or a person authorised by the appropriate chief officer;
(b) in relation to premises in respect of which a local authority Part 1A closure order has effect, means a person authorised by the local authority.

11D Closure of premises associated with persistent disorder or nuisance: offences

(1) A person who remains on or enters premises in contravention of a Part 1A closure notice commits an offence.

(2) A person who –

(a) obstructs a person acting under section 11A(7) or 11C(2),
(b) remains on closed premises, or
(c) enters closed premises, commits an offence.

(3) A person guilty of an offence under this section is liable on summary conviction –

(a) to imprisonment for a period not exceeding 51 weeks, or
(b) to a fine not exceeding level 5 on the standard scale, or to both.

(4) A person who has a reasonable excuse for entering or being on the premises does not commit an offence under subsection (1) or (2)(b) or (c) (as the case may be).

(5) In relation to an offence committed before the commencement of section 281(5) of the Criminal Justice Act 2003, the reference in subsection (3)(a) to 51 weeks is to be read as a reference to 6 months.

11E Part 1A closure order: extension and discharge

(1) At any time before the end of the period for which a Part 1A closure order is made or extended, a complaint may be made by –

(a) a constable if the order is a police Part 1A closure order, or
(b) the local authority if the order is a local authority Part 1A closure order,

to a justice of the peace for an extension or further extension of the period for which the order has effect.

(2) A complaint may not be made under subsection (1) in relation to a police Part 1A closure order unless the complaint is authorised by a police officer not below the rank of superintendent –

(a) who has reasonable grounds for believing that it is necessary to extend the period for which the order has effect for the purpose of preventing the occurrence of significant and persistent disorder or persistent serious nuisance to members of the public, and
(b) who is satisfied that the local authority has been consulted about the intention to make the complaint.

(3) A complaint may not be made under subsection (1) in relation to a local authority Part 1A closure order unless the local authority –

(a) has reasonable grounds for believing that it is necessary to extend the period for which the order has effect for the purpose of preventing the occurrence of significant and persistent disorder or persistent serious nuisance to members of the public, and
(b) is satisfied that the appropriate chief officer has been consulted about the intention to make the complaint.

(4) If a complaint is made to a justice of the peace under subsection (1), the justice may issue a summons directed to –

(a) any person on whom the Part 1A closure notice relating to the closed premises was served under subsection (7)(d) or (e) or (8) of section 11A, or
(b) any other person who appears to the justice to have an interest in the closed premises but on whom the Part 1A closure notice was not served, requiring such person to appear before the magistrates' court to answer to the complaint.

(5) If the court is satisfied that the order is necessary to prevent the occurrence of significant and persistent disorder or persistent serious nuisance to members of the public for a further period, it may make an order extending the period for which the Part 1A closure order has effect by a period not exceeding 3 months.

(6) But a Part 1A closure order must not have effect for more than 6 months.

(7) Any of the following persons may make a complaint to a justice of the peace for an order that a Part 1A closure order is discharged –

(a) a constable if the Part 1A closure order is a police Part 1A closure order;
(b) the local authority if the Part 1A closure order is a local authority Part 1A closure order;
(c) a person on whom the Part 1A closure notice relating to the closed premises was served under subsection (7)(d) or (e) or (8) of section 11A;
(d) a person who has an interest in the closed premises but on whom the Part 1A closure notice was not served.

(8) If a complaint is made under subsection (7) –

(a) in relation to a police Part 1A closure order, by a person other than a constable, or
(b) in relation to a local authority Part 1A closure order, by a person other than the local authority, the justice may issue a summons directed to such constable as the justice thinks appropriate or to the local authority (as the case may be) requiring the constable or authority to appear before the magistrates' court to answer to the complaint.

(9) The court may not make an order discharging a Part 1A closure order unless it is satisfied that the Part 1A closure order is no longer necessary to prevent the occurrence of significant and persistent disorder or persistent serious nuisance to members of the public.

(10) If a summons is issued in accordance with subsection (4) or (8), a notice stating the date, time and place at which the complaint will be heard must be served on –

(a) if the summons is issued under subsection (4), the persons to whom it is directed;
(b) if the summons is issued under subsection (8), the persons mentioned in subsection (7)(c) and (d) (other than the complainant);
(c) if the complaint relates to a police Part 1A closure order, such constable as the justice thinks appropriate (unless a constable is the complainant);
(d) if the complaint relates to a local authority Part 1A closure order, the local authority (unless it is the complainant).

11F Part 1A closure order: appeals

(1) This section applies to –

(a) an order under section 11B or 11E;
(b) a decision by a court not to make an order under either of those sections.

(2) An appeal against an order or decision to which this section applies must be brought to the Crown Court before the end of the period of 21 days beginning with the day on which the order or decision is made.

(3) An appeal against an order under section 11B or 11E(5) may be brought by –

(a) a person on whom the Part 1A closure notice relating to the closed premises was served under section 11A(7)(d) or (e), or
(b) a person who has an interest in the closed premises but on whom the Part 1A closure notice was not served.

(4) An appeal against the decision of a court not to make such an order may be brought by –

(a) a constable if the Part 1A closure order is (or, if made, would have been) a police Part 1A closure order, or
(b) the local authority if the Part 1A closure order is (or, if made, would have been) a local authority Part 1A closure order.

(5) On an appeal under this section the Crown Court may make such order as it thinks appropriate.

11G Part 1A closure order: access to other premises

(1) This section applies to any person who occupies or owns any part of a building or structure –

(a) in which closed premises are situated, and
(b) in respect of which the Part 1A closure order does not have effect.

(2) A person to whom this section applies may, at any time while a Part 1A closure order has effect, apply to –

(a) the magistrates' court in respect of an order made under section 11B or 11E, or
(b) the Crown Court in respect of an order made under section 11F.

(3) If an application is made under this section notice of the date, time and place of the hearing to consider the application must be given to –

(a) such constable as the court thinks appropriate;
(b) the local authority;
(c) any person on whom the Part 1A closure notice relating to the closed premises was served under subsection (7)(d) or (e) or (8) of section 11A; and
(d) any person who has an interest in the closed premises but on whom the Part 1A closure notice was not served.

(4) On an application under this section the court may make such order as it thinks appropriate in relation to access to any part of a building or structure in which closed premises are situated.

(5) It is immaterial whether any provision has been made as mentioned in section 11B(6).

11H Part 1A closure order: reimbursement of costs

(1) A police authority or a local authority which incurs expenditure for the purpose of clearing, securing or maintaining the premises in respect of which a Part 1A closure order has effect may apply to the court which made the order for an order under this section.

(2) On an application under this section the court may make such order as it thinks appropriate in the circumstances for the reimbursement (in full or in part) by the owner of the premises of the expenditure mentioned in subsection (1).

(3) But an application for an order under this section must not be entertained unless it is made before the end of the period of 3 months starting with the day the Part 1A closure order ceases to have effect.

(4) An application under this section must be served on –

(a) the police authority for the area in which the premises are situated if the application is made by the local authority;
(b) the local authority if the application is made by a police authority; and
(c) the owner of the premises.

11I Part 1A closure notice or order: exemption from liability

(1) A constable is not liable for relevant damages in respect of anything done or omitted to be done by the constable in the performance or purported performance of functions under this Part.

(2) A chief officer of police who has direction or control of a constable is not liable for relevant damages in respect of anything done or omitted to be done by the constable in the performance or purported performance of functions under this Part.

(3) Neither a local authority nor an employee of a local authority is liable for relevant damages in respect of anything done or omitted to be done by or on behalf of the authority in the performance or purported performance of functions under this Part.

(4) Subsections (1) to (3) do not apply –

(a) if the act or omission is shown to have been in bad faith;
(b) so as to prevent an award of damages made in respect of an act or omission on the ground that the act or omission was unlawful by virtue of section 6(1) of the Human Rights Act 1998.

(5) This section does not affect any other exemption from liability for damages (whether at common law or otherwise).

(6) In this section "relevant damages" means damages in proceedings for judicial review or for the tort of negligence or misfeasance in public office.

11J Part 1A closure notices and orders: compensation

(1) This section applies to any person who incurs financial loss in consequence of –

    (a)   the issue of a Part 1A closure notice, or
    (b)   a Part 1A closure order having effect.

(2) A person to whom this section applies may apply to –

    (a)   the magistrates' court which considered the application for a Part 1A closure order;
    (b)   the Crown Court if the Part 1A closure order was made or extended by an order made by that Court on an appeal under section 11F.

(3) An application under this section must not be entertained unless it is made not later than the end of the period of 3 months starting with whichever is the later of –

    (a)   the day the court decides not to make a Part 1A closure order;
    (b)   the day the Crown Court dismisses an appeal against a decision not to make a Part 1A closure order;
    (c)   the day the Part 1A closure order ceases to have effect.

(4) On an application under this section the court may order the payment of compensation out of central funds if it is satisfied –

    (a)   that the person is not associated with such use of the premises as is mentioned in section 11A(1)(b),
    (b)   if the person is the owner or occupier of the premises, that the person took reasonable steps to prevent such use of the premises,
    (c)   that the person has incurred financial loss as mentioned in subsection (1), and
    (d)   having regard to all the circumstances it is appropriate to order payment of compensation in respect of that loss.

(5) In this section "central funds" has the same meaning as in enactments providing for the payment of costs.

11K Guidance

(1) The Secretary of State may issue guidance relating to the discharge of any functions under or for the purposes of this Part.

(2) A person discharging a function to which guidance under this section relates must have regard to the guidance in discharging the function.

11L Interpretation

(1) This section applies for the purposes of this Part.

(2) "Anti-social behaviour" means behaviour by a person which causes or is likely to cause harassment, alarm or distress to one or more other persons not of the same household as the person.

(3) "The appropriate chief officer", in relation to –

    (a)   any premises, or
    (b)   a Part 1A closure order relating to any premises,

means the chief officer of police for the area in which the premises are situated.

(4) "Closed premises" means premises in respect of which a Part 1A closure order has effect.

(5) "Local authority", in relation to England, means –

    (a)   a district council;
    (b)   a London borough council;
    (c)   a county council for an area for which there is no district council;
    (d)   the Common Council of the City of London in its capacity as a local authority;
    (e)   the Council of the Isles of Scilly.

(6) "Local authority", in relation to Wales, means –

    (a)   a county council;
    (b)   a county borough council.

(7) References to the local authority in relation to –

    (a)   any premises,
    (b)   a Part 1A closure notice relating to any premises, or
    (c)   a Part 1A closure order relating to any premises,

are references to the local authority for the area in which the premises are situated

(8) "A local authority Part 1A closure order" means a Part 1A closure order made or extended on the application of the local authority.

(9) "The owner", in relation to premises, means –

    (a)   a person who is for the time being entitled to dispose of the fee simple in the premises, whether in possession or in reversion (apart from a mortgagee not in possession), or
    (b)   a person who holds or is entitled to the rents and profits of the premises under a lease which (when granted) was for a term of not less than 3 years.

(10) "A Part 1A closure notice" means a notice issued under section 11A.

(11) "A Part 1A closure order" means –

    (a)   an order made under section 11B;
    (b)   an order extended under section 11E;
    (c)   an order made or extended under section 11F which has the like effect as an order made or extended under section 11B or 11E (as the case may be).

(12) "A police Part 1A closure order" means a Part 1A closure order made or extended on the application of a constable.

(13) "Premises" includes –

    (a)   any land or other place (whether enclosed or not);
    (b)   any outbuildings which are or are used as part of premises."

Schedule 21

Section 122

Nuisance Or Disturbance On HSS Premises

1 Offence of causing nuisance or disturbance on HSS premises

(1) A person commits an offence if –

    (a)   the person causes, without reasonable excuse and while on HSS premises, a nuisance or disturbance to an HSS staff member who is working there or is otherwise there in connection with work,
    (b)   the person refuses, without reasonable excuse, to leave the HSS premises when asked to do so by a constable or an HSS staff member, and
    (c)   the person is not on the HSS premises for the purpose of obtaining medical advice, treatment or care for himself or herself.

(2) A person who commits an offence under this paragraph is liable on summary conviction to a fine not exceeding level 3 on the standard scale.

(3) For the purposes of this paragraph –

    (a)   a person ceases to be on HSS premises for the purpose of obtaining medical advice, treatment or care for himself or herself once the person has received the advice, treatment or care, and
    (b)   a person is not on HSS premises for the purpose of obtaining medical advice, treatment or care for himself or herself if the person has been refused the advice, treatment or care during the last 8 hours.

(4) In this paragraph –

"hospital grounds" means land in the vicinity of a hospital and associated with it, "HSS premises" means –
(a) any hospital vested in, or managed by, an HSS trust,
(b) any building or other structure, or vehicle, associated with the hospital and situated on hospital grounds (whether or not vested in, or managed by, an HSS trust), and
(c) the hospital grounds,

"HSS staff member" means a person employed by an HSS trust or otherwise working for it (whether as or on behalf of a contractor, as a volunteer or otherwise),
"HSS trust" means a Health and Social Services trust established under Article 10 of the Health and Personal Social Services (Northern Ireland) Order 1991 (S.I. 1991/194 (N.I. 1)), and
"vehicle" includes an air ambulance.

2 Power to remove person causing nuisance or disturbance

(1) If a constable reasonably suspects that a person is committing or has committed an offence under paragraph 1, the constable may remove the person from the HSS premises concerned.

(2) If an authorised officer reasonably suspects that a person is committing or has committed an offence under paragraph 1, the authorised officer may –
(a) remove the person from the HSS premises concerned, or
(b) authorise an HSS staff member to do so.

(3) Any person removing another person from HSS premises under this paragraph may use reasonable force (if necessary).

(4) An authorised officer cannot remove a person under this paragraph or authorise another person to do so if the authorised officer has reason to believe that –
(a) the person to be removed requires medical advice, treatment or care for himself or herself, or
(b) the removal of the person would endanger the person's physical or mental health.

(5) In this paragraph –

"authorised officer" means any HSS staff member authorised by an HSS trust to exercise the powers conferred on an authorised officer by this paragraph, and
"HSS premises", "HSS staff member" and "HSS trust" have the same meaning as in paragraph 1.

3 Guidance about the power to remove etc.

(1) The Department of Health, Social Services and Public Safety may from time to time prepare and publish guidance to HSS trusts and authorised officers about the powers in paragraph 2.

(2) Such guidance may, in particular, relate to –
(a) the authorisation by HSS trusts of authorised officers,
(b) the authorisation by authorised officers of HSS staff members to remove persons under paragraph 2,
(c) training requirements for authorised officers and HSS staff members authorised by them to remove persons under paragraph 2,
(d) matters that may be relevant to a consideration by authorised officers for the purposes of paragraph 2 of whether offences are being, or have been, committed under paragraph 1,
(e) matters to be taken into account by authorised officers in deciding whether there is reason to believe that a person requires medical advice, treatment or care for himself or herself or that the removal of a person would endanger the person's physical or mental health,
(f) the procedure to be followed by authorised officers or persons authorised by them before using the power of removal in paragraph 2,

(g)   the degree of force that it may be appropriate for authorised officers or persons authorised by them to use in particular circumstances,
(h)   arrangements for ensuring that persons on HSS premises are aware of the offence in paragraph 1 and the powers of removal in paragraph 2, or
(i)   the keeping of records.

(3) Before publishing guidance under this paragraph, the Department of Health, Social Services and Public Safety must consult such persons as the Department considers appropriate.

(4) An HSS trust and an authorised officer must have regard to any guidance published under this paragraph when exercising functions under, or in connection with, paragraph 2.

(5) In this paragraph –

"authorised officer" has the same meaning as in paragraph 2, and "HSS premises", "HSS staff member" and "HSS trust" have the same meaning as in paragraph 1.

Schedule 22

Section 126

Police Misconduct And Performance Procedures

PART 1
AMENDMENTS OF POLICE ACT 1996

1

The Police Act 1996 (c. 16) has effect subject to the following amendments.

2   General duty of Secretary of State

In section 36(2)(d) (general duty of Secretary of State) for "section 85" substitute "sections 84 and 85".

3   Regulations for police forces

(1) Section 50 (regulations for police forces) is amended as follows.

(2) For subsection (3) substitute –

"(3)   Without prejudice to the powers conferred by this section, regulations under this section shall –

(a)   establish, or
(b)   make provision for the establishment of, procedures for the taking of disciplinary proceedings in respect of the conduct, efficiency and effectiveness of members of police forces, including procedures for cases in which such persons may be dealt with by dismissal."

(3) In subsection (4) omit ", subject to subsection (3)(b),".

4   Regulations for special constables

(1) Section 51 (regulations for special constables) is amended as follows.

(2) In subsection (2)(ba) (conduct of special constables) after "conduct" insert ", efficiency and effectiveness".

(3) After subsection (2) insert –

"(2A)   Without prejudice to the powers conferred by this section, regulations under this section shall –

(a)   establish, or
(b)   make provision for the establishment of, procedures for the taking of disciplinary proceedings in respect of the conduct, efficiency and effectiveness of special constables,

5 Police Federations

In section 59(3) (representation only by another member of a police force except in certain circumstances) for "provided by" substitute "provided in regulations made in accordance with".

6 Police Advisory Board

(1) Section 63(3) (supply of draft regulations to the Police Advisory Board) is amended as follows.

(2) In paragraph (a), for "regulations under section 50 or 52" substitute "regulations or rules under section 50, 52, 84 or 85".

(3) After "a draft of the regulations" insert "or rules".

7 Representation at disciplinary and other proceedings

For section 84 substitute –

> **"84 Representation etc. at disciplinary and other proceedings**
>
> (1) The Secretary of State shall by regulations make provision for or in connection with –
>
> (a) enabling the officer concerned or a relevant authority to be represented in proceedings conducted under regulations made in pursuance of section 50(3) or section 51(2A);
>
> (b) enabling the panel conducting such proceedings to receive advice from a relevant lawyer or another person falling within any prescribed description of persons.
>
> (2) Regulations under this section may in particular make provision –
>
> (a) specifying the circumstances in which the officer concerned or a relevant authority is entitled to be legally represented (by a relevant lawyer);
>
> (b) specifying the circumstances in which the officer concerned or a relevant authority is entitled to be represented by a person (other than a relevant lawyer) who falls within any prescribed description of persons;
>
> (c) for securing that –
>
> (i) a relevant authority may be legally represented, and
>
> (ii) the panel conducting the proceedings may receive advice from a relevant lawyer,
>
> whether or not the officer concerned is legally represented.
>
> (3) Without prejudice to the powers conferred by this section, regulations under this section shall, in relation to cases where the officer concerned is entitled to legal or other representation, make provision –
>
> (a) for securing that the officer is notified of his right to such representation;
>
> (b) specifying when the officer is to be so notified;
>
> (c) for securing that proceedings at which the officer may be dismissed are not to take place unless the officer has been notified of his right to such representation.
>
> (4) In this section –
>
> "the officer concerned", in relation to proceedings within subsection (1)(a), means the member of a police force or special constable to whom the proceedings relate;
>
> "the panel", in relation to proceedings within subsection (1)(a), means the panel of persons, or the person, prescribed for the purpose of conducting the proceedings;
>
> "prescribed" means prescribed by regulations under this section;
>
> "relevant authority" means –
>
> (a) where the officer concerned is a member of a police force (other than a senior officer), or a special constable, the chief officer of police of the police force of which the officer is a member, or for which the officer is appointed as a special constable;
>
> (b) where the officer concerned is a senior officer, the police authority for the police force of which the officer is a member;
>
> "relevant lawyer" means a person who, for the purposes of the Legal Services Act 2007, is an authorised person in relation to an activity which constitutes the exercise of a right of audience (within the meaning of that Act);

"senior officer" means a member of a police force holding a rank above that of chief superintendent.

(5) But in prescribed circumstances "relevant authority" also includes the Independent Police Complaints Commission.

(6) Regulations under this section may make different provision for different cases and circumstances.

(7) A statutory instrument containing regulations under this section shall be subject to annulment in pursuance of a resolution of either House of Parliament.

(8) Subsection (7) does not apply to a statutory instrument containing (whether alone or with other provision) any regulations under this section coming into force at a time that is the earliest time at which any regulations under this section are to come into force since the commencement of paragraph 7 of Schedule 22 to the Criminal Justice and Immigration Act 2008.

(9) A statutory instrument within subsection (8) may not be made unless a draft of it has been laid before and approved by a resolution of each House of Parliament."

8 Appeals against dismissal etc.

(1) Section 85 (appeals against dismissal etc.) is amended as follows.

(2) For subsections (1) and (2) substitute –

"(1) The Secretary of State shall by rules make provision specifying the cases in which a member of a police force or a special constable may appeal to a police appeals tribunal.

(2) A police appeals tribunal may, on the determination of an appeal under this section, make an order dealing with the appellant in any way in which he could have been dealt with by the person who made the decision appealed against."

(3) For subsection (4) substitute –

"(4) Rules made under this section may, in particular, make provision –
- (a) for enabling a police appeals tribunal, in such circumstances as are specified in the rules, to determine a case without a hearing;
- (b) for the appellant or the respondent to be entitled, in a case where there is a hearing, to be represented –
  - (i) by a relevant lawyer within the meaning of section 84, or
  - (ii) by a person who falls within any description of persons prescribed by the rules;
- (c) for enabling a police appeals tribunal to require any person to attend a hearing to give evidence or to produce documents, and rules made in pursuance of paragraph (c) may apply subsections (2) and (3) of section 250 of the Local Government Act 1972 with such modifications as may be set out in the rules.

(4A) Rules under this section may make different provision for different cases and circumstances."

(4) For subsection (5) substitute –

"(5) A statutory instrument containing rules under this section shall be subject to annulment in pursuance of a resolution of either House of Parliament.

(5A) Subsection (5) does not apply to a statutory instrument containing (whether alone or with other provision) the first rules made under this section after the commencement of paragraph 8 of Schedule 22 to the Criminal Justice and Immigration Act 2008: such an instrument may not be made unless a draft of it has been laid before and approved by a resolution of each House of Parliament."

9 Guidance concerning disciplinary proceedings etc.

(1) Section 87 (guidance concerning disciplinary proceedings etc.) is amended as follows.

(2) For subsection (1) substitute –

"(1) The Secretary of State may issue relevant guidance to –
- (a) police authorities,
- (b) chief officers of police,
- (c) other members of police forces,

(d) special constables, and
(e) persons employed by a police authority who are under the direction and control of the chief officer of police of the police force maintained by that authority.

(1ZA) "Relevant guidance" is guidance as to the discharge of functions under regulations under section 50 or 51 in relation to the matters mentioned in section 50(2)(e) or 51(2)(ba)."

(3) In subsection (1A), after "section 50" insert "or 51".

(4) In subsection (5), after "section 50" insert "or 51".

10 Police officers engaged on service outside their force

(1) Section 97 (police officers engaged on service outside their force) is amended as follows.

(2) In subsection (6) –

(a) in paragraph (b), omit "or is required to resign as an alternative to dismissal";
(b) in paragraph (c), omit "or is required to resign as an alternative to dismissal".

(3) In subsection (7), omit ", or required to resign as an alternative to dismissal,".

11 Police Appeals Tribunals

(1) Schedule 6 (appeals to police appeals tribunals) is amended as follows.

(2) In paragraph 1(1) (appeals by senior officers) for paragraphs (b) and (c) substitute –

"(b) one shall be Her Majesty's Chief Inspector of Constabulary appointed under section 54(1) or one of Her Majesty's Inspectors of Constabulary nominated by the Chief Inspector, and
(c) one shall be the permanent secretary to the Home Office or a Home Office director nominated by the permanent secretary."

(3) In paragraph 2 (appeals by other members of police forces) for sub-paragraph (1) substitute –

"(1) In the case of an appeal by a member of a police force (other than a senior officer) or a special constable, the police appeals tribunal shall consist of four members appointed by the relevant police authority, of whom –

(a) one shall be a person chosen from the list referred to in paragraph 1(1)(a),
(b) one shall be a senior officer,
(c) one shall be a member of the relevant police authority, and
(d) one shall be a retired member of a police force who, at the time of his retirement, was a member of an appropriate staff association."

(4) Omit paragraph 6 (hearings).

(5) In paragraph 7 (effect of orders) for sub-paragraph (1) substitute –

"(1) Where on the determination of an appeal the tribunal makes such an order as is mentioned in section 85(2), the order shall take effect –

(a) by way of substitution for the decision appealed against, and
(b) as from the date of that decision."

(6) In paragraph 10 (interpretation) –

(a) for sub-paragraph (b) substitute –
"(b) "the relevant police authority" means the police authority which maintains –
(i) the police force of which the appellant is a member, or
(ii) the police force for the area for which the appellant is appointed as a special constable,
as the case may be."
(b) for sub-paragraph (c) substitute –
"(c) "appropriate staff association" means –
(i) where the appellant was, immediately before the proceedings from which the appeal is brought, of the rank of chief superintendent or superintendent, the Police Superintendents' Association of England and Wales; and
(ii) in any other case, the Police Federation of England and Wales."

PART 2
AMENDMENTS OF MINISTRY OF DEFENCE POLICE ACT 1987

12

The Ministry of Defence Police Act 1987 (c. 4) has effect subject to the following amendments.

13 Defence Police Federation

In section 3(4) (representation of a member of the Ministry of Defence Police by the Federation) for "on an appeal to the Secretary of State or as provided by" substitute "as provided in regulations made under".

14 Regulations relating to disciplinary matters

(1) Section 3A (regulations relating to disciplinary matters) is amended as follows.

(2) For subsection (1) substitute –

"(1) The Secretary of State may make regulations with respect to –

(a) the conduct of members of the Ministry of Defence Police and the maintenance of discipline;
(b) the suspension from duty of members of the Ministry of Defence Police.

(1A) Without prejudice to the powers conferred by subsection (1), regulations under this section shall –

(a) establish, or
(b) make provision for the establishment of,

procedures for the taking of disciplinary proceedings in respect of the conduct of members of the Ministry of Defence Police, including procedures for cases in which such persons may be dealt with by dismissal."

(3) For subsection (2) substitute –

"(2) The regulations may provide for decisions which would otherwise fall to be taken by the Secretary of State or the chief constable of the Ministry of Defence Police to be taken instead by –

(a) a person appointed in accordance with the regulations; or
(b) the Ministry of Defence Police Committee."

15 Representation etc. at disciplinary proceedings

For section 4 substitute –

"4 Representation etc. at disciplinary proceedings

(1) The Secretary of State shall by regulations make provision for or in connection with –

(a) enabling the officer concerned or the relevant authority to be represented in proceedings conducted under regulations made in pursuance of section 3A;
(b) enabling the panel conducting such proceedings to receive advice from a relevant lawyer or another person falling within any prescribed description of persons.

(2) Regulations under this section may in particular make provision –

(a) specifying the circumstances in which the officer concerned or the relevant authority is entitled to be represented by a relevant lawyer;
(b) specifying the circumstances in which the officer concerned or the relevant authority is entitled to be represented by a person (other than a relevant lawyer) who falls within any prescribed description of persons;
(c) for securing that –
   (i) the relevant authority may be legally represented, and
   (ii) the panel conducting the proceedings may receive advice from a relevant lawyer, whether or not the officer concerned is legally represented.

(3) Without prejudice to the powers conferred by this section, regulations under this section shall, in relation to cases where the officer concerned is entitled to legal or other representation, make provision –

(a) for securing that the officer is notified of his right to such representation;
(b) specifying when the officer is to be so notified;
(c) for securing that proceedings at which the officer may be dismissed are not to take place unless the officer has been notified of his right to such representation.

(4) In this section –

"the officer concerned", in relation to proceedings within subsection (1)(a), means the member of the Ministry of Defence Police to whom the proceedings relate;
"the panel", in relation to proceedings within subsection (1)(a), means the panel of persons, or the person, prescribed for the purpose of conducting the proceedings;
"prescribed" means prescribed by regulations under this section;
"relevant authority" means –
(a) where the officer concerned is a member of the Ministry of Defence Police (other than a senior officer), the chief constable for the Ministry of Defence Police;
(b) where the officer concerned is a senior officer, the Ministry of Defence Police Committee;

"relevant lawyer" means –
(a) in relation to England and Wales, a person who, for the purposes of the Legal Services Act 2007, is an authorised person in relation to an activity which constitutes the exercise of a right of audience (within the meaning of that Act), and
(b) in relation to Scotland or Northern Ireland, counsel or a solicitor;

"senior officer" means a member of the Ministry of Defence Police holding a rank above that of chief superintendent.

(5) But in prescribed circumstances "relevant authority" also includes –

(a) in relation to England and Wales, the Independent Police Complaints Commission;
(b) in relation to Scotland, the Police Complaints Commissioner for Scotland;
(c) in relation to Northern Ireland, the Police Ombudsman for Northern Ireland.

(6) A statutory instrument containing regulations under this section shall be subject to annulment in pursuance of a resolution of either House of Parliament.

(7) Subsection (6) does not apply to a statutory instrument containing (whether alone or with other provision) any regulations under this section coming into force at a time that is the earliest time at which any regulations under this section are to come into force since the commencement of paragraph 15 of Schedule 22 to the Criminal Justice and Immigration Act 2008.

(8) A statutory instrument within subsection (7) may not be made unless a draft of it has been laid before and approved by a resolution of each House of Parliament."

16 Appeals against dismissal etc.

For section 4A substitute –

"4A Appeals against dismissal etc.

(1) The Secretary of State shall by regulations –

(a) make provision specifying the cases in which a member of the Ministry of Defence Police may appeal to a police appeals tribunal;
(b) make provision equivalent, subject to such modifications as the Secretary of State thinks fit, to that made (or authorised to be made) in relation to police appeals tribunals by any provision of Schedule 6 to the Police Act 1996 (c. 16) or Schedule 3 to the Police (Scotland) Act 1967 (c. 77).

(2) A police appeals tribunal may, on the determination of an appeal under this section, make an order dealing with the appellant in any way in which he could have been dealt with by the person who made the decision appealed against.

(3) The Secretary of State may make regulations as to the procedure on appeals to police appeals tribunals under this section.

(4) Regulations under this section may, in particular, make provision –

- (a) for enabling a police appeals tribunal, in such circumstances as are specified in the regulations, to determine a case without a hearing;
- (b) for the appellant or the respondent to be entitled, in a case where there is a hearing, to be represented –
  - (i) by a relevant lawyer, or
  - (ii) by a person who falls within any description of persons prescribed by the regulations;
- (c) for enabling a police appeals tribunal to require any person to attend a hearing to give evidence or to produce documents, and regulations made in pursuance of paragraph (c) may apply subsections (2) and (3) of section 250 of the Local Government Act 1972 with such modifications as may be set out in the regulations.

(5) Any statutory instrument containing regulations under this section shall be subject to annulment in pursuance of a resolution of either House of Parliament.

(6) Subsection (5) does not apply to a statutory instrument containing (whether alone or with other provision) the first regulations made under this section after the commencement of paragraph 16 of Schedule 22 to the Criminal Justice and Immigration Act 2008: such an instrument may not be made unless a draft of it has been laid before and approved by a resolution of each House of Parliament.

(7) In this section –

"police appeals tribunal" means a tribunal constituted in accordance with regulations under this section;
"relevant lawyer" has the same meaning as in section 4."

PART 3
AMENDMENTS OF RAILWAYS AND TRANSPORT SAFETY ACT 2003

17

The Railways and Transport Safety Act 2003 (c. 20) has effect subject to the following amendments.

18 Police regulations: general

(1) Section 36 (police regulations: general) is amended as follows.

(2) In subsection (1) (power to make regulations about constables) after "conditions" insert "of service".

(3) For subsection (2) substitute –

"(2) The Authority shall also make regulations similar to the provision made by and under –

- (a) sections 84 and 85 of the Police Act 1996 (representation etc. at disciplinary and other proceedings, and appeal), and
- (b) Schedule 6 to that Act (appeals to police appeals tribunals)."

19 Police regulations: special constables

After section 37(1) (power to make regulations about special constables) insert –

"(1A) The Authority shall also make regulations similar to the provision made by and under –

- (a) sections 84 and 85 of the Police Act 1996 (representation etc. at disciplinary and other proceedings, and appeal), and
- (b) Schedule 6 to that Act (appeals to police appeals tribunals)."

20 Police regulations by Secretary of State

For section 42(3) substitute –

"(3) If regulations under this section make provision for a matter specified in section 50(3) or section 51(2A) of the Police Act 1996 (disciplinary proceedings), they must also make provision similar to that made by and under –

(a) sections 84 and 85 of that Act (representation etc. at disciplinary and other proceedings, and appeal), and
(b) Schedule 6 to that Act (appeals to police appeals tribunals)."

21 Regulations: further appeal

Omit section 43 (regulations: further appeal).

Schedule 23

Section 127

Investigation of complaints of police misconduct etc.

1

The Police Reform Act 2002 (c. 30) has effect subject to the following amendments.

2

In section 23(2) (regulations) after paragraph (q) insert –

"(r) for enabling representations on behalf of a person to whose conduct an investigation relates to be made to the Commission by a person who is not that person's legal representative but is of a description specified in the regulations."

3

Schedule 3 (handling of complaints and conduct matters etc.) is amended as follows.

4

In paragraph 6(4) (handling of complaints by appropriate authority: use of local resolution procedures) in each of paragraphs (a)(ii) and (b)(ii), for the words from ", a requirement to resign" to the end substitute "or the giving of a final written warning."

5

After paragraph 19 insert –

"**19A Special procedure where investigation relates to police officer or special constable**

Paragraphs 19B to 19E apply to investigations of complaints or recordable conduct matters in cases where the person concerned (see paragraph 19B(11)) is a member of a police force or a special constable.

19B Assessment of seriousness of conduct under investigation

(1) If, during the course of an investigation of a complaint, it appears to the person investigating that there is an indication that a person to whose conduct the investigation relates may have –

(a) committed a criminal offence, or
(b) behaved in a manner which would justify the bringing of disciplinary proceedings, the person investigating must certify the investigation as one subject to special requirements.

(2) If the person investigating a complaint certifies the investigation as one subject to special requirements, the person must, as soon as is reasonably practicable after doing so, make a severity assessment in relation to the conduct of the person concerned to which the investigation relates.

(3) The person investigating a recordable conduct matter must make a severity assessment in relation to the conduct to which the investigation relates –

(a) as soon as is reasonably practicable after his appointment or designation, or
(b) in the case of a matter recorded in accordance with paragraph 21A(5) or 24B(2), as soon as is reasonably practicable after it is so recorded.

(4) For the purposes of this paragraph a "severity assessment", in relation to conduct, means an assessment as to –

(a) whether the conduct, if proved, would amount to misconduct or gross misconduct, and
(b) if the conduct were to become the subject of disciplinary proceedings, the form which those proceedings would be likely to take.

(5) An assessment under this paragraph may only be made after consultation with the appropriate authority.

(6) On completing an assessment under this paragraph, the person investigating the complaint or matter must give a notification to the person concerned that complies with sub-paragraph (7).

(7) The notification must –

(a) give the prescribed information about the results of the assessment;
(b) give the prescribed information about the effect of paragraph 19C and of regulations under paragraph 19D;
(c) set out the prescribed time limits for providing the person investigating the complaint or matter with relevant statements and relevant documents respectively for the purposes of paragraph 19C(2);
(d) give such other information as may be prescribed.

(8) Sub-paragraph (6) does not apply for so long as the person investigating the complaint or matter considers that giving the notification might prejudice –

(a) the investigation, or
(b) any other investigation (including, in particular, a criminal investigation).

(9) Where the person investigating a complaint or matter has made a severity assessment and considers it appropriate to do so, the person may revise the assessment.

(10) On revising a severity assessment, the person investigating the complaint or matter must notify the prescribed information about the revised assessment to the person concerned.

(11) In this paragraph and paragraphs 19C to 19E –

"the person concerned" –
(a) in relation to an investigation of a complaint, means the person in respect of whom it appears to the person investigating that there is the indication mentioned in paragraph 19B(1);
(b) in relation to an investigation of a recordable conduct matter, means the person to whose conduct the investigation relates;

"relevant document" –
(a) means a document relating to any complaint or matter under investigation, and
(b) includes such a document containing suggestions as to lines of inquiry to be pursued or witnesses to be interviewed;

"relevant statement" means an oral or written statement relating to any complaint or matter under investigation.

19C Duty to consider submissions from person whose conduct is being investigated

(1) This paragraph applies to –

(a) an investigation of a complaint that has been certified under paragraph 19B(1) as one subject to special requirements, or
(b) an investigation of a recordable conduct matter.

(2) If before the expiry of the appropriate time limit notified in pursuance of paragraph 19B(7)(c) –

(a) the person concerned provides the person investigating the complaint or matter with a relevant statement or a relevant document, or
(b) any person of a prescribed description provides that person with a relevant document, that person must consider the statement or document.

19D Interview of person whose conduct is being investigated

(1) The Secretary of State may by regulations make provision as to the procedure to be followed in connection with any interview of the person concerned which is held during the course of an investigation within paragraph 19C(1)(a) or (b) by the person investigating the complaint or matter.

(2) Regulations under this paragraph may, in particular, make provision –

(a) for determining how the time at which an interview is to be held is to be agreed or decided,
(b) about the information that must be provided to the person being interviewed,
(c) for enabling that person to be accompanied at the interview by a person of a prescribed description.

19E Duty to provide certain information to appropriate authority

(1) This paragraph applies during the course of an investigation within paragraph 19C(1)(a) or (b).

(2) The person investigating the complaint or matter must supply the appropriate authority with such information in that person's possession as the authority may reasonably request for the purpose mentioned in sub-paragraph (3).

(3) That purpose is determining, in accordance with regulations under section 50 or 51 of the 1996 Act, whether the person concerned should be, or should remain, suspended –

(a) from office as constable, and
(b) where that person is a member of a police force, from membership of that force."

6

(1) Paragraph 20A (accelerated procedure in special cases) is amended as follows.

(2) In sub-paragraph (1) (application of paragraph) for "a person appointed or designated to investigate" substitute "the person investigating".

(3) In sub-paragraph (6) (investigation to continue after submission of report) for "appointed or designated to investigate" substitute "investigating".

(4) In sub-paragraph (7) (definition of special conditions) –

(a) for paragraphs (a) and (b) substitute –
"(a) there is sufficient evidence, in the form of written statements or other documents, to establish on the balance of probabilities that conduct to which the investigation relates constitutes gross misconduct;";
(b) in paragraph (c), for "is the subject matter of the investigation" substitute "it is".

(5) Omit sub-paragraph (8) (interpretation).

7

(1) Paragraph 20B (investigations managed or carried out by Commission: action by appropriate authority) is amended as follows.

(2) For sub-paragraphs (3) and (4) (action to be taken where special conditions are satisfied) substitute –

"(3) If the appropriate authority determines that the special conditions are satisfied then, unless it considers that the circumstances are such as to make it inappropriate to do so, it shall –

(a) certify the case as a special case for the purposes of regulations under section 50(3) or 51(2A) of the 1996 Act; and
(b) take such steps as are required by those regulations in relation to a case so certified."

(3) Omit sub-paragraph (5) (appropriate authority to notify DPP if special conditions are satisfied).

8

In paragraph 20D(2) (action by Commission on receipt of memorandum) for "appointed under paragraph 18 or designated under paragraph 19" substitute "investigating the complaint or matter".

9

(1) Paragraph 20E (other investigations: action by appropriate authority) is amended as follows.

(2) For sub-paragraphs (3) and (4) (action to be taken where special conditions are satisfied) substitute –

> "(3) If the appropriate authority determines that the special conditions are satisfied then, unless it considers that the circumstances are such as to make it inappropriate to do so, it shall –
>
> (a) certify the case as a special case for the purposes of regulations under section 50(3) or 51(2A) of the 1996 Act; and
> (b) take such steps as are required by those regulations in relation to a case so certified."

(3) Omit sub-paragraph (5) (appropriate authority to notify DPP if special conditions are satisfied).

(4) In sub-paragraph (7) (appropriate authority to notify person investigating if special conditions are not satisfied) for "appointed under paragraph 16 or 17" substitute "investigating the complaint or matter".

10

Omit paragraph 20G (special cases: Director of Public Prosecutions) and the cross-heading immediately preceding it.

11

(1) Paragraph 21A (procedure where conduct matter is revealed in course of investigation of DSI matter) is amended as follows.

(2) In sub-paragraph (5) (DSI matter is to be recorded as conduct matter) omit the words from "(and the other provisions" to the end.

(3) After sub-paragraph (5) insert –

> "(6) Where a DSI matter is recorded under paragraph 11 as a conduct matter by virtue of sub-paragraph (5) –
>
> (a) the person investigating the DSI matter shall (subject to any determination made by the Commission under paragraph 15(5)) continue the investigation as if appointed or designated to investigate the conduct matter, and
> (b) the other provisions of this Schedule shall apply in relation to that matter accordingly."

12

(1) Paragraph 22 (final reports on investigations) is amended as follows.

(2) In sub-paragraph (1) (cases where paragraph 22 applies) –

(a) after paragraph (a) insert "or";
(b) omit paragraph (c).

(3) In sub-paragraph (4) (meaning of appropriate authority in the case of a conduct matter which was formerly a DSI matter) for the words from "a DSI matter" to "or (4)" substitute "a matter that was formerly a DSI matter but has been recorded as a conduct matter in pursuance of paragraph 21A(5)".

(4) At the end insert –

"(7) The Secretary of State may by regulations make provision requiring a report on an investigation within paragraph 19C(1)(a) or (b) –

(a) to include such matters as are specified in the regulations;
(b) to be accompanied by such documents or other items as are so specified.

(8) A person who has submitted a report under this paragraph on an investigation within paragraph 19C(1)(a) or (b) must supply the appropriate authority with such copies of further documents or other items in that person's possession as the authority may request.

(9) The appropriate authority may only make a request under sub-paragraph (8) in respect of a copy of a document or other item if the authority –

(a) considers that the document or item is of relevance to the investigation, and
(b) requires a copy of the document or the item for either or both of the purposes mentioned in sub-paragraph (10).

(10) Those purposes are –

(a) complying with any obligation under regulations under section 50(3) or 51(2A) of the 1996 Act which the authority has in relation to any person to whose conduct the investigation related;
(b) ensuring that any such person receives a fair hearing at any disciplinary proceedings in respect of any such conduct of his."

13

(1) Paragraph 23 (action by Commission in response to investigation report) is amended as follows.

(2) In sub-paragraph (2) (action to be taken on receipt of report) –

(a) for paragraph (b) substitute –
"(b) shall determine whether the conditions set out in sub-paragraphs (2A) and (2B) are satisfied in respect of the report;";
(b) in paragraph (c), for "the report does so indicate" substitute "those conditions are so satisfied";
(c) in paragraph (d), after "appropriate authority" insert "and the persons mentioned in sub-paragraph (5)".

(3) After sub-paragraph (2) insert –

"(2A) The first condition is that the report indicates that a criminal offence may have been committed by a person to whose conduct the investigation related.

(2B) The second condition is that –

(a) the circumstances are such that, in the opinion of the Commission, it is appropriate for the matters dealt with in the report to be considered by the Director of Public Prosecutions, or
(b) any matters dealt with in the report fall within any prescribed category of matters."

(4) In sub-paragraph (5) (persons to be notified) for "Those" substitute "The".

(5) For sub-paragraphs (6) and (7) substitute –

"(6) On receipt of the report, the Commission shall also notify the appropriate authority that it must –

(a) in accordance with regulations under section 50 or 51 of the 1996 Act, determine –
   (i) whether any person to whose conduct the investigation related has a case to answer in respect of misconduct or gross misconduct or has no case to answer, and
   (ii) what action (if any) the authority is required to, or will in its discretion, take in respect of the matters dealt with in the report, and
(b) determine what other action (if any) the authority will in its discretion take in respect of those matters."

(7) On receipt of a notification under sub-paragraph (6) the appropriate authority shall make those determinations and submit a memorandum to the Commission which –

(a) sets out the determinations the authority has made, and (b) if the appropriate authority has decided in relation to any person to whose conduct the investigation related that disciplinary proceedings should not be brought against that person, sets out its reasons for so deciding."

(6) In sub-paragraph (8)(a) (action by Commission on receipt of memorandum) for "is proposing to take the action" substitute "has made the determinations under sub-paragraph (6)(a)".

14

(1) Paragraph 24 (action by the appropriate authority in response to investigation report) is amended as follows.

(2) In sub-paragraph (2) (action to be taken on receipt of report) –

- (a) for paragraph (a) substitute –
  - "(a) shall determine whether the conditions set out in sub-paragraphs (2A) and (2B) are satisfied in respect of the report;";
- (b) in paragraph (b), for "the report does so indicate" substitute "those conditions are so satisfied";
- (c) after paragraph (b) insert "and
  - (c) shall notify the persons mentioned in sub-paragraph (5) of its determination under paragraph (a) and of any action taken by it under paragraph (b)."

(3) After sub-paragraph (2) insert –

"(2A) The first condition is that the report indicates that a criminal offence may have been committed by a person to whose conduct the investigation related.

(2B) The second condition is that –

- (a) the circumstances are such that, in the opinion of the appropriate authority, it is appropriate for the matters dealt with in the report to be considered by the Director of Public Prosecutions, or
- (b) any matters dealt with in the report fall within any prescribed category of matters."

(4) In sub-paragraph (5) (persons to be notified) for "Those" substitute "The".

(5) After sub-paragraph (5) insert –

"(5A) In the case of a report falling within sub-paragraph (1)(b) which relates to a recordable conduct matter, the appropriate authority shall also notify the Commission of its determination under sub-paragraph (2)(a).

(5B) On receipt of such a notification that the appropriate authority has determined that the conditions in sub-paragraphs (2A) and (2B) are not satisfied in respect of the report, the Commission –

- (a) shall make its own determination as to whether those conditions are so satisfied, and
- (b) if it determines that they are so satisfied, shall direct the appropriate authority to notify the Director of Public Prosecutions of the Commission's determination and to send the Director a copy of the report.

(5C) It shall be the duty of the appropriate authority to comply with any direction given to it under sub-paragraph (5B)."

(6) For sub-paragraph (6) substitute –

"(6) On receipt of the report or (as the case may be) copy, the appropriate authority shall also –

- (a) in accordance with regulations under section 50 or 51 of the 1996 Act, determine –
  - (i) whether any person to whose conduct the investigation related has a case to answer in respect of misconduct or gross misconduct or has no case to answer, and
  - (ii) what action (if any) the authority is required to, or will in its discretion, take in respect of the matters dealt with in the report, and
- (b) determine what other action (if any) the authority will in its discretion take in respect of those matters."

(7) In sub-paragraph (7) (appropriate authority to give notice on making a determination under sub-paragraph (6)) for "a determination" substitute "the determinations".

(8) In sub-paragraph (8) (contents of notification authority is required to give of its determination) for paragraphs (b) and (c) substitute –

"(b) the determinations the authority has made under sub-paragraph (6);".

15

In paragraph 24A(2) (final reports on investigations into other DSI matters: obligation to submit report) for the words from "A person appointed" to "paragraph 19" substitute "The person investigating".

16

(1) Paragraph 24B (action in response to a report on a DSI matter) is amended as follows.

(2) In sub-paragraph (2) (circumstances in which appropriate authority must record matter as a conduct matter) omit the words from "(and the other provisions" to the end.

(3) After sub-paragraph (2) insert –

"(3) Where a DSI matter is recorded under paragraph 11 as a conduct matter by virtue of sub-paragraph (2) –

(a) the person investigating the DSI matter shall (subject to any determination made by the Commission under paragraph 15(5)) investigate the conduct matter as if appointed or designated to do so, and
(b) the other provisions of this Schedule shall apply in relation to that matter accordingly."

17

(1) Paragraph 25 (appeals to Commission with respect to an investigation) is amended as follows.

(2) In sub-paragraph (2) (rights of appeal) –

(a) for paragraph (a)(ii) substitute –
"(ii) about any determination of the appropriate authority relating to the taking (or not taking) of action in respect of any matters dealt with in the report on the investigation;";
(b) for paragraph (c) substitute –
"(ba) a right of appeal against any determination by the appropriate authority that a person to whose conduct the investigation related has a case to answer in respect of misconduct or gross misconduct or has no case to answer;
(c) a right of appeal against any determination by the appropriate authority relating to the taking (or not taking) of action in respect of any matters dealt with in the report; and
(d) a right of appeal against any determination by the appropriate authority under paragraph 24(2)(a) as a result of which it is not required to send the Director of Public Prosecutions a copy of the report;".

(3) In sub-paragraph (3) (power of Commission to require appropriate authority to submit memorandum on an appeal) –

(a) before paragraph (a) insert –
"(za) sets out whether the appropriate authority has determined that a person to whose conduct the investigation related has a case to answer in respect of misconduct or gross misconduct or has no case to answer;";
(b) for paragraphs (a) and (b) substitute –
"(a) sets out what action (if any) the authority has determined that it is required to or will, in its discretion, take in respect of the matters dealt with in the report;";
(c) in paragraph (c), for "any person whose conduct is the subject-matter of the report" substitute "a person to whose conduct the investigation related";
(d) after paragraph (c) insert "and
(d) if the appropriate authority made a determination under paragraph 24(2)(a) as a result of which it is not required to send the Director of Public Prosecutions a copy of the report, sets out the reasons for that determination;".

(4) In sub-paragraph (5) (determinations to be made by Commission on an appeal) –

(a) after "shall determine" insert "such of the following as it considers appropriate in the circumstances";
(b) for paragraph (c) substitute –
"(c) whether the appropriate authority –
(i) has made such a determination as is mentioned in sub-paragraph (3)(za) that the Commission considers to be appropriate in respect of the matters dealt with in the report, and
(ii) has determined that it is required to or will, in its discretion, take the action (if any) that the Commission considers to be so appropriate; and
(d) whether the conditions set out in paragraph 24(2A) and (2B) are satisfied in respect of the report."

(5) In sub-paragraph (9) (action to be taken by Commission when it determines appropriate authority is not taking appropriate action) for "is not proposing to take the action in consequence of" substitute "has not made a determination as to whether there is a case for a person to whose conduct the investigation related to answer that the Commission considers appropriate or has not determined that it is required to or will, in its discretion, take the action in respect of the matters dealt with in".

(6) After sub-paragraph (9) insert –

"(9A) If, on an appeal under this paragraph, the Commission determines that the conditions set out paragraph 24(2A) and (2B) are satisfied in respect of the report, it shall direct the appropriate authority –

(a) to notify the Director of Public Prosecutions of the Commission's determination, and
(b) to send the Director a copy of the report."

18

(1) Paragraph 27 (duties with respect to disciplinary proceedings) is amended as follows.

(2) In sub-paragraph (1) (application of paragraph) in each of paragraphs (a) and (b), for "proposing to" substitute "required to or will, in its discretion,".

(3) In sub-paragraph (3) (recommendations that may be made by Commission in certain circumstances) –

(a) before paragraph (a) insert –
"(za) that the person has a case to answer in respect of misconduct or gross misconduct or has no case to answer in relation to his conduct to which the investigation related;";
(b) for paragraph (a) substitute –
"(a) that disciplinary proceedings of the form specified in the recommendation are brought against that person in respect of his conduct to which the investigation related;";
(c) in paragraph (b), for "include such charges" substitute "deal with such aspects of that conduct".

19

After paragraph 28 insert –

"**29 Minor definitions**

In this Part of this Schedule –

"gross misconduct" means a breach of the Standards of Professional Behaviour that is so serious as to justify dismissal;
"misconduct" means a breach of the Standards of Professional Behaviour;
"the person investigating", in relation to a complaint, recordable conduct matter or DSI matter, means the person appointed or designated to investigate that complaint or matter;
"prescribed" means prescribed by regulations made by the Secretary of State;
"the Standards of Professional Behaviour" means the standards so described in, and established by, regulations made by the Secretary of State."

Schedule 24

Section 140

Section 327A of Criminal Justice Act 2003: meaning of "child sex offence"

The following is the Schedule to be inserted as Schedule 34A to the Criminal Justice Act 2003 (c. 44) –

"SCHEDULE 34A
Child Sex Offences For Purposes Of Section 327A

1 **Offences under provisions repealed by Sexual Offences Act 2003**

An offence under –

(a) section 5 or 6 of the Sexual Offences Act 1956 (intercourse with girl under 13 or 16), or
(b) section 28 of that Act (causing or encouraging the prostitution of, intercourse with or indecent assault on girl under 16).

2

An offence under any of –

(a) section 1 of that Act (rape),
(b) section 10 of that Act (incest by a man), and
(c) sections 12 to 16 of that Act (buggery, indecency between men, indecent assault and assault with intent to commit buggery),

where the victim or (as the case may be) the other party was under 18 at the time of the offence.

3

An offence under section 1 of the Indecency with Children Act 1960 (indecent conduct towards child under 14).

4

An offence under section 9 of the Theft Act 1968 of burglary with intent to commit rape where the intended offence was an offence against a person under 18.

5

An offence under section 54 of the Criminal Law Act 1977 (incitement of child under 16 to commit incest).

6

An offence under section 3 of the Sexual Offences (Amendment) Act 2000 (abuse of position of trust).

7 **Other offences**

An offence under any of –

(a) sections 5 to 8 of the Sexual Offences Act 2003 (rape and other offences against children under 13),
(b) sections 9 to 15 of that Act (child sex offences),
(c) sections 16 to 19 of that Act (abuse of position of trust),
(d) sections 25 and 26 of that Act (familial child sex offences), and
(e) sections 47 to 50 of that Act (abuse of children through prostitution and pornography).

8

An offence under any of –

(a) sections 1 to 4 of that Act (rape, assault and causing sexual activity without consent),
(b) sections 30 to 41 of that Act (persons with a mental disorder impeding choice, inducements etc to persons with a mental disorder, and care workers for persons with a mental disorder), and
(c) section 61 of that Act (administering a substance with intent), where the victim of the offence was under 18 at the time of the offence.

9

An offence under section 62 or 63 of that Act (committing an offence with intent to commit a sexual offence and trespass with intent to commit a sexual offence) where the intended offence was an offence against a person under 18.

10

An offence under section 66 or 67 of that Act (exposure and voyeurism) where the victim or intended victim of the offence was under 18 at the time of the offence.

11

An offence under –

(a) section 1 of the Protection of Children Act 1978 (indecent photographs of children), or
(b) section 160 of the Criminal Justice Act 1988 (possession of indecent photograph of child).

12

An offence under section 170 of the Customs and Excise Management Act 1979 (penalty for fraudulent evasion of duty etc) in relation to goods prohibited to be imported under section 42 of the Customs Consolidation Act 1876 (indecent or obscene articles) where the prohibited goods included any indecent photograph showing a person under 18.

13

An offence under section 63 of the Criminal Justice and Immigration Act 2008 (possession of extreme pornographic images) in relation to an image showing a person under 18.

14 General

A reference in this Schedule to an offence ("offence A") includes –

(a) a reference to an attempt to commit offence A,
(b) a reference to a conspiracy to commit offence A,
(c) a reference to incitement to commit offence A,
(d) a reference to an offence under Part 2 of the Serious Crime Act 2007 in relation to which offence A is the offence (or one of the offences) which the person intended or believed would be committed, and
(e) a reference to aiding and abetting, counselling or procuring the commission of offence A.

15

A reference in this Schedule to an offence ("offence A") includes –

(a) a reference to an offence under section 70 of the Army Act 1955, section 70 of the Air Force Act 1955 or section 42 of the Naval Discipline Act 1957 as respects which the corresponding civil offence (within the meaning given by the section in question) is offence A, and
(b) a reference to an offence under section 42 of the Armed Forces Act 2006 as respects which the corresponding offence under the law of England and Wales (within the meaning given by that section) is offence A; and section 48 of that Act (attempts etc. outside England and Wales) applies for the purposes of paragraph (b) as if the reference in subsection (3)(b) to any of the following provisions of that Act were a reference to that paragraph."

Schedule 25

Section 145

Amendments To Armed Forces Legislation Part 1 Courts-Martial (Appeals) Act 1968

1

The Courts-Martial (Appeals) Act 1968 (c. 20) has effect subject to the following amendments.

2 Power to dismiss certain appeals following references by the CCRC

After section 25B insert –

"Appeals following references by the CCRC

25C Power to dismiss certain appeals following references by the CCRC

(1) This section applies where there is an appeal under this Part following a reference by the Criminal Cases Review Commission under section 12A(1)(a), (7) or (8) of the Criminal Appeal Act 1995.

(2) Notwithstanding anything in section 12, 21 or 25 of this Act, the Appeal Court may dismiss the appeal if –

(a) the only ground for allowing it would be that there has been a development in the law since the date of the conviction or finding that is the subject of the appeal, and
(b) the condition in subsection (3) is met.

(3) The condition in this subsection is that if –

(a) the reference had not been made, but
(b) the appellant had made (and had been entitled to make) an application for an extension of time within which to seek leave to appeal on the ground of the development in the law, the Court would not think it appropriate to grant the application by exercising the power conferred by section 9(3)."

3 Interim hospital orders

Section 16(5) (effect of interim hospital order made by Appeal Court) is omitted.

4

Section 25B(3) (as substituted by the Armed Forces Act 2006) (effect of interim hospital order made by Appeal Court) is omitted.

5

Before section 36 (but after the cross-heading preceding it) insert –

"35A Effect of interim hospital orders

(1) This section applies where the Appeal Court –

(a) make an interim hospital order by virtue of any provision of this Part, or
(b) renew an interim hospital order so made.

(2) The Court Martial shall be treated for the purposes of section 38(7) of the Mental Health Act 1983 (absconding offenders) as the court that made the order."

6

In section 36 (powers of Court under Part 2 which are exercisable by single judge), in subsection (1) after paragraph (h) insert –

"(ha) to renew an interim hospital order made by them by virtue of any provision of this Part;".

7 Evidence

(1) Section 28 (evidence) is amended as follows.

(2) In subsection (1), at the beginning insert "For the purposes of an appeal or an application for leave to appeal,".

(3) In that subsection, for paragraph (b) substitute –

"(b) order any witness to attend for examination and be examined before the Court (whether or not he was called in the proceedings from which the appeal lies); and".

(4) After subsection (1) insert –

"(1A) The power conferred by subsection (1)(a) may be exercised so as to require the production of any document, exhibit or other thing mentioned in that subsection to –

(a) the Appeal Court;
(b) the appellant;
(c) the respondent."

(5) In subsection (4), at the beginning insert "For the purposes of an appeal or an application for leave to appeal,".

(6) After subsection (4) insert –

"(5) In this section, "respondent" includes a person who will be a respondent if leave to appeal is granted."

8 Appeals against procedural directions

In section 36C (appeals against procedural directions), subsections (1) and (2) are omitted.

9 Detention of accused pending appeal to Supreme Court

(1) Section 43 (as amended by the Armed Forces Act 2006) (detention of accused on appeal by Crown) is amended as follows.

(2) In subsection (1) for "may make an order under this section" substitute "shall make one of the orders specified in subsection (1A)".

(3) In subsection (1A) –

(a) for "An order under this section is" substitute "The orders specified in this subsection are",
(b) the word "or" at the end of paragraph (a) is omitted, and
(c) after paragraph (b) insert –
"(c) an order that the accused be released without bail."

(4) After subsection (1B) insert –

"(1C) The Appeal Court may make an order within subsection (1A)(c) only if they think that it is in the interests of justice that the accused should not be liable to be detained as a result of the decision of the Supreme Court on the appeal."

(5) In subsection (2) for "under this section" substitute "within subsection (1A)(a) or (b)".

(6) For subsection (5) substitute –

"(5) The accused shall not be liable to be detained again as a result of the decision of the Supreme Court on the appeal if –

(a) the Appeal Court have made an order within subsection (1A)(c), or
(b) the Appeal Court have made an order within subsection (1A)(a) or (b) but the order has ceased to have effect by virtue of subsection (2) or the accused has been released or discharged by virtue of subsection (3)."

PART 2
ARMED FORCES ACT 2006

10

The Armed Forces Act 2006 (c. 52) has effect subject to the following amendments.

11 Consecutive custodial sentences

In section 188(4) (consecutive custodial sentences), after "Part 12 of the 2003 Act" insert "or under Part 2 of the Criminal Justice Act 1991".

12 Dangerous offenders

In section 209 (offenders under 18 convicted of certain serious offences), in subsection (7) for "sections 221, 222 and 227" substitute "section 226(2) of the 2003 Act (as applied by section 221(2) of this Act) and section 227 of this Act".

13

(1) Section 219 (dangerous offenders aged 18 or over) is amended as follows.

(2) In subsection (1) for the words from "a person" to the end substitute " –

 (a) a person aged 18 or over is convicted by the Court Martial of an offence under section 42 (criminal conduct),
 (b) the corresponding offence under the law of England and Wales is a serious offence, and
 (c) the court is of the required opinion (defined by section 223)."

(3) For subsections (2) and (3) substitute –

"(2) Section 225(2) to (4) of the 2003 Act apply in relation to the offender.

(3) In section 225(2) and (3A) of the 2003 Act (as applied by subsection (2)), references to "the offence" are to be read as references to the offence under section 42 of this Act."

(4) For the italic cross-heading before section 219 substitute *"Required or discretionary sentences for particular offences"*.

14

(1) Section 220 (certain violent or sexual offences: offenders aged 18 or over) is amended as follows.

(2) In subsection (1) for the words from "a person" to the end substitute " –

 (a) a person aged 18 or over is convicted by the Court Martial of an offence under section 42 (criminal conduct),
 (b) the corresponding offence under the law of England and Wales is a specified offence,
 (c) the court is of the required opinion (defined by section 223), and
 (d) where the corresponding offence under the law of England and Wales is a serious offence, the case is not one in which the court is required by section 225(2) of the 2003 Act (as applied by section 219(2) of this Act) to impose a sentence of imprisonment for life."

(3) For subsection (2) substitute –

"(2) Section 227(2) to (5) of the 2003 Act apply in relation to the offender."

(4) In subsection (3) –

 (a) for "section 227" substitute "section 227(2) to (5)",
 (b) before paragraph (a) insert –

 "(za) the reference in section 227(2A) to "the offence" is to be read as a reference to the offence under section 42 of this Act;", and

 (c) in paragraph (a) for "subsection (2)(b)" substitute "subsection (2C)(b)".

(5) After subsection (3) insert –

"(3A) The power conferred by section 227(6) of the 2003 Act includes power to amend section 227(2B) as applied by this section."

15

(1) Section 221 (dangerous offenders aged under 18) is amended as follows.

(2) In subsection (1) for the words from "a person" to the end substitute " –
- (a) a person aged under 18 is convicted by the Court Martial of an offence under section 42 (criminal conduct),
- (b) the corresponding offence under the law of England and Wales is a serious offence, and
- (c) the court is of the required opinion (defined by section 223)."

(3) For subsection (2) substitute –

"(2) Section 226(2) to (4) of the 2003 Act apply in relation to the offender."

(4) In subsection (3) –
- (a) for the words from the beginning to "is" substitute "In section 226(2) of the 2003 Act (as applied subsection (2))", and
- (b) in paragraphs (a) and (b) the words "in section 226(2)" are omitted.

(5) Subsection (4) is omitted.

16

(1) Section 222 (offenders aged under 18: certain violent or sexual offences) is amended as follows.

(2) In subsection (1), in paragraph (d) for the words from "section 221" to the end substitute "section 226(2) of the 2003 Act (as applied by section 221(2) of this Act) to impose a sentence of detention for life."

(3) For subsection (2) substitute –

"(2) Section 228(2) to (5) of the 2003 Act apply in relation to the offender."

(4) In subsection (3) –
- (a) for "section 228" substitute "section 228(2) to (5)", and
- (b) in paragraph (a) for "subsection (2)(b)" substitute "subsection (2B)(b)".

(5) After subsection (3) insert –

"(3A) The power conferred by section 228(7) of the 2003 Act includes power to amend section 228(2A) as applied by this section."

17

(1) Section 223 (the required opinion for the purposes of sections 219 to 222) is amended as follows.

(2) In subsection (1) for "219(2), 220(2), 221(2)" substitute "219(1), 220(1), 221(1)".

(3) In subsection (2) for "section 229(2) to (4)" substitute "section 229(2) and (2A)".

(4) In subsection (3) the words "to (4)" are omitted.

18

(1) Section 228 (appeals where previous convictions set aside) is amended as follows.

(2) For subsection (1) substitute –

"(1) Subsection (3) applies where –

(a) a sentence has been imposed on any person under section 225(3) or 227(2) of the 2003 Act (as applied by section 219(2) or 220(2) of this Act),
(b) the condition in section 225(3A) or (as the case may be) 227(2A) of the 2003 Act was met but the condition in section 225(3B) or (as the case may be) 227(2B) of that Act was not, and
(c) any previous conviction of his without which the condition in section 225(3A) or (as the case may be) 227(2A) would not have been met has been subsequently set aside on appeal."

19

In section 237 (purposes of sentencing), in subsection (3)(b) –

(a) or "to 222" substitute ", 221", and
(b) for "any of sections 225 to 228" substitute "section 225(2) or 226(2)".

20

In section 256 (pre-sentence reports), in subsection (1)(c) for the words from "section" to the end substitute "section 219(1), 220(1), 221(1) or 222(1) (sentences for dangerous offenders)."

21

In section 260 (discretionary custodial sentences: general restrictions), in subsection (1)(b) for the words from "as a result" to the end substitute "under section 225(2) or 226(2) of the 2003 Act (as applied by section 219(2) or 221(2) of this Act) or as a result of any of sections 225 to 227 of this Act."

22

In section 261 (length of discretionary custodial sentences: general provision) –

(a) in subsection (1) for "falling to be imposed as a result of section 219(2) or 221(2)" substitute "imposed under section 225 or 226 of the 2003 Act (as applied by section 219(2) or 221(2) of this Act)", and
(b) in subsection (3) for "required minimum sentences" substitute "sentences that may or must be imposed".

23

In section 273 (review of unduly lenient sentences by Court Martial Appeal Court), in subsection (6)(b) for "section 219, 220, 221, 222, 225, 226 or 227" substitute "section 225(2) or 226(2) of the 2003 Act (as applied by section 219(2) or 221(2) of this Act) or by section 225, 226 or 227 of this Act".

24 Restrictions on imposing community punishment

In section 253(2)(h) (duties in complying with section 252) for "section 151(2) of the 2003 Act as applied by section 270 of this Act" substitute "section 270B(4)".

25

In section 254(1) (savings for powers to mitigate sentence etc.) for "and 270" substitute ", 270 and 270B".

26

(1) Section 270 (community punishments: general restrictions etc.) is amended as follows.

(2) After subsection (6) insert –

"(6A) The fact that by virtue of any provision of this section –

(a) a community punishment may be awarded in respect of an offence, or
(b) particular restrictions on liberty may be imposed by a community punishment,

does not require a court to award such a punishment or to impose those restrictions."

(3) Subsection (7) is omitted.

(4) In subsection (8) –

(a) the word "Accordingly" is omitted; and
(b) for "151(2) of the 2003 Act as applied by this section" substitute "270B(4)".

27

After section 270 insert –

"270A Community punishment available only for offences punishable with imprisonment or for offenders previously fined

The power to award a community punishment is only exercisable in respect of an offence if –

(a) a person who is guilty of such an offence is liable to imprisonment; or
(b) in any other case, section 270B(4) confers power to award such a punishment.

270B Community punishment for offender previously fined

(1) This section provides for the award of a community punishment by a court in respect of an offence ("the current offence") committed by a person to whom subsection (2) or (3) applies.

(2) This subsection applies to the offender if –

(a) a person guilty of the current offence is liable to imprisonment;
(b) the offender was aged 16 or over when he was convicted;
(c) on three or more previous occasions the offender has, on conviction by a court for an offence committed by him after attaining the age of 16, had passed on him a sentence consisting only of a fine; and
(d) despite the effect of section 238(1)(b), the court would not (apart from this section) regard the current offence, or the combination of the current offence and one or more offences associated with it, as being serious enough to warrant a community punishment.

(3) This subsection applies to the offender if –

(a) a person guilty of the current offence is not liable to imprisonment;
(b) the offender was aged 16 or over when he was convicted; and
(c) on three or more previous occasions the offender has, on conviction by a court for an offence committed by him after attaining the age of 16, had passed on him a sentence consisting only of a fine.

(4) The court may award a community punishment in respect of the current offence if it considers that, having regard to all the circumstances including the matters referred to in subsection (5), it would be in the interests of justice to award such a punishment.

(5) Those matters are –

(a) the nature of the offences to which the previous convictions mentioned in subsection (2)(c) or (3)(c) (as the case may be) relate and their relevance to the current offence; and
(b) the time that has elapsed since the offender's conviction of each of those offences.

(6) In subsections (2)(c) and (3)(c) "conviction by a court" means –

(a) a conviction by a civilian court in any part of the United Kingdom for a service offence or for an offence punishable by the law of that part of the United Kingdom; or
(b) a conviction in service disciplinary proceedings.

(7) For the purposes of subsections (2)(c) and (3)(c) a compensation order or a service compensation order awarded in service disciplinary proceedings does not form part of an offender's sentence.

(8) It is immaterial for the purposes of subsections (2)(c) and (3)(c) whether on previous occasions a court has passed on the offender a sentence not consisting only of a fine.

(9) This section does not limit the extent to which a court may, in accordance with section 238(1)(b) and (2), treat any previous convictions of the offender as increasing the seriousness of an offence.

(10) In this section –

(a) "service disciplinary proceedings" means proceedings (whether or not before a court) in respect of a service offence; and
(b) any reference to a conviction or sentence, in the context of such proceedings, includes anything that under section 376(1) to (3) is to be treated as a conviction or sentence."

28 Review of sentence on reference by Attorney General

In section 273 (reviews of unduly lenient sentencing by Court Martial Appeal Court) for subsection (7) substitute –

"(7) Where a reference under subsection (1) relates to a case in which the Court Martial made an order specified in subsection (7A), the Court Martial Appeal Court may not, in deciding what sentence is appropriate for the case, make any allowance for the fact that the offender is being sentenced for a second time.

(7A) The orders specified in this subsection are –

(a) an order under section 269(2) of the 2003 Act (determination of minimum term in relation to mandatory life sentence);
(b) an order under section 82A(2) of the Sentencing Act (determination of minimum term in relation to discretionary life sentences and certain other sentences)."

29 Compensation for miscarriages of justice

(1) Section 276 (compensation for miscarriages of justice) is amended as follows.

(2) In subsection (1) for "subsections (2) and (3)" substitute "subsections (2) to (3A)".

(3) At the end of subsection (3) insert "before the end of the period of 2 years beginning with the date on which the conviction of the person concerned is reversed or he is pardoned.

(3A) But the Secretary of State may direct that an application for compensation made after the end of that period is to be treated as if it had been made within that period if the Secretary of State considers that there are exceptional circumstances which justify doing so."

(4) For subsection (6) substitute –

"(6) Section 276A applies in relation to the assessment of the amount of the compensation."

(5) After subsection (7) insert –

"(7A) But in a case where –

(a) a person's conviction for an offence is quashed on an appeal out of time, and
(b) the person is to be subject to a retrial, the conviction is not to be treated for the purposes of subsection (1) as "reversed" unless and until the person is acquitted of all offences at the retrial or the prosecution indicates that it has decided not to proceed with the retrial."

30

After section 276 insert –

"**276A Miscarriages of justice: amount of compensation**

(1) This section applies where an assessor is required to assess the amount of compensation payable to or in respect of a person under section 276 for a miscarriage of justice.

(2) In assessing so much of any compensation payable under section 276 as is attributable to suffering, harm to reputation or similar damage, the assessor must have regard in particular to –

(a) the seriousness of the offence of which the person was convicted and the severity of the punishment resulting from the conviction, and
(b) the conduct of the investigation and prosecution of the offence.

(3) The assessor may make from the total amount of compensation that the assessor would otherwise have assessed as payable under section 276 any deduction or deductions that the assessor considers appropriate by reason of either or both of the following –

(a) any conduct of the person appearing to the assessor to have directly or indirectly caused, or contributed to, the conviction concerned; and
(b) any other convictions of the person and any punishment resulting from them.

(4) If, having had regard to any matters falling within subsection (3)(a) or (b), the assessor considers that there are exceptional circumstances which justify doing so, the assessor may determine that the amount of compensation payable under section 276 is to be a nominal amount only.

(5) The total amount of compensation payable to or in respect of a person under section 276 for a particular miscarriage of justice must not exceed the overall compensation limit.

That limit is –
(a) £1 million in a case to which section 276B applies, and
(b) £500,000 in any other case.

(6) The total amount of compensation payable under section 276 for a person's loss of earnings or earnings capacity in respect of any one year must not exceed the earnings compensation limit. That limit is an amount equal to 1.5 times the median annual gross earnings according to the latest figures published by the Office of National Statistics at the time of the assessment.

(7) The Secretary of State may by order amend subsection (5) or (6) so as to alter any amount for the time being specified as the overall compensation limit or the earnings compensation limit.

276B Cases where person has been detained for at least 10 years

(1) For the purposes of section 276A(5) this section applies to any case where the person concerned ("P") has been in qualifying detention for a period (or total period) of at least 10 years by the time when –

(a) the conviction is reversed, or
(b) the pardon is given,

as mentioned in section 276(1).

(2) P was "in qualifying detention" at any time when P was detained in a prison, a hospital or at any other place, if P was so detained –

(a) by virtue of a sentence passed in respect of the relevant offence,
(b) under mental health legislation by reason of P's conviction of that offence (disregarding any conditions other than the fact of the conviction that had to be fulfilled in order for P to be so detained), or
(c) as a result of P's having been ordered to be kept in service custody, or remanded for mental health purposes, in connection with the relevant offence or with any other offence the charge for which was founded on the same facts or evidence as that for the relevant offence.

(3) In calculating the period (or total period) during which P has been in qualifying detention as mentioned in subsection (1), no account is to be taken of any period of time during which P was both –

(a) in qualifying detention, and
(b) in excluded concurrent detention.

(4) P was "in excluded concurrent detention" at any time when P was detained in a prison, a hospital or at any other place, if P was so detained –

(a) during the term of a sentence passed in respect of an offence other than the relevant offence,
(b) under mental health legislation by reason of P's conviction of any such other offence (disregarding any conditions other than the fact of the conviction that had to be fulfilled in order for P to be so detained), or
(c) as a result of P's having been ordered to be kept in service custody, or remanded for mental health purposes, in connection with an offence for which P was subsequently convicted other than –
(i) the relevant offence, or
(ii) any other offence the charge for which was founded on the same facts or evidence as that for the relevant offence.

(5) But P was not "in excluded concurrent detention" at any time by virtue of subsection (4)(a), (b) or (c) if P's conviction of the other offence mentioned in that provision was quashed on appeal, or a pardon was given in respect of it.

(6) In this section –

"kept in service custody" means –
(a) kept in service custody under section 105(2) of the Armed Forces Act 2006, or
(b) kept in military, air-force or naval custody under section 75A(2) of the Army Act 1955 or of the Air Force Act 1955 or section 47G(2) of the Naval Discipline Act 1957 (as the case may be);

"mental health legislation" means –
(a) Part 3 of the Mental Health Act 1983, or
(b) the provisions of any earlier enactment corresponding to Part 3 of that Act;

"the relevant offence" means the offence in respect of which the conviction is quashed or the pardon is given (but see subsection (7));

"remanded for mental health purposes" means remanded or admitted to hospital under section 35, 36 or 38 of the Mental Health Act 1983 or under any corresponding provision of any earlier enactment;

"reversed" has the same meaning as in section 276 of this Act.

(7) If, as a result of the miscarriage of justice –
(a) two or more convictions are reversed, or
(b) a pardon is given in respect of two or more offences, "the relevant offence" means any of the offences concerned."

31

In section 373 (orders, regulations etc.) in subsection (3)(a), after "113," insert "276A(7),".

32 Imposition of unpaid work requirement for breach of service community order or overseas service community order

In paragraph 14(b) of Schedule 5 (modifications of Schedule 8 to the Criminal Justice Act 2003 as it applies to overseas community orders), for "(3)" substitute "(3A)".

33 Suspended prison sentences: further conviction or breach of requirement

In paragraph 9(1)(b) of Schedule 7 (which provides for paragraph 9 of Schedule 12 to the Criminal Justice Act 2003, as it applies to an order under paragraph 8 of that Schedule made by a service court, to have effect with substituted sub-paragraphs (2) and (3)) –

(a) in the substituted text of sub-paragraph (2), after "Part 12" insert "of this Act or under Part 2 of the Criminal Justice Act 1991"; and
(b) in the substituted text of sub-paragraph (3), after "287" insert "of the Armed Forces Act 2006".

PART 3
TRANSITIONAL PROVISIONS

34 Transitional provisions: compensation for miscarriage of justice

(1) Paragraph 29(3) has effect in relation to any application for compensation made in relation to –

(a) a conviction which is reversed, and
(b) a pardon which is given, on or after the commencement date.

(2) Paragraphs 29(4) and 30 have effect in relation to –

(a) any application for compensation made on or after the commencement date, and
(b) any application for compensation made before that date in relation to which the question whether there is a right to compensation has not been determined before that date by the Secretary of State under section 276(4) of the 2006 Act.

(3) Paragraph 29(5) has effect in relation to any conviction quashed on an appeal out of time in respect of which an application for compensation has not been made before the commencement date.

(4) Paragraph 29(5) so has effect whether a conviction was quashed before, on or after the commencement date.

(5) In the case of –

    (a)   a conviction which is reversed, or
    (b)   a pardon which is given,

before the commencement date but in relation to which an application for compensation has not been made before that date, any such application must be made before the end of the period of 2 years beginning with that date.

(6) But the Secretary of State may direct that an application for compensation in relation to a case falling within sub-paragraph (5) which is made after the end of that period is to be treated as if it had been made before the end of that period if the Secretary of State considers that there are exceptional circumstances which justify doing so.

(7) In this paragraph –

"the 2006 Act" means the Armed Forces Act 2006 (c. 52);
"application for compensation" means an application for compensation made under section 276(3) of the 2006 Act;
"the commencement date" means the date on which paragraphs 29 and 30 come into force;
"reversed" has the same meaning as in section 276(1) of the 2006 Act (as amended by paragraph 29(5)).

Schedule 26

Section 148

Minor And Consequential Amendments

PART 1
FINE DEFAULTERS

1 Magistrates' Courts Act 1980 (c. 43)

In section 81(3) of the Magistrates' Courts Act 1980 (enforcement of fines imposed on young offenders) for paragraph (a) substitute –

    "(a)   a youth default order under section 39 of the Criminal Justice and Immigration Act 2008; or".

2 Criminal Justice Act 2003 (c. 44)

(1) The Criminal Justice Act 2003 is amended as follows.

(2) In section 221(2) (provision of attendance centres) after paragraph (b) insert –

    "(c)   default orders under section 300 of this Act, or
    (d)   youth default orders under section 39 of the Criminal Justice and Immigration Act 2008."

(3) In section 300 (power to impose unpaid work requirement or curfew requirement on fine defaulter) –

    (a)   in subsection (1) –
        (i)   for "16" substitute "18", and
        (ii)   omit paragraph (b), and
    (b)   in subsection (2), omit from "or, as the case may be" to "young offender)".

(4) In Schedule 31 (modifications of community order provisions for purposes of default order) after paragraph 3 insert –

"**3A Attendance centre requirement**

In its application to a default order, section 214(2) (attendance centre requirement) is modified by the substitution for "not be less than 12 or more than 36" of "be –

(a) not less than 12, and
(b) in the case of an amount in default which is specified in the first column of the following Table, not more than the number of hours set out opposite that amount in the second column.

Amount	Number of hours
An amount not exceeding £200	18 hours
An amount exceeding £200 but not exceeding £500	21 hours
An amount exceeding £500 but not exceeding £1,000	24 hours
An amount exceeding £1,000 but not exceeding £2,5000	30 hours
An amount exceeding £2,500	36 hours"

(5) In paragraph 4(5)(a) of that Schedule (modifications of community order provisions for purposes of default order) omit ", (5)".

(6) In paragraph 5 of that Schedule, for "or 3" substitute ", 3 or 3A".

PART 2
OTHER AMENDMENTS

3 Prison Act 1952 (c. 52)

In section 43(1)(aa) of the Prison Act 1952 (provision by Secretary of State of young offender institutions), at the end insert "or other persons who may be lawfully detained there".

4 Criminal Justice Act 1961 (c. 39)

In section 38(3)(c) of the Criminal Justice Act 1961 (construction of references to imprisonment or detention in case of children and young persons) after "in accordance with" insert "a determination of the Secretary of State or of a person authorised by him, in accordance with arrangements made by the Secretary of State or in accordance with".

5 Children and Young Persons Act 1969 (c. 54)

(1) Section 23AA of the Children and Young Persons Act 1969 (electronic monitoring of remand conditions) is amended as follows.

(2) In subsection (4) –
(a) paragraph (a) is omitted; and
(b) in paragraph (b), for "those arrangements" substitute "arrangements currently available in each local justice area which is a relevant area".

(3) In subsection (8) for "Subsections (8) to (10) of section 3AA" substitute "Subsections (4) to (7) of section 3AC".

6 Criminal Appeal (Northern Ireland) Act 1980 (c. 47)

In section 13A(3) of the Criminal Appeal (Northern Ireland) Act 1980 (grounds for allowing appeal against finding of unfitness to be tried), in paragraph (a) for "the finding" substitute "a finding".

7 Wildlife and Countryside Act 1981 (c. 69)

In section 19XA(1) of the Wildlife and Countryside Act 1981 (constables' powers in connection with samples) for "by this section" substitute "by section 19".

8 Mental Health Act 1983 (c.20)

In section 37 of the Mental Health Act 1983 (powers of court to order hospital admission or guardianship), in subsection (1A)(c) for "any of sections 225 to 228" substitute "section 225(2) or 226(2)".

9 Repatriation of Prisoners Act 1984 (c. 47)

The Repatriation of Prisoners Act 1984 has effect subject to the following amendments.

10

Before section 1 insert –

"Transfer of prisoners to or from the United Kingdom".

11

(1) Section 1 (issue of warrant for transfer) is amended as follows.

(2) In subsections (2) and (3) for "warrant under this Act" substitute "warrant under this section".

(3) In subsection (4) –

    (a)   for "warrant under this Act" (in both places) substitute "warrant under this section";
    (b)   in paragraph (b) omit the words "under this Act".

(4) In subsection (5) (as it applies in cases in which the relevant Minister is the Scottish Ministers and in cases in which the relevant Minister is the Secretary of State) for "warrant under this Act" substitute "warrant under this section".

(5) In subsection (6) after "warrant" (in the first place it appears) insert "under this section".

(6) In subsection (7)(b) after "under" insert "any of".

(7) In subsection (8) –

    (a)   after "similar to" insert "any of";
    (b)   after "respect to" insert " –
            (a) "; and
    (c)   at the end insert "; or
        (b)   the transfer between different countries and territories (or different parts of a country or territory) of responsibility for the detention and release of persons who are required to be so detained in one of those countries or territories (or parts of a country or territory) but are present in the other country or territory (or part of a country or territory)."

12

(1) Section 2 (transfer out of the United Kingdom) is amended as follows.

(2) In subsection (1) after "warrant" insert "under section 1".

(3) In subsection (4) –

(a) in paragraph (a) for "warrant under this Act" substitute "warrant under section 1"; and
(b) in paragraph (b)(i) (as it continues to have effect in relation to prisoners sentenced for offences committed before 4th April 2005) after "33(1)(b)" insert ", (1A)".

(4) In subsection (7) for "warrant under this Act" substitute "warrant under section 1".

13

(1) Section 3 (transfer into the United Kingdom) is amended as follows.

(2) In subsection (1), after "a warrant" insert "under section 1".

(3) In subsections (2), (4) and (6), for "warrant under this Act" substitute "warrant under section 1".

(4) In subsection (7) –
(a) at the beginning insert "Part 1 of"; and
(b) for "warrant under this Act" substitute "warrant under section 1".

(5) Subsection (10) is omitted.

14

(1) Section 4 (temporary return) is amended as follows

(2) In subsection (1) –
(a) for "warrant under this Act" substitute "warrant under section 1";
(b) in paragraph (a), after "Kingdom" (in the second place it appears) insert ", or from which responsibility for his detention and release has previously been transferred to the United Kingdom,";
(c) in paragraph (b), after "transferred" insert ", or to which responsibility for his detention and release has previously been transferred,".

(3) In subsection (2) –
(a) for "a warrant under this Act" substitute "a warrant under section 1";
(b) for "earlier warrant under this Act" substitute "earlier warrant under section 1 or section 4A".

(4) In subsection (3) –
(a) for "issued under this Act" substitute "issued under section 1";
(b) after "an earlier warrant" insert "under section 1 or section 4A".

(5) In subsection (4) for "warrant under this Act" substitute "warrant under section 1".

(6) After subsection (5) insert –

"(6) Any reference in subsection (5)(a) to the prisoner having previously been transferred into or from Scotland includes a reference to responsibility for his detention and release having previously been transferred to or from the Scottish Ministers (as the case may be).".

15

Before section 5 (operation of warrant and retaking prisoners) insert –

"Supplementary and general provisions".

16

(1) Section 5 (operation of warrant and retaking prisoners) is amended as follows.

(2) In subsection (1) –
(a) for "under this Act" substitute "under section 1"; and

(b) after "this section" insert "(apart from subsection (9))".

(3) After subsection (8) insert –

"(9) Where –

(a) a warrant under section 4A has been issued, and
(b) the relevant person is a person to whom subsection (3) of that section applies,

subsections (2) to (8) above apply for the purposes of that warrant (but with the modifications contained in subsection (10)), except (without prejudice to section 4C(4) or any enactment contained otherwise than in this Act) in relation to any time when the relevant person is required to be detained in accordance with provisions contained in the warrant by virtue of section 4C(1)(b).

(10) In their application for the purposes of a warrant under section 4A those subsections shall have effect as if –

(a) any reference to the warrant under section 1 (however expressed) were a reference to the warrant under section 4A;
(b) any reference to the prisoner were a reference to the relevant person;
(c) in subsection (4) –
  (i) in paragraph (a) for "that person" there were substituted "the authorised person"; and
  (ii) paragraph (b) were omitted; and
(d) in subsection (8)(a) for "transfer of a prisoner to or from Scotland" there were substituted "transfer of responsibility for the detention and release of the relevant person to the Scottish Ministers"."

17

(1) Section 6 (revocation etc. of warrants) is amended as follows.

(2) In subsection (1) –

(a) for "warrant under this Act" (in the first place they appear) substitute "warrant under section 1";
(b) in paragraph (b) for "this Act" substitute "that section".

(3) After subsection (1) insert –

"(1A) Subject to section 4A(8), if at any time it appears to the relevant Minister appropriate, in order that effect may be given to any such arrangements as are mentioned in section 4A(5)(a) for a warrant under section 4A to be revoked or varied, he may as the case may require –

(a) revoke that warrant; or
(b) revoke that warrant and issue a new warrant under section 4A containing provision superseding some or all of the provisions of the previous warrant."

(4) In subsections (2) and (3) after "subsection (1)(b)" insert "or (1A)(b)".

(5) In subsection (5)(a), for the words from "where" to the end substitute "in a case where –

(i) the warrant was issued under section 1 and provides for the transfer of the prisoner to or from Scotland; or
(ii) the warrant was issued under section 4A and provides for the transfer of responsibility for the detention and release of the relevant person to those Ministers;".

18

(1) Section 8 is amended as follows.

(2) In subsection (1) after the definition of "the prisoner" insert "; and

"the relevant person" has the meaning given by section 4A(5)(b)."

(3) In subsection (3) –

(a) in paragraph (a) after "section 1(1)(a)" insert "or 4A(5)(a)";

(b) in paragraph (b) for "such a party" substitute "a party to such international arrangements as are mentioned in section 1(1)(a)";
(c) after paragraph (b) (but before the "or" after that paragraph) insert –
"(ba) that the appropriate authority of a country or territory which is a party to such international arrangements as are mentioned in section 4A(5)(a) has agreed to the transfer of responsibility for the detention and release of a particular person in accordance with those arrangements,".

19

(1) The Schedule (operation of certain enactments in relation to the prisoner) is amended as follows.

(2) For the cross-heading before paragraph 1 substitute –

"PART 1
WARRANTS UNDER SECTION 1

Application of Part 1".

(3) In paragraph 1 –

(a) at the beginning insert "This Part of";
(b) after "under" insert "section 1 of"; and
(c) after "; and in" insert "this Part of".

(4) In paragraph 2 (as it applies in England and Wales in relation to offences committed before 4 April 2005) –

(a) in sub-paragraph (1A)(a) (which defines the enactments relating to release on licence) after "33(1)(b) insert ", (1A)"; and
(b) after sub-paragraph (2) insert –

"(2A) If the warrant specifies that the offence or any of the offences in relation to which a determinate sentence is to be served corresponds to murder or an offence specified in Schedule 15 to the Criminal Justice Act 2003 (specified violent or sexual offences), any reference (however expressed) in Part 2 of the Criminal Justice Act 1991 to a person sentenced for an offence specified in that Schedule is to be read as including a reference to the prisoner."

(5) In paragraph 2 (as it applies in England and Wales in relation to offences committed on or after 4 April 2005), after sub-paragraph (3) insert –

"(3A) If the warrant specifies that the offence or any of the offences in relation to which a determinate sentence is to be served corresponds to murder or an offence specified in Schedule 15 to the Criminal Justice Act 2003 (specified violent or sexual offences), any reference (however expressed) in Chapter 6 of Part 12 of that Act to a person sentenced for an offence specified in that Schedule is to be read as including a reference to the prisoner."

(6) After paragraph 8 insert –

"PART 2
WARRANTS UNDER SECTION 4A TRANSFERRING RESPONSIBILITY TO THE RELEVANT MINISTER

9

This Part of this Schedule applies where a warrant is issued under section 4A providing for the transfer of responsibility for the detention and release of the relevant person to the relevant Minister (within the meaning of that section).

10

Paragraphs 2 to 8 above apply as they apply where a warrant is issued under section 1, but with the following modifications.

11

Any reference to "the relevant provisions" is to be read as a reference to the provisions contained in the warrant by virtue of section 4C(1)(b).

12

(1) Any reference to the prisoner is to be read as a reference to the relevant person.

(2) Sub-paragraph (1) does not apply to the words "a short-term or long-term prisoner" in paragraph 2(3) (as it applies in Scotland to repatriated prisoners any of whose sentences were imposed on or after 1 October 1993).

13

In paragraph 2 (as it applies in Scotland to repatriated prisoners any of whose sentences were imposed on or after 1 October 1993) the reference to prisoners repatriated to Scotland is to be read as a reference to any relevant person –

(a) in whose case the warrant under section 4A transfers responsibility for his detention and release from a country or territory outside the British Islands to the Scottish Ministers; and
(b) whose sentence or any of whose sentences in that country or territory were imposed on or after 1 October 1993.

14

The reference in paragraph 7 to the time of the prisoner's transfer into the United Kingdom is to be read as a reference to the time at which the warrant under section 4A was issued."

20 Police and Criminal Evidence Act 1984 (c. 60)

(1) In section 37B of the Police and Criminal Evidence Act 1984 (consultation with the Director of Public Prosecutions) in subsection (9) (meaning of caution) –

(a) after paragraph (a) (and before the word "and" immediately following it) insert –
"(aa) a youth conditional caution within the meaning of Chapter 1 of Part 4 of the Crime and Disorder Act 1998"; and
(b) in paragraph (b), for "of the Crime and Disorder Act 1998" substitute "of that Act".

(2) In section 63B of that Act (testing for presence of Class A drugs) in subsection (7) (disclosure of information obtained from drug samples) in paragraph (aa) after "Criminal Justice Act 2003" insert "or a youth conditional caution under Chapter 1 of Part 4 of the Crime and Disorder Act 1998".

21 Criminal Justice Act 1987 (c. 38)

In section 1(17) of the Criminal Justice Act 1987 (application of Serious Fraud Office provisions to Northern Ireland), for "Attorney General for Northern Ireland" substitute "Advocate General for Northern Ireland".

22 Criminal Justice Act 1988 (c. 33)

The Criminal Justice Act 1988 has effect subject to the following amendments.

23

In section 36 (reviews of sentencing), in subsection (2)(b)(iii) for "any of sections 225 to 228" substitute "section 225(2) or 226(2)".

24

In section 160(1) (offence of possession of indecent photographs of children) for "Subject to subsection (1A)," substitute "Subject to section 160A,".

25 Criminal Justice (Evidence, Etc.) (Northern Ireland) Order 1988 (S.I. 1988/1847 (N.I. 17))

In article 15(5) of the Criminal Justice (Evidence, Etc.) (Northern Ireland) Order 1988 (possession of indecent photographs of children) after "Article 2(2)" insert ", (2A)".

26 Football Spectators Act 1989 (c. 37)

In paragraph 1(c), (k) and (q) of Schedule 1 to the Football Spectators Act 1989 (offences) –

(a) for "Part III" substitute "Part 3 or 3A"; and
(b) for "(racial hatred)" substitute "(hatred by reference to race etc)".

27 Criminal Justice (International Co-operation) Act 1990 (c. 5)

In section 6(7) of the Criminal Justice (International Co-operation) Act 1990 (transfer of overseas prisoner to give evidence or assist investigation in the United Kingdom), for the words from "having been" to the end of paragraph (b) substitute " –

(b) having been transferred there, or responsibility for his detention and release having been transferred there, from the United Kingdom under the Repatriation of Prisoners Act 1984;
(c) having been transferred there, or responsibility for his detention and release having been transferred there, under any similar provision or arrangement from any other country or territory,".

28 Broadcasting Act 1990 (c. 42)

(1) Section 167 of the Broadcasting Act 1990 (power to make copies of recordings) is amended as follows.

(2) In subsection (4)(b), after "section 24" insert "or 29H".

(3) In subsection (5)(b), after "section 22" insert "or 29F".

29 Criminal Justice Act 1991 (c. 53)

(1) The Criminal Justice Act 1991 is amended as follows.

(2) In section 43(5) (young offenders), for "under this Part" substitute "under any provision of this Part other than section 33(1A)".

(3) In section 44(6) (disapplication of certain provisions for prisoners serving extended sentences) for "section 46" substitute "section 46(2)".

(4) In section 46(3) (definition of persons liable to removal from the United Kingdom) after "for the purposes of this section" insert "and the following provisions of this Part".

(5) In section 46B(5) (re-entry into United Kingdom of offender removed early from prison), after "subsections (1)" insert ", (1A)".

(6) In paragraph 10(3)(d) of Schedule 3 (reciprocal enforcement of certain orders) –

(a) for "references in paragraph 3 to a day centre were references to" substitute "in paragraph 3 "day centre" meant", and
(b) at the end insert "or an attendance centre provided under section 221 of that Act".

(7) Sub-paragraph (6) extends to England and Wales and Northern Ireland only.

30 Prisoners and Criminal Proceedings (Scotland) Act 1993 (c. 9)

In section 10 of the Prisoners and Criminal Proceedings (Scotland) Act 1993 (life prisoners transferred to Scotland), after subsection (4) insert –

"(4A) The reference in subsection (4)(b) above to a person who has been transferred to Scotland in pursuance of a warrant under the Repatriation of Prisoners Act 1984 includes a reference to a person who is detained in Scotland in pursuance of a warrant issued by the Scottish Ministers under section 4A of that Act (warrant transferring responsibility for detention and release of offender).

(4B) Such a person is to be taken to have been transferred when the warrant under section 4A of that Act was issued in respect of that person."

31 Crime (Sentences) Act 1997 (c. 43)

The Crime (Sentences) Act 1997 has effect subject to the following amendments.

32

(1) Schedule 1 (transfer of prisoners within the British Islands) is amended as follows.

(2) In paragraph 8(2)(a) (as it continues to have effect in relation to prisoners serving sentences of imprisonment for offences committed before 4th April 2005), after "46" insert ", 50A".

(3) In paragraph 8(4)(a) (as it continues to have effect in relation to prisoners serving sentences of imprisonment for offences committed before 4th April 2005), after "46" insert ", 50A".

(4) Any reference in paragraph 8(2)(a) or (4)(a) to section 39 of the 1991 Act is to be read as a reference to section 254(1) of the Criminal Justice Act 2003 (c. 44) in relation to any prisoner to whom paragraph 19 of Schedule 2 to the Criminal Justice Act 2003 (Commencement No. 8 and Transitional and Saving Provisions) Order 2005 (S.I. 2005/950) applies.

(5) In paragraph 9(2)(a) (as it continues to have effect in relation to prisoners serving sentences of imprisonment for offences committed before 4th April 2005), after "46" insert ", 50A".

(6) In paragraph 9(4)(a) (as it continues to have effect in relation to prisoners serving sentences of imprisonment for offences committed before 4th April 2005), after "46" insert ", 50A".

(7) Any reference in paragraph 9(2)(a) or (4)(a) to section 39 of the 1991 Act is to be read as a reference to section 254(1) of the Criminal Justice Act 2003 in relation to any prisoner to whom paragraph 19 of Schedule 2 to the Criminal Justice Act 2003 (Commencement No. 8 and Transitional and Saving Provisions) Order 2005 applies.

33

(1) Schedule 2 (repatriation of prisoners to the British Islands) is amended as follows.

(2) In paragraph 2(2) (as it continues to have effect in relation to persons to whom it applied before 4th April 2005), in the definition of enactments relating to release on licence, after "33(1)(b)," insert ", (1A),".

(3) In paragraph 3(2) (as it continues to have effect in relation to persons to whom it applied before 4th April 2005), in the definition of enactments relating to release on licence, after "33(1)(b)," insert ", (1A),".

(4) In paragraph 5 (which modifies paragraph 2 of the Schedule to the Repatriation of Prisoners Act 1984 (c. 47) in its application to certain descriptions of prisoner), after sub-paragraph (1)(b) insert –

> "(c) prisoners detained in Scotland in pursuance of warrants which –
> (i) are issued by the Scottish Ministers under section 4A of the Repatriation of Prisoners Act 1984 (warrant transferring responsibility for detention and release); and
> (ii) relate to sentences that were imposed before 1 October 1993."

34 Crime and Disorder Act 1998 (c. 37)

(1) Section 38(4) of the Crime and Disorder Act 1998 (which defines "youth justice services" for the purposes of sections 38 to 41) is amended as follows.

(2) After paragraph (a) insert –

"(aa) the provision of assistance to persons determining whether reprimands or warnings should be given under section 65 below;".

(3) After paragraph (b) insert –

"(ba) the provision of assistance to persons determining whether youth conditional cautions (within the meaning of Chapter 1 of Part 4) should be given and which conditions to attach to such cautions;
(bb) the supervision and rehabilitation of persons to whom such cautions are given;".

35 Youth Justice and Criminal Evidence Act 1999 (c. 23)

The Youth Justice and Criminal Evidence Act 1999 has effect subject to the following amendments.

36

(1) Section 35 (child complainants and other child witnesses) is amended as follows.

(2) In subsection (3) (offences to which section applies), in paragraph (a) –

(a) before sub-paragraph (v) insert –
"(iva) any of sections 33 to 36 of the Sexual Offences Act 1956,"; and
(b) in sub-paragraph (vi), at end insert "or any relevant superseded enactment".

(3) After that subsection insert –

"(3A) In subsection (3)(a)(vi) "relevant superseded enactment" means –

(a) any of sections 1 to 32 of the Sexual Offences Act 1956;
(b) the Indecency with Children Act 1960;
(c) the Sexual Offences Act 1967;
(d) section 54 of the Criminal Law Act 1977."

37

(1) Section 62 (meaning of "sexual offence" and other references to offences) is amended as follows.

(2) In subsection (1) at end insert "or any relevant superseded offence".

(3) After that subsection insert –

"(1A) In subsection (1) "relevant superseded offence" means –

(a) rape or burglary with intent to rape;
(b) an offence under any of sections 2 to 12 and 14 to 17 of the Sexual Offences Act 1956 (unlawful intercourse, indecent assault, forcible abduction etc.);
(c) an offence under section 128 of the Mental Health Act 1959 (unlawful intercourse with person receiving treatment for mental disorder by member of hospital staff etc.);
(d) an offence under section 1 of the Indecency with Children Act 1960 (indecent conduct towards child under 14);
(e) an offence under section 54 of the Criminal Law Act 1977 (incitement of child under 16 to commit incest)."

38

The amendments made by paragraphs 36 and 37 are deemed to have had effect as from 1 May 2004.

39

Where an order under section 61 of the Youth Justice and Criminal Evidence Act 1999 (c. 23) (application of Part 2 of Act to service courts) makes provision as regards the application of any provision of section 35 or 62 of that Act which is amended or inserted by paragraph 36 or 37, the order may have effect in relation to times before the making of the order.

40 Powers of Criminal Courts (Sentencing) Act 2000 (c. 6)

The Powers of Criminal Courts (Sentencing) Act 2000 has effect subject to the following amendments.

41

In section 12 (absolute and conditional discharge), in subsection (1) for "section 225, 226, 227 or 228" substitute "section 225(2) or 226(2)".

42

In section 24(5)(a) (first meeting: duration of contract), after "under paragraph" insert "9ZD,".

43

In section 28(a) (offender etc. referred back to court), for "Part I" substitute "Parts 1 and 1ZA".

44

In section 92 (detention under sections 90 and 91: place of detention etc.) omit subsection (3).

45

In section 116 (power to order return to prison where offence committed during original sentence) –

(a) in subsection (1)(b) for "under Part II of the Criminal Justice Act 1991 (early release of prisoners)" substitute "under any provision of Part 2 of the Criminal Justice Act 1991 (early release of prisoners) other than section 33(1A)", and

(b) in subsection (7), for "section 84 above" substitute "section 265 of the Criminal Justice Act 2003 (restriction on consecutive sentences for released prisoners)".

46

In section 130 (compensation orders), in subsection (2) for "section 225, 226, 227 or 228" substitute "section 225(2) or 226(2)".

47

In section 146 (driving disqualification for any offence), in subsection (2) for "section 225, 226, 227 or 228" substitute "section 225(2) or 226(2)".

48

In section 164 (further interpretative provisions), in subsection (3)(c) for "any of sections 225 to 228" substitute "section 225(2) or 226(2)".

49

(1) Schedule 1 (youth offender panels: further court proceedings) is amended as follows.

(2) In the heading for Part 1, at the end insert ": REVOCATION OF REFERRAL ORDER".

(3) In paragraphs 5(3), 9 and 14(2)(b), after "under paragraph" insert "9ZD,".

50 Criminal Justice and Court Services Act 2000 (c. 43)

In section 1 of the Criminal Justice and Court Services Act 2000 (purposes of the Chapter) –

(a) in subsection (1A)(a) for "authorised persons to be given assistance in" substitute "the giving of assistance to persons", and

(b) in subsection (4) for ""authorised person" and "conditional caution" have" substitute ""conditional caution" has".

51 Life Sentences (Northern Ireland) Order 2001 (S.I. 2001/2564) (N.I. 2)

In Article 10 of the Life Sentences (Northern Ireland) Order 2001 (life prisoners transferred to Northern Ireland), after paragraph (5) insert –

"(6) The reference in paragraph (4)(b) to a person transferred to Northern Ireland in pursuance of a warrant under the Repatriation of Prisoners Act 1984 includes a person who is detained in Northern Ireland in pursuance of a warrant under section 4A of that Act (warrant transferring responsibility for detention and release of offender)."

52 Crime (International Co-operation) Act 2003 (c. 32)

In section 48(2)(b) of the Crime (International Co-operation) Act 2003 (transfer of EU etc prisoner to assist UK investigation), for the words from "having been" to the end of paragraph (b) substitute " –

(a) having been transferred there, or responsibility for his detention and release having been transferred there, from the United Kingdom under the Repatriation of Prisoners Act 1984;
(b) having been transferred there, or responsibility for his detention and release having been transferred there, under any similar provision or arrangement from any other country or territory."

53 Sexual Offences Act 2003 (c. 42)

The Sexual Offences Act 2003 has effect subject to the following amendments.

54

(1) In section 83(6)(a) (notification requirements: initial notification) after "court" insert "or kept in service custody".

(2) This paragraph extends to England and Wales and Northern Ireland only.

55

(1) In section 85(4)(a) (notification requirements: periodic notification) after "court" insert "or kept in service custody".

(2) This paragraph extends to England and Wales and Northern Ireland only.

56v

(1) Section 133 (interpretation) is amended as follows.

(2) In subsection (1) –

(a) in paragraph (a) of the definition of "cautioned", for "by a police officer" substitute "(or, in Northern Ireland, cautioned by a police officer)";
(b) at the appropriate place insert –

""kept in service custody" means kept in service custody by virtue of an order under section 105(2) of the Armed Forces Act 2006 (but see also subsection (3));".

(3) After subsection (2) insert –

"(3) In relation to any time before the commencement of section 105(2) of the Armed Forces Act 2006, "kept in service custody" means being kept in military, air-force or naval custody by virtue of an order made under section 75A(2) of the Army Act 1955 or of the Air Force Act 1955 or section 47G(2) of the Naval Discipline Act 1957 (as the case may be)."

(4) This paragraph extends to England and Wales and Northern Ireland only.

57

(1) In section 138 (orders and regulations), at the end insert –

"(4) Orders or regulations made by the Secretary of State under this Act may –

(a) make different provision for different purposes;
(b) include supplementary, incidental, consequential, transitional, transitory or saving provisions."

(2) The amendment made by sub-paragraph (1), and the repeals in Part 4 of Schedule 28 of sections 86(4) and 87(6) of the Sexual Offences Act 2003 (which are consequential on that amendment), extend to England and Wales and Northern Ireland only.

58

(1) Schedule 3 (sexual offences in respect of which offender becomes subject to notification requirements) is amended as follows.

(2) After paragraph 35 insert –

"35A An offence under section 63 of the Criminal Justice and Immigration Act 2008 (possession of extreme pornographic images) if the offender –

(a) was 18 or over, and
(b) is sentenced in respect of the offence to imprisonment for a term of at least 2 years."

(3) After paragraph 92 insert –

"92A An offence under section 63 of the Criminal Justice and Immigration Act 2008 (possession of extreme pornographic images) if the offender –

(a) was 18 or over, and
(b) is sentenced in respect of the offence to imprisonment for a term of at least 2 years."

(4) In paragraphs 93(1) and 93A(1) (service offences) for "35" substitute "35A".

(5) This paragraph extends to England and Wales and Northern Ireland only.

59 Criminal Justice Act 2003 (c. 44)

The Criminal Justice Act 2003 has effect subject to the following amendments.

60

(1) Section 23A (financial penalties) is amended as follows.

(2) In subsection (5), for paragraphs (b) and (c) substitute –

"(b) the person to whom the financial penalty is to be paid and how it may be paid."

(3) In subsection (6), for "to the specified officer" substitute "in accordance with the provision specified under subsection (5)(b)."

(4) After subsection (6) insert –

"(6A) Where a financial penalty is (in accordance with the provision specified under subsection (5)(b)) paid to a person other than a designated officer for a local justice area, the person to whom it is paid must give the payment to such an officer."

(5) Omit subsections (7) to (9).

61

After section 23A insert –

"23B   Variation of conditions

A relevant prosecutor may, with the consent of the offender, vary the conditions attached to a conditional caution by –

(a)   modifying or omitting any of the conditions;
(b)   adding a condition."

62

In section 25 (codes of practice) in subsection (2) after paragraph (g) insert –

"(ga)   the provision which may be made by a relevant prosecutor under section 23A(5)(b),".

63

In sections 88(3), 89(9) and 91(5) (days to be disregarded in calculating certain time periods relating to bail and custody under Part 10), before paragraph (a) insert –

"(za)   Saturday,".

64

In section 142 (purposes of sentencing), in subsection (2)(c) for "any of sections 225 to 228" substitute "section 225(2) or 226(2)".

65

In section 150 (circumstances in which community sentence not available), in paragraph (d) for "any of sections 225 to 228" to the end substitute "section 225(2) or 226(2) of this Act (requirement to impose sentence of imprisonment for life or detention for life)".

66

In section 152 (general restrictions on imposing custodial sentences), in subsection (1)(b) for "any of sections 225 to 228" substitute "section 225(2) or 226(2)".

67

In section 153 (length of discretionary custodial sentences: general provision), in subsection (1), omit "falling to be".

68

In section 163 (general power of Crown Court to fine) for "any of sections 225 to 228" substitute "section 225(2) or 226(2)".

69

In section 224 (meaning of "specified offence" etc), in subsection (3) the definition of relevant offence is omitted.

70

Section 233 (offences under service law) is omitted.

71

In section 264 (consecutive terms), in subsection (6)(a)(i) after "means" insert "one-half of".

72

In section 305 (interpretation of Part 12), in subsection (4) –

(a) for paragraphs (c) and (d) substitute –
"(c) a sentence falls to be imposed under subsection (2) of section 225 if the court is obliged to pass a sentence of imprisonment for life under that subsection;
(d) a sentence falls to be imposed under subsection (2) of section 226 if the court is obliged to pass a sentence of detention for life under that subsection;", and
(b) paragraph (e) is omitted.

73

In section 273 (life prisoners transferred to England and Wales), after subsection (4) insert –

"(5) The reference in subsection (2)(b) above to a person who has been transferred to England and Wales in pursuance of a warrant issued under the Repatriation of Prisoners Act 1984 includes a reference to a person who is detained in England and Wales in pursuance of a warrant under section 4A of that Act (warrant transferring responsibility for detention and release of offender)."

74

(1) Section 325 (arrangements for assessing etc risks posed by certain offenders) is amended as follows.

(2) In subsection (8), for "section 326" substitute "sections 326 and 327A".

(3) After that subsection insert –

"(8A) Responsible authorities must have regard to any guidance issued under subsection (8) in discharging those functions."

75

In section 326(5)(a) (review of arrangements), for "and this section" substitute ", this section and section 327A".

76

In section 330(5)(a) (orders subject to the affirmative procedure) after "section 223," insert –

"section 227(6),
section 228(7)".

77

In Part 4 of Schedule 37, in the entry relating to the Magistrates' Courts Act 1980, in the second column, omit the words "In section 33(1), paragraph (b) and the word "and" immediately preceding it".

78 Criminal Justice Act 2003 (Commencement No. 8 and Transitional and Saving Provisions) Order 2005 (S.I. 2005/950)

In paragraph 14 of Schedule 2 to the Criminal Justice Act 2003 (Commencement No. 8 and Transitional and Saving Provisions) Order 2005 (saving from certain provisions of the Criminal Justice Act 2003 for sentences of imprisonment of less than 12 months), for "sections 244 to 268" substitute "sections 244 to 264 and 266 to 268".

79 Terrorism Act 2006 (c. 11)

(1) Schedule 1 to the Terrorism Act 2006 (Convention offences) is amended as follows.

(2) In the cross-heading before paragraph 6 (offences involving nuclear material), after "*material*" add "*or nuclear facilities*".

(3) In paragraph 6(1), after "section 1(1)" insert "(a) to (d)".

(4) For paragraph 6(2) and (3) substitute –

"(2) An offence mentioned in section 1(1)(a) or (b) of that Act where the act making the person guilty of the offence (whether done in the United Kingdom or elsewhere) –

(a) is directed at a nuclear facility or interferes with the operation of such a facility, and
(b) causes death, injury or damage resulting from the emission of ionising radiation or the release of radioactive material.

(3) An offence under any of the following provisions of that Act –

(a) section 1B (offences relating to damage to environment);
(b) section 1C (offences of importing or exporting etc. nuclear material: extended jurisdiction);
(c) section 2 (offences involving preparatory acts and threats).

(4) Expressions used in this paragraph and that Act have the same meanings in this paragraph as in that Act."

(5) After paragraph 6 insert –

"6A (1) Any of the following offences under the Customs and Excise Management Act 1979 –

(a) an offence under section 50(2) or (3) (improper importation of goods) in connection with a prohibition or restriction relating to the importation of nuclear material;
(b) an offence under section 68(2) (exportation of prohibited or restricted goods) in connection with a prohibition or restriction relating to the exportation or shipment as stores of nuclear material;
(c) an offence under section 170(1) or (2) (fraudulent evasion of duty etc.) in connection with a prohibition or restriction relating to the importation, exportation or shipment as stores of nuclear material.

(2) In this paragraph "nuclear material" has the same meaning as in the Nuclear Material (Offences) Act 1983 (see section 6 of that Act)."

80 Natural Environment and Rural Communities Act 2006 (c. 16)

In paragraph 7 of Schedule 5 to the Natural Environment and Rural Communities Act 2006 (powers of wildlife inspectors extended to certain other Acts) after paragraph (d) insert –

"(da) section 19XB(1) and (4) (offences in connection with enforcement powers);".

81 Police and Justice Act 2006 (c. 48)

(1) The Police and Justice Act 2006 is amended as follows.

(2) In subsection (1) of section 49 (orders and regulations) –

(a) at the end of paragraph (a) insert "or";
(b) omit paragraph (c) and the "or" preceding it.

(3) In paragraph 30 of Schedule 1 (National Policing Improvement Agency: inspections) omit sub-paragraph (3).

82 Armed Forces Act 2006 (c. 52)

(1) The Armed Forces Act 2006 has effect subject to the following amendments.

(2) In paragraph 12(ah) of Schedule 2 (offences) –

(a) for "and 18 to 23" substitute ", 18 to 23 and 29B to 29G", and
(b) for "racial or religious hatred" substitute "hatred by reference to race etc".

(3) In paragraph 1(2) of Schedule 5 (service community orders: general) –

(a) for "12, 13, 15, 16(5), 17(5) and (6)" substitute "13, 16(5), 17(6)", and
(b) after "21" insert ", 25A".

(4) In paragraph 10(2)(b) of Schedule 5 (overseas community orders: general) –

(a) for "12, 13, 15, 16(5), 17(5) and (6)" substitute "13, 16(5), 17(6)", and
(b) for "and 23(1)(a)(ii)" substitute ", 23(1)(a)(ii) and 25A".

83 Offender Management Act 2007 (c. 21)

In section 1 of the Offender Management Act 2007 (meaning of "the probation purposes") –

(a) in subsection (1)(b) for "authorised persons to be given assistance in" substitute "the giving of assistance to persons", and

(b) in subsection (4) for ""authorised person" and "conditional caution" have" substitute ""conditional caution" has".

Schedule 27

Section 148

Transitory, Transitional And Saving Provisions

PART 1
YOUTH JUSTICE

1 Abolition of certain youth orders and related amendments

(1) Section 1, subsections (1) and (2) of section 6, the amendments in Part 1 of Schedule 4 and the repeals and revocations in Part 1 of Schedule 28 do not have effect in relation to –

(a) any offence committed before they come into force, or
(b) any failure to comply with an order made in respect of an offence committed before they come into force.

(2) So far as an amendment in Part 2 of Schedule 4 relates to any of the following orders, the amendment has effect in relation to orders made before, as well as after, the amendment comes into force –

(a) a referral order made under the Powers of Criminal Courts (Sentencing) Act 2000 (c. 6);
(b) a reparation order made under that Act;
(c) a community order made under section 177 of the Criminal Justice Act 2003 (c. 44).

2 Reparation orders

(1) Sub-paragraph (2) applies if the amendments of Schedule 8 to the Powers of Criminal Courts (Sentencing) Act 2000 (action plan orders and reparation orders) made by paragraph 108(1) to (5) of Schedule 4 (reparation orders: court before which offender to appear or be brought) come into force before the amendments of Schedule 8 to that Act made by paragraph 62 of that Schedule.

(2) After paragraph 108(1) to (5) of Schedule 4 comes into force, and until paragraph 62 of that Schedule comes into force, paragraph 3 of Schedule 8 to the Powers of Criminal Courts (Sentencing) Act 2000 has effect as if –

(a) in sub-paragraph (5)(a) and (c), for "the appropriate court" there were substituted "a youth court", and
(b) in sub-paragraph (6), for "appropriate" there were substituted "youth".

(3) Sub-paragraph (4) applies if the amendments of Schedule 8 to the Powers of Criminal Courts (Sentencing) Act 2000 (action plan orders and reparation orders) made by paragraph 62 of Schedule 4 come into force before the amendments of Schedule 8 to that Act made by paragraph 108(1) to (5) of that Schedule (reparation orders: court before which offender to appear or be brought).

(4) After paragraph 62 of Schedule 4 comes into force, and until paragraph 108(1) to (5) of that Schedule comes into force, paragraph 1 of Schedule 8 to the Powers of Criminal Courts (Sentencing) Act 2000 has effect as if –

(a) for "an action plan order or" there were substituted "a", and
(b) the words "69(8) or, as the case may be," were omitted.

3 Making of youth rehabilitation orders: other existing orders

In paragraph 29(3)(c) of Schedule 1 (requirements not to conflict with other obligations), the reference to a youth rehabilitation order is to be read as including a reference to any youth community order within the meaning of section 147(2) of the Criminal Justice Act 2003 (c. 44) (as it has effect immediately before the commencement of paragraph 72 of Schedule 4 to this Act).

4 Instructions: other existing orders

In section 5(3)(c) (instructions not to conflict with other obligations), the reference to a youth rehabilitation order is to be read as including a reference to any youth community order within the meaning of section 147(2) of the Criminal Justice Act 2003 (as it has effect immediately before the commencement of paragraph 72 of Schedule 4 to this Act).

5 Fine default: section 35 of the Crime (Sentences) Act 1997

The amendments, repeals and revocations in section 6, Schedule 4 and Part 1 of Schedule 28 of provisions which are necessary to give effect to section 35 of the Crime (Sentences) Act 1997 (c. 43) (fine defaulters) do not have effect in relation to a sum ordered to be paid where –

(a) the sum is treated as adjudged to be paid on conviction, and
(b) the act or omission to which the sum relates occurred, or the order was made, before the commencement of those repeals and amendments.

6 Restrictions on imposing community sentences

In subsection (5) of section 148 of the Criminal Justice Act 2003 (restrictions on imposing community sentences), as inserted by section 10 of this Act, the reference to a youth rehabilitation order is to be read as including a reference to any youth community order within the meaning of section 147(2) of the Criminal Justice Act 2003 (as it has effect immediately before the commencement of paragraph 72 of Schedule 4 to this Act).

7 Attendance centre rules

The reference in paragraph 1(2)(a)(ii) of Schedule 2 to rules made under subsection (1)(d) or (e) of section 222 of the Criminal Justice Act 2003 includes a reference to rules made, or having effect as if made, before the coming into force of that section under section 62(3) of the Powers of Criminal Courts (Sentencing) Act 2000 (c. 6) (provision, regulation and management of attendance centres).

PART 2
SENTENCING

8 Release and recall of prisoners

Nothing in the amendments made by section 26 affects the operation of Part 2 of the Criminal Justice Act 1991 (c. 53) in relation to a long-term prisoner within the meaning of that Part who (for the purposes of that Part) has served one-half of his sentence before the commencement of that section.

9

Section 33(1A) of the Criminal Justice Act 1991 (c. 53) (which is inserted by section 26(2)) does not apply to a long-term prisoner serving a sentence (for one or more offences committed before 4th April 2005) by virtue of having been transferred to the United Kingdom in pursuance of a warrant under section 1 of the Repatriation of Prisoners Act 1984 (c. 47) if –

(a) the warrant was issued before the commencement of section 26(2); and
(b) the offence or one of the offences for which the prisoner is serving that sentence corresponds to murder or to any offence specified in Schedule 15 to the Criminal Justice Act 2003 (c. 44).

10

The amendments made by subsections (3) and (5) of section 28 do not apply in relation to any person who is released on licence under section 36(1) of the Criminal Justice Act 1991 before the commencement of section 28.

11

In section 255A and 255C of the Criminal Justice Act 2003 (which are inserted by section 29) "specified offence prisoner" is to be read as including a prisoner serving a determinate sentence by virtue of having been transferred to the United Kingdom in pursuance of a warrant under section 1 of the Repatriation of Prisoners Act 1984 if –

(a) the warrant was issued before the commencement of section 29; and
(b) the offence or one of the offences for which the prisoner is serving that sentence corresponds to murder or to any offence specified in Schedule 15 to the Criminal Justice Act 2003.

12

The amendment made by subsection (1) of section 32 applies in relation to any person who is recalled under section 254(1) of the Criminal Justice Act 2003 on or after the commencement of section 32 but it is immaterial when the person was released on licence under Part 2 of the Criminal Justice Act 1991.

13 Fine defaulters

(1) Section 39 and Schedule 7 do not apply –

(a) in relation to a sum adjudged to be paid by a conviction if the offence was committed before the commencement of that section, or
(b) where a sum ordered to be paid is treated as adjudged to be paid by a conviction, if the act or omission to which the sum relates occurred, or the order was made, before the commencement of that section.

(2) Section 40 and paragraph 2(4) and (6) of Schedule 26 do not apply –

(a) in relation to a sum adjudged to be paid by a conviction if the offence was committed before the commencement of that section, or
(b) where a sum ordered to be paid is treated as adjudged to be paid by a conviction, if the act or omission to which the sum relates occurred, or the order was made, before the commencement of that section.

PART 3
APPEALS

14 Appeals against conviction etc.

The amendment made by section 42 applies in relation to an appeal under Part 1 of the Criminal Appeal Act 1968 (c. 19) if the reference by the Criminal Cases Review Commission is made on or after the date on which that section comes into force.

15

The amendment made by section 43 applies in relation to an appeal under Part 1 of the Criminal Appeal (Northern Ireland) Act 1980 (c. 47) if the reference by the Criminal Cases Review Commission is made on or after the date on which that section comes into force.

16 Prosecution appeals

(1) The amendment made by section 44 applies in relation to an appeal under Part 9 of the Criminal Justice Act 2003 (c. 44) if the proceedings on appeal begin on or after the date on which that section comes into force.

(2) For the purposes of this paragraph, the proceedings on appeal begin –

(a) if the prosecution appeals with leave of the Crown Court judge, on the date the application for leave is served on the Crown Court officer or, in the case of an oral application, on the date the application is made, or
(b) if the prosecution appeals with leave of the Court of Appeal, on the date the application for leave is served on the Crown Court officer.

(3) In this paragraph, references to service on the Crown Court officer are to be read in accordance with the Criminal Procedure Rules 2005 (S.I.2005/384).

17

(1) The amendment made by section 45 applies in relation to an appeal under Part IV of the Criminal Justice (Northern Ireland) Order 2004 (S.I. 2004/1500 (N.I.9)) if the proceedings on appeal begin on after the date on which that section comes into force.

(2) For the purposes of this paragraph, the proceedings on appeal begin –

(a) if the prosecution appeals with leave of the Crown Court judge, on the date the application for leave is made,
(b) if the prosecution appeals with leave of the Court of Appeal, on the date the application for leave is served on the proper officer, or
(c) if leave to appeal is not required, on the date the prosecution informs the Crown Court judge that it intends to appeal.

(3) In this paragraph, "the proper officer" has the same meaning as in the Criminal Appeal (Prosecution Appeals) Rules (Northern Ireland) 2005 (S.R (N.I.) 2005/159).

PART 4
OTHER CRIMINAL JUSTICE PROVISIONS

18 Alternatives to prosecution for offenders under 18

The amendments made by Schedule 9 do not apply in relation to offences committed before the commencement of section 48.

19 Protection for spent cautions under Rehabilitation of Offenders Act 1974

(1) Subject to the following provisions of this paragraph, the Rehabilitation of Offenders Act 1974 (c. 53) (as amended by Schedule 10 to this Act) applies to cautions given before the commencement date as it applies to cautions given on or after that date.

(2) A caution given before the commencement date shall be regarded as a spent caution at a time determined in accordance with sub-paragraphs (3) to (8).

(3) A caution other than a conditional caution (as defined in section 8A(2)(a) of the 1974 Act) shall be regarded as a spent caution on the commencement date.

(4) If the period of three months from the date on which a conditional caution was given ends on or before the commencement date, the caution shall be regarded as a spent caution on the commencement date unless sub-paragraph (7) applies.

(5) If the period of three months from the date on which a conditional caution was given ends after the commencement date, the caution shall be regarded as a spent caution at the end of that period of three months unless sub-paragraph (7) applies.

(6) Sub-paragraph (7) applies if –

(a) before the date on which the caution would be regarded as a spent caution in accordance with sub-paragraph (4) or (5) ("the relevant date"), the person concerned is convicted of the offence in respect of which the caution was given, and
(b) the rehabilitation period for the offence ends after the relevant date.

(7) The caution shall be regarded as a spent caution at the end of the rehabilitation period for the offence.

(8) If, on or after the date on which the caution becomes regarded as a spent caution in accordance with sub-paragraph (4) or (5), the person concerned is convicted of the offence in respect of which the caution was given –

(a) the caution shall be treated for the purposes of Schedule 2 to the 1974 Act as not having become spent in relation to any period before the end of the rehabilitation period for the offence, and
(b) the caution shall be regarded as a spent caution at the end of that rehabilitation period.

(9) In this paragraph, "the commencement date" means the date on which section 49 comes into force.

20

In the application of subsection (7) of section 9A of the Rehabilitation of Offenders Act 1974 (as inserted by paragraph 4 of Schedule 10) to offences committed before the commencement of section 281(5) of the Criminal Justice Act 2003 (c. 44), the reference to 51 weeks is to be read as a reference to 6 months.

21 Extension of powers of non-legal staff

A designation made under section 7A of the Prosecution of Offences Act 1985 (c. 23) (powers of non-legal staff) which has effect immediately before the date on which section 55 comes into force continues to have effect on and after that date as if made under section 7A as amended by that section.

22 Compensation for miscarriages of justice

(1) Section 61(3) has effect in relation to any application for compensation made in relation to –

(a) a conviction which is reversed, and
(b) a pardon which is given, on or after the commencement date.

(2) Section 61(4), (6) and (7) have effect in relation to –

(a) any application for compensation made on or after the commencement date, and
(b) any application for compensation made before that date in relation to which the question whether there is a right to compensation has not been determined before that date by the Secretary of State under section 133(3) of the 1988 Act.

(3) Section 61(5) has effect in relation to any conviction quashed on an appeal out of time in respect of which an application for compensation has not been made before the commencement date.

(4) Section 61(5) so has effect whether a conviction was quashed before, on or after the commencement date.

(5) In the case of –

(a) a conviction which is reversed, or
(b) a pardon which is given,

before the commencement date but in relation to which an application for compensation has not been made before that date, any such application must be made before the end of the period of 2 years beginning with that date.

(6) But the Secretary of State may direct that an application for compensation in relation to a case falling within sub-paragraph (5) which is made after the end of that period is to be treated as if it had been made before the end of that period if the Secretary of State considers that there are exceptional circumstances which justify doing so.

(7) In this paragraph –

"the 1988 Act" means the Criminal Justice Act 1988 (c. 33);
"application for compensation" means an application for compensation made under section 133(2) of the 1988 Act;
"the commencement date" means the date on which section 61 comes into force;
"reversed" has the same meaning as in section 133 of the 1988 Act (as amended by section 61(5)).

PART 5
CRIMINAL LAW

23 Penalties for possession of extreme pornographic images

In section 67(4)(a) the reference to 12 months is to be read as a reference to 6 months in relation to an offence committed before the commencement of section 154(1) of the Criminal Justice Act 2003 (c. 44).

24 Indecent photographs of children

(1) Section 69(3) applies in relation to things done as mentioned in –

(a) section 1(1) of the Protection of Children Act 1978 (c. 37) (offences relating to indecent photographs of children), or
(b) section 160(1) of the Criminal Justice Act 1988 (c. 33) (offence of possession of indecent photographs of children),

after the commencement of section 69.

(2) Section 70(3) applies in relation to things done as mentioned in –

(a) Article 3(1) of the Protection of Children (Northern Ireland) Order 1978 (S.I. 1978/1047 (N.I. 17)) (offences relating to indecent photographs of children), or
(b) Article 15(1) of the Criminal Justice (Evidence, Etc.) (Northern Ireland) Order 1988 (S.I. 1988/1847 (N.I. 17)) (offence of possession of indecent photographs of children),

after the commencement of section 70.

25 Maximum penalty for publication etc. of obscene articles

Section 71 does not apply to offences committed before the commencement of that section.

26 Offences relating to nuclear material and nuclear facilities

The new section 2 inserted into the Nuclear Material (Offences) Act 1983 (c. 18) by paragraph 4 of Schedule 17 and the repeal in Part 5 of Schedule 28 of section 14 of the Terrorism Act 2006 (c. 11) do not apply in relation to anything done before the date on which Schedule 17 comes into force.

27 Reasonable force for purposes of self-defence etc.

(1) Section 76 applies whether the alleged offence took place before, or on or after, the date on which that section comes into force.

(2) But that section does not apply in relation to –

(a) any trial on indictment where the arraignment took place before that date, or
(b) any summary trial which began before that date,

or in relation to any proceedings in respect of any trial within paragraph (a) or (b).

(3) Where the alleged offence is a service offence, that section similarly does not apply in relation to –

(a) any proceedings before a court where the arraignment took place before that date, or
(b) any summary proceedings which began before that date,

or in relation to any proceedings in respect of any proceedings within paragraph (a) or (b).

(4) For the purposes of sub-paragraph (3) summary proceedings are to be regarded as beginning when the hearing of the charge, or (as the case may be) the summary trial of the charge, begins.

(5) In this paragraph –

"service offence" means –
(a) any offence against any provision of Part 2 of the Army Act 1955 (3 & 4 Eliz. 2 c. 18), Part 2 of the Air Force Act 1955 (3 & 4 Eliz. 2 c. 19) or Part 1 of the Naval Discipline Act 1957 (c. 53); or
(b) any offence under Part 1 of the Armed Forces Act 2006 (c. 52);

"summary proceedings" means summary proceedings conducted by a commanding officer or appropriate superior authority.

28 Unlawfully obtaining etc. personal data: defences

The amendment made by section 78 does not apply in relation to an offence committed before the commencement of that section.

PART 6
INTERNATIONAL CO-OPERATION IN RELATION TO CRIMINAL JUSTICE MATTERS

29 Mutual recognition of financial penalties

(1) The amendments made by subsection (1) of section 80, and subsection (2) of that section, do not apply in relation to financial penalties (within the meaning of that section) imposed before that section comes into force.

(2) Section 82 does not apply in relation to financial penalties (within the meaning of that section) imposed before that section comes into force.

(3) Section 84 does not apply in relation to financial penalties (within the meaning of that section) imposed before that section comes into force.

(4) Section 87 does not apply in relation to financial penalties (within the meaning of that section) imposed before that section comes into force.

30 Repatriation of prisoners

The amendment made by section 93 does not apply to warrants under section 1 of the Repatriation of Prisoners Act 1984 issued before the commencement of that section.

PART 7
VIOLENT OFFENDER ORDERS

31 Penalties for offences

In section 113(7)(a) in its application in relation to England and Wales the reference to 12 months is to be read as a reference to 6 months in relation to an offence committed before the commencement of section 154(1) of the Criminal Justice Act 2003 (c. 44).

32 Service custody and detention

(1) In relation to any time before the commencement of section 105(2) of the Armed Forces Act 2006 (c. 52) –

(a) the definition of "kept in service custody" in section 117(1) of this Act does not apply; and
(b) any reference in Part 7 to being kept in service custody is to be read as a reference to being kept in military, air-force or naval custody by virtue of an order made under section 75A(2) of the Army Act 1955 (3 & 4 Eliz. 2 c. 18) or of the Air Force Act 1955 (3 & 4 Eliz. 2 c. 19) or section 47G(2) of the Naval Discipline Act 1957 (c. 53) (as the case may be).

(2) In relation to any time before the commencement of the definition of "service detention" in section 374 of the Armed Forces Act 2006 –

(a) the definition of "service detention" in section 117(1) of this Act does not apply; and
(b) any reference in Part 7 to service detention is to be read as a reference to detention under section 71(1)(e) of the Army Act 1955 or of the Air Force Act 1955 or section 43(1)(e) of the Naval Discipline Act 1957.

PART 8
ANTI-SOCIAL BEHAVIOUR

33 Review of anti-social behaviour orders etc.

(1) The amendments made by section 123 do not apply in relation to an antisocial behaviour order, or a section 1B or 1C order, made more than 9 months before the day on which that section comes into force, unless the order has been varied by a further order made no more than 9 months before that day.

(2) In sub-paragraph (1) "section 1B or 1C order" means an order under section 1B or section 1C of the Crime and Disorder Act 1998 (c. 37).

34 Individual support orders

(1) The amendments made by section 124 do not apply in relation to an antisocial behaviour order, or a section 1B or 1C order, made more than 9 months before the day on which that section comes into force, unless the order has been varied by a further order made no more than 9 months before that day.

(2) In sub-paragraph (1) "section 1B or 1C order" means an order under section 1B or section 1C of the Crime and Disorder Act 1998 (c. 37).

PART 9
POLICE

35 Police misconduct and performance procedures

(1) This paragraph applies if paragraphs 7, 8(3), 15 and 16 of Schedule 22 come into force before the relevant provisions of the Legal Services Act 2007 (c. 29) come into force.

(2) Until the relevant provisions of the Legal Services Act 2007 come into force –

(a) section 84 of the Police Act 1996 (c. 16) (as substituted by paragraph 7 of that Schedule and as referred to in the subsection (4) of section 85 of that Act substituted by paragraph 8(3) of that Schedule) has effect as if, in subsection (4), for the definition of "relevant lawyer" there were substituted –

" "relevant lawyer" means counsel or a solicitor;"; and

(b) section 4 of the Ministry of Defence Police Act 1987 (c. 4) (as substituted by paragraph 15 of that Schedule and as referred to in subsection (7) of the section 4A of that Act substituted by paragraph 16 of that Schedule) has effect as if, in subsection (4), for the definition of "relevant lawyer" there were substituted –

" "relevant lawyer" means counsel or a solicitor;".

(3) In this paragraph "the relevant provisions of the Legal Services Act 2007" means the provisions of that Act which provide, for the purposes of that Act, for a person to be an authorised person in relation to an activity which constitutes the exercise of a right of audience (within the meaning of that Act).

PART 10

SPECIAL IMMIGRATION STATUS

36 Conditions on designated persons

In the application of section 133 to England and Wales in relation to an offence committed before the commencement of section 281(5) of the Criminal Justice Act 2003 (c. 44) (51 week maximum term of sentences) the reference in section 133(6)(b) to 51 weeks is to be read as a reference to six months.

PART 11

MISCELLANEOUS

37 Persistent sales of tobacco to persons under 18

The new sections 12A and 12B inserted into the Children and Young Persons Act 1933 (c. 12) by section 143 do not apply where any of the offences mentioned in those new sections were committed before the commencement of that section.

38 Sexual offences

The amendment made by sub-paragraph (1) of paragraph 57 of Schedule 26 is not to be read as affecting the validity of any supplementary, incidental, consequential, transitional, transitory or saving provisions included in orders or regulations made by the Secretary of State under the Sexual Offences Act 2003 (c. 42) before the commencement of that sub-paragraph.

Schedule 28

Section 149

Repeals And Revocations

PART 1
YOUTH REHABILITATION ORDERS

Title	Extent of repeal or revocation
Children and Young Persons Act 1933 (c. 12)	In section 34(7), the words "section 163 of the Powers of Criminal Courts (Sentencing) Act 2000 or". In section 49 – (a) in subsection (4A), paragraph (d) (but not the word "and" immediately following it); (b) in subsection (13)(c), sub-paragraph (i) together with the word "and" immediately following it.
Social Work (Scotland) Act 1968 (c. 49)	In section 94(1), in the definition of "supervision order", the words "the Powers of Criminal Courts (Sentencing) Act 2000 or".
Children and Young Persons Act 1969 (c. 54)	Section 25. In section 70(1), the definition of "supervision order".
Northern Ireland (Modification of Enactments — No. 1) Order 1973 (S.I. 1973/2163)	In Schedule 1, the entry relating to section 25(2) of the Children and Young Persons Act 1969.
Transfer of Functions (Local Government, etc.) (Northern Ireland) Order 1973 (S.R. & O. 1973 No. 256)	In Schedule 2, the entry relating to section 25 of the Children and Young Persons Act 1969.
Bail Act 1976 (c. 63)	In section 4(3), the words "to be dealt with"
Magistrates' Courts Act 1980 (c. 43)	In Schedule 6A, the entries relating to Schedules 3, 5 and 7 to the Powers of Criminal Courts (Sentencing) Act 2000 (c. 6).
Contempt of Court Act 1981 (c. 49)	In section 14, the subsection (2A) inserted by the Criminal Justice Act 1982 (c. 48)
Criminal Justice Act 1982 (c. 48)	In Schedule 13 – (a) in paragraph 7(2)(b), the words "(within the meaning of Part 12 of the Criminal Justice Act 2003)"; (b) in paragraph 7(3)(b), the words "within the meaning of Part 12 of the Criminal Justice Act 2003";

	(c) in paragraph 9(3)(a), the words "under section 177 of the Criminal Justice Act 2003";
	(d) in paragraph 9(4)(a), the words "(within the meaning of Part 12 of the Criminal Justice Act 2003)";
	(e) in paragraph 9(5), the words "(within the meaning of the Part 12 of the Criminal Justice Act 2003)";
	(f) in paragraph 9(6), the words "(within the meaning of Part 12 of the Criminal Justice Act 2003)".
	In Schedule 14, paragraph 60
Mental Health Act 1983 (c. 20)	In section 37(8)(c), the words "a supervision order (within the meaning of that Act) or".
Health and Social Services and Social Security Adjudications Act 1983 (c. 41)	In Schedule 2, paragraphs 15(b) and 16.
Children Act 1989 (c. 41)	In section 21(2)(c), in sub-paragraph (i), the words "paragraph 7(5) of Schedule 7 to the Powers of Criminal Courts (Sentencing) Act 2000 or" and the word "or" at the end of that sub-paragraph.
	In section 105(6), in paragraph (b), the words from "or an" to the end of that paragraph. In Schedule 13, paragraph 35(3)
Criminal Justice Act 1991 (c. 53)	In paragraph 11 of Schedule 3 –
	(a) in sub-paragraph (2)(a), the words "under section 177 of the Criminal Justice Act 2003";
	(b) in sub-paragraph (4), the words "under section 177 of the Criminal Justice Act 2003".
	In Schedule 11, paragraph 3.
Children (Prescribed Orders—Northern Ireland, Guernsey and Isle of Man) Regulations 1991 (S.I. 1991/2032)	In regulation 8(1) –
	(a) sub-paragraph (a)(ii);
	(b) sub-paragraph (b)(i), (ii), (iv) and (v);
	(c) sub-paragraph (c)(ii) and (iii).
Prisoners (Return to Custody) Act 1995 (c. 16)	Section 2(2)
Children (Northern Ireland Consequential Amendments) Order 1995 (S.I. 1995/ 756)	Article 7(2) and (3)

Crime and Disorder Act 1998 (c. 37)	In section 38(4) – (a)　paragraph (g); (b)　in paragraph (h), the words "or a supervision order". In Schedule 8, paragraph 13(1)
Powers of Criminal Courts (Sentencing) Act 2000 (c. 6)	Chapters 1, 2, 4 and 5 of Part 4 In section 74(3)(a), the words "or with the requirements of any community order or any youth community order to which he may be subject". In section 75, the words "action plan orders and" and "so far as relating to reparation orders". In section 137(2) – (a)　paragraphs (a) to (c); (b)　in paragraph (d), the words "action plan order or". In section 159, the words "paragraph 3(1), 10(6) or 18(1) of Schedule 3 to this Act,", "paragraph 1(1) of Schedule 5 to this Act," and "paragraph 7(2) of Schedule 7 to this Act, or". In section 160 – (a)　subsection (2); (b)　in subsection (3)(a), "40(2)(a)"; (c)　subsection (5). In section 163, the definitions of – (a)　"action plan order"; (b)　"affected person"; (c)　"attendance centre"; (d)　"attendance centre order"; (e)　"community sentence"; (f)　"curfew order"; (g)　"exclusion order"; (h)　"supervision order"; (i)　"supervisor"; (j)　"youth community order"; and paragraphs (a), (aa) and (f) of the definition of "responsible officer". Schedules 3 and 5 to 7 In Schedule 8 – (a)　in the heading, the words "action plan orders and"; (b)　paragraph 1 and the heading preceding that paragraph;

	(c) in the cross-heading before paragraph 2, the words "action plan order or";
	(d) in paragraph 2 –
	(i) in sub-paragraph (2), in paragraph (a), sub-paragraphs (ii) and (iii) and in paragraphs (b) and (c) the words "action plan order or";
	(ii) in sub-paragraphs (5) and (7), the words "action plan order or";
	(iii) in sub-paragraph (8), the words "or action plan order" in both places;
	(d) paragraphs 3 and 4;
	(e) in the cross-heading before paragraph 5, the words "action plan order or";
	(f) in paragraph 5(1)(a), the words "action plan order or";
	(g) in paragraph 6(9)(a), (b) and (c), the words "action plan order or".
	In Schedule 9, paragraphs 1, 2(2), (3)(a) and (4), 28(2), 33, 34(b), 39, 41, 42, 49, 80, 93(a), 126(b), 127, 129, 131 and 132.
	In Schedule 10, paragraphs 4 to 6 and 12 to 15.
	In Schedule 11, paragraphs 4(1)(a), (2) and (3) and 5.
Care Standards Act 2000 (c. 14)	In Schedule 4, paragraph 28(3).
Criminal Justice and Court Services Act 2000 (c. 43)	Section 46.
	Section 52.
	Section 70(5).
	In Schedule 7 –
	(a) in paragraph 4(2), in the entry relating to the Powers of Criminal Courts (Sentencing) Act 2000, the entries beginning "sections 63(1)(b)" and "in section 69";
	(b) paragraphs 37(b), 69, 163, 164, 174, 175 and 192;
	(c) in paragraph 196, paragraphs (a), (b), (c)(i) and (iii) and (d);
	(d) in paragraph 197 –
	(i) paragraph (a);
	(ii) paragraph (d);

	(iii) in paragraph (f), the definitions of "affected person" and "exclusion order";
	(iv) paragraph (g)(i);
	(e) paragraphs 201, 202(2) and 204
Anti-social Behaviour Act 2003 (c. 38)	Section 88. Schedule 2.
Criminal Justice Act 2003 (c. 44)	In section 147, subsections (1)(b) and (2). In section 148 – (a) in subsection (2), the words "which consists of or includes a community order"; (b) subsection (3). In section 156(2), "or (3)(a)". In section 161 – (a) in subsection (1), the words "aged 14 or over"; (b) subsection (7). In section 176, the definition of "youth community order". In section 197(1)(b), the words "the offender is aged 18 or over and". Section 199(4). Section 211(5). In section 221(2), paragraph (b) together with the word "or" immediately preceding it. Section 279. In Schedule 8 In section 330(5)(a), the entry relating to section 161(7)., paragraphs 12, 15 and 17(5). Schedule 24. In Schedule 32, paragraphs 2(2), 8(2)(a), 14, 64(3)(a)(ii), 70(5)(a) and (7), 73, 89(2), 95 to 105, 106(2), 107, 122, 123(3), (5) and (8), 125, 127, 128, 129, 131(3) and 138.

PART 2
SENTENCING

Title	Extent of repeal or revocation
Criminal Justice Act 1991 (c. 53)	In section 45 – (a) in subsection (3), subsection (2) of the substituted text, and (b) subsection (4). Section 46(1). In section 46A – (a) in subsection (1), the words "Subject to subsection (2) below,"; (b) subsection (2); (c) subsection (8). In section 50(2), the words from "but nothing" to the end.
Crime (Sentences) Act 1997 (c. 43)	In section 31(1), "(1) or (2)" In Schedule 5, in paragraph 7, the words "the corresponding subsection of".
Powers of Criminal Courts (Sentencing) Act 2000 (c. 6)	In section 17 – (a) in subsection (1), paragraph (c) together with the word "and" immediately preceding it; (b) subsection (5) Section 92(3)
Criminal Justice Act 2003 (c. 44)	In section 142(2)(a), the words "at the time of conviction". In section 153(1), the words "falling to be". In section 224(3), the definition of "relevant offence". In section 227(1)(a), the words ", other than a serious offence," In section 228 – (a) in subsection (1)(b)(ii), the words from "or by section 226(3)" to the end, and (b) subsection (3)(a) and the word "and" immediately following it. In section 229 – (a) in subsection (2) the words from the beginning to "18", and (b) subsections (3) and (4). Sections 233 and 234.

Criminal Justice Act 2003 (c. 44)—cont.	In section 247 – (a) in subsection (2), the word "and" (at the end of paragraph (a)) and paragraph (b), and (b) subsections (3), (4), (5) and (6). Section 254(3) to (5).
	In section 256 – (a) in subsection (2), the words "or (b)"; (b) subsections (3) and (5). In section 260 – (a) subsections (3) and (3A); (b) in subsection (6), in paragraph (a), the words "or (3)(e)" and paragraph (b). In section 264A(3), the words from "and none" to the end In section 300 – (a) in subsection (1), paragraph (b) together with the word "or" immediately preceding it; (b) in subsection (2) – (a) the words from "or, as the case may be" to "young offender)"; (b) the word "or" at the end of paragraph (a) Section 305(4)(e). Schedules 16 and 17. In Schedule 31, in paragraph 4(5)(a), ", (5)".
Referral Orders (Amendment of Referral Conditions) Regulations 2003 (S.I. 2003/1605)	Regulation 2(2) and (3).
Criminal Justice Act 2003 (Commencement No. 8 and Transitional and Saving Provisions) Order 2005 (S.I. 2005/950	Paragraph 30 of Schedule 2

Armed Forces Act 2006 (c. 52)	In section 221 – (a) in subsection (3)(a) and (b) the words "in section 226(2)", and (b) subsection (4). In section 223(3), the words "to (4)". In section 270 – (a) subsection (7), and (b) in subsection (8), the word "Accordingly". In Schedule 16, paragraphs 218 and 225.

PART 3
APPEALS

Title	Extent of repeal
Criminal Appeal Act 1968 (c. 19)	In section 4(2), the words "for the offence of which he remains convicted on that count". In section 6 – (a) subsection (5); (b) in subsection (7), the definition of interim hospital order. Section 11(6). In section 14 – (a) subsection (5); (b) in subsection (7), the definition of interim hospital order. Section 16B(3). In section 31, in the heading, the words "under Part 1". Section 31C(1) and (2).
Courts-Martial (Appeals) Act 1968 (c. 20)	Section 16(5). Section 25B(3). Section 36C(1) and (2). In section 43(1A), the word "or" at the end of paragraph (a)
Judicature (Northern Ireland) Act 1978 (c. 23)	In section 49 – (a) in subsection (2), the words from "or, where subsection (3) applies" to the end; (b) subsection (3).

Criminal Appeal (Northern Ireland) Act 1980 (c. 47)	Section 10(6).
Mental Health Act 1983 (c. 20)	In Schedule 4, paragraph 23(d)(ii).
Criminal Justice Act 1988 (c. 33)	In section 36(9), the word "and" at the end of paragraph (ab).
Powers of Criminal Courts (Sentencing) Act 2000 (c. 6)	In section 155 – (a) in subsection (1), the words from "or, where subsection (2) below applies" to the end; (b) subsections (2) and (3).
Criminal Justice Act 2003 (c. 44)	Section 272(1).

PART 4

OTHER CRIMINAL JUSTICE PROVISIONS

Title	Extent of repeal
Children and Young Persons Act 1969 (c. 54)	Section 23AA(4)(a).
Bail Act 1976 (c. 63)	Section 3AA(6) to (10) and (12).
Magistrates' Courts Act 1980 (c. 43)	Section 13(5) Section 24(1B).
Prosecution of Offences Act 1985 (c. 23)	Section 7A(6).
Criminal Justice (Terrorism and Conspiracy) Act 1998 (c. 40)	Section 8.
Access to Justice Act 1999 (c. 22)	Section 17A(5)
Powers of Criminal Courts (Sentencing) Act 2000 (c. 6)	In section 3 – (a) in subsection (2), paragraph (b) and the word "or" immediately preceding it; (b) in subsection (5), in paragraph (b), the words "paragraph (b) and".
Sexual Offences Act 2003 (c. 42)	Section 86(4) Section 87(6)

Criminal Justice Act 2003 (c. 44)	Section 23A(7) to (9).
	In Schedule 3, paragraphs 13, 22 and 57(2).
	In Schedule 36, paragraph 50.
	In Part 4 of Schedule 37, in the entry relating to the Magistrates' Courts Act 1980, in the second column, the words "In section 33(1), paragraph (b) and the word "and" immediately preceding it".

PART 5
CRIMINAL LAW

Title	Extent of repeal
Criminal Libel Act 1819 (60 Geo. 3 & 1 Geo. 4 c. 8)	In section 1, the words "any blasphemous libel, or".
Law of Libel Amendment Act 1888 (c. 64)	In section 3, the words "blasphemous or".
	In section 4, the words "blasphemous or".
Nuclear Material (Offences) Act 1983 (c. 18)	Section 1(2).
	In section 6(1), the words "in this Act".
Public Order Act 1986 (c. 64)	Section 29B(3).
	In section 29H –
	(a) in subsection (1), the words "in England and Wales";
	(b) subsection (2).
	In section 29I –
	(a) in subsection (2)(a), the words "in the case of an order made in proceedings in England and Wales,";
	(b) subsections (2)(b) and (4).
	In section 29L(1) and (2), the words "in England and Wales".
Sexual Offences Act 2003 (c. 42)	In Schedule 2, in paragraph 1(d), the words "in relation to a photograph or pseudophotograph showing a child under 16".
Terrorism Act 2006 (c. 11)	Section 14.

PART 6
INTERNATIONAL CO-OPERATION IN RELATION TO CRIMINAL JUSTICE MATTERS

Title	Extent of repeal
Commissioners for Revenue and Customs Act 2005 (c. 11)	In Schedule 2, paragraph 14.
Repatriation of Prisoners Act 1984 (c. 47)	In section 1(4)(b) the words "under this Act".Section 3(10).In section 8(1) the word "and" after the definition of "order".
Police and Justice Act 2006 (c.48)	Section 44(4).

PART 7
ANTI-SOCIAL BEHAVIOUR

Title	Extent of repeal
Police and Justice Act 2006 (c. 48)	In Schedule 14, paragraph 55(5)

PART 8
POLICING

Title	Extent of repeal
Police Act 1996 (c. 16)	In section 50(4), the words ", subject to subsection (3)(b),".
	In section 54(2), the words "and the Central Police Training and Development Authority".
	In section 97—
	(a) in subsection (6), in each of paragraphs (b) and (c), the words "or is required to resign as an alternative to dismissal";
	(b) in subsection (7), the words ", or required to resign as an alternative to dismissal,"
	In Schedule 6, paragraph 6.
Greater London Authority Act 1999 (c. 29)	In Schedule 27, paragraphs 95 and 107.
Criminal Justice and Police Act 2001 (c. 16)	In section 125 –
	(a) subsections (3) and (4);
	(b) in subsection (5), paragraph (b), together with the word "and" immediately preceding it.

Police Reform Act 2002 (c. 30)	In Schedule 3 – (a) paragraphs 20A(8), 20B(5) and 20E(5); (b) paragraph 20G together with the cross heading immediately preceding it; (c) in paragraphs 21A(5) and 24B(2), the words from "(and the other provisions" to the end; (d) paragraph 22(1)(c) (together with the word "or" immediately preceding it); (e) in paragraph 25, the word "and" immediately after each of sub-paragraphs (2)(b), (3)(b) and (5)(b).
Railways and Transport Safety Act 2003 (c. 20)	Section 43.
Police and Justice Act 2006 (c. 48)	In section 49(1), paragraph (c) together with the word "or" immediately preceding it. In Schedule 1, paragraph 30(3). In Schedule 2, paragraph 19.
Legal Services Act 2007 (c. 29)	In Schedule 21, paragraphs 73 and 119.

INDEX

References are to paragraph numbers.

Absence of accused
  sentencing   2.12, 2.13, 2.14
  trial   2.12, 2.13, 2.14
Adoption   8.35, 8.37
  meaning   8.37
Allocation of cases triable either way   2.2, 2.3, 2.4, 2.5
  commencement   2.3
  committal for sentence   2.4, 2.5
Anti-social behaviour   7.1
Anti-social behaviour orders   7.16, 7.17, 7.18, 7.19
  background   7.17
  guidance as to use   7.17
  new provisions   7.18, 7.19
  review   7.18, 7.19
Appeal   10.2, 10.3, 10.4, 10.5, 10.6, 10.7, 10.9, 11.17
  background   10.2, 10.3
  consultation process   10.2, 10.3
  detention of defendant pending appeal to Supreme Court   10.9
  evidence   10.9
  power to dismiss following references by Criminal Cases Review Commission   10.4, 10.5
  powers of Court of Appeal to re-sentence   10.9
  powers of single judge   10.9
  prosecution, by   10.6, 10.7
  special immigration status   11.17
  time for issue of certificates of fitness to appeal   10.9
  unsafe conviction   10.2, 10.3
Attendance centre   5.25
  requirement on fine defaulter   3.9
  youth rehabilitation order, and   5.25
Attorney-General   10.8
  review of sentence on reference by   10.8
Audience, rights of   2.21, 2.22, 2.23
  magistrates' courts   2.21, 2.23
  background rationale   2.22

Bail   2.6, 2.7, 2.8, 2.9, 2.10, 2.11, 3.29, 3.30
  credits for remand on   3.29, 3.30
  electronic monitoring condition   2.7, 2.8
  persons aged 17 or above   2.9

Bail—*continued*
  offences tried summarily   2.10, 2.11
  summary offences   2.10, 2.11
Blasphemy   9.19
  abolition   9.19

Cautions   4.6, 4.7, 4.9, 4.10, 4.11, 4.12, 4.13, 4.14, 4.15
  conditional   4.6, 4.7, 4.9, 4.10, 4.11, 4.12, 4.13, 4.14, 4.15
Child sex offenders   12.2, 12.3, 12.4, 12.5, 12.6, 12.7
  information about   12.2
  background   12.3, 12.4, 12.5
  consideration of disclosure of data   12.6, 12.7
  new provisions   12.6, 12.7
  Megan's Law   12.4, 12.5
  Sarah's Law   12.3, 12.4, 12.5
Children   8.31
  indecent photographs   8.31
Children and young persons
  electronic monitoring condition   2.8
Closure orders   7.2, 7.3, 7.4, 7.5, 7.6, 7.7, 7.8, 7.9, 7.10, 7.11, 7.12, 7.13, 7.14, 7.15
  Consultation Paper   7.5, 7.6
  premises associated with persistent disorder or nuisance   7.2, 7.3, 7.4, 7.5, 7.6
  appeals   7.14
  criminal offence   7.12
  discharge   7.13
  extension   7.13
  preconditions   7.8, 7.9, 7.10, 7.11
  reimbursement of costs or compensation   7.15
  when application may be made   7.7
  who may apply   7.7
Committal for sentence   2.4, 2.5
Community sentences   3.5, 3.6, 3.7, 3.8
  unpaid work requirement for breach   3.8
Compensation   12.15, 12.16, 12.17
  miscarriages of justice   12.15, 12.16, 12.17
Conditional cautions   4.6, 4.7, 4.9
  Code of Practice   4.13
  conditions   4.11, 4.12
  non-compliance with conditions   4.14
  preconditions   4.10

Conditional cautions—*continued*
restrictions on sentencing on
  subsequent conviction   4.15
Convention on the Rights of the Child   4.5
Crack house orders   7.4, 7.5, 7.6
Criminal Cases Review Commission 10.4, 10.5
powers to dismiss appeal following
  references by   10.4, 10.5
**Criminal Justice and Immigration Act
2008**   1.1, 1.2, 1.3, 1.4, 1.6, 1.7
commencement   1.3, 1.4
outline   1.6
Parliamentary history   1.2
passage of   1.7
Criminal legal aid   2.16, 2.17, 2.19, 2.20
Criminal offences   9.1
Curfew   5.27, 5.28
youth rehabilitation order   5.27, 5.28

Default order   3.9
Defence statement   2.15
contents   2.15
Defences   9.1
Detention for public protection   4.22
Drug treatment   5.34
youth rehabilitation order   5.34

Education requirement   5.36
youth rehabilitation order   5.36
Electronic monitoring   2.7, 5.37, 11.19
children and young persons   2.8
persons aged 17 or above   2.9
special immigration status   11.19
youth rehabilitation order   5.37
Extended sentence   3.33, 3.43, 4.22
recall   3.43
release on licence   3.33
violent or sexual offences, for   4.22
Extreme pornography   8.2, 8.3, 8.4, 8.5, 8.6,
  8.7, 8.8, 8.9, 8.10, 8.11, 8.12, 8.13,
  8.14, 8.15, 8.16, 8.17, 8.18, 8.19,
  8.20, 8.21, 8.22, 8.23, 8.24, 8.25,
  8.26, 8.27, 8.28, 8.29, 8.30
background   8.3, 8.4, 8.5, 8.6, 8.7, 8.8
classified work   8.22, 8.23, 8.24
concept   8.9
defences   8.25, 8.26, 8.27
excluded material   8.22, 8.23, 8.24
extreme image   8.16, 8.17, 8.18
grossly offensive, disgusting or
  otherwise of an obscene
  character   8.19, 8.20
human rights, and   8.28
image   8.10
offence   8.9, 8.10, 8.11, 8.12, 8.13, 8.14,
  8.15, 8.16, 8.17, 8.18, 8.19, 8.20,
  8.21, 8.22, 8.23, 8.24
pornographic   8.11, 8.12, 8.13, 8.14, 8.15,
  8.16, 8.17, 8.18, 8.19, 8.20
portray   8.17, 8.18
possession   8.21
producer   8.13, 8.14, 8.15
rationale   8.3, 8.4, 8.5, 8.6, 8.7, 8.8

Extreme pornography—*continued*
special rules relating to providers of
  information society services   8.29,
    8.30

Fine defaulter
attendance centre requirement   3.9
Foreign prisoners   3.36, 3.37
licence provisions   3.36, 3.37
Fostering   5.17, 5.18, 5.32
youth rehabilitation order, and   5.32
youth rehabilitation orders   5.17, 5.18

Grooming   8.35, 8.36
offences   8.36

Hatred on grounds of sexual orientation   9.2,
  9.3, 9.4, 9.5, 9.6, 9.7, 9.8, 9.9
background   9.4
new provisions   9.3, 9.4
offence   9.6, 9.7, 9.8, 9.9
sexual orientation   9.5
Home detention curfew scheme   3.31, 3.32
Hospital premises   7.21, 7.22, 7.23, 7.24, 7.25,
  7.26, 7.27, 7.28, 7.29, 7.30, 7.31
nuisance or disturbance on   7.21
background   7.22, 7.23
justification for offence   7.24
diagnosis or treatment   7.29
guidance   7.31
offence   7.25, 7.26, 7.27
power to remove   7.30
reasonable excuse   7.28
Human rights   8.28, 11.7
extreme pornography   8.28
special immigration status, and   11.7

Imprisonment   3.10, 3.11, 3.12, 3.13, 3.15,
  3.16, 3.17, 3.18, 3.19, 3.20, 3.21,
    3.22, 3.23, 3.24
consecutive terms   3.10, 3.11, 3.12, 3.13
Imprisonment for public protection   3.15, 3.16
dangerousness   3.24
preconditions   3.17, 3.18, 3.19, 3.20, 3.21,
    3.22, 3.23
Incitement   9.20, 9.21, 9.22
inciting commission of nuclear
  offence   9.20, 9.21, 9.22
Inciting commission of nuclear offence   9.20,
  9.21, 9.22
Indecent photographs of children   8.31
Indeterminate sentences   3.25, 3.26, 3.27
determination of tariffs   3.25, 3.26, 3.27
Individual support orders   7.20
Intensive supervision and surveillance   5.16
youth rehabilitation orders   5.16
Interim hospital orders   10.9
International co-operation   12.13, 12.14
mutual recognition of financial
  penalties   12.13, 12.14

Index

Intoxicating substance treatment
    requirement   5.35
    youth rehabilitation order   5.35

Legal aid
    criminal   2.16, 2.17, 2.19, 2.20
Life prisoners
    revocation of licence   3.44, 3.45
Long-term prisoners   3.34, 3.35
    release on licence   3.34, 3.35

Magistrates' courts
    rights of audience   2.21, 2.22, 2.23
Mental health treatment   5.33
    youth rehabilitation order   5.33
Miscarriages of justice   12.15, 12.16, 12.17
    compensation   12.15, 12.16, 12.17
Miscellaneous changes   12.1
    summary   12.1
Mutual recognition of financial
    penalties   12.13, 12.14

Nuisance or disturbance   7.21, 7.22, 7.23, 7.24, 7.25, 7.26, 7.27, 7.28, 7.29, 7.30, 7.31
    hospital premises   7.21, 7.22, 7.23, 7.24, 7.25, 7.26, 7.27, 7.28, 7.29, 7.30, 7.31
    meaning   7.26, 7.27

Obscenity   8.1, 8.2, 8.3, 8.4, 8.5, 8.6, 8.7, 8.8, 8.9, 8.10, 8.11, 8.12, 8.13, 8.14, 8.15, 8.16, 8.17, 8.18, 8.19, 8.20, 8.21, 8.22, 8.23, 8.24, 8.25, 8.26, 8.27, 8.28, 8.29, 8.30, 8.32

Persistent disorder or nuisance   7.2, 7.3, 7.4, 7.5, 7.6, 7.7, 7.8, 7.9, 7.10, 7.11, 7.12, 7.13, 7.14, 7.15
    closure of premises associated with   7.2, 7.3, 7.4, 7.5, 7.6, 7.7, 7.8, 7.9, 7.10, 7.11, 7.12, 7.13, 7.14, 7.15
Personal data   9.23, 9.24
    penalty for unlawfully obtaining   9.23, 9.24
Policing   12.11, 12.12
    discipline   12.12
Pornography   8.2, 8.3, 8.4, 8.5, 8.6, 8.7, 8.8, 8.9, 8.10, 8.11, 8.12, 8.13, 8.14, 8.15, 8.16, 8.17, 8.18, 8.19, 8.20, 8.21, 8.22, 8.23, 8.24, 8.25, 8.26, 8.27, 8.28, 8.29, 8.30
    extreme   8.2, 8.3, 8.4, 8.5, 8.6, 8.7, 8.8, 8.9, 8.10, 8.11, 8.12, 8.13, 8.14, 8.15, 8.16, 8.17, 8.18, 8.19, 8.20, 8.21, 8.22, 8.23, 8.24, 8.25, 8.26, 8.27, 8.28, 8.29, 8.30
Pre-sentence reports   3.4, 5.10
    youth rehabilitation order   5.10

Prisoners   3.28, 3.33, 3.34, 3.35, 3.36, 3.37, 3.38, 3.39, 3.40, 3.41, 3.42
    foreign
        licence provisions   3.36, 3.37
    life
        revocation of licence   3.44, 3.45
    long-term
        release on licence   3.34, 3.35
    recall   3.28
        extended sentences   3.43
    release   3.28
        automatic   3.40, 3.41
        ineligible or unsuitable
            prisoners   3.42
    release after recall   3.38, 3.39
    release on licence   3.33
Procedural changes   2.1
Prosecution   10.6, 10.7
    appeals by   10.6, 10.7
Publication of obscene articles   8.32
    maximum penalty   8.32

Reasonable force   9.10, 9.11, 9.12, 9.13, 9.14, 9.15, 9.16, 9.17, 9.18
    self-defence, and   9.10
    background   9.11
    common law defence   9.12, 9.13, 9.14, 9.15, 9.16, 9.17, 9.18
Recall of prisoners   3.28
    extended sentences   3.43
Referral orders   4.16, 4.17, 4.18, 4.19, 4.20
    background   4.16
    changes   4.17, 4.18
    changes in length   4.19, 4.20
    compulsory reference   4.17
    discretionary reference   4.18
    power to revoke   4.19, 4.20
Release of prisoners   3.28
    automatic   3.40, 3.41
    ineligible or unsuitable prisoners   3.42
    recall, after   3.38, 3.39
Reprimands   4.8
Review of sentence   10.8
    reference by Attorney-General   10.8

Self-defence   9.10, 9.11, 9.12, 9.13, 9.14, 9.15, 9.16, 9.17, 9.18
    reasonable force, and   9.10
    background   9.11
    common law defence   9.12, 9.13, 9.14, 9.15, 9.16, 9.17, 9.18
Sentencing   3.1, 3.2, 3.3, 3.4, 3.5, 3.6, 3.7, 3.8, 3.9, 3.10, 3.11, 3.12, 3.13, 3.25, 3.26, 3.27, 3.31, 3.32, 3.33, 4.4, 4.5
    absence of accused   2.12, 2.13, 2.14
    attendance centre requirement on
        fine defaulter   3.9
    background   3.2, 3.3
    community sentences   3.5, 3.6, 3.7
    consecutive terms of imprisonment   3.10, 3.11, 3.12, 3.13
    enforcement   3.8, 3.9
    home detention curfew scheme   3.31, 3.32

Sentencing—*continued*
   indeterminate sentences
      determination of tariffs   3.25, 3.26, 3.27
      offenders under age of 18   4.4, 4.5
      pre-sentence reports   3.4
      range of sentences   3.3
   release on licence of prisoner
      serving extended sentence   3.33
   unpaid work requirement for
      breach of community order   3.8
   wider context   3.2, 3.3
Sexual offences   4.22, 8.1, 8.2, 8.3, 8.4, 8.5, 8.6, 8.7, 8.8, 8.9, 8.10, 8.11, 8.12, 8.13, 8.14, 8.15, 8.16, 8.17, 8.18, 8.19, 8.20, 8.21, 8.22, 8.23, 8.24, 8.25, 8.26, 8.27, 8.28, 8.29, 8.30, 8.32, 8.33, 8.34, 8.38
   committed outside UK   8.33, 8.34
   extended sentences   4.22
   information concerning sex
      offenders   8.38
Sexual offences prevention orders   12.8
   relevant sexual offences   12.8
Sexual offenders   3.14, 3.15, 3.16, 3.17, 3.18, 3.19, 3.20, 3.21, 3.22, 3.23, 3.24
   imprisonment for public protection   3.15, 3.16, 3.17, 3.18, 3.19, 3.20, 3.21, 3.22, 3.23, 3.24
Sexual orientation   9.2, 9.3, 9.4, 9.5, 9.6, 9.7, 9.8, 9.9
   hatred on grounds of   9.2, 9.3, 9.4, 9.5, 9.6, 9.7, 9.8, 9.9
   meaning   9.5
Special immigration status   11.1, 11.2, 11.3, 11.4, 11.5, 11.6, 11.7, 11.8, 11.9, 11.10, 11.11, 11.12, 11.13, 11.14, 11.15, 11.16, 11.17, 11.18, 11.19, 11.20, 11.21, 11.22
   background   11.2, 11.3, 11.4, 11.5
   conditions   11.19, 11.20
      failure to comply   11.20
   designated person   11.1
   designation
      end of   11.22
   effect of designation   11.18
   electronic monitoring   11.19
   family member   11.14
   foreign criminal   11.8, 11.9
      condition 1   11.10, 11.11
      condition 2   11.12
      condition 3
         acts contrary to purposes and principles of UN   11.13
         crimes against peace   11.13
         serious non-political crimes   11.13
   human rights, and   11.7
   necessary, whether   11.6, 11.7
   preconditions   11.8, 11.9, 11.10, 11.11, 11.12, 11.13, 11.14, 11.15, 11.16
   right of appeal   11.17

Special immigration status—*continued*
   S v Secretary of State for the Home Department   11.2, 11.3, 11.4, 11.5
   social security   11.21
   support   11.21
   time limits on designation   11.15, 11.16
Summary offences
   bail   2.10, 2.11

Tobacco   12.9, 12.10
   persistent sales to persons aged under 18   12.9, 12.10
   restricted premises order   12.9, 12.10
Trial
   absence of accused   2.12, 2.13, 2.14

Unlawfully obtaining personal data   9.23, 9.24
   penalty   9.23, 9.24

Violent offences
   extended sentences   4.22
Violent offender orders   6.1, 6.2, 6.3, 6.4, 6.5, 6.6, 6.7, 6.8, 6.9, 6.10, 6.11, 6.12, 6.13, 6.14, 6.15, 6.16, 6.17, 6.18, 6.19, 6.20, 6.21
   appeals   6.19
   application   6.6, 6.7
   ASBOs, and   6.4
   background   6.2
   burden of proof   6.8, 6.9, 6.10, 6.11, 6.12, 6.13, 6.14
   civil nature   6.3, 6.4
   conditions   6.16
   contents   6.16
   custodial sentence, and   6.15
   definition   6.3, 6.4
   discharge   6.17
   gap in supervision arrangements   6.2
   hearing   6.6, 6.7
   interim   6.18
   making order   6.8, 6.9, 6.10, 6.11
      'necessary'   6.12, 6.13, 6.14
      when order can be made   6.15
   notification requirements   6.20
   offences   6.21
   preconditions for making   6.5
   prohibitions   6.16
   protecting the public   6.3, 6.4
   qualifying offender   6.5
   renewal   6.17
   restrictions   6.16
   'serious violent harm'   6.13, 6.14
   specified offenders   6.5
   standard of proof   6.8, 6.9, 6.10, 6.11, 6.12, 6.13, 6.14
   variation   6.17
Violent offenders   3.14, 3.15, 3.16, 3.17, 3.18, 3.19, 3.20, 3.21, 3.22, 3.23, 3.24
   imprisonment for public protection   3.15, 3.16, 3.17, 3.18, 3.19, 3.20, 3.21, 3.22, 3.23, 3.24

Index

Warnings 4.8

Young offenders 4.1, 4.2, 4.3, 4.4, 4.5, 4.6, 4.7, 4.8, 4.9, 4.10, 4.11, 4.12, 4.13, 4.14, 4.15
- alternatives to prosecution 4.6, 4.8, 4.9, 4.10, 4.11, 4.12, 4.13, 4.14, 4.15
- background 4.7
- conditional cautions 4.6, 4.7, 4.9, 4.10, 4.11, 4.12, 4.13, 4.14, 4.15
- general changes 4.1, 4.2, 4.3
- purposes of sentencing 4.4, 4.5
- Convention on the Rights of the Child 4.5
- reprimands 4.8
- statistics 4.2, 4.3
- warnings 4.8
- wider background 4.2, 4.3

Youth default orders 4.21

Youth rehabilitation order 5.1, 5.2, 5.3, 5.4, 5.5, 5.6, 5.7, 5.8, 5.9, 5.10, 5.11, 5.12, 5.13, 5.14, 5.15, 5.16, 5.17, 5.18, 5.19, 5.20, 5.21, 5.22, 5.23, 5.24, 5.25, 5.26, 5.27, 5.28, 5.29, 5.30, 5.31, 5.32, 5.33, 5.34, 5.35, 5.36, 5.37, 5.38, 5.39, 5.40, 5.41
- activity requirement 5.19, 5.20
- alternatives to custody 5.15
- amendment 5.39, 5.40
- attendance centre requirement 5.25
- background 5.2, 5.3
- breach 5.38
- Consultation Paper 5.3
- curfew requirement 5.27, 5.28
- drug treatment requirement 5.34
- education requirement 5.36

Youth rehabilitation order—*continued*
- electronic monitoring 5.37
- exclusion requirement 5.29, 5.30
- fostering requirement 5.32
- fostering, with 5.17, 5.18
- intensive supervision and surveillance 5.16
- intoxicating substance treatment requirement 5.35
- length 5.6, 5.7
- local authority residence requirement 5.31
- making order 5.11, 5.12, 5.13
- meaning 5.4
- mental health treatment requirement 5.33
- powers of court following conviction 5.41
- pre-sentence reports 5.10
- preconditions 5.19, 5.20, 5.21, 5.22, 5.23, 5.24, 5.25, 5.26, 5.27, 5.28, 5.29, 5.30, 5.31, 5.32, 5.33, 5.34, 5.35, 5.36, 5.37
- programme requirement 5.24
- prohibited activity 5.26
- requirements 5.1
- requirements that may be imposed 5.8, 5.9
- restrictions on community sentences, and 5.5
- restrictions on making 5.14
- revocation 5.39
- supervision requirement 5.21
- unpaid work requirement 5.22, 5.23